Educational Research

Educational Research

Quantitative and Qualitative Approaches

Burke Johnson
University of South Alabama

Larry Christensen
University of South Alabama

Allyn and Bacon
Boston   London   Toronto   Sydney   Tokyo   Singapore

Vice President and Editor-in-Chief: Paul A. Smith
Series Editorial Assistant: Shannon Morrow
Senior Marketing Manager: Brad Parkins
Production Editor: Christopher H. Rawlings
Editorial-Production Service: Omegatype Typography, Inc.
Composition and Prepress Buyer: Linda Cox
Manufacturing Buyer: Megan Cochran
Cover Administrator: Linda Knowles
Electronic Composition: Omegatype Typography, Inc.

Internet: www.abacon.com

Between the time Website information is gathered and published, some sites may have
closed. Also, the transcription of URLs can result in typographical errors. The publisher
would appreciate notification where these occur so that they may be corrected in
subsequent editions.

Many of the designations used by manufacturers and sellers to distinguish their products
are claimed as trademarks. Where those designations appear in this book, and Allyn and
Bacon was aware of a trademark claim, the designations have been printed in initial or all
caps.

Library of Congress Cataloging-in-Publication Data

Johnson, Burke.
    Educational research : quantitative and qualitative approaches /
  Burke Johnson, Larry Christensen.
      p.   cm.
  Includes bibliographical references and indexes.
  ISBN 0-205-26659-2
    1. Education—Research.   I. Christensen, Larry B.
  II. Title.
  LB1028.J59   2000
  370'.7'2—dc21
                                      99-33623
                                         CIP

Printed in the United States of America

10 9 8 7 6 5 4 3 2   03 02

Brief Contents

Contents

**PART II
PLANNING THE RESEARCH STUDY   35**

CHAPTER 2   Problem Identification and Hypothesis Formation   **35**

CHAPTER 5   Methods of Data Collection   125

CHAPTER 6   Sampling   155

CHAPTER 7   Validity of Research   **186**

PART IV
SELECTING A RESEARCH METHOD   **219**

CHAPTER 8   Experimental Research   **219**

CHAPTER 9   Quasi-Experimental and Single-Case Designs   254

CHAPTER 10   Nonexperimental Quantitative Research   280

CHAPTER 11   Qualitative Research   311

CHAPTER 12   Historical Research   341

PART V
ANALYZING THE DATA   **359**

CHAPTER 13   Descriptive Statistics   359

Preface

AUDIENCE

This book was written for the masters-level, introductory research methods course that is required in most colleges of education in the United States. It can also be used as an undergraduate text or for more advanced graduate-level courses. Instructors should be able to cover the material in one semester.

PURPOSE

We had several purposes in writing this textbook. Our first purpose was to write an introductory research methods book that was accurate and up-to-date. This purpose evolved from Burke Johnson's experience teaching educational research for several years, and, in the process, reviewing popular educational research methods textbooks. Review and use of these textbooks repeatedly revealed errors of omission and commission. These errors motivated Burke to begin the project of writing a new textbook. Burke discussed this project with a colleague, Larry Christensen, who agreed that a new textbook was needed, and Larry agreed to collaborate on the project.

We come from interdisciplinary backgrounds and have attempted to incorporate our respective insights into this book. Burke is an educational research methodologist and program evaluator, with additional graduate training in sociology, and Larry is a psychological research methodologist and author of a highly successful book entitled *Experimental Methodology*. We have kept up with the changes taking place in the field of research methods, and this textbook incorporates the latest information. We also provide references throughout the book for readers who want to examine original sources.

Second, we have provided a research methods textbook that takes an evenhanded approach to the different types of educational research. It seems to us that many texts emphasize one method at the expense of others. We believe that all the major approaches to research discussed in this text have merit when they are employed carefully and properly. We show the strengths and appropriateness of each method. We also show how the experts in each area conduct high-quality research and how they view their approach to research.

Third, we have provided a textbook that assumes no prior research background, is highly readable, and makes learning about research fun. Believe it or not, learning about research methods can be exciting. We are excited about research methods, and we have tried to share our enthusiasm with you. At the same time, we have tried to write a textbook that is at least as rigorous as other texts currently in use.

Fourth, we have tried to enable our readers to become critical *consumers* of research and potential *users* of research. Reading research articles is commonplace in graduate programs; this text will help you become adept at reading empirical articles. We also suspect that most of our readers will be called on at some point in their careers to summarize a research literature, to write a research proposal, to develop a data collection instrument, or to empirically test an idea. You should be well prepared for these kinds of activities after carefully studying the material in this book and from reading published examples of high-quality research.

ORGANIZATION OF THE BOOK

We chose to organize the textbook to follow the steps involved in the research process. Specifically, the textbook is organized into six parts.

Part I: Introduction

In this section we introduce the reader to the field of educational research, including the concept and philosophy of research, the differences between quantitative and qualitative research, and the different methods of research.

Part II: Planning the Research Study

In this section we carefully explain how to come up with a research problem, how to formulate research hypotheses, and how to write a research proposal. We also emphasize the importance of ethics in educational research.

Part III: Foundations of Research

In this section we first provide an introduction to measurement. Measurement is so important in research that nothing else really matters if you don't have good measurement. Next we discuss the major methods of collecting data: standardized tests, questionnaires, interviews, focus groups, observations, and previously collected data (secondary data). Then we provide an explanation of how to select (sample) people to participate in a quantitative or qualitative research study. We also explain the important issue of validity in quantitative and qualitative research, showing the various threats to good research and some techniques used to prevent mistakes.

Part IV: Selecting a Research Method

In this section we provide extensive discussion of the major research methods. We explain the following types of research: experimental research, quasi-experimental research, single-case research, nonexperimental quantitative research, historical research, phenomenology, ethnography, case study, and grounded theory research.

Part V: Analyzing the Data

In this section we provide two chapters on how to analyze quantitative research data (descriptive and inferential statistics) and one chapter on how to analyze qualitative research data.

Part VI: Writing the Research Report

In this final chapter we explain how to write quantitative and qualitative research manuscripts in a form that can be submitted to an educational journal for publication. We explain how to use the guidelines provided in the 1994 edition of the *Publication Manual of the American Psychological Association.* These important guidelines are used by the vast majority of journals in education and psychology.

Appendixes: Examples of Research Articles

We include two full-length articles published in respected educational research journals. One article is an example of experimental research; the other article is an example of an ethnography.

FEATURES OF THE TEXT

We have included several features in this text to make the task of learning about research easier. Each chapter begins with a list of objectives to get the student thinking about what he or she is going to be learning. We have also placed the definitions of all key terms in the margins of the text to make them stand out clearly. Throughout the text we try to provide multiple examples of concepts, many from published research studies. At the end of each chapter is a chapter summary, study questions about the most important ideas in the chapter, a set of exercises that instructors can assign to enrich the learning experience of their students, and a list of key terms.

SUPPLEMENTARY MATERIALS

The instructor's manual was written by Dr. James Van Haneghan. Jim has many years of experience teaching educational research methods. Burke will make available on his homepage some supplementary materials for teachers and students. Burke's World Wide Web address is http://www.coe.usouthal.edu/faculty/RBJ/Burke.html.

NOTE TO STUDENTS

You are probably wondering how to study research methods. We suggest you begin each chapter by reading the chapter objectives at the beginning of each chapter and the chapter summary at the end of the chapter. This will give you a good idea about where you are going. Then skim through the chapter, noticing the section headings and the key terms. This will help you see how the material is organized. Now you are ready to read the chapter. After finishing reading the chapter, read the chapter summary again and answer the study questions. As you prepare for tests, make sure that you know the definitions to all the key terms because they are the basic building blocks for learning about research. Try to think of your own examples of the ideas presented in the chapter. Don't get lost in the details, however. Write out the chapter section headings (or go to Burke's homepage) so you can see how things are organized into the big picture. Finally, as we point out several times in the text, one of the best ways to learn how to design an educational research study is to read high-quality, published research articles in your research area. We believe that if you do these things, you will be able to learn from the ideas presented in this book. If you want more help, look at Burke's homepage for additional learning aids.

NOTE TO INSTRUCTORS

We have included two full-length research articles in the text. Rather than include an article at the end of every chapter, we have listed articles that can be read as examples. These articles are listed in the exercises at the end of the chapters. We chose only to include two full articles, rather than five or six, because we wanted to keep the cost of the book down for students, and we assumed that instructors would want to use different articles over time. We highly recommend, however, that your students read high-quality examples of published research. Dr. James Van Haneghan has also included many class exercises for each chapter, a set of overheads, and a set of exam questions in the instructor's manual for your use.

ACKNOWLEDGMENTS

First and foremost, Burke Johnson would like to thank his wife, Dr. Lisa A. Turner, for putting up with the late hours and for being the first reviewer of everything he wrote. We want to thank Nancy Forsyth of Allyn and Bacon for believing in our new ideas and for making publication of this text possible. We thank our Allyn and Bacon editors Sean Wakely and Paul Smith, editorial assistants Jill Jeffreys and Shannon Morrow, and the editorial-production staff of Omegatype Typography for all their help. We thank Professors Bill Gilley, University of South Alabama; Joe Newman, University of South Alabama; and Bikas Sinha, Indian Statistical Institute, Calcutta, India, for reviewing the chapters in their areas of expertise. Burke also thanks his students, who put up with reading much of the book in manuscript form, for their insightful thoughts on how to improve the book. Larry would like to thank Jennifer Rowe for her assistance in preparing many of the figures that appear in the book. Last, but certainly not least, we thank the reviewers selected by Allyn and Bacon who provided invaluable input: Amy Gillett, University of Wisconsin–Stout; Bryan Griffin, Georgia Southern University; Beverly A. Joyce, Dowling College; Robert W. Lissitz, University of Maryland at College Park; Doris L. Prater, University of Houston, Clear Lake; Joan Quilling, University of Missouri, Columbia; Thomas A. Romberg, University of Wisconsin; and Paul Westmeyer, The University of Texas at San Antonio.

COMMENTS

We hope that you (students and instructors) will send your comments to us so that we can continually improve our textbook. You can contact us at the following e-mail addresses: bjohnson@usamail.usouthal.edu (Burke Johnson) and lchriste@usamail.usouthal.edu (Larry Christensen).

Educational Research

1
PART

INTRODUCTION

CHAPTER 1

Introduction to Educational Research

LEARNING OBJECTIVES

To be able to

- explain the importance of educational research.
- list at least five areas of educational research.
- explain the difference between basic and applied research.
- describe action research and evaluation research.
- discuss the different sources of knowledge.
- explain the scientific approach to knowledge generation.
- list the five objectives of educational research and provide an example of each.
- describe the characteristics of quantitative research.
- list and explain the different types of variables used in research.
- describe the characteristics of qualitative research.
- list and explain the differences among the different methods of research.
- explain the idea of a correlation coefficient.
- describe the multimethod perspective of research.

Welcome to the world of educational research. Research has been conducted in virtually every area in the field of education. In fact, the research techniques described in this book are used all over the world to help many fields advance and solve problems. As you know, researchers in academic disciplines, including education, have been trying to answer difficult questions and improve our society for a long time. The search for better answers to important questions will always continue. In this book we will discuss the way in which research is conducted in an attempt to provide answers to important questions. We hope you will enjoy learning about research, and we hope it opens up new ways of thinking for you.

As you read this book you will learn how to think about research, how to evaluate the quality of published research reports, and how to conduct research on your own. In a sense you will also be learning a new language, because researchers use a specialized language or jargon. But remember, don't be afraid of new words. The words have definitions that represent ideas you can understand, and you have been learning new words all of your life. On a lighter side: You can use the new words to impress your friends, right? Just kidding. In sum, we welcome you to the world of research and hope you will enjoy it. Because this is likely to be a required course for you, we will begin by discussing a few reasons for taking a course on educational research methods.

WHY STUDY EDUCATIONAL RESEARCH?

You may have asked, Why do I have to take a class on educational research? First of all, research can be more interesting than you might think. We hope in time you will find that the material and the ways of thinking are interesting and beneficial. Second, throughout this book you will be learning critical thinking skills. Rather than assuming that what is written in a book or what someone says is "fact" or undeniable "truth," we will show you some techniques for evaluating arguments. In all cases, the question is one of evidence. As a start, we suggest that you take the word *proof* and eliminate it from your vocabulary this semester or quarter when you talk about research results. That's because proof exists in the realms of mathematics and deductive logic. In science and research, the best we can do is to provide evidence. Sometimes the evidence is very convincing; at other times it may not be. You must use your critical thinking skills to judge the evidence available on any given topic. Critical thinking is a skill that will be helpful in your studies and professional work as long as you live. Learning about research methods should help sharpen your critical thinking skills.

Another important reason to study research is to help you better understand discussions of research you hear in the media, such as television and radio, or hear in person at professional meetings. Examples of research in our society abound. For example, when you watch a television program what comes in between those short segments of actual programming? Commercials! Do you ever wonder about those "research studies" that claim to "prove" that one laundry detergent is better than another? As you know, the purpose of commercials is to influence your behavior. Advertisers spend millions of dollars each year on marketing research to understand your thinking and behavior. If you watch a sporting event, you will likely see commercials for beer, cars, trucks, food, and tennis shoes. If you watch soap operas in the afternoon, you likely see very different commercials. The reason for this variation is that advertisers generally know who is watching what programs at what times. The actual commercials are developed so that they are likely to appeal to your ways of thinking about what is fun, exciting, and important. Also, did you know that every major presidential candidate has a research consultant who explains the best ways to get your vote and win the election? The point is that other people study you all of the time, and in this book you will learn about the techniques they use. Understanding these techniques should help you to be more aware of their efforts.

You will learn here that not all research is created equal. That is, some research studies are more defensible than others. You will learn how to ask the right questions about research studies and you will know when to put confidence in a set of research findings. You will learn to ask questions like, Was the study an experiment or was it a nonexperimental research study? Were control groups included in the design? Did the researcher randomly assign participants to the different comparison groups? How did the researchers control for the influence of extraneous variables? How were the participants in the research selected? Did the researcher use techniques that help reduce the effects of human bias?

One day you may need to examine the research on a topic and make an informed judgment on what course of action to take or to recommend to someone else. Therefore, it is important that you understand how to evaluate research, because understanding research terminology, the characteristics of the different types of research, and how research can be designed to provide solid evidence will allow you to critically evaluate research results and make informed decisions based on research literatures. A **research literature** is the set of published research studies on a particular topic. One important point to remember is that you should always place more confidence in a research finding when several different researchers in different places have found the same result. Furthermore, you should not treat a single research study as the final word on any topic.

Research literature
Set of published research studies on a topic

On a practical level, understanding research techniques may even help you in your career as a student and as a professional teacher, counselor, or coach. Perhaps one day you will be asked to write a proposal to obtain a grant or conduct a research study on your own. If you study the contents of this book, you will learn how to design and conduct a defensible study and you will learn about the different sections in a research grant proposal. Furthermore, if you look at the bibliographies in the books you use in your other education courses, you will see that many of these references are to research studies. After learning about research, you will be able to go back and evaluate the research studies your textbooks are based on. In other words, you will not have to accept something as true just because someone said it was true.

AREAS OF EDUCATIONAL RESEARCH

Let's start off by examining some areas of research in education. In Figure 1.1 you will find a list of the major divisions and the special interest areas in the American Educational

Research Association (AERA). The AERA is the largest and most prestigious research association in the field of education, and it includes approximately 24,000 members. It is composed of university professors from all areas of education, governmental employees, teachers, and professionals from educational think tanks and testing companies. Each year, approximately 11,000 of the members of the AERA, and many nonmembers, attend a national conference sponsored by the AERA, where many attendees present the results of their latest research.

You can see in Figure 1.1 that education is a broad field that includes many different research areas. Do you see any areas of research in Figure 1.1 that sound especially interesting? If you are writing a research paper, you might pick one of these areas as your starting point. The areas of research listed in Figure 1.1 are still, however, fairly general. To see the specific areas and topics of current interest to educational researchers, go to the library and browse through the education journals.

EXAMPLES OF EDUCATIONAL RESEARCH

The majority of journal articles in education include an abstract on the front page of the article. An abstract is a brief summary of what is included in the article. We have reproduced the abstracts of four research articles here so that you can get a better feel for what is done in an actual research study. We recommend that you read some research articles as soon as possible so that you will see some full-length examples of research. As you read the following abstracts, try to determine (1) the purpose of the study, (2) how the researchers studied the phenomenon, and (3) what the results were.

I. Giving Voice to High School Students: Pressure and Boredom, Ya Know What I'm Saying? by Edwin Farreil, George Peguero, Rashed Lindsey, and Ronald White (1988). The concerns of students identified as at-risk of dropping out of school in an urban setting were studied using innovative ethnographic methods. Students from the subject population were hired to act as collaborators rather than informants and to collect taped dialogues between themselves and their peers. As collaborators, they also participated in the analysis of data and contributed to identifying the research questions of the inquiry. Data indicated that pressure and boredom were most often mentioned as negative factors in the lives of the students, with pressure emanating from social forces outside of school but contributing to boredom inside. (p. 489)

II. Creativity and Cooperation in the Elementary Music Classroom by Lynda Baloche (1994). The author examines attitudes towards, and the effects of focus on, creativity and cooperation in the elementary music classroom. First, elementary music teachers were interviewed regarding their values towards creativity and cooperation. Then, a curriculum was field tested that utilized cooperative learning and emphasized activities designed to encourage creative thinking and problem solving. A pretreatment-posttreatment study, with experimental and control group, was conducted to measure actual changes in student

FIGURE 1.1 Divisions and special interest groups in the American Educational Research Association. Note the special interest groups change slightly year to year.

Major Divisions in the AERA

Administration, Curriculum Studies
Counseling and Human Development
Education in the Professions
History and Historiography
Learning and Instruction

Measurement and Research Methodology
Postsecondary Education
School Evaluation and Program Development
Social Context of Education
Teaching and Teacher Education

Special Interest Groups in the AERA

Accelerated Schools
Action Research
Adolescence
Advanced Studies of National Databases
American Indian/Alaskan Native Education
Artificial Intelligence and Education
Arts and Learning
Associates for Research on Private Education
Basic Research in Reading and Literacy
Bilingual Education Research
Brain and Education
Business Education and Information Systems Research
Career Development
Classroom Management
Computer Applications in Education
Constructivist Theory, Research, and Practice
Critical Issues in Curriculum
Early Education and Child Development
Economics Education
Education and Student Development in the Cities
Education in Science and Technology
Educational Enterprises
Educational Statisticians
Electronic Networking
Faculty Evaluation and Development
Families as Educators
Fiscal Issues, Policy, and Educational Finance
Futures Research and Strategic Planning
Instructional Supervision
Instructional Technology
International Studies
John Dewy Society
Language and Social Processes
Law and Education
Leadership Development, Training and Research
Lesbian and Gay Studies
Literature
Measurement Services
Media, Culture, and Curriculum
Middle Level Education
Military Education and Training
Moral Development and Education
Motivation in Education
Multiple Linear Regression
Occupational Stress and Health

Organizational Theory
Peace Education
Philosophical Studies of Education
Politics of Education
Professional Licensure and Certification
Professors of Educational Research
Qualitative Research
Rasch Measurement
Religion and Education
Research Focus on Black Education
Research in Mathematics Education
Research in Social Studies Education
Research on Education of Asian and Pacific Americans
Research on Education of Deaf Persons
Research on Evaluation
Research on Giftedness and Talent
Research on Learning and Instruction in Physical Education
Research Using NAEP Data
Research Utilization
Restructuring Public Education
Rural Education
School Effectiveness and School Improvement
School-University Collaborative Research
Second Language Research
Self-Study of Teacher Education Practices
Semiotics in Education
Society of Professors of Education
Sociology of Education
Special Education Research
State and Regional Educational Research Associations
Structural Equation Modeling
Study of Learning Environments
Studying and Self-Directed Learning
Subject Knowledge and Conceptual Change
Survey Research in Education
Teacher as Researcher
Teacher's Work and Teachers' Unions
Teaching in Educational Administration
Textbooks, Textbook Publishing, and Schools
Training in Business and Industry
Vocabulary
Vocational Education
Writing

levels of creativity and attitudes towards cooperation. A follow-up of creativity measures was conducted for many years later. Results indicate that elementary music teachers can adapt cooperative learning models to their teaching and can, short-term, influence students' levels of creativity and attitudes towards cooperation. (p. 255)

III. A Grounded Theory of Counselors' Construal of Success in the Initial Session by Kenneth Frontman and Mark Kunkel (1994). Counselors (N=69) in 5 mental health fields provided written descriptions of their experience of success in an initial counseling session. Grounded theory analysis of these descriptions suggested that counselors tend to construe success of initial sessions through collaboration (i.e., adherence to desired interactional norms, establishment of rapport, and progress in problem solving) and positive awareness (client display of strengths and counselor self-evaluation of performance). Findings are discussed as they relate to counseling theory and practice. (p. 492)

IV. Gender Differences in Mathematics Performance: A Meta-Analysis by Janet Hyde, Elizabeth Fennema, and Susan Lamon (1990). Reviewers have consistently concluded that males perform better on mathematics tests than females do. To make a refined assessment of the magnitude of gender differences in mathematics performance, we performed a meta-analysis of 100 studies. . . . We conclude that gender differences are small. (p. 139) [A meta-analysis is a statistical technique for literature summarization.]

BASIC AND APPLIED RESEARCH

Basic research
Research about fundamental processes

Applied research
Research about practical questions

Research studies can be placed along a continuum with the words **basic research** at one end and the words **applied research** at the other end. The word *mixed* can be placed in the center. Basic research is aimed at generating fundamental knowledge and theoretical understanding about basic human processes. Research examining the effect of "priming" in memory is an example of basic research. Priming is "an enhancement of the processing of a stimulus as a function of prior exposure" (Anderson, 1995, p. 459). Assume that a researcher asks you to name a fruit and you say "pineapple." Then on the second trial, the researcher either asks you to name another type of fruit *or* the researcher asks you to name a type of dog. Which response do you think you could provide more quickly? It turns out that research participants could name another type of fruit faster than they could name a type of dog when they were asked to name a type of fruit first (Loftus, 1974, cited in Anderson). The naming of the fruit on the first trial "primed" the research participants' mental processing to name another fruit. It is hypothesized that priming operates because the first exposure activates the complex of neurons in long-term memory, where the concept is being stored. Basic research is usually conducted using the most rigorous research methods (e.g., experimental) under tightly controlled "laboratory" conditions. The key purpose of basic research is to develop a solid foundation of reliable knowledge on which future research can be built.

At the other end of the continuum is applied research. Applied research is focused on answering "real world," or practical, questions in order to provide immediate solutions.

Topics for applied research are often driven by current problems in education and by policymakers' concerns. Applied research is often conducted in more natural settings (i.e., more realistic or real-world settings) than basic research. An applied research study might focus on the effects of retaining low-performing elementary school students in their present grade level or on the relative effectiveness of two approaches to counseling (e.g., behavior therapy versus cognitive therapy). In the former, the results would potentially have practical implications for education policy; in the latter, the results would potentially have implications for practicing counselors.

ACTION RESEARCH

Action research
Applied research
focused on solving
practitioner's
problems

Action research is a form of applied research focused on solving local problems that practitioners face (Lewin, 1946; Stringer, 1996). For example, action research is typically conducted by teachers, administrators, counselors, and other educational professionals to answer questions they have and help solve problems such as teacher burnout, classroom discipline, parental involvement with the PTA, and so on. Action research involves the process of diagnosing a local problem, planning and carrying out a research study, developing new knowledge based on the research, and implementing the research findings to solve or improve a local problem. Action research recommendations are typically used in decision making by educational professionals. Action research is a cyclical process because problems are rarely solved through one research study. Many school districts have departments set up to conduct research affecting the school district. Although action research is geared toward solving local problems, the research results are sometimes presented at regional or national conferences or are published in the research literature, and, therefore, action research can add to the general body of scientific knowledge.

EVALUATION RESEARCH

Evaluation
Determining the
worth, merit, or
quality of an
evaluation object

Another type of applied research is program evaluation, or simply evaluation. **Evaluation** involves determining the worth, merit, or quality of an evaluation object. An evaluation object is the thing being evaluated (a program, a person, or a product) (Guba & Lincoln, 1981; Scriven, 1967; Worthen, Sanders, & Fitzpatrick, 1997). An educational program might be an after-school program for students with behavioral problems or a new curriculum at school. A person might be your new school district superintendent. A product might be a new textbook or a new piece of equipment a school is considering purchasing.

Evaluation involves the conduct of research activities by an evaluator to provide information about an evaluation object. The four key questions evaluators frequently ask at this point are (1) Did the evaluation object have its intended impact? (Did it work?) (2) How does the evaluation object operate? (3) Is the evaluation object cost effective? (Is there a cheaper alternative available?) (4) How can the evaluation object be improved? In addition,

*Formative
evaluation*
Evaluation
focused on
improving the
evaluation object

based on the research evidence collected, evaluators typically make two kinds of decisions. First they state how the evaluation object can be improved; this is called **formative evaluation.** Second, evaluators make judgments about whether the evaluation object is effective and whether it should be continued; this is called **summative evaluation.** Formative evaluation is very important for improving and fine tuning programs over time, and summative evaluation is very important for policymakers making funding decisions.

SOURCES OF KNOWLEDGE

*Summative
evaluation*
Evaluation
focused on
determining
overall
effectiveness of
the evaluation
object

Take a moment now to consider how you have learned about the world around you. Try to identify the source or sources of one of your particular beliefs. For example, consider your political party identification (i.e., Democrat, Republican, Independent, or something else). Political scientists have shown that college students' party identification can often be predicted by their parents' party identification. Obviously there are many additional influences that affect party identification. Can you identify some of them? Let's examine some of the ways people in general learn about the world around them. We group the sources of knowledge into three areas: experiences, expert opinion, and reasoning. Perhaps you can think of some additional sources.

Experience

Empiricism
Idea that
knowledge comes
from experience

Empiricism is the idea that knowledge comes from experience. We learn by observing, and when we observe, we rely on our sense perception. Each day of our lives, we look, feel, hear, smell, and taste so that we can understand our surroundings. According to the philosophical doctrine of empiricism, what we observe with our senses is said to be true. John Locke (1632–1704), a proponent of this idea, said that our mind at birth is a *tabula rasa,* a blank slate ready to be written on. Throughout our lives, our slate is filled up with knowledge based on our experiences. The statement "I know the car is blue because I saw it" is an example of an **empirical statement.** *Empirical* is a fancy word meaning "based on observation or experiment." The word *empirical* denotes that a statement is verifiable by means of observation. In the next paragraph we try to trace some of the sources of experiences you may have had during your lifetime.

*Empirical
statement*
A statement based
on observation or
experiment

Throughout our lives we participate in and learn about the world around us. We interact with people and generate our personal knowledge. In the beginning, we are born at a certain time, in a certain place, into a specific family that uses a specific language. When we are young, for example, our family is the most important source of our knowledge, our attitudes, and our values. As we grow older, other people and social institutions around us influence us more and more, including our peers, our religion, our schools (and libraries), our economy, and the various media we are exposed to or seek out. We learn the customs, beliefs, and traditions of the people around us. We learn "how things are," and our personal knowledge continues to be constructed. Over time, many of our actions and beliefs may seem to become "instinctual." That is, they may become automatic and unquestioned.

Expert Opinion

In an information-rich society like the United States, another source of our knowledge is what experts say. We rely on experts or authorities because we don't have time to sift through all of the information needed to answer each and every question. Listening to experts can be informative; however, experts don't always agree. And don't forget that some experts are not experts on the topic for which they are quoted. Some purported "experts" speak far beyond their fields of expertise, and they may actually know no more than you or I. For a humorous example, during the 1980s there was a television commercial that went something like this: "Hi. I'm not a doctor. I just play one on [soap opera]. And I recommend using Brand-X aspirin. It works." We always need to check the credentials of an expert, and we need to determine whether the expert has a vested interest in the particular statement being purported.

Reasoning

Rationalism
Idea that reason is
the primary source
of knowledge

Rationalism is the philosophical idea that reason is the primary source of knowledge. The idea is most often associated with René Descartes (1596–1650) and Benedict de Spinoza (1632–1677). Reason involves thinking about something and developing an understanding of it through reasoning. In its extreme form, rationalism means that some truths are knowable independent of observation. In its less extreme form, rationalism simply refers to the use of reason in developing understandings about the world. Deductive reasoning and inductive reasoning are two important forms of reasoning.

Deductive
reasoning
Drawing a
specific
conclusion from a
set of premises

    Deductive reasoning is the process of drawing a specific conclusion from a set of premises. In deductive reasoning, a conclusion will be true if the premises are true.

    One form of deductive reasoning is the syllogism. Here is an example:

Major Premise:	All schoolteachers are mortal.
Minor Premise:	John is a schoolteacher.
Conclusion:	Therefore, John is mortal.

According to this deductive argument, John must be a mortal. Keep in mind, however, that reasoning like this is dependent on the validity of the premises. Just try replacing the word *mortal* with the word *Martians* and then you will conclude that John is a Martian. In deductive reasoning the conclusion will be false if any of the premises are false. In our Martian example, the conclusion is false because the major premise stating "All schoolteachers are Martians" is false. Deductive reasoning can be very useful in helping us to understand things in our world, but we must always make sure that our premises are true. We need to be careful about what we assume when we draw our conclusions.

Inductive
reasoning
Reasoning from
the particular to
the general

    Inductive reasoning involves reasoning "from particular instances of something to a general statement about them, from individuals to universals" (Angeles, 1992, p. 144). We engage in inductive reasoning frequently in our lives when we observe many specific instances of some phenomenon and draw conclusions about it. For example, you have certainly observed all of your life that the sun appears every morning (except on cloudy days).

Probabilistic
Stating what is
likely to occur

Based on your observations you probably feel comfortable in concluding that the sun will make its appearance again tomorrow (if it is not cloudy). In this case you are indeed likely to be correct. But notice that when you use inductive reasoning you are using a **probabilistic** form of reasoning. That is, you are stating what is likely to occur, not what will necessarily occur. Because of this, you are taking a risk (albeit a small one in this case) because induction involves making conclusions that go beyond the evidence in the premises. This is not necessarily a problem, but you should be aware that it could be one.

Problem of
induction
Things that
happened in
the past may
not happen in
the future

The potential problem in inductive reasoning is known as the **problem of induction:** Although something may have happened many times in the past, it is still possible that it will not happen in the future. In short, the future may not resemble the past. Let's say that every cat you have ever seen had a tail. Using inductive reasoning, you may be led to conclude that "all cats have tails." You can see the problem here because one day you might run across a Manx cat, which has no tail. The point is that inductive reasoning can be useful in helping us to come up with generalizations about the world; however, we must remember that we have not proven our generalizations to be true. Our generalizations are only statements of probability.

THE SCIENTIFIC APPROACH TO KNOWLEDGE GENERATION

Science
An approach for
the generation of
knowledge

In this book, science is defined in a way that is inclusive of the different approaches to research discussed in this book. In particular, we define **science** as an approach for the generation of knowledge. The root of the word science is the Latin *scientia,* which means "knowledge." We define science as any systematic or carefully done actions carried out to answer questions or meet other needs of a developing research domain (e.g., describing things, exploring, experimenting, explaining). Science often involves the application of the scientific method; however, as philosophers and historians of science have pointed out, science can also include other methods and activities that are carried out by researchers as they attempt to generate scientific knowledge. Science goes beyond "taken for granted" knowledge (i.e., things assumed to be true) and is used to uncover more accurate descriptions and explanations of the world around us. In this book we will generally treat the term *science* (as just defined) and the term *research* as synonyms.

Dynamics of Science

Over time science results in an accumulation of specific findings, theories, and other knowledge. As a result, science is said to be progressive. When researchers conduct new research studies, they try to build on and extend current research theories and results. Sir Isaac Newton expressed it well when he stated, "We stand on the shoulders of giants." Newton's point was that researchers generally do not start from scratch, and Newton knew that he was no exception to this rule. In short, researchers usually build on past findings and understandings.

At the same time, science is dynamic and open to new ideas and theories that show promise. Different researchers approach research differently, and they often describe, explain, and interpret things in different, but perhaps complementary, ways. New ideas emerge. As new ideas are generated and evidence is obtained, results are presented at conferences and are published in monographs, books, and journals so that other members of the scientific community can examine them. Before findings are published in journals, the studies are usually evaluated by a group of experts called referees to make sure there are no major flaws and that the procedures are defensible. Researchers are usually required to report exactly how they conducted their research so that other researchers will have the opportunity to evaluate the procedures or even replicate the study. Once published, research findings are openly discussed and are critically evaluated by members of the scientific community. Overall, we can say that science is a never-ending process that includes rational thinking, the reliance on empirical observation, constant peer evaluation and critique, and, very important, active creativity and discovery.

Basic Assumptions of Science

Educational researchers must make a few general assumptions so that they can go about their daily business of doing research. At the most basic level, researchers assume there is a world out there that can be studied. Second, researchers assume there is some degree of "regularity" in the world that can be determined through research. For example, the next time you go to your research class, note the seats you and a few people around you are sitting in. When the class meets again, see whether you and the others sit in the same seats as during the previous meeting. You will probably notice that many of the people do. Why is this? This happens because humans are to some degree predictable, and because they are, many researchers hope to generalize their findings beyond the people and places used in their studies. Third, researchers not only believe that there is some regularity in the world, but also that there is "discoverability"—that is, it is possible to discover the regularity in human behavior. This does not mean that the task of discovering the nature of a phenomenon will be simple. Nature is very reluctant to reveal its secrets. For example, although significant progress has been made, we still do not know the exact causes of many learning disabilities. Research must continue, and over time we will find more and more pieces to the puzzle. One day we hope we will see the whole picture and be able to put the puzzle together.

Scientific Method

Hypothesis
A prediction or educated guess

Theory
An explanation or an explanatory system

Science is not a perfectly orderly process. Solso and Johnson put it well when they say science progresses in a "slow, fumbling, bumbling manner" (1994, p. 8). Science is a dynamic process that includes a countless number of activities. However, several of the key features of science are as follows: (1) making empirical observations, (2) generating and testing **hypotheses** (predictions or educated guesses), (3) building and testing **theories** (explanations), and (4) attempting to predict and influence the world to make it a better place to live (American Association for the Advancement of Science, 1990; Angeles, 1992). These four features are best understood as part of the scientific method.

Deductive method
A top-down or confirmatory approach to science

Inductive method
A bottom-up or generative approach to science

There are two important forms of the scientific method that need to be distinguished, the **deductive method** and the **inductive method.** Although both methods involve empirical observation, the observation occurs at different points. The basic deductive method includes three steps. First, the researcher states a hypothesis, which is frequently based on existing theory (i.e., currently available scientific explanations). Second, the researcher collects data to be used to test the hypothesis empirically. Third, the researcher makes the decision to tentatively accept or to reject the hypothesis based on the data. The basic inductive method also includes three steps. First, the researcher starts by making observations. Second, the researcher studies the observations and searches for a pattern (i.e., a statement of what is occurring). Third, the researcher makes a tentative conclusion about how some aspect of the world operates; that is, the researcher makes a generalization.

Sometimes the deductive method is called a top-down approach because it starts with a theory or hypothesis. The steps move from the general to the specific (theory—hypothesis—data). The inductive approach is sometimes called the bottom-up approach because it moves from the specific to the general: it starts with specific observations and then moves to a tentative generalization about how some aspect of the world operates. The deductive method is the traditional theory or hypothesis testing approach. The inductive method is known as the theory or hypothesis generation approach. Again, the deductive scientific method is used to test hypotheses (or test theories), and the inductive scientific method is used to discover or generate new hypotheses and tentative theoretical explanations that can be tested at a later time.

Theory

The inductive and deductive scientific methods both involve the concept of theory. The inductive approach focuses on *generating* or building theory and the deductive approach focuses on *testing* theory. The term *theory* as used in this book refers to an explanation or an explanatory system that discusses "how" a phenomenon operates and "why" it operates as it does. Theory refers to a generalization or set of generalizations used systematically to explain some phenomenon. In other words, a theory explains how something operates in general (i.e., for many people) and it moves beyond the findings of any single research study. Using a theory, you should be able to explain a phenomenon, make sense out of it, and be able to make predictions.

Rule of parsimony
Preferring the most simple theory that works

Criterion of falsifiability
Statements and theories should be "refutable"

One criterion sometimes used to judge theories is the **rule of parsimony.** A theory is parsimonious when it is simple, concise, and succinct. If two competing theories both explain and predict a phenomenon equally well, then the more parsimonious theory is to be preferred according to the rule of parsimony. In other words, simple theories are preferred over highly complex ones, other things being equal. Another important criterion for evaluating theories is the **criterion of falsifiability** (Popper, 1985). This is "the property of a statement or theory that it is capable of being refuted by experience" (Blackburn, 1994, p. 135). This idea was originally provided by Sir Karl Popper (1902–1994), who was one of the most important philosophers of science of the twentieth century. Popper also points out that we should not jump too quickly to reject a theory when one instance of it appears to falsify it. He says that we should "Propose theories which can be criticized. Think about possible decisive falsifying experiments—crucial experiments. But do not give up your theories too easily, not, at any rate, before you have critically examined your criticism" (Popper, 1974, p. 984). The key idea of the criterion of falsifiability is that if it is impossible to ever refute a statement or theory, then that statement or theory is not useful for science.

Now let's examine a theory. Several research studies have examined techniques for promoting attitude change. Dissonance theory was originally developed by Leon Festinger (1957) and has received some empirical support. According to dissonance theory, creating mental contradictions in people can lead them to change their attitudes. Dissonance is an uncomfortable state or form of mental anxiety that is caused by these contradictions. It is created when an individual holds contradictory beliefs or behaves in ways that contradict his or her beliefs. Because dissonance creates discomfort, people are motivated to reduce it. Festinger points out that people often rationalize in order to reduce their dissonance. They may, for example, change a belief or an attitude, reinterpret the situation that caused the dissonance, or add new beliefs. This theory was used to explain the surprising research finding that the more money people are paid to argue for a position that they oppose, the less they will change their attitudes toward it (Linder, Cooper, & Jones, 1967). This result is counterintuitive according to everyday thinking, which might predict that greater pay would result in greater attitude change.

Another more educational theory is called expectation theory. According to this theory, teachers' expectations about their students affect their behavior toward their students, which, in turn, affects their students' behavior. The theory is based on the self-fulfilling prophecy (Merton, 1948). Robert Rosenthal and Lenore Jacobson (1968) studied the effects of teachers' expectations and found that students whom teachers expected to perform well had higher increases in IQ than other students. These authors called this the Pygmalion effect. Rosenthal also found that "those children in whom intellectual growth was expected were described as having a significantly better chance of becoming successful in the future, as significantly more interesting, curious, and happy" (Rosenthal, 1991, p. 6). Students who had IQ increases, but had not been expected to have increases by the teachers, were not viewed more favorably by the teachers. These results suggest that teacher expectations can sometimes affect student performance. Note, however, that recent research has suggested that the power of expectations is not as great as had originally been concluded (Goldenberg, 1992). Nonetheless, the theory of expectations is a useful idea.

There are many other theories in education. A few are attribution theory, constructivism, critical theory, labeling theory, Kohlberg's theory of moral development, open systems theory, operant conditioning, parallel distributed processing, proximal development, rational emotive therapy, site based management, situated learning, and social learning theory. If you want to find out more about any of these theories, just go to the library and conduct a search using ERIC or one of the other computerized search tools located in your school library. (These tools are discussed in Chapter 2.) You will find plenty of references to get you started. Keep in mind as you read research articles that you will not always find the word *theory* in the article because there will often not be a well-developed theory available to the researcher or the researcher may not have a fancy name for his or her theory.

Still, you can view the authors' explanations of their findings as their attempts to develop a theory: theory most simply means "explanation."

Science and the Idea of Proof

Many beginning students believe that science and research are processes in which researchers constantly prove what is true. You may be surprised to learn that researchers rarely use the word *prove* when discussing their research findings. In fact, as we mentioned earlier, we recommend that you eliminate the word *prove* from your vocabulary when you are talking about research because most researchers hold knowledge to be ultimately tentative. They recognize that things that are believed to be true today may change eventually and that some findings may be found later to have only been partially true or even patently false. What we obtain in research is scientific "evidence." It is essential that you understand this point. An important educational methodologist, the late Fred Kerlinger (1986), made this point very clearly:

> The interpretation of research data culminates in conditional probabilistic statements of the "If *p*, then *q*" kind. We enrich such statements by qualifying them in some such way as: If *p*, then *q*, under conditions *r, s,* and *t. . . . Let us flatly assert that nothing can be "proved" scientifically. All one can do is to bring evidence to bear that such-and-such a proposition is true.* Proof is a deductive matter, and experimental methods of inquiry are not methods of proof. [emphasis added] (p. 145)

Replication
Research examining the same variables with different people

As you learn more about research, keep Kerlinger's point in mind. You should never place too much weight on a single research study. **Replication** by other researchers should make you more confident about a research finding because the resulting evidence is much stronger. When you are tempted to use the word *prove,* stop and think—you will learn more about the fundamental nature of research.

Objectives of Science

Exploration
Attempting to generate ideas about phenomena

Discussions of science often focus on the importance of explanation. However, there are several additional objectives that are also important if the field of educational research is to continue to operate effectively and progress. The first objective is **exploration.** Exploration is especially important in the early phases of research because researchers must generate ideas about phenomena before additional research can progress. To determine whether exploration was the objective of a research study, answer the following questions: (1) Were the researchers studying a phenomenon or some aspect of a phenomenon about which little was previously known? (2) Did the researchers choose to ignore previous research or explanations so that they could study a phenomenon without any preconceived notions? (3) Were the researchers trying to "discover" important factors or "generate" new ideas for further research? If you answer yes to any of these questions, then the researchers were probably operating in the exploratory mode of research.

As implied in questions 2 and 3, exploration does not always have to be done in the early phases of research. Sometimes researchers may want to enter the field without fixed or preconceived notions about what they are studying so that they can explore a phenomenon in a new way and so that they can avoid being biased or "blinded" by previous findings or theories. One of the articles mentioned earlier in this chapter (under Examples of Educational Research), titled "Giving Voice to High School Students," was exploratory because the researchers tried to uncover what at-risk students thought was important in their lives, why the students acted in the ways they did, and how they viewed various formal and informal groups (e.g., teachers). The researchers tried to describe the at-risk adolescents' beliefs and circumstances to explain why they acted as they did. One finding was that some at-risk students formed subcultures that were in conflict with the teachers' culture; that is, the groups differed on criteria such as values, beliefs, and activities that were considered appropriate. These differences made it difficult for the teachers and the students to communicate, which resulted in student apathy and boredom in the classroom.

The key to exploration is induction. In particular, the researcher explores the specifics of something or some situation in order to develop tentative hypotheses or generalizations about it. Exploration is similar to basic descriptive activities in that it often includes description. However, attempts are also frequently made in exploratory research to generate preliminary explanations or theories about how and why a phenomenon operates as it does.

Description
Attempting to describe the characteristics of a phenomenon

The second objective is **description.** To determine whether description was the main objective of a research study, answer the following questions: (1) Were the researchers primarily describing a phenomenon? (2) Were the researchers documenting the characteristics of some phenomenon? Description is one of the most basic activities in research. It may simply involve observing a phenomenon and recording what one sees. For example, a seasoned teacher may observe the behavior of a student teacher and take notes. At other times, description may rely on the use of quantitative measuring instruments such as standardized tests. For example, a researcher may want to measure the intangible construct called IQ, or intelligence quotient. To do this, the researcher must rely on some type of test that has been constructed specifically for this purpose. At other times, description may involve reporting attitudes and opinions about certain issues. For an example, see the September 1996 issue of *Phi Delta Kappan,* which reports national attitudes toward education each year. The study is conducted by the Gallup Organization and is commissioned by the education honor society Phi Delta Kappa. Two questions and their responses are shown in Figure 1.2 on page 16.

Explanation
Attempting to show how and why a phenomenon operates as it does

The third objective is **explanation.** According to many writers, this is the key purpose of science. To determine whether explanation was the primary objective of a research study, answer the following questions: (1) Were the researchers trying to develop a theory about a phenomenon to explain how and why it operates as it does? (2) Were the researchers trying to explain how certain phenomena operate by identifying the factors that produce change in them? More specifically, were the researchers studying cause-and-effect relationships? If the answer to any of these questions is yes, then the researchers' primary objective is probably explanation. The objective of the majority of educational research is explanation. An example of a research study focusing on explanation was the study mentioned above, titled "Creativity and Cooperation in the Elementary Music Classroom," by Baloche (1994). In that study Baloche was interested in determining the effect of a new curriculum on student creativity and cooperation levels; the focus was on cause and effect. In a study like this, the cause is used to "explain" the effect (i.e., the outcome).

FIGURE 1.2   Items from Phi Delta Kappa/Gallup Poll (September 1996).

Question: Would you favor or oppose a requirement for high school graduation that all students in the local public schools perform some kind of community service?

	National Totals %	No Children in School %	Public School Parents %	Nonpublic School Parents %
Favor	66	66	67	75
Oppose	32	32	32	25
Don't know	2	2	1	*

Question: Just your impression, do you think that the national dropout rate of students in high school is higher today than it was twenty-five years ago, lower today, or about the same as it was twenty-five years ago?

	National Totals %	No Children in School %	Public School Parents %	Nonpublic School Parents %
Higher	64	62	66	73
Lower	15	15	15	8
About the same	18	19	17	16
Don't know	3	4	2	3

*Less than one-half of 1%.

Prediction
Attempting to predict or forecast a phenomenon

The fourth objective is **prediction.** To determine whether prediction was the primary objective of a research study, answer the following question: Did the researchers conduct the research so that they could predict or forecast some event in the future? A researcher is able to make a prediction when certain information known in advance can be used to determine what will happen at a later point in time. Sometimes predictions can also be made from research studies in which the primary focus was on explanation. That is, when researchers determine cause-and-effect operations (explanations), they can use this information to form predictions.

One research study in which the focus was on prediction was conducted by Fuertes, Sedlacek, and Liu (1994). These researchers conducted a ten year research study and found that Asian American university students' academic performance and retention could be predicted using the Scholastic Assessment Test (SAT) and another instrument called the Noncognitive Questionnaire. The strongest predictor of the students' GPAs was their SAT math scores. Other useful predictors (from the Noncognitive Questionnaire) were community service, realistic self-appraisal, academic self-concept, nontraditional knowledge, and handling racism. The strongest predictors of enrollment (i.e., retention) were self-concept, realistic self-appraisal, and SAT math score.

Influence
Attempting to apply research

The fifth objective is called **influence.** This objective is different from the previous ones because it refers to the application of research knowledge rather than the generation of research knowledge. Here you should ask the following question: Were the researchers applying research knowledge to make something useful happen in the world? The ultimate objective of most social, behavioral, and educational research is to improve the world. Therefore, influence is important. For teachers, "influence" involves things like helping students to learn more than they previously knew, helping children with special needs, and preventing negative outcomes such as dropping out of school or disruptive behavior in the classroom. For counselors, influence may involve helping clients to overcome psychological problems such as depression, personality disorders, and dysfunctional behaviors.

As you work through this book and learn about the different methods of research, you will be learning more about these objectives. At this point you should be able to examine a research article and determine what the researcher's objectives were. Don't be surprised if there appears to be more than one objective. That is not at all uncommon. You should also be aware that researchers often use the terms *descriptive research, exploratory research, explanatory research,* and *predictive research.* When they do this, they are simply describing the primary objective of the research.

QUANTITATIVE AND QUALITATIVE RESEARCH

Quantitative research
Research relying primarily on the collection of quantitative data

Qualitative research
Research relying primarily on the collection of qualitative data

Our description of science and research so far has been general. For example, we suggest that all researchers hope to generate useful knowledge about the world. We also suggest that, taken as a whole, science involves at least five key objectives. Now you will learn about the two major approaches to research called quantitative research and qualitative research. **Quantitative research** is defined as research relying primarily on the collection of quantitative data (i.e., numerical data). On the other hand, **qualitative research** is research relying primarily on the collection of qualitative data (i.e., nonnumerical data such as words and pictures). Although our definitions of quantitative and qualitative research are straightforward, researchers following these approaches tend to have different views of research, and they typically go about studying the world in different ways. Although the approaches are different, we believe that both approaches can be used to generate important and useful knowledge. Figure 1.3 on page 18 provides an overview of some of the typical differences between quantitative and qualitative research.

First, the quantitative research approach focuses on the deductive component of the scientific method because the focus is generally on hypothesis testing and theory testing. Quantitative research is also sometimes said to be "confirmatory" because researchers test or attempt to "confirm" their hypotheses. On the other hand, qualitative research relies more on the inductive form of the scientific method and is therefore used to come up with or generate new hypotheses and theories. Qualitative research is often exploratory; that is, it is frequently used when little is known about a certain topic or when an inductive approach is deemed more appropriate.

You should understand that the inductive–deductive distinction is somewhat artificial because at some point in the research process, quantitative and qualitative researchers use both induction and deduction. In particular, scientific reasoning is a cyclical process of induction *and* deduction. In quantitative research, hypotheses are typically deduced from a

FIGURE 1.3 Emphases of qualitative and quantitative research.

	Quantitative Research	*Qualitative Research*
Scientific method	Deductive method; used to test hypotheses and theory	Inductive method; used to generate hypotheses and theory
View of human behavior	Behavior is lawlike	Behavior is fluid and dynamic
Most common research objective	Explanatory	Exploratory
Focus	Narrow-angle lens	Wide-angle lens
Nature of observation	Study behavior under tightly controlled conditions	Study behavior naturalistically; study the context of behavior
Nature of reality	Objective	Socially constructed
Form of data collected	Collect quantitative data based on precise measurement (e.g., rating scales, response time)	Collect qualitative data (interviews, observations, field notes); researcher is the principal data collection instrument.
Nature of data	Numbers	Words
Data analysis	Statistical relationships	Search for themes, patterns, holism
Form of final report	Statistical report	Narrative report

theory or currently available explanations, and the predicted observable outcomes are deduced from the hypotheses. Data are then collected to determine whether the hypotheses, and as a result the theory or explanation, are supported. However, it is common for unanticipated outcomes to appear in quantitative research findings. When this happens, quantitative researchers commonly enter the inductive mode of generating new or revised hypotheses and explanations, which will be put to test during a future research study. Likewise, in qualitative research, after inductive hypotheses and a tentative theory are generated from observations, the observable consequences of these are often deduced and then tested through additional observations. Overall, when we say that quantitative research is more deductive and qualitative research is more inductive, it is really a matter of emphasis, not exclusion.

Quantitative and qualitative research are also distinguished by different views of human behavior. It is generally assumed in quantitative research that behavior is lawlike. The assumption of **determinism** is made, which means all events have a cause (Salmon, 1984). For example, the process by which children learn to read is determined by one or more causes. Likewise, there are causes for adolescents dropping out of school. Because quantitative research has not identified any unerring laws of human behavior, most contemporary quantitative researchers search for **probabilistic causes** (Humphreys, 1989). A probabilistic statement may go, "Adolescents who become involved with drugs and alcohol are more likely to drop out of high school than adolescents who do not become involved with drugs and alcohol." The point is that most quantitative researchers try to identify

Determinism
All events have causes

Probabilistic causes
Causes that usually produce an outcome

cause-and-effect relationships that enable them to make probabilistic predictions and generalizations. On the other hand, qualitative researchers often focus on the fluid and dynamic dimensions of behavior. Behavior is seen to be more situational and context bound than generalizable across contexts. Different groups are said to construct different realities, and, as a result, patterns of behavior are found but may vary from group to group. These views are not, however, set in stone. For example, quantitative researchers also sometimes study the influence of context and the dynamic processes of behavior (e.g., social psychologists examine individuals as they interact in social situations). Likewise, qualitative researchers often try to develop explanations of behavior (theories) that sometimes include causal-type language and attempt to make generalizations. Still the distinctions between quantitative and qualitative research generally hold and are used to define and distinguish the two approaches.

Quantitative research often uses a narrow-angle lens in the sense that only one or a few factors are studied at the same time. Often, through experimental control, researchers attempt to hold constant the factors not being studied. This is often accomplished under laboratory conditions, in which an experimenter randomly assigns participants to groups, manipulates only one factor, and then examines the outcome. For example, a researcher might first randomly assign research volunteers to two groups. Random assignment helps achieve experimental control because it makes the two groups similar. Then the researcher might expose one group to a new teaching method and use the traditional lecture method on the other group. The researcher examines which teaching approach results in the most learning and attributes the difference to the teaching method received. The researcher is able to make a causal attribution because the two groups were similar at the start of the experiment and the only factor they differed on was which teaching method they received.

On the other hand, qualitative research uses a wide-angle lens, examining behavior as it occurs naturalistically in all of its detail. Qualitative researchers do not want to intervene in the natural flow of behavior because they believe that this intervention would change the behavior. Qualitative researchers study behavior holistically. They try to look at many dimensions and layers of behavior, such as the types of people in a group, how they interact, and what kinds of agreements or norms they have, and how these dimensions come together to describe the group. For example, perhaps a qualitative researcher wants to study the social climate and culture of a highly successful school. He or she would probably spend a great deal of time studying the many aspects and dimensions of the school in order to come up with an analysis of how the school operates and why it is successful.

Quantitative researchers operate under the assumption of objectivity. First, they assume that there is an objective reality "out there" to be observed. It is assumed that rational observers who look at the same phenomenon in the world will basically agree on its existence. Second, quantitative researchers claim to remain objective when they carry out their research. They try to remain "value-free," and they attempt to avoid human bias whenever possible. For example, standardized questionnaires and other quantitative measuring tools are often used to measure carefully what is observed. In experiments researchers frequently use a random process to assign participants to different groups in order to eliminate the possibility of human bias while constructing different groups for comparison. In judging results, statistical criteria are often used to form conclusions.

Qualitative researchers sometimes challenge the concept of objective reality and argue that reality is constructed differently by different groups of people through the operation of language and common experiences, values, concerns, and beliefs. Some qualitative researchers suggest that "reality is socially constructed" (e.g., Guba & Lincoln, 1989). An example of this viewpoint is that Eskimos may "see" many types of snow, whereas the average person will probably only see a few types. The Eskimos' experiences may allow them to see something real (to them) that we do not see. In terms of the importance of remaining objective during the collection of data, many qualitative researchers would agree with the quantitative researchers. However, in qualitative research the researcher is said to be the "instrument of data collection." Rather than using a standardized instrument, the researcher must collect the data, ask the questions, and make the interpretations about what is observed. In addition, the researcher must try to understand the people he or she is observing from their viewpoint. This is the concept of "empathetic understanding" (what Max Weber called *verstehen*)—understanding something from that person's viewpoint (Taylor & Bogdan, 1984; Weber, 1968). This is similar to the familiar idea of putting yourself into someone else's shoes.

Quantitative research generally reduces measurement to numbers. In survey research, for example, attitudes are usually measured using rating scales. The following five-point agreement scale is an example: (1) Strongly Disagree, (2) Disagree, (3) Neutral, (4) Agree, (5) Strongly Agree. The interviewer makes a statement and the respondents reply with one of the five allowable response categories. After all respondents are asked a question, the researcher typically calculates and reports an average for the group of respondents. Let us say, for example, that a researcher asks a group of teachers for their degree of agreement with the following statement: "Teachers need more training in the area of child psychopathology." The researcher might then calculate the average response for the whole group, which might be 4.15 based on a five-point scale. The researcher might also determine whether the ratings vary by years of teaching experience. Perhaps the average agreement for new teachers is 4.5 and the average for teachers with five or more years of experience is 3.9. As you might guess, quantitative data are usually analyzed using statistical analysis programs on a computer.

On the other hand, qualitative researchers do not usually collect data in the form of numbers. Rather, they frequently conduct observations and in-depth interviews, and the data are usually in the form of words. For example, a qualitative researcher may conduct a focus group discussion with six or seven new teachers to discuss the adequacy of their undergraduate educational programs in preparing them to deal with real-world problems that they face in schools. The facilitator of the focus group would probably videotape the group and tape record what was said. Later, the recording would be transcribed into words, which would then be analyzed using the techniques of qualitative data analysis (see Chapter 15). Also, when a qualitative researcher enters the field and makes observations, he or she will write down what he or she sees, as well as relevant insights and thoughts. The data are again in the form of words. During qualitative data analysis, the researcher will try to identify categories that describe what happened as well as general themes appearing again and again in the data.

Finally, qualitative and quantitative research reports tend to differ. Quantitative reports are commonly reported in journal articles ranging from five to fifteen pages. The reports will include many numbers and results of statistical significance testing (to be explained later). In contrast, qualitative research reports are generally longer, and they are written in narrative form describing what was found and including interpretations to make sense out of it. Qualitative journal articles are frequently twenty to thirty pages long, and the results of qualitative research are often published in the form of books or monographs rather than journal articles.

QUANTITATIVE RESEARCH METHODS: EXPERIMENTAL AND NONEXPERIMENTAL RESEARCH

You now know some of the characteristics of quantitative and qualitative research. We save further discussion of qualitative research for later chapters. Here, we introduce some of the different methods of quantitative research. Before doing so, however, you need to know about variables, because quantitative researchers usually describe the world by using variables, and they attempt to explain and predict aspects of the world by demonstrating the relationships among variables.

Variables

Variable
A condition or characteristic that can take on different values or categories

A **variable** is defined as a condition or characteristic that can take on different values or categories. A much-studied educational variable is intelligence, which varies from low to high for different people. Age is another variable that varies from low to high (e.g., from 1 minute old to 130 years old or so). Another variable is gender, which is either male or female. To better understand the concept of a variable, it is helpful to compare it with a **constant,** its opposite. A constant is a single value or category of a variable. A constant is a single condition or characteristic. Here's the idea: the variable gender is a marker for two constants—male and female. The category (i.e., constant) "male" is a marker for only one thing; it is one of the two constants forming the variable called gender. Gender varies but "male" does not vary. Therefore, gender is a variable, and male is a constant. In the case of the variable called age, all of the ages make up the values (i.e., constants) of the variable, and each value (e.g., twelve years old or thirteen years old) is a constant. If you are still having a hard time with the distinction between a variable and a constant, think of it like this: a variable is like a set of things, and a constant is *one* of those things.

Constant
A single value or category of a variable

The variables we just used, age and gender, are actually different types of variables. Age is an example of a quantitative variable, and gender is an example of a categorical variable. A **quantitative variable** is a variable that varies in degree or amount. It usually involves numbers. A **categorical variable** is a variable that varies in type or kind. It usually involves different groups. As described in the previous paragraph, age takes on numbers (e.g., number of years old) and gender takes on two types or kinds (male and female). Now consider the variable annual income. How does it vary? It varies in amount, ranging from no income at all last year to some very large amount of income. Therefore, income is a

Quantitative variable
A variable that varies in degree or amount

Categorical variable
A variable that varies in type or kind

Independent variable
A variable that is presumed to cause a change in another variable

Dependent variable
A variable that is presumed to be influenced by one or more independent variables

Cause-and-effect relationship
Relationship in which one variable affects another variable

quantitative variable. If you think about how much money you made last year, you can determine your value on the variable annual income. Now think about the variable religion. How does this variable vary? It varies in kind or type. It can take on any of the categories standing for the different world religions (e.g., Christianity, Judaism, and Islam). If you need a little more practice identifying quantitative and categorical variables, take a look at the examples in Figure 1.4.

Yet another categorization scheme for variables is to speak of independent and dependent variables. An **independent variable** is a variable *presumed* to cause a change in another variable. Sometimes the independent variable is manipulated by the researcher (i.e., the researcher determines the value of the independent variable); at other times, the independent variable is studied by the researcher but is not directly manipulated (i.e., the researcher studies what happens when an independent variable naturally changes). The independent variable is also called an antecedent variable because it must come before another variable if it is to produce a change in it. A **dependent variable** is the variable that researchers study to determine the influence of one or more independent variables. The dependent variable is the variable that is "dependent on" the antecedent (i.e., independent) variable(s). A **cause-and-effect relationship** between an independent variable and a dependent variable is present when changes in the independent variable tend to cause changes in the dependent variable. Sometimes researchers call the dependent variable an outcome variable or a response variable because it is used to measure the impact of one or more independent variables.

FIGURE 1.4   Examples of quantitative and categorical variables.

Quantitative Variables	*Categorical variables*
Height	Gender
Weight	Religion
Temperature	Ethnicity
Annual income	Method of therapy
Most aptitude tests	College major
Most achievement tests	Political party identification
School size	Type of school
Class size	Marital status of parents
Self-esteem level	Student retention (retained or not)
Grade point average	Type of teacher expectation
Teacher-pupil ratio	Native language
Time spent on homework	Teaching method
Age	Personality type
Anxiety level	Learning style
Job satisfaction score	Type of feedback
Number of behavioral outbursts	Computer use (or not)
Reading performance	Type of reading instruction
Spelling accuracy	Inclusion (or not)
Number of performance errors	Problem solving strategy used
Rate of cognitive processing	Memory strategy used

Here is a simple example of a cause-and-effect relationship. Think about the U.S. Surgeon General's warning written on cigarette packages: "Smoking Causes Lung Cancer, Heart Disease, Emphysema, and May Complicate Pregnancy." Can you identify the independent and dependent variables in this relationship? It is smoking that is presumed to cause lung cancer and several other diseases. (You should be aware that extensive research beyond simply observing that smoking and lung cancer were associated was conducted to establish that the link between smoking and cancer was causal.) In this example, smoking is the independent variable (with the values corresponding to the number of cigarettes smoked a day) and presence of lung cancer is the dependent variable (with the values being lung cancer present and lung cancer not present). For shorthand we could use *IV* to stand for independent variable and *DV* to stand for dependent variable. We also sometimes use an arrow: *IV* → *DV*. The arrow (→) means "tends to cause changes in" or "affects." In words, this says that the researcher believes "changes in the independent variable tend to cause changes in the dependent variable." In the smoking example, we write Smoking → Presence of Lung Cancer.

Intervening variable
A variable that occurs between two other variables

Another type of variable is an **intervening variable.** An intervening variable occurs between two other variables in a causal chain. In the case *X* → *Y* we have only an independent variable and a dependent variable. In the case *X* → *I* → *Y* we have an intervening variable (*I*) occurring between the two other variables. In the case of smoking, perhaps an intervening variable is the development of cancer cells. It is helpful to identify intervening variables because these variables may help explain the process by which an independent variable causes a change in a dependent variable. As another example, let *X* stand for teaching approach (perhaps the levels of the variable are lecture and cooperative groups) and let *Y* stand for test score on class exam (varying from 0 to 100 percent correct). Research may show that *X* → *Y*; that is, test scores depend on which teaching approach is used. In this case, an intervening variable might be enjoyment of school (varying from strong dislike to strong liking for school). Therefore, the full causal chain is *X* → *I* → *Y*, where *X* is teaching approach, *I* is enjoyment of school, and *Y* is test scores. So that you don't get confused when you read research articles, you also need to know that intervening variables are sometimes called *mediator variables* (Baron & Kenny, 1986). Don't be alarmed, because the words are synonyms.

Experimental Research

Experimental research
Research in which the researcher manipulates the independent variable

The purpose of **experimental research** is to determine cause-and-effect relationships. The experimental research method enables us to identify causal relationships because it allows us to observe, under controlled conditions, the effects of systematically changing one or more variables. Specifically, in experimental research the researcher actively intervenes in the world and then observes what happened. Thus, **manipulation** is the key defining characteristic of experimental research. The use of manipulation in determining cause-and-effect relationships is based on the activity theory of causation (Collingwood, 1940; Cook & Shadish, 1994). Active manipulation is not involved in any other type of research. Because of this (and because of experimental control), experimental research provides the strongest evidence of all the research methods about the existence of cause-and-effect relationships.

Manipulation
An intervention studied by an experimenter

In a simple experiment, a researcher will systematically vary an independent variable and assess its effects on a dependent variable. For example, perhaps an educational researcher wants to determine the effect of a new teaching approach on reading achievement. The researcher could perform the new teaching approach with one group of participants and perform the traditional teaching approach with another group of participants. After the treatment, the experimenter would determine which group showed the greatest amount of learning (reading achievement). If the group receiving the new teaching approach showed the greatest gain, then the researcher would tentatively conclude that the new approach is better than the traditional approach.

Although the type of experiment just described is sometimes done, there is a potential problem with it. What if the two groups of students differed on variables such as vocabulary, reading ability, age, and so on? More specifically, what if the students in the new teaching approach group happened to be older, had better vocabularies, and were better readers than the students in the traditional teaching approach group? Furthermore, perhaps the students with better vocabularies, who were older, and who were better readers also tended to learn more quickly than other students. If this were true, then it is likely that the students in the new teaching approach group would have learned faster regardless of teaching approach. In this example, the variables age, vocabulary, and reading ability are called extraneous variables. **Extraneous variables** are variables other than the independent variable of interest (e.g., teaching approach) that may be related to the outcome. When extraneous variables are not "controlled for," or dealt with in some way, an outside reviewer of the research study may come up with competing explanations for the research findings. These competing explanations are sometimes called *alternative explanations.* They are also frequently called *rival hypotheses* by many researchers. In our example, the researcher is not able to know whether the students in the new teaching approach performed better because of the teaching approach or because they had better vocabularies, were older, or were better readers. All these factors are said to be "confounded"; that is, these factors are entangled with the independent variable and the researcher can't state with any degree of confidence which is the most important factor. Sometimes we call these uncontrolled extraneous variables confounding variables.

Extraneous variable A variable that may compete with the independent variable in explaining the outcome

Because the presence of extraneous variables makes the interpretation of research findings very difficult, the effective researcher attempts to control them whenever possible. The best way to control for extraneous variables in an experiment like the one above is to randomly assign research participants to the groups to be compared; that is, random assignment is the most effective technique of experimental control. *Random assignment helps ensure that the people in the groups to be compared are similar prior to the intervention or manipulation.* For example, if the researcher wants to randomly assign thirty people to two groups, then the researcher might put thirty slips of paper, each with one name on it, into a hat and randomly pull out fifteen pieces. The fifteen names pulled out will become one of the two groups and the fifteen names remaining in the hat will become the other group. When this is done, the only differences between the groups will be due to chance. In other words, the people in the groups will be "similar" at the start of the experiment. After making the groups similar, the researcher administers the levels of the independent variable, making the groups different *only* on this variable. Perhaps teaching method is the independent variable and the levels are cooperative learning and lecture. The administration of the independent variable, or manipulation, would involve exposing one group to cooperative learning and the other group to lecture. Then, if the two groups become different after the manipulation, the researcher will know that the difference was due to the independent variable. In summary, (1) the experimenter uses random assignment to make the groups similar; (2) the experimenter does something different with the groups; and (3) if the groups then become different the experimenter concludes that the difference was due to what the experimenter did (i.e., it was due to the independent variable). We will introduce you, in later chapters, to additional methods used to control for extraneous variables when you are not able to use random assignment. For now, remember that random assignment to groups is the most effective way to make the groups similar and therefore control for extraneous variables.

Nonexperimental Research

Nonexperimental research
Research in which the independent variable is not manipulated and there is no random assignment to groups

In **nonexperimental research,** random assignment to groups is not possible, and there is no manipulation of an independent variable by the researcher. As a result, evidence gathered in support of cause-and-effect relationships is severely limited. Nonetheless, when important questions need to be answered, research must still be conducted, even if an experiment cannot be done. It is important to remember that *your research question should determine what you study, not your preference for a particular research method.* For example, during the 1960s extensive research linking cigarette smoking to lung cancer was conducted. Experimental research with humans was not possible because it would have been unethical. Therefore, in addition to experimental research with laboratory animals, medical researchers relied on nonexperimental research methods for their extensive research with humans.

Causal-comparative research
A form of nonexperimental research in which the primary independent variable of interest is categorical

One type of nonexperimental research is called **causal-comparative research.** Typically, in this type of research the researcher studies the relationship between one or more *categorical* independent variables and one or more quantitative dependent variables. In the most basic or "simple" case, there is a single categorical independent variable and a single quantitative dependent variable. Because the independent variable is categorical in causal-comparative research (e.g., males versus females; parents versus nonparents; or public school teachers versus private school teachers), the different groups' average scores on a dependent variable are "compared" to determine whether a relationship is present between the independent and dependent variables. For example, if the independent variable is student retention (where the categories of the variable are retained in the first grade and not retained in the first grade) and the dependent variable is level of achievement, then the retained students' average achievement would be compared to the nonretained students' average achievement. (Which group do you think would have higher achievements, on average, the retained or the nonretained students?)

Despite the presence of the term *causal* included in the title of "causal-comparative research," you must keep in mind that causal-comparative research is a nonexperimental research method, which means that there is *no manipulation* of an independent variable by a researcher. Furthermore, techniques of controlling for extraneous variables are more limited compared to experimental research (in which random assignment may be possible).

Because of the lack of manipulation and weaker techniques of controlling for extraneous variables, it is difficult to make statements about cause and effect. In short, do not be misled by the word *causal* in the name of this type of research, and remember that experimental research is virtually always better for determining cause and effect than is causal-comparative research or any other type of nonexperimental research.

An example of causal-comparative research is a study titled "Gender Differences in Mathematics Achievement and Other Variables among University Students" (Rech, 1996). Rech compared the average performance levels of males with the average performance levels of females in intermediate algebra and college algebra courses at a large urban commuter university. In the intermediate algebra course, Rech found that women did slightly better than males. The average percentage correct for females was 75 percent, and the average percentage correct for males was 73.8 percent. In the college algebra course, the difference in female and male performance was even smaller (74.3 percent versus 73.9 percent). The data were collected from more than 2,300 research participants over six semesters.

It was mentioned earlier that the most basic case of causal-comparative research involves a single categorical independent variable and a single quantitative dependent variable. To "design" a basic causal-comparative study as an exercise, look at Figure 1.4 and find a categorical variable that can serve as your independent variable and find a quantitative variable that can be your dependent variable. As an example, we can select retention for an independent variable and self-esteem as a dependent variable. We hypothesize that student retention (retained versus nonretained) has an influence on self-esteem. More specifically, we predict that retained students will have lower self-esteems than nonretained students. We would have to go to a school and collect data if we actually wanted to conduct a research study to see whether there is any support for this hypothesis.

You may ask why a researcher would use a causal-comparative study rather than an experiment since experiments are more effective in determining cause and effect relationships. Gay (1996) provides a nice answer: "Independent variables in causal-comparative studies are variables which cannot be manipulated (e.g., sex, male-female), should not be manipulated (e.g., prenatal care), or simply are not manipulated, but could be (e.g., method of instruction)" (p. 17). Because there is no manipulation, the results of causal-comparative research can provide only limited or preliminary evidence about causality. Furthermore, to obtain evidence about causality, the researcher must always make careful attempts to control for extraneous variables. You will learn more about this issue in later chapters.

Another nonexperimental research method is called **correlational research.** Like causal-comparative research, there is *no manipulation* of an independent variable in correlational research. Rather, in correlational research the researcher typically studies the relationships among two or more quantitative variables. That is, in most correlational research the independent and dependent variables are quantitative. The purposes of correlational research are typically to learn about the relationships among variables and to make predictions based on an understanding of the relationships. To understand how to study the relationship between two variables when both variables are quantitative, you need a basic understanding of a correlation coefficient.

A **correlation coefficient** is an index that provides information about the strength and direction of the relationship between two variables. It provides information about how

---

Correlational research
A form of nonexperimental research in which the primary independent or predictor variable of interest is quantitative

Correlation coefficient
An index indicating the strength and direction of relationship between two variables

two variables are associated. More specifically, a correlation coefficient is a number that can range from –1 to 1, with zero standing for no correlation at all. If the number is greater than zero, you have a positive correlation. If the number is less than zero, you have a negative correlation. If the number is equal to zero, then there is no correlation between the two variables being correlated. If the number is equal to +1.00 or if it is equal to –1.00, the correlation is called perfect; that is, it is as strong as possible. Now we provide an explanation of these points.

Positive correlation Two variables move in the same direction

A **positive correlation** is present when scores on two variables tend to move in the same direction. For example, consider the variables high school GPA and SAT (the college entrance exam). How do you think scores on these two variables are related? A diagram of this relationship is shown in Figure 1.5(a). As you can see in Figure 1.5(a), the students who have high GPAs tend also to have high scores on the SAT, and students who have low GPAs tend to have low scores on the SAT. That's the relationship. We say that GPA and SAT are positively correlated because as SAT scores increase, GPAs also tend to increase (i.e., the variables move in the same direction). Because of this relationship, researchers can use SAT scores to help make predictions about GPAs. However, because the correlation is not "perfect" the prediction is also far from perfect.

Negative correlation Two variables move in opposite directions

A **negative correlation** is present when the scores on two variables tend to move in opposite directions. For example, consider the variables amount of daily cholesterol consumption and life expectancy. How do you think these variables are related? Do you think the relationship meets the definition of a negative correlation? A diagram of this relationship is shown in Figure 1.5(b). You can see that as daily cholesterol consumption increases, life expectancy tends to decrease. That is, the variables move in the opposite direction. As one variable goes up, the other tends to go down, and vice versa. Therefore, researchers can

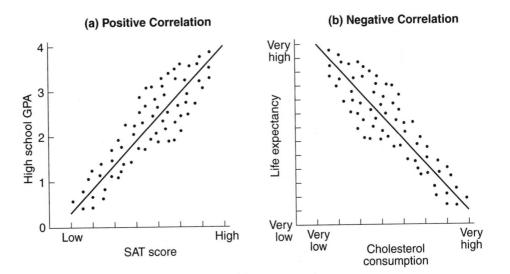

FIGURE 1.5   Examples of positive and negative correlation.

use information about cholesterol consumption to help predict life expectancies. High values on one variable are associated with low values on the other variable, and vice versa. This is what we mean by a negative correlation.

At this point you know the difference between a positive correlation (the variables move in the same direction) and a negative correlation (the variables move in opposite directions). There is, however, one more point about a correlation coefficient that you need to know. In addition to the "direction" of a correlation (positive or negative), we are interested in the strength of the correlation. By "strength," we mean "How strong is the relationship?" Remember this point: zero means no relationship at all, and +1.00 and −1.00 mean the relationship is as strong as possible.

The larger the size of the number, *ignoring the sign if it is negative,* the *stronger* the relationship. For example, if you have a negative correlation of −.5, then ignore the negative sign and you have .5, which shows the *strength* of the correlation. Therefore, a correlation of −.5 and a correlation of +.5 have the same strength. The only difference between the two is the direction of the relationship (−.5 is a negative correlation and +.5 is a positive correlation). *It does not matter whether a correlation is positive or negative when you are interested in its strength.* The strength of a correlation operates like this: zero stands for no correlation at all (i.e., it is the smallest possible strength) and +1.00 and −1.00 are as strong as a correlation can ever be. That is, +1.00 and −1.00 are equally strong; in research jargon, we say that both +1.00 and −1.00 are "perfect correlations." The only difference between +1.00 and −1.00 is the direction of the relationship, not the strength. (If you want to see some diagrams of correlations of different strengths and directions, take a look at Appendix C.)

If you didn't like the previous paragraph, here is a different way to determine how strong a correlation is. Simply check to see how far away the number is from zero. The farther the number is from zero the stronger the correlation. A correlation of .9 is stronger than a correlation of .2 because it is farther from zero. Likewise, a correlation of −.9 is stronger than a correlation of −.2 because it, too, is farther from zero. Now for a trick question. Which correlation do you believe is stronger: −.90 or +.80? The answer is −.90 because −.90 is farther from zero than +.80. (I think you've got it!)

This is only a brief introduction to the idea of a correlation coefficient. You will become more comfortable with the concept the more you use it, and we will be using the concept often in later chapters. For now, you should clearly understand that you can have positive and negative correlations or no correlation at all, and that some correlations are stronger than other correlations. You have learned more already than you thought you would, haven't you!

In the most basic form of correlational research, the researcher examines the correlation between two quantitative variables. For example, perhaps an educational psychologist has a theory stating that global self-esteem (which is a relatively stable personality trait) should predict class performance. More specifically, it is predicted that students entering a particular history class with high self-esteem will tend to do better than students entering the class with low self-esteem, and vice versa. To test this hypothesis, the researcher could collect the relevant data and calculate the correlation between self-esteem and performance on the class examinations. We would expect a positive correlation (i.e., the higher the self-esteem, the higher the performance on the history exam). In our hypothetical example, let's say that the correlation was +.5. That is a medium-size positive correlation, and it would support our hypothesis of a positive correlation.

The researcher would be able to say very little about cause and effect based on the correlation of .5 in our example of self-esteem and class performance. About all that one can claim is that there is a relationship between self-esteem and class performance—the higher the self-esteem the better the class performance. This is similar to the basic case of the causal-comparative research, where there is one independent variable and one dependent variable. There are three main problems with the basic cases of correlational and causal-comparative research described in this chapter: (1) there is no manipulation of the independent variable by the researcher, (2) it is difficult to determine the temporal order of the variables (i.e., which variable occurs first), and (3) there are usually too many other reasons why we might observe the relationship; that is, there are usually too many extraneous variables that are unexplained.

Remember this important point: you must *not* jump to a conclusion about cause and effect in a nonexperimental research study in which the researcher has examined only the relationship between two variables, such as examining a correlation coefficient in correlational research or comparing two group means in causal-comparative research. Simply finding a relationship between self-esteem and class performance (correlational research) or between gender and class performance (causal-comparative research) is *not sufficient evidence for concluding that the relationship is causal.* Therefore, you must not jump to that conclusion. We will discuss the issue of cause and effect more in later chapters. For now, make sure you remember that experimental research with random assignment is the single best method for determining cause-and-effect relationships and that nonexperimental research methods are much weaker.

> *Ethnography*
> A form of qualitative research focused on describing the culture of a group of people

QUALITATIVE RESEARCH METHODS: ETHNOGRAPHY AND HISTORICAL RESEARCH

Ethnography

> *Culture*
> The shared attitudes, values, norms, practices, language, and material things of a group of people

> *Holistic description*
> The description of how members make up a group

Ethnography is one of the most popular approaches to qualitative research used by educational researchers. The word **ethnography** literally means "writing about people." When ethnographers conduct research, they are usually interested in describing the **culture** of a group of people and learning what it is like to be a member of the group from the perspective of the members of the group. That is, they are interested in documenting things like the attitudes, values, norms, practices, patterns of interaction, perspectives, meanings, interpretations, and language of a group of people. They may also be interested in the material things that the group members either produce or use, such as clothing styles, ethnic foods, and architectural styles. Ethnographers try to be **holistic;** they try to describe how the individual members of a group interact and how they come together to make up the group as a whole. In other words, the group is more than just the sum of its parts. Just a few of the many groups recently studied by educational ethnographers are poor and working-class white and African American men (Weis & Fine, 1996), teachers in Mohawk communities in Canada (McAlpine, Eriks-Brophy, & Crago, 1996), collegiate basketball players (Adler & Adler, 1991), Puerto Rican American parents with children in special education (Harry, 1992), Native American students who drop out of school (Deyhle, 1992), and teachers suffering from burnout (Dworkin, 1987).

Historical Research

Historical research Research about events in the past

The last general type of research used by educational researchers and discussed in this introductory chapter is **historical research**. Historical research is done so that researchers can better understand events that occurred in the past. Educational historians have been able to find historical data that lend themselves to data analysis and can be used to study how various educational phenomena operated in the past. For example, educational researchers document the history of education and important events that occurred in the past, they study trends in education occurring over time, they study the multiple factors that led to certain events in the past, and they study how things operated in the past (e.g., different teaching practices and the different outcomes resulting from those practices). They may also study the origin of current practices and document any changes over time. *Historiography* is the word historians often use to mean "research methods." As you will learn in Chapter 12, historiography involves the posing of questions, the collection of authentic source materials, the analysis and interpretation of those materials, and the composition of the results into a final report. Historical research, like the other methods of research, has an important place in education.

MULTIMETHOD RESEARCH

The forms of research we have covered in this introductory chapter are shown in Figure 1.7. We will discuss each of these types of research in more depth in later chapters. In addition, we will add several more types of research to this list. It is important to understand that *all of the major types of research we discuss in this textbook have value*. It is not uncommon for an educational researcher to use several different types of research at different times. A researcher will select the appropriate research method based on a consideration of the research question(s) of interest, the objective(s) of the research, time and cost constraints, available populations, the possibility (or not) of the manipulation of an independent variable, and the availability of data. Sometimes a researcher will use more than one research approach within a single study. However, even if researchers never used more than one method in a single study, published research literatures would still tend to include articles based on different approaches and methods because of the diversity of the researchers working in the area.

Multimethod approach The use of more than one research method

We view the use of multiple perspectives, theories, and research methods as a strength in educational research. According to the **multimethod approach** to research, the use of more than one method of research can be beneficial. In fact, we view the quantitative

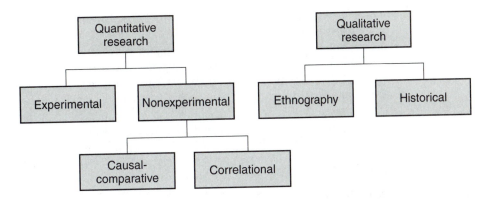

FIGURE 1.7 Major types of research discussed in Chapter 1. We will add more methods to this list in later chapters.

and qualitative research approaches and the specific quantitative and qualitative research methods as complementary. A tenet of the multimethod approach is that it is wise to collect multiple sets of data using different research methods with "nonoverlapping weaknesses in addition to their complementary strengths" (Brewer & Hunter, 1989; Webb, Campbell, Schwartz, Sechrest, & Grove, 1981). This often helps to improve the quality of research because the different research methods have different strengths and different weaknesses.

By combining two (or more) research methods with different strengths and weaknesses in a research study, you can make it less likely that you will make a mistake. Lincoln and Guba (1985) explain this idea using the metaphor of fish nets. Perhaps a fisherman has several fishing nets, each with one or more holes. In order to come up with one good net, the fisherman decides to overlap the different fishing nets, forming one overall net. All the nets have holes in them; however, when the nets are put together there will probably no longer be a hole in the overall net. In the case of research methods, an experimental research study may demonstrate causality well but it may be limited in realism because of the confines of the research laboratory. On the other hand, an ethnographic research study may not demonstrate causality especially well, but it can be done in the field, which enables a researcher to observe behavior as it naturally takes place and, therefore, increase realism. By using both methods, causality is strong and realism is no longer a big problem.

While it is often not practical to use more than one research method in a single research study, you should be aware of the potential benefit of using multiple methods. Furthermore, even if a researcher does not use multiple methods in a single research study, the relevant set of published research studies will usually include research based on several different research methods. The research "literature" is therefore multimethod. As a result, the multimethod (or "multifishing net") advantage will be gained in the overall area of research.

When a research finding has been demonstrated using more than one type of research, one can place more confidence in it. We say that a finding has been "corroborated" if the same result is found using different types of research. Conversely, if different data sources or types of research result in conflicting information, then additional research will be needed to explore the nature of the phenomenon more completely and determine the source of conflict. That is, if different types of research result in different findings, then the researcher should study the phenomenon in more depth to determine the exact reason for the conflicting findings. The world is a complex and ever-changing place. As we study it, it is helpful to be equipped with the best methods and approaches currently available. You will probably find that some methods and approaches fit your style or personality better than others. However, we hope that you will keep an open mind as you learn about the other kinds of research. All the research methods can be useful if used properly. In short, we hope you will enjoy your journey through this book, and we will try to make it as interesting and exciting as possible.

SUMMARY

It is important that educators and counselors be research literate because of the importance of research in education and society. By learning about research you will be able to evaluate published research articles successfully and conduct well-designed research studies on your own. Educational researchers generally generate evidence about educational phenomena by collecting empirical data and utilizing the inductive and deductive forms of the scientific method. The five general objectives of science are exploration, description, explanation, prediction, and influence. Qualitative and quantitative research are the two major research traditions in educational research. Both traditions are important. Qualitative research tends to use the inductive form of the scientific method to generate hypotheses and develop theory about phenomena in the world. It is typically conducted in naturalistic settings. Quantitative research is typically done under more tightly controlled conditions and tends to use the deductive form of the scientific method, focusing on hypothesis testing and theory testing. Several research methods (experimental, causal-comparative, correlational, ethnography, and historical) were introduced here and will be covered in more depth in later chapters.

STUDY QUESTIONS

1. Why should we study educational research?
2. Why is it important that both basic and applied research be done?
3. What is the difference between formative and summative evaluation?
4. What are the different sources of knowledge? Which ones are especially important for educational researchers?
5. What is the key difference between inductive and deductive reasoning?
6. Describe the two forms of the scientific method, and explain why both are important.
7. Explain why researchers do not use the word *proof* when they write up the results of their research in journal articles.
8. What are the five main objectives of science? (*Hint:* The first letters form the acronym EDEPI.) Explain why all the objectives are important.

9. Describe the key features of quantitative and qualitative research. Explain why both types of research are important.
10. What is the difference between a categorical variable and a quantitative variable? Think of an example of each.
11. Why is experimental research more effective than nonexperimental research when a researcher is interested in studying cause and effect?
12. Think of an example of a positive correlation and an example of a negative correlation.

EXERCISES

1. Select one categorical independent variable and one quantitative dependent variable from Figure 1.4 and design your own simple causal-comparative research study. List some potential extraneous variables.
2. Select two quantitative variables from Figure 1.4 and design your own simple correlational research study. List some potential extraneous variables.
3. A full-length example of quantitative research is provided in Appendix A, and a full-length example of qualitative research is provided in Appendix B. Examine these two articles so that you can see some examples of educational research published in academic journals.
4. Read the quantitative research study given in Appendix A and write a two-page summary of the article. Organize your paper into the following three sections: (1) Purpose (What was the research study about? What did the researchers hope to learn?); (2) Methods (How did the researchers carry out their research study? What did they actually do?); (3) Findings (What were the key results of the research study?). Don't worry about the technical jargon in the research article. Just try to get the main ideas.
5. Read the qualitative research study given in Appendix B and write a two-page summary of the article. Organize your paper into the three sections previously described (Purpose, Methods, and Findings).

KEY TERMS

action research (7)

applied research (6)

basic research (6)

categorical variable (21)

causal-comparative research (25)

cause-and-effect relationship (22)

constant (21)

correlation coefficient (26)

correlational research (26)

criterion of falsifiability (12)

culture (29)

deductive method (12)

deductive reasoning (9)

dependent variable (22)

description (15)

determinism (18)

empirical statement (8)

empiricism (8)

ethnography (29)

evaluation (7)

experimental research (23)

explanation (15)

exploration (14)

extraneous variable (24)

formative evaluation (8)

historical research (30)

holistic description (29)

hypothesis (11)

independent variable (22)

inductive method (12)

inductive reasoning (9)

influence (16)

intervening variable (23)

manipulation (23)

multimethod approach (30)

negative correlation (27)

nonexperimental research (25)

positive correlation (27)

prediction (16)

probabilistic (10)

probabilistic causes (18)

problem of induction (10)

qualitative research (17)

quantitative research (17)

quantitative variable (21)

rationalism (9)

replication (14)

research literature (3)

rule of parsimony (12)

science (10)

summative evaluation (8)

theory (11)

variable (21)

CHAPTER 2

Problem Identification
and Hypothesis Formation

LEARNING OBJECTIVES

To be able to

- identify research problems.
- explain why it is necessary to conduct a literature search.
- explain how a literature search is conducted.
- explain the purpose of a literature search when conducting a "grounded theory" study.
- explain the purpose and necessity of stating your research problem and hypothesis.
- explain the difference in the problem statement in a qualitative and quantitative study.
- specify the components that must be included in written preparation of a research plan.

Up to this point in the text we have discussed the basic characteristics of research and the different models, quantitative and qualitative, used in the research process. The research process, however, begins when you have a problem in need of a solution, because a research study is conducted in an attempt to solve a problem. The veteran researcher typically has identified more problems than he or she has the time to solve. The beginning researcher, however, frequently has trouble identifying a research problem.

Identifying a research problem should be relatively simple in the field of education because of the numerous problems that need to be solved and because of the exposure and experience we have all had in this arena. All of us have participated in the educational system, first as students and then, perhaps, as teachers or instructors. Some of you are probably participating in the educational system in the capacity of both student and teacher. In one or both of these capacities you have probably observed and discussed a host of problems with our current educational system and been exposed to the implementation of new techniques and methods of instruction. For example, at some point you may have been exposed to "computer-assisted instruction," "team teaching," or the "open classroom" and either thought it was a great concept that assisted the instructional process or thought that it impeded learning. In other instances you may have questioned the value of activities such as field trips and extracurricular programs, or some new approach to teaching biology, chemistry, or physics. From a research perspective each of these issues represents a potential legitimate research problem. All you have to do is adjust your thinking a little bit. For example, assume you know of individuals who take students on field trips or bring local "experts" into the classroom on the assumption that these activities and events enhance the educational process. You, however, do not, because you believe experts and field trips add little and the time spent on these activities could be spent more effectively on other types of instruction. You may have even gotten into arguments with your colleagues regarding the value of such activities and found that you could not change their opinion. Such an argument or disagreement is, however, the legitimate subject matter for a research study. All you have to do is convert the argument into a research question and ask, for example, What benefits are derived from taking students on field trips? or, What benefit is derived from having local experts talk to a class of students?

Once you have converted the argument into a question that is researchable, you have taken the first step in developing a research study. As you can see, researchable questions are numerous in education. To identify them, all you have to do is develop an inquisitive attitude and ask questions. For example, if your school system is implementing a new method of teaching reading, you may or may not think the new method represents an improvement. From a research perspective you must take an inquisitive and questioning approach and ask, Does the new method represent an improvement in teaching reading over the old method? rather than just state your opinion regarding the new instructional method.

SOURCES OF RESEARCH IDEAS

Where do ideas and research problems originate? Where should you look for a researchable problem? In all fields research problems may grow out of existing theories and prior research. In education we are fortunate in that we have our own experience and the experience of others to draw from. Typically, research ideas originate from one of four sources: everyday life, practical issues, past research, or theory.

Everyday Life

One of the most fruitful sources of ideas for beginning researchers is their own experience as educators. In the course of conducting your job as an educator, you continuously have to make decisions about such things as the best method of teaching students, how to maintain discipline in the classroom, how best to use technology in the classroom, and how to motivate a bright but underachieving student. Students want to know how to learn the assigned material quickly and with the least effort. You also observe that some students aggressively pursue their studies whereas others procrastinate and do anything but study. Some students are very aggressive and constantly disrupt the classroom whereas others are model students. Experiences such as these can be turned into research problems. For example, you could ask why some strategies of instruction work better with some students than with others or why some students use one method of study and others use another and whether there is any relationship between the method of study and grades made. In the course of reading the local paper Christensen encountered an article (Jones, 1997) discussing the effect of the mayors of several large cities having taken over the operation of the school system in their city. For example, the Illinois legislature handed Mayor Richard Daley total control of Chicago's 400,000-student system in 1995. In New York Mayor Rudolph Giuliani has consistently pushed for more influence over the schools. In each instance the mayors have tried to implement reforms in an attempt to improve the school system.

Although some of these reform efforts, such as those implemented by Mayor Daley in Chicago, have been applauded, there has been little improvement in student performance. Additionally, there has been some concern over the loss of autonomy and independence that may be needed to effectively run a school system. These are all issues that could potentially be converted to a research study. For example, you could ask a question such as, Why are some mayor-controlled school systems more effective than others? All that is required is the inquisitive approach that converts a problem into a question in need of an answer.

Practical Issues

Many research ideas can arise from practical issues that require a solution. Educators are constantly faced with such problems as the instruction of our youth, disruptive behavior in the classroom, selection of textbooks, and providing instruction for the culturally diverse, as well as issues such as salaries and burnout. One controversial issue that has recently been in the news is the decision of the school board in Oakland, California, to teach ebonics (a term derived from the words *ebony* and *phonics* that refers to the African American speech pattern) as a second language. This decision was based on the apparently favorable results of several teachers who taught English using a "contrastive analysis" technique, in which the teacher used books written in both ebonics and standard English to point out differences in syntax. This decision by the Oakland school board created a swell of rhetoric, particularly because it suggested that schools might seek federal funds earmarked for bilingual programs. Most of the reaction, including that from the black community, was negative and nonsupportive. A decision was also made that federal funds could not be used to support the instruction of ebonics. Note that this reaction and decision was made with very little research data although the limited data available were supportive (Leland & Joseph, 1997). Clearly this is a practical issue that deserves investigation, and one that easily lends itself to the formulation of a research question such as, Is learning standard English enhanced among African American students if they are taught using the contrastive analysis technique involving ebonics and standard English?

Past Research

The research literature of previously conducted studies represents an excellent source of research ideas and may represent the source that produces the most research ideas. This may sound like a contradiction because a research study is designed to answer a research question or questions. One of the interesting features of research is that it tends to generate more questions than it answers. Although each well-designed study does provide an advancement in knowledge, phenomena are multidetermined. Any study can investigate only a limited number of variables, and the investigation of the variables selected may lead to hypotheses about the effects of other variables. The multidimensional nature of phenomena is also the frequent cause of a lack of agreement between the results of two or more studies. For example, there are several studies demonstrating that depressed individuals consume more carbohydrates than nondepressed individuals. Some investigators (Wurtman & Wurtman, 1989) have proposed that this added carbohydrate consumption is beneficial to the depressed individuals because it provides a temporary amelioration of the depression. Other investigators (Christensen, 1993) have suggested that the carbohydrate consumption is detrimental and contributes to the depression. Some variable that was not investigated in either of the prior studies may represent the source of the conflict. This variable would represent the hypothesized cause of the conflict, and another study must be conducted to determine whether this additional variable provides an explanation for the apparent contradiction. For example, Christensen (1991) has proposed that a time variable might explain the contradiction between the Wurtman and Christensen studies. It is possible that carbohydrate consumption creates an initial improvement in depressed mood but the longer term effect is a deterioration in mood and maintenance of the depressed state. Another study must be conducted that investigates this time variable to determine whether it is the cause of the contradiction between these two studies. Because each study conducted tends to generate more questions than it answers, a researcher can continue to investigate a given problem area for years. This fact has resulted in some researchers spending their entire professional life conducting research on one given topic.

To illustrate the way in which past research leads to subsequent research ideas, consider the study conducted by Imich (1994). Imich (1994) investigated the issue of students being excluded or expelled from school in Great Britain. Prior research had indicated that student exclusions from school were increasing. Because of this increase, student exclusions from school became an issue of national concern in Great Britain in the early 1990s. However, the prior studies that had been conducted did not separate students that were temporarily and permanently expelled. Therefore, no information existed that would identify whether the increase in exclusions was owing to students being temporarily or permanently expelled. In an attempt to obtain a clearer picture of the nature of school exclusions, Imich (1994) first identified three types of exclusions: fixed-term (exclusion for a fixed period of time), indefinite (exclusion for an unspecified time period), and permanent, as specified under the 1986 Education Act. Based on an analysis of data obtained from a population of approximately 225,000 students over a three-year period, he found that permanent exclusions rose about 50 percent, fixed-term exclusions almost doubled, and indefinite exclusions tripled. Imich (1994) also found that the rate of exclusion of students from school depended on the area in which the student lived and the school attended. However, the rate of exclusion was not related to the level of social disadvantage within a school, the size of the school, or the academic performance of the students in the school.

The Imich (1994) study did provide a clearer picture of the rate of exclusion of students from schools in Great Britain, but the study really generated more questions than it answered. The study demonstrated that exclusions of all types were rising, with the indefinite exclusions rising most rapidly. However, the pattern of exclusions varied considerably between areas and schools, and no clear picture emerged to explain these differences. Further studies are needed to identify the causes of this variability. These further studies might investigate the attitudes, policies, and practices of the various schools toward disruptive behavior of their students to determine whether these are the variables causing the variability in exclusion rates. The Imich study also demonstrated that there are still unanswered questions, which provide the stimulus and the research ideas for another study. Each research study leads to a subsequent study. Research is an ongoing and continuous process.

Theory

Theory
A generalization
or set of
generalizations used
systematically to
explain some
phenomenon

Theory was defined in Chapter 1 as a generalization or set of generalizations used systematically to explain some phenomenon. Regardless of the way in which theory is defined, it serves the purpose of making sense out of current knowledge by integrating and summarizing this knowledge. This is referred to as the goal function of theory. Theory also guides research by making predictions. This is the tool function of theory. It is the tool function that is of interest to us. A good theory goes beyond the goal function of summarizing and integrating what is currently known to suggest new relationships and make new predictions. It is in this manner that theories guide research. The suggested relationships and new predictions have to be tested or subjected to a research study to verify their authenticity. The suggested relationships and new predictions represent the research ideas for investigation.

Weiner's (1974) attributional theory of success and failure is an example of a theory that suggests a way of thinking about and explaining test anxiety. Attribution theory has therefore been used to stimulate a number of research studies investigating test anxiety. From this theory Bandalos, Yates, and Thorndike-Christ (1995) hypothesized and validated the prediction that test anxiety was related to the type of attribution a student made for his or her good or bad grade on a test. Individuals who attributed failure on a test to a lack of effort on their part reported lower levels of test anxiety than did those who cited a lack of ability or some external cause such as the difficulty of the test. Similarly, students who attributed successful performance on a test to some external factor such as the test being easy or to luck reported higher levels of test anxiety.

These four sources of research ideas—everyday life, practical issues, past research, and theory—barely scratch the surface of the situations and circumstances that can inspire a creative research idea. The important issue is not the identification of sources of research ideas but the generation of researchable ideas from these sources. Generation of research ideas represents the initial stage of a research project and development of these research ideas requires the development of a way of thinking. As we have previously stated, you have to develop a questioning and inquisitive approach to life to formulate a research idea. For example, Edwin H. Land invented the Polaroid Land Camera after his three-year-old daughter asked him why a camera could not produce pictures instantly. He could have dismissed this question and merely told her that this was not possible. However, Land asked himself why it couldn't be done. While out for a stroll, he thought about this issue and came up with the idea of a camera that could produce developed photographs.

Ideas That Can't Be Empirically Researched

Research ideas originate from a variety of sources. All ideas that may be developed are not appropriate for a research study. Some ideas are very important, are debated vigorously, and consume inordinate amounts of time and energy, but are not appropriate for a research study. These ideas typically revolve about issues of value, morality, and religion. Consider, for example, the issue of school prayer, which has been debated for years, has polarized a segment of the U.S. population, and has even been debated in the courts, ultimately resulting in the ruling that prayer should not be a regular part of school activities. This ruling was based on the opinion of members of the judicial system and did not arise as a result of a research study because the issue of school prayer is a value and moral issue. As such, it implies notions of what is right and wrong or proper and improper and does not have any final answer. Research cannot provide answers to such questions although it can provide information on opinions, attitudes, and behaviors of individuals. Research cannot resolve the issue of which position is the morally best or correct one.

REVIEW OF THE LITERATURE

After you have identified a research idea, the next step in the research process is to become familiar with the information available on the topic. For example, assume you want to conduct research on the effect of students' self-concept on academic achievement. Before beginning to design this research project, you should first become familiar with the available information on self-concept and academic achievement. A lot of work has been conducted on both topics and you need to review the literature to become familiar with what has already been done that relates to this research problem. Sometimes the beginning researcher is too eager to start collecting data that will provide information about his or her research problem and views the literature review as a necessary evil that delays the all-important data-collection stage. This feeling is most frequently owing to a lack of understanding concerning both the purpose and value of a literature review. Rather than being a relatively useless exercise imposed by an unsympathetic professor, the literature review is a very important part of the research process.

The general purpose of the literature review is to gain an understanding of the current state of knowledge about your selected research topic. Specifically, a review of the literature will tell you whether the problem you have identified has already been researched. If it has, you should either revise the problem in light of the results of other studies or look for another problem. If the problem you have identified has not been investigated, related studies may give you ideas as to how to proceed and design your study so that you can obtain an answer to the problem. A literature review can also point out methodological problems specific to the research problem you are studying. Are special groups or special pieces of equipment needed to conduct the research? If so, the literature can give clues as to where to find the equipment or how to identify the particular groups of participants needed.

Gaining familiarity with the literature will also help you after you have collected your data and analyzed your results. One of the last stages of a research project is to prepare a research report in which you communicate the results of the study to others. In doing so you not only have to describe the study you conducted and the results you found but also have to explain or interpret the results of your study. For example, Baer, Tishelman, Degler, Osnes, and Stokes (1992) found that modification of preschoolers' behavior was more effective if someone other than the preschoolers, such as the researcher, selected a reward for them. Conversely, there was no difference in self-selection versus researcher-selected rewards for first graders. Baer et al. (1992) had to try to explain why preschoolers' and first graders' responses differed depending on who selected their reward. In trying to make sense out of data collected from a study such as this, it is often valuable to be aware of the literature because it can frequently provide clues as to why the effects occurred. If you are familiar with the literature, you can also discuss your results, in terms of whether they support or contradict prior studies. If your study is at odds with other studies, you can speculate as to why this difference occurs, and this speculation then forms the basis for another study to attempt to resolve the contradictory findings.

Up to this point we have discussed the necessity of conducting a literature review prior to designing your study and beginning data collection. This is the procedure you would follow if you were conducting a quantitative study and most qualitative studies. However, for some qualitative research studies, such as a **grounded theory** (Glaser, 1978) study (a qualitative research approach we discuss in depth later), a comprehensive review of the literature prior to data collection may not be recommended because researchers using the grounded theory approach attempt to develop a set of constructs, relationships, and theory uncontaminated by knowledge of prior research or theory. It is assumed that the researcher following the grounded theory approach will be able to take a fresh and uncontaminated perspective of the data collected and develop a set of constructs, relationships, and theories that could not be developed if the researcher's perspective were contaminated with a prior knowledge of the relationships, constructs, and theories discovered and elaborated upon by other researchers. This does not mean that the literature does not

Grounded theory
A qualitative
research approach

have a place in the grounded theory approach. Glaser (1978) recommends that the literature should be reviewed after the theory is sufficiently grounded and developed so that the prior literature can be related to it and in this way show additional support for the developed theory or show how the developed theory and the literature conflict. In this way ideas for further investigation will be developed.

While Glaser (1978) recommended not reviewing the literature until the theory was sufficiently grounded and developed, this approach is not recommended by others. The current position among qualitative researchers seems to be that a literature review can be of value, although it should not constrain and stifle the discovery of new constructs, relationships, and theory. Strauss and Corbin (1990) specify several different ways in which a literature review conducted prior to data collection can be of value.

The literature review can be used to stimulate theoretical sensitivity of concepts and relationships that prior literature has repeatedly identified and thus appear to be meaningful and significant. Because of their apparent significance, you may want to bring these concepts into the situation you are studying to identify the role they may play. For example, if the concept of isolation is repeatedly identified in the literature as being significantly related to creative achievement and you are studying creative achievement in underprivileged children, you may want to look for evidence of how isolation relates to creative achievement in your study.

The literature can stimulate questions. In conducting a grounded theory study, you will be collecting data by asking the research participants a variety of questions and/or observing them. The literature can assist you in deriving an initial list of pertinent questions to ask or behaviors that you may want to observe. The questions asked or observations made may change as the study progresses, but the prior literature can help in formulating the basis for getting started on the research project.

Finally, the literature can provide some information about the situations and populations that you need to study so that you can uncover phenomena that are important to the development of your theory. For example, in a study of creativity the literature may indicate that you should look at individuals experiencing various emotional states because this may represent an important variable in the development of your theory of creativity.

As a general rule, you should remember that the literature review serves a slightly different purpose in quantitative and qualitative research. In quantitative research the literature review is conducted prior to the actual conduct of the study because it serves the purpose of giving you familiarity with the literature and may assist you in specifying the research question and hypothesis as well as designing the research study. In qualitative research the literature review is also important, but it is not always performed prior to the conduct of the study. Sometimes it is conducted before data collection, but it may also be conducted after the study is completed or during data collection. This is because the literature review in qualitative research is used not only to explain the theoretical underpinnings of the research study and assist in formulation of the research question and selection of the study population, but also to stimulate new insights and concepts throughout the study. Qualitative researchers often integrate the literature review throughout their study, working back and forth between the literature and the completion of the research study (LeCompte, Preissle, & Tesch, 1993).

Sources of Information

Assuming you are convinced of the necessity of conducting a literature review, you now need to find the pertinent information in the library. The two primary sources of tracking down information relevant to any research topic are books and journals, although information can also be found in technical reports and academic theses and dissertations.

Books   Books have been written about most, if not all, areas in education. This is actually a good place to start your literature search because it will provide you with a general overview of your research topic and a summary of the literature published up to the time the book was written. Most books focus on a specific topic such as "team teaching" or "Head Start." If you have selected a research topic focusing on one of these issues, then a book written about that topic will give you a good overview of the subject matter. Remember, however, that the literature cited in books is generally several years old, so they do not provide the most up-to-date information. Even books that have just been published do not contain the most recent information because there is a delay between when the book was written and when it is available for consumers to buy.

There are also books that provide integrative reviews and summaries of studies on a number of specific educational topics. For example, the *Encyclopedia of Educational Research* provides a review of the research literature on several hundred topics in education. It would therefore be advisable to obtain a copy of this book to see whether your research topic is included. If it is, you may obtain valuable information that can assist you in your research project. Some of the books that provide a review of education-related literature are listed in Table 2.1 on page 44.

Although books are excellent for giving you a good introduction and overview of the issues of importance in the research area you have chosen, they do not provide a comprehensive review of all the research conducted on any specific topic. Any book author has to be selective and present only a small portion of the literature. To be sure that you have not read a biased orientation, you should select and examine several books on your chosen research topic.

Journals   After you have examined several books on your research topic, your next step is to identify relevant articles contained in any of the numerous journals that publish educational research. Most of the pertinent information about a research topic is usually found in educational journals. Frequently, a review that started with books leads to the journals. Books are generally the outgrowth of work cited in journals, so the progression from books back to journals is a natural one.

How should you go about identifying the relevant work cited in journals? There are numerous journals that publish educational research. It would be impossible to go through each journal looking for relevant information. This is where periodical indexes, abstract journals, and citation indexes become valuable. The indexes of most value and importance to educational researchers are the *Current Index to Journals in Education* (**CIJE**), and *Resources in Education* (**RIE**), which are produced by the Educational Resources Information Center (**ERIC**). CIJE provides an index and short annotation of articles from over 800 education-related journals spanning the period from 1966 to the present. RIE provides abstracts of re-

CIJE
An annotated index of articles from educational journals

RIE
An index of abstracts of research reports

ERIC
A database containing information from CIJE and RIE

TABLE 2.1 Books That Contain Reviews of Education-Related Literature

Book	Content
Encyclopedia of Educational Research	Brief summary of the research on several hundred topics in education
The International Encyclopedia of Educational Evaluation	Contains discussions on the basic concepts in all areas of educational evaluation including evaluation studies, curriculum evaluation, measurement theory and application, tests, and educational policy and planning
The International Encyclopedia of Education: Research and Studies	Provides a scholarly and professional discussion of educational problems, practices, and institutions around the world
International Encyclopedia of Higher Education	A ten-volume series that provides a discussion of contemporary topics in higher education
Encyclopedia of Higher Education	Contains articles and essays that attempt to integrate the current international knowledge about higher education
Handbook of Research on Teaching	Contains articles by specialists who list, summarize, and critically discuss the research on selected topics in the field of education
Encyclopedia of Special Education	Provides information on the special needs, characteristics, and problems in the education of exceptional children
Handbook of Reading Research	Provides a summary of research related to the teaching and learning of reading
Handbook of Research on Curriculum	A summary of research on topics and issues related to curriculum development
Handbook of Research on Educational Administration	A summary of research on issues related to educational administration
Handbook of Research on Mathematics Teaching and Learning	A summary of research on topics dealing with the teaching and learning of mathematics
Handbook of Research on Social Studies Teaching and Learning	A summary of research on topics related to the teaching and learning of social studies
Handbook of Research on Teacher Education	A summary of research on topics related to issues of concern in teacher education
Handbook of Research on the Teaching of English	A summary of research on topics related to the teaching and learning of English
Handbook of Research on the Education of Young Children	A summary of research on the development and education of young children

search reports from sources other than journals. These may include progress reports of ongoing research studies, technical reports of federally sponsored research programs, and reports of studies conducted by local agencies such as school districts or Title III centers.

In the past, literature reviews were conducted by manually searching through indexes such as these to identify relevant journal articles and research reports. However, this approach has become unwieldy and very impractical given the vast amount of information and number of journal articles and research reports in existence. At the present time the available volumes of CIJE and RIE contain over 800,000 entries, and this number is growing at a rate of over 30,000 a year. Fortunately, there are various information retrieval systems available that permit us to more efficiently and rapidly complete a literature search.

Computer Database Search

With advancements in computer technology it has become possible to store and access large data sets such as the entries published in CIJE and RIE. In an effort to expedite and improve the accuracy of literature searches, a number of comprehensive computerized information storage and retrieval systems, such as OVID online search and DIALOG (Dialog Information Services), have been developed. Information retrieval systems like these have access to many databases, and each database is generally specific to a given field. For example, the information of primary interest to educational researchers would be found in the ERIC database, which produces the entries for CIJE and RIE. Educational researchers may also be interested in other databases, such as the *Psychological Abstracts* or *Sociological Abstracts* database, if their study deals with a psychological or sociological as well as an educational issue. In such an instance the educational researcher would want to use the PsychINFO or the SocioFILE information retrieval source because they would access the psychological and the sociological literature. There are times when you may want to search several databases. However, the ERIC database is the one most widely used in education.

A search of these databases can be done online or by using a personal computer equipped with a CD-ROM drive. Most libraries are equipped with the technology that will enable you to perform a search using the ERIC database that exists on CD-ROM. If your library has the capability available, this method is probably most efficient for searching the literature because you can sit down at the personal computer and conduct the search yourself, perhaps with some initial instruction by the librarian or someone familiar with conducting such a search. If the CD-ROM capability is not available, your library will probably be able to conduct an online search. This typically means that the librarian will have to conduct the search using information you have given him or her. Obtaining references from an online search can take more time than a CD-ROM search and may cost you some money, although it typically will be no more than $25 to $50. Some universities even provide access to databases through use of a personal computer in your room or an office in your department. If your university provides this service, you have an efficient and rapid means of conducting your literature search. You should consult your librarian to obtain information regarding the resources available to you for conducting your literature search. In this day and age it is unlikely that you will be confined to manually searching the CIJE and RIE volumes to identify the reference sources pertinent to your research topic.

LITERATURE SEARCH AND THE INTERNET

Internet
A network of millions of computers joined to promote communication

In addition to online and CD-ROM based searches, you should also consider making use of the **Internet,** particularly because you can search ERIC on it. The Internet is a "network of networks" consisting of millions of computers and tens of millions of users all over the world, all of which are connected to a single network to promote communication. Many, if not most, universities subscribe to the Internet and make its services available to faculty, staff, and students.

There are several ways to use the Internet to assist in your literature review. Many groups, organizations, and corporations have developed databases that they make available on the Internet. For example, you can obtain access to databases that provide statistical data, library catalogs, and journal entries. Some of these databases are free and can be accessed once you log on to the Internet. Others require that your library subscribe to their services. InfoTrac SearchBank is one such service that accesses over 1,500 journals and magazines. The CARL corporation markets the CARL system, which is a library management system that networks large libraries across the nation. Check with your library to determine the databases to which they have subscribed, because these are the databases that are available for your use.

There are also conferences, debates, journals, and lists of references as well as the results of research studies on the Internet. Educational researchers have formed computer networks that enable them to carry on electronic discussions and inform each other of upcoming events as well as results of their research projects. One general bulletin board sponsored by the American Educational Research Association is the *Educational Research List* (ERL-L). This general bulletin board contains specialized "bulletin boards," or discussion groups, covering topics ranging from curriculum studies to postsecondary education. Accessing one or more of these bulletin boards may provide valuable information regarding your research topic.

The Internet is potentially a valuable resource. It definitely gives you access to a wealth of information. The challenge is to learn how to "mine" the Internet and effectively use its vast array of information. There are books that describe the Internet and provide some instruction in searching for information, such as *A Student's Guide to the Internet,* by C. L. Clark, which is a Prentice-Hall publication. However, these books provide only a basic introduction. The best way to learn more about the Internet is to use it. As you spend more and more time navigating the Internet, you will become proficient at locating information and maximizing the tremendous resources available at your fingertips.

FEASIBILITY OF THE STUDY

After you have completed your literature review you are ready to synthesize this wealth of material and formulate the specific research questions and research hypotheses you are going to investigate. Prior to taking this step you must make a decision as to whether the study you want to conduct is feasible. Every research study that is conducted varies with respect to the amount of time required to gather the data, type of research participants needed, expense, expertise of the researcher, and ethical sensitivity. Studies that are either too time consuming, require skills that you, the researcher, may not have, or are too expensive should not be initiated.

Assume, for example, that you want to investigate the efficacy of a new instructional program for teaching reading to children with attention deficit hyperactive disorder

(ADHD). Think about some of the requirements of such a study. First, you must have access to a population of children with ADHD and ensure that each child in the study has met the diagnosis of ADHD. Next you must obtain the cooperation of the children's parents, the children themselves, the school system, and the teacher in order to conduct the study. Even if you have this cooperation, the study will take time because you are investigating a reading instruction program. Therefore, you must be prepared to spend six months to a year in data collection. Finally, conducting such a study may entail some expense in providing the diagnosis of ADHD and obtaining the instructional materials and the assessment instruments. Overall, this would seem to be an ambitious study out of reach of most students.

Studies such as this are very interesting and important. However, you must make an intelligent decision and make sure that you have the resources to complete the study you want to conduct before proceeding further. If the study you would like to conduct is not feasible, maybe you can scale down or alter your study so that it does not require extensive resources. At this point it would be desirable for you to discuss your study with your professor. He or she can probably give you some valuable suggestions as to how to alter the study so that it is feasible for you to complete.

STATEMENT OF THE RESEARCH PROBLEM

After you have completed the literature review and have read and digested the literature, you should be able to make an exact statement of the specific problem you wish to investigate. In most studies, the problem statement tends to be stated as the "purpose of research study." Regardless of whether you make an exact statement of the research problem or a statement of the purpose of the research, this statement needs to be made, because making it ensures that you have a good grasp of the specific problem you wish to investigate. A specific problem statement will also enable you to communicate your research project to others. Providing a specification of the study purpose at the outset also has the advantage of guiding the research process by, for example, indicating how and by what methods the data will be collected. However, the nature of this statement will differ somewhat depending on whether you are conducting a qualitative or quantitative study because of the different methodologies employed by each paradigm.

Problem Statement in a Qualitative Study

The problem statement in a qualitative study represents, in most instances, a statement of the purpose of the study. This statement of purpose should express the assumptions of a qualitative paradigm (Creswell, 1994). This means that a qualitative study's statement of purpose should

1. Convey a sense of an emerging design by stating that the purpose of the study is to describe, understand, develop, or discover something

2. State and define the central idea that you want to describe, understand, or discover
3. State the method by which you plan to collect and analyze the data by specifying whether you are conducting an ethnographic study, grounded theory study, case study, or phenomenological study
4. State the unit of analysis and/or the research site, such as fourth-grade students participating in a specific program

For example, Drew (1986) stated the following purpose of her study:

> The focus of the present study was to explore distressing and nurturing encounters of patients with caregivers and to ascertain the meanings that are engendered by such encounters. The study was conducted on one of the surgical units and the obstetrical/gynecological unit of a 374-bed community hospital. (p. 40)

This purpose statement contains several of the essential ingredients characterizing a qualitative study. It conveys the sense of an emerging design and defines the central idea by stating that the researcher intends to "explore distressing and nurturing encounters." It also states that the research site will be a specific unit in a community hospital. Although this statement of purpose does not explicitly state the method used to collect and analyze the data, it does contain most of the elements of a statement of purpose for a qualitative study. This example also demonstrates that not every statement of purpose will contain all the fundamental characteristics of a good, qualitative purpose statement. However, good purpose statements will contain most of these characteristics.

Problem Statement in a Quantitative Study

Problem
An interrogative sentence that asks about the relation that exists between two or more variables

When making a statement of a research problem in a quantitative study, you are really asking a question. According to Kerlinger (1986, p. 17) a **problem** is "an interrogative sentence that asks 'What relation exists between two or more variables?' " Kerlinger believes that a research problem must be stated in question form. Many quantitative researchers do prefer the question form because this aids in focusing the problem. However, it is also appropriate to state the research problem in declarative form, which is frequently done. For example, Butler and Neuman (1995, p. 262) used the declarative form and stated that

> Our main proposal is that perceptions of help seeking and therefore actual help seeking behaviors will also differ in task-involving and ego-involving settings.

However, using the declarative form makes the statement of the research problem appear similar to a statement of a research hypothesis (which we will discuss later). For this reason, it is recommended that the question form be used to differentiate the statement of the research problem from the statement of the research hypothesis. Butler and Neuman's statement of the research problem could easily have been stated in question form as follows:

Will perceptions of help-seeking behaviors and therefore actual help-seeking behaviors differ in task-involving versus ego-involving settings?

Note that both the declarative and question form are making the same statement of the research problem, and each statement conforms to Kerlinger's definition of a problem because it contains at least two variables—help seeking and type of settings—and it asks about the relation between these two variables. The form used, question or declarative, is a matter of preference as long as it meets the criteria for a research problem. However, for the beginning researcher, it is probably best if you use the research question format because this form presents the problem directly, providing greater assurance that you understand exactly what you are investigating.

You should also be aware that not all problems that conform to Kerlinger's definition represent research problems. There are many moral, ethical, and religious problems that are valid and in need of solution but are not good research problems. Consider, for example, the problem of whether schools should teach sex education or whether prayer should be permitted in public schools. These are valid questions and problems that the country has wrestled with on numerous occasions. However, they are not good research problems primarily because they cannot be investigated. The criterion that distinguishes a researchable from a nonresearchable problem is whether it is capable of being empirically tested. There are many interesting and important questions that cannot be empirically tested, which means that they cannot be considered research questions. For example, consider the problem of whether sex education should be taught in school. This is a valid problem and one that has been debated many times. However, it is a value judgment based on one's beliefs as to where children should receive their sex education. How do you design a study to determine the answer to such a value judgment? The answer is you don't, because it is not possible to gather data that will provide an answer to this question.

There are many questions surrounding the issue of teaching sex education in the classroom that *are* good research problems. For example, you could ask the question, Do children who are taught sex education in the classroom have fewer out-of-wedlock children than those who do not receive this form of sex education? However, now you are asking about the effect of having taught sex education in the classroom and not whether it should be taught. These are two very different questions. One is capable of being empirically tested and the other is not. Only those problems that meet the criterion of "capable of empirically testing" are research problems.

Specificity of the Research Problem   In formulating your research problem you should make sure that you formulate it in very specific terms because a research problem stated in very specific terms ensures that you, the researcher, have a good understanding of the variables you are investigating. It also aids in the design and conduct of your research study. To drive these points home, consider the difficulties you would encounter if you asked the question, What is the effect of participation in extracurricular activities on academic performance? This question meets the criterion of a good research problem in that it should be capable of empirical testing. However, it is worded so vaguely that it is difficult to pinpoint what is being investigated. The concepts of extracurricular activities and academic performance are vague. What type of extracurricular activity and what type of academic performance? There are many different types of extracurricular activity, and it would be inappropriate to assume that each type would have a similar effect. Similarly, academic performance could refer to overall average performance or to performance in specific subject areas. Now contrast this question with the following: What effect does playing football have on a student's overall grade point average during the football season? This question specifies exactly the variables that are to be investigated: the extracurricular activity of playing football and academic performance as measured by overall grade point average.

As you should be able to see from this example, making a specific statement of the research problem helps ensure that you, the researcher, understand the problem you are investigating. If the problem is stated vaguely, you probably don't have a good grasp of the variables you want to study, which means that you may design a study that does not provide an answer to your research question. Making a specific problem statement also helps you make decisions about factors such as who the research participants will be and what materials or measures you will need to conduct the study. A vaguely stated research problem gives no such assistance. To drive this point home, go back and reread the two research questions stated above and ask yourself, What research participants should I use? What outcome measures should I use?

Now you might be asking yourself, How specific should I be in formulating the research problem? Remember that the purpose of formulating a specific research question is to ensure that you have a good grasp of the variables being investigated and to assist you in designing and completing your research study. If the formulation of your research questions is specific enough to serve these purposes, you have probably been specific enough. If these purposes have not been met, you need to rethink your research question and add additional specificity.

FORMULATING HYPOTHESES

Hypothesis
A prediction or guess of the relation that exists among the variables being investigated

After you have completed your literature review and have made a specific statement of your research problem, preferably in question form, you are ready to formulate your hypotheses. This is because the research problem has made a specific statement of the variables you will investigate, and you typically have some expectation or prediction of the relationship between these variables. The **hypothesis** represents the formal statement of your best guess or your prediction of the relation that exists among these variables. Therefore, it logically follows the statement of the research problem because you could not formulate the hypothesis without having first stated, either explicitly or implicitly, the research problem. For example, the research problem that Butler and Neuman (1995) formulated was that the perceptions and actual help-seeking behaviors of children will differ in task (an instructional set that told the children that they would learn to solve puzzles) versus ego-involving (an instructional set that told children that kids who solve the puzzles are very smart) settings. From this research problem they formulated several hypotheses, one of which stated that children in an ego-involving setting will be less likely to request help than children in task-involving settings.

Note that this hypothesis took the two variables stated in Butler and Neuman's research problem—help-seeking behaviors and type of setting—and made a prediction of how help-seeking behaviors would differ depending on the type of setting the children were in.

This progression from the statement of the research problem to the hypothesis should seem logical because the hypothesis merely represents a statement of the predicted relation between the variables stated in the research problem. However, in reading the journal articles you have identified in your literature review, you will probably have difficulty finding a statement of the research problem in every study because many authors do not make such an explicit statement. It seems that experienced researchers have such familiarity with their field that they often consider the research problem to be self-evident. Their predicted solutions to these problems, or their hypotheses, are not apparent, so they must be stated.

At this point you might wonder how to get the information you need to make your hypothesis or prediction of the relation that should exist between the variables you are investigating. The stated hypothesis typically emerges from the literature review or from theory. As we stated earlier, one of the functions of theory is to guide research. One of the ways in which a theory accomplishes this function is to make predictions of possible relations between variables. Similarly, the research literature you have read may suggest the relation that should exist between the variables being investigated. However, hypotheses can also come from reasoning based on casual observation of events. For example, you may have noticed that some children get very nervous when they take a test, and these children seem to be the ones that make the poorest grades. From this observation you may formulate a research problem that asks the question, How does test anxiety affect performance on a test? and hypothesize that performance on the test will decrease as test anxiety increases.

Regardless of the source of the hypothesis, it must meet one criterion: A hypothesis must be stated so that it is capable of being either refuted or confirmed. A hypothesis that fails to meet this criterion, or is nontestable, removes the problem from the realm of empirical research. This is why moral, ethical, and religious problems and the hypotheses that follow from them are outside the realm of empirical research. One can neither confirm nor refute hypotheses focusing on such issues because it is not possible to collect data that will resolve these issues. For example, it is not possible to collect data that would support or refute a hypothesis stating that students get a better education if they are taught both an evolutionary and Christian perspective on the origin of humans.

Now that we have talked about hypotheses and their importance in a research study, we also need to point out that their importance exists primarily in quantitative studies. Remember that quantitative and qualitative research are somewhat different and have different goals. Quantitative research has the goal of identifying the relations that exist between sets of variables whereas qualitative research attempts to discover, explore, or describe a given setting, event, or situation. Therefore hypothesis formulation is appropriate at the outset of a quantitative research study. In this type of study we not only specify the variables being investigated, but we also conduct the study to determine whether the relation we predict among these variables actually exists. In a qualitative study we do not have such knowledge of the variables. The study is generally conducted to describe or discover the significant variables. Therefore hypotheses in qualitative studies are usually generated as the data are accumulated and the researcher gains insight into the phenomenon being investigated.

THE RESEARCH PLAN

Research hypothesis
The hypothesis of interest to the researcher and the one he or she would like to see supported by the study results

Research plan
The outline or plan that will be used in conducting the research study

After you have completed your literature review and formulated your **research hypothesis,** the next step is to prepare a written **research plan.** This is another one of those steps that you may think is just busy work required by your professor. However, there are very good reasons for preparing a written, detailed research plan. The primary advantage is that it forces you not only to spell out the rationale for your research study, but also to specify each step in detail. In doing so you will definitely encounter issues that you had not thought of and need to plan for in order to complete your study. Also, after you have completed the written form of the research plan, you can give it to your professor or others for comments. This will typically generate questions that may improve your research plan. Remember that you want to identify any difficulties with the research plan before you start the study and not afterwards, because this is the stage in which you can correct any problems so that your research study will result in the accumulation of knowledge that is uncontaminated by confounding variables. Most research plans include the following components:

Introduction
1. The reason for conducting the study
2. How the study fits in with and is an extension of prior research
3. The purpose of the study
4. The hypotheses of the study

Method
1. Research participants
2. Apparatus and/or instruments
3. Procedure

Data analysis

Other additional headings may be included if they provide clearer communication of the research study and its results. For example, some research plans may include a separate section labeled Design that details the design used in the study. A separate design section would be included if it was complicated. Dissertations often include a separate Literature Review section.

Introduction

The introduction to any research study is generally funnel shaped in that it is broad at the beginning and narrow at the end. It should begin with a very general introduction to the problem area, which may include a statement of the research problem. The introduction should then start to narrow by citing the results of prior studies that bear on the specific issue you are investigating. This discussion of the prior literature should provide the rationale for conducting the study. It should lead directly into a statement of the purpose of your study and in this way show the continuity between what you are investigating and prior research. After stating the purpose of the study, you should state the hypothesis of the study.

Method

The purpose of the method section is to specify exactly how you are planning to conduct the study. In this section you must be sufficiently exact that someone else can read your method section and conduct exactly the same study that you are going to conduct. If another researcher can read the method section and replicate the study you are going to conduct, you have adequately described this section. Although this section may vary depending on whether you are conducting a quantitative or qualitative study, it generally consists of a description of the research participants, any apparatus or instruments used in data collection, and the design and procedure to be followed in collecting the data.

Research Participants   In this section you should specify exactly who the research participants will be, how many will participate in the study, their characteristics (e.g., age, gender), and how they are going to be selected for inclusion in your study. Any other information relating to the research participants should also be included in this section. For example, you should mention if you are going to give the research participants an inducement to participate. A description of the research participants might be as follows:

> The research participants will be 140 randomly selected children from those attending grades 2 and 6 in three Midwestern schools serving a primarily middle-class neighborhood. There will be an equal number of male and female children from each grade. Each child will be given a free ticket to one of the local theaters when he or she completes the research study.

Apparatus and/or Instruments   In this section you describe the instruments (such as intelligence tests, achievement tests, a measure of self-concept or attitude) and any materials (such as booklets or training manuals) or apparatus (such as a computer or biofeedback equipment) that you plan to use to collect your data. The apparatus should be described in sufficient detail to enable someone else to obtain comparable equipment. Similarly, any instruments or materials should be described, and this description should include information regarding their validity and reliability as well as where they can be obtained. Following the description of the apparatus and/or instruments, you should explain why each item is being used. For example, this section might read as follows:

> The Information and Block Design subtest of the Wechsler Preschool and Primary Scale of Intelligence—Revised (WPPSI-R) [Wechsler, 1989] will be used to estimate the research participants general level of intellectual functioning. The Information subtest . . . [briefly explain what it is and what type of response is required of the

child]. The Block Design subtest . . . [briefly explain what it is and what type of response is required of the child]. Test-retest reliability of the Information subtest ranges from .74 to .84 and .79 to .86 for the Block Design subtest.

The research participants' aggression will be measured using the Bass pounding device (Bass, 1997) [this is a fictitious reference]. This device measures aggression by recording the force with which children hit a strike plate. The research participants are instructed to strike the plate after completing each task and the force of the strike is recorded in terms of pounds per square inch of force. The validity of this instrument has been assessed by demonstrating that violent juvenile offenders strike the plate with significantly greater force than do nonviolent juvenile offenders.

Procedure   In the procedure section you describe not only the design of the study but also how you are going to implement it. Some studies provide a separate subsection in which the overall design of the study is presented as well as a procedure section that presents the implementation of the study design. This typically occurs when the design is complex and would not be readily apparent from the procedure section. In most studies these two components are integrated. Therefore, in the procedure section you must describe how you are going to execute the study from the moment you meet the first research participant to the moment you terminate contact. In providing this description you must present a step-by-step account of what both you and the research participant will do. This should include any instructions or conditions to be presented to the participants and the responses that are required of them, as well as any control techniques used, such as randomization. One criterion you can use to determine whether you have adequately described the procedure section is to ask someone else to read it and then have them explain to you how the study will be conducted. If they can read your procedure section and conduct the study you designed, you have adequately communicated the procedure you will use to collect the data. Look at Manthei and Gilmore's (1996) description of the procedure used in their study investigating teacher stress.

> The *Stress in Teaching Questionnaire* was administered to all eight schools five times; at the end of term 1 and near the end of term 3 in years 1987 and 1988; and at the end of term 3 of 1990 (the end of the first year of the implementation of the Tomorrow's Schools administrative reforms). In each instance, the purpose of the questionnaire was explained to the whole staff. Teachers either completed them during a scheduled staff meeting or individually over the next few days. Completed questionnaires were either handed directly to one of the researchers or were collected by a designated staff member and posted directly to a researcher. This procedure ensured that a high percentage (between 70 and 90 percent) of each school's teaching staff was included in each testing. (p. 6)

In the procedure section these researchers identified the type of questionnaire administered which identifies the type of information they received, and they specified when the questionnaire was administered. The procedure also specified how the questionnaires were handled after completion by the participants. From this description you should be able to collect data in the same manner as did Manthei and Gilmore. Although this represents a rather simple procedure section and one that was probably easy to write, it illustrates the detail that must be included and the characteristics of the section.

Data Analysis

After you have provided a description of how you are going to collect the data for your study, you need to specify how you are going to analyze that data to test the hypotheses that you formulated. The study design and the way in which you analyze your data are intimately related. In most instances the nature of the data analysis will evolve directly from the study design. As you develop your study design, you should ask yourself, How am I going to analyze the data collected to test the hypotheses I have formulated? This is necessary to ensure that the data you collect can be analyzed appropriately. It also provides a check on the design of your study, because if you cannot identify a way of analyzing the data collected so that they provide information about the study hypotheses, you must redesign the study.

The appropriate method of analyzing your data depends on whether you are conducting a qualitative or quantitative study and the specific components of each type of study. For example, if you were conducting a quantitative study in which the research participants were randomly assigned to one of three groups and each group of participants received a different method of instruction, you would probably use a one-way analysis-of-variance statistical test. Therefore, to specify the appropriate test for analyzing your data, you must have some knowledge of statistics. Only when you know something about both statistics and research methodology can you design a quantitative study from beginning to end.

Qualitative data analysis is much more eclectic, and there is no "one" or "right" way of analyzing the data because of the nature of the qualitative data collected. The data collected from a qualitative study comes from observations, interviews, documents, and audiovisual materials such as photographs, videotapes, and films. Data analysis requires the reduction and interpretation of the voluminous amount of information collected. Analysis of this volume of data requires reduction to certain patterns, categories, or themes, which are then interpreted using some schema. In general, qualitative data analysis requires separating the data into smaller pieces so that a larger, consolidated picture can emerge.

CONSUMER USE OF THE LITERATURE

In this book we attempt to give you detailed information on how to conduct a research study in the field of education. This chapter discussed issues such as how you can identify a research problem, the necessity and value of conducting a literature review, and the formulation of hypotheses. These are necessary and basic steps required in the conduct of a research study. However, the reality of the situation is that most of you will not be engaged in a lifetime of research and may never conduct a study. Even if you do not become an educational researcher, courses such as this one are valuable because they make you a better consumer of research. After taking this course you will have the basic information needed to evaluate a research study to determine whether the conclusions are valid or whether it was conducted correctly. If it was not, then you should immediately conclude that the results are suspect.

There are other issues that you must be aware of to be an effective consumer of research. One of the most important issues is that you should not and must not consider the results of any one study to be conclusive. This means that you need to look across studies to see whether they are repeatedly confirmed or replicated. For example, assume that you read a study demonstrating that computer-assisted instruction resulted in better performance than did instruction that did not have the aid of computers. Does this mean that you can definitely conclude that computer-assisted instruction is the superior mode of instruction? Of course not. One study does not produce a conclusive finding that you can rely on. In order to have faith in the results of a study the results *must* be replicated by other researchers on other populations in other locations. This means that you must look across studies to see whether a given effect is replicated or whether other investigators also find the same effect, because the phenomena that educational researchers investigate are too complex to be explained by a single study, and the ability to control the research environment, the research participant sample, and the procedures used vary considerably from study to study. Therefore many studies will be conducted on a given phenomenon, and each study will be conducted in a slightly different way on a slightly different participant sample. The results will vary slightly from study to study, and you must somehow integrate these studies. In the past the primary method was to review each study and categorize them in some manner, such as those that were methodologically sound versus those that contained obvious design problems, and then reach a conclusion based on the proportion of studies that suggested a given outcome. If most of these studies indicated that computer-assisted instruction, for example, was the more effective mode of instruction, then that was the conclusion you reached. However, reaching a conclusion in this manner maximizes the opportunity for introducing subjective judgments, preferences, and biases, which becomes obvious when two people review the same literature and reach different conclusions.

More recently a better technique has been developed and used to summarize the results of quantitative studies that have investigated a given phenomenon. This technique is *Meta-analysis*
A quantitative technique used to integrate and describe the results of a large number of studies
called meta-analysis. **Meta-analysis** is a term introduced by Glass (1976) to describe a quantitative approach that can be used to integrate and describe the results of a large number of studies. Meta-analysis gets around the problem of making subjective judgments and preferences in summarizing the research literature because it involves the use of a variety of quantitative techniques to analyze the results of studies conducted on a given topic. Therefore, when you are conducting your literature review and trying to reach some conclusion regarding a given phenomenon, pay particular attention to literature summaries that have made use of meta-analysis because the results of these summaries are more accurate in the conclusion reached.

To illustrate the use of meta-analysis, let us look at the meta-analysis conducted by Forness and Kavale (1996) on studies that attempted to investigate the efficacy of a social skills training program in children with learning disabilities. Fifty-three studies were identified from abstract and citation archives, reference lists from prior literature reviews, and bibliographies of research reports. Forness and Kavale applied standard meta-analytic statistical procedures to the results of these fifty-three studies to provide an overall integration and description of the findings of these studies. This analysis revealed that the social skills training programs applied to children with learning deficits had a very small but positive effect. This is the primary conclusion you should retain from the currently available literature. If you looked at individual studies, you might find some that indicated social skills training programs were totally ineffective and others that indicated they were very effective. Without the benefit of a meta-analysis, you may be influenced more by one or several of these studies and reach an inappropriate conclusion. Meta-analysis eliminates this type of bias and provides an overall synopsis of the available literature.

SUMMARY

The first step in conducting a research study is identifying a problem in need of a solution. Although the beginning researcher may have difficulty in identifying a research problem, the field of education has numerous problems in need of a solution. One of the primary components needed to identify a research problem is to develop an inquisitive attitude and ask questions. Once you develop this mental set, then problem identification is relatively easy.

Educational research problems arise from a number of traditional sources such as theories, practical issues, and past research. Additionally, in education we have our own experience to draw on, because educational research is concerned with the field of education, and we have all had experience with this field. However, many problems dealing with moral, ethical, and religious issues cannot be subjected to empirical research even though they are frequently significant issues that must be dealt with in education.

Once a researchable topic has been identified, you must conduct a literature search. A review of the literature will reveal the current state of knowledge about your selected topic and suggest ways in which you can investigate the problem as well as point out related methodological issues. However, if you are conducting a qualitative research study rather than a quantitative study, you may not need to conduct as thorough a literature review to ensure that you, as the researcher, can take a fresh and uncontaminated perspective of the data collected and hopefully develop a novel set of constructs, relationships, and theories.

In conducting the literature review, you should probably begin with books written on the topic and progress from there to actual research reports in journals. In reviewing the past research on a topic, the most efficient means is to make use of one of the various information retrieval systems, particularly one that has access to the ERIC database, because this database contains the information of primary interest to educational researchers. The Internet can also assist in your literature review because many groups, organizations, and corporations have developed databases that are available on the Internet. Additionally, there are conferences, debates, and journals as well as the results of research studies on the Internet.

After you have conducted the literature review, you must determine whether the study you want to conduct is feasible. This means that you must make an assessment of the amount of time, research participant population, expertise, and expense requirement, as well as the ethical sensitivity of the study. If this assessment indicates that the study is feasible to conduct, then you must make a clear and exact statement of the purpose of the research problem. If you are conducting a qualitative study, the problem statement should express the language and methodology of a qualitative paradigm. If you are conducting a quantitative study, you would formulate your statement of the research problem in either question or declarative format. Regardless of the format used, the statement of the research problem should make a statement of the relation that exists between two or more variables. This stated relation must be capable of being empirically tested. The statement must also be specific enough to assist you in making decisions about such factors as participants, apparatus, and the general design of the research study.

After you have formulated the statement of the research problem, you must formulate your hypotheses, because they represent the predicted relationship that exists among the variables under investigation. Often, hypotheses are a function of past research. If they are confirmed, the results not only answer the question asked but also provide additional support to the literature that suggests the hypotheses. There is one criterion that any hypothesis must meet: It must be stated so that it is capable of being either refuted or confirmed.

Remember also that hypotheses are used most frequently and are most important in quantitative research. In qualitative research the goal is to discover, explore, or describe a given setting, event, or situation. Therefore hypotheses are not formulated at the outset of the study. Rather, they are usually generated as the data are accumulated and insight is gained into the phenomenon being investigated.

STUDY QUESTIONS

1. What are the different sources of research ideas? Give an example of each.
2. What is the general purpose of a literature review, and how does this differ from a grounded theory study?
3. What sources of information are available to assist in the literature review?
4. What purpose does the statement of purpose of the research study serve, and how does this statement differ for a qualitative and quantitative study?
5. Why should you make a very specific statement of the research problem?
6. What is a hypothesis? What function does it serve, and what criteria must it meet?
7. What are the components of a research plan, and what is contained in each component?
8. What is a meta-analysis, and why is the conclusion reached in a meta-analysis study more valid than the conclusion reached in a single study?

EXERCISES

1. Formulate a research question for a quantitative study and identify the source of the idea.

2. Conduct a mini-literature review by identifying four published research articles related to the idea listed in exercise 1.
3. Formulate a research hypothesis for the research idea chosen in exercise 1.
4. Formulate a research question for a qualitative study.

KEY TERMS

CIJE (43)

ERIC (43)

grounded theory (41)

hypothesis (50)

Internet (45)

meta-analysis (56)

problem (48)

research hypothesis (52)

research plan (52)

RIE (43)

theory (39)

CHAPTER 3

Research Ethics

LEARNING OBJECTIVES

To be able to

- explain why it is necessary to consider ethical issues when designing and conducting research.
- state the guidelines that must be followed in conducting research with humans.
- explain the procedures that must be followed to obtain approval to conduct a study.
- specify the issues involved in conducting research with minors.

If you look at the journals in which educational researchers publish, you will see that these individuals are interested in a wide range of topics, such as learning strategies, factors affecting achievement, prediction of performance, types of instruction, and teacher effectiveness, all in an effort to acquire knowledge that will enhance the educational process. In pursuing these interests educational researchers make use of many different types of research approaches, such as interviews, surveys, ethnographic research, and experiments. In other words, to acquire knowledge about the educational process, educational researchers make use of the techniques that we are presenting in this book. In using these techniques researchers ask questions, observe behavior, and manipulate various stimuli such as different teaching techniques in order to obtain information that will ultimately improve the educational process.

If you just think about the potential good that will come out of an educational research study, it makes a lot of sense to interview or survey students and teachers or ask them to participate in an experiment. However, we live in a society in which we have the right to privacy and the right to expect freedom from surveillance of our behavior without our consent. We also have the right to know if our behavior is being manipulated and, if so, why.

Unfortunately, these basic rights can easily be violated when a research study is conducted. The possibility of such violation creates a problem for researchers because the public constantly demands to see improvements in the educational system. Whenever SAT scores decline or when survey results are publicized indicating that "Johnny can't read," the educational system is attacked and demands are made for improving instruction. Improvements in education are a result, however, of well-designed and well-conducted research studies. In conducting these research studies, it is sometimes necessary to infringe on people's right to privacy and ask personal questions or observe their behavior because this is the only way in which researchers can collect the information needed for improving the educational system as a whole. Additionally, for the educator trained in research techniques, a decision *not* to conduct research is a matter of ethical concern.

In order to advance knowledge and find the answers to our questions it is often necessary to impinge on well-recognized rights of individuals. Therefore, consideration of research ethics constitutes an integral part of the development and implementation of any research study. It would be very difficult, for example, to conduct a study investigating various strategies of teaching children with attention deficit hyperactive disorder (ADHD) without violating the children's right to privacy because it would be necessary first to identify and label certain children as having ADHD. This would be only one of the many ethical concerns to be considered in conducting such a study.

Such issues certainly create an ethical dilemma for the researcher, who must decide whether to conduct the research and violate certain rights of individuals for the purpose of gaining knowledge that could help others or to sacrifice such a gain in knowledge for the purpose of preserving human rights. As you can see, consideration of the ethics of any research study is necessary to assist the scientist in preventing abuses that could occur and in delineating the responsibilities of the investigator. This is why issues such as maintaining participants' anonymity and obtaining their informed consent prior to conducting the study are so important.

WHAT ARE RESEARCH ETHICS?

When most people think of ethics, they first think of moralistic sermons and endless philosophical debates. Whenever ethical issues are discussed, it is typical for individuals to differ about what does and what does not constitute ethical behavior. Most of the disagreements seem to arise because of the different approaches people take in attempting to resolve an ethical issue.

There are three basic approaches—deontology, ethical skepticism, and utilitarianism—that people tend to adopt when considering ethical issues in research. These approaches differ in terms of the criteria used to make decisions about what is right and wrong (Schlenker & Forsyth, 1977). The **deontological approach** takes the position that ethical issues must be judged on the basis of some universal code. From this point of view, certain actions are inherently unethical and should never be performed regardless of the circumstances. For example, Baumrind (1985) used the deontological approach to argue that the use of deception in research is morally wrong and should not be used under any circumstances because it involves lying to research participants and precludes obtaining their informed consent.

A person using **ethical skepticism** would argue that concrete and inviolate moral codes such as those used by the deontologist cannot be formulated. Such a skeptic would not deny that ethical principles are important but would claim that ethical rules are arbitrary and relative to one's culture and time. According to this approach an ethical decision must be a matter of the individual's conscience, and the researcher should do what he or she thinks is right and refrain from doing what he or she thinks is wrong. Research ethics are therefore a matter of the individual's conscience.

The third approach to assessing ethical issues is that of **utilitarianism.** This position maintains that judgments regarding the ethics of a particular research study depend on the consequences of that study for both the individual research participant and the larger benefit that may arise from the study results. From this position ethical decisions are based on weighing the potential benefits that might accrue from a research study against the potential costs, as illustrated in Figure 3.1. If the benefits are sufficiently large relative to the costs, then the decision is that the study is ethically acceptable. This is the primary approach used by the federal government, most professional organizations, and institutional review boards in reaching difficult ethical decisions about studies that place research participants at risk but also have the potential for yielding important knowledge and significant benefit to humans. This approach says that research ethics should be a set of principles to assist the researcher in deciding which goals are important in reconciling conflicting values (Diener & Crandall, 1978). The utilitarian approach seems to be the primary approach that permits a rational and logical basis for debating ethical issues that arise in the conduct of research and the only approach that permits reaching a decision as to whether to conduct the research or to forgo the research because the potential benefit does not outweigh the potential cost. Regardless of the approach one takes, research ethics should not be a set of moralistic dictates imposed on the research community. Rather, they should be a set of principles that will assist researchers in deciding which goals are most important in reconciling conflicting values (Diener & Crandall, 1978).

Deontological approach An ethical approach that says ethical issues must be judged on the basis of some universal code

Ethical skepticism An ethical approach that says concrete and inviolate moral codes cannot be formulated

Utilitarianism An ethical approach that says judgments of the ethics of a study depend on the consequences the study has for the research participants and the benefits that may arise from the study

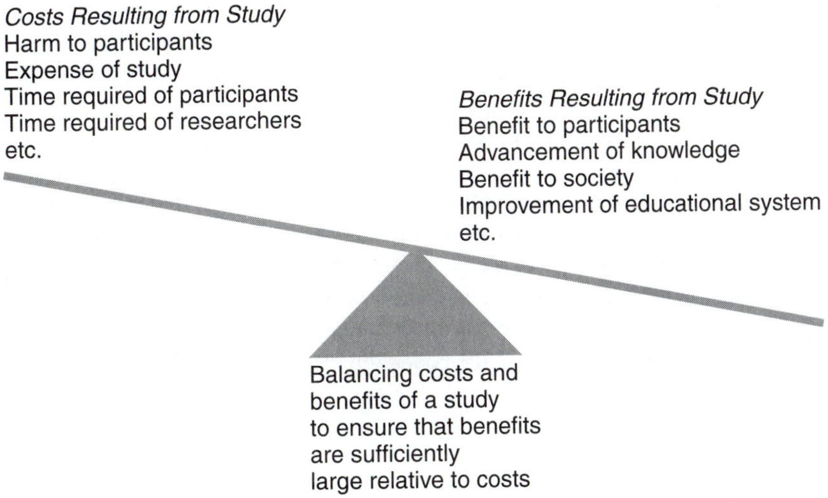

Costs Resulting from Study
Harm to participants
Expense of study
Time required of participants
Time required of researchers
etc.

Benefits Resulting from Study
Benefit to participants
Advancement of knowledge
Benefit to society
Improvement of educational system
etc.

Balancing costs and
benefits of a study
to ensure that benefits
are sufficiently
large relative to costs

FIGURE 3.1   Utilitarian approach to judging the ethical acceptability of a research study.

ETHICAL CONCERNS

Research ethics
A set of principles
to guide and assist
researchers in
deciding which
goals are most
important and
in reconciling
conflicting values

If **research ethics** refers to a guiding set of principles that are to assist researchers in establishing goals and reconciling conflicting values, it is important to first identify the ethical issues that are of importance to researchers. Diener and Crandall (1978) have identified three areas of ethical concern for social and behavioral scientists. These areas are (1) the relationship between society and science, (2) professional issues, and (3) the treatment of research participants.

Relationship between Society and Science

The ethical issue concerning the relationship between society and science revolves around the extent to which societal concerns and cultural values should direct the course of research. The society in which we live tends to dictate to a great extent the issues and research areas that are considered important and should be investigated. For example, the common cold is a condition that afflicts everyone at some point. However, little time is spent investigating ways to eliminate this common affliction, probably because a cold is typically a temporary discomfort that is not life threatening. There are many other issues that have more far-reaching implications, such as the education of our children. Society considers such problems much more important, and it encourages research on areas that are considered important.

One of the ways in which these priorities are communicated to researchers is through the numerous funding agencies that exist within our society. The largest funding agency is the federal government. The federal government spends millions of dollars every year on both basic and applied research. However, it also sets priorities for how the money is to be spent. To increase the probability of obtaining a portion of these research funds, investigators often orient their research proposals toward these same priorities, which means that the federal government at least partially dictates the type of research that is conducted. Every year these funding agencies announce "Requests for Proposals" in specific areas. For example, the U.S. Department of Education, Office of Educational Research and Development, recently issued a request for research proposals focused on field-initiated studies. These are studies that apply current knowledge to the field of education. This request for proposals was very broad and was looking for research proposals that range from those focusing on improving student achievement in core content areas to those that would promote excellence and equity in the education of children at risk for educational failure.

Professional Issues

The primary professional issue that has stimulated ethical concern is that of fraudulent activity by scientists. Researchers are trained to ask questions, to be skeptical, and to use the scientific method in seeking knowledge. This search for truth is completely antithetical to engaging in any form of deception. The most serious professional crime any researcher can commit is to cheat or present fraudulent results to the research community, such as that illustrated in Exhibit 3.1. Although there is an unwritten rule that scientists present uncontaminated results, there seems to be a disturbing increase in the tendency of some scientists to forge or falsify data, manipulate results to support a theory, or selectively report data. Between 1950 and 1979 there were only fourteen documented cases of serious scientific misconduct, whereas there were twenty-six cases between 1980 and 1987 (Woolf, 1988), and these data may reflect an underreporting of the actual incidence because of the repercussions that emerge from whistle blowing.

There seem to be both personal and nonpersonal factors that contribute to scientific misconduct (Knight, 1984). Nonpersonal factors include such things as the pressure to publish and the competition for research funding. Most research is conducted at research institutions, most of which are universities. These institutions evaluate researchers on the basis of the grants they receive and the articles they publish. Receiving a promotion or even keeping one's position may be contingent on the number of articles published and grants obtained. This pressure is frequently reported by researchers who engage in fraudulent activities. Other nonpersonal factors include inadequate supervision of trainees, inadequate procedures for keeping records or retaining data, and the diffusion of responsibility for jointly authored studies.

Personal factors focus on the psychological makeup of the individual. Fraudulent activity is attributed to the researcher's reaction to the extreme stress resulting from participation in a highly competitive academic research environment. Although there may be personal and nonpersonal factors contributing to a person's tendency to engage in fraudulent activity, there is never any justification for engaging in such behavior. The cost of fraudulent activity is enormous, both to the profession and to the researcher. Not only is the whole research enterprise discredited, but the professional career of the individual is destroyed.

EXHIBIT 3.1   A Case of Fraudulent Research

Steven E. Breuning received his doctorate from the Illinois Institute of Technology in 1977. Several years later he obtained a position at the Coldwater Regional Center in Michigan. At Coldwater, Breuning was invited to collaborate on an NIMH-funded study of the use of neuroleptics on institutionalized people who were mentally retarded. In January 1981 he was appointed director of the John Merck program at Pittsburgh's Western Psychiatric Institute and Clinic, where he continued to report on the results of the Coldwater research and even obtained his own NIMH grant to study the effects of stimulant medication on retarded subjects. During this time Breuning gained considerable prominence and was considered one of the field's leading researchers. In 1983, however, questions were raised about the validity of Breuning's work. The individual who had initially taken Breuning on as an investigator started questioning a paper in which Breuning reported results having impossibly high reliability. This prompted a further review of Breuning's published work, and contacts were made with personnel at Coldwater, where the research had supposedly been conducted. Coldwater's director of psychology had never heard of the study and was not aware that Breuning had conducted any research while at Coldwater. NIMH was informed of the allegations in December 1983. Following a three-year investigation, an NIMH team concluded that Breuning "knowingly, willfully, and repeatedly engaged in misleading and deceptive practices in reporting his research." He reportedly had not carried out the research that was described, and only a few of the experimental participants had ever been studied. It was concluded that Breuning had engaged in serious scientific misconduct (Holden, 1987).

Partial publication Publishing several articles from the data collected in one large study

Although fraudulent activity is obviously the most serious form of scientific misconduct, there are several other issues of a less serious nature that are beginning to receive attention (Hilgartner, 1990; Grisso et al., 1991). The two issues of concern with respect to research publication are partial publication and duplicate publication. **Partial publication** refers to collecting data for one study and then publishing several articles based on this one large set of data rather than publishing all the findings and data in one article. This piecemeal publication is generally considered to be undesirable (APA, 1994) unless it facilitates scientific communication. However, the author of such piecemeal publication typically benefits from it. Promotion and tenure as well as salary raises are partially contingent on the number of articles published, so it is to the benefit of the author to publish as many articles as possible in good journals—which promotes piecemeal publication.

Duplicate publication Publishing the same data and results in more than one journal or in other publications

Duplicate publication refers to publishing the same data and results in more than one journal or in other publications. According to William Russell, Executive Director of AERA, duplicate publication is explicitly forbidden by some organizations such as the Educational Research Association and generally discouraged (personal communication). However, different outlets such as research journals and books and articles for the popular press reach different audiences and serve different purposes. The ethical issue that must be considered is whether presenting the data to these different audiences represents an ethical violation or effective communication of scientific data.

In addition to partial and duplicate publication, the ethical issues surrounding the use and archiving of videotaped data, research with vulnerable populations, and financial conflicts of interests involving commercial applications that may arise from a research breakthrough are being discussed in organizations such as the American Psychological Association. Although some of these, such as the financial conflict of interest surrounding a commercial application of a study, would typically have little relevance for educational researchers, others would. For example, educational researchers frequently use minors in their studies. Children are considered vulnerable persons, and when investigating vulnerable populations, consideration must be given to concerns such as protecting their right to privacy and informed consent to participate in a study. This issue is discussed in further depth later in this chapter.

Treatment of Research Participants

Treatment of research participants is the most important and fundamental issue that researchers must confront. The conduct of research with humans has the potential for creating a great deal of physical and psychological harm. The grossly inhumane medical experiments conducted by Nazi scientists during World War II immediately come to mind. For example, individuals were immersed in ice water to determine how long it would take them to freeze to death. Bones were broken and rebroken to see how many times they could be broken before healing was not possible. These experiments were conducted by individuals living in what is thought to have been a demented society, and we seem to think that such studies could not be performed in our culture. Prior to the decade of the 1960s, comments about the ethics of research were virtually nonexistent. In the mid-1960s ethical issues became a dominant concern as it increasingly became clear that research did not invariably operate to benefit others and experiments were not always conducted in a manner that ensured the safety of participants. The most dramatic examples of unethical research have been conducted in the medical field, with the Tuskegee experiment (Jones, 1981) described in Exhibit 3.2 representing the most blatant example of a violation of human rights.

As recently as September 1995, *U.S. News and World Report* (Pasternak & Cary, 1995) published an article on once secret records of government-sponsored or -funded radiation experiments carried out between 1944 and 1974. In some of these experiments, cancer patients were exposed to radiation under the guise that it might cure their cancer. Documents, however, suggested that many of these experiments were conducted only to gather data on the effects of radiation on humans. These experiments caused the patients to become violently ill, bleed from various orifices, and plead to have the treatment stopped. However, Dr. Saenger, the principal investigator of these studies, would encourage the patient to continue, using the argument that radiation exposure was beneficial.

In December 1996 the Cleveland Plain Dealer reported on the results of its investigation of internal Food and Drug Administration records. This analysis revealed that some research is still conducted on unknowing people and in other cases the participants are not fully informed of the risks of their participation.

Both the radiation experiments and the Tuskegee experiment are clearly unethical and inflicted extensive harm and psychological pain on the research participants. Educational research does not appear to have the potential for inflicting a similar degree of physical or psychological harm to its research participants. It would be easy to become

---

EXHIBIT 3.2   The Tuskegee Syphilis Experiment

In July 1972 the Associated Press released a story that revealed that the U.S. Public Health Service (PHS) had for forty years been conducting a study of the effects of untreated syphilis on black men in Macon County, Alabama. The study consisted of conducting a variety of medical tests (including an examination) on 399 black men who were in the late stages of the disease and on 200 controls. Physicians employed by the PHS administered a variety of blood tests and routine autopsies to learn more about the serious complications that resulted from the final stages of the disease.

This was a study aimed strictly at compiling data on the effects of the disease and not on the treatment of syphilis. No drugs or alternative therapies were tested or ever used. The participants were never told the purpose of the study or what they were or were not being treated for. The PHS

nurse monitoring the participants informed the local physicians of the individuals who were taking part in the study and that they were not to be treated for syphilis. Participants who were offered treatment by other physicians were advised that they would be dropped from the study if they took the treatment.

The participants were not aware of the purpose of the study or the danger it posed to them, and no attempt was ever made to explain the situation to them. In fact, participants were enticed with a variety of inducements, physical examination, free rides to and from the clinic, hot meals, free treatment for other ailments, and a $50 burial stipend, and were followed to ensure that they did not receive treatment from other physicians. This study violated almost every standard of ethics for research with humans from informed consent to physical harm of the participants.

---

complacent and conclude that consideration of ethical issues is something that other fields have to contend with and that educational research is spared. Reaching such a conclusion is wrong because ethical issues are part and parcel of educational research. However, the ethical issues that educational researchers must face are often not as dramatic or blatant as those that frequently exist in medical or research. Consequently, the educational researcher frequently must be *more* rather than less attuned to the ethical issues that surround his or her research.

To illustrate the subtle ethical issues that can exist in a study that an educational researcher might conduct, consider the survey study conducted by Phillips (1994). Phillips was interested in studying adolescents' attitudes and behaviors related to HIV/AIDS prevention. Specifically, she was interested in collecting data that would provide insight into adolescents' thoughts about using condoms during sexual intercourse and how their thinking influenced their decision to either use or not use the condoms. Collecting the data involved surveying sexually related attitudes and behavior. This research did not inject, expose, medicate, touch, deceive, or assign the participants to treatment or control groups, nor did it require them to reveal their identity. Therefore, although it did investigate "sensitive" behavior, it did not, at least on the surface, seem to represent a study that had the potential for violating the participants' rights.

Fortunately, Phillips met with various groups prior to conducting her study, and these meetings revealed a number of ethical concerns that led her to alter her instrument and her procedures. For example, she met with a student peer group and a combined parent-teacher group to discuss the objectives of the research and the content of the questionnaire. In addition to asking questions about sexual attitudes and behavior, the questionnaire was initially constructed to inquire about the adolescents' drug use. In the combined parent-teacher group discussion, teachers and parents joked about how they would be glad to find out about the drug users because they had some children that were suspected of using drugs. Although Phillips had told the schools that she would provide them with aggregate data only for each school, there was still the potential that a teacher, after learning that her school had, say, ten drug users, would assume that she or he had guessed right and treat the suspected student differently. To avoid such a possibility, Phillips removed all questions regarding illicit drug use except one on alcohol and cigarette smoking. The same concern did not exist for sexual activity because many teachers seemed to assume that this was a widespread activity, which minimized the possibility for singling out a specific student.

Another subtle ethical issue Phillips had to contend with was the issue of privacy. Because the survey instrument focused on sexual behavior, students who had not experienced sexual intercourse would find many of the questions not applicable. These students would therefore skip most of the questions and finish more rapidly than their sexually active classmates. This more rapid completion could convey their sexual inexperience to their classmates. To avoid such a possibility Phillips constructed a second set of questions for the sexually inactive student designed to take about as long to complete as the sections for the sexually active student. This seemed to solve this problem. However, listening to students talk about completing surveys revealed that they would listen to or watch when their friends turned the page to branching questions in order to discern how they had answered the question. This is a sophisticated attempt to pry into another student's answers. To get around this privacy issue Phillips reorganized the questionnaire to ensure that all branching questions were at the bottom of the page and all students would have to turn a page.

Although the survey study Phillips conducted did not place the participants in any physical danger, there was the potential for some emotional harm. Some of the students volunteered that they had been raped and/or were incest victims. This was information that was not requested in the survey, but it would have been unethical to disregard it because the questionnaire created an environment in which these unpleasant events were recalled. Some of the questions on the sexual survey could also threaten the well-being of the adolescents. For example, a question asking the adolescents to identify their sexual preference may result in the student having to confront lesbian or homosexual tendencies, which could cause some emotional distress or discomfort. To deal with these issues, Phillips gave each student her office phone number and told them they could call her with any questions. During the administration of the questionnaire, students could ask questions in private and any other questions they might have would be answered after completion of the questionnaire. Additionally, each student was given a pamphlet, published by the American Red Cross, that included telephone numbers for counseling referral services.

These are some of the more subtle ethical issues Phillips had to contend with in conducting her study. You might think that such ethical concerns are limited primarily to sensitive research such as the issue of sexuality investigated by Phillips. However, similar issues can arise in many other types of studies. For example, educational researchers conducting qualitative research may make extensive use of interviews. In the course of these interviews the research participants can, and often do, reveal sensitive information that is not part of the goal of the study. Research participants often view the researchers as "experts" and frequently feel comfortable conveying confidential and sensitive information. For example, students may reveal that they are being abused, that they are having difficulty with a teacher, or that they are abusing drugs. When this information is revealed, the researcher must be prepared to address such issues rather than dismiss them as outside the confines of the purpose of the study. It is these types of ethical issues that can creep into a study, and the researcher must anticipate them and have a plan to conduct a study that is ethically sound. As you should be able to see, there are ethical issues surrounding virtually any study, and the investigator must consider the ethics of research prior to its conduct.

ETHICAL GUIDELINES FOR RESEARCH WITH HUMANS

We hope we have convinced you of the necessity of considering the ethics of your research study prior to actually collecting any data. Even so, a novice researcher may not be sophisticated enough to know what types of issues to consider even if he or she is motivated to make the study as ethical as possible and provide as much protection for participants as possible. To assist the researcher in conducting an ethically sound study, a number of organizations such as the American Educational Research Association, American Psychological Association, the Society for Research in Child Development, and the American Counseling Association have prepared a set of ethical guidelines that can be used by a researcher to assist in the conduct of the most ethically acceptable study. The American Educational Research Association (AERA, 1992) has developed a set of standards designed specifically to guide the work of researchers in education. This set of standards seems to be most appropriate for the educational researcher and appears in Exhibit 3.3 on pages 70–75.

In reading these guidelines you can see that it is the investigator's responsibility to ensure that the study he or she is planning is ethically acceptable and that research participants are treated ethically by everyone involved in the study. Assurance of the ethical acceptability of the study means that

1. You have to get the informed consent of the participant.
2. Any deception must be justified by the study's scientific, educational, or applied value.
3. The research participants must know that they are free to withdraw from the study at any time without prejudice.
4. The research participants are protected from physical and mental discomfort, harm, and danger that may arise from the research procedures.
5. The research participants have a right to remain anonymous, and the confidentiality of the participants and the data must be protected.

Let's look at each of these very important points in some detail.

Foreword

Educational researchers come from many disciplines, embrace several competing theoretical frameworks, and use a variety of research methodologies. AERA recognizes that its members are already guided by codes in the various disciplines and, also, by organizations such as institutional review boards. AERA's code of ethics incorporates a set of standards designed specifically to guide the work of researchers in education. Education, by its very nature, is aimed at the improvement of individual lives and societies. Further, research in education is often directed at children and other vulnerable populations. A main objective of this code is to remind us, as educational researchers, that we should strive to protect these populations, and to maintain the integrity of our research, of our research community, and of all those with whom we have professional relations. We should pledge ourselves to do this by maintaining our own competence and that of people we induct into the field, by continually evaluating our research for its ethical and scientific adequacy, and by conducting our internal and external relations according to the highest ethical standards.

The standards that follow remind us that we are involved not only in research but in education. It is, therefore, essential that we continually reflect on our research to be sure that it is not only sound scientifically but that it makes a positive contribution to the educational enterprise.

I. Guiding Standards: Responsibilities to the Field

A. Preamble.   To maintain the integrity of research, educational researchers should warrant their research conclusions adequately in a way consistent with the standards of their own theoretical and methodological perspectives. They should keep themselves well informed in both their own and competing paradigms where those are relevant to their research, and they should continually evaluate the criteria of adequacy by which research is judged.

B. Standards

1. Educational researchers should conduct their professional lives in such a way that they do not jeopardize future research, the public standing of the field, or the discipline's research results.

2. Educational researchers must not fabricate, falsify, or misrepresent authorship, evidence, data, findings, or conclusions.

3. Educational researchers must not knowingly or negligently use their professional roles for fraudulent purposes.

4. Educational researchers should honestly and fully disclose their qualifications and limitations when providing professional opinions to the public, to government agencies, and others who may avail themselves of the expertise possessed by members of AERA.

5. Educational researchers should attempt to report their findings to all relevant stakeholders, and should refrain from keeping secret or selectively communicating their findings.

6. Educational researchers should report research conceptions, procedures, results, and analyses accurately and sufficiently in detail to allow knowledgeable, trained researchers to understand and interpret them.

7. Educational researchers' reports to the public should be written straightforwardly to communicate the practical significance for policy, including limits in effectiveness and in generalizability to situations, problems, and contexts. In writing for or communicating with nonresearchers, educational researchers must take care not to misrepresent the practical or policy implications of their research or the research of others.

8. When educational researchers participate in actions related to hiring, retention, and advancement, they should not discriminate on the basis of gender, sexual orientation, physical disabilities, marital status, color, social class, religion, ethnic background, national origin, or other attributes not relevant to the evaluation of academic or research competence.

9. Educational researchers have a responsibility to make candid, forthright personnel recommendations and not to recommend those who are manifestly unfit.

10. Educational researchers should decline request to review the work of others where strong conflicts of interest are involved, or when such requests cannot be conscientiously fulfilled on time. Materials sent for review should be read

in their entirety and considered carefully, with evaluative comments justified with explicit reasons.

11. Educational researchers should avoid all forms of harassment, not merely those overt actions or threats that are due cause for legal action. They must not use their professional positions or rank to coerce personal or sexual favors or economic or professional advantages from students, research assistants, clerical staff, colleagues, or any others.

12. Educational researchers should not be penalized for reporting in good faith violations of these or other professional standards.

II. Guiding Standards: Research Populations, Educational Institutions, and the Public

A. Preamble. Educational researchers conduct research within a broad array of settings and institutions, including schools, colleges, universities, hospitals, and prisons. It is of paramount importance that educational researchers respect the rights, privacy, dignity, and sensitivities of their research populations and also the integrity of the institutions within which the research occurs. Educational researchers should be especially careful in working with children and other vulnerable populations. These standards are intended to reinforce and strengthen already existing standards enforced by institutional review boards and other professional associations.

B. Standards

1. Participants, or their guardians, in a research study have the right to be informed about the likely risks involved in the research and of potential consequences for participants, and to give their informed consent before participating in research. Educational researchers should communicate the aims of the investigation as well as possible to informants and participants (and their guardians), and appropriate representatives of institutions, and keep them updated about any significant changes in the research program.

2. Honesty should characterize the relationship between researchers and participants and appropriate institutional representatives. Deception is discouraged; it should be used only when clearly necessary for scientific studies, and should then be minimized. After the study the researcher should explain to the participants and institutional representatives the reasons for the deception.

3. Educational researchers should be sensitive to any locally established institutional policies or guidelines for conducting research.

4. Participants have the right to withdraw from the study at any time, unless otherwise constrained by their official capacities or roles.

5. Educational researchers should exercise caution to ensure that there is no exploitation for personal gain of research populations or of institutional settings of research. Educational researchers should not use their influence over subordinates, students, or others to compel them to participate in research.

6. Researchers have a responsibility to be mindful of cultural, religious, gender, and other significant differences within the research population in the planning, conduct, and reporting of their research.

7. Researchers should carefully consider and minimize the use of research techniques that might have negative social consequences, for example, negative sociometrics with young children or experimental interventions that might deprive students of important parts of the standard curriculum.

8. Educational researchers should be sensitive to the integrity of ongoing institutional activities and alert appropriate institutional representatives of possible disturbances in such activities which may result from the conduct of the research.

9. Educational researchers should communicate their findings and the practical significance of their research in clear, straightforward, and appropriate language to relevant research populations, institutional representatives, and other stakeholders.

10. Informants and participants have a right to remain anonymous. This right should be respected when no clear understanding to the contrary has been reached. Researchers are responsible for taking appropriate precautions to protect the confidentiality of both participants and data. Those being studied should be made aware of the capacities of the various data-gathering technologies to be used in the investigation so that they can make an informed decision about their participation. It should also

(continued)

EXHIBIT 3.3   *(continued)*

be made clear to informants and participants that despite every effort made to preserve it, anonymity may be compromised. Secondary researchers should respect and maintain the anonymity established by primary researchers.

III. Guiding Standards: Intellectual Ownership

A. Preamble.   Intellectual ownership is predominantly a function of creative contribution. Intellectual ownership is not predominantly a function of effort expended.

B. Standards

1. Authorship should be determined based on the following guidelines, which are not intended to stifle collaboration, but rather to clarify the credit appropriately due for various contributions to research.

   a) All those, regardless of status, who have made substantive creative contribution to the generation of an intellectual product are entitled to be listed as authors of that product.

   b) First authorship and order of authorship should be the consequence of relative creative leadership and creative contribution. Examples of creative contributions are: writing first drafts or substantial portions; significant rewriting or substantive editing; and contributing generative ideas or basic conceptual schemes or analytic categories, collecting data which require significant interpretation or judgment, and interpreting data.

   c) Clerical or mechanical contributions to an intellectual product are not grounds for ascribing authorship. Examples of such technical contributions are: typing, routine data collection or analysis, routine editing, and participation in staff meetings.

   d) Authorship and first authorship are not warranted by legal or contractual responsibility for or authority over the project or process that generates an intellectual product. It is improper to enter into contractual arrangements that preclude the proper assignment of authorship.

   e) Anyone listed as author must have given his/her consent to be so listed.

   f) The work of those who have contributed to the production of an intellectual product in ways short of these requirements for authorship should be appropriately acknowledged within the product.

   g) Acknowledgement of other work significantly relied on in the development of an intellectual product is required. However, so long as such work is not plagiarized or otherwise inappropriately used, such reliance is not ground for authorship or ownership.

   h) It is improper to use positions of authority to appropriate the work of others or claim credit for it.

   i) Theses and dissertations are special cases in which authorship is not determined strictly by the criteria elaborated in these standards. Students' advisors, who might in other circumstances be deserving of authorship based on their collaborative contribution, should not be considered authors. Their creative contributions should, however, be fully and appropriately acknowledged.

   j) Authors should disclose the publication history of articles they submit for publication; that is, if the present article is substantially similar in content and form to one previously published, that fact should be noted and the place of publication cited.

2. While under suitable circumstances, ideas and other intellectual products may be viewed as commodities, arrangements concerning the production or distribution of ideas or other intellectual products must be consistent with academic freedom and the appropriate availability of intellectual products to scholars, students, and the public. Moreover, when a conflict between the academic and scholarly purposes of intellectual production and profit from such production arises, preference should be given to the academic and scholarly purposes.

3. Ownership of intellectual products should be based upon the following guidelines:

   a) Individuals are entitled to profit from the sale or disposition of those intellectual products, they create. They may therefore enter into contracts or other arrangements for the publication or disposition of intellectual products, and profit financially from these arrangements.

b) Arrangements for the publication or disposition of intellectual products should be consistent with their appropriate public availability and with academic freedom. Such arrangements should emphasize the academic functions of publication over the maximization of profit.

c) Individuals or groups who fund or otherwise provide resources for the development of intellectual products are entitled to assert claims to a fair share of the royalties or other profits from the sale or disposition of these products. As such claims are likely to be contentious, funding institutions and authors should agree on policies for the disposition of profits at the outset of the research or development project.

d) Authors should not use positions of authority over other individuals to compel them to purchase an intellectual product from which the authors benefit. This standard is not meant to prohibit use of an author's own textbook in a class, but copies should be made available on library reserve so that students are not forced to purchase it.

IV. Guiding Standards: Editing, Reviewing, and Appraising Research

A. Preamble. Editors and reviewers have a responsibility to recognize a wide variety of theoretical and methodological perspectives and, at the same time, to ensure that manuscripts meet the highest standards as defined in the various perspectives.

B. Standards

1. AERA journals should handle refereed articles in a manner consistent with the following principles:

a) Fairness requires a review process that evaluates submitted works solely on the basis of merit. Merit shall be understood to include both the competence with which the argument is conducted and the significance of the results achieved.

b) Although each AERA journal may concentrate on a particular field or type of research, the set of journals as a whole should be open to all disciplines and perspectives currently represented in the membership and which support a tradition of responsible educational scholarship. This standard is not intended to exclude worthy innovations.

c) Blind review, with multiple readers, should be used for each submission, except where explicitly waived. (See #3.)

d) Judgments of the adequacy of an inquiry should be made by reviewers who are competent to read the work submitted to them. Editors should strive to select reviewers who are familiar with the research paradigm and who are not so unsympathetic as to preclude a disinterested judgment of the merit of the inquiry.

e) Editors should insist that even unfavorable reviews be dispassionate and constructive. Authors have the right to know the grounds for rejection of their work.

2. AERA journals should have written, published policies for refereeing articles.

3. AERA journals should have a written, published policy stating when solicited and nonrefereed publications are permissible.

4. AERA journals should publish statements indicating any special emphases expected to characterize articles submitted for review.

5. In addition to enforcing standing strictures against sexist and racist language, editors should reject articles that contain *ad hominem* attacks on individuals or groups or insist that such language or attacks be removed prior to publication.

6. AERA journals and AERA members who serve as editors of journals should require authors to disclose the full publication history of material substantially similar in content and form to that submitted to their journals.

V. Guiding Standards: Sponsors, Policymakers, and Other Users of Research

A. Preamble. Researchers, research institutions, and sponsors of research jointly share responsibility for the ethical integrity of research, and should ensure that this integrity is not violated. While it is recognized that these parties may sometimes have conflicting legitimate aims, all those with responsibility

(continued)

EXHIBIT 3.3 *(continued)*

for research should protect against compromising the standards of research, the community of researchers, the subjects of research, and the users of research. They should support the widest possible dissemination and publication of research results. AERA should promote, as nearly as it can, conditions conducive to the preservation of research integrity.

B. Standards

1. The data and results of a research study belong to the researchers who designed and conducted the study, unless specific contractual arrangements have been made with respect to either or both the data and results, except as noted in II B.4. (participants may withdraw at any stage.)
2. Educational researchers are free to interpret and publish their findings without censorship or approval from individuals or organizations, including sponsors, funding agencies, participants, colleagues, supervisors, or administrators. This understanding should be conveyed to participants as part of the responsibility to secure informed consent.
3. Researchers conducting sponsored research retain the right to publish the findings under their own names.
4. Educational researchers should not agree to conduct research that conflicts with academic freedom, nor should they agree to undue or questionable influence by government or other funding agencies. Examples of such improper influence include endeavors to interfere with the conduct of research, the analysis of findings, or the reporting of interpretations. Researchers should report to AERA attempts by sponsors or funding agencies to use any questionable influence.
5. Educational researchers should fully disclose the aims and sponsorship of their research, except where such disclosure would violate the usual tenets of confidentiality and anonymity. Sponsors or funders have the right to have disclaimers included in research reports to differentiate their sponsorship from the conclusions of the research.
6. Educational researchers should not accept funds from sponsoring agencies that request multiple renderings of reports that would distort the results or mislead readers.
7. Educational researchers should fulfill their responsibilities to agencies funding research, which are entitled to an accounting of the use of their funds, and to a report of the procedures, findings, and implications of the funded research.
8. Educational researchers should make clear the bases and rationales, and the limits thereof, of their professionally rendered judgments in consultation with the public, government, or other institutions. When there are contrasting professional opinions to the one being offered, this should be made clear.
9. Educational researchers should disclose to appropriate parties all cases where they would stand to benefit financially from their research or cases where their affiliations might tend to bias their interpretation of their research or their professional judgments.

VI. Guiding Standards: Students and Student Researchers

A. Preamble. Educational researchers have a responsibility to ensure the competence of those inducted into the field and to provide appropriate help and professional advice to novice researchers.

B. Standards

1. In relations with students and student researchers, educational researchers should be candid, fair, nonexploitative, and committed to their welfare and progress. They should conscientiously supervise, encourage, and support students and student researchers in their academic endeavors, and should appropriately assist them in securing research support or professional employment.
2. Students and student researchers should be selected based upon their competence and potential contributions to the field. Educational researchers should not discriminate among students and student researchers on the basis of gender, sexual orientation, marital status, color, social class, religion, ethnic background, national origin, or other irrelevant factors.

3. Educational researchers should inform students and student researchers concerning the ethical dimensions of research, encourage their practice of research consistent with ethical standards, and support their avoidance of questionable projects.
4. Educational researchers should realistically apprise students and student researchers with regard to career opportunities and implications associated with their participation in particular research projects or degree programs. Educational researchers should ensure that research assistantships be educative.
5. Educational researchers should be fair in the evaluation of research performance, and should communicate that evaluation fully and honestly to the student or student researcher. Researchers have an obligation to report honestly on the competence of assistants to other professionals who require such evaluations.
6. Educational researchers should not permit personal animosities or intellectual differences vis-a-vis colleagues to foreclose student and student researcher access to those colleagues, or to place the student or student researcher in an untenable position with those colleagues.

Informed Consent

Federal regulations as well as the guidelines established by the AERA state that research participants must give informed consent before they can participate in a study. Consent must also be given before a researcher can use individuals' existing records for research purposes. The Buckley Amendment, or the Family Education Rights and Privacy Act of 1974, protects the privacy of the records maintained by agencies such as a school system. This "privacy act" states that records maintained by an agency for one purpose cannot be released for another purpose without the consent of the individual. Records such as student grades that are collected and maintained for the purpose of recording student performance cannot be released to a researcher for research purposes without the student's consent.

Before a participant can participate in a research study, the researcher must give the prospective participant a description of all the features of the study that might reasonably influence his or her willingness to participate. If you are planning to conduct a survey of sexual attitudes, you must inform the prospective participants of the nature of the survey and the type of questions that they may have to respond to, because some of the participants may not want to answer explicit sexual questions. Similarly, if you are conducting a study pertaining to academic achievement and you are going to ask the students about their grades in other classes, you have to inform the students of this fact. In other words, you must look at the tasks you are going to ask your research participants to complete and ask yourself whether this task could hurt, embarrass, or in some other way create a reaction in the participants that would make them not want to participate in the study. As a general rule the following information should be given to each person in seeking his or her informed consent:

1. Purpose of the research along with a description of the procedures to be followed and the length of time it will take the participant to complete the study
2. A description of any risks or discomforts the participant may encounter

3. A description of any benefits the participant or others may expect from the research
4. A description of other procedures or treatment that might be advantageous to the participant
5. A statement of the extent to which the results will be kept confidential
6. Names of people the participant may contact with questions about the study or the research participant's rights
7. A statement indicating that participation is voluntary and the participant can withdraw and refuse to participate at any time with no penalty

Exhibit 3.4 provides an example of an informed consent form. It is only when you have given the participant this information and he or she still volunteers to participate in the study that you have obtained informed consent.

Although the general guideline is that informed consent must be obtained before a person can participate in a research study, it is also recognized that there are some types of research that cannot be conducted if the research participants are fully informed of all aspects of the research because this may invalidate the study. Resnick and Schwartz (1973) provided an excellent demonstration of this fact. They used a verbal conditioning task in which the experimenter merely says "good" or "okay" whenever the participant constructed a sentence beginning with either the pronoun "I" or "we." The experimenter's saying "good" or "okay" after sentences beginning with the "I" or "we" pronoun served as a reinforcer that encouraged the participant to increase the likelihood of selecting one of these two pronouns. In this study Resnick and Schwartz varied the amount of information they gave the participants. They gave the "uninformed" group a rationale for the study and told them of the type of task they were to complete. The "informed" group was informed totally about the nature of the study. They were told that it was a verbal conditioning study and that the experimenter would say "good" or "okay" whenever they selected an "I" or "we" pronoun in an attempt to increase their frequency of using these pronouns. Figure 3.2 (page 78) shows that the uninformed group demonstrated verbal conditioning whereas the informed group did not. The uninformed group appeared enthusiastic and arrived at their scheduled time. The informed participants were uncooperative and "often haughty, insisting that they had only one time slot to spare which we could take or leave" (Resnick & Schwartz, 1973, p. 13).

From this study you can see clearly that informing participants of all aspects of the research can, in some studies, totally alter the results. Federal as well as AERA guidelines recognize the necessity of sometimes forgoing the requirement of informed consent. Whenever a judgment is made that informed consent would alter the outcome of a study or that the study could not be conducted if informed consent is required, the investigator incurs an added ethical obligation to ensure that the benefits of the research outweigh the risks. Generally, in studies that present no more than minimal risk of harm to the participants, informed consent may be waived. Fortunately, most educational research would seem to fall under the category of minimal or no risk, which reduces the problem of the requirement of obtaining informed consent. However, whenever informed consent can be obtained, it should and must. Only in instances when it cannot should the researcher seek a waiver.

EXHIBIT 3.4   Consent Form

Informed Consent

Title: Predictors of speech rate in normally fluent children

Principal Investigator: Sally Smith

Department: Education

Telephone Number: 111–123–4567

You are invited to participate in a research study investigating the things that affect how fast normal children of different ages speak. If you volunteer to participate in this research study, we will test the clarity of your hearing, language, and speech.

The research will involve asking you to talk about different things such as telling what you see on picture cards, saying words and sounds as fast as you can, and repeating words and sentences. You will be asked to name animals, colors, letters, and numbers as fast as you can and to read a paragraph. If you get tired before the tests are finished, you can rest and finish the study later. Your speech will be recorded so we can study that later.

The study will take between one and one-and-one-half hours.

You may not get any benefit from participating in the study, but the tests we give you may help us understand how different things affect how fast children speak.

If you volunteer to participate in this study, you should always remember that you may withdraw and stop participating in the study at any time you wish. You will not be penalized in any way if you withdraw and stop participating in the study.

There are no risks from participating in this study other than perhaps you may get tired of doing the tests.

All information that you provide to us will be kept strictly confidential. At no time will we give any information to anyone outside the research staff. The recordings of your speech will be erased when the research is finished. The results of this study may be presented at professional meetings or published in a professional journal, but your name and any other identifying information will not be revealed.

If you have any questions about this study or if you have any questions regarding your rights as a research participant, you may call the Institutional Review Board of the university at 111–123–5678. You may also contact Dr. Sally Smith at 123–4567.

AGREEMENT TO PARTICIPATE IN RESEARCH

I have read, or have had read to me, and understand the above study and have had an opportunity to ask questions which have been answered to my satisfaction. I agree voluntarily to participate in the study as described.

_____
Participant's Name

_____
Date

_____
Signature of Consenting Party

_____
Date

_____
Signature of Investigator

_____
Date

_____
Signature of Witness

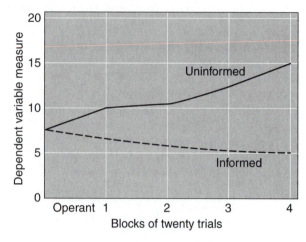

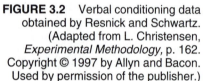

FIGURE 3.2   Verbal conditioning data obtained by Resnick and Schwartz. (Adapted from L. Christensen, *Experimental Methodology*, p. 162. Copyright © 1997 by Allyn and Bacon. Used by permission of the publisher.)

Informed Consent and Minors as Research Participants

The principle of informed consent refers to the fact that a person, once given the pertinent information, is competent and legally free of the desire of others to make a decision as to whether to participate in a given research study. Minors, however, are presumed to be incompetent and cannot give consent. Consent has to be obtained from parents (or the minor's legal guardian) after they have been informed of all features of the study that may affect their willingness to allow their child to participate (see Exhibit 3.5). Once consent has been obtained from the minor's parent or guardian, assent must be obtained from the minor. This means that the minor has to agree to participate in the research after being informed of all the features that may affect his or her willingness to participate.

Federal regulations state that the assent of the minor should be obtained when he or she is capable of providing assent. However, the age at which a person is capable of providing assent can differ among children. To provide assent the child must be able to understand what is being asked, to realize that permission is being sought, and to make choices free from outside constraints. This depends on the cognitive capabilities of the child. Unfortunately, the cognitive capabilities of children develop at different rates, making it difficult to state an age at which a child is capable of providing assent. Individuals over the age of nine generally have sufficient cognitive ability to make a decision concerning participation in research while individuals over the age of fourteen seem to make the same decisions as adults (Leikin, 1993). This should not be taken to mean that assent should definitely be obtained from individuals over age fourteen, possibly from individuals over age nine, and not from individuals age nine or less. Rather, most individuals (e.g., Leikin, 1993) and the ethical guidelines provided by the Society for Research in Child Development (1993) state that assent should be obtained from all children. This is the guideline that we also recommend. Not only is it more ethically acceptable to obtain the assent of minors, but it may also enhance the validity of the study. Insisting that minors participate when they clearly state that they do not want to can alter their behavioral responses and represent a confounding influence on the data collected.

EXHIBIT 3.5 Example of a Parental Consent Form for Use with Minors

Dear Parent or Legal Guardian:

I am doing research about children's ideas about effort. I would like to know whether ideas about effort are related to how children study and remember in learning and testing situations. I am asking for your permission to let your child be in this research.

There will be two 30-minute sessions alone with your child or in small groups. The sessions will be held in a room at your child's school during school hours. The time will be selected by your child's teacher. The first session will include two questionnaires. The Students' Perception of Control Questionnaire will be given to small groups. The questionnaire has sixty questions about why things happen in school. It measures the students' beliefs about whether they can make good grades if they try. The second questionnaire is a measure of self-esteem. It measures how a child feels about himself or herself in different situations such as at school and with friends.

In the second session your child will be asked to put together a difficult puzzle. Each child will be shown the solution to the puzzle and then will be asked to study and remember some pictures. Some children will be told that the memory task is a test to see how well they remember, and others will be told it is a chance to learn how to remember better. Finally, children will be asked to rate how well they did, how they feel about what they just did, and whether they would like to do something like this again.

I would also like to look at your child's intelligence and achievement test scores. I am asking permission to use your child's records. Any personal information about you or your child will be confidential. The results from this research may be presented at a professional meeting or published in a professional journal, but your child's name and other identifying information will not be revealed.

You are under no obligation for your child to participate in this project. If you give your consent, you are free to change your mind and remove your child at any time without negative consequences. Also, your child is free to refuse to participate at any time without negative consequences.

If you are willing for your child to participate, and your child wants to participate, please sign below and return this form to school with your child. If you have any questions, please contact me at 765–4321.

Sincerely,

Jane Doe, Ph.D.
Assistant Professor

I give my permission for my child to be tested on the memory task described in this letter, and to complete the questionnaires concerning beliefs about effort and self-esteem. I grant the County Public School System permission to release to Dr. Jane Doe or her assistant my child's test scores and/or access to my child's files.

_____	_____
Child's Name	Birthdate
_____	_____
Signature of Parent/Legal Guardian	Date

ADDITIONAL CONSENT

There are many educational research studies that are conducted within the confines of a school system. These studies require the cooperation of a number of individuals such as the teacher, principal, and superintendent. These individuals must give their approval to the study, which means that informed consent must also be received from them. This is a very important step in the conduct of a successful study and the researcher must not underemphasize the importance of this cooperation. All questions posed by these individuals must be answered, and their right to choose to participate or not or to discontinue participation at any time should be respected.

DECEPTION

The principle of informed consent refers to the fact that research participants are to receive information about the purpose and nature of the study in which they are asked to participate so that they can evaluate the procedures to be followed and make an informed judgment as to whether they want to participate. Sometimes, however, providing a full disclosure of the nature and purpose of the study will alter the outcome and invalidate the study, as we illustrated earlier in the Resnick and Schwartz study. In such instances it is necessary to mislead or withhold information from the research participants. In other words it is necessary to engage in **deception** to conduct a valid study.

Deception
Misleading or
withholding
information from
the research
participant

Although the AERA ethical guidelines discourage the use of deception, these guidelines do recognize that some research studies cannot be conducted without its use. For example, Butler and Neuman (1995) investigated some of the variables that influenced help-seeking behaviors among children. In conducting this study the experimenters did not inform the children that they were studying the variables that influence whether they would seek help. Rather, the children were invited to try out some materials that consisted of completing several puzzles. They were not given any information suggesting that the variable of interest was help seeking, but were given instructions as to how to seek help if they were so inclined. Obviously, in this study it was necessary to make use of deception in the form of withholding information because if the true purpose of the study had been revealed, it could have altered the outcome and invalidated the results.

Debriefing
A poststudy
interview in which
all aspects of the
study are revealed,
any reasons for
deception are
explained, and any
questions the
participant has
about the study
are answered

The form of deception used by Butler and Neuman consisted of withholding information. Withholding information represents one of the milder forms of deception. However, even use of this mild form of deception violates the principle of informed consent and therefore is of ethical concern. This is why the AERA ethical guidelines explicitly state that deception is discouraged unless it is necessary for the integrity of the study.

If deception is used, the reasons for the deception should be explained to the participants in the debriefing session held after the study has been completed. **Debriefing** refers to an interview conducted with each research participant after the participant has completed the study. In this interview the experimenter and research participant talk about the study. It is an opportunity for each research participant to comment freely about any part of the study and express any concerns that he or she may have had about the study. Phillips (1994), for example, realized that her survey of adolescents' attitudes and behavior related to HIV/AIDS prevention was bound to raise questions not only about the survey but also about other related issues. Consistent with Phillips' expectations, the student research participants asked numerous questions regarding HIV/AIDS specifically and sexuality more generally.

Debriefing is also an opportunity for the researcher to reveal aspects of the study that were not disclosed at the outset. Holmes (1976a; 1976b) has pointed out that debriefing should meet the two goals of dehoaxing and desensitizing. **Dehoaxing** refers to informing the participants about any deception that may have been used in the study. Not only can any deception used be revealed, but the reasons for its use can also be explained. **Desensitizing** refers to helping the participants, during the debriefing interview, deal with and eliminate any stress or other undesirable feeling that the study may have created, as may exist if you are studying cheating behavior or failure. Desensitizing is typically done by suggesting that the undesirable behavior was the result of some situational variable rather than some characteristic of the participant. Another tactic used by experimenters is to point out that the participant's behavior was normal and expected.

The important question is whether a debriefing session is effective in desensitizing or dehoaxing the participants. In Holmes's (1976a; 1976b) review of the literature relating to these two techniques, he concluded that they were generally effective. However, this means only that effective debriefing is possible. These results hold only if debriefing is carried out properly. A sloppy or improperly prepared debriefing session may have a very different effect. Therefore, it is necessary not only to include a debriefing session after each study, but also to ensure that the debriefing session is appropriately conducted.

Dehoaxing
Informing participants about any deception used and the reasons for its use

Desensitizing
Reducing or eliminating any stress or other undesirable feelings the participant may have as a result of participating in the study

FREEDOM TO WITHDRAW

The AERA ethical standards explicitly state that research "participants have the right to withdraw from a study at any time, unless otherwise constrained by their official capacity or roles" (p. 24). This principle seems very straightforward and easily accomplished. Merely inform the participant that he or she is free to withdraw from the study at any time. From the researcher's perspective such a statement should be sufficient to comply with the "freedom to withdraw" principle. However, from the participant's perspective such a statement may not be sufficient because he or she may feel coercive pressure to participate. Such pressure may arise if a teacher requests students to participate or if a principal or superintendent asks teachers to participate in a study. Students may feel coercive pressure by thinking that their grades may be affected if they don't participate, or teachers may believe that their jobs are in jeopardy if they refuse participation. In such instances the participant is not completely free to withdraw, and the researcher must make a special effort to ensure that the research participants are convinced that refusing to participate or withdrawing from the experiment will have no adverse effect on them.

Special consideration should be given to minors and their freedom to dissent. Minors are generally viewed as not having the ability to provide informed consent to participate or to decline participation. This is why consent is sought from the minor's legal parent or guardian. However, the minor can provide assent or dissent to participate. The ethical issue that must be considered here is whether parents or guardians can overrule the dissent of children. The *Ethical Standards for Research with Children* published by the Society for Research in Child Development (1993) states that the child's freedom to choose not to participate should be respected. As a general rule, dissent from participation should always be honored unless the study provides a benefit to the child that he or she could not get elsewhere.

Although it seems most appropriate to respect the wishes of a child to dissent, there is obviously an age at which it does not seem reasonable to seek assent or dissent. The most obvious situation involves infants. Here it is important for the researcher to be sensitive to any indicators of discomfort in the infant. With older children the situation is more difficult, because they have varying cognitive capabilities. There is some evidence (see Pence, 1980) to suggest that researchers should honor the dissent of children down to the age of seven. However, if children below that age seem disturbed or uncomfortable with participation, the researcher should seriously consider excusing the child from the study and in such a way as to ensure that no adverse effects are incurred.

PROTECTION FROM MENTAL AND PHYSICAL HARM

The most important and fundamental issue confronting the researcher is the treatment of the research participants. Earlier we provided several examples of medical studies that inflicted both physical and mental harm on the participants. Fortunately, studies conducted by educational researchers seldom if ever run the risk of inflicting such severe mental and physical harm on participants. In fact, educational research has historically engaged in research that typically imposes either minimal or no risk to the participants and has enjoyed a special status with respect to formal ethical oversight. A large portion of this research has been singled out for exempt status in the Code of Federal Regulations for the Protection of Human Subjects (OPRR Reports, 1991). Paragraph 46.101(b)(1) of this code states that "Research conducted in established or commonly accepted educational settings involving normal educational practices such as (i) research on regular and special educational instructional strategies, or (ii) research on the effectiveness of or the comparison among instructional techniques, curricula, or classroom management methods" (p. 5) are exempt from oversight.

The problem with this statement lies in its ambiguity. It is worded so vaguely as to leave considerable room for competing interpretations as to what represents "commonly accepted educational settings involving normal educational practices." Additionally, educational research is not a static entity but one that is constantly changing. One of the more notable changes is the increased use of qualitative research methods.

Qualitative research, as Howe and Dougherty (1993) have pointed out, has two features, intimacy and open-endedness, that muddy the ethical waters and exclude it from the special exempt status reserved for many educational research studies. Qualitative research is an ongoing and evolving process, with the data collection process proceeding more like a friendship between the participant and the researcher. Interviewing, for example, requires contact on a one-to-one basis and removes the participant from his or her normal activities. Video and audio taping create permanent records that can pose a threat to confidentiality and anonymity. It is these activities as well as the ambiguity of the wording identifying "exempt" that indicate a need for some type of ethical oversight of educational research. The ethical oversight provided by virtually any institution that conducts research is the Institutional Review Board (**IRB**).

IRB
The institutional review committee that assesses the ethical acceptability of research proposals

CONFIDENTIALITY AND ANONYMITY

Anonymity
Keeping the identity of the participant from everyone, including the researcher

Confidentiality
Not revealing the identity of the participant to anyone other than the researcher and the researcher's staff

AERA ethical guidelines state that research participants have the right to remain anonymous and the confidentiality of both the participants and the data must be protected. Confidentiality and anonymity are two of the ways researchers protect participants. **Anonymity** means that the identity of the participants is not known to the researcher. Anonymity, for example, could be achieved in a survey on the frequency with which high school students cheated on examinations if this survey did not ask the students for any information that could be used to identify them, and the survey administered was conducted in large groups of, say, 100 students. **Confidentiality** means that the participant's identity, although known to the research group, is not revealed to anyone other than the researcher and his or her staff. Confidentiality would be maintained if, for example, you were conducting a study on children with learning disabilities. Although the research staff would know which children were in the study, and, therefore, had a learning disability, this information would not be revealed to anyone outside the research staff. Confidentiality and anonymity are important to avoid connecting the participant with any information that would be embarrassing or harmful. Because it is impossible to know how people might interpret responses, or what responses may have adverse consequences for the participant, maintaining the participant's anonymity is recommended. When anonymity cannot be maintained, confidentiality of the participant's responses and identity is essential.

INSTITUTIONAL REVIEW BOARD

The legal requirement of having all human research reviewed by the IRB dates back to 1966. At that time there was a concern for the way in which medical research was designed and conducted. As a result of this concern, the Surgeon General initiated an institutional review requirement at the Department of Health, Education, and Welfare (DHEW). This policy was extended to all investigations funded by the Public Health Service that involved human participants, including those in the social and behavioral sciences. By 1973 the DHEW regulations governing human research required a review by an IRB for all research receiving Public Health Service funds. This meant that virtually all institutions of higher education had to establish an IRB and file an assurance policy with the Office for Protection from Research Risks of the Department of Health and Human Services. This assurance policy articulates the responsibilities and purview of the IRB within that institution. Although the Public Health Service mandated only that federally funded projects be reviewed by the IRB, most institutions extended the scope of the IRB to include all research involving human participants, even those falling into the exempt category. Once this institutional assurance policy is approved, it becomes a legal document to which the institution and researchers must comply. If your institution has such an assurance policy, you, as an educational researcher, must submit a proposal to the IRB to determine whether your study is exempt from ethical oversight. In this proposal you should state whether you believe it falls into the exempt category. A member of the IRB makes the decision as to whether the study is exempt and can proceed as proposed or must be reviewed by the full IRB. In short, this means that <u>"exempt" refers to being exempt from certain requirements and full committee review, not exempt from IRB oversight altogether.</u>

In reviewing the research proposals, members of the IRB are required to make judgments regarding the ethical appropriateness of the proposed research by ensuring that research protocols are explained to the research participants and that the risks of harm are reasonable in relation to the hoped-for benefits. To make this judgment, the IRB members must have sufficient information about the specifics of the research protocol. This means that the investigator must submit a research protocol that the IRB can review. This research protocol must provide provide the following information:

1. Information regarding the purpose and rationale of the research
2. Information about the research participants to be used in the study
3. The location of the research
4. The tasks or variables and procedures to be used
5. Whether the procedures are experimental
6. The research design used to answer the research question
7. The potential benefits to the research participants or general knowledge acquired from the study
8. Any risks or hazards from participation in the research
9. Precautions taken to reduce the risks and hazards
10. A description of how confidentiality will be ensured
11. A consent form for participation

A sample protocol (not including the consent form) appears in Exhibit 3.6.

Once the research protocol has been submitted, the IRB administrators must determine whether the protocol should be reviewed by the full board. There are actually seven different categories of review. The three most frequently used are exempt studies, studies that receive expedited review, and studies that receive review by the full board. Exempt studies are those that appear to involve no risk to the participants and do not require review by the full IRB. However, studies involving fetal participants, prisoners, and children are never exempt unless the study involves observing these participants in the absence of any

---

EXHIBIT 3.6 Example of a Research Protocol Submitted to the IRB

Title of Protocol: The Relationship of Attributional Beliefs, Self-Esteem, and Ego Involvement to Performance on Cognitive Tasks in Students with Mental Retardation.

Primary Investigator: Jane A. Donner, Department of Psychology, University of the Southeast, 460-6321.

Co-Investigator: Carolyn L. Pickering, Graduate Student, Department of Psychology, University of the Southeast, 460-6321.

Relevant Background and Purpose Recent research suggests that the way in which a cognitive task is presented influences performance on the task. Nicholls (1985) suggested that ego involvement would often result in diminished task performance. He describes ego involvement as a task orientation in which the goal is to either demonstrate one's ability relative to others or avoid demonstrating a lack of ability. This ego orientation is in contrast to task involvement where the goal is simply to learn or improve a skill. In support of the Nicholls position, Graham and Golan (1991) found that ego-involving instructions resulted in poorer recall in a memory task than task-orienting instructions. Apparently, the focus on performance detracted from the necessary information processing.

The present investigation is designed to determine potential individual differences in the ego-involvement effect. It is possible that some persons are more at risk for the debilitating effects of ego-involving instructions than others. It is predicted that students with mental retardation who have low self-esteem and negative attributional beliefs will be influenced negatively by ego-involving instructions.

Subject Population Forty students with mental retardation will be recruited from special education classrooms at approximately three elementary schools in the Mobile County Public School System. Students will be recruited from the intermediate classes (fourth–sixth grades). The students' participation will be voluntary and they will have parental consent.

Materials and Procedure

Overview The research will be conducted at the students' school and will include two sessions, each approximately a half-hour long. In the first session, students will first complete attributional and self-esteem questionnaires, which will be read aloud to them, in small groups of about three. Students will be read pretraining exercises and provided guidance in answering the questions to be sure they understand how to answer the actual questionnaires.

In the next session, students will be tested individually. They will first work on a geometric puzzle task which they will not have time to finish. The examiner will then show them how to finish the puzzle. Next, half the subjects will receive a categorization memory task with ego-orienting instructions and the other half will receive the same task with task-orienting instructions.

Questionnaires The attributional questionnaire (attached) is designed to assess the students' beliefs about the importance of different casual factors (e.g., effort, ability, luck, and powerful others) in academic performance. The self-esteem questionnaire (attached) is designed to measure global self-worth and self-esteem in four domains.

Experimental Tasks The geometric puzzle task will use a difficult block design task from an intelligence test for children. One pattern on a card, which is not included in the intelligence test, will be shown to children for them to copy with their blocks, and they will be given 60 seconds to work on the design. It is not expected that the children will be able to finish the puzzle, and the examiner will then show the students how to finish the puzzle.

The categorization memory task will be used to assess students' performance. Each child will be presented with sixteen pictures classifiable according to categories (e.g., clothes, vehicles, animals)

(continued)

EXHIBIT 3.6 *(continued)*

with four items in each category. Relatively typical items (e.g., car, truck, boat, motorcycle) are used as stimuli. Children will first be given 60 seconds to arrange the pictures in any way that will help them remember. If a student does not touch the items, he or she will be reminded that he or she can arrange them in any way he or she would like. After 60 seconds students will be given an additional 60 seconds to study their arrangement of the items, after which they will recall the items in any order. Students will be given three trials of the task. This task will yield three measures: (a) clustering (ARC) at organization (Roenker, Thompson, & Brown, 1971), (b) ARC at recall, and (c) recall accuracy. ARC scores indicate the amount of clustering relative to chance. An ARC score of 1 reflects perfect clustering, whereas an ARC score of 0 reflects the degree of clustering that would be expected by chance.

Instructional Formats   The categorization memory task will be presented in two instructional formats (adapted from Graham and Golan, 1991). Students will be randomly assigned to receive either the task-involvement format or the ego-involvement format. The instructions for the task-involvement format are as follows:

> You will probably make mistakes on this memory task at first but you will probably get better as you go on. If you think about the task and try to see it as something you can learn from, you will have more fun doing it.

The instructions for the ego-involvement format are as follows:

> You are either good at this memory task compared to others or you are not. How well you do in this task will tell me something about your memory ability in this kind of activity.

After being read the instructions, the students will begin the task. At the end of the session students will be asked to rate from 1–5 how well they think they

did, how much fun they thought the task was, whether they would like to do the memory task again in the future, and whether they felt certain emotions (such as happy, sad, proud, and ashamed) during the task. Following this questionnaire, students will be told that since they performed so well on the tasks, they will receive a prize, such as a sticker or piece of candy.

Design and Methodology   Following approval by the appropriate school personnel, the attached consent form will be distributed by the classroom teacher. Students who return the consent form, signed by their parent or guardian are then invited to participate in the research. Parental consent will also be requested to obtain students' IQ scores from their school files. These scores will be used to determine whether students' scores are within the range specified by the American Association of Mental Retardation and to obtain a group mean for the students. The data will be analyzed through multiple regression with attributions, self-esteem, and instructional format as predictors of performance.

Potential Benefit   The present literature on ego- and task-involvement indicates that ego instructions can negatively affect performance. It is important to determine the individual differences in this phenomenon. It is possible that children with mental retardation and with low self-esteem and with negative attributional beliefs may be especially at risk for the debilitating effects of ego-involving instructions. If this is the case, one could reduce these individual differences in performance and support optimal learning by presenting tasks primarily in a task-involvement format.

Risks   The risks are minimal. It is possible that students will be discouraged by not having time to complete the puzzle and by not remembering all of the pictures. However, at the end of the session, we will make it clear to each student that the tasks were designed to be difficult for everyone. In addition, all students will be told at the end of the session that they did very well on the task.

Confidentiality   All personal information will remain confidential. All data will be stored securely in a locked laboratory on campus. Only the principal investigator and her assistants will have access to these data.

Signatures:

_____

Department Chairperson

_____

Primary Investigator

Used by permission of the author.

type of intervention. Studies receiving expedited review are those involving no more than minimal risk. Its name suggests that the study is reviewed rapidly and by fewer members than constitute the full board. This is typically the case and the study receives more rapid turnaround than exists when the full board reviews a protocol. Studies receiving full board review would be all other studies.

If the IRB staff reviews a protocol and places it in the exempt category, it is typically returned to the investigator within a few days, and the investigator is free to begin his or her research project. Remember that it is the IRB staff and not the researcher that must make the decision as to whether the protocol is exempt. In making this decision, the IRB staff makes use of the exempt categories set forth in the OPRR Reports (1991), which are as follows:

1. Research conducted in established or commonly accepted educational settings, involving normal educational practices, such as (i) research on regular and special education instructional strategies, or (ii) research on the effectiveness of or the comparison among instructional techniques, curricula, or classroom management methods.
2. Research involving the use of educational tests (cognitive, diagnostic, aptitude, achievement), survey procedures, interview procedures, or observation of public behavior, unless:
    (i)   information obtained is recorded in such a manner that human subjects can be identified, directly or through identifiers linked to the subjects; and
    (ii) any disclosure of the human subjects' responses outside the research could reasonably place the subjects at risk of criminal or civil liability or be damaging to the subjects' financial standing, employability, or reputation.
3. Research involving the use of educational tests (cognitive, diagnostic, aptitude, achievement), survey procedures, interview procedures, or observation of public behavior that is not exempt under (2) above if
    (i)   the human subjects are elected or appointed public officials or candidates for public office, or
    (ii) Federal statute(s) require(s) without exception that the confidentiality of the personally identifiable information will be maintained throughout the research and thereafter.
4. Research involving the collection or study of existing data, documents, records, pathological specimens, or diagnostic specimens if these sources are publicly

available or if the information is recorded by the investigator in such a manner that subjects cannot be identified, directly or through identifiers linked to the subjects.

5. Research and demonstration projects that are conducted by or subject to the approval of Department or Agency heads, and that are designed to study, evaluate or otherwise examine:

   (i)   Public benefit or service programs
   (ii)   Procedures for obtaining benefits or services under those programs
   (iii) Possible changes in or alternatives to those programs or procedures
   (iv)   Possible changes in methods or levels of payment for benefits or services under those programs (p. 5)

In reading these exempt categories, it seems as though a large portion of educational research would fall into the exempt category, and much of it does. Even if a study does fall into the exempt category and receives approval from the IRB, it does not mean that there are no other ethical issues to be considered. Phillips (1994) submitted her survey of adolescents' attitudes and behaviors related to HIV/AIDS prevention to the IRB and received approval pending only minor changes in the vocabulary of the consent form. Phillips requested a full board review of her research protocol even though she felt it would fall into exempt category except for the fact that the research participants were minors. The study was an anonymous survey of adolescents' attitudes. The study did not inject, expose, medicate, or even touch the participants, and their responses could not be traced back to any specific individual. However, even with the IRB approval Phillips identified a number of ethical concerns ranging from privacy to potential harm of the participants. This example illustrates that the investigator must remain attuned to the ethics of his or her research and not become complacent just because IRB approval has been received. One final point needs to be made with respect to IRB oversight. Many of the studies that educational researchers conduct use children as their research participants. Any time a study uses children as research participants, it must be reviewed by the IRB. There is no exception to this.

SUMMARY

When conducting educational research, it is necessary to ask questions and observe the behavior of students, teachers, and administrators. In doing so, researchers must be careful not to impinge on the well-recognized rights of these individuals to privacy and freedom from surveillance without consent. Research ethics are necessary to assist researchers in conducting ethically sound studies by providing a set of principles that will assist in establishing appropriate goals and resolving conflicting values.

There are three areas of ethical concern for the educational researcher. These include

1. *The relationship between society and science.* The society in which we live influences the research issues that are important and that need to be investigated. The most influential agency is the federal government because this agency not only provides most of the funds for research but also identifies priority areas.

2. *Professional issues.* The primary professional issue of ethical importance is fraudulent activity by scientists. In recent years there has been a rise in the presentation of fraudulent results. This increase seems to be due primarily to the pressure to obtain grants and publish articles because these activities are frequently tied to promotions, raises, and tenure, although psychological makeup and other nonpersonal factors may contribute. Other less serious professional issues include partial and dual publication, the use and archiving of videotaped data, and the conduct of research with vulnerable populations such as minors.

3. *Treatment of research participants.* Treatment of the research participants is the most fundamental ethical issue. Although most educational research does not run the risk of physical harm, there are subtle ethical issues that must be addressed relating to the potential for emotional harm, deception, and protecting the privacy of research participants.

The AERA has developed a set of ethical guidelines, specifically directed toward the educational researcher, which need to be followed when conducting a research study. Some of the important points included in these guidelines are

1. *The necessity of obtaining informed consent.* This means that a person can participate in a research study only when he or she has agreed to participate and has been given all information that would influence his or her willingness to participate. Providing full disclosure of the nature or purpose of the research will alter the outcome and invalidate the results of some studies. In these cases deception may be used but the investigator must justify the use of the deception. If deception is used, it must be revealed and any negative effects occurring from it must be eliminated during a debriefing session.

2. *Assent and dissent with minors.* Minors cannot provide informed consent, but when they are capable of providing assent, it must be obtained.

3. *Freedom to withdraw.* It must be communicated to the research participants that they are free to withdraw from the research study at any time without penalty. As a general rule, the dissent of a minor should also be respected even if the guardian or parent has provided informed consent. Children below the age of being able to provide consent or infants should be excused from the research study if they seem to be disturbed or uncomfortable with the procedures.

4. *Confidentiality and anonymity.* Ideally, the research participant's identity is not known to the researcher (anonymity). In cases where it is not possible to maintain anonymity, the identity of the participant and his or her responses must not be revealed to anyone other than the research staff (confidentiality).

In all cases it is necessary to present a research proposal to the IRB for approval even if the guidelines presented by the AERA have been followed and the proposal seems to fall into the exempt category. Most institutional assurance policies state that *all* research involving humans is to be reviewed by the IRB, which means that it is the IRB that makes the decision as to whether a study falls into the exempt category.

STUDY QUESTIONS

1. Define research ethics and the approaches used in considering ethical issues.
2. What are the areas of ethical concern for educational researchers, and what are the primary issues of concern in each area?
3. What are the primary guidelines to follow in conducting an ethical study as outlined by the AERA?
4. What does informed consent mean, what information should be given to a research participant prior to obtaining his or her informed consent, and what are the issues involved in obtaining the consent of minors?
5. Under what circumstances can deception be used in a research study, and what specific procedure should the researcher follow if deception is used in a study?
6. What are the important issues to consider in ensuring that research participants feel free to withdraw from a study at any time?
7. What is the purpose of the IRB, and why must all studies receive IRB approval?

KEY TERMS

anonymity (83)

confidentiality (83)

debriefing (80)

deception (80)

dehoaxing (81)

deontological approach (62)

desensitizing (81)

duplicate publication (65)

ethical skepticism (62)

IRB (83)

partial publication (65)

research ethics (63)

utilitarianism (62)

3
PART

FOUNDATIONS OF RESEARCH

CHAPTER 4

Standardized Measurement and Assessment

LEARNING OBJECTIVES

To be able to

- explain the meaning of measurement.
- explain the different scales of measurement, including the type of information communicated by each one.
- articulate the twelve assumptions underlying testing and assessment.
- explain the meaning of reliability.
- explain the differences among each of the methods for computing reliability.
- explain the meaning of validity.
- explain the different methods of collecting validity evidence and realize that construct validity embraces all forms of validity evidence.
- identify the different types of standardized tests and the sources of information on these tests.

Think for a moment about what you have learned about conducting an educational research study. All research studies begin with a research question and hypotheses relating to this research question. After the research question is formulated, you have to develop a way of providing an answer to that research question by collecting information, or data, that will give you the answer you are looking for. Whenever you collect data, you are measuring or assessing something. For example, assume that you are going to conduct a quantitative experimental research study investigating the effect of an accelerated reading rate on memory for a text in children with dyslexia. In conducting this study you would have to first identify a group of children with dyslexia. You could select these children, as Breznitz (1997) did, by measuring them on a number of variables such as reading ability and selecting those with impaired reading but normal intelligence, visual acuity, motivation, educational opportunity, and instruction. After the children with dyslexia are identified, the study can be conducted. In conducting the study you have to measure the dependent variable of memory for the text the children with dyslexia had read. Therefore, to conduct this study, measurement would be required to identify the participant sample and to collect the dependent variable data.

As you can see, conducting an educational research study requires the measurement of one or more variables. From your own experience, you have probably had exposure to the measurement of many different types of variables. Students are frequently given some type of achievement test, some of which are constructed by teachers and others by measurement professionals. Tests are often used to diagnose learning and/or behavior problems, intelligence, aptitude, and/or interests. More recently, students in some areas of the country are being evaluated at the end of their high school education to determine whether they have acquired the minimal knowledge and skills expected of a high school graduate. Measurement, therefore, is something that exists in many areas, and educational research is one of them.

Measuring variables of interest to educational researchers is often a rather difficult task. Educational researchers investigate variables such as memory, dyslexia, motivation, and educational achievement. When we measure these variables, we frequently express them as numbers. However, converting variables such as these to numbers or dimensions is difficult, and considerable time and energy is often devoted to this process. Because of this difficulty, we briefly discuss the nature of measurement and the various scales of measurement.

SCALES OF MEASUREMENT

Measurement
The act of measuring by assigning symbols or numbers to something according to a specific set of rules

Measurement refers to the act of measuring. When we measure something, we are making an evaluation in which we attempt to identify the dimensions, quantity, capacity, or degree of something. This measurement or evaluation process operates by assigning symbols or numbers to objects, events, people, characteristics, and so forth according to a specific set of rules. Actually, this is something we do all the time. For example, whenever you determine how tall a person is or how much they weigh, you are engaged in measurement because you are assigning numbers according to a given set of rules. If you are measuring height in inches, the rule you are using is that you are assigning the number 1 to a length that is exactly 1 inch on a standard ruler. Height in inches is determined by counting the number of these 1-inch lengths it takes to span the length or height of the person whom you are measuring. If you are measuring or evaluating the gender of a person, you use the rule of assigning the symbol of female to individuals that have female characteristics and the symbol of male to individuals that have male characteristics. The result of any measurement is that you have a guideline for representing the dimensions or magnitude of something, such as the height or gender of a person. Stating that a person is 68 inches tall communicates the exact height of that person, just as the symbol of female communicates the gender dimension of that person.

Educational researchers might be interested in variables such as aggression, shyness, depression, dyslexia, gender, and intelligence. To conduct a study investigating these variables, some procedure or technique is needed for representing their dimensions and/or magnitude. These procedures or techniques exist in many forms. The number derived from an intelligence test represents an index of the magnitude of intellect. The number of times a child hits another has been used as an index of the magnitude of aggression. The biological makeup of a child is used as an index of gender.

Measurement can be categorized in terms of the type of information communicated by the symbols or numbers that are assigned. It is generally agreed that there are four different levels or scales of measurement; nominal, ordinal, interval, and ratio. Each of these scales of measurement conveys different kinds of information, as illustrated in Table 4.1. It is important to know and understand the scale of measurement being employed because it suggests the type of statistical manipulations of the data that are appropriate and identifies the type of information being communicated.

Nominal scale
A scale of measurement that uses symbols or numbers to label, classify, or identify people or objects

Nominal Scale

Nominal scales are the simplest form of measurement. These scales involve using symbols or numbers to label, classify, or identify the people or objects you are studying. For example, we use the nominal scale when we use a symbol or a number to identify the room in which a class is being taught. A student may have a history class in room A or in room 112 and an English class in room B or in room 224. These symbols or numbers are used

TABLE 4.1 Scale of Measurement

Scale	Characteristics
Nominal	Ability to categorize, label, classify, name, or identify
Ordinal	Rank order objects or individuals from first to last or best to worst
Interval	Ability to rank order objects or individuals; has equal intervals or distances between adjacent numbers
Ratio	Ability to rank order objects or individuals; has equal intervals between adjacent numbers and has an absolute zero point that permits forming ratio statements

exclusively for identification purposes. They do little else. They cannot be added, subtracted, ranked, or averaged. Similarly, the symbol A or the number 112 does not stand for instruction in history. In another school year mathematics may be taught in this classroom. However, it is possible to count the frequency with which something is identified by a given symbol or number. For example, it is possible to count the number of classrooms in which English or history was taught. These frequency data could then be statistically analyzed.

Even though the nominal scale is so simple, many observations made by educational researchers exist at this level. For example, educational researchers frequently create an independent variable by categorizing people by some characteristic such as gender or the presence or absence of a disorder such as ADHD and then compare the performance of the people placed in the different categories. Wang and Staver (1997), for example, compared the performance of male and female children in China on science achievement. In analyzing the data collected in this study, they could have labeled males "1" and females "2" or kept the symbols for male and female. In this study Wang and Staver also analyzed the science achievement data by province as well as gender, as illustrated in Table 4.2.

Ordinal Scale

Ordinal scale
A rank-order scale
of measurement

The **ordinal scale** of measurement is a rank-order scale. This scale of measurement is frequently used to determine which students will be accepted into graduate programs because most graduate programs receive many more applicants than they can accept. Therefore, applicants are frequently rank ordered from the one with the most outstanding credentials to the one with the least outstanding credentials. A specified number of students with the highest ranks are selected for admission. In another situation, students might be rank ordered in terms of their need for remedial instruction. In both examples, the key characteristic is that individuals are compared with others in terms of some ability or performance and assigned a rank with, perhaps, "1" being assigned to the person with the most ability or the person who performs best, "2" to the next best, and so forth.

From this example you should be able to see that an ordinal scale of measurement allows you to make ordinal judgments; that is, it allows you to determine which person is better or worse than another person. However, it does not give you any indication as to how

TABLE 4.2 Science Achievement of Male and Female Students in Five Provinces in China

	Mean		Standard Deviation	
Province	*Female*	*Male*	*Female*	*Male*
Gansu	15.405	17.657	4.556	4.296
Guangxi	15.264	17.195	4.318	4.291
Hubci	15.701	18.160	4.276	4.099
Inner Mongolia	15.460	17.772	4.525	4.305
Jiangshu	15.306	17.834	4.253	3.994

Based on data presented by Wang and Staver (1997).

TABLE 4.3   Ranking of Students on Need for Remedial Instruction

Student	Ranking	Student	Ranking
Tommy	1	William	6
Jerry	2	Joyce	7
Sally	3	Bob	8
Suzie	4	Pam	9
Nancy	5	Ben	10

much better one person is than another. If you ranked ten students in terms of their need for remedial instruction, as illustrated in Table 4.3, you would know that the person receiving a rank of "1" is the person needing remedial instruction the most. However, you would not know how much more the person ranked first needed remedial instruction than the person who was ranked second. An ordinal scale of measurement says nothing about how much greater one ranking is than another. Although numbers are used to represent the rank ordering, these numbers do not say anything about the magnitude of difference that exists between the individuals holding two different ranks. If the only information you had was the rank order of a group of individuals, you could not tell whether the difference between the individuals ranked first and second was the same as the difference that existed between the individuals ranked second and third. All you can do with ordinal-level data is rank individuals on some characteristic according to their position on that characteristic.

Interval Scale

Interval scale
A scale of measurement that has equal intervals of distances between adjacent numbers

The **interval scale** of measurement has the rank-order feature of ordinal scales and also possesses the additional characteristic of equal distances, or equal intervals, between adjacent numbers. In other words, the difference between any two adjacent numbers on the scale is equal to the difference between any two other adjacent numbers.

Clear illustrations of an interval scale are the Celsius temperature scale (illustrated in Figure 4.1) and the Fahrenheit temperature scale, because all points on these scales are equally distant from one another. A difference in temperature between 0 and 20 degrees Fahrenheit is the same as the difference between 40 and 60 degrees Fahrenheit. However, you must remember that the zero point on an interval scale is arbitrary. The zero point on the Celsius scale refers to the point at which water freezes at sea level, not an absence of heat, which is what a true zero point would designate. Actually, the absence of heat is approximately –273 degrees Celsius, not the zero point on this temperature scale.

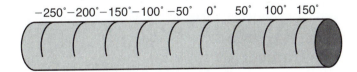

−250° −200° −150° −100° −50°   0°   50°   100° 150°

FIGURE 4.1   A Celsius temperature scale.

This absence of an absolute zero point restricts the type of information that is conveyed by interval-level measurements. Specifically, it eliminates the ability to form ratio statements. For example, it seems logical that you should be able to state that 20 degrees Celsius is twice as warm as 10 degrees Celsius because the difference between 0 and 20 degrees is twice as great as the difference between 0 and 10 degrees, or $20/10 = 2$. However, these ratio statements cannot be made because interval scales do not contain absolute zero points. To illustrate this point, consider the two temperatures 40 and 80 degrees Fahrenheit. If ratio statements could be made, 80 degrees Fahrenheit should be twice as warm as 40 degrees Fahrenheit. If this relationship is true, it should exist regardless of whether we are talking about temperature measured according to the Fahrenheit scale or the Celsius scale. However, 40 degrees Fahrenheit converts to approximately 4.4 degrees Celsius and 80 degrees Fahrenheit converts to approximately 26.7 degrees Celsius. This is the apparent paradox of an interval scale, a function of the absence of an absolute zero point.

Once the interval level of measurement has been reached, it is possible to engage in arithmetic operations such as computing an average and getting a meaningful result. Many of the scores (e.g., IQ, personality, attitude, aptitude, educational level, reading achievement) we use in educational research are taken to be at the interval level of measurement. However, for most of the characteristics we investigate, zero does not mean an absence of that characteristic. If a person got a science achievement score of zero, that would not necessarily mean that there was a complete absence of achievement in science, just as an IQ score of zero would not necessarily mean an absence of intelligence.

Ratio Scale

Ratio scale
A scale of measurement that has a true zero point as well as all the characteristics of the nominal, ordinal, and interval scales

The **ratio scale** of measurement has all the properties of the nominal, ordinal, and interval scales plus a true zero point. Therefore the number zero represents an absence of the characteristic being measured. Something weighing zero pounds means that it has no weight or is weightless, an absence of weight. Because a ratio scale of measurement has the characteristics of equal intervals between the numbers and a true or absolute zero point, all mathematical operations can meaningfully be performed.

In education, ratio-level measurement is occasionally used. For example, if you are interested in the number of test items a student got correct or the amount of time taken to complete an assignment, you have ratio-level measurement. However, most of the characteristics we measure in education are not at this level because educational researchers deal with attributes such as educational attainment, learning disorders, personality, attitudes, opinions, and learning strategies. Such attributes and characteristics do not possess the characteristics of a ratio scale of measurement. Therefore, ratio-level measurement, desirable as it is, is not the level of measurement used in most educational research studies.

Level of Measurement in Education

If ratio-level measurement is infrequently used in educational research, just what level of measurement is used? Actually, most of the characteristics and attributes measured in educational research exist at the ordinal level of measurement. Characteristics that we measure, such as IQ, reading achievement, evaluations of learning disability, and so on, are, strictly speaking, ordinal. However, Kerlinger (1986) and most educational researchers seem to agree that educational scales and the characteristics they measure approximate interval-level measurement fairly well. If you consider the characteristics of an ordinal and interval scale of measurement when you read educational research articles, you should be able to see that researchers operate as though the scales they have used are interval-level measurement. Educational researchers do this because interval-level data can be manipulated in ways that are not possible with ordinal-level data, such as computing meaningful averages.

ASSUMPTIONS UNDERLYING TESTING AND ASSESSMENT

As they go about the process of conducting their research studies, educational researchers engage in a variety of procedures in an attempt to obtain measures of characteristics that are often considered subjective and difficult to assess, such as personality or teacher morale. Measuring these characteristics involves both testing and assessment. The distinction between testing and assessment is often somewhat ambiguous and has been slow in developing and becoming integrated into everyday parlance. However, there is a difference in spite of this overlap, and this difference needs to be made salient. For our purposes, we will follow the lead of Cohen, Swerdlik, and Philips (1996) and define testing as "the process of measuring . . . variables by means of devices or procedures designed to obtain a sample of behavior" and assessment as "the gathering and integration of . . . data for the purpose of making . . . *an educational* evaluation, accomplished through the use of tools such as tests, interviews, case studies, behavioral observation, and specially designed apparatus and measurement procedures" (p. 6; italics are ours).

In assessing the characteristics of interest to educational researchers, any of a variety of tools ranging from educational and psychological tests to interviews and behavioral observations are used. In many cases very innovative tools are devised to assess people with disabilities. Wilson, Thompson, and Wylie (1982), for example, devised a dental plate that could be activated by the tongue for individuals who lacked the capacity for speech or control of their hands or limbs. This dental plate made it possible for these individuals to provide five different types of responses by depressing the tongue on different areas of the plate.

Educational researchers have been very creative in attempting to assess the multitude of characteristics of interest to them. They have devised assessment tools, used existing tools, or adapted existing tools previously developed for use in the measurement of some characteristic. In testing and assessing these characteristics, a number of assumptions have been, and are, made. Cohen, Swerdlik, and Phillips (1996) have identified twelve assumptions that are basic to the testing and assessment enterprise. These assumptions are as follows:

Traits
Distinguishable, relatively enduring ways in which one person differs from another

1. *Psychological traits and states exist.* This assumption basically states that we agree that psychological traits and states such as anxiety, motivation, shyness, and aggressiveness actually exist and are not a fabrication of some mad scientist. **Traits** are defined as

States
Distinguishable,
but less enduring
ways in which
people differ

"any distinguishable, relatively enduring way in which one individual varies from another" (Guilford, 1959, p. 6). **States** refer to distinguishable ways in which individuals vary, but they differ from traits in that they are less enduring (Chaplin, John, & Goldberg, 1988), or are more transient characteristics. For example, the psychological trait of anxiety would indicate an enduring or constant level of anxiety that persists both over time and across situations. The psychological state of anxiety would indicate a more temporary condition, such as might exist if you were walking in the woods and saw a snake on the path in front of you. Actually, few people would deny that psychological traits and states exist. The controversy surrounding traits and states is just how they exist, a debate beyond the scope of this textbook.

2. *Psychological traits and states can be quantified and measured.* This assumption states that it is possible to assign numbers to psychological traits and states and that these numbers are representative of the properties of the states and traits being measured. In other words, the numerical test score obtained to represent a state or trait is presumed to represent the nature or strength of the state or trait being measured. This means that the higher the test score, the higher the test taker is presumed to be on the targeted trait or state.

3. *Various approaches to measuring aspects of the same thing can be useful.* The same trait, state, interest, ability, or aptitude can be measured using a number of different measurement techniques and tests. Tests vary on a number of dimensions, such as the extent to which they are linked to theory; the extent to which the stimulus materials are verbal or nonverbal; whether they were derived on an empirical or a rational basis; how the test items are presented; and the way in which they are administered, scored, and interpreted. These differences do not imply that there is confusion in the field in terms of how some characteristic should be measured. Rather, it indicates that there are many different ways of measuring the characteristics of interest to educational researchers. This is similar to the different ways of measuring distance. You can measure distance in terms of feet, yards, miles, kilometers, or the amount of time taken to go from the starting to the ending point. Each measure of distance, just as each measure of a characteristic, provides different information.

4. *Assessment can provide answers to some of life's most momentous questions.* Educational researchers are asked to provide answers to questions ranging from the most effective way to teach to determining which children should be targeted for special educational attention. These are not trivial questions, and users of assessment tools need to know when the tools they use provide answers to these questions.

5. *Assessment can pinpoint phenomena that require further attention or study.* Assessment tools are frequently used for making diagnoses. Educational researchers frequently conduct studies on special populations such as children with learning disabilities or children with ADHD. To study such populations, children with these disorders must be identified; this identification is made using some type of assessment tool.

6. *Various sources of data enrich and are part of the assessment process.* The information received from one test or assessment tool is only one source of information from which a decision is made. In most situations, information from various sources must be ob-

tained to make an accurate and informed decision. For example, to diagnose ADHD you need information from psychological tests measuring this disorder as well as information from teachers, parents, a physician, and a psychologist.

7. *Various sources of error are always part of the assessment process.* Error in the assessment process refers to the fact that the scores obtained in any assessment are influenced by variables other than the trait or characteristic being assessed. For example, if you are trying to assess students' intelligence by giving them an intelligence test, the IQ score obtained on the test would be a result of these persons' actual intellectual level plus a variety of other factors, such as how tired they were when they took the test, whether they were physically sick, or whether they were experiencing some interpersonal difficulty such as going through a divorce. These "other" variables partially determine the score obtained from the assessment and introduce "error" into the assessment. The greater the amount of error, the more inaccurate the assessment.

8. *Tests and other measurement techniques have strengths and weaknesses.* It probably seems like common sense to state that every assessment technique has its own unique strengths and weaknesses. The important issue is not a recognition of the fact that these strengths and weaknesses exist, but that the user of the assessment recognizes and understands these strengths and weaknesses so he or she can appropriately interpret the results of the assessment.

9. *Test-related behavior predicts non-test-related behavior.* Every test or assessment is conducted on the assumption that the information obtained from the assessment will say something about some behavior outside the testing situation. For example, achievement tests are given to children on the assumption that their performance on the test will say something about their level of achievement in mathematics, reading, or comprehension.

10. *Present-day behavior sampling predicts future behavior.* Whenever a person takes a test or some other assessment tool, he or she is demonstrating a certain level of performance on the testing day. This performance is frequently used to make a prediction about some future behavior. Performance on an IQ test is, for example, used to predict a person's future level of ability and, perhaps, how well he or she may do in school or in some other intellectually stimulating task.

11. *Testing and assessment can be conducted in a fair and unbiased manner.* All test publishers attempt to develop tests that are fair and unbiased. Fairness and biasing issues arise when a test is administered to people whose background and experience are different from those for whom the test was intended. In cases such as this, the test or assessment probably will be unfair and biased, which just emphasizes that any assessment device can be used inappropriately. This is why the person administering the assessment device must be aware of its strengths and weaknesses so that it can be applied appropriately and a valid assessment can be obtained.

12. *Testing and assessment benefit society.* Many critical decisions are made on the basis of tests and other assessments. Minimal teacher competency in some states is established on the basis of tests. Tests are used to determine whether a person has a learning

disability, to assess teacher morale, and to evaluate the mental competency of a person. Without the existence of tests and assessment, the world would be much more unpredictable.

IDENTIFYING A GOOD TEST OR ASSESSMENT PROCEDURE

When we conduct a research study, we want to select measuring instruments that give us the best and most accurate measure of the variables we are investigating. If we are conducting a study investigating the usefulness of a reading program in teaching reading to children with dyslexia, we want a good assessment of dyslexia to ensure that the children included in our study are truly dyslexic. We also want a good measure of reading so that we can document any change in reading ability of the children with dyslexia as a result of having participated in the reading program. Reliability and validity are the two most important psychometric properties of a test or assessment procedure.

Reliability

Reliability
Consistency
or stability

Reliability refers to consistency or stability. With respect to psychological and educational testing and assessment, reliability refers to the consistency or stability of the scores we get from our tests and assessment procedures. If a test or assessment procedure is reliable, it will produce similar scores or responses on every occasion. For example, if the scores from a test of intelligence are reliable, the same, or just about the same, IQ scores will be obtained every time it is administered to a particular group of people.

It doesn't take much thought to realize that reliability is necessary for any measure to be useful. Assume you gave John Doe an IQ test today and he scored 120, six months later he scored 100, and twelve months later he scored 130. Given these results you would have little idea as to what John Doe's "true" IQ score is because there is little consistency between the scores, meaning that any one measure of IQ using this intelligence test could be very inaccurate. However, if the IQ scores on the three occasions were 120, 122, and 119, you would know that the test John Doe was given was producing consistent results. This reliability makes the measure useful.

The reliability of a measure must be determined empirically. Table 4.4 summarizes the different ways of assessing reliability. Each way provides a slightly different index of reliability. You must select the method that provides the index needed for the measure you are using. Many times several different ways of computing reliability will be used to demonstrate the different ways in which the measure is reliable.

Test-retest
reliability
A measure of the
consistency of
scores over time

Test-Retest Reliability   **Test-retest reliability** refers to the consistency of test scores over time. For example, if we were to assess the reliability of an intelligence test using the test-retest method, we would give the test to a group of, say, 100 individuals on one occasion, wait a period of time, and then give the same intelligence test to the same 100 individuals again. Then we would correlate the scores on the first testing occasion with the scores on

TABLE 4.4   Summary of Methods for Computing Reliability

Type of Reliability	Number of Testing Sessions	Number of Test Forms	Statistical Procedure
Test-retest	2	1	Correlation coefficient
Equivalent-forms	1 or 2	2	Correlation coefficient
Split-half	1	1	Correlation coefficient
Internal consistency	1	1	Kuder-Richardson or coefficient alpha
Inter-scorer	1	1	Correlation coefficient

the second testing occasion. If the individuals who received high IQ scores on the first testing occasion received high IQ scores on the second testing occasion, and the individuals who received low IQ scores on the first testing occasion also received low IQ scores on the second testing occasion, the correlation between the scores on the two testing occasions would be high, indicating that the test is reliable according to the test-retest method. If these individuals received very different scores on the two testing occasions, the correlation between the two sets of scores would be low, indicating that the test is unreliable according to this method of assessing reliability.

If you look at Table 4.5 you can see the type of scores that might be obtained from a reliable and unreliable intelligence test. For the reliable intelligence test, the scores from the first and second testing period are about the same, which means that the test is providing about the same measure of intelligence on both testing occasions. For the unreliable intelligence test, the rank order of the scores from the first and second testing period are quite different. This means that the assessment of intelligence would be very different depending on which assessment time was used.

TABLE 4.5   Illustration of Reliable and Unreliable Intelligence Tests Using the Test-Retest Reliability Procedure

Reliable Test		Unreliable Test	
First Testing	Second Testing	First Testing	Second Testing
110	112	110	95
123	120	123	103
115	116	115	147
109	113	109	100
99	95	99	120
103	102	103	110
131	128	131	125
128	130	128	142
119	114	119	111
121	124	105	135

One of the major problems with assessing test-retest reliability is knowing how much time should elapse between the two testing occasions. If the time interval is too short, the scores obtained from the two testing occasions may be partially due to individuals remembering how they responded when they took the test the first time. In this case the reliability of the test is artificially inflated. On the other hand, if the time interval is too long, the response to the test may be due to changes in the individual that affect his or her response to the test. As time passes, people change. They may, for example, learn new things, forget some things, or acquire new skills. Unfortunately, there does not seem to be an ideal time interval in which to administer a test. Although it is probably safe to say that less than a week is too short a time interval for most tests, the best time interval to use depends on the kind of test involved. Generally, as the length of time increases, the correlation between the scores obtained on each testing decreases.

As you can see, the time interval between the first and second testing occasion can have an effect on the reliability coefficient obtained. Because the time interval can be critical, this information is always provided in addition to the actual reliability coefficient.

Equivalent Forms Reliability   Have you ever taken an examination in which some people got one form of the test and other people got a different form of the test? If so, you have experienced the use of alternative forms. In constructing alternative forms the instructor attempts to make them equivalent in all respects. If you have ever wondered whether alternative forms are really equivalent, you have wondered about equivalent-forms reliability. **Equivalent-forms reliability** refers to the consistency of a group of individuals' scores on two equivalent forms of a test designed to measure the same characteristic. Equivalent forms means that two tests are constructed so that they are identical in every way except for the specific items asked on the test. This means that they have the same number of items, the items are of the same difficulty level, the items measure the same construct, and the test is administered, scored, and interpreted in the same way. Once the two equivalent tests are constructed, they are administered concurrently to a group of individuals or the second test is administered shortly after the first test. Either way, each person will have taken both tests and will have scores on both tests. The scores made by the group of participants on both tests are then correlated; this correlation coefficient represents the consistency or reliability of the test. Not only does this method provide a measure of reliability, but it also avoids the memory problem encountered when using the test-retest method.

Although the equivalent-forms-reliability method is an excellent way of assessing reliability, the success of this method depends on the ability to construct two equivalent forms of the same test. It is difficult, however, to construct two equivalent tests that measure the same construct, especially when the two tests cannot use the same items. To the extent that they are not equivalent, measurement error is introduced, which lowers the reliability of the test. In addition, the participants have to take essentially the same test twice in a short period of time. Sometimes this is difficult. Just think about the reaction you might have if you were told that you had to take the GRE twice in the same day just for the purpose of assessing the consistency of your responses. Because of these problems, particularly the necessity of having to construct two equivalent forms, this method of assessing reliability is seldom used.

Equivalent-forms reliability
A measure of the consistency of a group of individuals' scores on two equivalent forms of a test measuring the same construct

Split-Half Reliability   **Split-half reliability,** as the name implies, involves splitting a test into two equivalent halves and then assessing the consistency of the scores obtained from each half of the test. This method of computing reliability can be used when it is impractical or undesirable to assess reliability using the test-retest or equivalent-forms methods because of factors such as time or expense.

Inherent in this method is the necessity of dividing a test into two halves. There are several ways of accomplishing this. The first procedure is to divide the test in the middle. This procedure is not recommended because factors such as different levels of fatigue influencing the first versus the second half of the test, different amounts of test anxiety, and differences in item difficulty as a function of placement in the test could spuriously raise or lower the reliability coefficient. A more acceptable way to split a test is to use the odd-numbered items for one half of the test and the even-numbered items for the other half of the test. Randomly assigning the items to one or the other half of the test is also acceptable. A third way is to divide the test by content so that each half contains an equal number of items equivalent in content and difficulty. In this case one must make a decision as to how to divide the test in half. The criterion to apply is to use the method that is most likely to produce two equivalent forms of the test. For example, if the first twenty items of a mathematical skills test deal with fractions and the second twenty items deal with decimals, you will not want to use the first twenty items for one half and the second twenty items for the other half. Rather, you would split the test using the odd-even technique or some other technique that ensures that both halves of the test contain items dealing with fractions and decimals. In general, you want each half equal to the other in format, style, content, and other aspects.

Once you have created the two halves, reliability can be determined using the following steps:

1. Score each half of the test for every person to whom it was administered.
2. Compute a correlation between scores on the two halves of the test.
3. Adjust the computed correlation coefficient using the Spearman-Brown formula (explained in the following).

The adjusted correlation represents the split-half estimate of reliability. A low correlation indicates that the test was unreliable and contained considerable measurement error, and a high correlation indicates that the test was reliable.

The split-half method has effectively reduced the length of the test by 50 percent, so reliability is determined for a test half the length of the whole test. However, longer tests tend to be more reliable. Fortunately, there is a statistical way of correcting for the shortened test length. The statistical correction, the **Spearman-Brown formula** (r_{sb}), is as follows:

$$r_{sb} = \frac{2r_{\text{split half}}}{1 + r_{\text{split half}}}$$

where

r_{sb} = the Spearman-Brown reliability coefficient
$r_{\text{split half}}$ = the split-half reliability coefficient

To illustrate the use of the Spearman-Brown formula, assume that you have a 100-item test that you administer to a group of 200 participants. You then split this 100-item test into two equal halves of 50 items each by using the odd-even method and then score each half. The scores on each half of the test are correlated. Assume that this correlation is .75. This correlation has to be corrected for the reduced length as follows:

$$r_{total} = \frac{2\,(.75)}{1 + .75} = \frac{1.50}{1.75} = .81$$

When the correction formula is applied, the reliability coefficient is .81, which is a more accurate indication of the reliability of the 100-item test. However, there is one caution to follow in using the Spearman-Brown formula. It is appropriate for use only with homogeneous tests, which measure one construct or characteristic. It is not appropriate for measuring the reliability of heterogeneous tests, which measure more than one construct or characteristic, or speed tests, which must be completed within a specified amount of time.

Internal consistency The consistency with which a test measures a single construct

Internal Consistency **Internal consistency** refers to how well a test measures a single construct or concept. The test-retest and equivalent-forms methods of assessing reliability are general methods that can be used with just about any test. Some tests, however, are homogeneous. A test is homogeneous when all the items measure a single construct or a single factor such as reading comprehension or spelling ability. This is in contrast to test heterogeneity, which refers to the degree to which a test measures more than one construct or factor. A heterogeneous test is composed of items that measure several different constructs. For example, contrast a test that is constructed to measure academic performance of sixth-grade students with a test designed to measure reading comprehension of sixth-grade students. A test of academic performance would be more heterogeneous in content than a test of reading comprehension because academic performance involves many skills, one of which is reading comprehension. Homogeneous tests have more inter-item consistency—internal consistency—than heterogeneous tests because the items focus on one construct and, therefore, sample a relatively narrow content area. Test homogeneity is generally desirable because it allows straightforward test-score interpretation. Measures of internal consistency provide a measure of the homogeneity of a test.

Kuder-Richardson formula 20 A statistical formula used to compute an estimate of the reliability of a homogeneous test

Kuder-Richardson. Many years ago G. Frederic Kuder and M. W. Richardson (1937; Richardson & Kuder, 1939) developed a number of formulas for estimating the reliability of a homogeneous test. Of the many formulas developed, their **Kuder-Richardson formula 20** or KR-20 (named because it is the twentieth formula developed in the series), is the most widely known and used. When test items are highly homogeneous, the KR-20 and the split-half reliability estimates give similar values. With heterogeneous test items the split-half method yields a higher reliability estimate. However, the KR-20 formula is the preferable method when the test consists of dichotomous items, particularly those items that can be scored right or wrong, as exists with multiple-choice or true-false items. The formula for computing a KR-20 reliability estimate is as follows:

$$r_{kr20} = \frac{k}{k-1}\left[1 - \frac{\sum pq}{\sigma^2}\right]$$

where

r_{kr20} stands for the Kuder-Richardson formula 20 reliability coefficient
k refers to the number of test items
p is the proportion of test takers who pass the items
q is the proportion of test takers who fail the items
σ^2 is the variance of the total test scores

Coefficient alpha
A variant of the
Kuder-Richardson
formula that
provides an
estimate of the
reliability of a
homogeneous test

Coefficient Alpha.   Through the years the Kuder-Richardson formulas have been the subject of many modifications. Probably the one variant that has received the most acceptance is a statistic called ***coefficient alpha.*** Coefficient alpha, originally developed by Cronbach (1951) and elaborated upon by others such as Cliff (1984), provides a reliability estimate that can be thought of as the mean of all possible split-half correlations, corrected by the Spearman-Brown formula. While the KR-20 formula is appropriate for use on dichotomously scored items, coefficient alpha can be used on tests with dichotomous or nondichotomous items, such as might exist on attitude measures or essay and short-answer tests, where partial credit can be given.

The formula for coefficient alpha is as follows:

$$r_\alpha = \frac{k}{k-1}\left[1 - \frac{\sum \sigma^2}{\sigma^2}\right]$$

where

r_α is coefficient alpha
k is the number of items
$\sum \sigma^2$ is the sum of the variances of each item
σ^2 is the variance of the total test scores

Computation of coefficient alpha is rather complicated and time consuming. Today, because of the availability of mainframe and personal computers, coefficient alpha seems to be the preferred statistic for obtaining an estimate of internal consistency reliability (Keith & Reynolds, 1990).

Inter-Scorer Reliability   There are many instances in which an evaluation of a research participant's performance is made by someone such as an instructor, a teacher, or some other professional. For example, we have all taken essay examinations. We would like to believe that a teacher is an objective evaluator and that the score we receive is the same regardless of who is doing the evaluation. However, the score we receive on such an examination is partially a function of our performance and partially a function of the person doing the scoring. This fact was vividly demonstrated many years ago when Starch and Elliott

(1912) revealed that the grade given to one student's English composition ranged from a low of 50 percent to a high of 98 percent depending on the teacher or volunteer who graded the paper. Because of the wide variability that can occur in the scoring of performance, it is important to determine the consistency of such an evaluation. Evaluation of the degree of agreement that exists between two or more scorers, judges, or raters is referred to as **inter-scorer reliability,** although it has also been referred to as judge reliability, inter-rater reliability, and observer reliability.

Probably the simplest way to determine the degree of consistency between two scorers in the scoring of a test or some other performance measure is to have each scorer independently evaluate the test or performance measure and then compute a correlation coefficient between the scores provided by the different scorers. For example, assume you had each student in a class read a passage and had two scorers score the reading ability of each of these students. The scores provided by each scorer on the students' reading ability are then correlated and the correlation between these scorers represents the inter-scorer reliability.

Frequently the agreement between two or more scorers is not very good unless some degree of training and practice precedes the scoring. Fortunately, with training, the degree of agreement can improve. The important issue is that training is often required and that a measure of the reliability of an evaluation of performance by scorers is necessary.

Validity

When we select a test or some other assessment procedure for use in a research study, we obviously want to select the one that will give us the information we want. If we want to measure a child's IQ, we obviously want some assessment that will provide a score that is indicative of the child's intellectual level. In other words, we want a valid assessment procedure because validity is "an evaluative judgment of the degree to which empirical and theoretical rationales support the adequacy and appropriateness of interpretations and actions on the basis of test scores or other modes of assessment" (Messick, 1989). **Validity,** therefore, is a judgment of the appropriateness of the interpretations and actions we make based on the score or scores we get from a test or assessment procedure.

Whenever we make an assessment we get one or more scores from each individual. The assessment procedure could be a psychological or educational test, a behavioral observation, a performance rating, data such as the number of school dropouts, or any of many other assessment procedures. Each of these assessment procedures produces one or more scores, and we make inferences from these scores. The number of school dropouts occurring in an academic year may be used to make inferences about the quality of education delivered or the extent to which the families of the students value education. If the assessment procedure was a measure of intelligence, the score obtained from this test would be used to infer the person's intellectual level. Based on this interpretation of a person's intellectual level, we may even take some specific action such as placing the child in a special program for gifted children.

When we make such inferences or when we take some action on the basis of scores, we want the inferences to be accurate and we want the action we have taken to be the correct one. Whether the inferences and the actions are appropriate and accurate is an em-

---

Inter-scorer reliability
The degree of agreement between two or more scorers, judges, or raters

Validity
A judgment of the appropriateness of the interpretations and actions made on the basis of a test score or scores

pirical question. This means that we must collect data to determine whether the inferences we have made about the meaning and interpretation of a score or set of scores, and the action we have taken on the basis of the score or scores, are correct. Validity refers to the empirical evidence and theoretical rationales that support the interpretations and actions we take based on the score or scores we get from an assessment procedure. Validity, therefore, is not a property of the assessment instrument, and it would be inappropriate to state that a given test is valid because this implies that validity is a property of the test. Rather, it is the interpretation and actions taken based on the obtained scores that are or are not valid.

Validation
The process of gathering evidence that supports an inference based on a test score or scores

To validate the inference that we make from a score requires collecting evidence that indicates that the inference is accurate. For example, if we give a student an intelligence test and that student gets a score of 130, we might infer from that score that the student is bright and can master any academic skill attempted. To validate this inference, we would have to collect evidence indicating that a person obtaining a score of 130 on this test is a very bright person who can master subjects ranging from chemistry to philosophy. **Validation,** therefore, is the process of gathering evidence supporting the score inference. There are many different ways this evidence can be collected. Focusing on tests for simplicity and presentation, we present the three main ways in which validity evidence is collected. As we discussed above, tests are only one assessment procedure. The discussion of ways of collecting validity evidence also applies to any other assessment procedure, so don't assume that the discussion that follows applies to tests only.

Content Validity   **Content validity** refers to a judgment of the degree to which the items, tasks, or questions on a test adequately sample the domain of interest, which can include educational achievement, teacher morale, shyness, or any other area of interest to an educational researcher. In other words, content validity involves examining the content of a test to determine whether the items represent the thing you are trying to measure. To illustrate content validity, let us assume that you are interested in investigating the efficacy of a new instructional method on the ability of students to acquire knowledge of statistics. In conducting this study you obviously need some measure of statistical knowledge. Statistical knowledge is typically measured by administering a test and using the test score to infer a person's mastery of statistics.

Content validity
A judgment of the degree to which the items, tasks, or questions on a test adequately sample the domain of interest

If the statistics test has content validity, the test questions, items, and tasks must sample the domain of information covered during the instructional period. If the instruction covered the theory, rationale, and computational procedure of Pearson product moment correlation, t-tests, and analysis of variance; the items, questions, and tasks on the statistics test should also cover this material. Additionally, in general the proportion of material covered during the instructional period should match the proportion of material covered in the statistics test. If 20 percent of the instruction time was spent covering correlation, 30 percent of the time was spent on t-tests, and 50 percent of the time was spent on analysis of variance, 20 percent of the test questions and tasks should be devoted to correlation, 30 percent to t-tests, and 50 percent to analysis of variance. In other words, there should be agreement between what is covered during instruction and what is covered in the test based on the assumption that more time is spent on those topics that are more important, difficult, and/or extensive.

Generally, evidence of content validity is obtained by expert judgment. Individuals who are experts in the area covered by the test review the test to determine whether it adequately samples the content area. In accomplishing this task the experts will generally review the content domain, such as the material covered during the instruction in statistics and the general procedure used in developing the test. This may include a review of the course syllabus, the text, the objectives, and the notes used by the instructor. From this review experts make a judgment concerning how well the items, questions, and tasks included on the test sample the content. In the case of the new method of instruction in statistics, the experts would probably review the syllabi, text, objectives, and notes used by the instructor and then look at the test questions and tasks. The experts would make a judgment as to whether the test adequately sampled and represented the material covered during course instruction. If in the judgment of the experts, the test adequately sampled the content domain, the test would have content validity.

Criterion-related validity
A judgment of the extent to which scores from a test can be used to predict or infer performance in some activity

Criterion-Related Validity   **Criterion-related validity** refers to a judgment of the extent to which scores from a test can be used to infer, or predict, the examinees' performance in some specific activity. The specific activity can be anything that we might want to predict, such as grades in school, teacher morale, job satisfaction, attitudes toward athletics, and self-concept. These specific activities are referred to as the criterion, which is the standard that we want to predict. For example, if we want to determine the criterion-related validity of a test of mathematical ability, we could use grades in mathematics classes as the criterion; the criterion of teacher morale might be the teachers' ratings of morale; and the criterion measure of violence in schools could be the number of fights.

Concurrent validity
Validity evidence obtained from assessing the relationship between test scores and criterion scores obtained at the same time

Once the criterion is established, criterion-related validity is demonstrated by determining how accurately the performance criterion can be predicted from the scores on the test. Establishing this predictive relationship between the criterion and the test scores can be accomplished using a criterion measure that is collected at the same time as the test scores or with a criterion measure that is collected after some stated time interval. **Concurrent-validity** studies are criterion-related studies in which the test scores and the criterion scores are obtained at the same time. These studies might be used for achievement tests or diagnostic tests. For example, a test that is purported to be capable of identifying children with dyslexia should have concurrent validity evidence because you will want to be able to infer dyslexia immediately after getting the test score. Similarly, if you want to assess a child's level of mathematical ability, you want to give a test designed to assess mathematical achievement and be able to infer the child's level of mathematical ability immediately after giving and scoring the test. Therefore, whenever a test score is used to infer a concurrent criterion measure, concurrent validity evidence is needed because it gives evidence of the degree to which an assessment score predicts a concurrent criterion measure.

Predictive validity
Validity evidence obtained from assessing the relationship between test scores collected at one point in time and criterion scores obtained at a later time

Predictive validity studies are criterion-related studies in which the test scores are collected at one point in time and the criterion measure is obtained at a future time, generally after some intervening event has taken place, such as completion of high school. For example, an educational researcher might want to obtain evidence of the validity of a test in predicting school dropout. To obtain this evidence the researcher would conduct a predictive validity study in which he or she would administer the test to students at the beginning of the school year. The criterion measure of whether students did or did not drop out of school would be collected at the end of the school year and then the scores that the students got at the beginning of the school year would be compared with the dropout data to determine whether students who dropped out got certain scores and students who did not drop out got other scores.

Judgments of both concurrent and predictive criterion-related validity are based on either a **validity coefficient** or expectancy data. The validity coefficient is a correlation coefficient that provides a measure of the degree of relationship between the scores on the test and the criterion measure. For example, if you want to obtain evidence of the validity of using a mathematics aptitude test in predicting who will do well in an algebra course, you may use grades in algebra class as the criterion. Evidence of predictive validity is obtained by correlating the scores on the mathematics aptitude test with the final grades in the algebra class. This correlation coefficient is the validity coefficient and represents evidence you can use to make a judgment of the predictive criterion-related validity of the mathematics aptitude test. Evidence of concurrent criterion-related validity is similarly obtained. The only difference is that the criterion measure is obtained at about the same time as the scores on the test.

A second way of getting evidence of criterion-related validity is to use expectancy data. **Expectancy data** represent data illustrating the number or percentage of people that fall into various categories on a criterion measure. The categories established typically represent intervals of scores on the criterion measure. For example, a number of states have instituted proficiency tests for teachers and have dictated that graduating education majors must take a proficiency test and obtain a certain score in order to apply for and get their teaching certificate. Let's assume for the moment that the range of scores one can get on the proficiency test range from 0 to 60 and that a score ≥ 40 has to be obtained to pass the proficiency test. This means that there are two categories—pass (≥ 40) and not pass (≤ 39)—for the proficiency test and everyone who takes the proficiency test is placed into one of these two categories.

Now let us assume further that the legislators in the state are considering using this proficiency test as a licensing test that has to be passed before a student can get his or her teaching certification. However, prior to passing this legislation, the legislators want some evidence as to the validity of using this proficiency test (this is an extremely astute group of legislators), so a group of researchers has all graduating seniors during one academic year take the proficiency test. Three years later these same researchers have the principals of the schools in which these students are teaching rate their teaching performance using a scale with categories of unacceptable, below average, average, above average, and superior. Data will now exist on each student in terms of whether they passed the proficiency test and how they rated on their teaching performance. These data can be placed in an expectancy table such as appears in Table 4.6. From this table you can see that 51 percent of the students who passed the proficiency test were also given a superior rating by their principal, whereas only 7 percent of the students who failed the proficiency exam were given a superior rating. As the rating of teaching ability declined, the percentage of students who failed the proficiency

---

Validity coefficient
A correlation coefficient computed between test scores and criterion scores

Expectancy data
Data illustrating the number or percentage of people that fall into various categories on a criterion measure

TABLE 4.6   Example of an Expectancy Table Using Hypothetical Proficiency Test Data and Principals' Ratings of Teachers (Showing Percentage of Students Passing the Proficiency Test for Each Rating Category)

	Proficiency Test Performance	
Rating Categories	*Pass*	*Fail*
Superior	51%	7%
Above average	26%	9%
Average	17%	17%
Below average	3%	24%
Unacceptable	3%	43%

exam increased and the percentage who passed decreased, giving evidence of the validity of the proficiency exam in predicting the success and quality of the student's later teaching ability. Such data represent evidence of the criterion-related validity of a test, such as the proficiency test, and can support the decision to use the test for determining which students should be granted a teaching certificate.

Construct validity
Evidence that a theoretical construct can be inferred from the scores on a test

Construct
An informed, scientific idea developed or "constructed" to describe or explain behavior

Construct Validity   **Construct validity** refers to the extent to which we can infer some theoretical construct from the scores on a test. A **construct** is "an informed, scientific idea developed or 'constructed' to describe or explain behavior" (Cohen, Seredllk, & Phillips, 1996). Examples of some constructs of interest to educational researchers are scholastic aptitude, intelligence, anxiety, self-esteem, emotional adjustment, morale, fear, and learning disability. Intelligence is a construct that may be used to describe why one student performs well in school and another cannot seem to grasp the material presented. The construct of emotional adjustment may be used to explain why a student cries easily or acts out in class. The construct of fear may be evoked to explain why a student will not try out for a school play or stand up to a bully. We use constructs to describe or explain a whole host of behaviors. These constructs, however, are unobservable, so a test that provides an indication that a construct exists is evidence of its construct validity.

Furthermore, evidence of construct validity involves formulating hypotheses about the expected behaviors that should occur from individuals who score high or low on a test and a tentative theory about why high and low scorers should behave differently. If the high and low scorers behave as predicted, then evidence exists supporting the construct validity of the test. If they behave differently, then the researcher must reexamine the hypotheses and his or her tentative theory or even the nature of the construct itself. For example, assume that you have developed a test for measuring intelligence. You predict that high scorers on the test will do better scholastically than low scorers because high scorers should be able to grasp academic material better than low scorers, leading to better academic success. If this prediction is supported, you have some evidence for the validity of the test you have developed. Actually, this is only one of many means of collecting evidence of construct validity.

Homogeneity. **Homogeneity,** as we discussed earlier in this chapter, refers to how well a test measures a single construct such as academic achievement, intelligence, or morale. One type of evidence that can be used to indicate that the score made on a test measures the intended construct is to demonstrate that all the items or parts of the test are measuring the same thing. For example, if you demonstrate that all parts of a test designed to measure academic achievement are measuring the same thing, you have one bit of evidence supporting the construct validity of the test.

In most instances, evidence of the homogeneity of a test is obtained by correlating the scores on each test item with the scores on the total test. For example, if you want to obtain evidence of the homogeneity of a test of student morale, you can give the test to a group of students and then correlate the scores on each test item with the total test scores. If the item scores correlated with the total test scores, you have evidence that the test was internally consistent. An item that correlated poorly with the total test score can be eliminated or revised because the low correlation indicates that it did not measure the same thing as the total test.

It is important to recognize that the contribution homogeneity makes to construct validity is limited. Evidence of homogeneity does not provide direct evidence that the construct is being measured by the test. However, it does indicate the degree to which the items on the test are measuring the same thing, and this has some relevance to construct validity. However, additional information must be gathered to demonstrate that the construct the test intends to measure can be inferred from the score a person gets on the test.

Developmental Changes. Many constructs of interest to educational researchers can be expected to change over time, particularly during infancy and childhood. Most scholastic abilities such as reading, spelling, and arithmetic ability are expected to increase yearly from about age six or earlier to the early teens. If a test were developed to measure a construct that is expected to change over time, such as we would expect with the construct of intelligence or scholastic ability, evidence of construct validity would exist if the test scores increased with advancing age. Obviously, this method of developing construct validity evidence is inappropriate to use with constructs that are not expected to demonstrate age-related changes, as you might expect with a construct such as emotional stability.

Correlations with Other Tests. The correlation between a new test and other previously developed tests is frequently used as evidence of the construct validity. There are actually two ways in which correlations with other tests are used. One is to develop convergent evidence and the other is to develop discriminant evidence. **Convergent evidence** exists if the scores on a test previously developed to measure the same construct as the new test and the new test are correlated. For example, if you develop a new test of intelligence, you may correlate the scores obtained from the new test with the scores obtained from a previously developed test that has been demonstrated to measure the construct of intelligence. If the scores on the new test are similar to the scores on the old previously validated test, evidence exists indicating that the new test is also measuring the construct of intelligence.

When using correlations with other tests as construct validity evidence, you want the correlations to be moderately high, but not too high. If the new test correlates too highly, then the two tests are probably just duplicates of each other and the new test is a needless

---

Homogeneity
In test validity, refers to how well a test measures a single construct

Convergent evidence
Evidence that the scores on prior tests and the current test designed to measure the same construct are correlated

duplication unless, of course, the new test has advantages such as brevity or ease of administration.

Discriminant evidence
Evidence that the scores on the newly developed test are not correlated with the scores on tests designed to measure theoretically different constructs

Discriminant evidence exists if it can be demonstrated that the scores on a newly developed test are not correlated with the scores on tests designed to measure constructs that should theoretically not be related to the construct measured on the new test. For example, a new test of intelligence should not be related to a measure of student morale or attitudes toward contraception. If the scores on the new test of intelligence are not correlated, or correlated very low, with the scores on measures of theoretically different constructs (e.g., attitudes toward contraception), discriminant validity evidence exists and this could be used as evidence of the construct validity of the new test. If you want to learn more about convergent and discriminant validity, see Campbell and Fiske (1959).

Factor analysis
A statistical procedure that identifies the minimum number of "factors," or dimensions, measured by a test

Factor Analysis.   **Factor analysis** is a statistical procedure that was developed to identify the minimal number of "factors," or dimensions, that are measured by a test. For example, assume that you develop a test of scholastic ability. In constructing this test you attempt to measure each facet of scholastic ability, so you construct subtests of every academic area you think is important. However, rather than constructing, for example, one subtest of mathematical ability, you construct several subtests: one for measuring addition, one for measuring subtraction, and one for measuring multiplication. You also attempt to construct subtests for additional areas of scholastic ability. Factor analysis can provide evidence indicating whether each of these subtests actually measures a different construct or whether, for example, all arithmetic subtests measure just the one construct of arithmetic. If all arithmetic subtests are correlated, they all "load" on one factor, which indicates that they are all measuring the same academic ability and should be combined into one construct called mathematical ability.

Unified View of Construct Validity   We have presented several ways of obtaining evidence of construct validity. There are many additional ways of collecting construct validity evidence and no one way is considered the definitive or best way. The current view is that construct validity is the unifying concept for all validity evidence and that all types of validity, including content and criterion-related validity, are forms of construct validity. Construct validity refers to any evidence that bears on the interpretation or meaning of test scores. This evidence comes from all sources. We have identified three different ways of collecting validity evidence. However, construct validity embraces all forms of validity evidence and construct validation should be viewed as an evolving and never-ending process (Messick, 1995).

Using Reliability and Validity Coefficients

Earlier in this chapter we stated that any good test or assessment procedure provides information that indicates just what type of inferences can be made from the test scores. We stated that the type of score inferences that can be made is based on the reliability and validity of the test or assessment procedure. Although this is true, there is another important issue that must be considered. To legitimately use reliability and validity information, the participants on which this information was collected must be similar to the participants on which you are conducting your study. For example, if you are conducting a study investigating the academic achievement of fifth- and sixth-grade students with IQs below the normal range, the reliability and validity coefficients of the academic achievement tests you select for this study must be the "norms" based on fifth- and sixth-grade students of below normal intelligence. If the reliability and validity coefficients are derived from fifth- and sixth-grade students with normal or higher IQs, these coefficients will give little information about the reliability and validity of the scores of fifth- and sixth-grade students with below normal intelligence. Therefore, before you make use of any assessment procedure, you must look at the characteristics of the "norming group" or the participants in the studies on which the reliability and validity coefficients are computed. If the characteristics of the participants in your study match the characteristics of the participants in the reliability and validity studies, you can use these coefficients to assess the quality of the assessment procedure. If they do not, you have no information on which to assess the quality of the assessment procedure. You can still get scores from using the assessment procedures. However, you will not know what they mean, so you essentially will be collecting data that you cannot interpret.

EDUCATIONAL AND PSYCHOLOGICAL TESTS

Whenever an educational researcher conducts a study, measurements must be taken on a number of variables. For example, if you are conducting an experimental study investigating the effect of exposure to a headstart program on later academic achievement of disadvantaged children, you have to have some way of identifying children that are disadvantaged and some measure of academic achievement. One way of doing this is to administer a test designed to measure the extent to which a child is disadvantaged and a test designed to measure a child's level of academic achievement. Fortunately, educational and psychological tests have been developed to measure most situations, characteristics, and types of performance and educational researchers make extensive use of these tests in their research projects. Although there are too many tests to mention in this textbook, we identify the primary areas in which tests have been developed and we mention some of the more popular tests in each of these areas.

Intelligence Tests

Intelligence tests have probably received the most attention and are the ones people are most familiar with because most of us have completed one at some time in our life. Intelligence, however, is an interesting construct because of the difficulty in coming up with an agreed-on definition. For example, what does intelligence mean to you? If you have difficulty answering this question, you are not alone. Sternberg, Conway, Ketron, and Bernstein (1981) asked 476 people, including students, commuters, and supermarket shoppers, to identify behaviors they considered intelligent and unintelligent. Behaviors most often associated with intelligence included "reasons logically and well," "reads widely," "displays common sense," "keeps an open mind," and "reads with high comprehension." Unintelligent behaviors most frequently included "does not tolerate diversity of views," "does not display curiosity," and "behaves with insufficient consideration of others." Do these examples fit your conception of intelligent and unintelligent behaviors? If they do not, don't be alarmed, because even the experts cannot agree on a definition.

Intelligence
The ability to think abstractly and to learn readily from experience

One general definition is that **intelligence** is the ability to think abstractly and to learn readily from experience (Flynn, 1987). However, this is a general definition and not one that is universally accepted. Neisser (1979) has even concluded that intelligence, because of its nature, cannot be explicitly defined because, for certain constructs, a single prototype does not exist. This is certainly true of intelligence. However, just because a universally accepted definition of intelligence does not exist does not mean that the concept does not exist, that it lacks utility, or that it cannot be measured. Indeed, it is a multifaceted construct and many tests have been developed to measure intelligence. Table 4.7 provides a summary of some of the tests of intelligence that have been developed and used in educational research as well as other settings.

TABLE 4.7 Examples of Intelligence Tests

Test	Description
Stanford-Binet Intelligence Test	Individually administered test for anyone from the ages of two through adulthood
Wechsler Scales	A series of three different scales to assess intellectual abilities of people from preschool through adulthood
Wechsler Adult Intelligence Scale	Assess the intellectual abilities of people from the ages of sixteen through adulthood
Wechsler Intelligence Scale for Children	Assess the intellectual abilities of people from the ages of six through sixteen
Wechsler Preschool and Primary Scale of Intelligence	Assess the intellectual abilities of people from the ages of three to seven years, three months
Slosson Intelligence Test	Individually administered test used as a quick screening device
Otis-Lennon School Ability Test	A group-administered intelligence test for use in grades kindergarten through thirteen
California Test of Mental Maturity	A group-administered intelligence test available for use in school settings
Kuhlmann-Anderson Intelligence Tests	A group-administered intelligence test available for use in school settings

Personality Tests

Personality
A multifaceted
construct that does
not have a
generally agreed
on definition

Personality is a construct that, like intelligence, has been defined in many different ways. These definitions have ranged from ones that are all-inclusive, such as Menninger's (1953, p. 23) definition of **personality** as "the individual as a whole, his height and weight and love and hates and blood pressure and reflexes; his smiles and hopes and bowed legs and enlarged tonsils. It means all that anyone is and that he is trying to become," to a statement that personality cannot be defined with any generality (Hall & Lindzey, 1970, p. 9). This disagreement is probably because, similar to intelligence, a single prototype does not exist. What this disagreement or confusion regarding the definition of personality does indicate is that it is a multifaceted construct. Many tests have been developed to measure the different facets of this construct, such as the emotional, motivational, interpersonal, and attitudinal characteristics representative of this construct. Examples of several different types of personality tests are illustrated in Table 4.8.

TABLE 4.8   Examples of Personality Tests

Type of Test	Measure	Description
Self-Report Measures of Traits and Clinical States	Minnesota Multiphasic Personality Inventory	A 550-item inventory providing scores on 10 clinical scales and several other scales such as "lie" and "validity" scales
	California Psychological Inventory	A 462-item inventory providing scores on 20 scales measuring a variety of traits in adults such as dominance and self-control
	NEO-Personality Inventory	A factor-analytically derived scale to test for five personality factors; often called the "big five"
Self-Report Measures of Attitudes, Interests, and Values	Strong Vocational Interest Blank	A 325-item inventory providing scores on 25 interest scales and 207 occupational scales
	Work Values Inventory	Explores sources of satisfaction a person seeks in his or her work
Self-Report Measures of Self-Concept	Minnesota School Attitude Survey	Assesses students' attitudes and feelings toward aspects of their school experience
	Tennessee Self-Concept Scale	Provides an overall measure of self-esteem and five self-concept categories for individuals age 12 and above
	Self-Description Questionnaire	Provides a measure of self-concept of children of less than adolescent age
Projective Techniques	Holtzman Inkblot Technique	Provides scores to 22 response variables such as anxiety and hostility derived from responses to 45 inkblots
	Thematic Apperception Test	Analyzes stories constructed from vague pictures in terms of needs such as achievement, affiliation, and aggression

Many personality tests are of the self-report variety in which the test taker is asked to respond, either on a pencil-and-paper format or on a computer, to a series of questions asking about his or her motives and feelings. These self-reports provide a window into the test taker's behavioral tendencies, feelings, and motives, which are in turn summarized with a specific label. Some of these labels are clinical labels such as neuroticism while others are trait labels such as dominance or sociability. Still other labels refer to attitudes, interests, or the values a person holds. The numerous summary labels that are used to portray and measure a person's "personality," and the numerous self-report inventories that have been developed to measure these, further reflect the fact that personality is a multifaceted construct.

Although self-report measures of personality can be a valuable source of information, they are always subject to contamination. In some instances a person may be motivated to "fake good" and in other instances he or she may be motivated to "fake bad" to obtain his or her goals. For example, assume you want your child to attend an elite private school that will not take children with negative attitudes on the assumption they might be prone to violent behavior. If you are asked to report on your child's behavioral tendencies and attitudes, you may not tell the truth ("fake good") to enhance the probability of your child being admitted into the school. Additionally, different individuals have different response styles that can influence the impression communicated by the responses to the personality test. For example, some people have a greater tendency to answer yes or true rather than no or false to short-answer items. Yet others may not have the insight into their own behavior or thinking to answer a question in a way that will accurately communicate information about them. These limitations of self-report inventories always have to be considered when using them to collect information.

In addition to self-reports, dimensions of personality have been measured using projective techniques. The major feature of projective techniques is that the test taker has to make a response to a relatively unstructured task using test stimuli that are usually vague or ambiguous. For example, the test taker may be asked to tell what he or she sees in a blot of ink that appears on a piece of paper or to make up a story from a card providing an ambiguous picture of several people who may be in a specific environment such as what appears to be a surgical room. The underlying assumption is that the way in which the test taker structures and interprets the ambiguous test stimuli will reflect fundamental aspects of his or her personality or psychological functioning and in this way reveal his or her needs, anxieties, and conflicts.

Projective techniques offer a number of advantages in that they may be less susceptible to faking than are self-report inventories because their purpose is not as apparent. Additionally, the task is often intrinsically interesting and entertaining, so it may represent a good "ice breaker" during the initial contact with the examiner. However, projective techniques have a number of potential problems that cause some individuals to question their effectiveness. Most projective techniques are inadequately standardized with respect to both administration and scoring, which means that the reliability and validity information is very important. Studies of most projective techniques have had difficulty demonstrating that the information obtained from these techniques is reliable and valid. In spite of this, these techniques have been used for years and continue to be used.

Educational Assessment Tests

One of the things many people associate with education is testing because it seems to be an inherent part of the educational process. The type of testing that many people think of is some type of performance or knowledge testing, because one of the most common ways of identifying whether a person has mastered a set of material is to determine whether they can answer questions about the material or engage in some type of performance indicative of mastery. However, many other types of tests are administered in public and private schools: intelligence tests, personality tests, tests of physical and sensory abilities, diagnostic tests, and so forth. In this section we look at the general categories of educational assessment tests and mention some of the tests that fall into each of these categories.

Preschool Assessment Tests   Many of the tests used with preschool children are referred to as screening tests rather than intelligence tests or academic achievement tests primarily because the predictive validity of many of the preschool tests is weak. During the preschool years many factors other than children's cognitive capacity influence their later development and ability. A child's health, the characteristics of the family environment, and temperament differences all influence the child's development. Therefore, testing at a young age typically fails to yield sufficient information about later performance in the classroom. When tests are used as screening tests, they are used to identify children "at risk" and in need of further evaluation. The definition of "at risk" is, however, not clearly defined. For example, it could be a child that may be in danger of not being ready for the first grade, or it may describe a level of functioning that is not within normal limits. It may even refer to a child who has difficulties that might not have been identified were it not for routine screening. Preschool assessment tests do have a place. However, they must be used with caution and not overinterpreted.

Preschool tests include tests such as the Early Screening Profile (Lasee & Smith, 1990) and the Miller Assessment for Preschoolers (Schouten & Kirkpatrick, 1993). The Early Screening Profile focuses on developmental functioning of children age two to just under seven and includes cognitive/language, motor, and self-help/social subtests. The Miller Assessment for Preschoolers focuses on the detection of developmental problems of children age two years nine months to five years eight months by making use of verbal, coordination, and a nonverbal foundations subtest. These are just two of many tests that assess the various behaviors and cognitive skills of young children.

Achievement tests
Tests designed to measure the degree of learning that has taken place after being exposed to a specific learning experience

Achievement Tests   **Achievement tests** are designed to measure the degree of learning that has taken place after a person has been exposed to a specific learning experience. This learning experience can be virtually anything. In the context of education, the learning experience most frequently encountered is classroom learning experience. After a teacher has covered a certain amount of material in a course such as American history, he or she wants to measure how much of this material the students have learned. The typical way of doing this is to give a test covering the material. This test is an achievement test because it is designed to measure the degree to which the students have learned the material covered.

Teacher-constructed tests such as the history test just mentioned are legitimate achievement tests, but they are not the only variety. Other achievement tests are the more standardized tests, such as the Metropolitan Achievement Test, which have been produced by a test publisher (e.g., Psychological Corporation) and contain normative data (data indicating how certain groups of individuals, such as sixth-grade white females, perform on the test). These tests may be given at the end of a school year so that the performance of the students who took the achievement test can be compared to the normative group. The comparison with the normative group is often used to measure accomplishment or achievement in various academic areas such as biology, English, mathematics, and comprehension. These standardized achievement tests can be used for a variety of purposes ranging from gauging the quality of instruction of a teacher, school district, or even a state to screening for academic difficulties to identify areas in need of remediation.

The primary difference between teacher-constructed achievement tests and standardized achievement tests is their psychometric soundness. Reliability and validity studies are seldom if ever computed on teacher-constructed tests for rather obvious reasons. Teachers do not have the luxury of having the time to collect validity and reliability data. They must cover a given segment of material and then construct a test that seems to sample the content area and represent a reasonable measure of achievement. Reliability and validity data can be collected on standardized achievement tests because these tests can go through a typical developmental process that permits the collection of such data.

Achievement tests can vary from measuring general achievement to measuring achievement in a specific subject area. Measures of general achievement cover a number of academic areas and are typically referred to as achievement batteries because they consist of a number of subtests. Each subtest typically focuses on a different academic area or skill. Measures of achievement in specific subject areas are tests designed to gauge achievement in specific areas such as reading, arithmetic, and science. Table 4.9 presents a sample of both general and specific standardized achievement tests.

Aptitude tests
Tests that focus on information acquired through the informal learning that goes on in life

Aptitude Tests **Aptitude tests** focus on information acquired through the informal learning that goes on in life as opposed to the formal learning that exists in the educational system. The differing mental and physical abilities of each individual allow him or her to acquire different amounts of information through everyday life experiences as well as through formal learning experiences such as course work in school. Aptitude tests attempt to tap the information we acquire under the uncontrolled and undefined conditions of life. This is in contrast to achievement tests, which attempt to measure information acquired in a formal and relatively structured environment, such as a French or computer programming class. Aptitude test performance, therefore, reflects the cumulative influence of all of our daily living experiences. There is an overlap and a sometimes blurry distinction between achievement and aptitude tests. If you remember that achievement tests are more limited in scope and reflect the learning that takes place in definable conditions such as a specific class designed to teach a specific subject matter, and aptitude tests reflect the learning that takes place in all life's uncontrolled conditions, you should be able to maintain the distinction between the two.

TABLE 4.9   Examples of Standardized Achievement Tests

Measure	Description
General Achievement Tests	
Metropolitan Achievement Tests	A group-administered test spanning the grades from kindergarten through twelfth grade and consisting of five subtests that can provide diagnostic information in the areas of reading, mathematics, and language.
Peabody Individual Achievement Test	An individually administered test spanning the grades from kindergarten through twelfth grade and consisting of six subtests.
Achievement Tests in Specific Subareas	
Nelson Reading Skills Test	A group administered test spanning third through ninth grades consisting of subtests measuring word meaning, and comprehension.
Cooperative Achievement Test	Used at the secondary school level, this test consists of separate achievement tests in diverse areas from literature and science to foreign language.
Basic English Skills Test	A test of basic language skills for use with any adult with limited English proficiency. Designed for use as a diagnostic and vocational counseling tool.

Another distinction that is often made between achievement and aptitude tests is that aptitude tests are typically used to make predictions whereas achievement tests are used to measure accomplishment. This does not mean that achievement tests are never used to make predictions, because they can and sometimes are. For example, achievement-test performance in a first-semester foreign language course may be considered predictive of achievement in subsequent foreign language courses. However, future predictions are most frequently made from aptitude tests.

Aptitude tests are used to make predictions about many things ranging from readiness for school and aptitude for college-level work to aptitude for work in a given profession such as law or medicine. For example, the Metropolitan Readiness Tests are several group-administered tests that assess the development of reading and mathematics skills in kindergarten and first grade. The Scholastic Aptitude Test is a group-administered test divided into verbal and mathematics sections. It is used in the college selection process and for advising high school students as to what might be their best course of action. Other aptitude tests consist of the Graduate Record Examination, used as a criterion for admission to many graduate schools; the Medical College Admission Test, which is required of students applying to medical school; and the Law School Admission Test, which is required of students applying to law school.

Diagnostic tests
Tests designed to
identify where a
student is having
difficulty with an
academic skill

Diagnostic Tests   In the field of education, **diagnostic tests** are designed to identify where a student is having difficulty with an academic skill. For example, a diagnostic mathematics test consists of subtests measuring the different types of knowledge and skills needed in mathematics. Poor performance on one or more subtests identifies the nature of the difficulty the student is having with mathematics, and attention can be directed to these areas to ameliorate the difficulty. These tests are generally administered to students who are suspected of having difficulty with a specific subject area because of poor performance either in the classroom or on an achievement test. For example, the Woodcock Reading Mastery Test is an individually administered test designed to measure skills inherent in reading. Its five subtests consist of letter identification, word identification, word attack, word comprehension, and passage comprehension. The KeyMath Revised test is an individually administered test for assessing difficulties with mathematical concepts, operations, and applications.

It is important to recognize that diagnostic tests are useful only in identifying where a student is having a problem with an academic skill. They do not give any information as to why the difficulty exists. The difficulties could stem from physical, psychological, or situational difficulties or some combination of these. Educators, psychologists, and physicians must provide the answers to the question of why.

SOURCES OF INFORMATION ABOUT TESTS

The information we have presented so far has focused on things such as the types of tests that have been constructed and the characteristics that a test or any other type of assessment measure must have to be considered a "good" test or assessment measure. Throughout the twentieth century educators, psychologists, and sociologists have been constructing tests to measure just about any construct you might be interested in. This means that if you are planning a research study investigating a construct such as "teacher morale," you do not have to worry about developing a measure of this construct because one probably exists. However, you have to know where to find such a measure. Fortunately, there are a number of reference sources that provide information about both published and unpublished tests.

*Mental
Measurements
Yearbook*
One of the
primary sources of
information about
published tests

Tests in Print
A primary source
of information
about published
tests

Probably the most important source of information about published tests is the ***Mental Measurements Yearbook*** (MMY) and ***Tests in Print*** (TIP), both of which are published by the Buros Institute of Mental Measurements at the Department of Educational Psychology of the University of Nebraska—Lincoln. If you are attempting to locate and learn about a test, you should consider consulting TIP first because TIP is a comprehensive volume that describes every test currently published as well as references to these tests. There are currently four volumes of TIP, of which TIP IV (Murphy, Conoley, & Impara, 1994) is the most recent. Each volume describes tests currently available for purchase, so you should select the most recent volume. Between editions of MMY, reviews of new and revised tests are accessible through an online computer service. Additionally, the institute publishes supplements to each volume during intermediate years; these supplements contain reviews of new and revised tests.

TABLE 4.10   Sources of Information about Tests and Test Reviews

Source	Description
Dictionary of Behavioral Assessment Techniques (Hersen & Bellack, 1988)	Presents a description, purpose, development, psychometric characteristics, clinical use, and future directions of behavioral assessment techniques.
Test Critiques (Keyser & Sweetland, 1994)	A series of 10 volumes which provide a description, practical application, use, psychometric characteristics, and reviewer's critique of over 700 tests.
ETS Test Collection, Princeton, NJ, 08541	A collection of published and unpublished educational tests and measurement devices. A brief annotation including the scope, target audience, and availability of each test is provided.
Handbook of Research Design and Social Measurement (Miller, 1991)	A source book presenting many sociological and psychological tests as well as a discussion of the steps involved in conducting a social science research study.
Measures of Personality and Social Psychological Attitudes (Robinson, Shaver, & Wrightsman, 1991).	Reviews measures of personality and attitudes, including not only a brief description of each scale and its psychometric properties but also a brief presentation of its liabilities.

Although the MMY and TIP are probably the most comprehensive resource for information on published tests, tests and reviews of tests can also be found in a number of other sources. Table 4.10 lists several sources of information that can be consulted.

Information about tests can also be obtained from the published literature and from catalogues distributed by test publishers. Sometimes a test will be published in a journal article prior to its being mentioned in the MMY. Such a journal article typically describes the development of the test and its psychometric characteristics. Publishers' catalogs describing tests are easy to obtain by merely calling the publisher. They are, however, limited in that they typically contain only a brief description of each test without the detailed critical review that would exist in a publication such as the MMY. Remember that publishers are in the business of selling tests and a critical review will be omitted.

SUMMARY

Measurement refers to the act of assigning symbols or numbers to objects, events, people, and characteristics according to a specific set of rules. There are four different scales of measurement, which communicate different kinds of information. The nominal scale is a "name" scale that typically uses symbols to label, classify, or identify people or objects. The ordinal scale rank orders the people, objects, or characteristics being studied. The interval scale has the characteristic of equal distances between adjacent numbers. The ratio scale has the property of a true zero point as well as the characteristics of the other scales of measurement.

In measuring the characteristics of interest to educational researchers, twelve assumptions are made. These assumptions are that (1) psychological traits and states being measured exist, (2) they can be quantified and measured, (3) the various approaches to measuring aspects of the same thing can be useful, (4) assessment can provide answers to some of life's most momentous questions, (5) assessment can pinpoint phenomena that require further attention or study, (6) various sources of data enrich and are part of the assessment process, (7) various sources of error are part of the assessment process, (8) tests and other assessment techniques have strengths and weaknesses, (9) test-related behavior predicts non-test-related behavior, (10) present-day behavior sampling predicts future behavior, (11) testing and assessment can be conducted in a fair and unbiased manner, and (12) testing and assessment benefit society.

A good test or assessment procedure must be reliable and valid. Reliability refers to the consistency or stability of a response. Reliability of a test or assessment procedure can be determined in several ways. Test-retest reliability refers to the consistency of scores over time. Equivalent forms reliability refers to the consistency of scores on two equivalent forms of a test. Split-half reliability refers to the consistency of scores obtained from two equivalent halves of the test or assessment procedure. Internal consistency refers to the homogeneity of a test, and the Kuder-Richardson formula 20 and coefficient alpha provide reliability estimates for homogeneous tests. Inter-scorer reliability refers to the consistency of scores provided by two or more people scoring the same performance.

Validity refers to the appropriateness of the interpretations and actions we make based on the scores we get from a test or assessment procedure. We must collect evidence to determine whether the inferences and actions taken are appropriate. Validity evidence can be collected in many ways. Content validity evidence refers to a judgment of the degree to which the items, tasks, or questions on a test sample the domain of interest. Criterion-related validity evidence refers to a judgment of the extent to which a test score can be used to infer, or predict, a person's performance in some specific activity. Concurrent criterion-related validity evidence is based on collecting the test scores and the criterion performance at the same time and determining whether the test scores predict the concurrent criterion. Predictive criterion-related validity evidence is based on test scores obtained at one point in time and criterion performance scores obtained at a later point in time and later determination of whether the test scores predict the subsequent criterion. Construct validity refers to the extent to which a theoretical construct can be inferred from the scores on a test. Evidence of construct validity is collected in many ways, such as collecting evidence of the homogeneity of the test, determining whether predicted changes in test scores do actually change, determining whether test scores correlate with scores of other tests designed to measure similar constructs, determining whether test scores do not correlate with scores of other tests designed to measure different constructs, and factor analyzing test items or subtest responses to determine whether the hypothesized constructs are being measured.

Although several procedures are listed as methods for collecting construct-validity evidence, it must be remembered that construct validity is the unifying construct for all validity evidence. All types of validity, including content- and criterion-related validity, are forms of construct validity.

Reliability and validity evidence can be used to select the test or assessment procedure that will provide interpretable scores. Being able to use this information is necessary because many tests and assessment procedures have been developed by the educational researcher. The educational researcher can consult a number of resource books, such as the *Mental Measurements Yearbook,* to identify intelligence tests, personality tests, and different educational assessment tests that can be used for his or her research study. Reliability and validity evidence should always be used in making the selection of the test or assessment procedure to use in any study because this is the information that permits the researcher to select the test or assessment procedure that gives the best and most accurate results.

STUDY QUESTIONS

1. Define measurement.
2. Define the four different levels or scales of measurement and explain the characteristics of each one.
3. List and explain the twelve assumptions underlying testing and measurement.
4. Define reliability and list the different ways of assessing it.
5. Explain each of the different ways of assessing reliability.
6. Under what conditions should each of the different ways of assessing reliability be used?
7. Define validity and validation.
8. Compare and contrast the different ways of obtaining validity evidence.
9. Explain what is meant by the "unified view of construct validity."
10. Define each of the types of tests discussed in your textbook, explain the purpose of each of these tests, and give an example of each one.

EXERCISES

To illustrate the type of research one would conduct in the field of testing and measurement, go to the library and get a copy of the following article: Moore, R. W., and Foy, L. H. (1997). The Scientific Attitude Inventory: A revision (SAI II). *Journal of Research in Science Teaching, 34,* 327–336.

As you read this article, you should answer the following questions:

1. How was the scale constructed and scored?
2. How was the scale validated?
3. How was the reliability of the scale assessed?

KEY TERMS

achievement tests (117)

aptitude tests (118)

coefficient alpha (105)

concurrent validity (108)

construct (110)

construct validity (110)

content validity (107)

convergent evidence (111)

criterion-related validity (108)

diagnostic tests (120)

discriminant evidence (112)

equivalent-forms reliability (102)

expectancy data (109)

factor analysis (112)

homogeneity (111)

intelligence (114)

internal consistency (104)

inter-scorer reliability (106)

interval scale (95)

Kuder-Richardson formula 20 (104)

measurement (92)

Mental Measurements Yearbook (120)

nominal scale (93)

ordinal scale (94)

personality (115)

predictive validity (108)

ratio scale (96)

reliability (100)

Spearman-Brown formula (103)

split-half reliability (103)

states (98)

test-retest reliability (100)

Tests in Print (120)

traits (97)

validation (107)

validity (106)

validity coefficient (109)

CHAPTER 5

Methods of
Data Collection

LEARNING OBJECTIVES

To be able to

- list the six methods of data collection.
- explain the difference between "method of data collection" and "research method."
- list the names of at least four different research methods.
- define and explain the characteristics of each of the six methods of data collection.
- explain each of the fourteen principles of questionnaire construction.
- know when open-ended questions and closed-ended questions are used.
- explain the concept of standardization.
- explain the key characteristics of the four different types of interviews.
- describe the four roles the researcher can take in qualitative interviewing.
- give multiple examples of response categories used for completely anchored rating scales.
- list at least five commonly used probes.

In Chapter 4 we introduced you to the concept of measurement. We also discussed the different kinds of tests used for collecting data in educational research. If an already constructed test is available for the topics of interest to you, you should strongly consider using that test because reliability and validity information will usually be available. However, an already developed data-collection instrument may not be available for your particular research needs. In this case you must construct a new test or another type of data collection instrument such as a questionnaire or an interview protocol, and this takes a lot of time and effort if you plan to do it properly.

The purpose of this chapter is to help you understand the different ways to collect research data and to show you how to construct a data-collection instrument. You will learn how to answer these two questions:

What data collection method or methods will allow me to obtain the information I need to answer my research questions?

How can I construct a data collection instrument when the need arises?

The following list shows the most common methods of data collection that are used by educational researchers:

1. Standardized tests
2. Questionnaires
3. Interviews
4. Focus groups
5. Observation
6. Secondary data

You learned about standardized tests in Chapter 4. In this chapter, we will cover the other methods of data collection. In addition to using standardized tests, researchers can have research participants fill out self-report instruments (questionnaires); researchers can talk to participants in person or over the telephone (interviews); researchers can discuss issues with multiple research participants at the same time in a small-group setting (focus groups); researchers can examine how research participants act in natural and structured environments (observation); and researchers can use data that came from an earlier time for a different purpose than the current research problem at hand (secondary data).

Research method
Overall research design and strategy

Method of data collection
Technique for physically obtaining data to be analyzed in a research study

In a typical research study, researchers begin by identifying the important research problems and research questions that they want to address. Then they select the most appropriate **research method** or methods (experimental research, qualitative research, correlational research, causal-comparative research, etc.) that will help them to decide on a research design and a research strategy that will allow them to answer their research questions. Researchers next decide how they are going to collect their empirical research data. That is, they decide what **methods of data collection** (tests, questionnaires, interviews, focus groups, observations) they are going to use to physically obtain research data from their research participants.

Additionally, it is important for you to understand that more than one method of data collection can be used with virtually every research method. For example, a researcher using the experimental research method could have his or her research participants fill out a questionnaire during both the pretest and posttest (i.e., before and after the "experimental manipulation"). The experimental researcher could also interview his or her participants during the pretest and posttest. Finally, the experimental researcher may choose to systematically observe his or her research participants before, during, and after the experimental manipulation.

Remember that in this chapter we are concerned with how research data are collected from research participants, not with the different research methods. In a typical published journal article, the methods of data collection are discussed in the procedures section; the research method is usually discussed in the design section. You will learn more about the different research methods in Chapters 8–12. Now we will explain the different methods of data collection.

QUESTIONNAIRES

Questionnaire
A self-report data-collection instrument filled out by research participants

A **questionnaire** is a self-report data-collection instrument that each research participant fills out as part of a research study. Researchers use questionnaires so that they can obtain information about the thoughts, feelings, attitudes, beliefs, values, perceptions, personality, and behavioral intentions of research participants. In other words, researchers attempt to measure many different kinds of characteristics using questionnaires.

We view the term *questionnaire* broadly, meaning that questionnaires are not restricted to a single research method. Questionnaires can be used to collect data with multiple research methods (experimental, qualitative, correlational, etc.). Furthermore, the content and organization of a questionnaire will correspond to the researcher's research objectives. The key point is that the questionnaire is a versatile tool available to you and other educational researchers.

Questionnaires typically include multiple questions and statements. For example, a researcher might ask a question about the present (Do you support the use of corporal punishment in elementary schools?), the past (Have you ever used corporal punishment with one of your students?), or the future (Do you think that you will use corporal punishment sometime in the future?). Questionnaires can also include statements that participants consider and respond to. For example, when filling out the Rosenberg Self-Esteem Scale in Figure 5.1, research participants must indicate their degree of agreement or disagreement with ten statements measuring their attitudes toward themselves.

How to Construct a Questionnaire

The most important principles of questionnaire construction are shown in Table 5.1. Take a moment to examine this list of fourteen principles so you will have an overview of what

FIGURE 5.1   The Rosenberg Self-Esteem Scale.

Circle one response for each of the following ten items.

	Strongly Agree	Agree	Disagree	Strongly Disagree
1. I feel that I am a person of worth, at least on an equal basis with others.	1	2	3	4
2. I feel that I have a number of good qualities.	1	2	3	4
*3. All in all, I am inclined to feel that I am a failure.	1	2	3	4
4. I am able to do things as well as most other people.	1	2	3	4
*5. I feel I do not have much to be proud of.	1	2	3	4
6. I take a positive attitude toward myself.	1	2	3	4
7. On the whole, I am satisfied with myself.	1	2	3	4
*8. I wish I could have more respect for myself.	1	2	3	4
*9. I certainly feel useless at times.	1	2	3	4
*10. At times I think I am no good at all.	1	2	3	4

Morris Rosenberg's "Self-Esteem Scale" from pp. 325–327 of *Society and Adolescent Self-Image* © 1989 by Morris Rosenberg, Wesleyan University Press.

Items marked with an asterisk have reversed wording. The numbers on items with reversed wording should be reversed before summing the responses for the ten items. For example, on item 3, "strongly agree" becomes 4, "agree" becomes 3, "disagree" becomes 2, and "strongly disagree" becomes 1.

is important to consider when constructing a questionnaire. We explain each of these principles in more detail.

Principle 1. Make sure the questionnaire items match your research objectives. This cardinal principle should be obvious. You must always determine why you intend to conduct your research study before you can write a questionnaire. If you plan on conducting an exploratory research study (i.e., you want to collect some preliminary information about a research problem), your questionnaire will usually not need to be as detailed as when you plan on conducting a confirmatory research study (i.e., when you intend on collecting data that will enable you to test research hypotheses). In both cases, you should carefully review the existing research literature as well as any related instruments that

TABLE 5.1   Principles of Questionnaire Construction

Principle 1	Make sure the questionnaire items match your research objectives.
Principle 2	Understand your research participants.
Principle 3	Use natural and familiar language.
Principle 4	Write items that are clear, precise, and relatively short.
Principle 5	Do not use "leading" or "loaded" questions.
Principle 6	Avoid double-barreled questions.
Principle 7	Avoid double negatives.
Principle 8	Determine whether an open-ended or a closed-ended question is needed.
Principle 9	Use mutually exclusive and exhaustive response categories for closed-ended questions.
Principle 10	Consider the different types of response categories available for closed-ended questionnaire items.
Principle 11	Use multiple items to measure abstract constructs.
Principle 12	Reverse the wording in some of the items to prevent response sets.
Principle 13	Develop a questionnaire that is easy for the participant to use.
Principle 14	Always pilot test your questionnaire.

have already been used for your research objectives before deciding to construct your own questionnaire.

Principle 2. Understand your research participants. A key to effective questionnaire construction is understanding your research participants. Remember that they, not you, are the ones filling out the questionnaire. A useful strategy when writing a questionnaire is to try to develop an empathetic understanding, or an ability to "think like" your potential research participants. If you can effectively consider how your research participants will interpret and react to each item on your questionnaire, then it is very likely to provide useful information.

Principle 3. Use natural and familiar language. You should use language that is understandable to the types of people that are going to fill out your questionnaire. Try to avoid the use of jargon or technical terms. Consider the age of your participants, their educational level, and any relevant cultural characteristics of your participants when deciding the kind of language you need to use. Remember that it is very possible that not everyone uses the same everyday language as you. If you are reading this book, you are probably a college graduate and you are also working on a graduate degree. Using natural and familiar language makes it easier for participants to fill out a questionnaire and helps participants feel more relaxed and less threatened by the task of filling it out.

Principle 4. Write items that are clear, precise, and relatively short. Each item on your questionnaire should be understandable to you (the researcher) and to the participant (the person filling out the questionnaire). Because each item is measuring something, it is important for it to be clear and precise. The GIGO principle is relevant here: "garbage in, garbage out." If the participants are not clear about what is being asked of them, their responses will result in data that cannot or should not be used in a research study. Your goal is for each research participant to interpret the meaning of each item in the questionnaire in exactly the same way. You should also avoid technical terms; if you must use a technical term, remember to define it for the participants. Finally, try to keep most items relatively short because long items can be confusing and stressful for research participants.

Loaded question
A question containing loaded, or emotionally charged, words

Leading question
A question that suggests a researcher is expecting a certain answer

Principle 5. Do not use "leading" or "loaded" questions. A leading or loaded question biases the response the participant gives to the question. A **loaded question** is one that contains loaded words (words that create a positive or negative reaction). For example, the word *liberal* was often avoided by politicians during the 1980s, even by liberals, because the word created a negative reaction in some people regardless of the content of the statement. A **leading question** is one that is phrased in a way that suggests to the participant that the researcher is expecting a certain answer. Here is an example of a leading question:

Don't you agree that teachers should earn more money than they currently earn?

☐ Yes, they should earn more.
☐ No, they should not earn more.
☐ Don't know/no opinion.

The phrase "Don't you agree" leads the participant here. A more neutral wording of this question would be as follows:

Do you believe teacher salaries are a little lower than they should be, a little higher than they should be, or about right?

☐ Teacher salaries are a little lower than they should be.
☐ Teacher salaries are a little higher than they should be.
☐ Teacher salaries are about right.
☐ Don't know/no opinion.

Always remember that your goal is to write questionnaire items that help participants feel free to provide their natural and honest answers. You want to obtain responses that are undistorted by the particular question wording.

Double-barreled question
A question that combines two or more issues or attitude objects

Principle 6. Avoid double-barreled questions. A **double-barreled question** combines two or more issues or attitude objects in a single item. Here is an example: Do you think that teachers should have more contact with parents and school administrators? As you can see, this single question asks about two different issues. The question is really asking, Do you think that teachers should have more contact with parents? *and* Do you think that teachers should have more contact with school administrators? Each of these two issues may elicit a different attitude, and combining them into one question makes it unclear which attitude or opinion is being measured. Therefore, it is a good rule to avoid double-barreled questions. As a general rule, if the word *and* appears in a question or statement, you should check to see whether it is double-barreled.

Principle 7. Avoid double negatives. When participants are asked for their agreement with a statement, double negatives can easily occur. For example,

Do you agree or disagree with the following statement?

Teachers should not be required to supervise their students during library time.

Double negative
A sentence construction that includes two negatives

If you disagree with the statement, you must construct a **double negative** (a sentence construction that includes two negatives). If you disagree, you are saying that you do *not* think that teachers should *not* supervise students during library time (Converse & Presser, 1986). In other words, you probably believe that teachers should supervise students during library time. If you use a negative item, you should consider underlining the negative word or words to catch the participant's attention.

Open-ended question
A question that allows participants to respond in their own words

Closed-ended question
A question that forces participants to choose a response

Principle 8. Determine whether an open-ended or a closed-ended question is needed. An **open-ended question** enables participants to respond in any way that they please. Open-ended questions provide primarily qualitative data. In contrast, a **closed-ended question** requires participants to choose from a limited number of responses predetermined by the researcher. Closed-ended questions provide primarily quantitative data.

To determine someone's marital status you could use the question, What is your current marital status? and leave sufficient space for participants to write in their answers. In this case the question is called an open-ended question because the participants must provide answers in their own words. On the other hand, you could use a closed-ended question to determine someone's marital status. Here is an example of a closed-ended question:

What is your marital status? (Check one box.)

☐ Single
☐ Married
☐ Divorced
☐ Separated
☐ Widowed

Item stem
The set of words forming a question or statement

You will notice that the **item stem** (the words forming the question or statement) is the same in our open-ended and closed-ended question examples (both ask, What is your marital status?). The key difference between an open-ended question and a closed-ended question is in the way the participants are allowed to respond. In open-ended questions participants must come up with their own answers, and in closed-ended questions participants must select from the predetermined categories provided by the researcher.

Open-ended questions are usually used in exploratory research (i.e., when the researcher knows little about the topic) and closed-ended questions are usually used in confirmatory research (i.e., when the researcher plans on testing specific hypotheses). Open-ended questions are valuable when the researcher needs to know what people are thinking and when the dimensions of a variable are not well defined. Because the participants respond by writing their answers in their own words, open-ended questions can provide rich information. For example, the following open-ended question would provide some interesting information: What do you think teachers can do to keep students from using illicit drugs? It can be difficult, however, to analyze the data obtained from open-ended questions. Closed-ended questions should be used when the dimensions of a variable are already known. Closed-ended questions expose all participants to the same response categories and allow more quantitative statistical analysis.

Principle 9. Use mutually exclusive and exhaustive response categories for closed-

Mutually *ended questions.* Categories are **mutually exclusive** when they do not overlap. For example,
exclusive the following categories for a question about the participant's age are *not* mutually exclusive:
Response
categories that
don't overlap
       10 or less
       10 to 20
       20 to 30
       30 to 40
       40 to 50
       50 to 60
       60 to 70
       70 to 80
       80 or greater

Do you see the problem with these response categories? The problem is that they overlap.
For example, a person who is 20 years old could be placed into two categories. In fact, persons aged 10, 20, 30, 40, 50, 60, 70, and 80 can all be placed into more than one category.
In short, the response categories are not mutually exclusive. In a moment we will show you
how to fix this problem.

Exhaustive   A set of response categories are **exhaustive** when there is a category available for all
Response legitimate responses. For example, what is the problem with the following categories from
categories that a question asking you for your current age?
include all
possible responses
       1 to 4
       5 to 9
       10 to 14

The problem is that these three categories are not exhaustive because there is no category
available for anyone over the age of fourteen or anyone less than one year old. A set of categories is not exhaustive unless there is a category available for all potential responses.
        Putting the ideas of mutually exclusive and exhaustive categories together, you can
see that the following set of response categories are mutually exclusive and exhaustive:

Which of the following categories includes your current age? (Check one box.)
     ☐ Less than 18
     ☐ 18 to 29
     ☐ 30 to 39
     ☐ 40 to 49
     ☐ 50 to 59
     ☐ 60 to 69
     ☐ 70 to 79
     ☐ 80 or older

The principle of mutually exclusive categories applies because none of the categories overlap. The principle of exhaustive categories applies because there is a category available for

all possible ages. Whenever you write a standard closed-ended question (a question with an item stem and a set of predetermined response categories), remember to make sure that your response categories are mutually exclusive and exhaustive.

Principle 10. Consider the different types of response categories available for closed-ended questionnaire items. In this section we introduce several popular types of closed-ended response categories by explaining the ideas of rating scales, rankings, semantic differentials, and checklists.

Rating Scales Researchers often obtain data from research participants by providing them with questions or statements (the item stem) and rating scales (the response choices) with instructions to make judgments about each item stem using the rating scale that is provided. A **rating scale** is a continuum of response choices that participants are told to use in indicating their responses. Rating scales produce numerical (quantitative) data rather than qualitative data (nominal-level data). Rating scales have been used by researchers for quite a long time. In an early review of the history of rating scales, Guilford (1936) provides examples from as early as 1805 and many other examples shortly after 1900. Some important early developers of rating scales are Sir Francis Galton (1822–1911), Karl Pearson (1857–1936), and, somewhat later, Rensis Likert (1903–1981).

Rating scale
A continuum of response choices

A **numerical rating scale** consists of a set of numbers and "anchored" endpoints. When you **anchor** a point on a rating scale, you label the point with a written descriptor. Here is an example of an item stem and a numerical rating scale with anchored endpoints:

Numerical rating scale
A rating scale with anchored endpoints

Anchor
A written descriptor for a point on a rating scale

How would you rate the overall job performance of your school principal?

1	2	3	4	5	6	7
Very Low						Very High

As you can see, the first endpoint ("1") is anchored with the words "Very Low." The other endpoint ("7") is anchored with the words "Very High." This is a seven-point rating scale because there are a total of seven points on the scale.

A similar type of rating scale is called a fully anchored rating scale. A **fully anchored rating scale** has all points anchored with descriptors. Here is an example of an item stem followed by a fully anchored rating scale:

Fully anchored rating scale
All points are anchored on the rating scale

My principal is an effective leader.

1	2	3	4	5
Strongly Agree	Agree	Neutral	Disagree	Strongly Disagree

This scale is a five-point rating scale because there are five points on the scale. Some researchers prefer to exclude the numbers and provide just the descriptors in a fully anchored rating scale. This scale is sometimes called an "agreement" rating scale because the participants report on their agreement or disagreement with the statement provided by the researcher in the item stem.

You may be wondering how many points a rating scale should have. Basically, research suggests that you should use somewhere from four points to eleven points on a rating scale (e.g., McKelvie, 1978; Nunally, 1978). Rating scales with fewer than four points are not as reliable as rating scales with more points. On the other hand, rating scales with more than eleven points can be confusing because most participants have limited abilities to make fine discriminations when there are a great number of scale points. Exhibit 5.1 includes four-point and five-point rating scales because these are very popular with educational researchers and have been shown to work quite well.

You may also wonder whether you should include a center or middle category in your rating scale. Research suggests that omitting the middle alternative ("neutral," "about the same," "average," "no difference," etc.) does not appreciably affect the overall pattern of results (Converse & Presser, 1986, pp. 36–37; Schuman & Presser, 1981, Chap. 6). As a result, some researchers choose to include a middle alternative and others choose not to include it. You can see in Figure 5.1 that Rosenberg used four-point rating scales (i.e., he omitted the middle alternative) in his Self-Esteem Scale. Some researchers, such as Rosenberg, prefer to omit the middle alternative because it forces research participants to lean one way or the other.

Take a moment now to examine Exhibit 5.1 and you will see some other rating scales commonly used by researchers and practitioners. As you can see, you can ask participants for many different kinds of ratings. For example, you might ask participants about agreement, approval, importance, satisfaction, or frequency.

Rankings   Sometimes you may want your research participants to rank order their responses. A **ranking** indicates the importance or priority assigned by a participant to an attitudinal object. Rankings can be used with open-ended and closed-ended questions. For example, you might first ask an open-ended question such as, In your opinion, who are the three top teachers in your school? Then you could follow up this question with a ranking item such as, Please rank order the teachers you just mentioned. Rankings can also be used with closed-ended items. For example, you might use the following closed-ended item:

Ranking
The ordering
of responses
into ranks

> Please rank the importance of the following qualities in a school principal. (Fill in your rank order in the spaces provided using the numbers 1 through 5.)
>
> _____ A principal that is sincere.
>
> _____ A principal that gets resources for the school.
>
> _____ A principal that is an advocate for teacher needs.
>
> _____ A principal that is a strong disciplinarian.
>
> _____ A principal that is a good motivator.

As you can see, this is a closed-ended item because predetermined response categories are provided. As a general rule, you should not ask participants to rank more than three to five responses or response categories because ranking can be a difficult task for participants.

EXHIBIT 5.1   Examples of Response Categories for Rating Scales

---

Agreement
(1) Strongly Agree   (2) Agree   (3) Disagree   (4) Strongly Disagree
(1) Strongly Agree   (2) Agree   (3) Neutral   (4) Disagree   (5) Strongly Disagree

Amount
(1) Too Much   (2) About the Right Amount   (3) Too Little
(1) Too Many   (2) About the Right Amount   (3) Not Enough

Approval
(1) Strongly Approve   (2) Approve   (3) Disapprove   (4) Strongly Disapprove
(1) Strongly Approve   (2) Approve   (3) Neutral   (4) Disapprove   (5) Strongly Disapprove

Belief
(1) Definitely True   (2) Probably True   (3) Probably False   (4) Definitely False

Comparison
(1) Much Better   (2) Better   (3) About the Same   (4) Worse   (5) Much Worse
(1) Much More   (2) Somewhat More   (3) About the Same   (4) Somewhat Less   (5) Much Less

Effectiveness
(1) Very effective   (2) Somewhat Effective   (3) Not Very Effective   (4) Not at All Effective

Evaluation
(1) Excellent   (2) Good   (3) Fair   (4) Poor
(1) Very Good   (2) Good   (3) Fair   (4) Poor   (5) Very Poor
(1) Very Good   (2) Somewhat Good   (3) Somewhat Bad   (4) Very Bad

Frequency
(1) Always   (2) Frequently   (3) Sometimes   (4) Never
(1) Regularly   (2) Fairly Often   (3) Seldom   (4) Never
(1) Very Often   (2) Fairly Often   (3) Seldom   (4) Hardly Ever   (5) Never

Importance
(1) Very Important   (2) Fairly Important   (3) Not Very Important   (4) Not at All Important

Knowledge
(1) Very Familiar   (2) Somewhat Familiar   (3) Not Very Familiar   (4) Not at All Familiar

Probability
(1) A Lot More Likely   (2) Somewhat More Likely   (3) No Difference
(4) Somewhat Less Likely   (5) A Lot Less Likely

Satisfaction
(1) Very Satisfied   (2) Satisfied   (3) Not Very Satisfied   (4) Not at All Satisfied

Semantic differential
A scaling technique in which participants rate a series of objects or concepts

Semantic Differential   The **semantic differential** is a scaling technique used to measure the meaning that participants give to various attitudinal objects or concepts (Osgood, Suci, & Tannenbaum, 1957). The participants are asked to rate each object or concept provided in the item stem on a series of seven-point, bipolar rating scales. The scales are "bipolar" because they have contrasting adjectives anchoring the endpoints. The contrasting adjectives are often antonyms. Some attitudinal objects you may wish to have your research participants rate are principal, teacher, student, disabled, and gifted. You can see an example of a semantic differential in Exhibit 5.2.

Semantic differentials are useful when you want to "profile" or describe the multiple characteristics associated with attitudinal objects. In Exhibit 5.2 you are asked to rate your school principal on twenty different bipolar rating scales. If you used this semantic differential with all the teachers in a school, you could average all the responses and profile the teachers' view of the principal. You may find that different groups produce different profiles. For example, males and females may view the principal differently. If you need to develop a semantic differential, it is helpful to look at a book of antonyms for contrasting word pairs. You can also find some useful lists of commonly used semantic differential word pairs in Isaac and Michael (1995) and in Jenkins, Russell, and Suci (1958).

Checklist
A list of response categories that respondents check if appropriate

Checklists   Researchers sometimes provide a list of response categories (a **checklist**) and ask the research participants to check the responses that apply to them. Multiple responses may be allowed. Here is an example of a checklist:

Where do you get your information about the most recent advances in teaching? (Please check all categories that apply to you.)

_____ Other teachers

_____ Professors

_____ Principal

_____ Parents

_____ Superintendent

_____ Academic journals

_____ Professional journals

_____ Magazines

_____ Television

_____ Other. Please list: _____

Summated rating scale
A multi-item scale that has the responses for each person summed into a single score

Likert scale
A summated rating scale

Principle 11. Use multiple items to measure abstract constructs. A **summated rating scale** (also called a **Likert scale**) is different from the numerical rating scales and the fully anchored rating scales that we discussed earlier. Rather than being composed of a single item stem and one rating scale, a summated rating scale is composed of multiple items that are designed to measure the same idea or the same construct. The ratings on the multiple items are then summed for each research participant, providing a single score for each person.

EXHIBIT 5.2   Example of Semantic Differential Scaling Technique

---

Please rate your school principal on each of the following descriptive scales. Place a checkmark on the space between each pair of words that best indicates how you feel.)

Your School Principal

Sociable	_____	_____	_____	_____	_____	_____	_____	Unsociable
Kind	_____	_____	_____	_____	_____	_____	_____	Cruel
Hard	_____	_____	_____	_____	_____	_____	_____	Soft
Successful	_____	_____	_____	_____	_____	_____	_____	Unsuccessful
Wise	_____	_____	_____	_____	_____	_____	_____	Foolish
Strong	_____	_____	_____	_____	_____	_____	_____	Weak
Severe	_____	_____	_____	_____	_____	_____	_____	Lenient
Masculine	_____	_____	_____	_____	_____	_____	_____	Feminine
Active	_____	_____	_____	_____	_____	_____	_____	Passive
Excitable	_____	_____	_____	_____	_____	_____	_____	Calm
Fast	_____	_____	_____	_____	_____	_____	_____	Slow
Good	_____	_____	_____	_____	_____	_____	_____	Bad
Predictable	_____	_____	_____	_____	_____	_____	_____	Unpredictable
Clear	_____	_____	_____	_____	_____	_____	_____	Confusing
Traditional	_____	_____	_____	_____	_____	_____	_____	Progressive
Authoritarian	_____	_____	_____	_____	_____	_____	_____	Democratic
Flexible	_____	_____	_____	_____	_____	_____	_____	Rigid
Happy	_____	_____	_____	_____	_____	_____	_____	Sad
Genuine	_____	_____	_____	_____	_____	_____	_____	False
Work	_____	_____	_____	_____	_____	_____	_____	Fun

The summated rating scale was developed by Rensis Likert (pronounced LICK-ert), who published the results of his dissertation in an article in 1932 (Likert, 1932). Since this time, summated rating scales have been extensively used by researchers. The key advantages of multiple-item rating scales compared to single-item rating scales is that multiple-item scales provide more reliable (i.e., more consistent or stable) scores and they produce more variability, which helps the researcher to make finer distinctions among the respondents. If you want to measure a complex construct (such as self-esteem, self-efficacy, locus of control, temperament, etc.), the use of a multiple-item scale is pretty much a necessity.

The Rosenberg Self-Esteem Scale shown in Figure 5.1 is a good example of a Likert scale (i.e., a summated rating scale). It consists of ten items designed to measure self-esteem. The lowest possible total score on the full scale for a person is ten, and the highest possible total score for a person is forty. A score of ten occurs when the participant obtains the lowest possible score on all the items. A score of forty occurs when the participant obtains the highest possible score on all the items. Most participants will score somewhere in between these two extremes (i.e., between the minimum and the maximum scores).

Principle 12. Reverse the wording in some of the items to help prevent response sets. When participants rate multiple items using the same or similar rating scale, an "acquiescence response set" may occur. A **response set** is the tendency for a research participant to respond to a series of items in a specific direction regardless of their content. One type of response set is called the **acquiescence response set,** which is the tendency to say yes rather than no or to agree rather than to disagree on a whole series of items. Another response set, called the **social desirability response set,** is the tendency to provide answers that are socially desirable. One technique used to prevent response sets (especially the acquiescence response set) is to reverse the wording in some of the items. This technique encourages participants to read each item on the questionnaire more carefully. An example of reversed wording is shown in Figure 5.1. You can see that items 3, 5, 8, 9, and 10 of the Rosenberg Self-Esteem Scale are "reversed" (i.e., agreement indicates *low* self-esteem). The items that have not been reversed (items 1, 2, 4, 6, and 7) indicate *high* self-esteem.

Principle 13. Develop a questionnaire that is easy for the participant to use. The ordering, or sequencing, of questionnaire items is one consideration. For example, Roberson and Sundstrom (1990) found that placing the important questions first and demographic questions (age, gender, etc.) last in an employee attitude survey resulted in the highest return rate. It is usually a good idea to begin a questionnaire with positive or nonthreatening items to obtain some commitment from the participant to fill out the questionnaire. The questionnaire should also not be overly long for the types of people in your target population. Otherwise they may not fill out the questionnaire properly, or they may refuse to complete the entire questionnaire.

It is also a good idea to limit the number of filter questions used in a questionnaire because participants may become confused or agitated. A **filter question** (also called a contingency question) is an item that directs participants to different followup questions depending on their response. It allows the researcher to "filter out" participants from questions that these participants cannot or should not attempt to answer. Here is an example of an item operating as a filter question:

Question 1: What is your gender?

    Male   → (IF MALE, GO TO QUESTION 5)
    Female → (IF FEMALE, GO TO QUESTION 2)

You should also include clear instructions throughout your questionnaire. If a questionnaire has several different topical sections, you need to provide transitional or "lead-in" statements to orient the participants to each new topic. Finally, always try to make your questionnaire look professional because participants are more likely to fill it out. Remember that the appearance and quality of your questionnaire is also a reflection on you and your organization.

Response set
Tendency to respond in a specific direction regardless of content

Acquiescence response set
Tendency to either agree or to disagree

Social desirability response set
Tendency to provide answers that are socially desirable

Filter question
An item that directs participants to different followup questions depending on their response

Pilot test
A preliminary test of your questionnaire

Principle 14. Always pilot test your questionnaire. It is a cardinal rule in research that you must "try out," or **pilot test,** your questionnaire to find out whether it operates properly. You should conduct your pilot test with a minimum of five to ten people. You may want to start with colleagues or friends, asking them to fill out the questionnaire. Then you will need to pilot test the questionnaire with several individuals similar to those who will be in your research study.

Think-aloud technique
Has participants verbalize their thoughts and perceptions while engaged in an activity

One useful technique to use during your pilot test is called the **think-aloud technique** which requires participants to verbalize their thoughts and perceptions while they engage in an activity. When this technique is used as part of a pilot test, you ask the participants to verbalize their thoughts and perceptions about the questionnaire while they are filling it out. You must record or carefully write down exactly what they say. It is also helpful to make audio-video tape recordings of the pilot test sessions for later review. The think-aloud technique is especially helpful for determining whether participants are interpreting the items the way you intended.

You will want to use the think-aloud technique with some of the participants in your pilot test, but you should have some others in the pilot test fill out the questionnaire under circumstances as similar as possible to the actual research study. When you conduct a pilot test you need to think about several issues. For example, be sure to check how long it takes participants to complete the questionnaire under circumstances similar to the actual research study. This will help you know if the questionnaire is too long. Writing overlong questionnaires is something you must be careful to avoid because you will always be able to think of some additional items that you would like to add.

Using the think-aloud technique, you can listen to how the participants think about the instructions and the items in your questionnaire. Try to determine whether any of the questionnaire items are confusing or threatening. Ask your participants to tell you when they reach an item that is difficult to understand, and then ask them to paraphrase what they believe the problem item is intended to measure. Determine whether your participants understand the items in a consistent way. Be sure to also check the veracity of the responses of your participants (i.e., whether their answers are true and accurate). These strategies will help you determine whether the items actually measure what they are intended to measure. When the participants are filling out the questionnaire, check to see whether they skip to the correct place if you have filter questions in your questionnaire.

After the participants finish filling out the questionnaire, you may discuss the questionnaire with them individually or in group sessions. Explain the purpose of your questionnaire to them and ask them whether they believe anything important was left out, whether the instructions were clear, whether there were any items that stood out for any reason, and probe for an explanation. If the questionnaire has an experimental manipulation embedded in it, be sure to check to see that the manipulation is working as intended. For example, if a statement or a vignette is supposed to increase empathy toward minority groups, ask your participants whether they understood it and whether they felt empathetic afterwards. After completing your pilot test, revise your questionnaire and then pilot test it again! Remember that you do not want to use a questionnaire in a research study until all of the kinks have been worked out.

INTERVIEWS

Interview
A data-collection
method in which
interviewer asks
interviewee
questions

Interviewer
The person asking
the questions

Interviewee
The person being
asked questions

*In-person
interview*
An interview
conducted
face-to-face

*Telephone
interview*
An interview
conducted over
the phone

Probes
Prompts to obtain
response clarity
or additional
information

You learned in the last section that you can collect data from research participants by having them fill out a questionnaire. Another way to collect data is to interview research participants. An **interview** is a data-collection method in which an **interviewer** (the researcher or someone working for the researcher) asks questions of an **interviewee** (the research participant). That is, the interviewer collects the data from the interviewee, who provides the data. Interviews that are done face-to-face are called **in-person interviews,** and interviews conducted over the telephone are called **telephone interviews.** A strength of interviews is that a researcher can freely use **probes** (prompts used to obtain response clarity or additional information). Some commonly used probes are given in Table 5.2.

An interview is an interpersonal encounter. It is important that you (the interviewer) establish rapport with the person you are interviewing (the interviewee). The interview should be friendly. At the same time, you must be impartial to whatever the interviewee says to you. If you react positively or negatively to the content of the interviewee's statements, you may bias the responses. It is also important that the interviewee trusts you because without trust you are likely to obtain biased research data.

Some techniques for establishing trust and rapport are to explain who the sponsoring organization is, to explain why you are conducting the research, and to point out to the participant that his or her responses are either anonymous (no name or identification will be attached to the respondent's data) or confidential (the respondent's name or identification will be attached to the respondent's data, but the researcher will never divulge the respondent's name to anyone). You want each potential participant to understand that your research is important and that his or her participation is important for the integrity of your study.

In Table 5.3 you can see four types of interviews (Patton, 1987; 1990). They are called the closed quantitative interview, the standardized open-ended interview, the interview guide approach, and the informal conversational interview. These four types can be

TABLE 5.2   Commonly Used Probes and Abbreviations

Standard Interviewer's Probe	*Abbreviation Used on Interview Protocol*
Repeat question.	(RQ)
Anything else?	(AE or Else?)
Any other reason?	(AO?)
Any others?	(Other?)
How do you mean?	(How mean?)
Could you tell me more about your thinking on that?	(Tell more)
Would you tell me what you have in mind?	(What in mind?)
What do you mean?	(What mean?)
Why do you feel that way?	(Why?)
Which would be closer to the way you feel?	(Which closer?)

From University of Michigan Survey Research Center, (1976). *Interviewer's manual* (rev. ed.). Ann Arbor, MI: University of Michigan Survey Research Center.

TABLE 5.3   Patton's Classification of Types of Interviews

Type of Interview	Characteristics	Strengths	Weaknesses
Informal conversational interview	Questions emerge from the immediate context and are asked in the natural course of things; there is no predetermination of question topics or wording.	Increases the salience and relevance of questions; interviews are built on and emerge from observations; the interview can be matched to individuals and circumstances.	Different information collected from different people with different questions. Less systematic and comprehensive if certain questions do not arise "naturally." Data organization and analysis can be quite difficult.
Interview guide approach	Topics and issues to be covered are specified in advance, in outline form; interviewer decides sequence and wording of questions in the course of the interview.	The outline increases the comprehensiveness of the data and makes data collection somewhat systematic for each respondent. Logical gaps in data can be anticipated and closed. Interviews remain fairly conversational and situational.	Important and salient topics may be inadvertently omitted. Interviewer flexibility in sequencing and wording questions can result in substantially different responses from different perspectives, thus reducing the comparability of responses.
Standardized open-ended interview	The exact wording and sequence of questions are determined in advance. All interviewees are asked the same basic questions in the same order. Questions are worded in a *completely* open-ended format.	Respondents answer the same questions, thus increasing comparability of responses; data are complete for each person on the topics addressed in the interview. Reduces interviewer effects and bias when several interviewers are used. Permits evaluation users to see and review the instrumentation used in the evaluation. Facilitates organization and analysis of the data.	Less flexibility in relating the interview to particular individuals and circumstances; standardized wording of questions may constrain and limit naturalness and relevance of questions and answers.
Closed quantitative interview	Questions and response categories are determined in advance. Responses are fixed; respondent chooses from among these fixed responses.	Data analysis is simple; responses can be directly compared and easily aggregated; many questions can be asked in a short time.	Respondents must fit their experiences and feelings into the researcher's categories; may be perceived as impersonal, irrelevant, and mechanistic. Can distort what respondents really mean or experience by so completely limiting their response choices.

Adapted from M. Q. Patton, *How to Use Qualitative Methods in Evaluation,* pp. 116–117, copyright © 1987 by Sage Publications, Inc. Used by permission of Sage Publications, Inc.

further subdivided into quantitative interviews (which include the closed quantitative interview) and qualitative interviews (which include the standardized open-ended interview, the interview guide approach to interviewing, and the informal conversational interview). We first discuss quantitative interviews.

Quantitative Interviews

Interview protocol
Data-collection instrument used in an interview

When carrying out quantitative interviews you must carefully read the words as they are provided in the interview protocol. The **interview protocol** is the data-collection instrument that includes the items, the response categories, the instructions, and so forth. The interview protocol in a quantitative interview is basically a script written by the researcher and read by the interviewer to the interviewees. The interviewer also records the interviewee's responses on the interview protocol. The interview protocol is usually written on paper for in-person interviews and shown on a computer screen for telephone interviews.

Standardization
Presenting the same stimulus to all participants

The goal of the quantitative interview is to standardize what is presented to the interviewees. **Standardization** has been achieved when what is said to all interviewees is the same or as similar as possible. Researchers want to expose each participant to the same stimulus so that the results will be comparable. Not surprisingly, quantitative interviews result in mostly quantitative data that are later analyzed using quantitative statistical procedures. The reason we say "mostly" is because quantitative interview protocols will often include a few open-ended items. If an open-ended question is asked in a quantitative interview, however, it is asked in exactly the same way for each participant in the study.

In Exhibit 5.3 you can see a section taken from an interview protocol. The exhibit includes five closed-ended items (items 25–30) from the 1998 Phi Delta Kappa/Gallup Education Poll. Note that DK stands for "don't know." Question 27 asks the participants to make their ratings using a four-point rating scale. The instruction provided at the end of question 27 tells the interviewer to go to item 28 *if* the respondent has one or more children in a public, parochial, or private school. *Otherwise,* the interviewer is instructed to go directly to item 30 (skipping items 28 and 29). (The participants are asked early in the interview whether they have one or more children in a public, parochial, or private school.) As you can see, this instruction operates just like a filter question.

The interview protocol used in the quantitative interview looks very similar to a questionnaire. In fact, many researchers call their interview protocol a questionnaire (e.g., Babbie, 1998; Converse and Presser, 1986; Frankfort-Nachmias and Nachmias, 1992). Although the data collection instruments are similar in interviews and questionnaires, there is a key difference in how the instruments are used. When conducting an interview, an *interviewer* reads the questions or statements exactly as written on the interview protocol and he or she records the interviewee's answers in the spaces that are provided. When using a questionnaire, the *research participant* reads and records his or her own answers in the spaces provided on the questionnaire.

The fourteen principles of questionnaire construction discussed earlier also apply to the construction of interview protocols. You may want to examine the list of principles shown in Table 5.1 again to convince yourself that the principles apply to interview protocols. When writing an interview protocol, the key point to remember is that the interviewer will read what you write and the research participant will hear what the interviewer reads. You will therefore need to make sure that your interview protocol operates properly for that purpose. You must also make sure that your interviewers are well trained in interviewing techniques and the proper use of an interview protocol.

EXHIBIT 5.3   Example of a Section of a Telephone Interview Protocol
(Questions 25–30 Are from the Phi Delta Kappa/Gallup Poll Education Poll, 1998)

---

25. There is always a lot of discussion about the best way to finance the public schools. Which do you think is the best way to finance the public schools—by means of local property taxes, by state taxes, or by taxes from the federal government in Washington, D.C.?
    1. Local property taxes   4. (DK)
    2. State taxes   5. (Refused)
    3. Federal taxes   _____

26. In your opinion, is the quality of the public schools related to the amount of money spent on students in those schools, or not?
    1. Yes   3. (DK)
    2. No   4. (Refused)   _____

27. How serious a problem would you say each of the following is in the public schools in your community? Would you say *(read and rotate A-G)* (is/are) a very serious problem, fairly serious, not very serious, or not at all serious?
    1. Very serious   A. Discipline   _____
    2. Fairly serious
    3. Not very serious   B. Drugs   _____
    4. Not at all serious   C. Alcohol   _____
    5. (DK)   D. Smoking   _____
    6. (Refused)
                                 E. Fighting   _____

                                 F. Gangs   _____

                                 G. Teenage pregnancy   _____

    (If code "1" in S4 or S5, continue; otherwise, skip to #30)

28. Thinking about your oldest child when he or she is at school, do you fear for his or her physical safety?
    1. Yes   3. (DK)
    2. No   4. (Refused)   _____

29. When your oldest child is outside at play in your own neighborhood, do you fear for his or her physical safety?
    1. Yes   3. (DK)
    2. No   4. (Refused)   _____

30. In your opinion, should children with learning problems be put in the same classrooms with other students, or should they be put in special classes of their own?
    1. Yes, same classrooms   3. (DK)
    2. No, should be put in   4. (Refused)
       special classes   _____

Used with permission of Phi Delta Kappa.

Qualitative Interviews

Qualitative interviews consist of open-ended questions and provide qualitative data. Qualitative interviews are also called depth interviews because they can be used to obtain in-depth information about a participant's thoughts, beliefs, knowledge, reasoning, motivations, and feelings about a topic. Qualitative interviewing allows a researcher to enter into the inner world of another person and to gain an understanding of that person's perspective (Patton, 1987). The interviewer must establish trust and rapport, making it easy for the interviewee to provide information about his or her inner world.

The interviewer should listen carefully and be the repository of detailed information. The interviewer should also be armed with probes or prompts to use when greater clarity or depth is needed from the person being interviewed. For example, the interviewer should freely use the probes shown in Table 5.2. The interviewer can also ask followup questions that may naturally emerge during the qualitative interview. A qualitative interview will typically last anywhere from thirty minutes to more than one hour.

Not surprisingly, qualitative interviews are very popular with qualitative researchers. It is not uncommon, however, for quantitative researchers also to conduct some qualitative interviews as part of their overall research study. The three different types of qualitative interviews are shown in Table 5.3. They are the informal conversational interview, the interview guide approach, and the standardized open-ended interview. The key characteristics of these three types of qualitative interviews are also given in Table 5.3.

The **informal conversational interview** is the most spontaneous and loosely structured of the three types of qualitative interviews. The interviewer discusses the topics of interest and follows all leads that emerge during the discussion. Because there is no interview protocol in the informal conversational interview, it is a good idea to tape record the interview so that no important information will be lost. Many times this will not be possible, however, if the interview occurs at an unexpected or unscheduled time. You should always take some field notes either during the interview and/or immediately after conducting the informal conversational interview.

In the next approach to qualitative interviewing, the **interview guide approach,** the interviewer enters the interview session with a plan to explore specific topics and to ask specific open-ended questions of the interviewee. These topics and questions are provided on an interview protocol written by the researcher before the interview session. The interviewer, however, does not have to follow these topics and questions during the interview in any particular order. The interviewer can also change the wording of any questions listed in the interview protocol. In short, the interview session is still a relatively unstructured interaction between the interviewer and the interviewee. At the same time, because of the interview protocol, the interviewer will cover the same general topics and questions with all of the interviewees. The interviewer must try to keep the interview on track, bringing the respondent back when he or she goes off on a topic that is not relevant to the research purpose.

Cross and Stewart (1995) used the interview guide approach in their study of what it is like to be a gifted student attending a rural high school. They were interested in studying gifted students attending rural high schools because gifted students attending urban schools had been examined in previous research. Here is Cross and Stewart's discussion of the qualitative interviewing process that they used in their research study:

> To obtain highly elaborated descriptions, the researchers asked subjects to situate their experiences in specific settings. The process attempted to get subjects to regress to the actual experience so that pure descriptions would emerge. The interviews consisted of a beginning question, which asked subjects:
>
> - When you think of your experience of being a student in your high school, what stands out in your mind?
>
> Followup questions included:
>
> - Can you think of a particular situation and describe it to me?
>
> After the subject described the situation, the researcher would follow up with prompts like:
>
> - Tell me more about that; or
> - What were you aware of at that time?
>
> When subjects exhausted their depictions, the researcher asked:
>
> - Can you think of another time when that happened?
>
> At this point, the aforementioned process would repeat. The researcher attended to the ideas conveyed by the subjects and tried not to lead the interviews in any direction. The interviews ranged in length from 40 to 90 minutes. All interviews were recorded on cassette tape and later transcribed. (p. 275)

Standardized open-ended interview
A set of open-ended questions are asked in a specific order and exactly as worded

In the third approach to qualitative interviewing, the **standardized open-ended interview,** the interviewer enters the interview session with a standardized interview protocol similar to the interview protocol used in quantitative interviewing. The key difference is that the interview protocol in the quantitative interview includes primarily closed-ended items, but the interview protocol in the standardized open-ended interview includes primarily open-ended items. The standardized open-ended interview is more structured than the interview guide approach to qualitative interviewing because the interviewer does not vary from the interview protocol in the former but can vary from the interview protocol in the latter. In the standardized open-ended interview, the questions are all written out, and the interviewer reads the questions exactly as written and in the same order to all interviewees.

FOCUS GROUPS

Focus group
A moderator leads a discussion with a small group of people

A **focus group** is a type of group interview in which a moderator (working for the researcher) leads a discussion with a small group of individuals (e.g., students, teachers, teenagers) to examine, in detail, how the group members think and feel about a topic. It is called a "focus" group because the moderator keeps the individuals in the group "focused" on the topic being discussed. The moderator generates discussion through the use of open-ended questions, and he or she acts as a facilitator of group process. Focus groups are used to collect qualitative data that are in the words of the group participants. The origin of focus groups is usually attributed to sociologist Robert K. Merton. He and his Columbia University students published the earliest works on focus groups (Merton & Kendall, 1946; Merton, Fisk, & Kendall, 1956).

Focus groups can be used for multiple purposes. Here are some of the many uses of focus groups identified by Stewart and Shamdasani (1998):

1. Obtaining general background information about a topic of interest.
2. Generating research hypotheses that can be submitted to further research and testing using more quantitative approaches.
3. Stimulating new ideas and creative concepts.
4. Diagnosing the potential for problems with a new program, service, or product.
5. Generating impressions of products, programs, services, institutions, or other objects of interest.
6. Learning how respondents talk about the phenomenon of interest (which may, in turn, facilitate the design of questionnaires, survey instruments, or other research tools that might be employed in more quantitative research).
7. Interpreting previously obtained quantitative results. (pp. 506–507)

A focus group is composed of six to twelve participants who are purposively selected because they can provide the kind of information of interest to the researcher. A focus group is usually homogeneous (composed of similar kinds of people) because the use of a homogeneous group promotes discussion. Homogeneous groups are less likely than heterogeneous groups to result in the formation of cliques and coalitions. The conduct of two to four focus groups as part of a single research study is quite common because it is unwise to rely too heavily on the information provided by a single focus group. Although each focus group is usually homogeneous, the set of focus groups used by the researcher may include some heterogeneity depending on the purpose of the research.

Group moderator
The person leading the focus group discussion

The **group moderator** (the person leading the focus group discussion) must have good interpersonal skills and he or she must know how to facilitate group discussion. He or she needs to get everyone involved in discussing the researcher's questions and not allow one or two people to dominate the discussion. If conflicts or power struggles occur, the moderator must skillfully bring the group back to task. The moderator must know when to probe or ask for more information and know when the discussion about a particular topic has been exhausted. It is not uncommon for the moderator to have an assistant who observes the group process, provides information to the moderator when needed, and takes notes during the session.

The moderator needs to cover all the open-ended questions included in the focus group interview protocol. The interview protocol is basically an interview guide. It typically consists of a sheet of paper with approximately ten open-ended questions typed on it. The more general questions are often placed early and the more specific questions are placed later in the interview protocol. The moderator may have anywhere from one to three hours to complete the group session. The moderator does not have to take many notes during the session because focus groups are almost always recorded (using audio- and/or videotapes) so that the data can be analyzed at a later time.

Focus groups are usually part of a larger research study. In other words, researchers usually do not rely solely on focus groups to collect their research data (unless the research is highly exploratory). Focus groups are especially useful as a complement to other methods of data collection. They are very useful for providing in-depth information in a relatively short period of time. In addition, the results are usually easy to understand. Researchers must, however, be very careful in making generalizations from focus groups because the sample size is too small and because the participants are usually not randomly selected from any known population. If you need more information about focus groups, examine *The Focus Group Kit* (Morgan & Krueger, 1998), a six-volume set of books examining just about every aspect of focus groups that you can imagine.

OBSERVATION

Observation
Unobtrusive
watching of
behavioral
patterns

The next method of data collection involves something that you do most of your waking hours—observe things. Researchers are also observers of things in the world. In research, **observation** is defined as the unobtrusive watching of behavioral patterns of people in certain situations to obtain information about the phenomenon of interest. Observation is an important way of collecting information about people because people do not always do what they say they do. It is a maxim in the social and behavioral sciences that attitudes and behavior are not always congruent.

A classic study done by a social scientist named Richard LaPiere (1934) demonstrated many years ago that attitudes and behaviors are not always congruent. LaPiere traveled over 10,000 miles in the United States over a two-year period (1930–1931) with a Chinese couple. LaPiere usually had the Chinese male secure the lodging and restaurant accommodations so that he could observe behavior toward the Chinese. LaPiere reported that he and his friends were denied service only once. LaPiere later sent a questionnaire to the same establishments asking whether a Chinese person would be accepted a guest. Fully 92 percent reported that they would *not* accept Chinese customers. This reported attitude was clearly at odds with the behavior that was observed by LaPiere.

Laboratory
observation
Observation done
in lab or other
setting set up by
the researcher

Because of the potential incongruence between attitudes and behavior, it is helpful when researchers collect observational data in addition to self-report data (e.g., tests, questionnaires, interviews, and focus groups). An advantage of observation over self-report methods is the researcher's ability to record actual behavior rather than obtain reports of preferences or intended behavior. Observation is not, however, without weaknesses, some of which are that it generally takes more time than self-report approaches, it usually costs more money than self-report approaches, it may not be possible to determine exactly why people behave as they do (i.e., to determine their inner states) through the use of observations, and people may act differently when they know they are being observed.

Observational data are collected in two different types of environments. **Laboratory observation** is carried out in settings that are set up by the researcher and inside the confines of a research lab. An example would be a researcher observing the behavior of children through a one-way window in the researcher's laboratory. A one-way window is a mirror on one side and a window through which the researcher can observe, on the other. **Naturalistic observation** is carried out in the real world. To make a naturalistic observation, you must go to wherever the behavior naturally occurs. LaPiere made naturalistic observations because he observed the behavior of hotel and restaurant proprietors in natural settings. Observing the behavior of children in their classrooms is another example of naturalistic observation. We now contrast how quantitative and qualitative researchers collect observational data.

Naturalistic observation
Observation done in real-world settings

Quantitative Observation

Quantitative observation
Standardized observation

Quantitative (or **structured**) **observation** involves the standardization of all observational procedures in order to obtain reliable research data. Quantitative observation frequently involves the standardization of each of the following: who is observed (what kinds of people are to be studied, such as teachers or students); what is observed (what variables are to be observed by the researcher, such as time on task or out of seat behavior); when the observations are to take place (during the morning hour, during break time); where the observations are to be carried out (in the laboratory, in the classroom, in the lunchroom, in the library, on the playground); and how the observations are to be done (this involves the extensive training of observers so that they use the same procedures and so that high interrater reliability can be obtained). Quantitative observation usually results in quantitative data such as counts or frequencies and percentages.

Different events may be of interest in quantitative observation (Weick, 1968). First, the researcher may observe nonverbal behavior (body movements, facial expressions, posture, eye contact, etc.). Second, the researcher may observe spatial behavior (the distance between different people and the distance between people and objects). Third, the researcher may observe extralinguistic behavior (characteristics of speech such as rate, tone, and volume). Fourth, the researcher may choose to observe linguistic behavior (what people say and what they write).

Time-interval sampling
Checking for events during specific time intervals

Quantitative observation may also involve observational sampling techniques. One technique is called **time-interval sampling,** which involves checking for events during time intervals specified in advance of the actual data collection. An example of time-interval sampling is a researcher observing student behavior for the first ten minutes of every hour. Another technique is called **event sampling,** which involves making observations only after a specific event has occurred. An example of event sampling is observing the behavior of students in a classroom after the teacher sends a student to the principal's office. For more information on quantitative observation sampling, see Dane (1990) and Suen and Ary (1989).

Event sampling
Observing only after specific events have occurred

Researchers conducting quantitative observation usually use checklists or other types of data-collection instruments, such as a laptop computer to record the research data or a videotape recorder for later coding. The content of the data-collection instrument will depend on the research problem and objectives of interest to the researcher. Data-collection instruments in quantitative observation are usually more specific and detailed than those used in qualitative observation. Usually, data-collection instruments are closed-ended in quantitative observation and open-ended in qualitative observation because quantitative observation tends to be used for confirmatory purposes (i.e., to test hypotheses), and qualitative observation tends to be used for exploratory purposes (i.e., to generate new information).

Qualitative Observation

Qualitative observation
Observing all potentially relevant phenomena

Qualitative observation involves observing all relevant phenomena and taking extensive field notes without specifying in advance exactly what is to be observed. In other words, qualitative observation is usually done for exploratory purposes. Qualitative observation is usually done in natural settings. In fact, the terms *qualitative observation* and *naturalistic observation* are frequently treated as synonyms in the research literature. Not surprisingly, qualitative observation is usually carried out by qualitative researchers.

Whenever you conduct qualitative observations, you must remember exactly what you have observed. In fact, the researcher is said to be the data-collection instrument in qualitative observation because it is the researcher who must decide what is important and what data are to be recorded. If you are wondering what to observe when you conduct a qualitative observation, you can consider the Guidelines for Directing Observation provided in Exhibit 5.4. In addition, you need to look for anything and everything to observe that may be relevant to your research questions.

Field notes
Notes taken by observer

Researchers record what they believe is important in their **field notes** (notes taken by the observer during and after making observations). It's a good idea to correct and edit any notes you write down during an observation as soon as possible after they are taken because that is when your memory is best. If you wait too long, you may forget important details and not be able to make sense of your handwritten, scribbled, field notes. In addition to taking field notes during your observations, consider audiotaping and videotaping the important scenes.

The form of interaction or type of role taken by the researcher during the conduct of a qualitative observation (called "fieldwork") varies along the following continuum (Gold, 1958):

Complete Participant	Participant-as-Observer	Observer-as-Participant	Complete Observer

Complete participant
Researcher becomes member of group being studied and does not tell members they are being studied

Although one role may be primary, the researcher may play all four roles at different times and in different situations during the conduct of a single qualitative research study. This is especially true when the researcher is in the field for an extended period of time.

The **complete participant** takes on the role of an insider, essentially becoming a member of the group being studied and spending a great deal of time with the group. For example, you might spend a year teaching at a "model school" that you want to learn about. During the year you would take extensive field notes, documenting what you observe and what you experience. Because the complete participant does not inform the group members that they are in a research study, many researchers question the use of this approach on

---

EXHIBIT 5.4   Guidelines for Directing Qualitative Observation

---

1. *Who* is in the group or scene? How many people are there, and what are their kinds, identities, and relevant characteristics? How is membership in the group or scene acquired?
2. *What* is happening here? What are the people in the group or scene doing and saying to one another?
   A. What behaviors are repetitive, and which occur irregularly? In what events, activities, or routines are participants engaged? What resources are used in these activities, and how are they allocated? How are activities organized, labeled, explained, and justified? What differing social contexts can be identified?
   B. How do the people in the group behave toward one another? What is the nature of this participation and interaction? How are the people connected or related to one another? What statuses and roles are evident in this interaction? Who makes what decisions for whom? How do the people organize themselves for interactions?
   C. What is the content of participants' conversations? What subjects are common, and which are rare? What stories, anecdotes, and homilies do they exchange? What verbal and nonverbal languages do they use for communication? What beliefs do the content of their conversations demonstrate? What formats do the conversations follow? What processes do they reflect? Who talks and who listens?
3. *Where* is the group or scene located? What physical settings and environments form their

contexts? What natural resources are evident, and what technologies are created or used? How does the group allocate and use space and physical objects? What is consumed, and what is produced? What sights, sounds, smells, tastes, and textures are found in the contexts that the group uses?
4. *When* does the group meet and interact? How often are these meetings, and how lengthy are they? How does the group conceptualize, use, and distribute time? How do participants view the past, present, and future?
5. *How* are the identified elements connected or interrelated, either from the participants' point of view or from the researcher's perspective? How is stability maintained? How does change originate, and how is it managed? How are the identified elements organized? What rules, norms, or mores govern this social organization? How is power conceptualized and distributed? How is this group related to other groups, organizations, or institutions?
6. *Why* does the group operate as it does? What meanings do participants attribute to what they do? What is the group's history? What goals are articulated in the group? What symbols, traditions, values, and world views can be found in the group?

---

ethical grounds. It is a cardinal rule in research ethics that research participants should know that they are involved in a research study, that they have the right *not* to participate, and that they are free to withdraw at any time during a research study if they do choose not to participate. You should therefore be very careful about doing "undercover" research except in legally open and accessible places such as a mall, a playground, a sporting event, and so forth.

Participant-as-observer
Researcher spends extended time with the group as an insider and tells members they are being studied

The **participant-as-observer** attempts to take on the role of an insider (a participant), similar to the complete participant. The participant-as-observer also spends a good deal of time in the field participating and observing. The participant-as-observer, however, explains to the people in the group being studied that he or she is a researcher and not a bonafide group member. The previous example of someone spending a year in a model school would be a participant-as-observer if the researcher informed the people in the school that he or she was conducting research and then participated in the school functions. An advantage of this approach is that, for ethical reasons, the researcher can request permission to collect and record data as needed. In addition, the researcher can obtain feedback about the researcher's observations and tentative conclusions from the people in the research study. A weakness is that the participants may not behave naturally because they are aware that they are being observed. Fortunately, this problem usually disappears as the people begin to trust the researcher and as they adjust to his or her presence.

Observer-as-participant
Researcher spends limited amount of time observing group members and tells members they are being studied

The **observer-as-participant** takes on the role of observer much more than the role of participant. The participants are fully aware that they are part of a research study. The observer-as-participant does not spend very much time in the field. Rather, the observer-as-participant has more limited and briefer interactions with the participants. For example, the researcher may negotiate entry to one faculty meeting, to one PTA meeting, and one or two classes as part of a research study. The researcher may also conduct several planned one-visit interviews with research participants. Compared to the complete participant and participant-as-observer roles, a disadvantage of the observer-as-participant role is that it is more difficult to obtain an insider's view. On the other hand, it is easier to maintain objectivity and neutrality.

Complete observer
Researcher observes as an outsider and does not tell the people they are being observed

The **complete observer** fully takes on the role of outside observer. He or she does not inform the people in the group being studied that they are being observed. The people usually will not know that they are being observed. For example, the complete observer may view people through a one-way window or he or she may sit in the back of the room at an open meeting. The advantage of this approach is that there is minimal **reactivity** (changes in the behavior of people because they know they are being observed). On the other hand, you can only take the role of complete observer in open settings because of ethical concerns.

Reactivity
Changes occurring in people because they know they are being observed

Perhaps the most useful styles of observation are the participant-as-observer and the observer-as-participant. These are generally preferred because they allow voluntary consent by research participants. In addition, they allow the researcher to take on a mix of the insider's role and the outsider's role. The complete participant always runs the risk losing his or her objectivity, and the complete observer always runs the risk of not understanding the insider perspective. Not surprisingly, the participant-as-observer and observer-as-participant styles of observation are the most commonly used by researchers.

Frontstage behavior
What people want or allow us to see

If you are going to enter the field and carry out qualitative observation, you should carry with you the general research question, a desire to learn, and an open mind. Good social skills are a must (Shaffir & Stebbins, 1991). Trust and rapport with the group being studied are essential if valid data are going to be obtained. Keep in mind, however, Goffman's warning (1959) that much social behavior observed is **frontstage behavior** (what people want or allow us to see) rather than **backstage behavior** (what people say and do with their closest friends, when "acting" is at a minimum). After getting in the field, the

Backstage behavior
What people say and do only with their closest friends

researcher must learn the ropes, maintain relations with the people being studied, and, at the end of the study, leave and keep in touch (Shaffir & Stebbins, 1991).

SECONDARY DATA

Secondary data
Data originally collected at an earlier time by a different person for a different purpose

Primary data
Original data collected a part of a research study

Personal documents
Anything written, photographed, or recorded for private purposes

Official documents
Anything written, photographed, or recorded by an organization

Archived research data
Data originally used for research purposes and then stored

The last major method of data collection involves the collection of secondary data for use in a research study. **Secondary data** are data originally collected or recorded at an earlier time, usually by a different person or researcher, for a different purpose than the current research problem at hand. Secondary data can include almost any kind of information, such as census records, archived research data, and even someone's personal diary. Some research studies are based entirely on secondary data; other research studies are based entirely on **primary data** (original data collected as part of a research study). Other research studies may be based on primary and secondary data because a researcher may choose to supplement his or her primary data with secondary data. You can think of it like this: when you collect original data for your research study, you are using primary data, but if you use data that were collected or recorded at an earlier time, you are using secondary data.

Documents are one major type of secondary data. **Personal documents** include anything that is written, photographed, or otherwise recorded for private purposes. Some examples of personal documents are letters, diaries, correspondence, family videos, and pictures. **Official documents** are written, photographed, or recorded by some type of public or private organization. Some examples are newspapers, educational journals and magazines, curriculum guides, annual reports, minutes of school board meetings, student records, student work, books, yearbooks, published articles, speeches, personnel files, and videos of things like news programs and advertisements. Documents are frequently used by qualitative researchers and by historical researchers.

The other major type of secondary data is **archived research data,** which include any form of data that were originally used for the purpose of public or private research. Archived research data may be in print form, but are usually stored in a computer-usable form (floppy disks, computer tapes, and CD-ROM). Some examples of archived research data are census tapes, including census data; and social science research data stored and kept by researchers or research-related organizations such as the Institute for Survey Research at the University of Michigan, the National Opinion Research Center in Chicago, and the Gallup Organization. You may want to visit the web sites of these organizations. Archived research data are usually quantitative and are used in quantitative research.

The largest repository of archived social science data is kept by the Inter-university Consortium for Political and Social Research (ICPSR). Although based in Ann Arbor, Michigan, the ICPSR is a consortium that includes the membership of over 500 colleges and universities in the United States and across the world. The ICPSR currently houses over 20,000 computer-readable data files, and faculty at member institutions (such as your local university) can obtain the data sets at very modest costs. Typically, the data were part of a research study by an academic researcher. Many studies were grant funded. After a researcher has finished with the data, he or she provides a copy to the ICPSR, which makes it available to member institutions or anyone else who has a legitimate reason to use it. If you want to see some of the many data files that are available, visit the ICPSR web site or go to your library and browse through the *ICPSR Guide to Resources and Services,* a book that includes descriptions of hundreds of research data files.

SUMMARY

A method of data collection is the procedure that a researcher uses to physically obtain research data from research participants. The method of data collection used in a research study is usually discussed in the procedures section of a research report. There are six major methods of data collection. In addition to using standardized tests (discussed in Chapter 4), researchers can have research participants fill out self-report instruments (questionnaires); researchers can talk to participants in person or over the telephone (interviews); researchers can discuss issues with multiple research participants at the same time in a small-group setting (focus groups); researchers can examine how research participants act in natural and structured environments (observation); and researchers can use data that came from an earlier time for a different purpose than the current research problem at hand (secondary data). Questionnaires, interviews, observation, and secondary data can be used to collect both quantitative and qualitative research data. Focus groups are used to collect qualitative data. The researcher must pay particular attention to the construction of the data collection instrument that is used to collect the research data.

STUDY QUESTIONS

1. What is a "method of data collection"?
2. What are the six main methods of data collection? (*Hint:* The first letters make the rather awkward acronym SQIFOS.)
3. What principles should you follow when constructing a questionnaire?
4. Think of an example of a leading or loaded question.
5. What is an "item stem"?
6. If you are conducting an exploratory research study, are you more likely to use closed-ended questions or open-ended questions?
7. How many points should a rating scale have?
8. When should you use a filter question?
9. Explain how to pilot test a questionnaire or an interview protocol.
10. What is the difference between a quantitative and a qualitative interview?
11. Why would a researcher want to conduct a focus group?
12. What are the main differences between quantitative and qualitative observations?
13. What are the four main roles that can be taken by a researcher during qualitative observation?
14. What is the difference between frontstage and backstage behavior?
15. What are some examples of secondary data?

EXERCISES

1. Fill out the Rosenberg Self-Esteem Scale shown in Figure 5.1. Then sum your responses to the ten items to obtain your overall score (i.e., your summated score). Be sure that you "reverse score" items 3, 5, 8, 9, and 10 (i.e., a 4 becomes a 1; a 3 becomes a 2; a 2 becomes a 3; and a 1 becomes a 4) before you add up your item scores to obtain your overall score. After doing this, you will know how to score a summated (Likert) scale.

2. Pick a topic and construct a five-item questionnaire. Collect data from five of your classmates. Have them evaluate your data-collection instrument based on what they have learned in this chapter. Revise your questionnaire.

KEY TERMS

acquiescence response set (138)

anchor (133)

archived research data (152)

backstage behavior (151)

checklist (136)

closed-ended question (131)

complete observer (151)

complete participant (149)

double-barreled question (130)

double negative (131)

event sampling (148)

exhaustive (132)

field notes (149)

filter question (138)

focus group (145)

frontstage behavior (151)

fully anchored rating scale (133)

group moderator (146)

informal conversational interview (144)

in-person interview (140)

interview (140)

interviewee (140)

interviewer (140)

interview guide approach (144)

interview protocol (142)

item stem (131)

laboratory observation (147)

leading question (130)

Likert scale (136)

loaded question (130)

method of data collection (126)

mutually exclusive (132)

naturalistic observation (148)

numerical rating scale (133)

observation (147)

observer-as-participant (151)

official documents (152)

open-ended question (131)

participant-as-observer (151)

personal documents (152)

pilot test (139)

primary data (152)

probes (140)

qualitative interview (144)

qualitative observation (149)

quantitative observation (148)

questionnaire (127)

ranking (134)

rating scale (133)

reactivity (151)

research method (126)

response set (138)

secondary data (152)

semantic differential (136)

social desirability response set (138)

standardization (142)

standardized open-ended interview (145)

summated rating scale (136)

telephone interview (140)

think-aloud technique (139)

time-interval sampling (148)

CHAPTER 6

Sampling

LEARNING OBJECTIVES

To be able to

- explain the difference between a sample and a census.
- define the key terms used in sampling (representative sample, generalize, element, statistic, parameter, and so forth).
- compare and contrast the different random sampling techniques.
- know which sampling techniques are equal probability selection methods.
- draw a simple random sample.
- draw a systematic sample.
- explain the difference between proportional and disproportional stratified sampling.
- explain the characteristics of one-stage and two-stage cluster sampling.
- list and explain the characteristics of the different nonrandom sampling techniques.
- explain the difference between random selection and random assignment.
- list the factors that you should consider when determining the appropriate sample size to be selected when using random sampling.
- discuss sampling in qualitative research and compare and contrast the different sampling techniques used in qualitative research.

Sampling
The process of
drawing a sample
from a population

Generalize
Make statements
about a population
based on sample
data

Survey research
A term sometimes
applied to
nonexperimental
research based on
questionnaires or
interviews

Census
A study of the
whole population
rather than a
sample

*Representative
sample*
A sample that
resembles the
population

In this chapter we examine the idea of sampling. **Sampling** is the process of drawing a sample from a population. When we sample, we study the characteristics of a subset (called the sample) selected from a larger group (called the population) in order to understand the characteristics of the larger group (the population). After researchers determine the characteristics of the sample, they **generalize** from the sample to the population; that is, researchers make statements about the population based on their study of the sample. A sample is usually much smaller in size than a population; hence, sampling can save time and money. For a real-world example of sampling and an introduction to the concept of representative samples, see Exhibit 6.1.

Random sampling is frequently used in **survey research,** which is a form of nonexperimental research in which questionnaires or interviews are used to gather information, and the goal is, typically, to understand the characteristics of a population. A well-known example of survey research is any of the many studies done to determine national voter attitudes and opinions about political candidates or various issues of national interest (education, family, crime, foreign affairs, and so on). The random sampling techniques discussed in this chapter are also used in most other types of quantitative research. Later in the chapter we devote an entire section to the special sampling techniques that are currently used in *qualitative* research. For now, however, our focus is on sampling in quantitative research.

If you study *every individual* in a population, you are actually conducting a census and not a survey. In a **census** the whole population is studied, not just a sample, or subset, of the population. A well-known example of a census is the United States Decennial Census conducted by the Census Bureau every ten years. The purpose of this census is to determine the demographic characteristics (age, gender, race, income level), educational characteristics (educational attainment, school enrollment), family characteristics (number of children, age at marriage, family structure), and work characteristics (e.g., type of job, occupational prestige of job, number of hours worked per week) of *all* individual citizens of the United States. That's about 260,000,000 people! As you can probably imagine, a census is quite expensive and very difficult to conduct.

When we conduct research using sampling techniques, we do *not* study every individual in the population of interest. Instead, we usually study a sample of the population. The use of random sampling saves time and money compared to a census, and resources are virtually always limited. Using the random sampling techniques discussed in this chapter, characteristics of the United States population can be estimated within a small margin of error (plus or minus a few percentage points) using only 1000 to 1500 individuals. Conducting a census for large populations is generally too difficult and too expensive. On the other hand, if a population is very small (e.g., all twenty-five teachers at a single elementary school), including all of the individuals in your research study is your best bet. The real power of random sampling comes when you are studying large populations.

In this chapter we discuss random (also called probability) sampling techniques and nonrandom (also called nonprobability) sampling techniques. Random sampling techniques are based on the mathematical theory of probability and usually produce "good" samples. A good sample is one that is representative of the population it came from. That is, *a representative sample resembles the population that it came from on all characteristics* (the proportions of males and females, teachers and nonteachers, young and old people,

EXHIBIT 6.1 Sampling in Action, by Dr. John Morrow

The concepts of sampling presented in this chapter have important applications to your daily life. For example, most farm products grown in the United States are subject to inspection by people employed by the Federal-State Inspection Service. Because it is not possible for each apple, each ham, or each peanut to be inspected individually, the Inspection Service has developed procedures for taking representative samples of each farm commodity for inspection. Analyses of these representative samples are used to infer the characteristics of large quantities of various farm products. Inspections, or analyses, of farm products by these government officials serve the purpose of protecting the general public by ensuring that the products in grocery stores are safe for public consumption. These inspections also serve the purpose of establishing the prices to be paid for the food products.

Let's look at the example of peanuts more closely. As you might imagine, thousands of tons of peanuts are grown in the United States annually. As with other farm products, these peanuts are subject to analysis by the Inspection Service before they can be put on the market. The Service inspectors need to know the percentages of specified components in each load of peanuts. These components include whole peanut kernels, half-kernels, shriveled kernels, hulls, foreign material (e.g., hay, sand, and pebbles), and the percentage of moisture in the peanuts. How can such a massive quantity of peanuts be inspected for these components without requiring an unrealistic amount of time and resources? The answer is *random sampling* techniques because they produce representative samples. For samples of peanuts to be representative of the full load from which they are drawn (population), they must contain all the components of the load, *and* contain each component *in the*

same proportion as in the total load. *A representative sample is a sample that is similar to the population on every characteristic except size*—a sample is always smaller than the population.

A typical truckload of peanuts brought to market by an American farmer ranges in size from approximately 2,000 to 6,000 pounds. The Inspection Service is allowed to draw a sample of only about 2 pounds from each load. Therefore, it is important that the Service inspectors use the best sampling procedures available to them. Service inspectors draw a sample of peanuts from each load with the use of a special tool called a peanut auger. The auger is a hollow, stainless-steel cylinder approximately 4 inches in diameter and 7 feet in length. The inspector pushes the auger into the peanuts from the top surface to the very bottom of the load. This procedure allows the auger to take a sample of peanuts from every level in the load. But, how does this ensure that most samples are representative? Enter mathematical probability. The inspectors use a computer-generated graph of the top surface of the load of peanuts, which designates *randomly selected* positions for inserting the auger. In this way, the Inspection Service has established a random sampling procedure for taking peanuts from each load. Theoretically, each peanut (and other components of the load) has an *equal chance* to be included in the sample. Thus, this random sampling technique produces samples that are representative of the loads of peanuts.

The next time you prepare a peanut butter and jelly sandwich for yourself, remember the inspectors with the Inspection Service. They had much to do with making the peanut butter, the jelly, and the wheat flour for the bread used in your sandwich safer and cheaper for your consumption.

Democrats and Republicans, and so forth) *except size. A representative sample is like the population except that it is smaller.* Although a random sample is rarely perfectly representative, random samples are almost always more representative than nonrandom samples. Nonrandom samples are said to be "biased" samples because they are almost always systematically different from the population on certain characteristics. In contrast, random samples are said to be "unbiased" samples because they tend to be representative of the populations from which they come.

As you read the rest of this chapter, remember that the main purpose of sampling is to enable the researcher to "generalize" to a population; that is, sampling should enable a researcher to understand and make probability statements about a population based on the analysis of a sample. In short, obtaining a sample is a means to an end. We focus here on helping you conceptually understand sampling in quantitative research, know about the most important sampling methods, and understand how to draw samples. If you need to learn more about sampling in quantitative research than is covered in this chapter, you should explore a sampling text (e.g., Henry, 1990; Jaeger, 1984; Kalton, 1983; Kish, 1965; Scheaffer, Mendenhall, & Ott, 1996; Sudman, 1976; Tryfos, 1996) or go to a consultant for help. We conclude the chapter with a discussion of sampling methods used in qualitative research. For more information on sampling in qualitative research, see LeCompte and Preissle (1993) and Patton (1987, 1990).

TERMINOLOGY USED IN SAMPLING

Sample
A set of elements taken from a larger population

Element
The basic unit that is selected from the population

N
The population size

n
The sample size

Population
The large group to which a researcher wants to generalize the sample results

Statistic
A numerical characteristic of a sample

Parameter
A numerical characteristic of a population

To understand sampling better, it is helpful to know some specialized terms that are commonly used by researchers when they describe sampling. A **sample** is a set of elements taken from a larger population according to certain rules. An **element** is the basic unit selected from the population. "Individuals" are the most common element sampled; however, other types of elements are possible, such as "groups" (e.g., schools, classrooms, clinics) or "objects" (e.g., textbooks, school records, television commercials, calculators produced on a production line). A sample is always smaller than a population, and it is often much smaller. In sampling, the letter N stands for the population size (the total number of people or elements in a population), and n stands for the sample size (the number of people or elements in a sample). For example, if we selected a sample of 500 people from a population of 150,000, then n would be 500 and N would be 150,000. Sampling rules tell you how to select a sample. The methods of sampling discussed in this chapter follow different rules for selection.

A **population** (sometimes called a target population) is the set of all elements. It is the large group to which a researcher wants to generalize his or her sample results. It is the total group that you are interested in learning more about. A few possible populations are the citizens of the United States, all the students attending public and private schools in Los Angeles, all middle school teachers in the city of Atlanta, and all counselors working at a mental health center in Ann Arbor, Michigan.

A **statistic** is a numerical characteristic of a sample. For example, based on the people included in a sample, a researcher might calculate the average reading performance, the correlation between two variables (e.g., test grades and study time), or the percentage of students receiving A grades. A **parameter** is a numerical characteristic of a total population. For example, it could be an average, a correlation, or a percentage that is based on the complete population rather than on a sample. We rarely know the values of the population parameters of interest. Therefore, we collect sample data so that we can estimate the probable values of the population parameters. A sample statistic will rarely be exactly the same as the population parameter, but most of the time it will not be very far off (assuming that the sample is a random sample of adequate size). The actual difference between a sample statistic value (let's say you calculated an average for the sample) and the population parameter (the actual average in the population) is called **sampling error.** Sampling error will fluctuate randomly over repeated sampling when a random sampling method is used. That is, a sample statistic (e.g., an average or a percentage) will sometimes be a little larger than a population parameter and it will sometimes be a little smaller. However, it will *not* be consistently too large or too small. That is, it will not be biased.

Sampling error
The difference between the value of a sample statistic and a population parameter

When we draw a sample, we typically begin by locating or constructing a **sampling frame,** which is a list of all the elements in the population. For example, if we are interested in drawing a sample of college students from Ohio State University, then the sampling frame is the list of all students attending Ohio State University. The researcher draws the sample from the sampling frame using one of the sampling methods discussed later. After the sample is selected, the members of the sample are contacted and asked if they will participate in the research study.

Sampling frame
A list of all the elements in a population

Typically some of the people in a sample will refuse to participate in the research study. You can determine the percentage that actually participates by calculating the response rate. The **response rate** is the percentage of people in a sample that participates in the research study. The response rate will usually be less than 100 percent. If you select, for example, a sample size of 200 people and only 183 of the 200 individuals participate, then the response rate is 91.5 percent ($183/200 \times 100$). The formula for the response rate is

Response rate
The percentage of people in a sample that participate in a research study

$$\text{Response rate} = \frac{\text{Number of people in the sample who participate in the research}}{\text{Total number of people in the sample}} \times 100$$

If you want a sample to be representative of a population, then it is essential that the response rate be as high as possible. Response rates around 70 percent and higher are generally considered acceptable. However, the sample may still be *biased* (not representative of the population) even when the response rate is high because the kinds of people who drop out of the sample may be different from the kinds of people who remain in the sample. Researchers should discuss the issues of sample selection procedures, response rates, and sample integrity when they write up their reports. Generally, you should not trust research reports in which this is not done.

RANDOM SAMPLING TECHNIQUES

Simple Random Sampling

A simple random sample is what researchers are usually referring to when they say they have a random sample or a probability sample. Simple random sampling is the most basic form of random sampling. It is the cornerstone of sampling theory. In fact, all the other random sampling methods use simple random sampling at some point during the sampling process. A simple random sample is formally defined as a sample drawn by a procedure in which every possible sample of a given size (e.g., size 100) has an equal chance of being selected from the population. More simply, a **simple random sample** is a sample drawn by a procedure in which every member of the population has an equal chance of being selected for the study. When every member has an equal chance of being selected, the sampling method is called an **equal probability selection method** (EPSEM).

One way to visualize the drawing of a simple random sample is to think about the "hat model." Here is how it works. First, go to a good old hat store and buy a big top hat. Next, make one slip of paper for each individual in the population and place all of the slips in the hat. Make sure you use standard sized slips of paper so they will all be the same shape, size, and weight. If there are 1,000 people in the population of interest, you will need 1,000 slips of paper. Now, let's say you want to obtain a simple random sample of 100 people. In order to make sure all the pieces of paper are thoroughly mixed in the hat, cover the top of the hat and shake it up rigorously. Next, select one slip of paper from the hat. After selecting the slip of paper, shake the hat up again to be sure the remaining slips are well mixed and then select another slip of paper. After you have selected all 100 names, you will have a simple random sample size of 100 ($n = 100$) from a population size of 1,000 ($N = 1,000$). After you finish selecting the sample, you can look at the names to see who is included in the sample. These are the people you will study.

There are actually two forms of simple random sampling. One form is called **sampling with replacement** and the other is called **sampling without replacement.** In sampling *with* replacement, after selecting a slip of paper from the hat, you write down the name and then place the slip back in the hat. Because the slip of paper can potentially be drawn again, the sample might not be composed of a set of unique elements; there could be some redundancy (a person may appear in the sample more than once). In sampling *without* replacement, after you select a slip of paper from the hat, you do not put it back. In this case all the elements in the sample will necessarily be distinct. If you select 100 names from the hat, you will have 100 different individuals in the sample. Following two leading samplers, Graham Kalton (1983) and Leslie Kish (1965), we use the term **simple random sampling** to refer to sampling without replacement and the term **unrestricted sampling** to refer to sampling with replacement. Therefore, in the remainder of this chapter, when we say we have a simple random sample, we will be referring to a sample generated without replacement.

From a technical standpoint, simple random sampling is slightly better than unrestricted sampling (Kalton, 1983).[1] In particular, you will not need to include quite as many people in a sample selected without replacement as you will in a sample selected with replacement. Think about it for a moment. If you have already included a person in your sample, do you want him or her in there again? Remember, you want your sample to be representative of a large population that is composed of many different people. The best route is to select a sample of different individuals, including as many people from the population as possible. Think of it like this: What if, by chance, an individual was included many times in a small sample? Wouldn't you have a sample that is heavily weighted toward a single individual rather than a sample that is representative of the population? "Double counting"

Simple random sample
A sample drawn by a procedure in which every member of the population has an equal chance of being selected

Equal probability selection method
Any sampling method where each member of the population has an equal chance of being selected

Sampling with replacement
It is possible for elements to be selected more than once

Sampling without replacement
It is not possible for elements to be selected more than once

Simple random sampling
The term usually used for sampling without replacement

Unrestricted sampling
The technical term used for sampling with replacement

selections (or triple counting, for example) makes sampling less efficient (i.e., you will need more people in an unrestricted sample than in a simple random sample). It should not be surprising to learn, therefore, that sampling without replacement is virtually always used by practicing researchers.

The goal in sampling is to get a sample that is as representative as possible of a target population at the lowest cost possible, and it costs money to increase the sample size. Therefore, simple random sampling (sampling without replacement) is generally preferred to unrestricted sampling (sampling with replacement). Unrestricted sampling does, however, have an important place in statistical theory. Nonetheless, experts on sampling make it clear that sampling without replacement is more efficient and preferred over sampling with replacement.[2]

Drawing a Simple Random Sample   Now let's get a little more practical and see how practicing researchers actually draw random samples. Although the hat model was a convenient metaphor for thinking about simple random sampling, it is rarely used in practice.

Table of random numbers
A list of numbers that fall in a random order

A more common approach is to use a **table of random numbers,** which is a list of numbers that fall in a random order. This means no number will appear more often than any other number in the long run. All numbers have an equal chance of appearing. Furthermore, there will be no systematic pattern in the table. If you ever think you see a pattern in a table or that some number occurs more frequently than it should, you need only look farther in the table. The apparent pattern will disappear.

An excerpt of a table of random numbers is given in Figure 6.1. The numbers in Figure 6.1 were generated by a computer using a random number generator (a computer program). If you need a larger set of random numbers, most computers will do this or you can go to the library and check out a book of random numbers (e.g., Kendall & Smith, 1954). A book of random numbers includes nothing but random numbers. (Talk about dry reading!) Before drawing a simple random sample, you should keep in mind that when a sample is not large enough, random sampling may not work very well. Basically, the more numbers you select, the better the process operates. Random selection cannot work magic, but if you

FIGURE 6.1   Table of random numbers.

Line/Column	1	2	3	4	5	6	7	8	9	10
1	10480	15011	01536	02011	81647	91646	69179	14194	62590	36207
2	22368	46573	25595	85393	30995	89198	27982	53402	93965	34095
3	24130	48360	22527	97265	76393	64809	15179	24830	49340	32081
4	42167	93093	06243	61680	07856	16376	39440	53537	71341	57004
5	37570	39975	81837	16656	06121	91782	60468	81305	49684	60672
6	77921	06907	11008	42751	27756	53498	18602	70659	90655	15053
7	99562	72905	56420	69994	98872	31016	71194	18738	44013	48840
8	96301	91977	05463	07972	18876	20922	94595	56869	69014	60045
9	89579	14342	63661	10281	17453	18103	57740	84378	25331	12565
10	85475	36857	53342	53988	53060	59533	38867	62300	08158	17983

use it properly, it has been shown repeatedly, both mathematically and empirically, that it works. In a later section, we will talk more about how large samples should be.

To use a table of random numbers, all of the elements in the sampling frame must have a number attached to them. Remember, a sampling frame is just a list of all the people (elements) in a population. If you are sampling from a list of your students or your clients, then you need to give each person a unique number. These numbers serve as an index. An example of a sampling frame is shown in Figure 6.2. This is a list of people in a small population with their associated identification numbers. The information on gender (a categorical variable) and age (a quantitative variable) are provided in the sampling frame because we want to be able to calculate the average age and the percent male and female later. This way we can see how well the sample we draw compares with the actual population shown in Figure 6.2. Usually you would have to collect this kind of information (data) before you would know how good the sample is. That is, a sampling frame usually contains only the names and the identification numbers.

Now let's draw a sample of size ten from this population of size sixty in Figure 6.2. First we need to select ten numbers from the table of random numbers. But how is this done? The answer is that you can do it in many different ways as long as you are consistent.

FIGURE 6.2   A sampling frame with information on gender and age included.[a]

Number	Name	Age	Number	Name	Age	Number	Name	Age
01	Johnny Adams (M)	64	21**	Scott House (M)	21	41	Beth Sanders (F)	63
02*	Fred Alexander (M)	18	22	Jan Hoffman (F)	60	42*	Lena Schmitt (F)	33
03**	Kathy Anderson(F)	57	23	Robert Johnson (M)	43	43	Cindy Scott (F)	31
04	Larry Barnes (M)	30	24	John Jones (M)	18	44	Sam Shepherd (M)	20
05	Hasem Basaleh (M)	38	25	John Locke (M)	52	45**	Max Smart (M)	47
06*	Tom Baxter (M)	31	26	Carlton Lawless (M)	35	46	Rhonda Smith (F)	23
07*	Barry Biddlecomb (M)	52	27*, **	Pam Mackey (F)	35	47	Kin Sullivan (F)	29
08	Don Campbell (M)	42	28	Ronald May (M)	20	48	Jimmy Thompson (M)	42
09**	Martha Carr (F)	21	29	Mike McNuty (M)	64	49	Susan Tyler (F)	23
10*	Eugene Davis (M)	21	30*	John Mills (M)	19	50	Lisa Turner (F)	57
11	Marion Dunn (F)	55	31	Doug Morgan (M)	33	51**	Velma Vandenberg (F)	43
12	James East (M)	44	32	Jean Neal (F)	33	52	Richard Viatle (M)	20
13	Greg Ellis (M)	50	33**	Anh Nguyan (M)	40	53*	Larry Watson (M)	26
14	Alex Evans (M)	65	34	David Payne (M)	57	54	Melvin White (M)	29
15**	Donna Faircloth (F)	27	35	Susan Poole (F)	28	55	Mark Wiggens (M)	46
16*	Barbara Flowers (F)	37	36	Brenda Prine (F)	38	56	Leon Wilson (M)	31
17	Kirk Garner (M)	37	37	Andrea Quinn (F)	30	57**	Andrew Young (M)	39
18*	Marie Gaylord (F)	46	38	Mohamed Rashid (M)	64	58	Hun Yu (F)	51
19	William Gilder (M)	30	39**	Anneke Reeves (F)	32	59	Alex Zellars (F)	42
20	Mark Harris (M)	63	40	Charlie Rogers (M)	46	60	Ellen Zimmer (F)	46

[a]Data on variables such as age and gender are usually not included in a sampling frame. Data are obtained after they are collected from the sample respondents. In order to do a couple of calculations, data on age and gender are provided in the columns and parentheses.

* indicates elements selected in simple random sampling example discussed in the text.

** indicates elements selected in systematic sampling example discussed in the text.

You can start anywhere in the table of random numbers, and then you can go in any direction (up, down, across, forward, or backward) as long as you keep going in that direction. It is important that you select a different starting point every time you use a table of random numbers so that you don't end up with the same numbers every time. If you decide to start at the top and move down in the table until you hit the bottom of the list, then go to the top of the next column and continue moving down. Generally speaking, moving either down or across is the easiest. The key is that once you pick a direction you must stick with it. There are only two digits in 60 (i.e., N), so we will need to find two-digit numbers in the table.

Let's pick our starting point at the top of column 4 and move downward using the first two digits listed. Look at Figure 6.1 as you read this paragraph. The first two-digit random number is 02. Do you see it at the top of column 4? Because 2 is a "valid" number (it is between 1 and 60), it is included in the sample. The second number is 85. It is outside the range (1–60), so just ignore it and move down to the next two-digit number. The next two numbers are 97 and 61. They are also out of range, so ignore them. The next number, 16, is a usable number so use it. We now have selected two numbers. Look at the table and find the next usable number. If you said 42 you are right. The next three usable numbers after that are 7, 10, and 53. Since you are now at the bottom of column 4 and still need more numbers, go to the top of column 5 and continue. The first number, 81, is not usable; however, the second number, 30, is. After 30, the next number in the usable range of 1–60 is 7. However, do not use this number because person 7 is already in the sample. Remember, we are sampling without replacement. Keep moving. The final three usable numbers are 6, 27, and 18. The sample is therefore composed of persons 2, 16, 42, 7, 10, 53, 30, 6, 27, and 18.

The final step is to see who these people are so you can go and see whether they will participate in your research study. As you can see in Figure 6.2, the sample is composed of Fred Alexander (element 2), Barbara Flowers (element 16), Lena Schmitt (element 42), Barry Biddlecomb (element 7), Eugene Davis (element 10), Larry Watson (element 53), John Mills (element 30), Tom Baxter (element 6), Pam Mackey (element 27), and Marie Gaylord (element 18). This is your sample of size 10. Single asterisks are placed by these names in Figure 6.2.

After collecting data (e.g., age) from the individuals in the sample, you would conduct a statistical analysis. Let's do a very simple calculation. The age was given for each individual. (Generally data would have been collected on many additional variables/characteristics besides age.) Now, calculate the average age for the individuals in the sample. Just add the ages for the 10 people and divide that number by 10. That is, $(18 + 31 + 52 + 21 + 37 + 46 + 35 + 19 + 33 + 26)/10 = 31.8$. The average age of the individuals in the sample is 31.8, and this is our estimate (best guess) of the average age of all of the individuals in the population.

In this case we know the population average is 38.95 or about 39 years old. To get 38.95 just add up the ages for all 60 people in the population and divide that number by 60. The sample value of 31.8 was off by approximately 7 years. Don't be alarmed if this seems like a big sampling error because a sample size of 10 is actually quite small. The difference between the sample average and the population average occurred because of chance. That is how random sampling works. If you were to select another sample of size 10, the average age in the sample would probably also be different from the population average. Try it. Draw another sample of size 10 from the sampling frame and make sure you can draw a simple random sample on your own. Basically, sampling error follows a normal, bell-shaped, curve. The vast majority of the time the sample mean will be relatively near the population mean, but it is possible for it to be far from the population mean.

We conclude this section with an excerpt from an actual journal article that relied on simple random sampling (Lance, 1996):

> Participants were selected from the 1992 Membership Directory of the Association on Higher Education and Disability (AHEAD), a professional organization for service providers to students with disabilities at institutions of higher education. Entries in the directory were assigned numbers, excluding those members who were students, were specialists in only one type of disability, did not reside in the United States, or were not affiliated with an institution of higher education. A statistical computer program was used to select a random sample of 250 of the members deemed eligible for participation in the study. . . . The final sample included 190 members from 47 states and the District of Columbia. (p. 280)

As you can see, the Membership Directory of the AHEAD was the researcher's sampling frame. Also, the researcher used a computer program to generate the random numbers rather than taking the numbers from a table of random numbers.

Systematic Sampling

Systematic sample
A sample obtained by determining the sampling interval, selecting a random starting point between 1 and *k,* and then selecting every *k*th element

Systematic sampling is an adaptation of simple random sampling.[3] It uses a shortcut for selecting the elements to be included in the sample. A **systematic sample** is defined as a sample that is obtained by determining the **sampling interval** (i.e., the population size divided by the desired sample size, *N/n,* which is symbolized by *k*), selecting at random a **starting point** (a number between 1 and *k,* including 1 and *k*), and then selecting every *k*th element in the sampling frame. Systematic sampling is generally easier than simple random sampling when you are selecting from lists (e.g., lists of names, lists of schools).

Sampling interval
The population size divided by the desired sample size

Let's hypothetically say that there are 50 teachers in your middle school and we have a list of these 50 middle school teachers, with the teachers numbered from 1 through 50. You have decided that you want to select 5 teachers to be on a PTA committee. We can select a systematic sample from our list of 50 teachers by following the three steps given in the definition of systematic sampling. First, determine the sampling interval (symbolized by the letter *k*). To obtain *k* you need the population size and the desired sample size. Then just divide the population size by the desired sample size. In this case, the population size is 50 and we want a sample of size 5. If you divide 50 by 5, you will see that *k* is equal to 10 (i.e., 50/5 = 10).[4]

k
The size of the sampling interval

Starting point
A randomly selected number between 1 and *k*

Second, randomly select one number between 1 and *k* (including 1 and *k*). You should use a table of random numbers for this step because we want the sample to be a random sample. In our example we want to randomly select a number between 1 and 10 because *k* equals 10. Therefore, go to the table of random numbers (Figure 6.1) and select a random number between 1 and 10. To do this you need to pick a place in a table of random numbers to begin sampling for a number in the range of 1 to 10 and then select the first usable number (i.e., the first number in the 1–10 range). If you start at the top of column 2 in Figure 6.1 and move down the column examining two-digit numbers, you will see that the first 5 numbers are not usable (15, 46, 48, 93, and 39). The next number, however, is 6, which is usable. Therefore, the teacher with the ID number 6 will be the first person selected to be in our sample. The number 6 also has a special name in our systematic sampling; it is called the starting point.

Third, after you have determined k (the sampling interval) and the starting point, you can select the rest of the systematic sample. In our example we randomly selected the number 6, which is our starting point. This is also the first person to be included in the sample. We now need 4 more people so that we will have a sample of size 5. To get the rest of the elements in our sample, you need to select every kth element starting at the starting point. In this example, our starting point is 6 and $k = 10$; therefore, the second person to be included in the sample is person 16 because we started at 6 and we added 10 (i.e., 6 + 10 = 16). To get the third person, you start with the second person's number (i.e., 16) and add k (i.e., 10). Therefore, the third person is person 26 (16 + 10 = 26). Continue adding k to get the other two people in the sample. The other two people in the sample will be person 36 (26 + 10 = 36) and person 46 (36 + 10 = 46). Summarizing, we started with 6 and continued adding 10 until we obtained our desired sample of size 5 (6, 6 + 10 = 16, 16 + 10 = 26, 26 + 10 = 36, and 36 + 10 = 46). The systematic random sample is composed of persons 6, 16, 26, 36, and 46. That is 5 people.

Now let's select a systematic sample from the sampling frame given in Figure 6.2. Earlier, we selected a simple random sample from this sampling frame. Specifically, we selected a simple random sample of size 10 from the population of size 60 shown in Figure 6.2. The 10 people chosen in the simple random sample are marked with single asterisks in Figure 6.2. Now we will select a systematic sample of size 10 from this same population, and we will calculate the average age so that we can compare it with the average age in the simple random sample (31.9) and with the average age in the population (38.95).

What do we do first? Remember, there are three steps and in the first step we must find k. In this case k is 60/10 = 6. Now we select a random number between 1 and 6 (with 1 and 6 also being possible selections). To do this go to the table of random numbers in Figure 6.1. This time let's start at column 10 and move downward, examining only one-digit numbers (since 1 through 6 are all one-digit numbers). As it turns out, the first number is 3 so we need not go farther. Three is our starting point. What are the remaining 9 numbers in our sample? Just keep adding 6 and you will see that they are 9, 15, 21, 27, 33, 39, 45, 51, and 57. The sample is, therefore, composed of persons 3, 9, 15, 21, 27, 33, 39, 45, 51, and 57. Specifically it is composed of Kathy Anderson, Martha Carr, Donna Faircloth, Scott House, Pam Mackey, Anh Nguyan, Anneke Reeves, Max Smart, Velma Vandenberg, and Andrew Young. These 10 people are marked in Figure 6.2 with double asterisks. Now calculate the average age for the 10 individuals in this systematic sample. It is 57 + 21 + 27 + 21 + 35 + 40 + 32 + 47 + 43 + 39 divided by 10. That's 362 divided by 10, which is 36.2. Since the population value is 38.95, 36.2 is a pretty good estimate, especially with such a small sample size ($n = 10$).

In this case, the average age in our systematic sample (36.2) is a better estimate of the population average (i.e., it is closer to 38.95) than the average age in the simple random sample selected (31.8). This will not, however, always be the case. Sometimes simple random sampling will work better and sometimes systematic sampling will work better. Basically, if a list (a sampling frame) is randomly ordered, then the results of a simple random sampling and systematic sampling will tend to be very similar (Tryfos, 1996). If lists are ordered according to the levels of a categorical variable (e.g., females are listed and then males are listed) or according to the values of a quantitative variable (e.g., the list is ordered in ascending or descending order on age), then systematic sampling will tend to perform a little better than simple random sampling (Kalton, 1983; Scheaffer, Mendenhall, and Ott, 1996).[5] By "better" we mean it will tend to be a little more representative of the population, given a certain sample size. Systematic sampling produces representative samples in general because it is an equal probability selection method (EPSEM); that is, each individual in the population has an equal chance of being included in the sample (Kalton, 1983).

If the list is ordered in a way that there are "cycles" in the data that coincide with the sampling interval (k), then systematic sampling can fail dramatically. You must watch out for this potentially serious problem. Look at the sampling frame given in Figure 6.3. The principal and assistant principals at 10 schools making up a hypothetical local school district are listed. Each school is assumed to have one principal and one assistant principal (i.e., there are 10 assistant principals and 10 principals). Let's say that we want to select a systematic sample of 5 of these 20 school administrators. Because the population size is 20 ($N = 20$), and we want a sample size of 5 ($n = 5$), the sampling interval k is 20/5, which is 4. Therefore we will select every fourth person (i.e., element) after randomly selecting a starting point between 1 and 4. Let the randomly selected starting point be 2; that is, assume you went to the table of random numbers and selected the number 2. As a result, element 2 is included in the sample. Now select every fourth element after 2 until you have 5 elements. That would be 6, 10, 14, and 18. The sample is composed of elements 2, 6, 10, 14, and 18.

But look at what happened this time. We included only assistant principals in the sample. All of the principals were excluded! This is obviously a major problem because our selected sample is not at all representative of the population; it is a biased sample that includes only assistant principals and no principals. The sampling frame in this case is said to have a cyclical pattern; it is sometimes said to be "periodic." The cyclical pattern in the sampling frame is obvious because each assistant principal is directly preceded and followed by a principal. In this case the **periodicity** (the presence of a cyclical pattern in a sampling frame) has caused a major problem. What should we learn from the bad experience we just had? Basically, always examine your sampling frame carefully. If you believe there is a cyclical pattern in the list, then do not use systematic sampling.

Periodicity
The presence of a cyclical pattern in the sampling frame

Stratified Random Sampling

Stratified sampling
Dividing the population into mutually exclusive groups and then selecting a random sample from each group

Stratified sampling is a technique in which a population is divided into mutually exclusive groups (called strata) and then a simple random sample or a systematic sample is selected from each group (each stratum). For example, we could divide a population into males and

Element 1	Principal 1
*Element 2	Assistant Principal 1
Element 3	Principal 2
Element 4	Assistant Principal 2
Element 5	Principal 3
*Element 6	Assistant Principal 3
Element 7	Principal 4
Element 8	Assistant Principal 4
Element 9	Principal 5
*Element 10	Assistant Principal 5
Element 11	Principal 6
Element 12	Assistant Principal 6
Element 13	Principal 7
*Element 14	Assistant Principal 7
Element 15	Principal 8
Element 16	Assistant Principal 8
Element 17	Principal 9
*Element 18	Assistant Principal 9
Element 19	Principal 10
Element 20	Assistant Principal 10

FIGURE 6.3   A periodic or cyclical sampling frame. Elements marked by an asterisk are in the example discussed in the text.

Stratification variable
The variable on which the population is divided

females and take a random sample of males and a random sample of females. The variable that we divide the population on is called the **stratification variable.** In the case of males and females, the stratification variable is gender. If you are wondering why this approach is called stratified sampling, it is probably because the strata can be viewed metaphorically as being similar to the discrete levels or layers below our earth's surface. The word was probably borrowed from the field of geology.

Proportional stratified sampling
Type of stratified sampling in which the sample proportions are made to be the same as the population proportions on the stratification variable

Proportional Stratified Sampling   The most commonly used form of stratified sampling is called **proportional stratified sampling.** If the stratification variable is gender, then the proportions of males and females in the sample are made to be the same as the proportions of males and females in the population. For example, if the population is composed of 70 percent females and 30 percent males, then 70 percent of the people in the sample will be randomly selected from the female subpopulation (i.e., all females in the total population) and 30 percent of the people in the sample will be randomly selected from the male subpopulation (i.e., all males in the total population). That is why it is called "proportional" stratified sampling. The proportions in the sample are made to be the same as the proportions in the total population on certain characteristics. (We tell you how to do this shortly.)

Proportional stratified sampling tends to be a little more efficient (it requires fewer people) than simple random sampling (Kalton, 1983, p. 21). When you draw a proportional stratified sample, the proportions in the sample on the stratification variable will be perfectly or almost perfectly representative of the proportions on that same stratification variable in the population. For example, if the stratification variable is gender, then the proportions of males and females in the sample will be the same as the proportions in the population. Other possible stratification variables can be used (e.g., grade level, intelligence, education, type of school attended), and you can use more than one stratification variable at the same time if you want (e.g., gender, education). A stratified random sample will also be representative of the population on the other variables that are not included as stratification variables because random samples are selected from each population group (i.e., from each subpopulation) or stratum. Proportional stratified sampling is an equal probability selection method (EPSEM), which means that every individual in the population has an equal chance of being included in the sample. That's why proportional stratified sampling produces representative samples.

As an example, suppose that you are interested in selecting a sample of students in grades one through three in an elementary school. We will use grade level as our stratification variable (rather than gender). The levels of the stratification variable are grade one, grade two, and grade three. Because we are using proportional stratified sampling, we want to make sure that the percentages of students in grades one through three in the sample are the same as the percentages in grades one through three in the school, while making sure that our sample is random in every other respect. As you can see, you have to know the percentages of students in grades one through three in the school *before drawing your sample* so that you can select the right number of students from each grade to be in your sample. Therefore, proportional stratified sampling requires that you know certain information before drawing a sample. If you have the required information, you can randomly select the right numbers of people so that your sample will be proportional to the population on the stratification variable and random in every other way. In our current example, assume that you know beforehand that 30 percent of the students in grades one through three are in the first grade, 35 percent are in the second grade, and 35 percent are in the third grade. This type of information may be available on the principal's computer files. If you know this information, you can then use proportional stratified sampling to make sure that you obtain the correct percentages of students in grades one through three in your sample.

Now let's use a more specific example. Suppose we want to select a sample of 100 students from a high school composed of 1,000 students. In order to select a stratified sample, you know that you must have information about the stratification variable(s) before selecting the sample. For this example, assume that based on information obtained before selecting the sample we know that 53 percent of the students in the high school are female and 47 percent are male. That means there are 530 females and 470 males in the high school (530 + 470 = 1,000). Next, we need to develop separate lists of the females and males so we can take a random sample from each list. One list will include all the female students, and the other list will include all the male students. Together, these two subpopulations (all females and all males) make up the total population of 1,000 students.

Again, there are 530 females and 470 males in the high school and we want a sample of size 100. How many females and how many males do you think we need to select if we want the percentages of females and males in our sample to be the same as the percentages in the high school? If you said 53 females and 47 males, you are correct. If we randomly select 53 females and 47 males, then the percentages of females (53 percent) and males (47 percent) in the sample will be the same as the percentages of females (53 percent) and males (47 percent) in the high school. In addition, our sample will be a random sample in every other respect. That is how proportional stratified sampling improves on the simple random sampling method. The sample will be exactly (or almost exactly, depending on rounding) representative of the population on gender composition, and since we are taking random samples from each group, we are still generating a random sample, which means that the sample will also be approximately representative of the population in every other respect. Proportional stratified random sampling is, therefore, very similar to simple random sampling, except it is usually a little better.

How many females and how many males would you select from our hypothetical high school of 530 females and 470 males *if you wanted a sample of size 500,* rather than a sample of size 100 as demonstrated in the previous example? The answer is 265 females and 235 males. To determine the number of females you need, just take 53 percent of 500, which is 265. To see how many males you need, take 47 percent of 500, which is 235. As you can see, 265 plus 235 is 500, which is your desired sample size. This is how you get a proportional stratified sample. You make sure that the proportions (or percentages) in your sample are the same as the proportions (or percentages) in the population, and you use random sampling within the groups.

If you are still not confident about selecting a stratified sample, we have provided one more example in Figure 6.4. We assume that you have a list of the males in the population and a list of the females in the population. That is, we assume you have two lists: a list of all males and a list of all females.

Up to this point we have shown that once you determine the number of people to select in each stratum (group), you can take a simple random sample of the appropriate size from each group. There is, however, a way to select a proportional stratified sample without having to worry about the number of people to select from each group (strata). Here's what you do. First, make sure that your list (your sampling frame) is ordered by group (strata). If, for example, gender is your stratification variable, then order the list by gender; that is, list all of the females first, and then list all of the males second. Second, simply take a *systematic sample* from the list. Kalton (1983) shows that systematic sampling from ordered lists is the way to proceed rather than determining the sample sizes and taking simple random samples. We agree that this is certainly easier in practice, and we also recommend this procedure in general because when a list is ordered by a stratification variable, it is unlikely that the problem of periodicity (a cyclical pattern in the list) will be present.

The sampling frame in Figure 6.5 is ordered by administrative status, with the 10 principals listed first and the 10 assistant principals listed second. In other words, the sampling frame is stratified by administrative status. Let's take a *systematic sample* of size 10 from the 20 school administrators listed in the sampling frame in Figure 6.5. Because there are 10 principals and 10 assistant principals, a proportional stratified sample would include 5 principals and 5 assistant principals. Because the population size is 20 and we want 10 people in our sample, $k = 2$ ($20/10 = 2$). (Remember: k is the sampling interval, which is the population size, 20, divided by the desired sample size, 10.) Since k is 2, we next randomly select a number from 1 to 2. Assume that we randomly selected the number 2. Therefore, the 10 people in the sample will be persons 2, 4, 6, 8, 10, 12, 14, 16, 18, and 20. The sampled elements are marked by asterisks in Figure 6.5. That includes 5 principals and 5 assistant principals. We have a proportional stratified sample with 10 people.[6]

FIGURE 6.4 How to obtain a proportional stratified sample.

Assume that there are 1,500 first graders in your school district. Also assume that you want to obtain a sample of 100 first graders. You decide that it is essential for your sample to be representative on gender, so you decide to use gender as a stratification variable. You can obtain a stratified sample by following these six steps:

1. Write down the names of the groups making up the stratification variable (gender) in column 1 (see columns below).
2. Write down the number of elements in each population group in column 2. In this example, we wrote down the number of males and the number of females in column 2. These are the sizes of the male and female subpopulations.
3. Determine the *sampling fractions* for males and females, and write these down in column 3. In this example, the sampling fractions show what proportion of the population is male and what proportion is female. To get the sampling fractions, divide the numbers in column 2 by the total population size (which is 1,500), and write these numbers down in column 3. In this example the sampling fractions are .29 (435/1,500 = .29) and .71 (1,065/1,500 = .71).
4. Multiply the numbers in column 3 by the total sample size desired (100), and place the results in column 4. In this example, the appropriate sample sizes are 29 (100 × .29) and 71 (100 × .71).
5. Now look at the numbers in column 4. These are the samples sizes to use when selecting males and females.
6. Last, take a simple random sample of 29 males from the males, and a simple random sample of 71 females from the females. That will give you a total sample size of 100 people. Furthermore, the proportions of males and females in the sample will be the same as the proportions in the population.

1 Gender	2 Population Sizes	3 Sampling Fractions	4 Sample Sizes
Male	435	.29	29
Female	1,065	.71	71
	1,500 (Total Population Size)	1.00	100 (Total Sample Size)

Disproportional Stratified Sampling So far we have focused on proportional stratified sampling. Sometimes, however, you may need to select a **disproportional stratified sample.** That is, you may want to select a larger percentage of certain groups of people than you would obtain if you used proportional stratified sampling. For example, you may want 50 percent of your sample to be African Americans and 50 percent to be European Americans. Because only 12 percent of the general population in the United States is African American, and because European Americans are a much larger percent than 50, you would definitely not get a 50/50 split using proportional stratified sampling. Therefore, you would oversample African Americans and undersample European Americans if you decided to obtain a 50/50 split. Notice that you will be selecting individuals disproportional to their sizes in the population—that's why they call it disproportional stratified sampling. Disproportional stratified sampling in often used when the research interest lies more in comparing groups than in making generalizations about the total population. As we will mention

Disproportional stratified sampling Type of stratified sampling in which the sample proportions are made to be different from the population proportions on the stratification variable

FIGURE 6.5   A sampling frame set up for proportional stratified sampling using systematic sampling.[a]

Element 1	Principal 1
[b]Element 2	Principal 2
Element 3	Principal 3
Element 4	Principal 4
Element 5	Principal 5
[b]Element 6	Principal 6
Element 7	Principal 7
Element 8	Principal 8
Element 9	Principal 9
[b]Element 10	Principal 10
Element 11	Assistant Principal 1
Element 12	Assistant Principal 2
Element 13	Assistant Principal 3
[b]Element 14	Assistant Principal 4
Element 15	Assistant Principal 5
Element 16	Assistant Principal 6
Element 17	Assistant Principal 7
[b]Element 18	Assistant Principal 8
Element 19	Assistant Principal 9
Element 20	Assistant Principal 10

[a]Notice how all of the principals are listed first and then all of the assistant principals are listed in this sampling frame. The sampling frame has been ordered according to administrative status (a categorical variable composed of principals and assistant principals).

[b]These are the elements selected in the example discussed in text.

later, if you use disproportional stratified sampling and also want to generalize to the total population, weighting procedures must be used. Disproportional stratified sampling is also sometimes used when certain groups in the population are very small; hence you oversample these groups to ensure that you have adequate sample sizes.

Here is an example where a disproportional stratified sample may be needed. Suppose you work at a traditionally female college of 5,000 students that recently started accepting males, and the number of females still far outweighs the number of males. Let's assume that 90 percent of the students (4,500) are female and only 10 percent of the students (500) are male. If you are mainly interested in comparing males and females or in obtaining large samples of both females and males, then you may wish to select the same number of males as females. That is, you may opt for a disproportional stratified sample. Let's say you have the resources to obtain a sample size of 300. In this case, you might decide to select an equal number of females and males (150 females and 150 males). This way, comparisons between females and males will be based on similar sample sizes for both groups. Furthermore, we have fully 150 males and 150 females, which may be considered adequate sample sizes given your monetary resources.

It is important to understand that when disproportional stratified sampling is used, statements cannot be made about the total population without weighting because the relative sizes of the sample strata do not represent the relative sizes of the groups in the population. Weighting is something statisticians do to provide less weight to the smaller strata so they better represent the smaller strata in the population. Without weighting you can make statements only about separate groups and make comparisons between the groups. Sometimes this is all researchers want to do.

An example should show the problem of trying to generalize to a total population from a disproportional stratified sample. If 150 females and 150 males are asked for their opinions about, say, female sports, it is quite possible that females and males will have different opinions on the subject. For example, assume that based on interviews with the females we find out that fully 75 percent support equal funding for men's and women's basketball teams. However, based on our interviews with the males, we find only 25 percent of them support equal funding. At this point we can state that, based on our sample, we believe that 75 percent of the females in the population support equal funding and only 25 percent of the males support equal funding. To find out what percent of the support applies to the total population without specifying gender, a novice researcher might try to use the 300 people in the sample and calculate the total support. The conclusion would be that 50 percent of the people in the student population support equal funding. However, this number does not represent the total population of 5,000 students because we had far too many males in our sample. To get a more accurate reading of the population using our sample, we have to weight the sample to make it representative by giving females a weight of 90 percent and males a weight of 10 percent. When this is done, the new estimate of support in the population becomes fully 70 percent in support. The earlier estimate was much too low. The point here is that you cannot generalize to the full population using disproportional stratified sampling unless you adjust the sample sizes' weights.

Cluster Random Sampling

Cluster sampling
Type of sampling in which clusters are randomly selected

Cluster
A collective type of unit that includes multiple elements

Cluster sampling is a form of sampling in which **clusters** (a collective type of unit that includes multiple elements, such as schools, churches, classrooms, universities, households, and city blocks) rather than single unit elements (such as individual students, teachers, counselors, administrators, and parents) are randomly selected. For example, a school is a cluster because it is composed of many individual students. At some point, cluster sampling always involves randomly selecting clusters (multiple-unit elements) rather than single-unit elements. For example, in cluster sampling one might randomly select classrooms. A classroom is a cluster because it is a collective unit composed of many single units (i.e., students). In the other sampling techniques discussed in this chapter, single units (individuals) were always the objects of selection, rather than collective units (clusters). Cluster sampling is just like simple random sampling except that rather than taking a random sample of *individuals* you take a random sample of *clusters*.

Cluster sampling requires a larger sample size than simple random sampling, systematic sampling, or stratified sampling. Nonetheless, there are many occasions when cluster sampling is preferred. In general, cluster sampling will be less accurate than simple random sampling, but at the same time, cluster sampling can be less costly. The tradeoff between cost and accuracy is prominent in cluster sampling situations. Often the importance of cost and time outweigh the loss in accuracy. For example, cluster sampling is often used when the elements in the population are geographically spread out. When you need to conduct in-person interviews, cluster sampling will result in reduced travel costs, reduced interviewer costs, and a reduced time period needed to physically interview all the people in the sample. If a population is geographically dispersed (like in the United States), the physical act of driving to every person's house in a simple random sample to conduct an interview will be very difficult to carry out. On the other hand, if you were conducting telephone interviews, you would *not* need to use cluster sampling. You could easily call from virtually anywhere in the United States.

An additional reason for cluster sampling is that sometimes a sampling frame of all the people in the population will not be available. When this is the case, you may be able to locate naturally occurring groups of sampling elements, such as classrooms, mental health agencies, census blocks, street maps, and voting districts. Lists of these clusters are usually available or they may be developed without too much effort. After a sample of clusters is randomly selected from the list of all the clusters in the population, you only need to develop lists of the elements in the randomly selected clusters that were selected. There is no need to identify everyone in the entire population. Developing a list of the people in a subset of population clusters is much easier than developing a list of *all* people in all clusters (i.e., the entire population).

One-stage cluster sampling
A set of randomly selected clusters in which all the elements in the selected clusters are included in the sample

Now let's do some examples of cluster sampling. In the most simple case of cluster sampling, **one-stage cluster sampling,** a set of clusters is randomly selected from the larger set of all clusters in the population. For example, you might take a random sample of 10 schools from all of the schools in a city. Typically, simple random sampling, systematic sampling, or stratified random sampling is used to select the clusters. After the clusters are selected, all the elements (e.g., people) in the selected clusters are included in the sample. Sampling is therefore only conducted at one stage. Here's an example. Let's say you are interested in getting a sample of 250 fifth-grade students in a public school system composed of 80 classrooms. Further, assume there are 2,000 fifth-grade students in the system. Finally, assume that there are approximately 25 students in each classroom. To reduce interviewing and travel time you may choose to randomly select 10 clusters (10 fifth-grade classrooms) and interview all the students in these classes. You will have to visit only 10 classrooms. This will result in a sample including approximately 250 fifth-grade students (with completed sample size depending on the response rate). If, on the other hand, you had taken a simple random sample of students (rather than classrooms), you would have needed to go to far more than 10 classrooms.

Two-stage cluster sampling
A set of clusters is randomly selected and then a random sample of elements is drawn from each of the clusters selected in stage one

In **two-stage cluster sampling,** sampling is done at two stages rather than at one. In stage one, a set of clusters is randomly selected from all of the clusters. In stage two, a random sample of elements is drawn from each of the clusters selected in stage one. For example, 25 classrooms (clusters) could be randomly sampled from the list of clusters. If all students in the 25 classrooms were included as in a one-stage cluster sample, the sample size would be 625 (25 classrooms times 25 students per classroom = 625). Just as before, however, we want to select a sample of size 250. Therefore, at stage two, 10 students could be randomly selected from each of the 25 classrooms. The outcome would be a cluster random sample of 250 students.

*Probability
proportional
to size*
A type of two-
stage cluster
sampling in which
each cluster's
chance of being
selected in stage
one depends on its
population size

At this point it is important to note that we have assumed that all the classrooms are composed of approximately 25 students. However, it is often *not* the case that clusters are of approximately equal sizes. As a result, when selecting clusters a technique called **probability proportional to size** (PPS) is frequently utilized. Basically, this more advanced technique is used to give large clusters a larger chance of being selected and smaller clusters a smaller chance of being selected. Then a fixed number of individuals (e.g., 10) is randomly selected from each of the selected clusters. This approach, though more advanced, is the route that has to be taken to ensure that all people in the population have an equal chance of being selected. In other words, PPS is an equal probability selection method technique. And remember, equal probability selection methods produce representative samples. To use this advanced technique, you will need to go to a more advanced book on sampling or get help from a statistical consultant at your college or university. The important point for you to remember here is that if you want a representative sample, then probability proportional to size must be used when the clusters are unequal in size.

NONRANDOM SAMPLING TECHNIQUES

Convenience Sampling

*Convenience
sampling*
People who
are available,
volunteer, or can
be easily recruited
are included in the
sample

Researchers use **convenience sampling** when they include in their sample people that are available or volunteer or can be easily recruited and are willing to participate in the research study. That is, the researcher selects individuals who can be "conveniently selected." It should be noticed that technically speaking we cannot generalize from a convenience sample to a population. First, and most importantly, not everyone in a population has an equal chance of being included in the sample. Second, it is often not clear what specific population a convenience "sample" comes from.

When convenience samples are used, it is especially important that researchers describe the characteristics of the people participating in their research studies. Sometimes, researchers will even describe the "hypothetical population" that they believe most closely corresponds to their convenience sample. Ultimately, however, it is up to you, the reader of a research article, to examine the characteristics of a convenience sample and decide whom you believe the group of people may represent.

You may be surprised to learn that the majority of experimental researchers do not select random samples. Rather, they tend to use convenience samples. For example, some published research is conducted with undergraduate students enrolled in introductory psychology or educational psychology classes. Here is an example from a study by Turner, Johnson, and Pickering (1996):

> Seventy-nine college students (47 women and 32 men) were recruited from introductory psychology courses. Students participated in research as an option for course credit. The average of the sample was 23.7 yr. (Range = 17 to 52). Seventy-three percent ($n = 58$) of the participants were Caucasian, 18% (or 14) were black, and the remaining 9% (or 7) were of other ethnic origins. (p. 1053)

Here is another example of a convenience sample:

> Fifty-five fourth-grade and 39 fifth-grade students from two public schools in western New York were included in the study, because their two principals and six teachers agreed to allow them to be pulled out of class individually and their parents gave written permission for their participation. (Gentile, Voelkl, Mt. Pleasant, & Monaco, 1995, p. 190)

Convenience samples are not the optimal way to go, especially when the researcher wants to generalize to a population based on a single study. Nonetheless, researchers are often forced to use convenience samples because of practical constraints.

Quota Sampling

Quota sampling The researcher determines the appropriate sample sizes or quotas for the groups identified as important and takes convenience samples from those groups

In **quota sampling** the researcher identifies the major groups or subgroups of interest, determines the number of people to be included in each of these groups, and then selects convenience samples of people for each group. Quota sampling is so named because once the researcher decides how many of certain types of people to include in the sample, he or she then tries to "meet the quotas"; that is, the researcher tries to get the right number of people. If the researcher decides to make the sample proportional to the population on certain characteristics (e.g., gender), then this method of quota sampling will have an apparent similarity to proportional stratified sampling. For example, if a school is composed of 60 percent females and 40 percent males, the researcher may decide to make sure that his or her sample is also 60 percent female and 40 percent male. However, an important difference between quota sampling and stratified random sampling is that once the researcher decides how many people to include in each group, random sampling is *not* used. Although a quota sample may look similar to a population on some characteristics (e.g., the percentage of females and males), it is not a probability sample, and, as a result, one's ability to generalize is severely limited.

Purposive Sampling

Purposive sampling The researcher specifies the characteristics of the population of interest and locates individuals with those characteristics

In **purposive sampling** (sometimes called judgmental sampling) the researcher specifies the characteristics of a population of interest and then tries to locate individuals who have those characteristics (e.g., Johnson, 1995). For example, a researcher may be interested in adult females over the age of 65 who are enrolled in a continuing education program. Once the group is located, the researcher asks those who meet the inclusion criteria to participate in the research study. When enough participants are obtained, the researcher does not ask anyone else to participate. In short, purposive sampling is a nonrandom sampling technique in which the researcher solicits persons with specific characteristics to participate in a research study. Here is an example of purposive sampling from a published research article:

> A purposive sample of adult returning graduate students in two schools at a large midwestern university was selected for this study. Criteria for the sample were threefold: adult students were 25 years of age and older, were returning to school

after an absence of at least 3 years, and were adding the student role to their other adult roles. Students in the sample were enrolled in a mix of day, evening, and weekend programs. (Flannery, 1991, p. 37)

Purposive sampling has the same limitations as any nonrandom sampling method. Specifically, the ability to generalize from a sample to a population based on a single research study is severely limited. The optimal situation would be where the researcher specifies the criteria potential participants must meet to be included in a research study but then attempts to obtain a random sample of these people. However, this is not always possible or practical.

Snowball Sampling

Snowball sampling Each research participant is asked to identify other potential research participants

In **snowball sampling** each research participant that volunteers to be in a research study is asked to identify one or more additional people who meet certain characteristics and may be willing to participate in the research study. Tallerico (1993) used snowball sampling to find 20 females who had once been school superintendents and four "informants" who had known a female superintendent, so that they could study why females left this position. Only a few individuals may be identified in the beginning of a research study as being appropriate, willing, and able participants. Over time, however, as each new participant suggests someone else who may participate, the sample becomes larger and larger. The sample can be viewed metaphorically as a snowball that is rolling down a hill, getting bigger and bigger. This sampling approach can be especially useful when you need to locate members of hard to find populations or when no sampling frame is available.

RANDOM SELECTION AND RANDOM ASSIGNMENT

Random selection Randomly selecting a group of people from a population

Random selection has been the focus of this chapter. Random selection is just another word that means random sampling. As you now know, simple random sampling is like pulling names from a hat. The names you pull out of the hat make up the random sample. We also discussed three specific methods of random sampling that are variations of simple random sampling (systematic sampling, stratified sampling, and cluster sampling). The purpose of random selection is to allow you to make generalizations from a sample to a population. Because the random selection methods produce representative samples, you are able to generalize from the sample to the population. This form of generalization is sometimes called statistical generalization.

Random assignment Randomly assigning a set of people to different groups

On the other hand, we briefly discussed **random assignment** in Chapter 1 when we described experimental research. Random assignment involves taking a set of people and randomly *assigning* them to the groups in the experiment. Recall that random assignment is used in experimental research to make the groups being compared similar on "all possible factors" at the beginning of the experiment. Then, if the groups differ after they receive the different treatments, the researcher can attribute the difference to the independent variable because this was the only factor on which the groups systematically differed (e.g., one group may receive a pill and another group may receive a placebo). As we explained earlier in this chapter when we discussed convenience samples, many experiments are not based on random samples. Rather, they are frequently based on convenience samples. Therefore, while you *can* make a statement about the effect of the independent variable on the dependent variable (e.g., the effect of the experimental pill on behavioral outbursts) in an experiment that has random assignment but does not have random selection, you will *not* be able to directly generalize from such an experiment. There is a way out of this problem in experimental research, however, through the use of replication logic.

When experimental findings are *replicated* in different places at different times with different people, the findings about the causal effect of the independent variable on the dependent variable can be generalized to some degree, even when random selection is not used. That is because when we repeatedly see the same causal result (e.g., the experimental pill consistently reduces behavioral disorders), evidence that the causal relationship is real and that it applies to many people is obtained. Nonetheless, the results from a *single* research study based on a convenience sample cannot be statistically generalized to any known population. The strongest possible experimental design is one in which the participants are randomly selected from a population *and* they are also randomly assigned to groups.

DETERMINING THE SAMPLE SIZE WHEN RANDOM SAMPLING IS USED

When you design a research study, you will inevitably ask how big your sample should be. The most simple answer is that the larger the sample size the better because larger samples result in smaller sampling errors, which means that your sample values (the statistics) will be closer to the true population values (the parameters). In the extreme case, sampling error would be zero if you included the complete population in your study rather than drawing a sample. As a rule of thumb, we recommend using the whole population when the population is 100 or less in size. That way, without too much expense, you can be completely confident that you know about the total population. Our second answer to the question of sample size is that you may want to examine the research literature that is most similar to the research you hope to conduct and see how many research participants are used.

We have provided a table with recommended sample sizes for your convenience in Figure 6.6. The sample sizes provided there are usually adequate. The recommended sample sizes are given for populations ranging in size from very small (e.g., 10) to extremely large (e.g., 500 million). All you need to know to use the table is the approximate size of the population you plan on drawing your sample from. You can see in the table that if the population is composed of 500 people, you need to randomly select 217 people. Likewise, if the

FIGURE 6.6   Sample sizes for various populations of size 10 to 500 million.

N stands for the size of the population. *n* stands for the size of the recommended sample. The sample sizes are based on the .05 confidence level. (Adapted from R. V. Krejecie and D. W. Morgan, "Determining Sample Size for Research Activities," *Educational and Psychological Measurement, 30*(3), p. 608, copyright © 1970 by Sage Publications, Inc. Reprinted by Permission of Sage Publications, Inc.)

N	n	N	n	N	n	N	n	N	n
10	10	110	86	300	169	950	274	4,500	354
15	14	120	92	320	175	1,000	278	5,000	357
20	19	130	97	340	181	1,100	285	6,000	361
25	24	140	103	360	186	1,200	291	7,000	364
30	28	150	108	380	191	1,300	297	8,000	367
35	32	160	113	400	196	1,400	302	9,000	368
40	36	170	118	420	201	1,500	306	10,000	370
45	40	180	123	440	205	1,600	310	15,000	375
50	44	190	127	460	210	1,700	313	20,000	377
55	48	200	132	480	214	1,800	317	30,000	379
60	52	210	136	500	217	1,900	320	40,000	380
65	56	220	140	550	226	2,000	322	50,000	381
70	59	230	144	600	234	2,200	327	75,000	382
75	63	240	148	650	242	2,400	331	100,000	384
80	66	250	152	700	248	2,600	335	250,000	384
85	70	260	155	750	254	2,800	338	500,000	384
90	73	270	159	800	260	3,000	341	1,000,000	384
95	76	280	162	850	265	3,500	346	10,000,000	384
100	80	290	165	900	269	4,000	351	500,000,000	384

population is composed of 1,500 people, you need to randomly select 306 people. We now make several additional points about random sampling from populations.

1. If you examine the numbers in Figure 6.6, you will notice that a researcher must randomly select a large percentage of the population when the population is small. However, as the population becomes larger and larger, the percentage of the population needed becomes smaller and smaller. For example, if the population is of size 100, you need to select 80 people randomly. That's 80 percent of the total population. If the population is of size 1,000, you need to randomly select 278 people. That's 27.8 percent of the total population. Finally, if the population is of size one million, you need to randomly select 384 people. That is only 0.0384 of one percent of the total population![7]

2. The more homogeneous a population, the smaller the sample size can be. A homogeneous population is one that is composed of similar people. In fact, if everyone were exactly alike, you would only need one person in your sample. Conversely, the more heterogeneous a population (the more dissimilar the people are), the larger the sample size needs to be.

3. The more categories or breakdowns you want to make in your data analysis, the larger the sample size needed. A researcher may be interested in determining the percentage of people in a city who plan on voting for a certain school superintendent candidate. But what if the researcher also wanted to know the percentage of females planning on voting for the candidate and the percentage of males planning on voting for the candidate? The original population has now been divided into two subpopulations of interest, and you would need an adequate sample size for each and every subpopulation. Therefore, a larger sample size would be needed. If you planned on making many additional breakdowns in your data analysis, the sample size would need to be increased quite sizeably.

4. In the later chapter on inferential statistics, we will explain the idea of confidence intervals. For now we will just say that sometimes researchers use a statistical procedure to estimate a population value, and they will provide an interval of values that they believe contains the population value. For example, you might hear a news reporter say that 55 percent of the people in a city support the school superintendent's decision to adopt school uniforms, *plus or minus 5 percent,* and that the "level of confidence" is 95 percent. The statement is that the true population value is probably somewhere between 50 and 60 percent. You will learn in a later chapter that the more people included in a sample, the smaller the confidence interval will be. For example, if more people were included in the sample, one might be able to say that 55 percent of the people support the decision, *plus or minus 3 percent.* That is, the true population value is probably somewhere between 52 and 58 percent. The rule is, the larger the sample size the greater the precision of statements about the population based on the sample. That is, the bigger the sample the better.

5. Assume that you are planning to measure a relationship or the effect of an independent variable on a dependent variable. If you expect the relationship or effect to be relatively *weak,* then you will need a *larger* sample size. That's because there is less "noise" or "random error" in larger samples.

6. The more efficient the random sampling method, the smaller the sample size needs to be. As we discussed earlier in this chapter, stratified random sampling tends to need slightly fewer people than simple random sampling. On the other hand, cluster random sampling tends to require slightly more people than simple random sampling.

7. The last consideration mentioned here is that some of the people in your original sample will refuse to participate in your research study. In other words, your final sample may end up being smaller than you had intended. If you can guess approximately what percentage of the people will actually participate (the response rate), you can use the following formula to adjust your original sample size. The numerator is the number of people you want to have in your research study. The denominator is the proportion of people you believe will agree to participate.

$$\frac{\text{Desired sample size}}{\text{Proportion likely to respond}} = \begin{array}{l}\text{Number of people to include} \\ \text{in your original sample}\end{array}$$

For example, say that you want a sample of size 75 and you expect that only 80 percent of the people in your original sample will actually participate in your research study when you ask them. All you need to do is to divide 75 by .80, and you have the number of people you need to include in your sample. You will need 94 people. As another example, you want a sample of size 50 people, and you expect that 70 percent of them will participate. Can you get the number of people you need to include in your original sample? The numerator is 50, your desired sample size. The denominator is .70. And 50 divided by .70 is equal to 71. You will need 71 people. Just get your calculator, and you will not find this too difficult.

SAMPLING IN QUALITATIVE RESEARCH

Qualitative researchers must first decide who or what they want to study. This initial task is based on consideration of which populations or phenomena are relevant to the research focus being proposed or developed. The researcher typically defines a set of criteria or attributes that the people to be studied must possess and uses these criteria to distinguish the people of potential interest from those people who should be excluded from consideration. Once these inclusion boundaries are set, the researcher knows who he or she wishes to study and can then attempt to locate and obtain the sample.

Two well-known qualitative researchers, Margaret LeCompte and Judith Preissle (1993), call the overall sampling strategy used in qualitative research *criterion-based selection* because the researcher develops inclusion criteria to be used in selecting people or other units (e.g., schools). Another well-known qualitative researcher, Michael Patton (1987, 1990), uses the term *purposeful sampling* to describe the same process because individuals or cases are selected that provide the information needed to address the purpose of the research. The terms criterion-based selection and purposeful sampling are synonyms, and both describe what we earlier called *purposive sampling*. Purposive sampling is used in both quantitative and qualitative research. In addition, the other forms of nonprobability sampling previously discussed (snowball sampling, quota sampling, and convenience sampling) are also used in qualitative research.

Although the goal is always to locate information-rich individuals or cases, decisions about whom to study are also affected by logistical constraints, such as the availability of appropriate participants, the accessibility of the potential participants, and the costs of locating the people and enlisting their participation. Researchers virtually always face practical constraints such as these when they decide who to include in their research studies. The researcher should pick a sample that can be used to meet the purpose of the research study and answer research questions while meeting cost and other constraints. Tradeoffs will always be present.

Comprehensive sampling
Including all cases in the research study

Many different types of sampling are used in qualitative research. We rely here mainly on the discussions by LeCompte and Preissle (1993) and Patton (1987, 1990). The first type is called **comprehensive sampling,** which means that all cases (individuals, groups, settings, or other phenomena) are examined in the research study. As you can see, this guarantees representativeness because everyone is included in the study. It can also be very expensive and quite impractical except for very small populations that are relatively easy to locate.

Maximum variation sampling
Purposively selecting a wide range of cases

Another form of sampling sometimes used by qualitative researchers is called **maximum variation sampling.** In this form of sampling a wide range of cases (individuals, groups, settings, or other phenomena) are purposively selected so that all types of cases along one or more dimensions are included in the research. One reason for using this approach is to help ensure that no one can claim you excluded certain types of cases. In addition, during data analysis the qualitative researcher can search for a central theme or pattern that occurs across the cases. Something all the cases have in common might be identified. For example, while studying the organizational culture of a local school, an ethnographic researcher might identify certain core values and beliefs common to most, if not all, of the teachers in the school. Here is another example from a journal article by Fisher (1993). Fisher was interested in describing the developmental changes experienced by older adults:

> Initially five sites were selected at which to conduct interviews: two senior centers in an urban county and two senior centers and a nursing home located in adjacent counties which combined suburban and rural characteristics. These sites were selected in order to increase the probability that persons available for interviewing would represent a broad age spectrum with diverse backgrounds and experiences. (p. 78)

Homogeneous sample selection
Selecting a small and homogeneous case or set of cases for intensive study

In **homogeneous sample selection** a relatively small and homogeneous case or set of cases is selected for intensive study. Focus group researchers commonly use this procedure. In focus group research a small homogeneous group of around six or seven people is interviewed in a group situation on a topic of common interest. The group interview and discussion typically last about two hours. The focus group facilitator is able to gain an in-depth understanding of how the people in the group think about a topic by generating group discussion through the use of open-ended questions and targeted followups. In general, when specific subgroups are targeted for a research study or as a component of a larger study, the researchers may have relied on homogeneous sample selection.

Extreme-case sampling
Identifying the extremes or poles of some characteristic and then selecting cases representing these extremes for examination

In **extreme case sampling** the extremes, or poles, of some characteristic are identified and then cases representing the extremes are selected for examination. The strategy is to select cases from the extremes and then to compare them. For example, you might examine a very large classroom and a very small classroom. Or, perhaps you are interested in teacher burnout so you decide to interview teachers with very high burnout and teachers with very low burnout. The logic is that these extreme cases may provide particularly rich sources of information. In general you might locate and compare "outstanding cases" with "notable failures" and attempt to determine what circumstances led to these outcomes (Patton, 1990). For example, you might compare the teaching environment created by an outstanding teacher with that created by a notably ineffective teacher.

Typical-case sampling
Selecting what are believed to be average cases

In **typical-case sampling** the researcher lists the criteria describing a typical or average case and then finds an example to study. The researcher should speak to several experts to try to get a consensus on what example(s) is(are) typical of the phenomenon and should, therefore, be studied. For example, you might interview several people at your school and ask them how they would describe the typical first-grade school teacher. They might describe this person in terms of characteristics such as age, gender, teaching style, and number of years of experience. Sometimes even in a research study in which many cases are examined, illustrating a typical case in the final report helps the reader to make more sense of the findings.

Critical-case sampling
Selecting what are believed to be particularly important cases

In **critical-case sampling** cases that can be used to make a point particularly well or are known to be particularly important are selected for study. According to Patton (1990) "a clue to the existence of a critical case is a statement to the effect that 'if it happens there, it will happen anywhere,' or, vice versa, 'if it doesn't happen there, it won't happen anywhere.' " For example, consider a counseling center director who wants to use a new testing procedure and wants to see whether counselors can be trained in the testing procedure in a two-hour training session. The director might check to see whether the least talented counselor can perform the test correctly after the two-hour training session. The director would be acting under the assumption that "if this person can do it, then I feel fairly confident that my other counselors will also be able to do it." Another example is a school superintendent who wants to make a change in a policy that may face resistance in the local schools. The superintendent may decide to select a school where he or she expects the greatest resistance to see whether enacting the policy is feasible in practice.

Negative-case sampling
Selecting cases that disconfirm the researcher's expectations and generalizations

In **negative-case sampling,** cases that disconfirm the researcher's expectations are purposively selected. For example, in the form of qualitative research called grounded theory, the qualitative researcher typically explores a phenomenon and attempts to inductively build a theory about it by checking out tentative hypotheses and hunches. As the researcher develops a tentative conclusion or generalization based on the data, however, it is important to search for instances in which the generalization does not hold in order to learn more about the boundaries of the generalization and about any potential problems that need to be addressed or qualifications that need to be made. If you are a careful and conscientious qualitative researcher, you must not overlook negative cases. You may find that your original expectation was not generally true and that you need to revise your generalization.

Opportunistic sampling
Selecting cases when the opportunity occurs

In **opportunistic sampling** the researcher takes advantage of opportunities during data collection to select important cases. The cases may be critical, negative, extreme, or even typical. The important point is that qualitative research is an ongoing and emergent process, and the researcher may not be able to state in advance of the research everyone and everything that will be included in the study. The focus may change and opportunities that could not be foreseen may occur. The effective researcher is one who is quick to discern whom to talk to and what to focus on while collecting the data in the field. The term opportunistic sampling was coined to refer to this process.

Mixed purposeful sampling
The mixing of more than one sampling strategy

The last form of sampling listed here is **mixed purposeful sampling.** This is a term that Patton coined to refer to the mixing of more than one sampling strategy. A researcher might, for example, conduct a quantitative survey research study based on a random sample, but also use typical case selection to obtain an illuminating case to describe in the final report. Or, a researcher might conduct a purely qualitative research study and start with maximum variation sampling, discover a general pattern or finding in the data, and then use negative-case selection to determine the generality of the pattern. Mixed purposeful sampling is also likely to be used when a researcher uses data triangulation—examining multiple data sources, which may be selected according to different sampling methods.

SUMMARY

Sampling is the process of drawing a sample from a population. When we sample, we study the characteristics of a subset (called the sample) selected from a larger group (called the population) in order to understand the characteristics of the larger group (the population). If the researcher selects a sample from a population by using a random sampling technique, then the sample will be representative of the total population—it will be similar to the population. Therefore, after the researcher determines the characteristics of a randomly selected sample, he or she can generalize from the sample to the population; that is, the researcher can make statements about the population based on the sample. A sample is usually much smaller in size than a population; hence, sampling can save time and money. The major random sampling methods are simple random sampling, systematic sampling, stratified random sampling, and cluster random sampling. Each of these random sampling methods is an equal probability selection method (EPSEM), which means each individual in the population has an equal chance of being included in the sample. Because each individual has an equal chance of being included in the sample, all of these sampling methods can be used to produce representative samples. Researchers do not always, however, use the most powerful sampling methods. Frequently nonrandom samples are drawn. The four types of nonrandom sampling discussed are convenience sampling, quota sampling, purposive sampling, and snowball sampling. In addition, several kinds of sampling primarily used by qualitative researchers are discussed: purposive sampling, comprehensive sampling, maximum variation sampling, homogeneous sampling, extreme-case sampling, typical-case sampling, critical-case sampling, negative-case sampling, opportunistic sampling, and mixed purposeful sampling.

STUDY QUESTIONS

1. What type of sampling produces representative samples?
2. What is a representative sample, and when is it important to obtain a representative sample?
3. What is the difference between a statistic and a parameter?
4. What is a sampling frame?
5. How do you select a simple random sample?
6. What do all of the equal probability selection methods (EPSEM) have in common?
7. What are the three steps for selecting a systematic sample?
8. How do you select a stratified sample?

9. What is the difference between proportional and disproportional stratified sampling?
10. When might a researcher want to use cluster sampling?
11. Are convenience samples used very often by experimental researchers?
12. If your goal is to generalize from a sample to a population, which is more important, random selection or random assignment?
13. If your population size is 250,000, how many participants will you need, at a minimum, for your research study? (*Hint:* Look at Figure 6.6.)
14. Sampling in qualitative research is similar to which type of sampling in quantitative research?

EXERCISE

1. Using the table of random numbers in Figure 6.1, draw a simple random sample of size 20 from the sampling frame in Figure 6.2. What is the average age of the 20 people in your sample? Next, draw a systematic sample of size 20 from the sampling frame in Figure 6.2 and calculate the average age. Compare the two sample averages you just obtained. Also compare the sample averages with the population parameter (i.e., the average age for all 60 people listed in Figure 6.2). What was the sampling error for your simple random sample? What was the sampling error for your systematic sample? (*Hint:* If you subtract the sample average from the population average, you obtain the sampling error.)

KEY TERMS

census (156)

cluster (172)

cluster sampling (172)

comprehensive sampling (180)

convenience sampling (174)

critical-case sampling (182)

disproportional stratified sample (170)

element (158)

equal probability selection method (160)

extreme-case sampling (181)

generalize (156)

homogeneous sample selection (181)

k (164)

maximum variation sampling (181)

mixed purposeful sampling (182)

N (158)

n (158)

negative-case sampling (182)

one-stage cluster sampling (173)

opportunistic sampling (182)

parameter (158)

periodicity (166)

population (158)

probability proportional to size (174)

proportional stratified sampling (167)

purposive sampling (175)

quota sampling (175)

random assignment (176)

random selection (176)

representative sample (156)

response rate (159)

sample (158)

sampling (156)

sampling error (159)

sampling frame (159)

sampling interval (164)

sampling without replacement (160)

sampling with replacement (160)

simple random sample (160)

simple random sampling (160)

snowball sampling (176)

starting point (164)

statistic (158)

stratification variable (167)

stratified sampling (166)

survey research (156)

systematic sample (164)

table of random numbers (161)

two-stage cluster sampling (173)

typical-case sampling (181)

unrestricted sampling (160)

ENDNOTES

1. If the population is large, the difference between sampling with and without replacement is of little consequence because when you select a sample from a large population, a single individual's chance of being included in the sample more than once is quite small.

2. Sampling with replacement and sampling without replacement are both equal probability selection methods (EPSEM) (Cochran, 1977, p. 18; Kish, 1965, pp. 39–40).

3. Systematic sampling is included as a type of random sampling for three reasons. First, the starting point is randomly selected. Second, it is an EPSEM (Kalton, 1983). Third, it is typically as good or better than a simple random sample of equal size (Scheaffer, Mendenhall, and Ott, 1996, pp. 252–254).

4. The sampling interval may not be a whole number in practice. A common solution is to round it off. If this does not work very well, see page 17 in Kalton (1983).

5. When lists are ordered in this way they are said to be stratified. Often the researcher will stratify the list in order to improve the sampling results. Sometimes the list is already stratified without the researcher doing anything at all. This usually improves the sample because of a process called *implicit stratification* (Jaeger, 1984; Sudman, 1976).

6. The stratification variable has been categorical in our examples (e.g., grade level, gender). You can also select a proportional stratified sample with quantitative stratification variables (e.g., age, IQ). Just reorder the list by the quantitative stratification variable and take a systematic sample. For example, in the case of age, reorder the names in your original list from the youngest person to the oldest person and take a systematic sample from your new list.

7. It has been erroneously suggested by some methodologists that researchers should sample 10 percent of a population, or 10 percent of the people in each group in a population. You should avoid this rule of thumb. Sampling experts make it clear that sample size should not be based on a percentage of a population. You can easily see the problem with the "10 percent rule" by applying it to a small population of 50 people and to a large population of 250 million people. In the former, the rule would say take a sample of size 5. In the latter, the rule would say take a sample of 25 million people!

CHAPTER 7

Validity of Research

LEARNING OBJECTIVES

To be able to

- explain the meaning of internal and external validity and their importance in the research process.
- identify and explain the types of evidence that are needed to reach a causal conclusion.
- explain the threats to internal validity and be able to identify when they might exist in a research study.
- explain the threats to external validity and when they might exist in a research study.
- explain the relationship that exists between internal and external validity and why, in most studies, the focus of attention is on internal validity.
- explain why it is important to select measures of the independent and dependent variables that are both reliable and valid.
- explain the role of operationalization of constructs in research.
- explain the types of validity used in qualitative research.

In order to conduct a research study that will provide an answer to your research question, you must develop a plan, outline, or strategy to use in data collection. You naturally want to develop a plan or strategy that will allow you to collect data leading to a valid conclusion. To accomplish this goal you must have knowledge of the factors that will lead to both valid and invalid conclusions. These factors are somewhat different depending on whether you are conducting a quantitative study or a qualitative study.

VALIDITY ISSUES IN THE DESIGN OF QUANTITATIVE RESEARCH

In Chapter 1 we state that description, exploration, explanation, prediction, and influence represent the objectives of research. To accomplish these objectives we must design research studies that allow us to collect uncontaminated data. This seems to be a straightforward requirement. In most quantitative studies we want to identify the effect created by some independent variable. However, in every study there is the possibility that some variable other than the independent variable influenced the dependent variable. For example, if you are investigating the effect of parents' involvement in their child's education (independent variable) on the child's achievement test scores (dependent variable), you probably want to conclude that greater parent involvement results in high achievement test scores. However, if the parents with the greater involvement also have the brightest children, the higher achievement test scores could be due to the child's greater intellect. In such an instance, intellect would be an **extraneous variable,** a variable other than the ones you are specifically studying, which may have confounded the results of the study.

Extraneous variable
Any variable other than the independent variable that may influence the dependent variable

Extraneous variables may or may not introduce a confound. Extraneous variables are confounded when they systematically vary with the independent variable and also influence the dependent variable. It is impossible to draw clear and valid conclusions from the data collected when a **confounding variable** also influences the dependent variable.

Confounding variable
An extraneous variable that systematically varies with the independent variable and also influence the dependent

To illustrate how extraneous variables can confound the outcome of a study and produce ambiguous results, consider a hypothetical "Pepsi challenge" study. Assume Pepsi wants to conduct a study demonstrating that its product is preferred over Coke. In conducting this study research participants are given, in random order, Pepsi in a cup marked with an M and Coke in a cup marked with a Q. The research participants are to drink the beverage in each cup and then identify the one they like most. Now assume that 80 percent of the participants indicate that they prefer the beverage in the cup marked with an M. Pepsi would take this as an indication that their product was preferred over Coke. On the surface this seems to be a valid conclusion until you look closer at the design of the study and ask yourself, Are there any extraneous variables in this study, other than the beverage consumed, that could have influenced and contaminated the outcome? One possible extraneous confounding variable is the letter that appears on each of the cups because the letter on the cup systematically varies with the type of beverage in the cup. If people are more likely to choose something with the letter M over the letter Q, this could influence their selection of the beverage of choice. If the letter on the cup does influence choice, the results are ambiguous because now it is impossible to tell whether the choice was due to the beverage, Coke or Pepsi, or to the letter that appeared on the cup. This is the type of subtle extraneous variable that can systematically confound the outcome of a study and lead to ambiguous results.

The key component here is that the extraneous variable has to systematically vary with the independent variable and influence the dependent variable to represent a confound. There are many extraneous variables surrounding a study but they do not represent a confounding influence. For example, the two beverages in the "Pepsi Challenge" study could be administered in glasses, paper cups, or Styrofoam containers. The type of container may influence a person's evaluation of the beverage, with glasses resulting in a more positive evaluation than Styrofoam containers. The type of container could, therefore, represent an extraneous variable that could influence the beverage of choice. However, it would not represent a confounding influence because both beverages would have been presented in identical containers. In other words, the influence of the extraneous variable of type of container is constant across all participants. Extraneous variables are not confounding variables when they have the same influence on everyone in the study or are held constant across everyone in the study. Only when they systematically influence one group and not the other, or have one influence on one research condition and another on another research condition, are they confounding extraneous variables. This type of potential confound can be seen in the "Pepsi Challenge" study because the Pepsi beverage was contained in the cup with the M and this resulted in people selecting this cup more than the cup with the Q, the one that contained the Coke beverage. Therefore the letter on the cup was not held constant across participants and systematically influenced the individuals' choice of the desired beverage.

It is this type of confound that must be eliminated from research studies. Unfortunately, when we conduct research, we do not know which extraneous variables may be confounding variables. Therefore we have to use our hunches, past research, and general intuition to identify potential confounding variables and then design a study that controls or eliminates the influence of these potential confounds. To eliminate such confounds and produce valid results, you must be aware of the criteria that must be met to conduct an uncontaminated study and have some knowledge of the type of variables that can represent confounding extraneous variables. In quantitative research there are two basic criteria, internal and external validity, that are used to evaluate the quality of a research design. We now discuss these two criteria in some depth.

INTERNAL VALIDITY

Internal validity
The ability to infer that a causal relationship exists between two variables

Internal validity is a term coined by Campbell and Stanley (1963). The concept was later refined by Cook and Campbell (1979) to refer to the "approximate validity with which we infer that a relationship between two variables is causal" (p. 37). Although research is conducted for the multiple purposes of description, exploration, explanation, prediction, and influence, most research focuses on the goal of explaining behavior. Most researchers are therefore attempting to determine whether a causal relationship exists between the variables being investigated.

Criteria for Inferring Causation

Three types of evidence are needed to reach a causal conclusion. First, you need some evidence that the independent and dependent variables are related. In other words, do changes in the independent variable correspond to changes in the dependent variable? For example, assume that you want to know whether being absent from school, the independent variable, has any effect on the grades students make, the dependent variable. If there is no relationship between these two variables, then one obviously cannot affect the other. However, if there is some relationship between the independent and dependent variables, it is possible that they are causally related. Note that we said that it is *possible* that the two variables are causally related. We used the word *possible* because evidence of covariation or correlation does not provide sufficient evidence of causation. Evidence of covariation is necessary but not sufficient to infer causation.

The second source of evidence needed to infer causation is the temporal ordering of the variables being investigated, because a cause must precede an effect. This means that you need some knowledge of the time sequence of the events. For example, if you are studying the causal relationship between grades and number of absences from school, you may want to determine whether grades cause absences from school or whether absence from school has a causal influence on grades. At first glance you might think that the direction of causality is from absence from school to grades, with fewer absences resulting in higher grades and more absences resulting in lower grades. However, it is also possible that the direction of causality is from grades to school absences. It may be that students with poor grades become frustrated and therefore miss school whereas students with good grades enjoy school so they demonstrate better attendance than do the students with poor grades. As you can see, the temporal order of the relationship has to be identified to reach a causal conclusion because the cause must precede the effect. It is logically impossible for an effect to occur prior to the existence of its cause.

The third type of evidence needed to reach a causal conclusion is that the variables being investigated are the ones that are causally related rather than being caused by some extraneous variable. In other words, we must look for variables other than the independent variable that may explain the change observed on the dependent variable. In the "Pepsi Challenge" experiment, the letter on the cup represents a logical explanation for participants' preference selection. In the example of student grades and attendance, it is possible that the grades students get and their attendance at school are caused by parents monitoring their children. Children whose parents do not monitor their children's behavior may have poorer grades and lower school attendance whereas children who are monitored by their parents may get better grades and have fewer absences. In this instance there is still a relationship between grades and school attendance, but the cause of this relationship is the third variable of parent monitoring. **Third variable** is simply another term to refer to a confounding extraneous variable.

Third variable
A confounding
extraneous
variable

This third-variable issue means that two variables may be correlated not because they are causally related, but because they are both related to some third variable. Consider the research that has attempted to relate coffee drinking to heart attacks (e.g., Brody, 1973). Some of these studies have found a positive correlation between the number of cups of coffee drunk and the incidence of heart attacks. From this positive relationship it is tempting to make a causal inference that coffee consumption is contributing to the risk of having a heart attack. This would be a tenuous assumption because cigarette smoking is related to both heart attacks and coffee drinking. Cigarette smoking, therefore, could be the third variable that is related to and possibly causing both coffee drinking and heart attacks, as illustrated in Figure 7.1. Nonsmokers not only do not consume much coffee, but they also have few heart attacks, whereas smokers consume large amounts of coffee and have heart attacks. Therefore, although there is a relationship between coffee consumption and heart attacks, this relationship could be caused by an underlying third variable of smoking.

As you can see from this example, a researcher cannot automatically assume causality just because two or more variables are related. Before making such a causal connection, the temporal ordering of the variables must be established and some assurance must be provided that an extraneous variable is not causing the observed relationship. Establishing the temporal ordering of variables is easily accomplished in experiments because the experimenter actively manipulates and has control over the presentation of the independent variable, the causal variable, and observes the effect of this manipulation on the dependent variable, the effect. Because the independent variable is presented first and the dependent

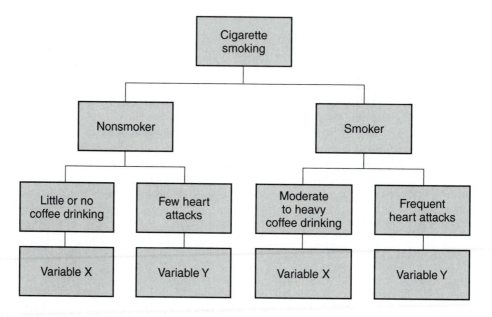

FIGURE 7.1   Illustration of the third variable problem.

variable is measured after the occurrence of the independent variable, the time sequence of the events is established in experimental research.

Research studies other than experimental studies also frequently attempt to infer causality. In these studies the direction of causality is more difficult to establish because of the difficulty in establishing the temporal sequencing of events and ruling out the influence of confounding extraneous variables. For example, assume you want to determine whether parental involvement in a child's education is related to the child's academic performance. To determine whether a relationship exists between these variables you conduct a survey that asks questions such as whether the parents monitor their children's completion of homework assignments, help their children with schoolwork, belong to the Parent Teachers Association, and so forth, and also obtain the children's grade point average. After collecting the data from the survey you obtain a measure of parent involvement by counting the number of things the parents do to assist in their children's education. This is then correlated with the children's GPA. Although these two variables may be correlated, this correlation does not, by itself, tell you anything about the direction of the effect. Does parent involvement precede the student's attainment of good grades or does the child's getting good grades precede the parents' involvement in the child's education? Additionally, this covariation does not say anything about a third variable causing both parent involvement and student achievement. It is possible that the parents' intelligence is causing both their involvement in their child's education and the child's educational achievement. Intelligent parents might be more attuned to the necessity of being involved in and monitoring their child's education than less intelligent parents. Similarly, bright parents should be more likely to have bright children, leading to greater educational attainment.

Attempts are often made to reach causal conclusions from nonexperimental studies. However, being able to validly make causal statements from these studies is difficult because it is difficult to identify the time order of the occurrence of the events and to rule out alternative explanations for the observed relationships. To make causal statements, the researcher must constantly be on the alert for extraneous confounding variables that could explain why two or more variables may be related. Internal validity is obtained when the influence of these confounding variables is ruled out or their influence is controlled. Although this problem is more acute in nonexperimental research, confounding extraneous variables can also creep into experimental studies and must be identified and controlled in the design of the study. The researcher must be on the alert for a confounding extraneous variable that would compromise internal validity in both experimental and nonexperimental research. The following represents some of the more obvious threats to internal validity. These threats are most applicable to experimental types of research but can also apply to nonexperimental research.

Threats to Internal Validity

Attempts must be made to control the threats to internal validity in any research study investigating causality because these threats represent rival and competing explanations for the results obtained. When these rival explanations exist, it is impossible to reach a causal

FIGURE 7.2   One-group pretest-posttest design.

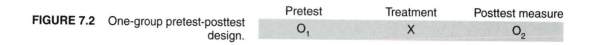

Pretest	Treatment	Posttest measure
O_1	X	O_2

One-group pretest-posttest design
A research design in which a treatment condition is administered to one group of participants after pretesting, but before posttesting on the dependent variable

explanation with any degree of certainty, leading to highly suspect results that cannot and should not be taken seriously. This is why it is necessary to control for and eliminate the systematic influence of these threats. These threats to the internal validity of a research study are greatest in a **one-group pretest-posttest design.** As Figure 7.2 illustrates, this is a research design in which one group of participants is pretested on some dependent variable and then administered a treatment condition. Some time after the treatment condition is administered, the group of participants is posttested on the dependent variable. For example, assume that you want to test the effects of a new drug on controlling the adverse behavior of children with ADHD. You first identify a group of children with ADHD and pretest them on some performance measure such as ability to perform a series of simple arithmetic computations in a 15-minute time period. You then give these children the treatment consisting of the new drug. After the children have taken the drug for two months you posttest them on the arithmetic computations task to see whether their posttest performance is superior to the pretest performance. Although it may be tempting to interpret any improvement in performance from pre- to posttesting as due to the new drug, there are a number of other variables that could exist during the interval between pre- and posttesting that could also affect the posttest performance. These other variables represent threats to the internal validity of the study.

Multigroup research design
A research design that includes more than one group of participants

There are also a number of variables that can threaten the internal validity of a study that uses a multigroup research design. The most basic **multigroup research design** is the two-group design. As illustrated in Figure 7.3, this design has two groups of participants, one of which receives a treatment condition while the other does not. Both groups are posttested on the dependent variable following administration of the treatment condition, and the posttest results are compared to see whether the group that received the treatment condition responds differently on the posttest than does the group that did not receive the treatment condition. This design could, for example, be used to test the effect of a drug on controlling the behavior problems of children with ADHD. One group of children with ADHD is given the drug and the other group is given a placebo (a pill that looks like the drug but does not contain the drug). Following drug administration, both groups of children with ADHD are posttested on measures such as the amount of time they spend out of their seat. The two groups are compared to determine whether the children that receive the drug

FIGURE 7.3   Two-group design comparing an experimental group that receives a treatment condition with a control group that does not receive the treatment condition.

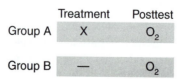

	Treatment	Posttest
Group A	X	O_2
Group B	—	O_2

stay in their seat for a longer period of time than do the children that do not receive the drug. There are a number of variables that can operate in this design and can threaten its internal validity, making it a very weak design. We now discuss some of the more obvious and common threats to the internal validity of the one-group pretest-posttest design and the multigroup design.

History   A **history** effect may occur in a one-group pretest-posttest research design in which the pre- and postmeasurements of the dependent variable are separated by a rather lengthy time interval. History refers to the specific events, other than any planned treatment event, that occur between the first and second measurement of the dependent variable, as illustrated in Figure 7.4. These events, in addition to any treatment effect, can influence the postmeasurement of the dependent variable; therefore, these events are confounded with the treatment effect and become rival explanations concerning the change that occurred between the pre- and postmeasurements.

Consider a study investigating the effect of a peer tutoring procedure on spelling performance. This is a procedure in which one student serves as a tutor and the other as a tutee. Tutors dictate words to a tutee and provide feedback as to whether the tutee correctly spells the word and the correct spelling if the word is spelled wrong. After a given number of words, the students reverse roles and continue the tutoring procedure. One approach to investigating the efficacy of such a tutoring procedure is to pretest the students on the speed with which they can learn to correctly spell a list of words prior to implementing the tutoring procedure. Then implement the tutoring procedure. After the students have had an opportunity to practice and become familiar with this procedure, test them again on the speed with which they learn to correctly spell a list of words equivalent to that which they had previously been asked to learn. If they require less time to learn to correctly spell the list of words after the tutoring procedure is implemented than before it is implemented, this should indicate that the peer tutoring system is a more efficient method of spelling instruction.

The difficulty with making this assumption is that a time interval elapsed between the pre- and postmeasurements. It is possible that some event other than just the tutoring system has an effect on the participants during this time and this event influences their performance on the spelling test. For example, to implement the peer tutoring system the teacher has to provide instruction to the students and constantly monitor their performance to ensure that they are conducting the peer tutoring correctly. This monitoring by the teacher can

History Any event, other than a planned treatment event, that occurs between the pre- and postmeasurement of the dependent variable and influences the postmeasurement of the dependent variable

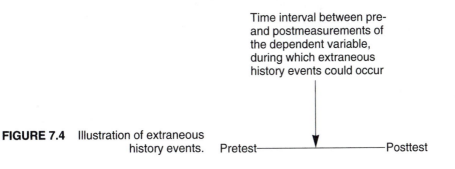

FIGURE 7.4   Illustration of extraneous history events.

increase the students' motivation to learn to spell the list of words and affect their spelling performance. If the monitoring does influence the students' motivation and, therefore, their spelling performance, it represents a history variable and functions as a rival explanation for the cause of the students' enhanced spelling performance. Such history events represent threats to the internal validity of studies because they represent plausible rival explanations for the outcome of the study.

Maturation
Any physical or mental change that occurs over time that affects performance on the dependent variable

Maturation   **Maturation**

refers to physical or mental changes that may occur within individuals over time, such as aging, learning, boredom, hunger, and fatigue. Such changes can affect an individual's performance on the dependent variable. Because such changes may alter performance on the dependent variable, they represent threats to the internal validity of a study.

Consider a study conducted by Snowling, Goulandris, and Defty (1996) in which they followed a group of children with dyslexia over a two-year period to track the development of their literary skills. Over this two-year time period, the children demonstrated an improvement in reading, spelling, and vocabulary, although this rate of improvement was not as large as children without dyslexia. This improvement in the literary skills of the children with dyslexia may represent a maturation effect that could threaten the internal validity of a study. (Snowling, Goulandis, and Defty included two control groups to rule out maturation effects. The inclusion of these groups is not mentioned here to illustrate the maturation threat to internal validity.)

For example, assume that Snowling, Goulandris, and Defty wanted to assess the effect of a special instructional program on the development of literary skills of children with dyslexia. To test the effect of this program, they pretested a group of children with dyslexia on reading, spelling, and vocabulary before they entered the special instructional program and then tested them a second time after they had been in the program for two years. In comparing the pretest with the posttest scores, the investigators found that the children with dyslexia made significant advancements in literary skills. Although it may be tempting to attribute the improvement in literary skills to the special instructional program, all or part of the improvement could have been due to a maturation effect, or the improvement in learning that would have taken place without the special instructional program. That this natural or normal improvement could result from a maturational effect represents a rival explanation for the advancement in literary skills of the children with dyslexia and represents a threat to the internal validity of the study. To conduct an internally valid study, such maturation threats must be controlled.

Testing
Any change in scores obtained on the second administration of a test as a result of having previously taken the test

Testing   **Testing**

refers to changes that may occur in participants' scores obtained on the second administration of a test as a result of previously having taken the test. In other words, the experience of having taken a pretest may alter the results obtained on the posttest independent of any treatment effect or experimental manipulation intervening between the pre- and posttest. Taking the pretest does a number of things that can alter a person's performance on a subsequent administration of the same test. Taking a test familiarizes you with the content of the test. After taking a test you may think about errors you made that could be corrected if the test were taken over. When the test is administered a second time, you are already familiar with it and may remember some of your prior responses. This can lead to an enhanced performance entirely tied to the initial or pretest administration. Any alteration in performance as a result of a testing effect threatens the internal validity of a one-group study because it serves as a rival hypothesis to some treatment effect or experimental manipulation intervening between the pre- and posttests. Whenever the same test is administered on multiple occasions, some control needs to be implemented for testing rival hypotheses.

Snowling, Goulandris, and Defty (1996), for example, administered a number of reading, spelling, and vocabulary tests to children with dyslexia at the beginning of their study and two years later. Some of these tests were a little unusual, such as the Rhyme Sensitivity Test, which presented children with a string of four words (e.g., cot, hot, fox, pot) for which they were to identify the odd word in the rhyme segment (fox in this example). The unusual nature of this test suggests that it may be subject to a testing effect because it would seem as though, after participating in this test once, children would be more familiar with it and would be able to perform better on a subsequent administration of the test. If this familiarization effect did exist, it would account for some of the improvement in performance demonstrated by the dyslexic children. It would therefore serve as a rival explanation for any improvement demonstrated over the two years and preclude a clear explanation of the observed improvement. Snowling et al. (1996) did attempt to control for such a pretesting effect by administrating two practice sessions in which the children could become familiar with the test and minimize a pretesting effect. Such practice sessions do not necessarily eliminate a pretesting effect. However, including control groups that also experienced any testing effect would have controlled for this potential threat to internal validity. (If you read the Snowling et al. study you will see that control groups were included. We did not mention them until now so that we could illustrate the testing threat to internal validity.)

Instrumentation
Any change that occurs in the way the dependent variable is measured

Instrumentation   **Instrumentation** refers to any change that occurs over time in the way in which the dependent variable is assessed. There are two primary ways in which an instrumentation threat may occur: An instrumentation threat can occur when the measurement instrument used during pretesting is different from that used during posttesting. If the tests used during pre- and posttesting are not completely equivalent, a difference can occur between the two performance measures that is strictly due to the difference in the way the two tests are assessing performance. For example, assume that children with dyslexia are tested at time 1 with one test of rhyme sensitivity, and two years later are tested with a different test of rhyme sensitivity. If a comparison is made of rhyme sensitivity from time 1 and two years later at time 2, any difference observed could be due to the children's enhanced development of rhyme sensitivity. However, it could also be due to the differences in the way the two tests measure rhyme sensitivity, which would be an instrumentation effect that would represent a rival explanation for any change observed in rhyme sensitivity. Instrumentation effects, therefore, represent threats to the internal validity of any study.

A second way in which an instrumentation effect could creep into a study is if the data were collected through observation. Many educational researchers use human observers to collect data. Human observers such as teachers are, unfortunately, subject to such influences as fatigue, boredom, and learning processes. In administering intelligent tests, the tester typically gains facility and skill over time and collects more reliable and valid data as additional tests are given. Observers and interviewers are also used to assess the effects of various experimental treatments. For example, Schafer and Smith (1996) had teachers and children view videotapes of children engaged in playful and real fights to make a judgment as to whether the fights were real or play. As the observers and interviewers assess more and more individuals, they gain skill. Interviewers may, for example, gain additional skill with the interview or with observing a particular type of behavior, producing changes in the data collected that cannot be attributed to either the participant or any experimental conditions being tested in the study. This is why studies that use human observers to collect data typically use more than one observer and have each observer go through a training program. In this way, some of the biases inherent in making observations can be minimized, and the various observers can serve as checks on one another to ensure that accurate data are being collected. Typically, the data collected by the various observers must coincide before they are considered reliable.

Statistical regression
The tendency of very high scores to become lower and very low scores to become higher on posttesting

Statistical Regression   **Statistical regression** refers to the fact that extreme scores will tend to regress or move toward the mean of a distribution on a second testing or assessment. Many educational research studies are designed in such a way that the research participants are tested before and after some experimental treatment condition is administered for the purpose of assessing change. Additionally, many of these studies investigate special groups of individuals such as children with learning disabilities or with a specific deficiency such as poor reading or mathematical ability. These special groups of research participants are typically identified by having extreme scores such as low reading comprehension scores. After the research participants are selected, they are given some experimental treatment condition to improve this deficiency or ameliorate the special condition. Any positive change from pre- to posttesting is frequently taken as evidence of the efficacy of the treatment program. However, the internal validity of a study such as this could be threatened because high-scoring research participants may score lower on posttesting or low-scoring research participants may score higher on posttesting not because of any experimental treatment effect but because of statistical regression.

Statistical regression is a phenomenon that can occur because the first and second measurements of performance are not perfectly correlated. This lack of perfect correlation occurs because a person's test-taking performance is influenced by many variables in addition to ability. Think about the variables that could influence the score you receive on a reading comprehension test. There will undoubtedly be some questions you cannot answer correctly. However, you guess and sometimes you guess correctly and at other times you guess incorrectly. In addition to chance factors such as guessing, your test-taking performance could also be influenced by other stresses in your life, such as not sleeping well the night before the test or having a fight with your spouse or significant other. You could also have misread questions, which may have led you to answer incorrectly. As you can see, there are many variables in addition to a person's ability that may influence the score obtained on a test.

To illustrate the statistical regression effect, assume you want to test a technique that is supposed to increase the reading comprehension of young children. To test this technique you give a reading comprehension test to a group of six- to ten-year-old children and select for your study all those children who received the lowest 10 percent of the scores on this test. Naturally, some of these individuals received low scores because they had very poor reading comprehension ability. However, others probably received low reading comprehension scores because they did not try very hard, were tired because they stayed up late the night before, or were especially stressed because of something like moving to another school or their parents' getting a divorce. These individuals would have artificially low scores because of these extraneous factors. On retesting, these children would be expected to do better because it is unlikely that these extraneous factors would again operate to the same extent to depress the reading comprehension scores. Consequently, the posttest scores would be higher. However, these higher scores would be the result of a statistical regression phenomenon and not because of the experimental treatment meant to improve reading comprehension. In this case, statistical regression would threaten the internal validity of the study.

Selection
Selecting
participants for
the various
treatment groups
that have different
characteristics

Selection   **Selection** is a threat to the internal validity of a study when a difference exists, at the outset of the research study, between the characteristics of the participants forming the various comparison groups. Participants in different comparison groups can differ in many ways, as illustrated in Table 7.1. One way in which this difference can occur is if you, as the researcher, have to use groups of participants that are already formed. For example, assume you want to test a procedure for enhancing young children's motivation to learn. To test this procedure you want to administer it to one group of fourth-grade children and compare their motivation to learn, after this procedure has been implemented, with a group of fourth-grade children who have not experienced this procedure. In conducting this study you obtain permission from the local school district. However, you have to administer the experimental procedure to one fourth-grade class and compare its performance with that of another fourth-grade class. This may not seem to be a problem because they both represent fourth-grade students. However, there is no guarantee that the students in these two classes have the same motivation to learn before the study is conducted. If the class that receives the experimental procedure had a greater motivation to learn prior to conducting the study, they naturally show up as having a greater motivation to learn after the experimental procedure is implemented. Any difference in motivation to learn between the two fourth-grade

TABLE 7.1   Characteristics on Which Research Participants Can Differ

Ability to do well on tests	Home environment	Reading ability
Age	Intelligence	Religious beliefs
Anxiety level	Language ability	Self-esteem
Attitudes toward research	Learning style	Socioeconomic status
Coordination	Maturity	Spelling ability
Curiosity	Motivation to learn	Stress level
Ethnicity	Personality type	Time spent on homework
Gender	Political beliefs	Vocabulary
Hearing ability	Quality of eyesight	

classes could, therefore, be due entirely to a selection bias. As you can see, using already formed groups runs the risk of a selection bias and must be controlled to reach a correct conclusion regarding the efficacy of a treatment condition.

Interaction with Selection   A number of the threats to internal validity we have just discussed, such as maturation, history, and instrumentation, can also interact with selection to produce an effect that looks like a treatment effect. To understand this you must have some understanding of the meaning of an interaction effect. An **interaction with selection** occurs in a multigroup comparison design when one of the threats affects the groups differently. In a two-group comparison design, a **selection by history interaction** would occur if the two comparison groups experienced a different history event and the history effect they experienced resulted in their responding in different ways to the dependent variable. For example, assume that a joke was cracked at some time during the study in one of the comparison groups. In the other comparison group one of the participants got very angry and frustrated at having to do the experimental task and voiced his disapproval aloud. These two experiences each represent a history effect, but the history effect occurring in each group would have been different. The different history effects, the joke or the expression of disapproval, would probably have affected the participants in each group very differently and may have also had a differential effect on their response to the dependent variable. If it did, this differential response would look like a treatment effect but would be a selection by history interaction effect.

To illustrate the **selection by maturation interaction,** suppose you want to teach the concepts of good and bad to five-year-old children with and without hearing difficulties. In doing so you find that the normal children learn these concepts much faster than do the children with hearing difficulties. From this study you might conclude that the ability of children who have hearing difficulties to learn these concepts is somehow impaired. However, as Figure 7.5 reveals, Kusche and Greenberg (1983) revealed that the ability of children with hearing difficulties to gain an understanding of the concepts of good and bad develops or evolves more slowly than it does in children who can hear normally. Five-year-old children who cannot hear have not matured to the point that they can understand these concepts as well as children who can hear normally. This difference in the evolution of the ability to understand these concepts is a maturational difference between the two groups of children and not an impairment in the ability of children who cannot hear to acquire these concepts. This indicates that a maturation by selection interaction exists, or that a maturational difference exists between these two groups of children in their ability to understand these two concepts. This maturational difference represents the most logical explanation for the difference observed in a study attempting to teach five-year-old children with and without hearing difficulties the concepts of good and bad and not a difference in ability to learn these concepts.

Mortality   A mortality bias sounds like a bias created from the fact that some of the research participants died. Although this is possible, it is not what it means. **Mortality** refers to a bias that can occur from the fact that some research participants who are scheduled to participate in the research study either do not show up at the scheduled time and place or do not participate in all phases of the research study. In conducting a research study, the typi-

---

Interaction with selection
Occurs when the different comparison groups are affected differently by one of the threats to internal validity

Selection by history interaction
Occurs when the different comparison groups experience a different history event

Selection by maturation interaction
Occurs when the different comparison groups experience a different rate of change on a maturation variable

Mortality
A differential loss of participants from the various comparison groups

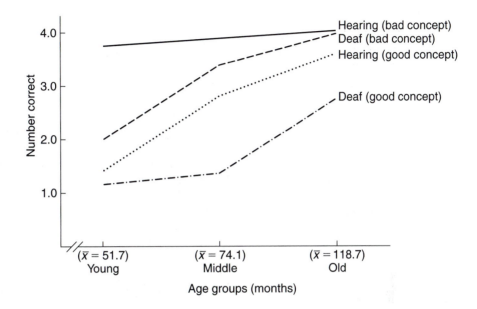

FIGURE 7.5   The evolution of good and bad concepts as a function of age and hearing status. (Adapted from C. A. Kusche and M. T. Greenberg, "Evaluative Understanding and Role Taking Ability: A Comparison of Deaf and Hearing Children," *Child Development, 54,* pp. 141–147, © 1983 by The Society for Research in Child Development, Inc.)

cal procedure is to identify the individuals who agree to participate and schedule them to participate at a specific time and place. However, people do not show up for a study for a variety of reasons ranging from just forgetting about the study to deciding that they don't want to participate.

The loss of research participants from the research study does not, in and of itself, produce a bias. The bias results because the loss, when using a multigroup design, may produce differences between the comparison groups that cannot be attributed to the experimental treatment condition. To attribute a difference between comparison groups to the experimental treatment, the comparison groups have to be the same on all variables except the independent variable. The loss of research participants from the various comparison groups can create differences on variables other than the independent variable, producing a mortality threat to the internal validity of the study.

For example, assume you want to test the efficacy of a new technique for teaching mathematics to students. To test this new technique you obtain permission from a school system to conduct the study. In conducting the study one teacher teaches mathematics to one group of students by the traditional method and to another group of students by the new technique for one selected week of the school year. You know that research has revealed that older students perform better than younger students on mathematics, so you try to control for the age influence by having an equal number of older and younger students in each experimental group. However, when you conduct the study, you find that half of the younger students assigned to the new technique group are sick and do not show up for class. When comparing the performance of the mathematical skills of the students in the two groups after the one week of instruction, you find that the new technique is superior to the traditional method. Can you conclude that the new technique is the superior teaching technique and that it should be used instead of the traditional method? This inference is incorrect because more older students were in the new technique group and past research has indicated that older students do better in mathematics. This age difference and not the method of instruction may have produced the difference in the mathematical performance of the students in the two groups. If it did, then a mortality bias existed and represents a rival explanation for the performance difference observed in the two groups of students. From this example, you can see that mortality is really a type of selection bias because mortality can result in the various comparison groups being composed of people that differ on variables other than the independent variable.

EXTERNAL VALIDITY

External validity
The extent to which the study results can be generalized to and across populations of persons, settings, and times

External validity is a term coined by Campbell and Stanley (1963) to refer to the extent to which the results of a study can be generalized to and across populations of persons, settings, and times. In Chapter 1 we state that one of the basic assumptions of science is that there are regularities in human behavior and these regularities can be discovered through systematic research. Whenever we conduct a research study, we are attempting to discover these regularities. However, each research study is conducted on a specific sample of individuals in a specific setting and at a specific point in time. External validity refers to the extent to which the results of our study can be generalized to individuals other than those who participated, at other points in time, and in other settings. If these generalizations can be made, the study has external validity.

To generalize the result of a study, you must identify a target group of individuals, settings, and times and then randomly select individuals from these populations so that you will have a sample representative of the target population of individuals, settings, and times. Most studies cannot randomly sample from the population of individuals, settings, and times because of the expense, time, and effort involved. Therefore, most studies contain characteristics that threaten their external validity.

There are three categories of threats to the external validity of a research study: lack of population validity, ecological validity, and time validity (Bracht & Glass, 1968; Wilson, 1981). We will discuss each of these so you can be aware of some of the factors that limit the generalizability of a study. Being aware of these factors will allow you to assess the extent to which the results of a study can be generalized and can help you design studies that circumvent these difficulties.

Population validity
The ability to generalize the study results to individuals not included in the study

Population Validity

Population validity refers to the ability to generalize from the sample of individuals on which a study was conducted to the larger target population of individuals and across dif-

Target population
The larger population to whom the study results are to be generalized

ferent subpopulations within the larger target population. The **target population** is the larger population, such as all children with a learning disability, to whom the research study results are to be generalized. Within this larger target population there are many subpopulations, such as male and female children with a learning disability. Population validity, therefore, has the two components of generalizing from a sample to a target population and generalizing from a sample across types of persons in the target population.

Generalizing from a sample of individuals to the larger target population is a two-stage process of defining the larger target population of individuals of interest and then randomly selecting a sample of individuals from this target population, as illustrated in Figure 7.6. Remember that random selection maximizes the probability that the sample will be representative of the target population. The characteristics of the population are then inferred from the characteristics of the sample. This is the ideal arrangement and the one that is sometimes achieved, primarily in survey research, as illustrated by several examples in Chapter 4 when we discussed sampling. It is also the type of sample that is needed when the goal of research is to identify population characteristics. Unfortunately, drawing a random sample from a target population is seldom possible because of practical considerations such as finances or practical limitations such as the fact that a list of all members of many target populations does not exist from which we can draw a sample (e.g., a list does not exist of all children with a learning disability). Therefore, we draw our sample from individuals that are accessible, which can be defined as the accessible population.

Accessible population
The research participants available for participation in the research

The **accessible population** is the group of research participants that are available to the researcher for participation in research. This may be the college students taking a class in the researcher's department or children with a learning disability attending school in a specific school district that has granted the researcher permission to conduct his or her research.

Two inferential steps must be made in generalizing from the study sample results to the larger target population, as illustrated in Figure 7.7. First we have to generalize from the sample of individuals participating in the study to the accessible population. This step is easily accomplished if the individuals participating in the research study have been

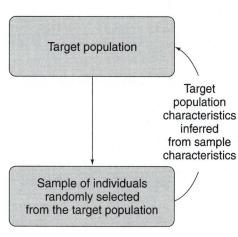

FIGURE 7.6 Two-step process involved in achieving external validity.

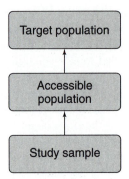

FIGURE 7.7   Inferential steps involved in generalizing from the study sample to the target population.

randomly selected from the accessible population. If the sample of participants is randomly selected, it should be representative, which means that the characteristics of the accessible population can be inferred from the sample. If a study is conducted on 50 children with learning disabilities randomly selected from the 200 attending the Cottage Hills School District, then the results obtained from the study can be generalized to all children with learning disabilities attending that school district. However, more typical is a study conducted on participants who not only are accessible but who volunteer.

The second step in the generalization process involves inferring from the accessible population to the target population. This is the generalization you want to make but the one that you can seldom make with any degree of confidence because the accessible population is seldom representative of the target population. For example, if the study you conducted demonstrated that you had developed a method for improving the reading skills of children with a reading disability, you would ideally want the results of your study to generalize to all children with a reading disability. To be able to make such a statement, the sample of children participating in your study would have had to have been randomly selected from the target population, which is rarely possible. Therefore, you probably have to settle for randomly selecting from an accessible population such as a specific school or a specific school district. One school, or even a school district, is seldom representative of the target population. For example, the school at which you conduct your study may consist primarily of children from an impoverished area of the city in which you work. Although this school may have a large percentage of children with learning disabilities, the children are certainly not representative of the target population consisting of all children in the United States with learning disabilities. Yet it is to the larger target population that you want to generalize. As you can see, generalizing the results of a study to the target population is frequently a tenuous process because the sample of participants used in most studies are not randomly selected from the target population.

Most of this discussion of external validity focuses on generalizing to a specific target population. However, we should not forget that external validity also focuses on the goal of generalizing across populations. In any target population there are many subpopulations, as we mentioned earlier. When we talk about generalizing across populations, we are really asking the question of whether the results hold for each of the subpopulations within the larger target population. Assume we conducted a study investigating a specific treatment enhancing the reading ability of children with dyslexia. Assume further that we did randomly select 500 children from the target population of children with dyslexia in the United States and found that the treatment was effective. Because we had randomly selected our sample (something that seldom occurs in this type of study), we could generalize back to the target population and conclude that children with dyslexia would, on the average, benefit from the treatment program.

The results would not, however, say anything about the effectiveness of the treatment for the many subpopulations with the larger target population. Can the results be generalized to both male and female children with dyslexia, to children with dyslexia coming from various socioeconomic groups, age groups, intellectual levels, and so forth? This is the issue of generalizing across populations. In fact, many studies that are conducted to test the generalization of a specific treatment across subpopulations, are attempting to identify the specific subpopulations to which a treatment can and cannot be generalized.

It is very important to understand the distinction between generalizing to and across populations. Survey research is the type of research that most often focuses on generalizing to target populations. Experimental and quasi-experimental research focuses more on generalizing across populations or identifying the populations to which a finding can and cannot be generalized.

Ecological Validity

Ecological validity
The ability to generalize the study results across settings

Ecological validity refers to the ability to generalize the results of a study across settings. For example, one study may be conducted in a rural school, in the South, using old computers that are slow and antiquated. If the results obtained from this study can be generalized to other settings, such as an urban school well equipped with state-of-the-art technology, then the study possesses ecological validity. Ecological validity, therefore, exists to the extent that the study results are independent of the setting in which the study was conducted. The following topics represent some of the characteristics of a research setting that can threaten ecological validity.

Multiple-treatment interference
Occurs when participation in one treatment condition influences a person's performance in another treatment condition

Multiple-Treatment Interference   The **multiple-treatment interference** effect occurs when a research participant's participation in one treatment condition has an effect on his or her participation in another treatment condition. It refers to the carryover effect from one treatment condition to another treatment condition in which participation in one treatment condition affects the participant's response to another treatment condition. The multiple-treatment interference effect is, therefore, a sequencing effect threatening both the generalization of the study and the internal validity of the study, because it is difficult to separate the effect of the order of the treatment conditions from the effect of the treatment conditions. When this effect occurs, any generalization of the study results is limited to the particular sequence of conditions that was administered.

Reactivity
An alteration in performance that occurs as a result of being aware of participating in a study

Reactivity   **Reactivity** refers to the alteration in performance that can occur as a result of being aware that one is participating in a research study. It is similar to the effect many people have of being on television: once you know the camera is on you, you shift to your "television" behavior. A similar phenomenon can occur in research studies. Once you know you are in a research study, you may change your behavior. A reactivity effect can therefore threaten both the internal and external validity of a study.

Experimenter effect
The unintentional effect that the researcher can have on the outcome of a study

Experimenter Effects   **Experimenter effect** refers to the unintentional effect that the experimenter or researcher can have on the outcome of a study. McGuigan (1963), for example, used nine different experimenters to test the effectiveness of four different methods of learning. Some of these nine experimenters found that performance differed depending on the method of learning used whereas other experimenters found that the method of learning did not influence performance. This indicates that the experimenter may unintentionally influence the outcome of a study, which is exactly what is implied by experimenter effects. These unintentional influences can threaten internal as well as external validity. Most studies use a comparison-group design that may control for the threat of experimenter effects on the internal validity of a study. However, even though controls may eliminate this threat of experimenter effect on the internal validity of a study, they do not control for that threat to the external validity of a study, because the results may be dependent, in part, on the characteristics of the experimenter.

Temporal Validity

Temporal validity
The extent to which the study results can be generalized across time

Temporal validity refers to the extent to which the results of a study can be generalized across time. Temporal validity is an issue because most educational research studies are conducted during one time period. For example, Thokildsen, Nolen, and Fournier (1994) assessed children's views of several practices teachers use to influence motivation to learn. The data for this study were collected by interviewing seven- to twelve-year-old children at one point in time. Although the data are valid for the time period in which they were collected, there is no assurance that the same results would hold true ten years later. Frequently, it is assumed that the results of studies are invariant across time. Although this may exist for the results of some studies, it almost certainly does not exist for the results of others. Walster (1964), for example, found that the attractiveness of job choice fluctuated from becoming less to more attractive shortly after making the choice. The important point is that research results can vary across time. Failure to consider the time variable can threaten the external validity of the study.

CONSTRUCT REPRESENTATION

Up to this point in the chapter we have discussed issues, such as internal validity, that are related to the validity of the design of an educational research study. Any educational research study involves the investigation of a set of variables such as televised instruction, the education of culturally diverse students, or the effect of stress on academic achievement. Additionally, we frequently want to conduct a study on a specific population of individuals such as children with attention deficit hyperactive disorder or dyslexia. Conducting a research study on variables or special populations such as these requires that they be assessed or measured. This creates some difficulty because many of the variables or characteristics of the special populations of interest represent abstract constructs. The educational researcher is faced with the task of identifying or devising some way of representing the constructs being investigated. Butler and Neuman (1995) were interested in help-seeking behaviors, which meant that they had to come up with a way of representing this construct. Similarly, Manthei and Gilmore (1996), in their study of teacher stress, had to come up with a way of representing the construct of stress. If you were interested in children with dyslexia, you would have to have some representation of the construct of dyslexia to determine which children were, in fact, dyslexic.

The difficulty in representing these constructs is that there is no one single behavior or operation that is a complete representation of the construct. For example, teacher stress could be manifested in displaying a short temper, physiological responses such as increased heart rate or blood pressure, or a score on a psychological stress inventory. Constructs such as these can manifest themselves in many different ways, and it is the researcher's task to identify the specific way in which a construct will be represented in the study he or she is conducting. This is where the concept of operationalism enters and is useful as a communication tool for the researcher. **Operationalism** means that terms or constructs are represented by a specific set of steps or operations. For example, if stress is measured by the Stress in Teaching Questionnaire, then stress is represented by a score on this questionnaire.

Operationalism
Representing constructs by a specific set of steps or operations

This is the technique that most researchers use when conducting their study. They select a specific operation or set of operations as their representation of the construct they are investigating. Manthei and Gilmore (1996) used the Stress in Teaching Questionnaire as their representation of teacher stress. Butler and Neuman's (1995) representation of help-seeking behaviors in second- and sixth-grade children was whether they asked the experimenter for assistance in solving puzzles.

Identifying the specific operations used to represent a construct is very convenient and is essential for communication. For example, Butler and Neuman's (1995) operationalization (i.e., their construct representation) of help-seeking left little room for interpretation or question as to the way in which they had conceptualized and interpreted help-seeking. Note, however, that this is not the only way in which a person can seek help. Help can also be obtained by asking peers for help or going to the library and looking for reference material that would provide assistance. Similarly, measuring teacher stress with the Stress in Teaching Questionnaire defines and communicates the way in which Manthei and Gilmore (1995) represented and measured the construct of teacher stress although there are obviously other ways of assessing teacher stress. The important point to remember is that specification of a set of operations is for accuracy in communication. This is the beauty of operationalizations. They specify, in a concrete and specific way, how a construct is conceptualized and measured in a given study. This degree of specificity permits an exact communication of the construct and allows anyone else to repeat the steps and represent the construct in the same way.

Although the operationalization of constructs is necessary for educational researchers to communicate the way in which a construct is represented in a given research study, this specificity is also a limiting factor because seldom, if ever, does a given operationalization completely represent the construct being investigated. Consider, for example, the study by Manthei and Gilmore (1995) in which they operationally represented teacher stress as the response teachers provided on the Stress in Teaching Questionnaire. Although this questionnaire probably does measure some component of teacher stress, it would be foolish to assume that this single measure provides a completely accurate representation of the construct of teacher stress. Rather, stress of any type probably includes physiological reactions, such as changes in heart rate and blood pressure, as well as behavioral changes such as being less tolerant of the students, both of which are probably not adequately assessed by a questionnaire. Additionally, Campbell (1969) has pointed out that every observation is affected by factors that bear no relation to the construct that is being measured. For example, the Stress in Teaching Questionnaire probably does, in part, measure teacher stress. However, it is also a function of events that are irrelevant to the stress that occurs as a result of teaching, such as the type of questions asked, the interpretation of the questions by the teacher completing the questionnaire, the tolerance a teacher has for stress, and stress factors influencing the teacher that are not related to the profession of teaching.

The important point to remember is that there are many different ways of operationally representing a construct and that each operationalization represents only a portion of the construct. The most accurate representation of a construct would involve measuring it in several different ways. For example, teacher stress could be measured by a questionnaire, by his or her reaction to students, and by having others rate or identify factors influencing teacher stress. As more and more measures of the same construct are included, the probability of obtaining a more complete representation of the construct increases. The use of multiple measures of a construct is called **multiple operationalism,** which is the recommended approach to use in research studies (Campbell, 1969).

Multiple operationalism The use of several measures of a construct

We also must point out that it is not sufficient to specify a set of operations as a representation of a construct and then assume that this represents a valid measure of the intended construct or even some component of the construct of interest. Any set of operations does not have any necessary relationship to the construct being investigated. All operations do is state in specific and concrete terms the way in which the construct is being represented in a particular study. To drive this point home with a ridiculous example, assume that you want to investigate the effect of intelligence on the ability to use three different ways of learning. In this study you operationally represent intelligence as a person's income on the assumption that more intelligent people make more money. This is obviously a poor representation of the construct of intelligence. However, it is operationalized in specific and concrete terms. This communicates the information and everyone will know how intelligence was represented in this study. However, it is a very poor measure, and therefore a poor way of representing intelligence. This should drive home the point that in addition to operationalizing the construct of interest in a particular study, you must also make sure that the operation or operations you are using are good, valid representations of the construct being investigated.

RESEARCH VALIDITY
IN QUALITATIVE RESEARCH

Discussions of the term *validity* have traditionally been attached to the quantitative research tradition. Not surprisingly, reactions by qualitative researchers have been mixed regarding whether or not this concept should be applied to qualitative research. At the extreme, some qualitative researchers have suggested that the traditional quantitative criteria of reliability and validity are not relevant to qualitative research (e.g., Smith, 1984). Smith contends that the basic assumptions of quantitative and qualitative research are incompatible, and therefore the concepts of reliability and validity should be abandoned. Most qualitative researchers, however, do not hold this viewpoint, and neither do we. Most qualitative researchers argue that some qualitative research studies are better than others, and they frequently use the term validity to refer to this difference. When qualitative researchers speak of research validity, they are usually referring to qualitative research that is plausible, credible, trustworthy, and, therefore, defensible. We believe it is important to think about the issue of validity in qualitative research and to examine some strategies that have been developed to maximize validity. A list of these strategies is provided in Table 7.2. Keep in mind that most of these strategies can also be used in quantitative research.

Researcher bias
Obtaining results consistent with what the researcher wants to find

One potential threat to validity that researchers must be careful to watch out for is called **researcher bias.** This problem is summed up in a statement a colleague of ours once made. She said, "The problem with qualitative research is that the researchers 'find' what they want to find, and then they write up their results." It is true that the problem of researcher bias is frequently an issue in qualitative research because qualitative research tends to be exploratory and is open-ended and less structured than quantitative research. (One would be remiss, however, to think that researcher bias is never a problem in quantitative research.) Researcher bias tends to result from selective observation and selective recording of information and also from allowing one's personal views and perspectives to affect how data are interpreted and how the research is conducted.

Reflexivity
Self-reflection by the researcher on his or her biases and predispositions

The key strategy used to understand researcher bias is called **reflexivity,** which means that the researcher actively engages in critical self-reflection about his or her potential biases and predispositions (Table 7.2). Through reflexivity, researchers become more self-aware, and they monitor and attempt to control their biases. Many qualitative researchers include a distinct section in their research proposals titled "Researcher Bias." In this section they discuss their personal background, how it may affect their research, and what strategies they will use to address the potential problem. Another strategy that researchers use to reduce the effect of researcher bias is called **negative-case sampling** (Table 7.2). This means that researchers attempt carefully and purposively to search for examples that disconfirm their expectations and explanations about what they are studying. If you use this approach, you will find it more difficult to ignore important information and you will come up with more credible and defensible results.

Negative-case sampling
Locating and examining cases that disconfirm the researcher's expectations

Now let's look at some types of validity that are important in qualitative research. We start with three types of validity that are especially relevant to qualitative research (Maxwell, 1992, 1996)—descriptive validity, interpretive validity, and theoretical validity. They

TABLE 7.2   Strategies Used to Promote Qualitative Research Validity

Strategy	*Description*
Researcher-as-detective	A metaphor characterizing the qualitative researcher as he or she searches for evidence about causes and effects. The researcher develops an understanding of the data through careful consideration of potential causes and effects and by systematically eliminating rival explanations or hypotheses until the final case is made beyond a reasonable doubt. The detective can utilize any of the strategies listed here.
Extended fieldwork	When possible, qualitative researchers should collect data in the field over an extended period of time.
Low-inference descriptors	The use of description phrased very close to the participants' accounts and researchers' field notes. Verbatims (i.e., direct quotations) are a commonly used type of low-inference descriptors.
Triangulation	Cross-checking information and conclusions through the use of multiple procedures or sources. When the different procedures or sources are in agreement you have corroboration.
Data triangulation	The use of multiple data sources to help understand a phenomenon.
Methods triangulation	The use of multiple research methods to study a phenomenon.
Investigator triangulation	The use of multiple investigators (i.e., multiple researchers) in collecting and interpreting the data.
Theory triangulation	The use of multiple theories and perspectives to help interpret and explain the data.
Participant feedback	The feedback and discussion of the researcher's interpretations and conclusions with the actual participants and other members of the participant community for verification and insight.
Peer review	Discussion of the researcher's interpretations and conclusions with other people. This includes discussion with a disinterested peer, (e.g., with another researcher not directly involved). This peer should be skeptical and play the devil's advocate, challenging the researcher to provide solid evidence for any interpretations or conclusions. Discussion with peers who are familiar with the research can also help provide useful challenges and insights.
Negative-case sampling	Locating and examining cases that disconfirm the researcher's expectations and tentative explanation.
Reflexivity	Involves self-awareness and critical self-reflection by the researcher on his or her potential biases and predispositions as these may affect the research process and conclusions.
Pattern matching	Predicting a series of results that form a pattern and then determining the degree to which the actual results fit the predicted pattern.

are important to qualitative research because description of what is observed and interpretation of participants' thoughts are two primary research activities. For example, ethnography produces descriptions and accounts of the lives and experiences of groups of people. Ethnographers also attempt to understand groups of people, from the insider's perspective (i.e., from the viewpoint of the people in the group). Developing a theoretical explanation of the behavior of group members is also of interest to qualitative researchers, especially qualitative researchers using the grounded theory perspective (discussed in Chapter 11). After discussing these three forms of validity, the traditional types of validity used in quantitative research, internal and external validity, are discussed. Internal validity is relevant when qualitative researchers explore cause and effect relationships. External validity is relevant when qualitative researchers generalize beyond their research studies.

Descriptive Validity

Descriptive validity
The factual accuracy of an account as reported by the researcher

The first type of validity in qualitative research is **descriptive validity,** which refers to the factual accuracy of the account as reported by the researchers. The key questions addressed in descriptive validity are, Did what was reported as taking place in the group being studied actually happen? and Did the researchers accurately report what they saw and heard? In other words, descriptive validity refers to accuracy in reporting descriptive information (description of events, objects, behaviors, people, settings, times, places, and so forth). This form of validity is important because description is a major objective in nearly all qualitative research.

Investigator triangulation
The use of multiple investigators in collecting and interpreting the data

One effective strategy used to obtain descriptive validity is **investigator triangulation** (Table 7.2). In the case of descriptive validity, investigator triangulation involves the use of multiple observers to record and describe the research participants' behavior and the context in which they were located. The use of multiple observers allows cross-checking of observations to make sure the investigators agree about what took place. When corroboration (agreement) of observations across multiple investigators is obtained, it is less likely that outside reviewers of the research will question whether something occurred. As a result, the research will be more credible and defensible.

Interpretive Validity

Interpretive validity
Accurately portraying the meaning given by the participants to what is being studied

Although descriptive validity refers to accuracy in reporting "just the facts," interpretive validity requires developing a "window" into the minds of the people being studied. **Interpretive validity** refers to accurately portraying the meaning attached by participants to what is being studied by the researcher. More specifically, it refers to the degree to which the research participants' viewpoints, thoughts, feelings, intentions, and experiences are accurately understood by the qualitative researcher and portrayed in the research report. An important part of qualitative research is understanding research participants' "inner worlds" (i.e., their subjective worlds), and interpretive validity refers to the degree of accuracy in presenting these inner worlds. Accurate interpretive validity requires that the researcher get inside the heads of the participants, look through the participants' eyes, and see and feel what they see and feel. In this way the qualitative researcher can understand things from the participants' perspectives and thus provide a valid account of these perspectives.

Participant feedback
Discussion of the researcher's conclusions with the actual participants

Some strategies for achieving interpretive validity are provided in Table 7.2. **Participant feedback** is perhaps the most important strategy (see Table 7.2). By sharing your interpretations of participants' viewpoints with the participants and other members of the group, you may clear up areas of miscommunication. Do the people being studied agree with what you have said about them? Although this strategy is not perfect because some participants may attempt to put on a good face, useful information is frequently obtained and inaccuracies are often identified.

Low-inference descriptors
Description phrased very close to the participants' accounts and the researchers' field notes

When writing the research report, using many **low-inference descriptors** is also helpful so that the reader can experience the participants' actual language, dialect, and personal meanings (Table 7.2). In this way, the reader can hear how the participants think and feel about issues and experiences. A verbatim is the lowest inference descriptor of all because the participants' exact words are provided in direct quotations. Here is an example of a verbatim from a high school dropout who was part of an ethnographic study of high school dropouts:

> I wouldn't do the work. I didn't like the teacher and I didn't like my Mom and Dad. So, even if I did my work, I wouldn't turn it in. I completed it. I just didn't want to turn it in. I was angry with my Mom and Dad because they were talking about moving out of state at the time (Okey & Cusick, 1995, p. 257).

This verbatim provides some description (i.e., what the participant did), but it also provides some information about the participant's interpretations and personal meanings (which is the topic of interpretive validity). The participant expresses his frustration and anger toward his parents and teacher and shares with us what homework meant to him at the time and why he acted as he did. By reading verbatims like this one, readers of a report can experience for themselves the participants' perspectives. Again, getting into the minds of research participants is a common goal in qualitative research, and Maxwell calls our accuracy in portraying this "inner content" interpretive validity.

Theoretical Validity

Theoretical validity
The degree to which a theoretical explanation fits the data

The third type of validity in qualitative research is called **theoretical validity.** You have theoretical validity to the degree that a theoretical explanation developed from a research study fits the data and is therefore credible and defensible. As we discuss in Chapter 1, theory usually refers to discussions of *how* a phenomenon operates and *why* it operates as it does. Theory is usually more abstract and less concrete than description and interpretation. Theory development moves beyond "just the facts" and provides an explanation of the phenomenon. In the words of Joseph Maxwell (1991):

> one could label the student's throwing of the eraser as an act of resistance, and connect this act to the repressive behavior or values of the teacher, the social structure of the school, and class relationships in U.S. society. The identification of the throwing as "resistance" constitutes the application of a theoretical construct . . . the connection of this to other aspects of the participants, the school, or the community constitutes the postulation of theoretical relationships among these constructs. (p. 291)

In this example, the theoretical construct called resistance is used to explain the student's behavior. Maxwell points out that the construct of resistance may also be related to other theoretical constructs or variables. In fact, theories are often developed by relating theoretical constructs.

Extended fieldwork
Collecting data in the field over an extended period of time

A strategy for promoting theoretical validity is **extended fieldwork** (Table 7.2), which means that you should spend a sufficient amount of time studying your research participants and their setting so that you can have confidence that the patterns of relationships you believe are operating are stable and so that you can understand why these relationships occur. As you spend more time in the field collecting data and generating and testing your interpretations, your theoretical explanation may become more detailed and intricate. You may decide to use the strategy called **theory triangulation** (Table 7.2; Denzin, 1989). This means that you would examine how the phenomenon being studied would be explained by different theories. The various theories might provide you with insights and help you develop a more cogent explanation. In a related way, you might also use investigator triangulation and consider the ideas and explanations generated by additional researchers studying the research participants.

Theory triangulation
The use of multiple theories and perspectives to help interpret and explain the data

Pattern matching
Predicting a pattern of results and determining if the actual results fit the predicted pattern

As you develop your theoretical explanation, you should make some predictions based on the theory and test the accuracy of those predictions. When doing this you can use the **pattern matching** strategy (Table 7.2). In pattern matching, the strategy is to make several predictions at once; then, if all of the predictions occur as predicted (i.e., if the pattern or "fingerprint" is found), you have evidence supporting your explanation. As you develop your theoretical explanation, you should also use the negative case sampling strategy mentioned earlier (Table 7.2). That is, you must always search for cases or examples that do not fit your explanation so that you do not simply find data that support your developing theory. As a general rule, your final explanation should accurately reflect the majority of the people in your research study. Another useful strategy for promoting theoretical validity is called **peer review** (Table 7.2), which means that you should try to spend some time discussing your explanation with your colleagues so that they can identify any problems in it. Each problem must then be resolved. In some cases you will find that you will need to go back to the field and collect additional data. Finally, when developing a theoretical explanation, you must also think about the issues of internal validity and external validity, to which we now turn.

Peer review
Discussing one's interpretations and conclusions with one's peers or colleagues

Internal Validity

You are already familiar with internal validity, which is the fourth type of validity in qualitative research of interest to us. As you know, internal validity refers to the degree to which a researcher is justified in concluding that an observed relationship is causal. Often qualitative researchers are not interested in cause-and-effect relationships. Sometimes, however, qualitative researchers are interested in identifying potential causes and effects. In fact, qualitative research can be very helpful in describing how phenomena operate (i.e., studying process) and in developing and testing preliminary causal hypotheses and theories (Campbell, 1979; Johnson, 1994; LeCompte & Preissle, 1993; Strauss, 1995; Yin, 1994). However, after potential causal relationships are studied using qualitative research, they should be tested and confirmed using experimental methods when this is feasible. In this way, more conclusive evidence about cause and effect can be obtained.

When qualitative researchers identify potential cause and effect relationships, they must think about many of the same issues discussed earlier in this chapter when we talked about internal validity and about the strategies used for obtaining theoretical validity. The qualitative researcher takes on the role of the "detective" searching for the true cause(s) of a phenomenon, examining each possible "clue," and attempting to rule out each rival explanation generated (see **researcher-as-detective** in Table 7.2). When trying to identify a causal relationship, the researcher makes mental comparisons. The comparison might be to a hypothetical control group. Although a control group is rarely used in qualitative research, the researcher can think about what would have happened if the causal factor had not occurred. The researcher can sometimes rely on his or her expert opinion, as well as published research studies when available, in deciding what would have happened. Furthermore, if the event is something that should occur again the researcher can determine whether the causal factor precedes the outcome. In other words, when the causal factor occurs again, does the effect follow?

Researcher-as-detective
Metaphor applied to researcher when searching for cause and effect

When a researcher believes that an observed relationship is causal, he or she must also attempt to make sure that the observed change in the dependent variable is due to the independent variable and not to something else (e.g., a confounding extraneous variable). The successful researcher will always make a list of rival explanations or rival hypotheses, which are possible or plausible reasons for the relationship other than the originally suspected cause. Be creative and think of as many rival explanations as you can. One way to get started is to be a skeptic and think of reasons why the relationship should *not* be causal. Each rival explanation must be examined after the list has been developed. Sometimes you will be able to check a rival explanation with the data you have already collected through additional data analysis. At other times you will need to collect additional data. One strategy would be to observe the relationship you believe to be causal under conditions in which the confounding variable is not present and compare this outcome with the original outcome. For example, if you concluded that a teacher effectively maintained classroom discipline on a given day but a critic maintained that it was the result of a parent visiting the classroom on that day, then you should try to observe the teacher again when the parent is not present. If the teacher is still successful, you have some evidence that the original finding was not because of the presence of the parent in the classroom.

Methods triangulation
The use of multiple research methods

All the strategies shown in Table 7.2 are used to improve the internal validity of qualitative research. Now we will explain the only two strategies not yet discussed: methods triangulation and data triangulation. When using **methods triangulation** (Table 7.2), the researcher uses more than one method of research in a single research study. We discuss this idea in Chapter 1 when we talk about multimethod research. (It is a good idea to review that material.) The word *methods* is used broadly here, and it refers to different methods of research (ethnography, correlational, experimental, and so forth) as well to different methods of data collection (e.g., interviews, questionnaires, focus groups, observations). You can intermix any of these methods (e.g., ethnography and survey research methods, interviews and observations, or experimental research and interviews). The logic is to combine different methods that have nonoverlapping weaknesses and strengths. The weaknesses (and strengths) of one method will tend to be different from those of a different method, which means that when you combine two or more methods you will have better evidence. In other words, the whole is better than its parts.

Here is an example of methods triangulation. Perhaps you are interested in why students in an elementary classroom stigmatize a certain student named Brian. A stigmatized student is an individual that is not well liked, has a lower status, and is seen as different from the "normal" students. Perhaps Brian has a different haircut from the other students, is dressed differently, or doesn't act like the other students. In this case, you might decide to observe how students treat Brian in various situations. In addition to observing the students, you will probably decide to interview Brian and the other students to understand their beliefs and feelings about Brian. A strength of observational data is that you can actually see the students' behaviors. A weakness of interviews is that what the students say and what they actually do may be different. However, using interviews you can delve into the students' thinking and reasoning, whereas you cannot do this using observational data. Therefore, the whole will likely be better than the parts.

Data triangulation
The use of multiple data sources

When using **data triangulation** (Table 7.2), the researcher uses multiple data sources in a single research study. "Data sources" does not mean using different methods. Data triangulation does refer to the use of multiple data sources using a single method. For example, the use of multiple interviews would provide multiple data sources while using a single method (i.e., the interview method). Likewise, the use of multiple observations is another example of data triangulation; multiple data sources would be provided while using a single method (i.e., the observational method). Another important part of data triangulation involves collecting data at different times, at different places, and with different people.

Here is an example of data triangulation. Perhaps a researcher is interested in studying why certain students are apathetic. It would make sense to get the perspectives of several different kinds of people. The researcher might interview teachers, interview students identified by the teachers as being apathetic, and interview peers of apathetic students. Then the researcher could check to see whether the information obtained from these different data sources was in agreement. Each data source may provide additional reasons as well as a different perspective on the question of student apathy, resulting in a more complete understanding of the phenomenon. The researcher should also interview apathetic students at different class periods during the day and in different types of classes (e.g., math and social studies). Through the rich information gathered (from different people, at different times, at different places), the researcher can develop a better understanding of why students are apathetic than if only one data source is used.

External Validity

As you know, external validity is important when you want to generalize from a set of research findings to other people, settings, and times. Typically, generalizability is not the major purpose of qualitative research. There are at least two reasons for this. First, the people and settings examined in qualitative research are rarely randomly selected, and, as you know, random selection is the best way to generalize from a sample to a population. As a result, qualitative research is virtually always weak in the form of population validity focused on "generalizing to" populations.

Second, some qualitative researchers are more interested in documenting "particularistic" findings than "universalistic" findings. In other words, in certain forms of qualitative research, the goal is to show what is unique about a certain group of people or a certain event, rather than generate findings that are broadly applicable. At a fundamental level, many qualitative researchers do not believe in the presence of "general laws" or "universal laws." General laws are things that apply to many people, and universal laws are things that apply to everyone. As a result, qualitative research is frequently considered weak on the "generalizing across populations" form of population validity (i.e., generalizing to different kinds of people), and on ecological validity (i.e., generalizing across settings), and temporal validity (i.e., generalizing across times).

Other experts argue that rough generalizations can be made from qualitative research. Perhaps the most reasonable stance toward the issue of generalizing is that we can generalize to other people, settings, and times to the degree that they are similar to the people, settings, and times in the original study. Stake (1990) uses the term **naturalistic generalization**[1] to refer to this process of generalizing based on similarity. The bottom line is this: The more similar the people and circumstances in a particular research study are to the ones that you want to generalize to, the more defensible your generalization will be and the more readily you should make such a generalization.

Naturalistic generalization
Generalizing based on similarity

To help readers of a research report know when they can generalize, qualitative researchers should provide the following kinds of information: the number and kinds of people in the study, how they were selected to be in the study, contextual information, the nature of the researcher's relationship with the participants, information about any "informants" who provided information, the methods of data collection used, and the data analysis techniques used. This information is usually reported in the methodology section of the final research report. Using the information included in a well-written methodology section, readers will be able to make informed decisions about to whom the results may be generalized. They will also have the information they will need if they decide to replicate the research study with new participants.

Some experts show another way to generalize from qualitative research (e.g., Yin, 1994). Qualitative researchers can sometimes use **replication logic,** just like the replication logic that is commonly used by experimental researchers when they generalize beyond the people in their studies, even when they do not have random samples. According to replication logic, the more times a research finding is shown to be true with different sets of people, the more confidence we can place in the finding and in the conclusion that the finding generalizes beyond the people in the original research study (Cook and Campbell, 1979). In other words, if the finding is replicated with different kinds of people and in different places, then the evidence may suggest that the finding applies very broadly. Yin's key point is that there is no reason why replication logic cannot be applied to certain kinds of qualitative research.[2]

Replication logic
The idea that the more times a research finding is shown to be true with different sets of people, the more confidence we can place in the finding and in generalizing beyond the original participants

Here is an example. Over the years you may observe a certain pattern of relations between boys and girls in a third-grade classroom. Now you decide to conduct a qualitative research study and you find that the pattern of relation occurs in your classroom and in two other third-grade classrooms you study. Because your research is interesting, you decide to publish it. Then other researchers replicate your study with other people and they find that the same relationship holds in the third-grade classrooms they study. According to replication logic, the more times a theory or a research finding is replicated with other people, the greater the support for the theory or research finding. Now assume that other researchers find that the relationship holds in classrooms at several other grade levels. If this happens, the evidence suggests that the finding generalizes to students in other grade levels, adding additional generality to the finding.

SUMMARY

When we conduct a study, we develop a plan, outline, or strategy to use that will allow us to collect data that will lead to a valid conclusion. In any study there are a number of extraneous variables that could systematically vary with the independent variable and confound the results making it impossible to assess the effect of the independent variable. To eliminate potentially confounding extraneous variables, we must design our study so that it is internally valid. A study has achieved internal validity when we can infer that there is a causal relationship between the independent and dependent variable.

To make this causal connection between the independent and dependent variables, we need evidence that they are related, that the direction of effect is from the independent variable (the cause) to the dependent variable (the effect), and that the observed effect on the dependent variable is due to the independent variable and not to some extraneous variable. Internal validity is related to the ability to rule out the influence of extraneous variables. A study is internally valid when the effect observed on the dependent variable is due to the independent variable. However, there are many extraneous variables that can creep into a study and confound the results. The influence of these extraneous variables must be controlled or eliminated. A number of the more obvious threats to the internal validity of a study are the following:

1. History—specific events, other than the independent variable, that occur between the first and second measurement of the dependent variable.
2. Maturation—the physical or mental changes that may occur in individuals over time such as aging, learning, boredom, hunger, and fatigue.
3. Testing—changes in the score a person makes on the second administration of a test that can be attributed entirely to the effect of having previously taken the test.
4. Instrumentation—any change that occurs in the measuring instrument between the pre- and posttesting.
5. Statistical Regression—the tendency of extreme scores to regress or move toward the mean of the distribution on a second testing.
6. Selection—differences that exist in the comparison groups at the outset of the research study and are not due to the independent variable.

7. Interaction with selection—differences that exist in the comparison groups because one of the threats, such as maturation or history, affects the groups differently.
8. Mortality—difference that exists in the comparison groups because the participants that drop out of the various comparison groups have different characteristics.

In addition to trying to meet the criteria of internal validity, the researcher must attempt to meet the criteria of external validity. In most studies we want to be able to generalize the results and state that they hold true for other individuals in other settings and at different points in time. External validity is achieved if we can generalize the results of our study to the larger target population, and at other points in time, and in other settings.

There are three categories that threaten the external validity of a study: lack of population validity, ecological validity, and time validity. Population validity refers to the ability to generalize to and across subpopulations in the target population. Ecological validity refers to the ability to generalize the results of a study across settings. Threats to ecological validity consist of the following:

1. Multiple-treatment interference—the effect that participation in one treatment condition has on participation in another treatment condition.
2. Reactivity effect—the alteration in performance that can occur from an awareness of being in a research study.
3. Experimenter effect—the unintentional effect that the experimenter or researcher has on the outcome of a study.

Temporal validity refers to the extent to which the results of a study can be generalized across time.

When we conduct a research study we also need to select measures of the variables we are investigating. This is frequently a difficult process because the variables we study often represent abstract constructs and we must devise some way of measuring these constructs. The technique used by most researchers is operationism or selecting a specific operation or set of operations as the representation of the construct they are investigating. Although operationism is necessary for communicating the way a construct is represented, seldom, if ever, does it provide a complete representation of the construct. Each operationalization of a construct represents only a portion of the construct.

The majority of this chapter focused on validity in traditional quantitative research, especially experimental research. However, validity is also an important issue in qualitative research. Three types of validity in qualitative research are descriptive validity, interpretive validity, and theoretical validity. Descriptive validity refers to the factual accuracy of the account as reported by the qualitative researcher. Interpretive validity is obtained to the degree that the participants' viewpoints, thoughts, intentions, and experiences are accurately understood and reported by the qualitative researcher. Theoretical validity is obtained to the degree that a theory or theoretical explanation developed from a research study fits the data and is, therefore, credible and defensible. Internal validity and external validity are also important to qualitative research when the researcher is interested in making cause and effect statements and generalizing, respectively. Twelve strategies used to promote validity in qualitative research were discussed.

STUDY QUESTIONS

1. What is a confounding extraneous variable and what must be done to eliminate its confounding influence?
2. Define internal validity.
3. What type of evidence is needed for inferring causation?
4. List the various threats to internal validity.
5. Describe each of the threats to internal validity and give an illustration of each.
6. Define external validity.
7. List the threats to external validity and explain each one.
8. What is the difference between the target population and the experimentally accessible population?
9. What are the various steps that are involved in achieving population validity?
10. Describe the threats to ecology validity.
11. What is meant by operationism?
12. What is meant by researcher bias in qualitative research?
13. What is reflexivity and why is it used?
14. List the different types of validity in qualitative research and explain each one.
15. What is meant by methods and data triangulation?
16. Explain the role of external validity in qualitative research.

KEY TERMS

accessible population (201)

confounding variable (187)

data triangulation (213)

descriptive validity (209)

ecological validity (203)

experimenter effect (204)

extended fieldwork (211)

external validity (200)

extraneous variable (187)

history (193)

instrumentation (195)

interaction with selection (198)

internal validity (188)

interpretive validity (209)

investigator triangulation (209)

low-inference descriptors (210)

maturation (194)

methods triangulation (212)

mortality (198)

multigroup research design (192)

multiple operationalism (206)

multiple-treatment interference (203)

naturalistic generalization (214)

negative-case sampling (207)

one-group pretest-posttest design (192)

operationalism (205)

participant feedback (210)

pattern matching (211)

peer review (211)

population validity (200)

reactivity (204)

reflexivity (207)

replication logic (214)

researcher-as-detective (212)

researcher bias (207)

selection (197)

selection by history interaction (198)

selection by maturation interaction (198)

statistical regression (196)

target population (201)

temporal validity (204)

testing (194)

theoretical validity (210)

theory triangulation (211)

third variable (189)

ENDNOTES

1. Donald Campbell (1986) makes a similar point, and he uses the term *proximal similarity* to refer to the degree of similarity between the people and circumstances in the original research study and the people and circumstances to which you wish to apply the findings. Using Campbell's term, your goal is to check for proximal similarity.
2. The late Donald Campbell, perhaps the most important research methodologist over the past 50 years, approved of Yin's (1994) book. See, for example, his introduction to this book.

PART 4

SELECTING A RESEARCH METHOD

CHAPTER 8

Experimental Research

LEARNING OBJECTIVES

To be able to

- explain the way in which the educational experiment produces evidence of causality.
- describe the different ways an independent variable can be manipulated.
- explain the importance of control in experimental research and how control is achieved.
- explain the different ways of controlling the influence of potentially confounding variables.
- explain why some experimental research designs are weak designs and others are strong designs.
- compare and contrast factorial and repeated measures designs.
- explain the concept of interaction.

In this chapter we discuss the experimental approach to conducting research. The experimental research approach, as discussed in Chapter 1, is the research method designed to ferret out cause-and-effect relationships. Causal relationships can be identified when using the experimental research approach because it allows us to observe, under controlled conditions, the effect of systematically changing one or more variables. It is this ability that represents the primary advantage of the experimental approach because it permits greater control over confounding extraneous variables. The greater the degree of control, the greater the degree of internal validity of the study, and the greater our confidence in our claims about causality. However, the more control that is exerted over confounding extraneous variables, the more unnatural the study becomes, which threatens the external validity of the study. Experimental research, therefore, frequently sacrifices external validity for enhanced internal validity. In spite of this disadvantage, experimental research is a valuable methodology for the educational researcher.

THE EXPERIMENT

Experiment
An environment in which the researcher objectively observes phenomena that are made to occur in a strictly controlled situation in which one or more variables are varied and the others are kept constant

Experimental research is carried out within the context of an experiment. An **experiment** is defined as the development of an environment in which the researcher, typically called the experimenter, objectively observes "phenomena which are made to occur in strictly controlled situations in which one *or more* variables are varied and the others are kept constant" (Zimney, 1961, p. 18; italics ours). This seems to be one of the better definitions, so let's take a closer look at what the definition is saying. First, it is saying that we must attempt to make impartial and unbiased observations. As we discuss in Chapter 7, this is not always possible because experimenters can unintentionally influence the outcome of an experiment. However, we must realize that we are capable of some unintentional influence and strive to make observations that are free of this bias.

In conducting experiments we make observations of "phenomena that are made to occur." *Phenomena* refers to some observable event. In educational research this means that we observe events such as responses to an interview, test, questionnaire, or actions or statements made by the participants in an experimental research study. These phenomena are "made to occur" because we present a set of conditions to the research participant and record the effect of these conditions on their behavior. This is the way in which we ferret out cause-and-effect relationships through use of the experiment. We present a set of stimulus conditions—the independent variable—and then observe the effect of this independent variable presentation on the dependent variable.

The observations must be made in a strictly controlled situation. This means that we must eliminate the influence of confounding extraneous variables. As we discuss in Chapter 7, controlling for variables confounded with the independent variable is necessary to achieve internal validity.

The last component of the definition of experiment that needs to be examined is that "one or more variables are varied and the others are kept constant." This means that we deliberately vary the independent variable(s) along a defined range and attempt to make sure that all other variables do not vary. For example, if you want to test the effect of eating breakfast on the ability to solve math problems, you may want to vary the independent variable of breakfast by having a group of participants that eats breakfast and a group that does not eat breakfast. On the other hand, you may want to vary the type of breakfast that the participants eat. You may feed some participants a high-carbohydrate, low-protein breakfast and feed others a high-protein, low-carbohydrate breakfast. The point is that you must vary the independent variable in some way, but the nature of the variation you create will depend on your research question and hypothesis. Regardless of the type of variation produced, you must keep all variables other than the independent variable constant. In other words, you must make sure that variables other than the independent variable do not vary. This is in effect saying that when you conduct an experiment, you must create a set of conditions in which extraneous variables are controlled and not confounded with the independent variable.

INDEPENDENT VARIABLE MANIPULATION

The independent variable is the variable that is manipulated by the experimenter and presumed to cause a change in the dependent variable. In any given study there are many possible independent variables that can be used. The independent variable or variables used in a given study are specified by the research question(s). For example, one of the research questions Breznitz (1997) asked was, "Does accelerated reading among dyslexic children partially account for changes in their short-term memory processing?" Breznitz wanted to determine the effect that increasing reading speed has on short-term memory, so reading speed has to be the independent variable. This means that reading speed has to be varied in some way. Breznitz hypothesized that readers with dyslexia who engaged in fast-paced reading relative to self-paced reading would show significant performance gains in short-term memory. This hypothesis specifies the nature of the variation that has to be created in the independent variable. There have to be at least two levels of variation of the independent variable of reading speed; these two levels are fast-paced and self-paced reading. Although the research question may identify the independent variable, it is not always easy to create the needed variation. For example, Breznitz had to develop a procedure that would allow for the manipulation of reading speed, and in such a way that the experimenter could increase the speed of reading over that of the self-paced reading of the children with dyslexia.

From this brief discussion, you should be able to see that there are many decisions that must be made regarding the manipulation of the independent variable. You must identify the variable that will represent the independent variable, and then you must decide how to manipulate the independent variable to provide an answer to your research question.

Ways to Manipulate an Independent Variable

The research question, as we have just discussed, identifies the independent variable. However, it does not specify the way in which the independent variable is to be manipulated.

There are at least three different ways, illustrated in Figure 8.1, in which you can manipulate an independent variable. The first way is by a **presence or absence technique.** This technique is exactly what the name implies. One group of research participants receives a treatment condition and the other group does not. For example, assume that you want to determine whether a review session will improve the mathematics test grades of high school students taking algebra. You can manipulate the independent variable using the presence or absence technique by having one group of algebra students take an examination without the aid of a review session and the other group take the same examination after they have participated in a review session.

A second way in which you can manipulate the independent variable is by an **amount technique.** This technique involves administering different amounts of the independent variable to several groups of participants. For example, you may think that a review session not only helps improve the examination scores of students taking an algebra test, but that several review sessions during the week preceding the examination provide an additional benefit. This would essentially involve varying the amount of review the students receive. You could manipulate the amount of review by having one group of students take the alge-

Presence or absence technique Manipulating the independent variable by presenting one group the treatment condition and withholding it from the other group

Amount technique Manipulating the independent variable by giving the various comparison groups different amounts of the independent variable

(a) Presence versus absence technique

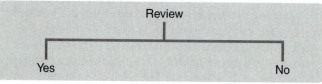

(b) Amount technique

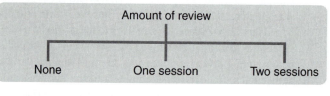

(c) Type technique

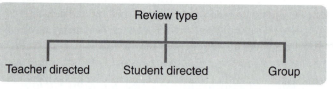

FIGURE 8.1   Three different ways of manipulating the independent variable.

bra examination without the aid of a review session. A second group would be given one review session, a third group would receive two review sessions, and a fourth group would receive three review sessions.

Type technique
Manipulating the independent variable by varying the type of variable presented to the different comparison groups

A third way of manipulating the independent variable is by a **type technique.** Using this technique involves varying the type of variable presented to the participants. For example, rather than vary the amount of review the participants received, you may think that the type of review is the important variable. You could, for example, have a teacher-directed review session, a student-directed review session, or a group review session. Once you have identified the types of review sessions you want to investigate, you would expose a different group of research participants to each type of review session prior to their taking the examination.

CONTROL OF CONFOUNDING VARIABLES

In Chapter 7 we discuss the importance of internal validity and controlling for the effect of confounding extraneous variables. We also discuss a number of the more obvious extraneous variables that can threaten the internal validity of an experiment. These are the types of extraneous variables that must be controlled within an experiment to enable us to reach causal conclusions. There are a number of ways in which confounding extraneous variables can be controlled. Before we discuss several of these control techniques, we want to briefly discuss the meaning of **experimental control.**

Experimental control
Eliminating any differential influence of extraneous variables

When you first consider controlling for potentially confounding extraneous variables, you probably think about totally eliminating the influence of these variables. For example, if noise is a potential confound in an experiment, you naturally consider controlling this potential confound by constructing an environment void of noise, perhaps by having the participants complete the experiment in a soundproof room. However, most variables that can influence the outcome of an educational experiment, such as intelligence, age, motivation, and stress, cannot be eliminated. Control of these variables comes through the elimination of any differential influence that they may have. **Differential influence** refers to influence that is different for different comparison groups of participants. For example, intelligence would have a differential influence if one comparison group was made up of bright individuals and the other comparison group was made up of individuals with average intelligence. We want to keep the influence of variables such as intelligence constant across the comparison groups, or equate the groups on such variables so that any difference noted on the dependent variable would be due to the manipulation of the independent variable. For example, Wade and Blier (1974), in their study of the effect of two methods of learning on the retention of a list of words, had to control for the association the participants had with these words because participants who had more association with the words would probably learn them faster and retain them longer. To control for association value, Wade and Blier selected words that had previously been shown to have the same average association value. In this way, they held the association value of the words constant across

Differential influence
When the influence of an extraneous variable is different for the various comparison groups

the two groups of participants and eliminated any differential influence this variable might have had.

As you can see from this example, control is frequently obtained by designing your study in such a way that the influence of the potential extraneous variables does not vary across the comparison groups. When constancy is obtained, the extraneous variable exerts an equal influence on the dependent variable across all comparison groups. When an equal influence in exerted, the effect of the extraneous variable on the dependent variable is the same for all comparison groups. Any difference noted on the dependent variable would, therefore, be attributable to the independent variable. Therefore, the influence of the extraneous variable would have been controlled. Control, as you can see, generally refers to achieving constancy. The question that must be answered is how to achieve this constancy. We now turn our attention to some of the more general techniques for achieving constancy of effect of potentially confounding variables.

Random Assignment

Random assignment A statistical control procedure that maximizes the probability that the comparison groups will be equated on all extraneous variables

Random assignment is a statistical control technique that maximizes the probability that potentially confounding extraneous variables, known and unknown, will not systematically bias the results of the study. Because random assignment has the ability to control for both known and unknown potentially confounding extraneous variables, it is a procedure that should be used whenever and wherever possible.

Ideally, in any research study you should select participants randomly from the population because this provides maximum assurance that a systematic bias does not exist in the selection process and that the selected participants are representative of the population. Remember that "representative" means that the sample participants have characteristics similar to that of the population and can, therefore, stand for the population. If the average IQ in the population is 110, then the average IQ in the sample should be about 110. The sample can say something about the population only when it is representative of the population.

Once participants have been randomly *selected* from the population, they should be randomly *assigned* to the various comparison groups, as illustrated in Figure 8.2. Although randomly selecting the sample of participants from the population and then randomly assigning the participants to the various comparison groups is the ideal arrangement, seldom is it possible to randomly select research participants from the population. Just think of the difficulty of randomly selecting a sample of high school English teachers from all English teachers within the United States. This would not only be difficult but next to impossible to do unless you had a large research grant that allowed you either to go to the high school in which they were teaching or pay to have them come to your university. Consequently, random selection of participants from the population is an ideal that is seldom achieved. Fortunately, random selection of participants is not the crucial element needed to achieve control over the influence of confounding variables in an experiment. Random assignment to the comparison groups provides maximum assurance that the extraneous variables are controlled because it makes the groups similar on all extraneous variables.

When research participants are randomly assigned to various comparison groups, as illustrated in Exhibit 8.1, each research participant has an equal probability of being as-

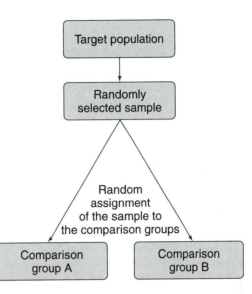

FIGURE 8.2   The ideal procedure for obtaining participants for an experiment.

signed to each group. This means that chance determines which person gets assigned to each comparison group. Remember that each person brings with him or her certain variables, such as intelligence. If we want to control for a variable such as intelligence, we want individuals with approximately the same intelligence level in each comparison group. This is exactly what random assignment does. When participants are randomly assigned, the variables they bring with them are also randomly assigned. The result is that variables such as intelligence are randomly assigned to the comparison groups when we randomly assign the participants. Therefore, the comparison groups are similar on these variables, and any differences that do exist will be due to chance. Random assignment, therefore, produces control by virtue of the fact that the variables to be controlled are distributed in approximately the same manner in all comparison groups. If the comparison groups are similar on the extraneous variables, the groups are expected to perform approximately the same on the dependent variable *when* the independent variable has no effect on the participants. If the participants respond differently on the dependent variable, this difference can be attributed to the independent variable.

Random assignment, as we point out in Chapter 1, is the most important technique to use to control potentially confounding extraneous variables. However, this does not mean that random assignment will always give us the needed control. It is possible that the comparison groups will not be similar even with random assignment because chance determines the way in which the variables are distributed. In most instances, particularly when you randomly assign a large number of individuals, the comparison groups will be similar. However, because chance determines which people are assigned to each comparison group, it is possible that the groups will not be similar. For example, it is possible that random assignment would result in the brightest individuals being assigned to one comparison group and individuals with average intelligence being assigned to another comparison group. The

---

EXHIBIT 8.1 Procedure for Randomly Assigning Participants to Comparison Groups

---

The most popular procedure for randomly assigning participants to comparison groups is to use a list of random numbers, such as the following list of 200 numbers. (Larger lists are contained in the appendixes of most statistics books.)

	1	2	3	4	5	6	7	8	9	10
1	8	1	4	5	5	6	9	8	7	3
2	2	7	9	6	5	4	6	4	8	3
3	0	0	0	5	5	8	9	7	6	9
4	7	8	3	4	7	0	7	7	5	2
5	8	5	8	6	3	5	4	2	2	2
6	7	3	5	3	6	8	0	7	3	3
7	1	8	6	0	1	0	7	4	4	7
8	7	9	5	3	0	1	5	5	5	1
9	5	6	6	7	8	5	8	1	1	9
10	3	0	3	3	9	1	9	9	1	9
11	9	7	4	7	8	4	7	1	0	9
12	5	6	4	5	1	4	5	4	1	1
13	5	7	4	0	4	2	5	9	6	7
14	8	6	0	5	6	9	4	4	3	2
15	6	7	6	7	3	3	7	1	8	9
16	2	6	0	6	7	3	3	0	6	9
17	6	7	5	5	1	4	7	4	1	2
18	6	3	0	9	9	9	5	3	8	0
19	0	3	7	3	0	3	0	6	8	6
20	7	1	6	8	2	0	5	3	2	1

This list consists of a series of twenty rows and ten columns. The number in each position is random because each of the numbers from 0 to 9 had an equal chance of occupying that position, and the selection of one number for a given position had no influence in the selection of another number for another position. Therefore, since each individual number is random, any combination of the numbers must be random.

Assume that you have fifteen participants in your sample and you want to randomly assign them to three comparison groups. First, you give each participant a number from 0 to 14. You then block the list of random numbers into columns of two to provide five pairs of columns since two columns are necessary to represent the total sample of participants.

Now you are ready to randomly assign the five participants to each of the three comparison groups.

The procedure usually followed is to randomly select the first five participants from the sample of fifteen and assign them to one comparison group. Then randomly select a second group of five participants from the sample of fifteen and assign them to another comparison group. Once these ten participants have been randomly selected and assigned, only five participants remain; these five participants are assigned to the third comparison group.

To randomly select the first participant for the first group, read down the first two columns until you encounter a number less than 15. From the list, we find that the first such number is 00. Consequently, the first randomly selected participant is the participant with the number 0. Proceed down the columns until you encounter the second number less than 15, which is 03. Participant number 3 represents the second randomly selected participant. Once you have reached the bottom of the first two columns, start at the top of the next two columns. With this procedure, the participant numbers 05, 06, and 09 are selected, which represent the remaining three of the first five randomly selected participants. Note that if you encounter a number that has already been selected (as we did with the number 05), you must disregard it.

To randomly select the second group of five participants, proceed down the columns and identify numbers less than 15 that have not already been chosen. Using this procedure, we find the numbers 10, 01, 14, 07, and 11. These numbers correspond to the second group of randomly selected participants. The third group represents the remaining participants.

We now have the following three randomly selected groups of participants.

00	01	02
03	07	04
05	10	08
06	11	12
09	14	13

Once each of the three groups has been randomly selected, they must be randomly assigned to one of the three experimental comparison groups.

This is accomplished by using only one column of the table of random numbers, since there are only three groups of participants. The three groups are numbered from 0 to 2. Proceed down the first column until you reach the first of these three numbers. In looking at column 1, you can see that the first number is 2. Consequently, group 2 (the third group of participants) is assigned to the first treatment condition and represents the first comparison group. The second number encountered is 0, so group 0 (the first group of participants) is assigned to the second treatment condition and represents the second comparison group. This means that group 1 (the second group of participants) is assigned to the third treatment condition and is the third comparison group. Now we have randomly assigned the sample of participants to three groups and have randomly assigned them to the three treatment or comparison conditions.

Treatment or Comparison Condition		
A_1	A_2	A_3
Group 2	Group 0	Group 1

smaller the number of research participants, the greater the risk that this will happen. However, random assignment minimizes the probability of this happening even with small samples. Since the probability of the groups' being equal is so much greater with than without random assignment, it is a very powerful method for generating similar groups and eliminating the threat of confounding variables. Because random assignment is the only method for controlling for the influence of unknown variables, it is necessary to randomize whenever and wherever possible, even when other control techniques are used.

Matching

Matching
Equating the comparison groups on one or more variables that are correlated with the dependent variable

Matching is a control technique for equating the comparison groups on one or more variables that are correlated with the dependent variable. The most commonly used matching procedure is to match participants in the various comparison groups on a case-by-case basis for each of the selected extraneous variables. For example, assume that you want to conduct an experiment testing the effectiveness of three different methods of instruction in algebra on algebra test performance. You know that variables such as IQ and gender are variables that probably affect test performance, so you want to control for the influence of these variables. One way to obtain the needed control is to match the participants in the three comparison groups so that each group contains individuals with about the same IQ and gender. In other words, if the first participant who volunteers for the study is a male with an IQ of 118, then we have to find two other males with IQs very close to 118. It would be very difficult to find individuals with exactly the same IQ, so the criterion is that the participants have to be very similar on the variables on which they are matched. Once you have identified three individuals who are similar on the matched variables, you randomly assign these three individuals to the three comparison groups. Note the use of random assignment even when we are using the control technique of matching. This follows the rule we stated earlier of randomizing whenever and wherever possible, even when other control techniques, such as matching, are used. Once these three individuals have been matched and randomly assigned, you would find another group of three individuals matched on IQ and gender and randomly assign them to the comparison groups. This procedure, as illustrated in Figure 8.3, is continued until you have the desired number of participants in each comparison group. The end result is that the participants in the comparison groups are identical or very similar on the matched variables. The influence of these variables on the dependent variable is, therefore, constant across the comparison groups. This is the desired type of control in an experiment.

Holding the Extraneous Variable Constant

Another frequently used technique is to hold the extraneous variable to be controlled constant across the comparison groups. This means that the participants in each comparison group will have approximately the same amount or type of the extraneous variable. For example, assume you want to test the efficacy of using ebonics in teaching reading. This approach was developed for use with African American individuals, so you would probably want to eliminate the extraneous variable of including other ethnic groups in the study by including only African American students. The extraneous variable of ethnic group would be controlled by holding the ethnic background of the research participants constant across

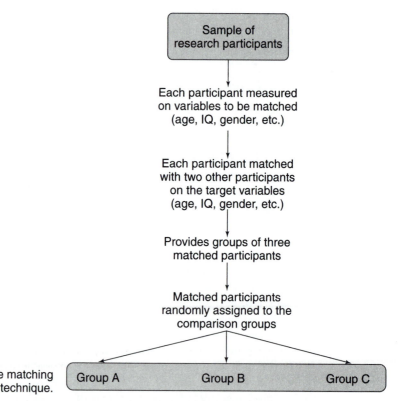

FIGURE 8.3   The matching control technique.

the comparison groups. After selecting a sample of only African American students, you should include the control technique of randomly assigning these students to the comparison groups, as illustrated in Figure 8.4. Again, this follows the principle of randomly assigning whenever and wherever possible.

Building the Extraneous Variable into the Research Design

Extraneous variables can be controlled by building them into the research design. When this is done, the extraneous variable becomes another independent variable. For example, in the hypothetical study investigating the use of ebonics in teaching reading to African American children, you want to control for the effects of intelligence. It would not make much sense to use the control technique of holding intelligence constant and include only individuals with IQs of a given range such as 105–110. It seems more appropriate to include individuals with a wider spectrum of intelligence levels. One way to accomplish this goal, and at the same time control for the extraneous variable of intelligence, is to select individuals with several IQ levels, such as 90–99, 100–109, and 110–119, and treat these IQ levels as an independent variable, as illustrated in Figure 8.5.

Although building the extraneous variable into the research design is an excellent technique for achieving control, it is recommended only if you are interested in the differences produced by the various levels of the extraneous variable. In the hypothetical ebonics study, you may be interested in seeing whether the efficacy of teaching reading using this method is more effective with individuals of different intellectual levels. In this case this control technique is excellent because it identifies the effect produced by the extraneous variable while, at the same time, controlling for its influence on the other independent

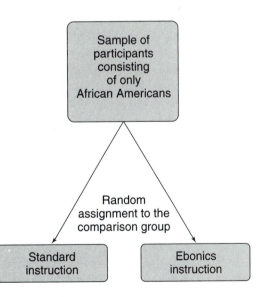

FIGURE 8.4   Control exercised by holding the extraneous variable constant.

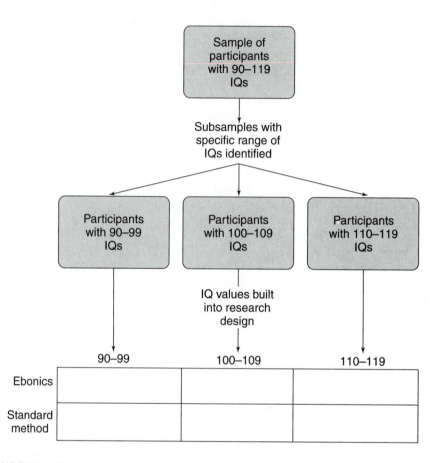

FIGURE 8.5   Control of an extraneous variable by building it into the research design.

Counterbalancing
Administering the experimental treatment conditions to all comparison groups, but in a different order

Sequencing effects
Biasing effects that can occur when each participant must participate in each experimental treatment condition

Order effect
A sequencing effect that occurs from the order in which the treatment conditions are administered

variable of interest. In other words, it takes an extraneous variable that could bias the experiment and makes it focal in the experiment as an independent variable.

Counterbalancing

Counterbalancing refers to administering the experimental treatments to all comparison groups, but in a different order. It is a technique used to control for **sequencing effects,** which are effects that can occur when the design of an experiment requires each participant to participate in each of several experimental comparison groups, as illustrated in Figure 8.6. This control technique is sometimes called *using the participants as their own control.* Two types of sequencing effects can occur when every person participates in each comparison group. The first is an **order effect,** which arises from the order in which the treatment conditions are administered. Supposed you are interested in the effect of caffeine on learn-

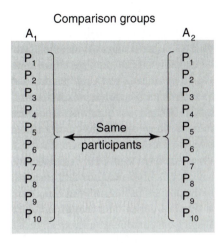

FIGURE 8.6 Type of design that may include sequencing effects.

ing to spell based on the fact that caffeine is assumed to increase attention and alertness. To test the effect of caffeine, you could administer caffeine on one day and a placebo on another day. This means that the research participants would get one of two possible orders of the treatment conditions: caffeine on the first day and placebo on the second day or placebo on the first day and caffeine on the second day.

In a study such as this, on the first experimental day the research participants may be unfamiliar with the experimental procedure, participating in an educational experiment, or the surroundings of the experiment. If they are administered the placebo condition on the first day, the participants might not perform effectively because their attention will not be focused totally on the spelling task. On the second day, when they are administered caffeine, this familiarity will exist, increasing the chances that the participant can focus more on the spelling task, which could enhance performance. The result is that the participants may perform better under the caffeine treatment condition administered on the second day not because it is any more effective, but because the participants are more familiar with the experiment and the experimental surroundings and can focus more attention on learning the list of spelling words. This type of effect is an order effect because it occurs strictly due to the order of presentation of the experimental treatment conditions.

Carryover effect
A sequencing effect that occurs when performance in one treatment condition is influenced by participation in a prior treatment condition(s)

The second type of sequencing effect that can occur is a carryover effect. A **carryover effect** occurs when performance in one treatment condition is partially dependent on the conditions that precede it. For example, if in the caffeine experiment caffeine was administered on the first day, it is possible that the caffeine was not completely metabolized and cleared from the body before the participants consumed the placebo on the next day. Any effect of the prior day's dose of caffeine would therefore carry over to the next day and affect performance. Therefore the performance on the day that participants consumed the placebo would be any placebo effect plus any carryover from the prior day's consumption of caffeine. This carryover effect was labeled a multiple-treatment effect in Chapter 7.

One of the ways of controlling for the carryover and order effects is to counterbalance the order in which the treatment conditions are administered to the participants. Basically, counterbalancing involves administering each experimental treatment condition to all groups of research participants but in a different order. For example, in the caffeine experiment, assume we wanted to test the effect of three different doses of caffeine (100, 200, and 300 mg of caffeine) against no caffeine or a placebo group. One way of counterbalancing would be to have groups of participants equal to the number of levels of the independent variable. In this caffeine experiment there are four levels of caffeine ranging from no caffeine to 300 mg, so there would be four experimental groups. Each group would receive the four treatment conditions but in a different order, as follows:

Group 1—placebo, 100 mg, 300 mg, 200 mg
Group 2—100 mg, 200 mg, placebo, 300 mg
Group 3—200 mg, 300 mg, 100 mg, placebo
Group 4—300 mg, placebo, 200 mg, 100 mg

This establishes the different counterbalanced orders. The important point to remember is that each group of participants takes each experimental treatment condition, so, in effect, the study is replicated as many times as there are groups of participants.

Analysis of Covariance

Analysis of covariance
A statistical method that can be used to statistically equate groups that differ on a pretest or some other variable

Analysis of covariance is a statistical method that can be used to equate groups that are found to differ on a pretest or some other variable or variables. It is useful when the participants in the various comparison groups differ on a pretest variable that is related to the dependent variable. If the pretest variable is related to the dependent variable, differences can be observed in the dependent variable that are due to the differences on the pretest variable. Analysis of covariance adjusts the scores on the dependent variable for the differences observed on the pretest variable and in this way statistically equates the participants in the various comparison groups. For example, if you are conducting a study on gender differences in solving mathematics problems, you will want to make sure that the male and female students are of equal ability level. If you measure the IQ of the participants and find that the male students are brighter than the female students, the mathematics performance could be due to this difference in ability and not anything related to gender. You could use analysis of covariance to adjust the mathematics scores for this difference in intelligence and in this way create two groups of participants that are equated, at least on this variable.

As you can see, analysis of covariance can be used to equate groups of participants on known variables that have been measured by the experimenter. However, as Glass and Hopkins (1984) point out, analysis of covariance is not a substitute for random assignment. Calculation of analysis of covariance is a rather complex statistical procedure that is beyond the scope of this book. The primary thing we want you to know is that this statistical procedure can be used to control for a measured variable or variables correlated with the dependent variable on which participants in the various comparison groups differ at the outset of an experiment.

EXPERIMENTAL RESEARCH DESIGNS

Research design
The outline, plan, or strategy used to answer a research question

Research design refers to the outline, plan, or strategy you are going to use to seek an answer to your research question(s). In other words, when you get to the stage of designing your experiment, you have to identify the plan or strategy to be used in collecting the data that will adequately test your hypotheses. Planning a research design means that you must specify how the participants are to be assigned to the comparison groups, how you are going to control for potentially confounding extraneous variables, and how you are going to collect and analyze the data.

There are many different research designs that can be developed for testing hypotheses. Some research designs are more effective than others at testing hypotheses because they differ in the extent to which they control for the effects of potentially confounding variables. In some instances there are practical constraints on the type of research design that can be developed, and these constraints can frequently limit the ability to control for potential confounds and, therefore, to adequately test the hypotheses. For example, it is always desirable to randomly assign participants to comparison groups. However, in a particular study we may have to use, as the comparison groups, previously formed classes of fifth-grade students. In terms of controlling for the effects of potential confounds, it would be best if we could randomly assign the students to the different fifth-grade classes. However, this is frequently not possible, which means that you have eliminated the ability to use a very important control technique. This does not mean that you should not do the study. Rather, it means that you must design the study so that it controls for the effect of as many potentially confounding variables as possible.

How do you go about designing an experiment that will test your hypotheses and provide an answer to your research questions? This is no simple task, and there is no set way to tell others how to do it. Designing a research study requires thought about the components to include and pitfalls to avoid. However, it helps to have some knowledge of the general types of research designs that can be used. Some of these research designs are weak in the sense that they do not provide for maximum control of potentially confounding variables. Others are strong in that they provide for the maximum control of potentially confounding variables. We will first discuss the weak designs and point out their deficiencies. We then discuss stronger experimental designs that represent ones that you should model when designing your research study.

Weak Experimental Research Designs

We present three experimental research designs that are designated weak designs because they do not control for many potentially confounding extraneous variables. Remember that in an experimental research study, we want to identify the effect produced by the independent variable. Any uncontrolled confounding variables threaten our ability to do this and can render the experiment useless in the worst case and, in the best of circumstances, jeopardize our ability to reach a valid conclusion. This is not to say that these weak experimental designs do not provide any valuable information. They can provide some useful

TABLE 8.1   Summary of the Threats to Internal Validity of Weak Experimental Designs

Designs	History	Maturation	Testing	Instrumentation	Regression	Selection	Mortality	Selection Interaction
One-group posttest-only design	–	–	NA	NA	NA	NA	–	NA
One-group pretest-posttest design	–	–	–	–	–	NA	NA	NA
Static-group comparison design	+	?	+	+	+	–	–	–

A negative sign (–) indicates a potential threat to internal validity; a positive sign (+) indicates that the threat is controlled; a question mark (?) indicates that the threat may or may not be controlled depending on the characteristics of the study; and NA indicates that the threat does not apply to that design.

information. However, whenever a researcher uses one of them, he or she must be alert to the influence of potentially confounding extraneous variables that can threaten the internal validity of the study. Table 8.1 provides a summary of some of the threats to internal validity that may operate in each of these three designs.

One-group posttest-only design
Administering a posttest to a single group of participants after they have been given an experimental treatment condition

One-Group Posttest-Only Design   In the **one-group posttest-only design,**[1] a single group of research participants is exposed to an experimental treatment and then measured on the dependent variable to assess the effect of the treatment condition, as illustrated in Figure 8.7. This design might be used if a school system wanted to find out whether implementation of a new reading program enhances students' desire to read. After implementation of the program for an entire school year, a survey is given to all students in the program to assess their attitude toward reading. If the results indicate that the students' attitude is positive, the program is assumed to engender a positive attitude toward reading.

The problem with reaching such a conclusion is that you cannot attribute the students' attitudes toward reading to the new reading program. It is possible that the students had a positive attitude toward reading prior to participating in the program and that the program actually had no impact on their attitude toward reading. The important point is that it is impossible to determine whether the new reading program had any effect or what that effect was without some sort of comparison. Because the students were not pretested, the re-

FIGURE 8.7   One-group posttest-only design.

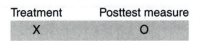

searcher does not know anything about what the students were like prior to implementation of the reading program. From a scientific point of view, this design is of almost no value because, without pretesting or comparing the students in the program to students who did not participate in the reading program, it is impossible to determine whether the treatment produced any effect. Even if it did produce an effect, it is impossible to determine whether that effect was caused by the treatment program or by some extraneous variable such as history, maturation, or statistical regression.

One-Group Pretest-Posttest Design   Most individuals quickly recognize that the one-group posttest-only design is ineffective because of the lack of some type of comparison. The first response in many instances is to state that a pretest is needed to be able to compare the pretreatment response with the posttreatment response. This design, illustrated in Figure 8.8, is an improvement over the one-group posttest-only design and is typically called the **one-group pretest-posttest design.** A group of research participants is measured on the dependent variable, O, prior to administration of the treatment condition. The independent variable, X, is then administered, and the dependent variable, O, is again measured. The difference between the pre- and posttest scores is taken as an index of the effectiveness of the treatment condition.

> *One-group pretest-posttest design* Administering a posttest to a single group of participants after they have been pretested and given an experimental treatment condition

Although the one-group pretest-posttest design does represent an improvement over the one-group posttest-only design, any change in the posttest scores over the pretest scores cannot automatically be taken as an index of an effect produced by the independent variable. Many potentially confounding extraneous variables, such as history, maturation, instrumentation, selection, and statistical regression, can influence the posttest results. To the extent that they do, these extraneous variables represent rival hypotheses explaining any difference between the pre- and posttest scores.

To illustrate the way in which these potential rival hypotheses can operate when using this design, consider a hypothetical study in which an educational researcher wants to test a new instructional program for teaching reading to slow learners in the fifth grade. At the beginning of the school year, slow learners are identified by administering the Metropolitan Achievement Tests to all fifth-grade students in the New Approach elementary school. Those fifth-grade students who score at least two years below the fifth-grade level (pre-O) are considered slow learners and placed in an experimental classroom where the new reading instructional program is administered. At the end of two years the Metropolitan Achievement Tests are again administered and the reading grade placement score received by the students at this time (post-O) is compared with their pre-O score. Now let's assume that this comparison indicates that the slow learners have improved an average of 2.2 years in reading grade placement, indicating that the students made nice advancement

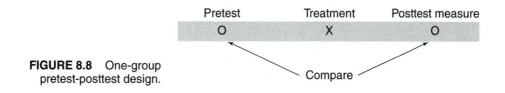

FIGURE 8.8   One-group pretest-posttest design.

during the two years that they were in the experimental classroom. It is tempting to attribute this improvement to the experimental reading program. However, if you think about it for a moment, you can probably identify several rival hypotheses that could have accounted for this change in performance.

History is a very real possibility. The students were placed in an experimental classroom, which means that they were singled out and given special attention. The special effort made by the school system may have motivated the parents of these children to encourage them to read and perform their homework assignments. This parental encouragement could have enhanced the students' reading performance in addition to the experimental program. Similarly, two years elapsed between the pre- and posttest assessments. The students were two years older and maturation would predict that some of the improvement would occur just because the students were older and thus had matured during the intervening two years. A testing effect could exist because the students took the Metropolitan Achievement Tests during pre- and posttesting, which means that the tests may have been more familiar on the second testing occasion. However, a testing effect would be more likely if a shorter time lapse had occurred between the pre- and posttesting. Finally, statistical regression is a very real possibility because the students selected for the experimental classroom were those who scored lowest on the initial pretest. Statistical regression would predict that some of these students would improve on posttesting because their low scores on the pretest were in part due to chance factors.

As you can see, the one-group pretest-posttest design is problematic in that many potentially confounding extraneous variables, in addition to the independent variable, can reasonably account for any change in behavior, making it a weak design. Although the one-group pretest-posttest design is weak, it does provide some information in that it lets you know if a change occurred between pre- and posttesting. However, it does not provide a reasonable explanation of the cause of this change because of the many threats that could also account for the behavioral change. When using this design, you should always be cautious about interpreting any effect as being due to the independent variable and constantly seek evidence that would rule out the existence of threats to the internal validity of the design.

Static-group comparison design
Comparing posttest performance of a group of participants who have been given an experimental treatment condition with a group that has not been given the experimental treatment condition

The Static-Group Comparison Design   The **static-group comparison design** is a design in which one group of research participants is administered a treatment and is then compared, on the dependent variable, with another group of research participants who did not receive the experimental treatment, as illustrated in Figure 8.9. The dashed line in Figure 8.9 indicates that intact or nonrandomly assigned groups are formed; X_1 indicates the experimental treatment condition; and X_2 indicates the control comparison condition. For example, if you want to determine whether including a computer-assisted drill and practice lab enhances learning and performance of students taking an educational statistics course, you might have one class take the statistics course without the computer laboratory (X_2) and the another class take statistics with the computer laboratory (X_1). Both classes would be taught by the same instructor, so there would not be an effect of different instructors. At the end of the course you would compare the two classes in terms of their statistics performance (O). If the class that includes the computer laboratory performs better than the class that does not have computer laboratory practice, this should indicate that the addition of the

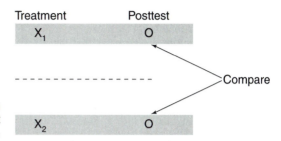

Treatment   Posttest

X_1 O

Compare

- - - - - - - - - - - - - - - - -

X_2 O

FIGURE 8.9   The static-group comparison design, where X_1 = experimental treatment and X_2 = control or standard treatment.

computer laboratory enhanced statistics performance. Unfortunately, this may not be true because there are some potentially confounding extraneous variables that can creep into this design and threaten its internal validity.

The static-group comparison design may seem to be adequate on the surface because a comparison group is included that provides for a comparison of the performance of participants who were and were not exposed to the computer laboratory. Additionally, the same instructor taught the two courses so there should be little difference in instructional quality. Why, then, is the design included as an example of a weak design? The reason is that the two classes of research participants were not equated on variables other than the independent variable. The two classes were formed based on the students that signed up for them at the two times offered and were not randomly assigned to the comparison groups, as the dashed line in Figure 8.9 illustrates. This could have resulted in having students in the two classes who were very different on many variables other than the presentation of the independent variable. For example, the students taking the course that included the computer laboratory may have been brighter, or older and more motivated to do well, than the students in the comparison group that did not have exposure to the computer laboratory. Either or both differences could have contributed to the final outcome and serve as rival hypotheses explaining the outcome.

To achieve maximum assurance that two or more comparison groups are equated, participants must be randomly assigned. There are, however, times when intact groups are the only groups available. In this instance the static-group comparison design may be the only type of design that can be used so you must be aware of the threats that exist to internal validity. Because a comparison group is included, threats such as history and instrumentation are probably controlled, and maturation may be. However, given that the two groups may not be equivalent, one group may be maturing faster than the other. Mortality could also influence the dependent variable and represent a possible threat to internal validity.

Strong Experimental Research Designs

The designs just presented are considered weak because they do not provide a way of isolating the effect of the independent variable from the influence of potentially confounding variables. A strong experimental research design is one in which the influence of confounding extraneous variables has been controlled. Table 8.2 summarizes the threats to internal validity that are controlled by the strong experimental designs. A strong experimental

TABLE 8.2   Summary of the Threats to Internal Validity That Are Controlled by the Strong Experimental Designs

Designs	History	Maturation	Testing	Instrumentation	Regression	Selection	Mortality	Selection Interaction	Sequencing
Pretest-posttest control-group design	+	+	+	+	+	+	?	+	NA
Posttest-only control-group design	+	+	+	+	+	+	?	+	NA
Factorial design	+	+	+	+	+	+	?	+	NA
Repeated-measures design*	?	?	?	?	?	NA	?	NA	?
Factorial design based on a mixed model	+	+	+	+	+	+	?	+	?

A positive sign (+) indicates that the threat is controlled; a question mark (?) indicates that the threat may or may not be controlled depending on the characteristics and control techniques included in the study; and NA indicates that the threat does not apply to that design.

*With counterbalancing, this design controls for all applicable threats except possibly mortality.

research design, therefore, is one that has internal validity. In most experimental research designs, the most effective way to achieve internal validity and eliminate rival hypotheses is to include one or more of the control techniques discussed earlier in this chapter and to include a control group.

Of the many control techniques available to the researcher, random assignment is the most important, and its importance cannot be overemphasized because it is the only means by which unknown variables can be controlled. Also, statistical reasoning is dependent on the randomization process, so we emphasize again, *randomize whenever and wherever possible.*

Control of confounding extraneous variables is also achieved by including a control group. In all strong experimental research designs, there are at least two comparison groups: an experimental group and a control group. The **experimental group,** as you might expect, is the group that receives the experimental treatment condition. The **control group** is the group that does not receive the experimental treatment condition. This might mean that nothing was done to the control group or that the control group got what might be viewed as a standard or typical condition. If you were investigating the efficacy of a new method of teaching reading, the experimental group would be exposed to the new reading method and the control group would be exposed to the typical or standard way of teaching reading. If you were testing a new drug on children with ADHD based on the hypothesis that it would reduce their level of ADHD and permit them to learn more effectively, the ex-

Experimental group
The group that receives the experimental treatment condition

Control group
The group that does not receive the experimental treatment condition

perimental group would receive the drug and the control group would receive either a placebo or the standard or commonly administered drug for treating ADHD. In this type of study you might even have three groups, a group that received the placebo, another that received the standard drug, and a third that received the experimental drug.

A control group is necessary because of the functions it serves. First, it serves as a comparison. To determine whether some treatment condition or independent variable had an effect, we must have a comparison or control group, assuming, of course, that all confounding extraneous variables are controlled. Consider a situation in which Tom, a student in your classroom, is repeatedly talking to other students seated around him. This is not only disruptive to these children but also to others in the classroom. To control this behavior you keep Tom in during recess and also move him to another area in the classroom. To your delight, this stops Tom from talking to others around him and allows you to continue teaching without this disruption. You attribute Tom's change in behavior to having kept him inside during recess. However, you also changed Tom's seating location, and it may be that he previously was seated around friends, which promoted his talking to them. When you moved him to another location in the classroom, you may have placed him in a spot where he was surrounded by people he knew but were not his friends, so a rival hypothesis is that the talking was prompted by his being surrounded by friends. To determine whether keeping him in during recess or being moved to another location was the factor in producing the change in behavior, a control student who would be moved to another location in the classroom but not be kept in during recess would have to be included. If both students changed their behavior and stopped talking to others around them, we would know that being kept in during recess was probably not the variable causing the elimination of talking behavior.

This hypothetical example also demonstrates that a control group serves to control for rival hypotheses. All variables operating on the control and experimental groups must be identical except for the independent variable manipulated by the experimenter. The change in location in the classroom variable was held constant across the student who was and the student who was not allowed to go out during recess and therefore did not confound the results. You must realize, however, that a control group can control for rival hypotheses only if the participants in the control and experimental groups are similar. If this condition does not exist, the control group cannot stand for the responses that members of the experimental group would have given if they did not receive the experimental treatment condition. The participants in the two groups must be as similar as possible so that theoretically they would yield identical scores in the absence of the introduction of the independent variable.

Pretest-posttest control-group design
A research design that administers a posttest to two randomly assigned groups of participants after both have been pretested and one of the groups has been administered the experimental treatment condition

Pretest-Posttest Control-Group Design   The **pretest-posttest control-group design,** as illustrated in Figure 8.10, is a design in which a group of research participants is randomly assigned to an experimental and control group and then pretested on the dependent variable, O. The independent variable, X, is then administered to the experimental group, and the experimental and control groups are posttested on the dependent variable, O. The pretest and posttest data can be analyzed using difference scores, analysis of covariance, or analysis of variance based on a mixed model to determine whether the independent variable produced an effect. The method that was used in the past was to compute a pre- to posttest difference score for both the experimental and control groups and then statistically compare

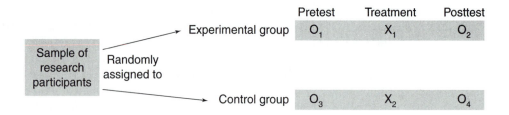

FIGURE 8.10   Pretest-posttest control-group design. X_1 and X_2 represent the two levels of the independent variable. O_1 to O_4 represent the pretest and posttest assessment of the dependent variable.

the difference scores to determine whether the experimental group's difference score is significantly different from the control group's difference score. This method has been criticized (e.g., Cronbach & Furby, 1970) as being inappropriate because such difference scores have low reliability. Although this view is not supported by all investigators (e.g., Rogosa, 1988), Cook and Campbell (1979) contend that the use of difference scores is less precise than either analysis of covariance or analysis of variance based on a mixed model (we will discuss this briefly later in this chapter). At the present time either of these latter two methods of analysis is the preferred method.

Figure 8.10 reveals that the pretest-posttest control-group design is a two-group design containing one control and one experimental group. However, this design could, and frequently is, expanded to include more than one experimental group, as illustrated in Figure 8.11. For example, if you want to determine which of three different ways of teaching reading was most effective, the standard way or two new, recently introduced ways, you would randomly assign the participants to three different groups and then pretest each prior to administering the different reading programs. After the reading programs have been administered, the participants are posttested and the data analyzed by one of the appropriate statistical techniques, such as analysis of covariance, to determine whether the different reading programs produced different results.

The pretest-posttest control-group design is an excellent experimental design because it does an excellent job of controlling for rival hypotheses that would threaten the internal validity of the experiment. History and maturation are controlled because any history event or maturation effect that occurred in the experimental group would also occur in the control group unless the history event affected only one of the two groups. In this case the history event would not be controlled because it would not have affected both groups. Instrumentation and testing are controlled because both the experimental and control groups were exposed to the pretest, so any effect of the pretest should exist in both groups. Regression and selection variables are controlled because participants were randomly assigned to the experimental and control groups. Random assignment provides maximum assurance that the two groups are equated at the outset of experiment. Although random assignment does not provide 100 percent assurance of initial equality of the experimental and control groups, it is the technique that provides the best assurance and, therefore, the technique that provides the best control for potential biases such as regression and selection.

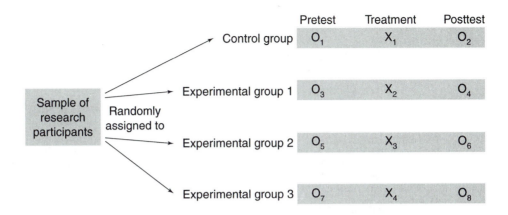

FIGURE 8.11   Pretest-posttest control-group design with more than one experimental group.

Now that we have discussed the pretest-posttest control group design, go back and look at the one-group pretest-posttest design. In comparing these two designs, you should be able to see that the one-group pretest-posttest design is essentially the equivalent of the experimental group in the pretest-posttest control-group design. The one-group pretest-posttest design was fraught with numerous extraneous variables that threatened the internal validity of this design. The pretest-posttest control-group design controls for these potential threats to internal validity by including two features, a control group and random assignment of participants to the experimental and control groups. This should provide some very convincing evidence of the value and necessity of incorporating random assignment and inclusion of a control group in experimental research designs.

Posttest-only control-group design
Administering a posttest to two randomly assigned groups of participants after one group has been administered the experimental treatment condition

Posttest-Only Control-Group Design   The **posttest-only control-group design,** illustrated in Figure 8.12, is an experimental design in which the research participants are randomly assigned to an experimental and a control group. The independent variable is administered to the experimental group and then the experimental and control groups are measured on the dependent variable. The posttest scores of the experimental and control groups are statistically compared to determine whether the independent variable produced an effect.

This is an excellent experimental design because of the control it provides to the threats to internal validity. Because the posttest-only control-group design includes a control group and randomly assigned participants to the experimental and control group, it controls for all potential threats to internal validity in the same way as the pretest-posttest control-group design did. Neither group, however, provides an effective control for mortality because this potential threat involves the differential loss of participants from the two comparison groups. If one group loses participants with characteristics that are different from those that are lost in the other comparison group, a difference could be found on post-testing because the differential loss produced two groups of participants who are no longer equivalent on all variables other than the independent variable. Because the pretest-posttest

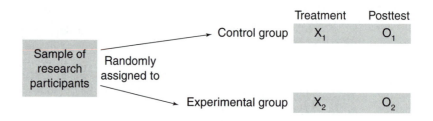

FIGURE 8.12 Posttest-only control-group design.

control-group design includes a pretest, it is possible to compare the control and experimental group participants who dropped out on this variable. If no difference existed, some basis would exist to argue that the mortality did not produce an inequality of the comparison groups. However, this argument is based only on a comparison of the pretest and not on other unknown variables that may also represent a confound. The bottom line is that there is no effective control for the potential threat that differential mortality can produce.

The two-group posttest-only control-group design presented in Figure 8.12 is only one variation of this design. There are many times when more than two groups are needed for comparison in a study; then the posttest-only control-group design can be expanded to include as many comparison groups as are needed. The same structure is maintained in that participants are randomly assigned to groups. After the experimental treatment is administered, the participants are posttested and compared, using analysis of variance, to determine whether a difference exists among the groups, as illustrated in Figure 8.13.

Factorial Designs

Factorial design
A design in which two or more independent variables are simultaneously studied to determine their independent and interactive effects on the dependent variable

A **factorial design** is one in which two or more independent variables are simultaneously studied to determine their independent and interactive effects on the dependent variable. The experimental designs we have discussed up to this point have all been limited to investigating only one independent variable. For example, assume you want to identify the most effective way of teaching mathematics and have identified four different types of instruction: computer-assisted, lecture, discussion, and programmed text. In designing this study you have one independent variable—method of instruction—and four different levels of that independent variable—the four types of instruction. Because there is only one independent variable, either the pretest-posttest control-group design or the posttest-only control-group design could be used. The design selected would depend on whether a pretest was included. In educational research we are often interested in the effect of several variables acting in concert. Most variables of significance to educators do not act independently. For example, one type of instruction may be more effective for large classes and another type for small classes. Similarly, a student's anxiety level may hinder effective performance when using a discussion format, whereas a computer-assisted format may allow the student to relax and perform better. This is where factorial designs come in because they allow us to investigate simultaneously several independent variables and the interaction between them.

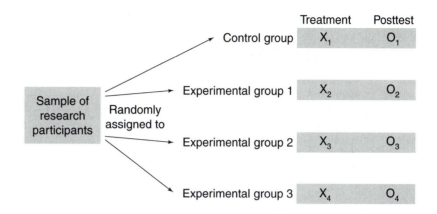

FIGURE 8.13   Posttest-only control-group design with more than one experimental group.

If you are interested in investigating the effect of anxiety level and type of instruction on teaching of mathematics, you are obviously investigating two independent variables. Let's further assume that you want to investigate the effect of two levels of anxiety—high and low—and four types of instruction—computer-assisted, lecture, discussion, and programmed-text. This means that you have two independent variables: anxiety level and type of instruction. The anxiety variable has two levels of variation—high and low—and the type of instruction variable has four levels of variation corresponding to the four different types of instruction. Figure 8.14 depicts this design, which reveals that there are eight combinations of the two independent variables: high anxiety and computer-assisted instruction, low anxiety and computer-assisted instruction, high anxiety and lecture, low anxiety and lecture, high anxiety and discussion, low anxiety and discussion, high anxiety and programmed text, and low anxiety and programmed text.

Each of these independent variable combinations is referred to as a **cell,** which means that there are eight cells to which research participants are randomly assigned. The participants randomly assigned to a given cell would receive the combination of independent variables corresponding to that cell. After the research participants have received their appropriate combination of independent variables and responded to the dependent variable, their dependent variable responses would be analyzed to identify two types of effects: main effects and interaction effects. A **main effect** refers to the influence of an independent variable. The design depicted in Figure 8.14 has two main effects: anxiety level and type of instruction. Statistical analysis of the main effect of anxiety level tells us whether anxiety level had a statistically significant influence on performance in mathematics or whether there was a statistically significant difference in performance depending on whether a person experienced high or low anxiety. The main effect of type of instruction tells us whether the method of providing mathematics instruction influenced performance or whether there was a statistically significant difference in performance depending on the type of mathematics instruction the research participants received.

A factorial design also allows us to investigate interaction effects. An **interaction effect** exists when the effect of one independent variable depends on the level of another

Cell
A combination of two or more independent variables in a factorial design

Main effect
The effect of one independent variable

Interaction effect
When the effect of one independent variable depends on the level of another independent variable

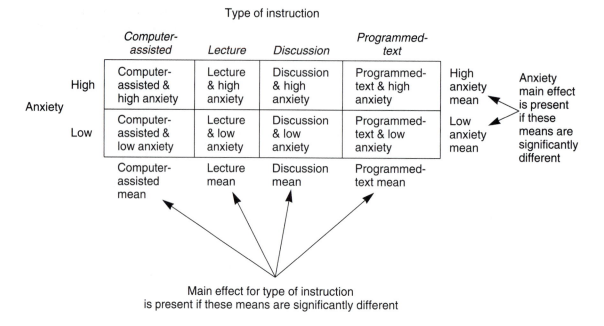

FIGURE 8.14   Factorial design with two independent variables.

independent variable. The concept of interaction is rather difficult for most students to grasp, so we will spend some time on this issue. First, we demonstrate an outcome in which the two main effects of anxiety level and type of instruction are present, but the interaction is not. Look at Figure 8.15(a). The scores in the cells represent the mean, or average, posttest score for each group of participants (e.g., the high-anxiety participants who received computer-assisted instruction had a mean score of 10). The hypothetical posttest scores represent the mean dependent variable score, such as number of mathematics problems correctly answered. The marginal row and column means outside the cells represent the mean posttest scores across the cells (e.g., the mean score of 17.5 for the high-anxiety participants is the average of the scores in the four cells of the high-anxiety participants). In this example, the mean score for the high-anxiety individuals is 17.5 and the mean score for the low-anxiety participants is 27.5, indicating that there is a main effect of participant anxiety level on performance. Similarly, there is a difference between the mean scores of individuals given different types of instruction, indicating that there is an instructional main effect that also influences performance. The difference in the mean mathematics performance scores of high- and low-anxiety individuals indicates that individuals with low anxiety performed better than individuals with high anxiety. The difference in the mean mathematics performance scores of individuals receiving the different types of instruction indicates that individuals receiving the computer-assisted instruction performed the worst and those receiving the programmed-text instruction performed the best.

Now look at Figure 8.15(b), which graphically illustrates the main effect for both independent variables. Particularly take note of the fact that <u>the two lines are parallel</u>. Whenever this happens, an interaction cannot exist, because an interaction means that the effect of one variable, such as anxiety level, depends on the level of the other variable being considered, such as the four different types of instruction, and this would produce nonparallel lines. In this example, individuals with low anxiety levels were always better than those

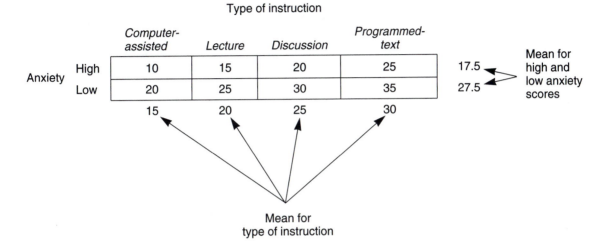

FIGURE 8.15(a)   Tabular representation of data showing significant main effect for both independent variables but not the interaction.

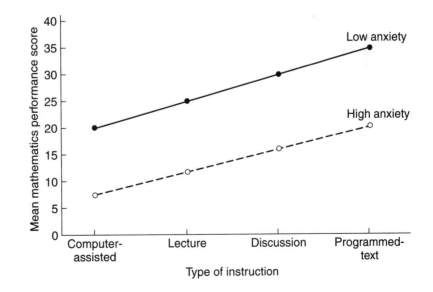

FIGURE 8.15(b)   Graphic illustration of a significant main effect for both independent variables.

with high anxiety levels regardless of the type of instruction received, indicating an anxiety main effect. Similarly, programmed-text instruction resulted in the best performance regardless of the participants' anxiety level, again indicating a main effect but no interaction effect.

Let us now look at an interaction effect. If you look at Figure 8.15(c), you will see that there is no difference between the marginal mean scores of individuals with different anxiety levels or with individuals receiving different types of instruction, indicating that these two main effects did not influence mathematics performance. However, if you look at the scores in the cells, you can see that high-anxiety participants received the highest scores when receiving computer-assisted instruction and the lowest scores when receiving programmed-text instruction. Low-anxiety participants, on the other hand, got the lowest scores under computer-assisted instruction and the highest scores when receiving programmed-text instruction. In other words, the effect of type of instruction depended on the participants' anxiety level, or an interaction existed between type of instruction and participant anxiety level. If you look at Figure 8.15(d), you will see that the lines for high- and low-anxiety individuals cross. Whenever the lines cross like this, you have an interaction effect. Performance increases under low anxiety levels and decreases under high anxiety levels as you move from computer-assisted instruction to programmed-text instruction. Therefore, the effectiveness of the type of instruction depends on whether a person has a high or low level of anxiety, which is an interaction effect.

Before leaving this section on interaction, we need to point out that a possible interaction exists whenever the lines on the graph are not parallel even if they do *not* cross. The classic interaction effect is one in which the lines cross, as we have illustrated in Figure 8.15(d). Now look at Figure 8.15(e) and you will see a graph in which the lines do not cross,

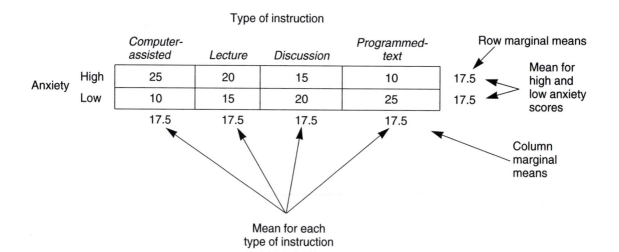

FIGURE 8.15(c)   Tabular representation of data showing nonsignificant main effects but a significant interaction effect.

but they are also not parallel, which also indicates an interaction effect. Equivalent performance exists for high- and low-anxiety individuals for computer-assisted instruction. However, performance increases under low anxiety levels and decreases under high anxiety levels as we move from computer-assisted instruction to programmed text. Again, the

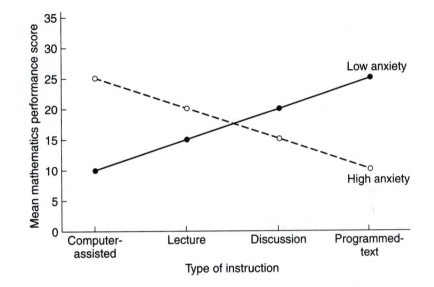

FIGURE 8.15(d)   Graphic illustration of a significant interaction effect.

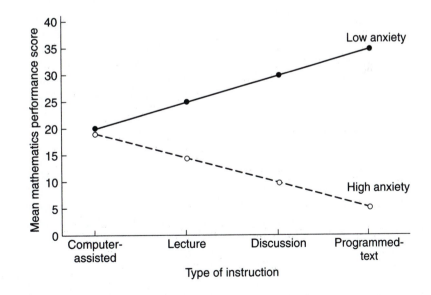

FIGURE 8.15(e)   Graphic illustration of a significant interaction.

effectiveness of type of instruction depends on the level of anxiety a person has, which is an interaction effect.

So far, the discussion of factorial designs has been limited to those with two independent variables. There are times when it would be advantageous to include three or more independent variables in a study. Factorial designs enable us to include as many independent variables as we consider important. Mathematically or statistically, there is almost no limit to the number of independent variables that can be included in a study. Practically speaking, however, there are several difficulties associated with increasing the number of variables. First, there is an associated increase in the number of research participants required. In an experiment with two independent variables, each of which has two levels of variation, a 2×2 arrangement is generated, yielding four cells. If ten participants are required for each cell, the experiment requires a total of forty participants. In a three-variable design, with two levels of variation per independent variable, a $2 \times 2 \times 2$ arrangement exists, yielding eight cells, and eighty participants are required in order to have ten participants per cell. Four variables mean that sixteen cells and 160 participants are required. As you can see, the required number of participants rapidly increases with an increase in the number of independent variables.

A second difficulty with factorial designs incorporating more than two independent variables arises when higher-order interactions are statistically significant. In a design with three independent variables, it is possible to have a significant interaction among the three variables. Consider a study that investigates the effect of the independent variables of type of instruction, anxiety level, and participant gender on performance in mathematics. A three-variable interaction means that the effect of type of instruction on mathematics performance depends on people's anxiety level and whether they are male or female. In other words, the two-way interaction between type of instruction and anxiety level is different for males and females If you conduct this study, you must look at this triple interaction and interpret its meaning, deciphering what combinations produce which effect, and why. Triple interactions can be quite difficult to interpret, and interactions of an even higher order tend to become unwieldy. Therefore, it is advisable to restrict a research design to no more than three variables. In spite of these problems, factorial designs are very popular because they permit the investigation of more than one independent variable and of the interactions that may exist among these variables.

Repeated-Measures Designs

Repeated-measures design A design in which all participants participate in all experimental treatment conditions

In a **repeated-measures design,** as illustrated in Figure 8.16, the same research participants participate in all experimental treatment conditions. Another way of stating this is that all participants are repeatedly measured under each treatment condition. Carr and Jessup (1997) used this design in one part of their study investigating variables that contributed to gender differences in first grader's mathematics strategy use. First-grade children were interviewed individually outside the classroom in October, January, and May of the school year to determine the strategies used when solving addition and subtraction problems. In other words, the participant's strategies (the dependent variable) were repeatedly investigated at three different times (the independent variable) during the school year to determine whether strategy use changed over the course of the school year.

Experimental treatment conditions

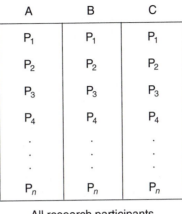

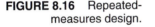

FIGURE 8.16 Repeated-measures design.

All research participants are in all conditions

The repeated-measures design has the benefit of requiring fewer participants than the factorial design because all participants participate in all experimental conditions. Remember that in the factorial design the number of participants needed is equal to the number needed in one cell or experimental condition × the number of experimental conditions or cells. In the repeated-measures design, the number of participants needed is equal to the number needed in one experimental condition because all participants participate in all experimental conditions, just as all the children in the Carr and Jessup (1997) study participated in the interviews conducted in October, January, and May.

With the repeated-measures design, the investigator does not have to worry about the participants in the different groups being equated because the same participants participate in all experimental conditions. The participants, therefore, serve as their own control, which means that the participants in the various experimental conditions are perfectly matched.

With all these advantages, you might think that the repeated-measures design would be used more than the factorial design. Actually, the reverse is true because the repeated measures design has the serious disadvantage of a confounding influence of a sequencing effect. Remember that this is an effect that can exist when participants participate in more than one experimental condition. Since this is the primary characteristic of a repeated-measures design, a sequencing rival hypothesis is a real possibility. In some studies, such as that by Carr and Jessup (1997), sequencing effects are not a problem and represent an integral part of the study. Carr and Jessup looked for changes in strategy use over the course of the year, so the sequencing effect was something they were studying. In other studies, sequencing would represent a confound. In order to overcome sequencing effects, investigators frequently use the counterbalancing control technique discussed earlier.

As you can see, there are some serious problems associated with the repeated-measures design. These problems are generally more difficult to control than those that exist with the factorial design. As a result, the factorial design is used more frequently.

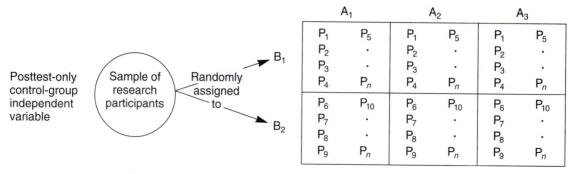

FIGURE 8.17   Factorial design based on a mixed model.

Factorial Designs Based on a Mixed Model

There are times in educational research when one or more of the variables of interest fits into a repeated-measures design and the other variable(s) of interest fits into a posttest-only control-group design. These variables can be combined into one study by using a factorial design based on a mixed model. The simplest form of this design involves an experiment using two independent variables. One independent variable requires several comparison groups, one for each level of variation of the independent variable. The other independent variable is constructed in such a way that all participants have to take each level of variation of the independent variable. Therefore, the first independent variable requires a posttest-only control-group design and the second independent variable requires a repeated-measures design. When the two independent variables are included in the same scheme, it becomes a **factorial design based on a mixed model,** as illustrated in Figure 8.17.

In this design, participants are randomly assigned to the different comparison groups required by the one independent variable. All participants then take each level of variation of the repeated-measures independent variable. This gives us the advantage of being able to test for the effects produced by each of the two independent variables as well as for the interaction between the two independent variables. Additionally, we have the advantage of needing fewer participants because all participants take all levels of variation of one of the independent variables.

We have limited our discussion of the factorial design based on a mixed model to two independent variables. This does not mean that the design cannot be extended to include more than two independent variables. As with the factorial design, we can include as many independent variables as are considered necessary.

Factorial design based on a mixed model
A factorial design in which different participants are randomly assigned to the different levels of one independent variable but all participants take all levels of another independent variable

SUMMARY

The experimental approach to conducting research is used to identify cause-and-effect relationships. This type of research is conducted within the context of an experiment, which is an environment in which the experimenter attempts to objectively observe phenomena that are made to occur in a strictly controlled environment in which one or more variables are varied and the others are kept constant.

Conducting an educational experiment involves manipulating the independent variable so that the effect of this manipulation can be observed on the dependent variable. The independent variable can be manipulated using a presence or absence technique, varying the amount of the independent variable that is administered, or varying the type of the independent variable.

Conducting an educational experiment necessitates control of the effect of potentially confounding extraneous variables. Control is achieved in most studies by eliminating any differential influence of the extraneous variables across the comparison groups. The most effective method for controlling the differential influence of potentially confounding extraneous variables is to randomly assign the research participants to the various comparison groups.

In addition to random assignment, control of potentially confounding extraneous variables is achieved by matching individual participants, holding extraneous variables constant, building the extraneous variable into the research design, counterbalancing, and using analysis of covariance. However, none of these control techniques takes the place of random assignment. Even if one or more of these other control techniques is used, you should still randomly assign whenever and wherever possible.

The dependent variable serves the purpose of measuring the effect produced by the independent variable. This means that you should select a dependent variable that is sensitive to the independent variable effect. There is generally more than one variable that could serve as the dependent variable. You must use judgment as to which variable is most sensitive and appropriate to use in your study.

The next step in conducting a research study is to design the study. Research design refers to the outline, plan, or strategy used in conducting the study. There are a number of research designs that can be used. Some of these designs are labeled weak designs because they do not control for the effect of potentially confounding extraneous variables. These designs include the one-group posttest-only design, the one-group pretest-posttest design, and the static-group comparison design. Other designs—the pretest-posttest control-group design and the posttest-only control-group design—are labeled strong experimental designs because they control for the effect of potentially confounding extraneous variables. This control is achieved primarily through the inclusion of a control comparison group and random assignment of participants to the comparison groups.

Factorial designs are frequently used in education research because they permit the simultaneous assessment of two or more independent variables. Use of a factorial design has the advantage of permitting us to investigate simultaneously the effect of several independent variables and the interaction between these independent variables. Investigation of the interaction allows us to determine whether the effect that one independent variable has on the dependent variable is dependent on the level of the other independent variable, which permits the investigation of complex relationships.

A repeated-measures design is used when the same research participants must participate in all experimental treatment conditions. Although the repeated-measures design has the advantage of needing fewer research participants and ensures that participants are equated across treatment conditions, it has the potentially major disadvantage of including sequencing effects. Counterbalancing can be used to control for sequencing effects in some but not all studies. Because sequencing effects are such a serious potential confound, this design is used less frequently than the factorial design.

There are times when one of the independent variables of interest would fit into a repeated-measures design and the other independent variable would fit into a posttest-only control-group design. When such an instance exists, a factorial design based on a mixed model is appropriate. When using this design, participants are randomly assigned to the different comparison groups required by the one independent variable. All participants then take each level of variation of the second independent variable.

STUDY QUESTIONS

1. Give a definition of an experiment and explain how it has the ability to identify causal relationships.
2. Define an independent and a dependent variable.
3. Identify and explain the different ways in which the independent variable can be manipulated.
4. How are potentially confounding extraneous variables controlled in experimental research?
5. Identify the different techniques that can be used to control for the influence of potentially confounding variables and explain how each of these techniques operates to produce this control.
6. Explain why you should randomly assign research participants whenever possible and why you should randomly assign even if another control technique is used.
7. Explain sequencing effects and identify the different sequencing effects that can occur in an educational experiment.
8. Identify and describe the weak experimental research designs.
9. Explain why the weak experimental research designs are considered weak.
10. For each of the weak experimental research designs, identify the potentially confounding extraneous variables that are not controlled and explain why these threats are not controlled.
11. Explain why the strong experimental research designs are considered strong.
12. What purpose is served by including a control group in experimental research?
13. Identify the strong experimental research designs and describe each one.
14. Explain how the strong experimental research designs control for the influence of each of the potentially confounding extraneous variables discussed in this chapter.
15. What is the advantage of the factorial design over the posttest-only control-group design?
16. Explain what is meant by an interaction effect.
17. Why is a factorial design used more frequently than a repeated-measures design?

EXERCISES

In studying research design, it is useful to read research articles published by other researchers and try to identify the type of designs they have used in reaching answers to their research questions. One exercise you can do to provide this experience is to go to the library and get the following research article:

Newman, E. J. & Tuckman, B. W. (1997). The effects of participant modeling on self-efficacy, incentive, productivity, and performance. *Journal of Research and Development in Education, 31,* 38–45.

After reading this article, answer the following questions:

1. What research questions and hypotheses are posed by the researchers?
2. What are the independent and dependent variables used in the research study?
3. What research designs were used by the researchers to test their research hypotheses?

KEY TERMS

amount technique (222)

analysis of covariance (232)

carryover effect (231)

cell (243)

control group (238)

counterbalancing (230)

differential influence (223)

experiment (220)

experimental control (223)

experimental group (238)

factorial design (242)

factorial design based on a
   mixed model (250)

interaction effect (243)

main effect (243)

matching (227)

one-group posttest-only
   design (234)

one-group pretest-posttest
   design (235)

order effect (230)

posttest-only control-
   group design (241)

presence or absence
   technique (222)

pretest-posttest control-
   group design (239)

random assignment (224)

repeated-measures design
   (248)

research design (233)

sequencing effects (230)

static-group comparison
   design (236)

type technique (223)

ENDNOTE

1. In some texts this design is called the one-shot case study, which is incorrect.

CHAPTER 9

Quasi-Experimental and Single-Case Designs

LEARNING OBJECTIVES

To be able to

- explain the difference between strong experimental research designs and quasi-experimental research designs.

- explain the limitations of quasi-experimental designs in making causal inferences.

- explain the characteristics of the nonequivalent control-group quasi-experimental design and how to search for rival hypotheses that may explain the obtained results.

- explain the characteristics of the interrupted and multiple time-series designs.

- explain how time-series and single-case research designs attempt to rule out confounding variables.

- explain how a treatment effect is demonstrated in single-case research designs.

- explain the limitations of each of the single-case research designs.

- explain the importance of measuring baseline performance and the desirable characteristics of a baseline.

- explain why only one variable should be changed at any one time in a single-case design.

- explain the relationship between single-case designs and group designs.

In the previous chapter we discussed the characteristics of experimental research and presented a number of strong experimental research designs that can be used to test causal hypotheses. However, there are times when educational researchers are confronted with situations in which all of the demands of experimental research cannot be met. For example, sometimes it is not possible to randomly assign participants to groups, a requirement of strong experimental research. On other occasions a researcher may have access to only a single intact group, such as a classroom of individuals with learning disabilities, or to only one or two participants, such as a student with school phobia. In these instances it would be impossible to use one of the strong research designs discussed in Chapter 8 because these designs require the random assignment of participants to at least two groups.

When this occurs, there are still a number of research designs that can be used to test your research hypotheses. When you have access to one or more intact groups of participants but the participants in the groups cannot be randomly assigned to treatment conditions, you can make use of a quasi-experimental design. When you have access to one or two participants, you can use a single-case experimental research design. These are the types of designs that are discussed in this chapter.

QUASI-EXPERIMENTAL RESEARCH DESIGNS

Quasi-experimental research design
An experimental research design that does not provide for full control of potential confounding variables primarily by not randomly assigning participants to comparison groups

A **quasi-experimental research design** is an experimental research design that does not provide for full control of potential confounding variables. In most instances, the primary reason that full control is not achieved is because participants cannot be randomly assigned to groups. For example, assume you want to conduct a study investigating the efficacy of several different ways of teaching reading to third-grade students. To control for the influence of confounding variables, ideally you want to randomly assign the third-grade students to the various groups or classrooms in which the different reading techniques are being taught. Sometimes it is not possible to randomly assign students to classrooms because of a variety of factors; for example, the school year may have already begun and the school system may not be willing to allow you to reassign students to different classrooms. This means that you would have to conduct the study making use of existing classes of students, which precludes the use of random assignment.

As we have previously discussed, random assignment of participants to groups is the most effective method of controlling for the influence of confounding variables. However, when random assignment is not possible, you need not abandon the study. Rather, you can construct a research design that controls for as many potentially confounding variables as possible. This typically means that you must make use of a quasi-experimental research design.

The important issue that must be considered when using a quasi-experimental design is whether it is possible to reach a valid causal conclusion using one of these designs, because they do not rule out the influence of all confounding variables. Causal inferences can be made using quasi-experimental designs, but these inferences are made only when data are collected that make rival explanations implausible. For example, assume you have a son that made a perfect score of 100 on a multiple-choice history test. If he had studied diligently for several days prior to taking the test, you would probably attribute the good grade to the diligent study. He could also have made the perfect score in a number of other ways (sheer luck in selecting the correct answer on each question, for example), but such alternative explanations may not be accepted because they are not plausible given their unlikely occurrence and the fact that your son had spent so much time studying. In like manner, causal interpretations are made from quasi-experiments only when rival explanations have been shown to be implausible. The difficulty is identifying the plausible rival explanations. As we illustrate later in this chapter, identification of plausible rival explanations frequently takes place by looking at the data and asking what variable(s) other than the independent variable could have produced the observed effect and then collecting data that render these rival explanations implausible.

Nonequivalent Control-Group Design

Nonequivalent control-group design
A design consisting of an experimental and a control group but participants are not randomly assigned to the comparison groups

Cook and Campbell (1979) identified a number of designs as being **nonequivalent control-group designs.** These designs are all similar in that they contain an experimental and a control group, but the participants are not randomly assigned to groups. This means that the participants in the experimental and control groups may not be similar on all variables that may affect the dependent variable. The variables on which the groups are not similar are potentially confounding variables that may operate as rival hypotheses to explain the outcome of the experiment, which makes these designs quasi-experimental designs. When it is not possible to randomly assign participants to the experimental and control groups, some form of the nonequivalent control-group design is frequently recommended. Probably the most frequently used version of the nonequivalent control group design is a scheme, depicted in Figure 9.1, consisting of giving an experimental and a control group a pretest and then a posttest after the experimental treatment condition has been administered to the experimental group. The responses of the two groups are then analyzed in one of two ways. The responses could be analyzed by comparing the pre- to posttest difference scores of the two groups or by comparing the experimental and control groups' posttest scores after they have been adjusted for any differences that may exist on their pretest scores using analysis of covariance (ANCOVA). Although both approaches have been used, ANCOVA is the one that is usually recommended, although pre- to posttest difference scores are still used to analyze the results of this design.

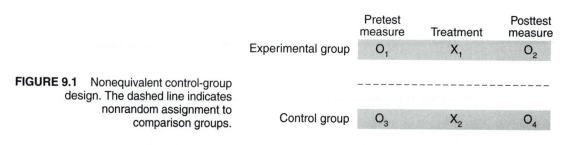

FIGURE 9.1   Nonequivalent control-group design. The dashed line indicates nonrandom assignment to comparison groups.

Consider the study conducted by Brown, Pressley, Van Meter, and Schuder (1996), which investigated the effect of using a specific type of instruction, called transactional strategies, for enhancing students' comprehension of the text that they read. In conducting this study the investigators identified a group of accomplished teachers who used the transactional-strategies instructional method in their classroom and a group of teachers in the same school district with reputations as excellent reading teachers who taught reading using the regular literacy curriculum. The investigators did not randomly assign the teachers to provide reading instruction by either the transactional strategy or the regular literacy curriculum because it takes several years to become an accomplished transactional-strategies instruction teacher. The researchers felt that it was inappropriate to ask these teachers to alter their instructional strategy for a year. Additionally, the second-grade students who participated in the study (those reading below a second-grade level at the beginning of the school year) were not randomly assigned to classes that taught the transactional-strategies or regular literacy curriculum. They did, however, select students from the various classes that were matched on reading comprehension at the beginning of the study. However, this equates the students only on initial reading comprehension. Because many teachers were used in the study and they, as well as the students, were not randomly assigned to groups, a quasi-experimental design had to be used.

Brown, Pressley, Van Meter, and Schuder (1996) selected the nonequivalent control-group research design with matching of participants in the two groups, as illustrated in Figure 9.2. Both groups, each consisting of several classes, were interviewed at the beginning of the academic year to identify the strategy used by the students to assist in their comprehension of the material read and were pretested on several outcome measures, such as a test of reading comprehension. After matched samples of students (students who had similar

FIGURE 9.2   Design of the Brown, Pressley, Van Meter, and Schuder study (1996).

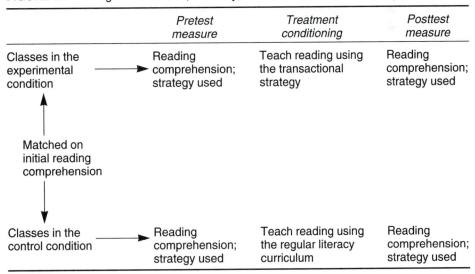

	Pretest measure	Treatment conditioning	Posttest measure
Classes in the experimental condition	Reading comprehension; strategy used	Teach reading using the transactional strategy	Reading comprehension; strategy used
Matched on initial reading comprehension			
Classes in the control condition	Reading comprehension; strategy used	Teach reading using the regular literacy curriculum	Reading comprehension; strategy used

reading comprehension scores) were identified, one group was taught reading using the transactional strategy and the other group was taught using the regular literacy curriculum. At the end of the academic year, the students in each group were posttested on the outcome measures. Analysis of the results revealed that the students who received transactional-strategies instruction improved in reading comprehension more than the students taught by the conventional reading method.

The results of the Brown, Pressley, Van Meter, and Schuder study (1996) demonstrated that the performance of the students receiving transactional-strategy instruction was superior to that of the students receiving conventional reading instruction. Because a quasi-experimental design was used, the question becomes one of interpreting the study results. The students in the two groups were matched in terms of initial reading comprehension, so some basis exists for asserting that the results were not due to the differences in initial reading comprehension. However, the teachers were not randomly assigned to the two groups, nor was there any attempt to equate the teachers in terms of teaching effectiveness. The authors state that the teachers who used the transactional-strategies method were excellent teachers who offered rich language arts experiences for their students. Consequently, these teachers would seem to represent very effective teachers. The investigators did select comparison teachers who were recommended by school principals and district reading specialists based on four criteria, such as fostering student involvement in reading and providing motivating learning activities. However, no attempt was made to ensure that the teachers providing instruction in the two methods were equated in ability to teach reading. Therefore there could be a difference in the ability of these teachers to motivate and/or provide instruction in reading, and such differences could have accounted for some or all of the difference in reading comprehension of the two groups of students.

Cook and Campbell (1979) have pointed out that the rival explanations arising from the use of designs such as the nonequivalent control-group design tend to be directly related to the results obtained. For example, look at Figure 9.3, which illustrates hypothetical results that might have been obtained from using the nonequivalent control-group design. This figure reveals that the control group did not change from pre- to posttesting. The experimental group, however, started at a higher level and showed a significant positive change. This outcome would seem to suggest that the experimental treatment was effective.

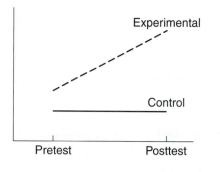

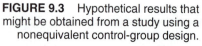

FIGURE 9.3 Hypothetical results that might be obtained from a study using a nonequivalent control-group design.

However, this outcome could also have been due to a selection-maturation effect or a local history effect.

Selection-maturation effect
When participants in one of two comparison groups grows or develops faster than participants in the other comparison group

A **selection-maturation effect** occurs when one of two groups of participants grows or develops faster than the other group. In the Brown, Pressley, Van Meter, and Schuder study (1996), a selection-maturation effect would have been present if the participants in the experimental condition were developing intellectually and motivationally more rapidly than the participants in the control group and increased their reading comprehension from pre- to posttesting because of these maturational factors and not because of the type of instruction they received. If this were the case, the posttest improvement in reading comprehension of the experimental group would be due to maturational factors and not to the experimental treatment effect.

Many investigators attempt to eliminate threat of bias from the selection-maturation effect by matching experimental and control participants on important variables. Brown, Pressley, Van Meter, and Schuder (1996) matched on initial reading comprehension, equating the groups on this variable. Ideally, this equality will persist over time, so any difference observed during a posttest is attributed to the experimental treatment condition. However, Campbell and Boruch (1975) have revealed that this assumption could be erroneous because a statistical regression phenomenon could occur within the two groups of matched participants, accounting for part or all of the difference observed between the two groups upon posttesting. This difference could be misinterpreted as being due to a treatment effect. If you conduct a study using a nonequivalent control group design with matching during pretesting, you should consult Campbell and Boruch's article (1975).

The outcome depicted in Figure 9.3 could also be the result of a local history effect (a history effect that affects only one of the comparison groups). A general history effect (a history effect that affects all comparison groups) is controlled in the nonequivalent control-group design by including a control group. However, the design is still susceptible to a local history effect, in which some event affects either the control or experimental group but not both. A local history effect could have occurred in the Brown, Pressley, Van Meter, and Schuder study if the students given the transactional-strategies instruction (the experimental instruction) were given more effective instruction than the students receiving the regular literary curriculum. This difference in instructional effectiveness could represent a rival explanation for any difference observed between the experimental and control groups because the better instruction could lead to enhanced learning and comprehension.

Interrupted Time-Series Design

In educational research there are times when it is difficult to find an equivalent group of participants to serve as a control group. When only one group of participants is available, you can make use of the one-group pretest-posttest design. However, as we discussed earlier, there are many confounding variables that threaten the internal validity of this design. To control for these potentially confounding variables in situations in which we have only one group of research participants, we must think of mechanisms other than the use of a control group. These other control mechanisms are part of the interrupted time-series design.

Interrupted time-series design
A design in which a treatment condition is assessed by comparing the pattern of pretest responses with the pattern of posttest responses obtained from a single group of participants

In the **interrupted time-series design,** a single group of participants is pretested a number of times during the A, or baseline phase, exposed to a treatment condition, and then posttested a number of times during the B, or treatment phase, as depicted in Figure 9.4. Baseline refers to the observation of a given behavior prior to the presentation of any treatment designed to alter behavior. The baseline phase is, therefore, the period during which the participants' behavior is recorded in its freely occurring state. After the baseline behavior is recorded, a treatment is implemented and behavior is recorded while this treatment is applied. The treatment effect is demonstrated by the discontinuity in the pretest versus the posttest responses. This discontinuity could be represented by a change in the level of the pre- and posttest responses. For example, pretest responses may consist of a group of children emitting an average of between eight and ten disruptive behaviors during a given class period, and the posttest responses may consist of an average of only three to five disruptive behaviors, indicating a change, or decline, in the level of response. This discontinuity could also be demonstrated by a change in the slope of the pre- and posttest responses. A change in the slope would occur if the pretest responses demonstrated a change in one direction, such as a gradual increase in the number of disruptive behaviors during a class period, and the posttest responses demonstrated a change in the opposite direction, such as a gradual decrease in these behaviors.

To illustrate this design, consider the study conducted by Mayer, Mitchell, Clementi, Clement-Robertson, and Myatt (1993). One of the variables they investigated was how making the classroom environment more positive affected the percentage of students who were engaged in their assigned activities. Mayer et al. identified ninth-grade students who had low grade point averages and were frequently absent from the schools. All these students attended an experimental classroom for at least one period each school day, so there was a single intact group of participants available for experimentation, which meant that some form of a time-series design had to be used. In this experimental classroom emphasis was placed on the positive. For example, classroom rules were stated positively (e.g., show courtesy and respect to others), and points and praise were given to the students when they followed the rules. While in this experimental classroom the experimenters assessed the percentage of students that were engaged in their assigned activities, defined as being "on-task," at ten and forty minutes into the class period. The percentage of students who were on-task was repeatedly measured before and after the teachers focused on making the classroom more positive.

Figure 9.5 illustrates the percentage of students who were on-task at both ten and forty minutes into the class period. From this figure you can see that the percentage of students who were on-task was assessed multiple times prior to and after implementation of the positive classroom environment, making it an interrupted time-series design. This assessment reveals that the percentage of students who were on-task remained rather constant during the first seven baseline class sessions, or the class sessions prior to the implementa-

FIGURE 9.4   Interrupted time-series design.

Multiple pretests	Treatment	Multiple posttests
$O_1 \ O_2 \ O_3 \ O_4 \ O_5$	X_1	$O_6 \ O_7 \ O_8 \ O_9 \ O_{10}$

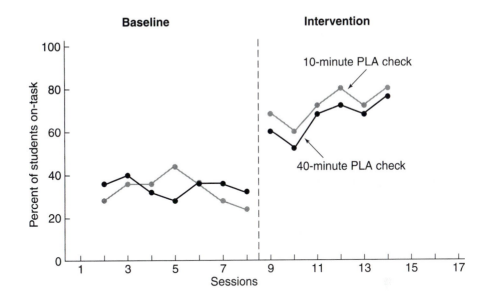

FIGURE 9.5   Percentage of students who are on-task at 10 minutes and 40 minutes into the class period. (Adapted from G. R. Mayer, L. K. Mitchell, T. Clementi, E. Clement-Robertson, & R. Myatt (1993). "A dropout prevention program for at-risk high school students: Emphasizing consulting to promote positive classroom climates," *Education and Treatment of Children, 16,* 135–146. Reprinted by permission.) The figure presented here depicts the results of one of five classrooms investigated by Mayer et al. Only one classroom is presented here to illustrate a time-series design, whereas Mayer et al. used five classrooms and a multiple-baseline design. PLA refers to planned activity.

tion of the positive classroom environment. After implementation of the positive classroom environment, the percentage of on-task students consistently rises over the next six class sessions, suggesting that the implementation of the positive approach had a beneficial effect on the students' behavior. This conclusion, however, is based on visual inspection. Now it is necessary to ask two questions. First, did a significant change occur following the introduction of the treatment condition? Second, can the observed change be attributed to the treatment condition?

Visual inspection of the pattern of pre- and postintervention behavior can be very helpful in ruling out some potentially confounding variables and in determining whether an experimental treatment had an effect. Figure 9.6 illustrates a number of possible patterns of behavior that can be obtained from time-series data. Look at the first three patterns, A, B, and C. Pattern A reveals a continuous increase in response prior to intervention, and this pattern of continuous increase is maintained during posttesting. Such a response pattern could reflect an instrumentation or a maturation effect rather than a treatment effect. Similarly, response patterns B and C reveal that the pattern of responses established during pretesting continued during posttesting. Response patterns A, B, and C, therefore, do not reveal a treatment effect because the postintervention pattern of responses represents a

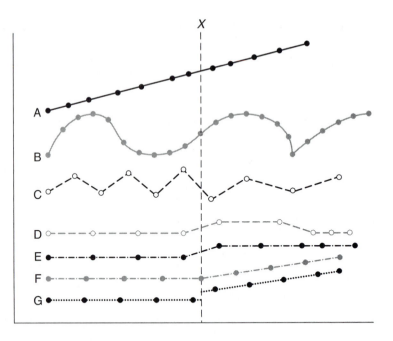

FIGURE 9.6 Possible pattern of behavior of a time-series variable. *X* designates introduction of the experimental intervention. (Adapted from J. T. Caporaso, *The structure and function of European integration,* © 1974 by Goodyear Publishing Company.)

continuation of the preintervention pattern of responses. If several pretests and posttests had not been obtained, it would be tempting to infer that a treatment effect had occurred. Look at the response immediately preceding and immediately following the intervention in patterns A and B. In these patterns you can see that the preintervention response was lower than the postintervention response, indicating an improvement in behavior. In pattern C the postintervention response was lower than the preintervention response, indicating a decline in response. Without taking repeated assessments before and after intervention, you would not know that the postintervention response represented a continuation of the preintervention pattern of response.

Response patterns D, E, F, and G appear to represent true changes in behavior because the posttest response pattern was different than the pretest response pattern. Additionally, the change in the response pattern continued, with the exception of pattern D, during the entire posttesting period. It is this change in the posttest pattern of responses, particularly if it is a continuous change, that gives some assurance of the fact that a change in response occurred.

Even with this visual inspection of the data, it is important to determine whether the change in response pattern is statistically significant, which involves a test of significance. The most widely used and appropriate significance test seems to be the autoregression moving average model (Box & Jenkins, 1970; Glass, Willson, & Gottman, 1975). Basically, this method consists of determining whether the pattern of postresponse measures differs from the pattern of preresponse measures. Use of this statistical method requires obtaining at least fifty data points (Glass, Willson, & Gottman, 1975), which frequently cannot be accomplished. Fortunately, Tryon (1982) and Cosbie (1993) have developed statistical procedures that can be used with as few as ten data points so that valid statistical analysis can be conducted on the data collected on most time-series studies.

After the data are analyzed and an assessment is made as to whether the preresponse pattern differs from the postresponse pattern, it is important to determine whether the change was due to the experimental intervention or to some confounding variable. For example, Mayer et al. (1993) had to determine whether the implementation of the positive classroom environment led to the increase in on-task behavior or whether some extraneous variable was responsible. This means that you have to look at the data and identify the possible confounding variables that could have produced the behavioral change. The primary rival hypothesis that exists in the interrupted time-series design is a history effect. If some extraneous variable that increased the percentage of students engaged in on-task behaviors occurred at the same time as the implementation of the positive classroom environment, this extraneous variable would serve as a rival explanation for the change in the students' behavior. A researcher using the interrupted time-series design must consider all other events taking place at the time of implementation of the experimental treatment and determine whether they might be rival explanations.

Multiple Time-Series Design

Multiple time-series design
An interrupted time-series design that includes a control group to rule out a history effect

The multiple time-series design is basically an extension of the interrupted time-series design. It has the advantage of eliminating the history effect by including an equivalent or comparable participant or group of participants that does not receive the treatment condition. As illustrated in Figure 9.7, the **multiple time-series design** consists of an experimental group that receives the treatment condition, X_1, and a comparable control group that receives some standard treatment or no treatment, X_2, after both groups have been repeatedly pretested. After the treatment condition is administered, both groups are posttested on multiple occasions. Although participants are not randomly assigned to the experimental and control conditions, including a control condition in addition to the multiple pre- and posttests increases control over some extraneous variables that could serve as rival hypotheses. The history effect, for example, is controlled because any history effect should influence the participants in the experimental and control conditions equally. Therefore, if the experimental participants demonstrated a change in performance and the control participants did

	Multiple pretests	Treatment	Multiple posttests
Experimental group	$O_1\ O_2\ O_3\ O_4$	X_1	$O_5\ O_6\ O_7\ O_8$
Control group	$O_9\ O_{10}\ O_{11}\ O_{12}$	X_2	$O_{13}\ O_{14}\ O_{15}\ O_{16}$

FIGURE 9.7   Multiple time-series design. The dashed line denotes a lack of random assignment to comparison groups.

not, evidence would exist for a treatment effect unconfounded by a history effect. Use of this design does, however, require identifying a comparable control group of participants, which frequently is difficult. Therefore, this design is seldom used.

SINGLE-CASE EXPERIMENTAL DESIGNS

Single-case experimental designs
Designs that use a single participant to investigate the effect of an experimental treatment condition

Single-case experimental designs use a single participant in the experimental design to investigate the efficacy of an experimental treatment condition. The necessity of conducting a study that investigates a single individual can occur any time you want to investigate some phenomenon but have access to only one or two individuals who demonstrate that phenomenon. For example, assume you have an unusually bright student in your class and you want to study this person's learning strategies. Because only one student with this ability level is in your class, you have to use a single-case design. Similarly, if you have one student in class that is being very disruptive and you want to demonstrate that a certain experimental procedure is effective in controlling such disruptive behavior, you have to use a single-case design.

As you can see, many instances worthy of investigation exist where only a single case may be available for study. Some people have the tendency, when encountering these designs for the first time, to equate them with case studies. This is incorrect. Single-case designs are designs that experimentally investigate the effect of an independent variable. However, single-case designs control for the influence of extraneous variables differently than do group comparison designs.

In the group comparison or strong research designs we have discussed so far, including the nonequivalent control-group designs, two groups of participants, an experimental group and a control group, were included. The experimental group is the group that gets the experimental treatment condition; the control group gets either no treatment or some standard or typical treatment. The control group is included in strong experimental research designs because it controls for a number of confounding variables and serves as a comparison to determine whether an experimental treatment produced an effect. However, a similar control condition does not exist with single-case experimental designs, which means we have to think of other strategies for controlling confounding extraneous variables and for obtaining comparison responses to determine whether an experimental treatment effect exists.

All single-case experimental designs are some form of a time-series design, as we illustrated with the interrupted time-series design, because these designs require repeated measurement on the dependent variable prior to and following implementation of the experimental treatment condition. The pretreatment responses are used as the comparison responses for assessing the effect of the independent variable. Additionally, the multiple pre- and posttreatment responses permit us to rule out many extraneous variables, such as history and maturation, that could confound the results. The way in which this is accomplished is identical to that which we discussed under the topic of interrupted time-series design earlier in this chapter. Remember that the pattern of posttreatment responses must not represent a continuation of the pattern of pretreatment responses for the independent variable to have caused a change in the response of the participant.

As we discuss the single-case experimental research designs, you should realize that these designs can be, and frequently are, used with an intact group of participants as well as with single participants. There are times when you cannot break a group of participants, such as a class, into a control and experimental group but still want to investigate the efficacy of an independent variable. In these instances you can treat the class as a single case and use one of the single-case experimental designs.

A-B-A and A-B-A-B Designs

A-B-A design
A single-case experimental design in which the response to the experimental treatment condition is compared to baseline responses taken before and after administering the treatment condition

The **A-B-A design** is a single-case design involving three phases, as illustrated in Figure 9.8. The first phase, the first A of this design, is the baseline condition during which the target response is repeatedly recorded prior to any experimental intervention. The second phase, the B part of this design, is the experimental treatment condition. During this phase some treatment condition is deliberately imposed to try to change the response of the participant. This treatment phase is typically continued for the same length of time as the original baseline phase, or until some substantial and stable change occurs in the behaviors being observed. After the treatment condition has been introduced and the desired behavioral change has occurred, the second A phase is introduced. The second A phase of this design represents a return to the baseline conditions. In other words, the treatment condition is withdrawn and whatever conditions existed during baseline are reinstated. This second A phase is reinstated to determine whether the behavior will revert back to its original pretreatment level. This reverting back to the original pretreatment level is very important for demonstrating that the treatment condition, and not some other extraneous variable, produced the behavioral change observed during the B phase when the experimental treatment condition was in effect. If the second A phase had not been included, the design would be the interrupted time-series design, which would include the potential rival hypothesis of history. However, if the response reverts back to the original baseline level when the treatment condition is withdrawn, rival hypotheses such as history become less plausible.

To illustrate the use of this design, consider the study conducted by Gunter, Shores, Jack, Denny, and DePaepe (1994). These researchers investigated the effect of using a teaching method that involved providing information that would ensure correct responses on the disruptive behavior of a twelve-year-old student named Tom. Tom was selected to participate in the study because his participation in a prior study identified him as having a high rate of disruptive behavior during academic instruction. A baseline rate of occurrence of disruptive behaviors (defined as making inappropriate noises, talking out without permission, walking away from the instructional area without permission, and making nondirected negative verbalizations) was recorded for ten class periods. Baseline recording

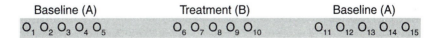

FIGURE 9.8   A-B-A time-series design.

for each class began when the teacher gave Tom his math assignment and ended with the completion of the math activity or the expiration of thirty minutes of continuous observation. Intervention was then implemented that consisted of the teachers providing Tom with the information that would ensure his getting a correct response prior to presenting him with the task he was to perform. For example, during intervention the teacher would say, "Tom, 6 × 4 is 24. What is 6 × 4?" if he had miscalculated this problem. After Tom had completed seventeen class periods under intervention conditions, the teacher reverted to her baseline behavior of not providing information that would ensure a correct response.

You can see a display of the per minute rate of disruptive behaviors Tom displayed for each session in Figure 9.9. From this figure you can see that Tom displayed a number of disruptive behaviors during every session of the first baseline (A) condition. When the treatment condition (B) of giving Tom information that ensured his giving a correct response was implemented, the disruptive behaviors declined, and during several of the sessions Tom did not display any disruptive behaviors. When baseline conditions (A) were reinstated and Tom no longer received the information he needed to provide a correct response, disruptive behaviors became more frequent.

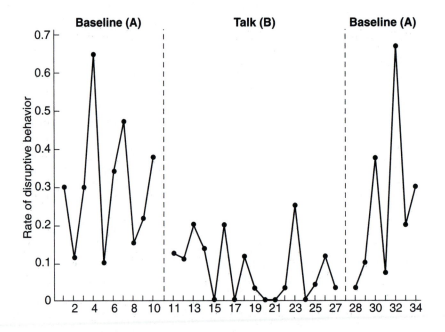

FIGURE 9.9   Rate of Tom's disruptive behaviors during baseline and intervention. (Adapted from P. L. Gunter, R. E. Shores, S. L. Jack, R. K. Denny, & P. A. DePaepe (1994). "A case study of the effects of altering instructional interactions on the disruptive behavior of a child identified with severe behavior disorders," *Education and Treatment of Children, 17,* 435–444. Reprinted by permission.) This figure depicts the first three phases of the design used by Gunter et al. to illustrate the A-B-A design.

In looking at the results of this study, it appears that the use of the A-B-A design provides a rather dramatic illustration of the influence of the experimental treatment condition. However, there are several problems with this design (Hersen & Barlow, 1976). The first problem is that the design ends with the baseline condition. From the standpoint of an educator who desires a positive behavioral change, this may be unacceptable because the benefits of the treatment condition are denied. Fortunately, this limitation can be handled easily by adding a fourth phase to the A-B-A design in which the treatment condition is reintroduced. This makes it an A-B-A-B design, as illustrated in Figure 9.10. When using the **A-B-A-B design**, the participant ends the experiment with the full benefit of the treatment condition. Actually, Gunter, Shores, Jack, Denny, and DePaepe (1994) used the A-B-A-B design. In Figure 9.10 you can see that they reinstated the treatment conditions. When the treatment condition was reinstated a second time, the disruptive behaviors declined once again. Tom, their experimental participant, did, therefore, end the study with the positive effects of the experimental treatment condition.

A second problem with using the A-B-A design is the necessity of the dependent variable response to revert to baseline conditions when the experimental treatment condition is withdrawn to rule out rival explanations such as history. If Tom's disruptive behav-

A-B-A-B design
An A-B-A design that is extended to include the reintroduction of the treatment condition

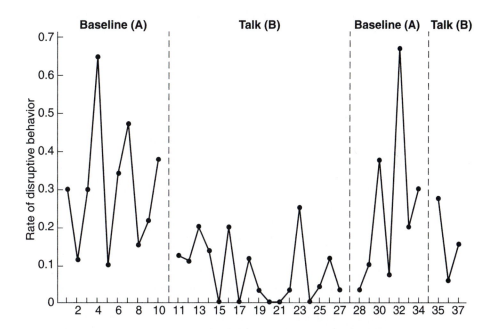

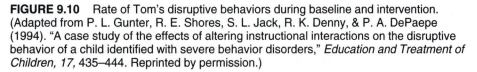

FIGURE 9.10   Rate of Tom's disruptive behaviors during baseline and intervention. (Adapted from P. L. Gunter, R. E. Shores, S. L. Jack, R. K. Denny, & P. A. DePaepe (1994). "A case study of the effects of altering instructional interactions on the disruptive behavior of a child identified with severe behavior disorders," *Education and Treatment of Children, 17,* 435–444. Reprinted by permission.)

ior did not revert to its baseline level when the treatment condition was withdrawn, it would have been impossible to determine whether the behavioral change was due to the treatment condition or to a history variable that occurred at the same time that the treatment condition was introduced. In other words, the behavior must change with the changing conditions of the design to demonstrate that the response being investigated is under the control of the researcher and not due to some extraneous variable. Reversal, therefore, is essential to rule out rival hypotheses.

The problem with the A-B-A and A-B-A-B designs is that a reversal to baseline does not occur with all dependent variable responses. Without the reversal, the researcher cannot be sure that the change in response following introduction of the treatment condition was not caused by some extraneous variable. Failure to reverse may be due to a carryover effect across phases, whereby the treatment condition was maintained so long that a relatively permanent change in behavior took place. For example, if you were investigating the effect of reinforcing students every time they correctly completed their mathematics homework, either by giving them praise, additional recess time, or allowing them to chat with their friends for ten minutes during class time, you may find that the reinforcer worked so well that the students found that successful completion of their homework and receiving a good grade was reinforcing by itself. This would sustain the behavior of completing homework without any teacher intervention. In such a case the teacher intervention could be removed and the students' behavior of completing their homework would continue, which would mean that the students' behavior would not reverse. Because of the possibility of such a carryover effect, Bijou, Peterson, Harris, Allen, and Johnston (1969) recommend that short experimental periods be used to facilitate obtaining a reversal effect. Once the influence of the experimental treatment has been demonstrated, attention can be placed on its persistence.

Before leaving the A-B-A design, we need to point out that when implementing this design, the return to baseline conditions sometimes involves a withdrawal of the treatment condition, and at other times it involves the implementation of another treatment condition in which the intent is to reverse the behavior. Reversing the behavior would involve attempting to create an alternative but incompatible behavior. For example, assume you want to increase the play behavior of a socially withdrawn female child. Baseline would consist of recording the percentage of time the child spends interacting with other children as well as with adults, such as the teachers, during a specific time period, such as during recess. Treatment might consist of praising the child whenever she interacted with other children and not with adults to see whether the percentage of time she spent with other children but not with adults increased over baseline. During the second A phase of the design, you could attempt to demonstrate the effect of the reinforcement by withdrawing the praise and seeing whether the child reverted to being socially withdrawn and interacting less with other children. You could also have implemented a reversal during this second A phase. If a reversal was implemented, you might praise the child whenever she interacted with teachers and ignore her whenever she interacted with other children. This reversal phase would be implemented to see whether the percentage of time the child spent with teachers would increase and the percentage of time the child spent with other children would decrease. If it did, then the child's behavior would have reversed from focusing on other children to focusing on teachers. If this reversal did take place, it would represent a dramatic demonstration of the power of the effect of reinforcement. Although a reversal to an alternative behavior can reveal dramatic results, it is more cumbersome and thus is used less frequently than the more adaptable withdrawal of the treatment condition.

Multiple-Baseline Design

Multiple-baseline design
A single-case experimental design in which the treatment condition is successively administered to different participants, or to the same participant in several settings, after baseline behaviors have been recorded for different periods of time

The primary limiting component of the A-B-A and the A-B-A-B designs is their inability to eliminate the rival hypothesis of history when the target behavior does not revert to baseline following withdrawal of the treatment condition. If you suspect that such a situation may exist, you should select a design that does control for a history rival hypothesis. In this situation the multiple-baseline design is a logical alternative because it does not entail withdrawing the treatment condition. Therefore, its effectiveness does not hinge on a reversal of behavior to baseline level.

The **multiple-baseline design,** as depicted in Figure 9.11, focuses on two or more different behaviors in the same individual, on the same behavior exhibited by two or more individuals, or on the same behavior exhibited by one individual but in different settings. To illustrate this design we focus on several different behaviors exhibited by one individual. Baseline data are collected on two or more different behaviors exhibited by the same research participant. After baseline data are collected, the experimental treatment is successively administered to each target behavior. If the behavior exposed to the treatment condition changes while all others remain at baseline, evidence exists supporting the efficacy of the treatment condition. It becomes increasingly implausible that extraneous variables could be contemporaneously influencing each target behavior at the same time as the treatment condition.

For example, assume that you had a student that repeatedly talked to others in class without permission, wrote notes to others in class, and would leave his desk at any time and wander around the room. These behaviors would tend to disrupt the class and compromise your teaching effectiveness. One of the ways you might think you could control these behaviors is to pay attention to and reinforce the student when he was not engaged in any of these behaviors and ignore him when he was performing these disruptive behaviors. Assume further, that you wanted to verify the efficacy of reinforcing positive behaviors and ignoring negative ones. To do this you could use a multiple-baseline design and collect baseline data on the frequency of occurrence of each of these behaviors for a specified

FIGURE 9.11   Multiple-baseline design.

		Phase 1	Phase 2	Phase 3	Phase 4	Phase 5
Different people, different behaviors, or different settings	A	Baseline	Treatment	Treatment	Treatment	Treatment
	B	Baseline	Baseline	Treatment	Treatment	Treatment
	C	Baseline	Baseline	Baseline	Treatment	Treatment
	D	Baseline	Baseline	Baseline	Baseline	Treatment

period of time, such as during one class period each day of a given week. Then you could systematically reinforce the absence of each of these behaviors. During the first week you could reinforce the student when he was not talking to others and attending to his work while at the same time recording the frequency of his talking to others as well as baseline behavior on the frequency of writing notes to others and walking around the room. During the second week you would continue reinforcing not talking but would also reinforce the absence of writing notes to others by, perhaps, praising the student when he avoided this behavior. During the third week you would continue to reinforce not talking and refraining from note writing, and also reinforce staying in his seat and not walking around the room. If each of these disruptive behaviors declined when and only when the student was reinforced for desirable behaviors, you would have evidence indicating that the reinforcement was effective in eliminating these disruptive behaviors.

Bro, Shank, McLaughlin, and Williams (1996) used the multiple-baseline design to investigate the effect of an in-school breakfast program on on-task behavior (i.e., engaging in the tasks consistent with the demands of each class, such as welding or silently reading) of at-risk students in a vocational and a learning-centered classroom. Note that in this study the multiple-baseline design is being used with two intact groups rather than different individual participants or behaviors. Baseline data consisted of recording the percentage of time the students were on-task. After five baseline days, the students in the vocational class were given the treatment condition of an in-school breakfast, which continued for the next thirty days. After nine baseline days the students in the learning-centered classroom were administered the in-school breakfast, which was continued for twenty-one days. Figure 9.12 shows that the percentage of time the students in the vocational class were on-task increased immediately following the in-school breakfast program. Similarly, the percentage of time the students in the learning-centered classroom were on-task increased following implementation of the breakfast treatment program, although not as dramatically as that which existed in the vocational class. The important point is that the change in behavior in both classes did not occur until the treatment condition was administered, providing evidence that the breakfast program was the cause of the increase in on-task performance.

Although the multiple-baseline design can provide convincing evidence for the efficacy of a treatment and avoids the problem of reversibility, it has another basic difficulty. For this design to be effective in evaluating of the efficacy of a treatment, the target behaviors must not be highly interrelated. This means that the behaviors must not be interdependent so that a change in one behavior alters the other behaviors. As you can imagine, independence does not always exist. Borden, Bruce, Mitchell, Carter, and Hall (1970), for example, used a multiple-baseline design and found that reinforcement not only changed the inattentive behavior of the target participant but also changed that of an adjacent peer. When interdependence exists, it destroys much of the power of this design because its power is dependent on its ability to demonstrate change when the treatment condition is administered to a given behavior, individual, or setting. If administering the experimental treatment to one behavior, individual, or setting results in a corresponding change in the other behaviors, individuals, or settings, then it will have less impact and produce less change in the remaining behaviors, individuals, or settings because the behavior had previously been altered. In this case, it would not be clear what caused the change in behavior. All this means is that, when considering the use of a multiple-baseline design, you must also de-

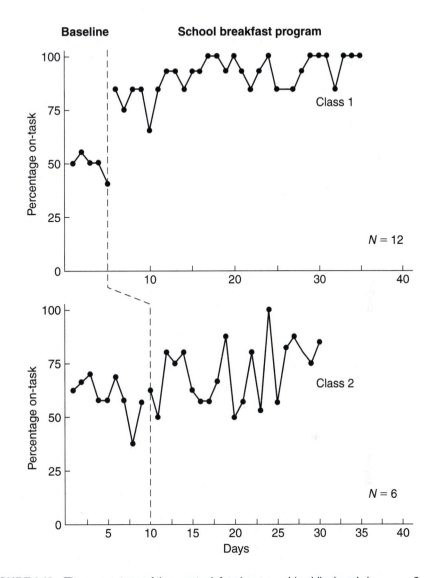

FIGURE 9.12   The percentage of time on-task for classroom 1 (welding) and classroom 2 (learning center) during baseline and school breakfast program. (Adapted from R. T. Bro, L. L. Shank, T. F. McLaughlin, & R. L. Williams (1996). "Effects of a breakfast program on on-task behaviors of vocational high school students," *The Journal of Educational Research, 90,* 111–115. Reprinted with permission of the Helen Dwight Reid Educational Foundation. Published by Heldref Publications, 1319 Eighteenth St., N.W., Washington, DC, 20036–1802. Copyright © 1996.)

termine whether the behaviors, individuals, or settings are independent, and if you think they may not be, you must collect data to ensure that they are independent. Different behaviors of the same individual are probably most likely to be interdependent. If you have data indicating that the target behaviors (e.g., talking-out and out-of-seat) are interdependent, you should use different individuals or different settings because these will probably be more distinct than different behaviors of the same individual.

Changing-Criterion Design

Changing-criterion design A single-case experimental design in which a participant's behavior is gradually altered by changing the criterion for success during successive treatment periods

The changing-criterion design is presented because it is particularly useful for investigating educational problems that require shaping of behavior over a period of time or in cases where a step-by-step increase in accuracy, frequency, or amount are the goals of the research. The **changing-criterion design,** depicted in Figure 9.13, requires an initial baseline measure on a single target behavior. A treatment condition is then implemented and continued across a series of intervention phases. During the first intervention or treatment phase, an initial criterion of successful performance is established. When the participant achieves the established level of performance, the experiment moves to the second phase, where a new and more difficult criterion level is established while the treatment condition is continued. When behavior reaches this new criterion level and is maintained, the next phase, with its more difficult criterion level, is introduced. In this manner, each successive phase of the experiment requires a step-by-step increase in the criterion measure. Experimental control and elimination of rival explanations are demonstrated by the successive change in the target behavior with each stepwise change in the criterion.

Hall and Fox (1977) provide a good illustration of the changing-criterion design in a study of a child named Dennis, who refused to complete arithmetic problems. To overcome this resistant behavior, the investigators first obtained a baseline measure of the average number of assigned arithmetic problems (4.25) that he would complete during a forty-five-minute session. Then Dennis was told that a specified number of problems had to be completed correctly during the subsequent session. If he completed them correctly, he could take recess and play with a basketball; if he did not, he would have to miss recess and remain in the room until they were correctly completed. During the first treatment phase, the criterion number of problems to be solved was set at five, which was about one more than the mean number completed during the baseline phase. After successfully achieving this criterion performance on three consecutive days, Dennis had to finish an additional problem to take recess and play with a basketball. The results of this experiment, shown in Figure 9.14, reveal that Dennis's performance increased as the acceptable criterion level was increased. When a change in behavior parallels the criterion change, it demonstrates the effects of the treatment.

Successful use of the changing-criterion design does require attention to the length of the baseline and treatment phases, the amount of change in criterion, and the number of changes in the criterion. Ideally, the treatment phases should be of different lengths, or if they are of a constant length, the baseline phase should be longer than the treatment phases.

FIGURE 9.13   Changing criterion design.

Phase A	Phase B	Phase C	Phase D
Baseline	Treatment and initial criterion	Treatment and criterion increment	Treatment and criterion increment

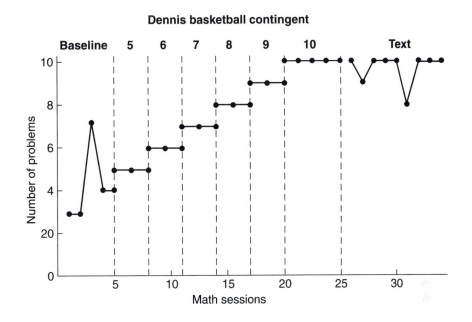

FIGURE 9.14   Number of math problems solved in a changing-criterion design. (Adapted from R. V. Hall, & R. G. Fox (1997). *Changing-criterion designs: An alternative applied behavior analysis procedure. New Developments in Behavioral Research: Theory, Method, and Application.* In honor of Sidney W. Bijou, edited by C. C. Etzel, G. M. LeBlanc, and D. M. Baer, 1977. Hillsdale, NJ: Lawrence Erlbaum Associates. Copyright © 1977 by Lawrence Erlbaum Associates. Reprinted by permission of the publisher and the authors.)

This is necessary to ensure that the step-by-step changes in behavior are caused by the experimental treatment and not by some history or maturational variable that occurs simultaneously with the criterion change. Each treatment phase should be long enough to allow the behavior to change to its new criterion level and then to stabilize. If the behavior fluctuates between the new and old criterion level, stability has not been achieved, and it is difficult to determine which criterion level has been achieved. The criterion change should be large enough to detect a behavioral change but small enough so that it can be achieved. This requirement is a logical one because an unachievable criterion change would doom the experiment to failure and not permit an assessment of the efficacy of the experimental treatment.

METHODOLOGICAL CONSIDERATIONS IN USING SINGLE-CASE DESIGNS

The discussion of the single-case experimental designs we have just presented by no means represents an exhaustive survey, but shows the most basic and commonly used designs. If you are interested in other single-case designs, you should consult Barlow and Hersen's

(1992) book. Regardless of the design used, there are several methodological issues that must be considered when attempting to conduct a single-case study.

Baseline

Baseline
The behavior of the participant prior to the administration of a treatment condition

We define **baseline** as observation of a dependent variable response prior to any attempt to change this response. Baseline, therefore, refers to the occurrence of a response in its freely occurring or natural state. This typically means that the behavior is recorded before anything is done to try to change it. The recording of a baseline is very important in single-case research because the baseline data serve as the standard against which change induced by the experimental treatment is assessed. You can most effectively determine whether the experimental treatment produced a change in dependent variable response when the baseline record is stable. This occurs when there is little variability in the recorded baseline response. The essential question is, When has a stable baseline been achieved? Kazdin (1978) suggests that a stable baseline is characterized by the absence of a trend and by only a slight amount of variability in the data. An absence of trend means that the baseline data do not increase or decrease over time. For example, if you were taking baseline data on the number of times a child exhibits disruptive behaviors during each of twenty 30-minute periods, a trend would exist if the number of disruptive behaviors tended to increase or decrease during each successive observational period. However, if the child consistently exhibited between six and ten disruptive behaviors during each of twenty observation periods, a trend would not exist.

If a trend present during baseline is opposite from what occurs during the experimental intervention phase, than the experiment demonstrates that the treatment condition is powerful enough not only to produce an effect, but also to reverse the previous trend. If the baseline trend is in the same direction as is expected from the intervention, it is difficult to draw an unambiguous conclusion regarding the influence of the treatment condition. In this case, it is best to wait for the baseline to stabilize before introducing the treatment condition. If the trend still persists, it is best to use another design that can more effectively demonstrate the effect of the treatment.

In addition to an absence of trend, a stable baseline, one that has only a slight degree of variability, must exist (Kazdin, 1978). Kazdin (1978) does not clarify the issue of what is meant by a slight degree of variability in the data. Sidman (1960) believes that the baseline response should be stable within a 5 percent range. In other words, if a student engages in an average of twenty disruptive behaviors during a thirty-minute observation period, stability would have been obtained if the number of disruptive behaviors varied from nineteen to twenty-one. However, this criterion is frequently difficult to attain with humans. McCullough, Cornell, McDaniel, and Mueller (1974), for example, found that the number of irrelevant comments made by high school students during a fifty-minute class period ranged from 17 to 104 during an eight-day period.

When extreme fluctuations or unsystematic variations exist in the baseline data, you can artificially reduce the variability by averaging data points across consecutive days or sessions. This averaging substantially reduces variability and allows the effect of the treatment condition to be accurately assessed. However, it does distort the day-to-day or session-to-session pattern of performance.

Changing One Variable at a Time

A cardinal rule in single-case research is that only one variable should be changed from one phase of the experiment to the next. You need to adhere to this rule so that you can isolate the variable that produced the observed behavioral change. For example, if you want to test the effect of reinforcement on increasing the amount of time a student, Cindy, spent working on her mathematics assignment, you could employ an A-B-A design. You first measure her baseline performance by recording the amount of time she spent working on mathematics during a specified observation period such as a class period. Following baseline, you could praise Cindy and give her a token she could trade for additional recess time when she worked on her mathematics assignment. At this point you are violating the rule of one variable because two types of reinforcement, praise and tokens, are being administered. If the amount of time spent working on mathematics assignments increases, you will not know whether it is due to the reinforcement of praise or to the reinforcement of having received a token she could trade for more recess time. In fact, it may not be either reinforcer independently but the combination of the two that is the catalyst. To isolate the effect of each variable, you have to conduct two separate A-B-A designs or use another type of single-case design known as an interaction design. For a discussion of the interaction design, see Christensen (1997).

Length of Phases

One of the issues that must be considered when designing a single-case study is the length of each phase of the study. Although there are few guidelines to follow, most researchers advocate continuing each phase until some degree of stability has been achieved. However, as discussed, in many studies stability of behavior is difficult to achieve. Additionally, waiting for stability leads to unequal phases, which some investigators, such as Barlow and Hersen (1992), consider to be undesirable. Unequal phases, particularly when the treatment phase is extended to demonstrate an effect, increase the possibility of a confounding influence of history or maturation. For example, assume you use praise in an attempt to increase in the amount of time spent on homework assignments. Baseline consists of recording time spent on homework for seven days and treatment consists of giving praise whenever time is spent doing homework for the next fourteen days. Now assume that an increase in time spent on homework assignments during the treatment phase is not evident until after the seventh day. Because a change in behavior does not exist until the eight day, a history or maturation effect may take place at this point in the experiment and account for the behavioral change. Because of the potentially confounding influence of such variables, Barlow and Hersen suggest using an equal number of data points in each phase of the study.

Assessment of Treatment Effect

After you have conducted your single-case experiment, you must determine whether the treatment condition was effective in producing a change in the dependent variable. Did the treatment reduce violent outbursts, increase mathematical skills, reduce disruptive classroom behavior, and so forth? Most single-case researchers have relied upon visual inspection to determine whether the treatment condition was effective in producing a behavioral change. Visual inspection is generally assumed to be sufficient if the behaviors during the baseline phase and the intervention phase do not overlap, or if the trend of the behavior during the baseline phase is different from that which exists during the intervention phase. If these conditions existed, reaching a conclusion that the treatment was effective in producing a change in the dependent variable would be very convincing if baseline behavior were stable. However, if there is a great deal of variability in the data, it is difficult to interpret without statistical analysis, which can analyze extremely variable data more objectively than can individuals. Statistical analysis can therefore provide a valuable supplement to visual inspection. We identified several types of statistical analysis in the section on interrupted time-series designs that can also be applied to the single-case experimental designs. At the present time there is no complete agreement as to which approach—statistical analysis or visual inspection—should be used. It is probably safe to say that statistical analysis adds little to the interpretation of data when a stable baseline and limited variability exists. When these two components do not exist, statistical analysis should be used in addition to visual analysis.

GROUP COMPARISON OR SINGLE-CASE DESIGNS

We have presented group and single-case designs in this and the last chapter, and in both instances we have discussed the designs from the perspective of testing the efficacy of some experimental treatment condition. In the past, the most frequently used designs were some type of group design. However, single-case designs are becoming more popular and are effective in demonstrating the efficacy of an experimental treatment. This might suggest that one type of design is more effective than the other or that one type of design should be used in some instances and the other in other instances. It is impossible to state that one type of design is preferred over the other. Rather, it seems as though the two types of designs should be complementary and integrated into an overall strategy for investigating a problem area.

A number of individuals (e.g., Kazdin, 1973) have suggested that the single-case study should be used in the beginning of an investigation because of its economy in research time and cost. The single-case study could be used as an initial probing procedure to investigate promising experimental treatment conditions to determine whether they may have an effect on specific dependent variables. However, the single-case design should probably serve only as a mapping device and not as a final indication of causality because of the possibility of confounding effects from extraneous variables that cannot be controlled. It is important to realize that the fact that a promising hypothesis is not supported with single-case designs does not discredit it. There is often a great deal of variability in the behavior of different individuals, and an experimental treatment condition that does not work on one individual may be effective on another. Therefore, if the hypothesis does not receive support from the individual on which it was tested, it should be tested on other individuals before it is discarded.

If an experimental treatment is demonstrated to be effective using the single-case approach, Kazdin (1973) and others believe that the treatment should be investigated using group comparison designs. Switching to group comparison designs allows us to more effectively control for the influence of potentially confounding variables and can enable us to examine the degree of generality of the findings. Use of the two types of designs in an integrated fashion allows us to investigate a problem area more effectively and economically. They are both very good designs and both can give us valuable information.

SUMMARY

Quasi-experimental designs are used when all the demands of experimental research cannot be met. For example, these designs are used when it is impossible to randomly assign research participants to the various comparison groups. This means that a confounding variable may be present that would make the interpretation of the results ambiguous. Therefore, whenever you use a quasi-experimental design you must be alert for the influence of extraneous variables that could confound the results.

There are many designs, such as the nonequivalent control-group design and the interrupted time-series design, that fall under the rubric of quasi-experimental designs. The most frequently used design is the nonequivalent control-group design, which consists of giving an experimental and a control group a pretest and then a posttest after an experimental treatment condition has been administered to the experimental group. The interrupted time-series design consists of taking multiple pretests, introducing a treatment condition, and then taking multiple posttests.

Single-case designs are all some type of a time-series design. Two of the most frequently used single-case designs are the A-B-A design and the multiple-baseline design. The A-B-A design assesses the effect of an independent variable by determining whether the dependent variable responses are different from the baseline responses following implementation of the experimental treatment and whether they revert to baseline level when the independent variable is removed. The A-B-A design rules out history by demonstrating that the dependent variable response reverts to baseline when the treatment condition is withdrawn. The multiple-baseline design assesses the effect of an independent variable by demonstrating that a change in behavior occurs only when the treatment effect is successively administered to different individuals, different behaviors, or to the same behavior in different settings.

The changing-criterion design can be used when the goal is to increase the amount, accuracy, or frequency of some behavior. After a baseline is established, a treatment condition is administered following attainment of a specific criterion of initial successful performance. When this performance criterion has been achieved, the criterion is progressively increased until the desired behavior is attained. The treatment condition is administered only after the criterion of successful performance is attained.

There are a number of methodological issues that must be considered when designing a single-case study. Ideally, the baseline must be stable. Although this generally means that there is little variability in the recorded baseline behavior, the definition of "little variability" has not been established. If extreme fluctuations in behavior exist, the researcher must attempt to identify and control the cause of the variation so as to reduce the variability of the participant's responses. Only one variable should be changed at a time when conducting a single-case design so that you can test the effect of that variable on the dependent variable. Additionally, you should consider the length of each phase of the single-case design. Although total agreement does not exist on this issue, one recommendation is to use an equal number of data points in each phase of the study.

After you have collected the data, you must determine whether the experimental treatment condition was effective in producing a behavioral change. Visual inspection of the data is sufficient if the pattern of behavior in the intervention phase is clearly different from the pattern in the baseline phase. If a great deal of variability exists in the data, statistical analysis should probably accompany the visual inspection.

STUDY QUESTIONS

1. What are quasi-experimental research designs and how do they differ from the strong experimental research designs?
2. Diagram the nonequivalent control-group design and explain how you might identify confounding variables that make interpretation of the results difficult.
3. What are single-case research designs?
4. How do single-case research designs rule out rival explanations?
5. How is the treatment effect identified in single-case research designs?
6. What is the multiple-time series design and how is it an improvement over the interrupted time-series design?
7. Diagram the A-B-A design and list its primary limitation.
8. Diagram the multiple-baseline design and discuss its primary limitation.
9. Diagram the changing-criterion design and discuss when you would use this design.
10. Identify and discuss the four methodological issues that must be considered when using a single-case research design.
11. Compare and contrast single-case and group designs.

EXERCISES

To provide you with some experience reading and identifying quasi-experimental and single-case designs, go to the library and get the following two articles.

Romano, J. L. (1996). School personnel prevention training: A measure of self-efficacy. *The Journal of Educational Research, 90,* 57–63.

Mayer, G. R., Mitchell, L. K., Clementi, T., Clement-Robertson, E., & Myatt, R. (1993). A dropout prevention program for at-risk high school students: Emphasizing consulting to promote positive classroom climates. *Education and Treatment of Children, 16,* 135–146.

Once you have the articles in hand, read them carefully and answer the following questions:

1. What is the primary research question addressed by each of these studies?
2. What were the independent and dependent variables in each of these research designs?
3. What type of design was used in each of these studies to answer the research question?
4. Why did the researchers have to use the design selected?
5. What limitations exist with regard to the type of research designs used?
6. What could the researchers have done to improve the research design?

KEY TERMS

A-B-A design (265)

A-B-A-B design (267)

baseline (274)

changing-criterion design (272)

interrupted time-series design (260)

multiple-baseline design (269)

multiple time-series design (263)

nonequivalent control-group design (256)

quasi-experimental research design (255)

selection-maturation effect (259)

single-case experimental designs (264)

CHAPTER 10

Nonexperimental Quantitative Research

LEARNING OBJECTIVES

To be able to

- state the definition of nonexperimental quantitative research.
- identify categorical and quantitative independent variables that cannot be manipulated by a researcher.
- describe the limitations of the simple cases of causal-comparative and correlational research.
- evaluate evidence for cause and effect using the three necessary conditions for cause-and-effect relationships.
- explain the third-variable problem.
- list and briefly describe the three major techniques of control that are used in nonexperimental research.
- compare and contrast cross-sectional research, longitudinal research, and retrospective research.
- compare and contrast the three types of longitudinal research.
- identify descriptive research studies, predictive research studies, and explanatory research studies when examining published research.
- explain the difference between a direct effect and an indirect effect.

Researchers are interested in the issue of causality because they want to learn how the world operates and obtain information about how to make it work better. You have learned in earlier chapters that experimental research is the strongest research method for providing evidence of a causal relationship between two variables. Sometimes, however, researchers are interested in causality but they cannot conduct an experiment, either because the independent variable cannot be manipulated or because it would be unethical to manipulate it. For example, let's say that you want to determine whether cigarette smoking causes lung cancer. What kind of research would you choose? Would you set up the following experiment? Select 500 newborn babies and randomly assign them to two groups, an experimental group ($n = 250$) that would be forced to smoke cigarettes and a control group ($n = 250$) that would not be allowed to smoke cigarettes. Then you would measure the rates of lung cancer in the two groups many years later. Obviously you could never conduct this experiment because it would be highly unethical. So what must you do instead? Should you give up on scientific research because you can't manipulate the independent variable? Of course not. The research problem is much too important. What you have to do in cases like this is use a *non*experimental research method and attempt to establish the best evidence that you can given your practical constraints.

Nonexperimental quantitative research (hereafter called nonexperimental research) is the topic of this chapter. To understand nonexperimental research, however, you need to recall the key characteristics of experimental research. You learned in earlier chapters that experimental and quasi-experimental research involves the *manipulation* of at least one independent variable. In other words, manipulation is the defining characteristic of experimental and quasi-experimental research. Manipulation is important because it allows the researcher to clearly determine who gets what levels of an independent variable. In addition, it allows the researcher to clearly establish the temporal sequence of the independent and dependent variables; that is, the researcher administers the independent variable and is then able to observe what happens to the participants after exposure to the independent variable.

You also know (especially since we are reminding you!) that the strongest experimental designs have *random assignment* to the groups forming the independent variable. Random assignment is the most powerful technique for controlling for extraneous variables. The purpose of random assignment is to make the groups (e.g., an experimental and a control group) approximately the same on all extraneous variables at the start of the experiment. Then, if a difference between the groups on the dependent variable is found *after* manipulation of an independent variable, the researcher can conclude that the observed difference is due to the independent variable rather than an extraneous variable. Random assignment is the best single way to make groups similar at the beginning of an experiment, and, therefore, it is the best way to isolate the influence of the independent variable. In short, manipulation and random assignment are the two most powerful things a researcher can do to make an experimental research study a strong design. In manipulation a researcher exerts direct control over the independent variable. In random assignment a researcher is able to eliminate extraneous variables as rival explanations of a reported finding because the groups will not systematically differ on any extraneous variable but will systematically differ on the independent variable.

Nonexperimental research
Research in which the independent variable is not manipulated by the researcher

You are now ready to understand nonexperimental research. Here is the formal definition of **nonexperimental research** used in this chapter (Kerlinger, 1986):

> Nonexperimental research is systematic empirical inquiry in which the scientist does not have direct control of independent variables because their manifestations have already occurred or because they are inherently not manipulable. Inferences about relations among variables are made, without direct intervention, from concomitant variation of independent and dependent variables. (p. 348)

You can see in Kerlinger's definition that the researcher does not manipulate the independent variable in nonexperimental research (i.e., "the scientist does not have direct control of independent variables"); the researcher can look back at what naturally happened in the past, or he or she can move forward and observe what happens over time (i.e., "because their manifestations have already occurred or because they are inherently not manipulable"); and the researcher observes how variables relate to one another (i.e., "Inferences about relations among variables are made . . . from concomitant variation of independent and dependent variables"). The independent and dependent variables can be categorical and/or quantitative in nonexperimental research. In this chapter you should assume that the dependent variable is quantitative unless we tell you otherwise. However, the logic explained in this chapter equally applies to a research study with a categorical dependent variable.[1]

Manipulation of an independent variable and random assignment to groups are missing in *non*experimental research studies. This means that nonexperimental researchers must study the world as it naturally occurs. Because nonexperimental researchers cannot directly manipulate their independent variables or randomly assign research participants to experimental and control groups, a red flag should always pop up in your mind reminding you that nonexperimental research cannot provide evidence for causality that is as strong as the evidence obtained in experimental research. Although we do not obtain final proof of the existence of causal relationships in either experimental or nonexperimental research, we do obtain much stronger evidence for causality in experimental research. In short, evidence for causality in nonexperimental research is more tentative, more exploratory, and less conclusive.

Despite its limitations, nonexperimental research is very important to the field of education because many important educational variables cannot be manipulated or created in the laboratory, and it is difficult if not impossible to create many real-life settings using experiments. Here is the way one leading research methodologist put it:

> It can even be said that nonexperimental research is more important than experimental research. This is, of course, not a methodological observation. It means, rather, that most social scientific and educational research problems do not lend themselves to experimentation, although many of them do lend themselves to controlled inquiry of the nonexperimental kind. Consider Piaget's studies of children's thinking, the authoritarianism studies of Adorno et al., the highly important study *Equality of Educational Opportunity,* and McClelland's studies of need for achievement. If a tally of sound and important studies in the behavioral sciences and education were made, it is possible that nonexperimental studies would outnumber and outrank experimental studies. (Kerlinger, 1986, pp. 359–360)

Kerlinger was trying to emphasize the importance of nonexperimental research in this quote despite the fact that he actually preferred experimental to nonexperimental research. He was careful to point out that his reasoning was not based on a methodological observation because, again, other things being equal, you should prefer an experiment when you are interested in studying causality. It is a cardinal rule in research, however, that *your research questions should drive your research.* This means that you first determine your research questions and then select the strongest research method available to address those questions. In education, this often means that we have to conduct nonexperimental research in order to address important questions.

STEPS IN NONEXPERIMENTAL RESEARCH

The typical steps in nonexperimental research are similar to the steps in experimental research. (1) The researcher determines the research problem and the research hypotheses to be tested. (2) The researcher selects the variables to be used in the study. (3) The researcher collects the data. (4) The researcher analyzes the data. (5) The researcher interprets the results of the study. The researcher specifically determines whether the hypotheses are supported. The researcher also typically explores the data to generate additional hypotheses to be tested in future research studies. It is important that the researcher follow these steps when conducting nonexperimental research in order to avoid the post hoc fallacy.

Post hoc fallacy
Making the argument that because A preceded B, A must have caused B

The **post hoc fallacy** reads *post hoc, ergo propter hoc.* (Now you know a little Latin!) In English this says, "after this, therefore because of this." We engage in the post hoc fallacy if we argue after the fact that since A preceded B, A must have caused B. For example, you get the flu and attribute it to your friend's sniffling child, who visited your home yesterday. This kind of reasoning is more informally known as "twenty-twenty hindsight." We are all pretty good at explaining, after the fact, why something happened. Although this kind of reasoning is fine for generating ideas, it is far from conclusive scientific evidence. An especially egregious form of the post hoc fallacy would occur if a researcher analyzed some data, found some statistically significant correlations or group differences, and then acted as if he or she had predicted those relationships. The point is that in explanatory research, you must test your hypotheses with empirical data to make sure that they work.

INDEPENDENT VARIABLES IN NONEXPERIMENTAL RESEARCH

We have pointed out that the independent variables used in nonexperimental research frequently cannot be manipulated, either because it is impossible to manipulate them or because it would be unethical to manipulate them. Nonexperimental research is also sometimes done on independent variables that can be but are not manipulated because the researcher wants to explore how the independent variable is related to other variables before doing an experiment or the researcher wants to replicate a result that has been previously demonstrated with experimental research. All these forms of nonexperimental research can make a contribution to the educational research literature.

Now let's look at some examples of categorical and quantitative independent variables that might be used in nonexperimental research because they cannot be manipulated. Some categorical independent variables that cannot be manipulated by the researcher are gender, parenting style, student learning style, ethnicity, retention in grade (i.e., retained or not retained), drug or tobacco use, any enduring personality trait that is operationalized as a categorical variable (e.g., high extroversion versus low extroversion), and so forth. You can probably think of some additional categorical independent variables that can't be manipulated by the researcher if you try. Some quantitative independent variables that cannot be manipulated by the researcher are intelligence, aptitude, age, GPA, any enduring personality trait that is operationalized as a quantitative variable (e.g., degree of extroversion varying from a low value of 1 to a high value of 100), and so forth. Again, you can probably think of some additional quantitative independent variables that can't be manipulated by the researcher if you think about it for a moment.

Researchers sometimes turn inherently quantitative independent variables into categorical independent variables. For example, you could take the quantitative variable aptitude and categorize it into three groups (high, medium, and low motivation). Another example is in the previous paragraph, where we pointed out that extroversion could be operationalized as either a categorical variable or a quantitative variable. Categorizing an independent variable makes the research study look like an experiment because the independent variable is usually categorical in experimental research studies. Do *not* be misled, however. If the independent variable is not manipulated, then it is not an experiment. Most experts contend that categorizing quantitative independent variables is a poor practice that should be discontinued (e.g., Kerlinger, 1986, p. 558; Pedhazur & Schmelkin, 1991, p. 308). The problem is that you lose some information about the relationship between the independent and dependent variables when you categorize a quantitative variable. Also, if only two categories are used (e.g., high versus low) then only linear (straight line) relationships can be examined. You can solve this last problem by simply using three categories rather than two categories. The problem of loss of information cannot be avoided. In short, we recommend that researchers generally avoid turning quantitative variables into categorical variables.

CAUSAL-COMPARATIVE AND CORRELATIONAL RESEARCH

You learned in Chapter 1 that the term causal-comparative research is sometimes applied to nonexperimental research in which the primary independent variable of interest is categorical, and the term correlational research is sometimes applied to nonexperimental research in which the primary independent variable of interest is quantitative (Fraenkel & Wallen, 1996). In practice, many published nonexperimental research studies are a cross between causal-comparative and correlational because the researchers include one or more categorical independent variables and one or more quantitative independent variables in the same research study. It is also important to realize that many published research studies are a cross between experimental and nonexperimental research. This happens when the researcher manipulates one variable (e.g., method of teaching) but includes another independent variable that is not manipulated (e.g., intelligence).

The distinction between causal-comparative and correlational research is artificial because one can easily transform a correlational research study into a causal-comparative research study by simply categorizing the independent variable. (We gave examples of categorizing the variables aptitude and extroversion earlier.) We recommend, however, that researchers do *not* categorize inherently quantitative independent variables. Students and researchers need to understand that what is *essential* when addressing the issue of causation is not whether an independent variable is categorical or quantitative, but how effectively the researcher deals with the three *necessary conditions for causation* (discussed later). Furthermore, we point out that many published research articles are a cross between causal-comparative and correlational. Nonetheless, it is instructive to learn about what are called the **simple cases** of causal-comparative and correlational research (i.e., nonexperimental research designs with only one independent variable and one dependent variable) when you are first learning about research because it allows you to start with the most basic forms of nonexperimental research.

In the **simple case of causal-comparative research,** there is one categorical independent variable and one quantitative dependent variable. For example, perhaps a researcher examined the relationship between gender and math performance and found out that, on average, the males did slightly better than the females. This is a simple case of causal-comparative research because there is one categorical independent variable (gender) and one quantitative dependent variable (math performance). In the simple case of causal-comparative research the researcher compares the two group means (males versus females) to see whether the groups differ on the dependent variable (math performance). The researcher also uses a statistical test to determine whether the relationship between the independent and dependent variables is statistically significant. The researcher would specifically use either a *t*-test or an ANOVA (explained in Chapter 14) to determine whether the difference between the two group means is **statistically significant** (i.e., Is the difference between the groups greater than what one would expect to see by chance?). Group means that are very different are usually statistically significant, and if they are, the researcher concludes that there is a relationship between the independent and dependent variables. (We will carefully explain the ideas of *t*-test, ANOVA, and statistical significance in Chapter 14. So don't worry about knowing any more than the basics for now! We just wanted to use these terms here to show you where they fit into the overall research process.)

In the **simple case of correlational research** there is one quantitative independent variable and one quantitative dependent variable. For example, perhaps a researcher examined the relationship between students' level of motivation and their math performance and found out that lower levels of motivation predicted lower math performance and higher levels of motivation predicted higher math performance (i.e., there was a positive correlation). In the simple case of correlational research, the researcher first plots his or her data to determine whether the relationship is linear or curvilinear. Examples of linear and curvilinear relationships are shown in Figure 10.1. As you can see, a linear relationship follows a

Simple cases
When there is only one independent variable and one dependent variable

Simple case of causal-comparative research
When there is one categorical independent variable and one quantitative dependent variable

Statistically significant
A research finding is probably *not* attributable to chance

Simple case of correlational research
When there is one quantitative independent variable and one quantitative dependent variable

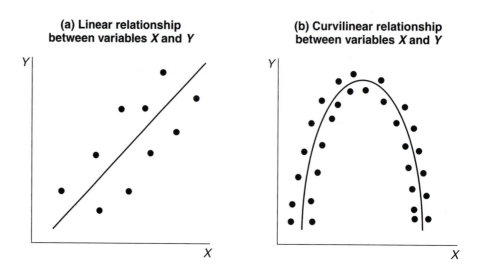

FIGURE 10.1   Linear and curvilinear relationships.

straight-line pattern and a curvilinear relationship follows a curved-line pattern. If the relationship between the variables is linear, then the researcher computes the Pearson Product Moment correlation coefficient. This is the most commonly used correlation coefficient (discussed in Chapter 1), and it is the one that researchers are usually referring to if they say they computed the "correlation" (without specifying the type of correlation). If the relationship is curvilinear, the researcher must rely on an alternative measure of the relationship between two variables known as η (Greek eta) (for details, see Howell, 1997, pp. 331–333) or use curvilinear regression (for details, see Pedhazur & Schmelkin, 1991, pp. 451–458).

After determining the correlation between the single independent variable and the single dependent variable in the simple case of correlational research, the researcher usually conducts a statistical test to determine whether the correlation is statistically significant. A correlation coefficient is said to be statistically significant when it is larger than would be expected by chance. Correlation coefficients that are much larger than zero are usually statistically significant.

Assume now that a researcher found that the relationship between the two variables was statistically significant in our examples of the simple cases of causal-comparative and correlational research. *It is important for you to remember that both of these simple cases of nonexperimental research are seriously flawed if you want to make a causal attribution* (i.e., if you want to conclude that gender affects math performance or if you want to conclude that level of motivation affects math performance). The biggest problem is that there are too many uncontrolled extraneous variables that may be the reason for the observed relationship. For example, can you think of some alternative explanations for an observed relationship between gender and math achievement (e.g., perhaps females are socialized to deemphasize mathematics and males are socialized to emphasize mathematics)? Can you think of some reasons why level of motivation might not be causally related to math achievement (e.g., perhaps math achievement is due to amount of time spent studying and ability rather than motivation)? These other reasons were not controlled or their influence was not held constant across the levels of variation of the independent variable. Therefore, they are rival explanations for any effect you believe you have observed on the dependent variable.

The key point is that you cannot draw a conclusion about cause and effect from either the simple case of causal-comparative research or the simple case of correlational research because *observing a relationship between two variables is not nearly enough evidence to conclude that the relationship is causal.* In the next sections we explain how you can establish firmer evidence of causation, and, as a result, you will be able to improve on the simple cases of causal-comparative and correlational research. For example, you can design superior nonexperimental research studies by also collecting data on extraneous variables that represent plausible alternative explanations. Then you can attempt to control for or rule out those extraneous variables as possible explanations for the results found in your research study. In practice, you should avoid the simple cases of causal-comparative and correlational research whenever you are interested in studying cause and effect.

THREE NECESSARY CONDITIONS FOR CAUSE-AND-EFFECT RELATIONSHIPS

Three necessary conditions
Three things that must be present if you are to contend that causation has occurred

Probabilistic cause
Changes in variable A tend to produce changes in variable B

Whenever your goal is to provide evidence about the existence of a cause-and-effect relationship between two variables, you must check for the presence of the **three necessary conditions** for concluding that changes in variable A tend to produce (cause) changes in variable B (Asher, 1983; Cook & Campbell, 1979). Notice that we said "tend to" in the previous sentence. We used those words to remind you that educational researchers are interested in **probabilistic cause** (i.e., changes in variable A tend to cause changes in variable B), not perfect causation (i.e., changes in variable A always produce the same changes in variable B). The idea of probabilistic cause should make sense to you because you know that, for example, a technique of teaching might work quite well for many students but it does not work well for a few of your students. Counselors know that a certain type of therapy may work well for many clients but not for a few of their clients. It is also true that the same individual might not always react the same way to the same stimulus. For these reasons, when educational researchers talk about causation, they are almost always talking about probabilistic causation rather than about perfect or absolute causation.

The three necessary conditions that you must always consider if you want to establish that changes in variable A tend to *cause* changes in variable B are discussed in Chapter 7. They are shown again in Table 10.1 for your review. As you can see in the table, condition 1 states that variable A and variable B must be related. This is the relationship condition: If there is no relationship whatsoever between two variables then one variable cannot affect the other variable. Condition 2 states that proper time order must be established. This condition should be obvious, because if changes in variable A are to cause changes in variable B, the changes in variable A must precede the changes in variable B.

TABLE 10.1   The Three Necessary Conditions for Causation

Researchers must establish three conditions if they are to conclude that changes in variable A cause changes in variable B.

Condition 1:	Variable A and variable B must be related (the relationship condition).
Condition 2:	Proper time order must be established (the temporal antecedence condition).
Condition 3:	The relationship between variable A and variable B must *not* be due to some confounding extraneous or "third" variable (the lack of alternative explanation condition).

Condition 3 says that the relationship between variable A and variable B must not be due to a confounding extraneous or third variable. This means that alternative or rival explanations must be eliminated. A common rival explanation states that an observed relationship was due to an extraneous variable (i.e., a third variable) that was not controlled for in the research study. This rival explanation is sometimes called the **third-variable problem** because it states that the relationship between A and B is actually due to C. We discuss the third-variable problem in more depth later. The key point for now is that because you want to conduct a strong research study, you must identify extraneous variables that operate as rival explanations, and you should identify those variables during the planning and designing phases of the study so the problem can be prevented. After a study has been completed, it is usually too late to do anything about an extraneous variable.

Third-variable problem
An observed relationship between two variables that may be due to an extraneous variable

Some terminology is potentially confusing. First, the terms *confounding variables* and *third variables* are used interchangeably in this chapter because they are synonyms. Both terms refer to extraneous variables that researchers need to identify before they collect their data so that they can attempt to eliminate the variables as rival explanations for an observed relationship. You can eliminate or minimize the influence of third variables by using one of the approaches discussed in the section on techniques of control in nonexperimental research. Second, the terms *alternative explanation, rival explanation, alternative hypothesis,* and *rival hypothesis* are also used interchangeably in this chapter because they also are synonyms. These terms are used to refer to new reasons for an observed relationship other than the reason originally stated by a researcher (i.e., the new reasons operate as alternatives or rivals).

Method of working multiple hypotheses
Attempting to identify all rival explanations

A technique for identifying rival explanations is called the **method of working multiple hypotheses** (Chamberlin, 1965). Chamberlin explains the method of working multiple hypotheses this way:

> The effort is to bring up into view every rational explanation of new phenomena, and to develop every tenable hypothesis respecting their cause and history. The investigator thus becomes the parent of a family of hypotheses; and, by his parental relation to all, he is forbidden to fasten his affections unduly upon any one. (cited in Kerlinger, 1986, p. 357)

If you conduct a research study, remember to use the method of working multiple hypotheses when you are *planning* the study, not after you have completed it and someone has identified the potential flaw. This way you can obtain conclusions that are defensible.

The three necessary conditions for cause and effect that we just discussed are truly general. They apply to both experimental and nonexperimental research. In fact, the criteria apply whenever you want to establish evidence that a relationship is causal, regardless of your research method (e.g., the conditions even apply in qualitative research if you are interested in causality). You have learned in previous chapters that strong experimental research designs (i.e., designs with manipulation and random assignment) perform extremely well on the three conditions for causation. Now we examine how well nonexperimental research performs on the three necessary conditions for causality.

APPLYING THE THREE NECESSARY CONDITIONS FOR CAUSATION IN NONEXPERIMENTAL RESEARCH

Neither manipulation nor random assignment is present in nonexperimental research. Let's examine the implications this fact has for establishing evidence of cause and effect. We start with the simple cases of causal-comparative and correlational research discussed earlier. Recall that in the simple cases there is a single independent variable and a single dependent variable. In an earlier example, we saw that a relationship was observed between gender and math performance in our causal-comparative example and a relationship was observed between level of motivation and math performance in our correlational example. The problem that we run into with the two simple cases is that observing a relationship is clearly not sufficient grounds for concluding that a relationship is causal. Let's more formally apply the three necessary conditions for causation to the two simple cases.

In the case of gender and math performance, a relationship was observed. This means that condition 1 is met (i.e., relationship between the two variables must be observed). We can also assume that gender occurs before math performance as measured in the research study if we assume that gender is a measure of one's biological sex. That's because biological sex is fixed at birth. In this case, condition 2 also appears to be met (i.e., gender comes before math performance). Note that one may argue that gender is much more than biological sex. If one makes this argument, however, it would be wise to specifically measure the important aspects of gender and study how they relate to the dependent variable. One would then have to consider the issue of time order for each new aspect studied.

Our biggest problem, based on the three necessary conditions, is with condition 3. There are many alternative explanations for an observed relationship between gender and math performance. As we pointed out earlier, perhaps males and females are socialized differently regarding mathematics. Or perhaps females are just as good at math as males except that they tend to have higher math anxiety than males, which lowers their math performance. Socialization and math anxiety represent uncontrolled third variables that are confounded (entangled) with the independent variable gender. Therefore, we cannot know for sure whether math performance is due to gender or whether it is due to socialization or to math anxiety (or to some other unnamed third variable). This problem is an example of the *third-variable problem* that is omnipresent in nonexperimental research. The third-variable problem is present whenever there are uncontrolled and, therefore, potentially confounding extraneous variables present.

Now let's move to the case of level of motivation and math performance. Once again, a relationship was observed (the higher the motivation, the higher the math performance). Therefore condition number 1 is met (relationship between the two variables is present). We can't know for sure whether level of motivation or math performance occurred first, since we assume that the researchers measured both variables at the same time in this example. (Later in this chapter we discuss some nonexperimental designs in which participants are studied at more than one time point.) We might assume on theoretical grounds that the level of motivation was to some degree present before the students took the test measuring their math performance. It is reasonable to assume, for example, that students who are more motivated will attend class regularly and study harder, and attending class and studying for exams occur before the actual exams. On the other hand, we cannot know time ordering for sure because it is also reasonable to believe that math performance has some impact on level of motivation. In short, condition 2 (proper time order) is only partially met because the proper time order is only assumed or hypothesized to occur, and no direct evidence exists that the proper time order did occur.

As was the case in the gender study example, condition 3 is a major problem. There are alternative explanations for the observed relationship between level of motivation and math performance. We listed two rival explanations earlier: perhaps the students' math performance was due to amount of time spend studying or to ability rather than to level of motivation. The problem of alternative or rival explanations is omnipresent in nonexperimental research. In a nonexperimental study, the researcher can never know for sure whether an observed relationship can be explained away by some uncontrolled extraneous or third variable that a researcher failed to identify.

The most serious problem that we run into in the simple cases of causal-comparative and correlational research is that the observed relationship may be due to an extraneous variable (condition 3). We have called this the third-variable problem. When the relationship between two variables is due to another variable, researchers sometimes call it a **spurious relationship.** A spurious relationship is a completely noncausal relationship. When the relationship between two variables is only partially due to another variable, the relationship is said to be **partially spurious** (Davis, 1985). If a third variable is to cause the third-variable problem, it must be related to both the independent and the dependent variable. The idea of a spurious relationship is shown in Figure 10.2. As you can see in the figure, the relationship between variable A and variable B is spurious because the relationship is due to the third variable.

Spurious relationship When the relationship between two variables is due to one or more third variables

Partially spurious When the relationship between two variables is partially due to one or more third variable

FIGURE 10.2 A spurious relationship. The observed relationship between variable A and variable B is "due to" a third variable, which is also called a confounding extraneous variable. The observed relationship between variable A and variable B will disappear after you control for the third variable.

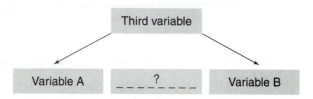

Did you know that the amount of fire damage to houses and the number of fire trucks responding to fires is positively related? However, we should not conclude based on this observed relationship that calling more fire trucks to a fire will cause more fire damage to occur because this is a spurious relationship. The real cause of the relationship between fire damage and the number of trucks responding is the *size of the fire.* More fire trucks respond to larger fires and more damage results from larger fires. However, if you only examined the relationship between number of fire trucks and amount of fire damage without considering the size of fire, you would find a clear, positive relationship [see part (a) in Figure 10.3].

Researchers frequently check to see whether relationships are due to third variables by controlling for these variables. You have controlled for a third variable when you have provided evidence that the relationship between two variables is not due to a third variable. In particular, *the original relationship between two variables will actually disappear when controlling for the third variable if the relationship is totally spurious,* as in the case of fire damage and fire trucks. In part (b) of Figure 10.3 we controlled for size of fire by examining

(a) Before controlling for size of fire

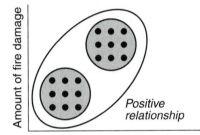

(b) After controlling for size of fire

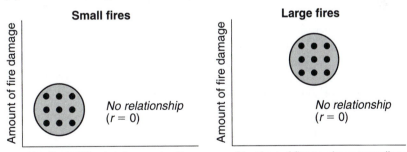

FIGURE 10.3   Relationship between amount of fire damage and number of trucks responding before and after controlling for size of fire. We controlled for size of fire by examining the original relationship at different levels of size of fire. The original relationship disappears.

the original relationship separately for small fires and large fires (i.e., we examined the relationship within levels of the extraneous variable). As you can see, there is no relationship between fire damage and number of trucks when you look only at small fires. Likewise, there is no relationship when you look only at large fires. Therefore, the original relationship between variables fire damage and number of fire trucks responding disappears when you control for the size of fire. In other words, there is no longer a relationship between the variables fire damage and number of fire trucks responding after you control for the third variable size of fire. Examining a relationship within the different levels of a third variable such as we just did is an important strategy of controlling for an extraneous variable. This strategy is one type of what we refer to as *statistical control.*

We have provided a list of some additional spurious relationships in Table 10.2. We think you will find the list quite entertaining! For example, did you know that there is a pos-

TABLE 10.2   Examples of Spurious Relationships

*Observed Spurious Relationship**	*Reason for the Relationship (the Third Variable)*
Amount of ice cream sold and deaths by drownings (Moore, 1993)	Season: Ice cream sales and drownings tend to be high during the warm months of the year.
Size of left hand and size of right hand	Genetics: The size of both hands is due to genetic makeup.
Height of sons and height of daughters (Davis, 1985)	Genetics: Heights of sons and daughters are both due their parents' genetic makeup.
Ministers' salaries and price of vodka	Area (i.e., urban or rural): In urban areas, prices and salaries tend to be higher.
Shoe size and reading performance for elementary school children	Age: Older children have larger shoe sizes and read better.
Number of doctors in region and number of people dying from disease	Population density: In highly dense areas, there are more doctors and more people die.
Number of police officers and number of crimes (Glass and Hopkins, 1996)	Population density: In highly dense areas, there are more police officers and more crimes.
Number of homicides and number of churches	Population density: In highly dense areas, there are more homicides and more churches.
Number of storks sighted and the population of Oldenburg, Germany, over a six-year period (Box, Hunter, and Hunter, 1978)	Time: Both variables were increasing over time.
Number of public libraries and the amount of drug use	Time: Both were increasing during the 1970s.
Teachers' salaries and the price of liquor (Moore and McCabe, 1993)	Time: Both tend to increase over time.

*Each of the spurious relationships in the first column shows a positive correlation. That is, as one of the variables increases, the other variable also increases.

itive relationship (i.e., a positive correlation) between the number of police officers in an area and the number of crimes in the area? Obviously, we cannot conclude based on this observed relationship that having more police officers causes crime. The completely spurious relationship is due to the third variable, population density. There are more crimes and more police officers in areas with many people, and there are fewer crimes and fewer police officers in areas with fewer people. Once the researcher controls for the third variable (population density), the original relationship will disappear. For example, if the researcher examined the relationship between police officers and crime within the different levels of population density (low, medium, and high population density), the relationship would disappear. Each of the spurious relationships shown in Table 10.2 will disappear if the researcher controls for the third variable causing the spurious relationship. None of the relationships is causal.

TECHNIQUES OF CONTROL IN NONEXPERIMENTAL RESEARCH

You learned in the previous section that the third-variable problem is usually present in nonexperimental research. This means that the threat of confounding extraneous variables is virtually always present in nonexperimental research. Now we discuss the major techniques that researchers use to control for extraneous variables in nonexperimental research. You have already been introduced to most of these ideas in earlier chapters (e.g., see Chapters 7 and 8).

Matching

Matching variable
The variable the researcher matches to eliminate it as an alternative explanation

As discussed in earlier chapters, one way to control for extraneous variables is to use matching. To perform matching you must first select one or more **matching variable.** The matching variable(s) are extraneous variable(s) that you want to eliminate as threats to the presumed causal relationship between your independent and dependent variables. The second step in matching is to select participants to be in your study in such a way that your independent and matching variables will be unrelated (i.e., uncorrelated, or unconfounded). If your independent variable is categorical, this simply involves constructing comparison groups that are similar on the matching variable but different on the independent variable. This is exactly the same goal that you had in experimental research.

For example, assume that your independent variable is gender and your dependent variable is math performance. Also assume that you want to match the groups on interest in mathematics because you think the relationship that is sometimes observed between gender and math performance is due to the fact that boys are socialized to be interested in mathematics. That is, perhaps boys are more interested in mathematics because of gender socialization, and, as a result, boys try harder and perform better in mathematics. In order to match on interest in mathematics, you could give an interest in mathematics test to all the students in your local high school. You could find twenty-five boys whose interest levels varied from low to high. Then, for each of these twenty-five boys, you would locate a girl with a similar score on the interest in mathematics test. When you were done, you would have twenty-five boys and twenty-five girls that were matched on interest in mathematics (for a total of fifty research participants). The two groups would be similar on the variable interest in mathematics (the extraneous variable you were worried about), but they would differ on gender (the independent variable). In order to complete this nonexperimental research study, you would measure the dependent variable math performance for the twenty-five boys and twenty-five girls to see whether they differed. If they did differ, it would not be because of interest in mathematics because the groups were similar on interest in mathematics.

Matching can also be used when the independent variable is quantitative. Assume that your independent variable is level of mathematics motivation (a quantitative variable varying from a low value of one to a high value of ten); your dependent variable is actual math performance; and the extraneous variable you want to eliminate as a rival explanation is grade point average (i.e., GPA is a proxy for overall academic achievement). Your research hypothesis is that higher motivation leads to higher math performance. In this example, you could match on the extraneous variable (GPA) by finding students with high, medium, and low GPAs at each of the ten levels of mathematics motivation. That is, for low-motivation students, you would locate students with high, medium, and low GPAs. Then for the next higher level of motivation, you would locate students with high, medium, and low GPAs. You would continue this process for all ten levels of motivation.[2] After completing this process you would have your research participants. Furthermore, your independent variable (motivation) and your matching variable (GPA) will be uncorrelated and, therefore, unconfounded. If you still observed a relationship between motivation and math performance, you conclude that it is not due to GPA because you eliminated GPA as a threat through the matching technique.

The key idea is that matching is used to strengthen nonexperimental research studies on condition 3 of the necessary conditions for causation (Table 10.1). That is, it is used to eliminate alternative explanations due to extraneous variables. Matching unfortunately has a number of weaknesses that limit its use. We conclude our discussion by listing the seven major limitations. (1) Matching can be cumbersome because you must search for individuals who meet the criteria for inclusion in the research study. This is a serious limitation unless you have a very large pool of potential participants to select from and you have access to information about them. (2) Researchers frequently cannot find matches for many potential research participants. These potential participants are eliminated or excluded from the research study. (3) There is usually more than one alternative explanation for the relationship of interest, so you need to match on more than one variable. (4) You must know what the relevant extraneous variables are in order to match. (5) You never know for sure that you have matched on all of the appropriate variables. (6) If you select people based on extreme scores, then the threat to internal validity, called regression to the mean, can be a problem in studies occurring over time (i.e., in longitudinal designs, discussed below). (7) Matching can create an unrepresentative sample because the participants are selected for the purpose of matching rather than for the purpose of being representative of a population. Therefore, the generalizability of the research (the external validity) may be compromised.

Holding the Extraneous Variable Constant

When using this technique of control, researchers turn the extraneous variable into a constant. They do this by restricting the research study to a particular subgroup. For example, if you are concerned that gender may operate as a confounding extraneous variable, then you can turn gender into a constant by including only female participants in your research study. If everyone is a female, then gender does not vary (it is a constant). Most importantly, if all participants are one gender, then gender cannot possibly confound the relationship between the independent and dependent variables. If you were concerned that age is a confounding extraneous variable, you could limit your research study to young people, middle-aged people, or older people. You could even limit the study to sixteen-year-old adolescents. Unfortunately, there is a serious problem with the technique of restricting your research study to a certain subpopulation. The researcher cannot generalize to the kinds of people that are excluded from the study. In other words, the generalizability (the external validity) of the study is restricted. For example, if the study were only done with sixteen-year-old adolescents, then the researcher could only generalize to sixteen-year-old adolescents.

Statistical Control

General linear model
A mathematical procedure that is the "parent" of many statistical techniques

Statistical control is the most commonly used technique for controlling for extraneous variables in nonexperimental research. When statistically controlling for one or more extraneous variables, the researcher uses a statistical technique to remove the influence of the extraneous variable(s). Most techniques of statistical control are spinoffs of a mathematical procedure called the **general linear model,** or the GLM (Knapp, 1978; Tabachnick & Fidell, 1996; Thompson, 1998). All you need to know about the general linear model is that it is the "parent" of many statistical techniques (i.e., the "children") that are used in education. More formally, many statistical procedures commonly used to control for extraneous variables are called special cases of the general linear model.

Special case of the general linear model
One of the "children" of a broader statistical procedure known as the general linear model (GLM)

One **special case of the general linear model** is called **partial correlation,** which is used to examine the relationship between two quantitative variables controlling for one or more quantitative extraneous variables (Cohen, 1968; Cohen & Cohen, 1983). It is called a partial correlation because the effect of the third variable is "partialled out" or removed from the original relationship. Typically, all the variables used in partial correlation analysis must be quantitative rather than categorical. Here is a relatively easy way to think about partial correlation. If you determine the regular correlation between your independent variable and your dependent variable *at each of the levels* of your extraneous variable, you will have several correlations (e.g., if your extraneous variable had ten levels, then you would have ten correlations; if your extraneous variable had one hundred levels, then you would have one hundred correlations). The partial correlation coefficient is simply the average of those correlations (Pedhazur, 1997). The range of a partial correlation coefficient is the same as a regular correlation coefficient (i.e., −1.00 to + 1.00, with zero signifying no relationship at all). As a general rule, if a researcher uses a regular correlation coefficient (the correlation between two variables) rather than a partial correlation coefficient (the correlation between two variables controlling for one or more additional variables), then you can

Partial correlation
Used to examine the relationship between two quantitative variables controlling for one or more quantitative extraneous variables

be pretty sure that he or she was not thinking about extraneous variables. On the other hand, if a researcher uses a partial correlation coefficient (or another control technique), you can be pretty sure that he or she was thinking about controlling for extraneous variables. As a general rule, you should upgrade your evaluations of research articles in which the authors controlled for extraneous variables.

Analysis of covariance Used to examine the relationship between one categorical independent variable and one quantitative dependent variable, controlling for one or more extraneous variables

Another special case of the general linear model is called **analysis of covariance,** which was discussed in earlier chapters. ANCOVA is used to determine the relationship between one categorical independent variable and one quantitative dependent variable controlling for one or more quantitative extraneous variables (Pedhazur & Schmelkin, 1991). For example, there is a relationship between gender (a categorical variable) and income (a quantitative variable) in the United States. Men earn more money, on average, than do women. You might decide, however, that you want to control for education; that is, you want to make sure that the difference is not due to education. You could eliminate education as a rival explanation (i.e., you could control for it) by comparing the average income levels of males and females at each of the levels of education in your data. You could also have the computer analyze your data using the ANCOVA technique to tell you whether gender and income are still related after controlling for education. If gender and income are still related, then the researcher can conclude that education has been eliminated as a rival hypothesis. The details of ANCOVA and partial correlation are beyond the scope of this book, but ANCOVA shows the relationship between a categorical independent variable (e.g., gender) and a quantitative dependent variable (e.g., income level) controlling for a quantitative extraneous variable (e.g., level of education).

An advantage of statistical control (compared to matching) is that researchers can base their research on samples of participants who are randomly selected from a population (Pedhazur & Schmelkin, 1991). (You don't have to throw out cases from the data as you do in matching when you can't find a match for an individual.) In order to statistically control for one or more extraneous variables, a researcher must collect data on the extraneous variables in addition to data on the independent and dependent variables (i.e., collect data on all the important variables). In effect, the researcher incorporates the extraneous variables into the design of the research study. Then, after collecting the data, the researcher controls for the extraneous variables during data analysis (using ANCOVA, partial correlation, or another technique).

TIME DIMENSION IN RESEARCH

It is important to have an understanding of the time dimension for at least two reasons. First, we often want to study how variables change over time (e.g., what happens to children as they get older). Second, the second necessary condition for establishing cause and effect is if variable A affects variable B, then variable A must occur before variable B. In other words, when studying cause and effect, researchers must establish proper time order. This means that we are concerned about the time dimension whenever we talk about a cause and effect. Nonexperimental research is classified into three types of research that address the time dimension issue quite differently. These three types of research are called cross-sectional research, longitudinal research, and retrospective research.

Cross-Sectional Research

Cross-sectional research
Data are collected at a single point in time and comparisons are made across the variables of interest

In **cross-sectional research,** data are collected from the research participants at a single point in time or during a single, relatively brief time period (i.e., a period long enough to collect data from all of the participants selected to be in the study). The data are typically collected from multiple groups or types of people in cross-sectional research. For example, data in a cross-sectional study might be collected from males and females, from persons in different socioeconomic classes, from multiple age groups, and from persons with different abilities and accomplishments. The major advantage of cross-sectional research is that data can be collected on many different kinds of people in a relatively short period of time.

Cross-sectional research has several weaknesses. One disadvantage is that it is difficult to establish time order (condition 2 of the necessary conditions for causality). If you collect data from research participants at a single time point only, you can't directly measure changes that are occurring in them over time. Time order can be partially established in cross-sectional research through theory, through past research findings, and through an understanding of the independent variable (e.g., you can safely assume that an adult's biological sex occurs before the amount of education they have because biological sex is set at birth). These techniques for establishing time order are weaker than actually observing people over time. A related disadvantage is that the study of developmental trends (changes in people as they get older) can be misleading when using cross-sectional data.

Suppose that you collected cross-sectional data from 1,000 adults who were ages 18 or older. When analyzing the data, suppose that you found that age and political conservatism were positively correlated (the older the participants are, the more conservative they tend to be). You cannot safely conclude in this case that aging causes conservatism because you have not established proper time order (necessary condition 2) and you have not ruled out rival explanations (necessary condition 3). Remember this important point: In a cross-sectional study people at different ages are not the same people. Therefore, you are not able to observe your participants change over time and properly establish time order. In addition, the older and younger people may differ on important extraneous variables (e.g., they might differ on education and experience of certain historical events). An alternative explanation for the relationship between age and political conservatism is that the people in the earlier generations of your data (the older people) have always been more conservative than the more recent generations (the younger people), perhaps because of some historical effect. The younger people lived in different historical times during their formative years, and they may turn out differently when they are older. Thus, you can't make a strong conclusion that age causes people to become more conservative.

Longitudinal research
Data are collected at multiple time points and comparisons are made across time

Longitudinal Research

In **longitudinal research,** the data are collected at more than one time point or data-collection period, and the researcher is interested in making comparisons across time.

Although longitudinal research requires a minimum of two time periods, data can be collected over as many time periods as needed to address the research questions. The term longitudinal research refers to research that occurs over time. There are three different variations of longitudinal research: trend studies, cohort studies, and panel studies. For some examples of longitudinal research, many of which are still ongoing, see Copeland, Savola, and Phelps' book *Inventory of Longitudinal Studies in the Social Sciences* (1991). Although not discussed in this chapter, longitudinal research can also be done in qualitative research (e.g., see Huber & Van de Ven, 1995).

Trend study
Independent samples are taken from a population over time and the same questions are asked

A **trend study** is a form of longitudinal research in which independent samples (samples composed of different people) are taken from a general population over time and the same questions are asked of the samples of participants. In a trend study you might, for example, take a new sample each year for five consecutive years of United States citizens who are eighteen years or older (i.e., adults). An example of a survey that has been used in many trend studies is the General Social Survey (GSS), which has been conducted annually since 1972 by interviewers working for the National Opinion Research Center, based in Chicago. The interviewers document the status of approximately 1,500 randomly selected adult (eighteen years or older) participants on an extensive number of variables each year (Davis & Smith, 1992).

Cohort study
Longitudinal research focusing specifically on one or more cohorts

The second type of longitudinal research is a **cohort study.** The focus in a cohort study is on one or more subpopulations or "cohorts." Researchers are usually interested in studying how and why cohort members change over time. A **cohort** is defined as any group of people with a common classification or common characteristic. For example, human development experts frequently study age cohorts, which are groups of people of the same age (six-year-old children or twelve-year-old children). Demographers frequently discuss birth cohorts, which are all people who are born during particular years (e.g., everyone born in 1970 is a birth cohort). A well-known cohort in the United States is the baby-boom generation, defined as everyone born in the United States between the years 1946 and 1964. You might base your own research study on the cohort of all persons majoring in science education who graduated from your college last year.

Cohort
Any group of people with a common classification or common characteristic

Cohort studies can take one of two forms (Glenn, 1977). In the first, independent (new) samples are selected from a cohort population (e.g., baby boomers) at successive points in time (e.g., years 2000, 2005, and 2010) and the cohort members in all of the samples are asked the same questions. As you can see, this is a type of trend study because independent (new) samples are selected from the cohort each time the study is done. In the second form of cohort study, the researcher does not select a new sample each time the study is done. Rather, the researcher selects some individuals from the cohort or cohorts the first year of the study and then follows these *same individuals* during the entire length of the study. This type of cohort study is a type of panel study, which is discussed next.

Panel study
Study in which the same individuals are studied at successive points over time

Prospective study
Another term applied to a panel study

The third major type of longitudinal research is a **panel study.**[3] The defining characteristic of a panel study is that the *same individuals* are studied at successive points over time. Because the researcher starts in the present and moves forward in time, the term **prospective study** is also applied by some researchers. For example, if you select 200 beginning teachers and follow them over the next ten years (e.g., interviewing them every other year), you have a panel, or prospective, study. You would be studying the same people over time. The individuals in a panel study are often selected from several age cohorts to strengthen the design. For example, a researcher might follow individuals from three age cohorts for three consecutive years. If the children in the study were ages five, seven, and nine in the first year of the study, they would be ages six, eight, and ten in the second year of the study (assuming the study was conducted at the same time of year), and they would be ages seven, nine, and eleven in the third year, or "third wave" of the study. As you can see, individuals in panel studies grow older over time. This means that the average age of the people in the study will increase over time, and at some point it will be impossible to continue a panel study because all of the participants will have died of old age!

Let's say that you interview 1,500 randomly selected participants who are representative of the United States in the year 2000. This group of people will become more and more unrepresentative of the United States at later dates (e.g., in 2005, 2010, and 2015) because the United States population is constantly changing (e.g., people are constantly born into and move in and out of the United States). No new people are added to the panel study over time.[4] The point is that even if no one ever dropped out of your panel study, the panel and the current population can become very different over time. This is a threat to external validity because it limits your ability to generalize from the panel to the current population.

Differential attrition
When participants do not drop out randomly

Perhaps an even greater problem is **differential attrition,** which occurs when participants do not drop out of the study randomly (i.e., when the people who drop out do not resemble the people who remain). In other words, the problem occurs when certain types of people drop out of the research study. Differential attrition can reduce external validity because after certain types of people drop out of the panel, the panel no longer resembles the population. Differential attrition can also reduce internal validity (the ability to firmly establish evidence of cause and effect). Assume, for example, that you are studying children's use of effective study strategies as they age. Your hypothesis is that age has a causal influence on effective strategy use (i.e., older children will use more effective study strategies than younger children). A problem might occur, however, if the less motivated and lower strategy users (i.e., children who use immature or inefficient strategies) drop out of your panel. You might erroneously conclude that effective strategy use increases with age simply because the lower strategy users drop out over time and the effective strategy users remain in the study. Because of the problems caused by differential attrition, researchers should always provide information about the kinds of people who dropped out of their research study and the potential implications this event has for their conclusions.

Panel studies also have some important strengths. First, you are better able to establish necessary condition 2 (proper time order) because you actually study the people over a period of time. Therefore, panel studies are superior to cross-sectional studies (studies in which data were collected at a single time point). Panel studies are also more powerful than trend studies because changes can be measured at the level they occur (within the individuals who change). Remember that in a trend study you are limited to comparing different people at different times, but in a panel study you can study the same individuals over time. One strategy in panel studies is to divide the original sample into groups based on the independent variable, follow the participants over time, and document what happens to them. Another strategy is to identify participants who change on a variable and the participants who do not change on the variable and then investigate the factors that help explain this change or lack of change.

You might, for example, decide to test the research hypothesis that students who begin using drugs in the tenth grade are more likely to drop out of high school than are students who do not use drugs during their high school years. To test this hypothesis you could select a sample of ninth-grade students and then interview them each year for the next five years. You could identify the students who begin drug use during the tenth grade and compare them with the other students over the next several years, looking for differences between the two groups. You might also want to test that hypothesis that students who start drug use earlier in high school (e.g., the ninth or tenth grade) are more likely to drop out than students who start drug use later in high school or students who never use drugs at all during the high school years. You would divide your sample during data analysis, as before, this time to see whether the early users were more likely to drop out than the later users or the nonusers to determine whether the hypotheses are supported. You could also analyze the data to test additional hypotheses or to locate additional behaviors and attitudes that are associated with drug use (e.g., peers who use drugs, poor grades, low self-esteem, family problems).

Medical researchers have effectively used prospective panel studies to help establish that smoking causes lung cancer (Gail, 1996). In a typical study, two groups of individuals (smokers and nonsmokers) are matched on multiple extraneous variables and are then followed forward in time. Researchers use matching to make the two groups as similar as possible, with the ultimate (but probably unattainable) goal being that the only important difference between the two groups is the participants' status on the independent variable. Then they follow these two groups over time, documenting their relative rates of lung cancer. The researchers also check for a dose/response relationship; that is, they check to see whether there is a positive correlation between the number of cigarettes smoked and the onset of lung cancer.

Prospective studies such as this cancer study are relatively strong on the first two conditions of causation. The relationship between smoking and lung cancer can be clearly established because different rates of lung cancer are found in the two groups and because a dose/response relationship is found. Time order is fairly well established because individuals are observed before and after the onset of cancer. Researchers use a variety of control techniques to help establish condition 3 (i.e., to rule out alternative explanations). As noted earlier, matching is used to create similar groups. Then, during data analysis, statistical control is used to further control for extraneous variables. Although prospective studies can be used to rule out many alternative explanations, they cannot rule out all of them. The key is that no *plausible* alternative explanation exists for the relationship between smoking and lung cancer.

The scientific opinion that smoking causes lung cancer (Gail, 1996) is based on the evidence obtained from a multitude of research studies. The most important human studies used in establishing this causal relationship have been prospective panel studies. Remember that the panel study is a relatively powerful nonexperimental method for examining causality. Unfortunately, prospective research is usually quite expensive and can take a long time to complete. Therefore, it should not be surprising that longitudinal studies are less common than cross-sectional studies. Prospective studies are often done at large universities by faculty members with federal funding and large staffs to help them conduct their research.

Retrospective Research

Retrospective research
The researcher starts with the dependent variable and moves backward in time

In **retrospective research,** the researcher typically starts with the dependent variable (i.e, with an observed result or outcome) and then "moves backward in time," locating information on variables that help explain individuals' status on the dependent variable. Retrospective research was one of the earliest kinds of research used to suggest smoking led to lung cancer (Gail, 1996). Medical researchers compared the smoking habits of people who currently had lung cancer with people who did not currently have lung cancer and found that smokers had higher rates of cancer than nonsmokers (Wynder & Graham, 1950). Retrospective research frequently uses retrospective questions to learn about the participants'

Retrospective questions
Questions asking people to recall something from an earlier time

pasts. **Retrospective questions** ask people to recall something from an earlier time in their life. In a smoking study, a retrospective question might ask current smokers how old they were when they first started smoking cigarettes. Another question might ask participants how many cigarettes they typically smoked each day during the past three weeks.

Here are some retrospective questions you might ask if you are studying drug use among high school students: Did you use drugs when you were in high school? What drug did you use most often? How frequently did you use that drug? Who first introduced you to the drug? Did your grades decline after you began using drugs? What was your grade level when your grades started declining? You must be careful when using retrospective questions because individuals' accounts of their past are not always entirely accurate. If possible, you should try to verify retrospective accounts by collecting additional corroborative information. For example, if someone said that his or her grades started declining in the tenth grade, you could check the student's school records for corroboration. Obviously, researchers cannot always corroborate each finding. You should, however, upgrade your evaluation of research studies in which corroboration was done for some or many of the research findings.

CLASSIFYING NONEXPERIMENTAL RESEARCH METHODS BY RESEARCH OBJECTIVE

A very useful way to classify nonexperimental research is by the primary objective or research purpose. After determining that a research study is nonexperimental (because there is no manipulation or random assignment), you should try to determine the primary research objective.[5] We discuss five major research objectives in Chapter 1: exploration, description, prediction, explanation, and influence. Nonexperimental quantitative research often takes one of three forms: descriptive research, predictive research, or explanatory nonexperimental research. We now explain each of these kinds of research and provide some examples.

Descriptive Research

Descriptive research Research focused on providing an accurate description or picture of the status or characteristics of a situation or phenomenon

The primary purpose of **descriptive research** is to provide an accurate description or picture of the status or characteristics of a situation or phenomenon. The focus is not on how to ferret out cause-and-effect-relationships but rather on describing the variables that exist in a given situation, and, sometimes, on how to describe the relationships that exist among those variables. An examination of the research questions or the author's stated purpose in each research article you look at will help you know when you should apply the label *descriptive research*. Researchers doing descriptive research commonly follow these three steps: (1) randomly select a sample from a defined population, (2) determine the sample characteristics, and (3) infer the characteristics of the population based on the sample.

Educators sometimes conduct descriptive research to learn about the attitudes, opinions, beliefs, behaviors, and demographics (e.g., age, gender, ethnicity, education) of people. Although the survey method of data collection is commonly used in descriptive research, keep in mind that this method (i.e., the use of questionnaires and/or interview protocols as discussed in Chapter 5) can also be used in predictive and explanatory research (see Babbie, 1990; Finkel, 1995; Kerlinger, 1986; Kiecolt & Nathan, 1985; Rosenberg, 1968; Stolzenberg & Land, 1983). Another research area that is primarily descriptive is in the field of tests and measurement. Test developers are constantly developing and refining tests and other measurement instruments, and they base many decisions on validity and reliability coefficients. Based on this descriptive information, they establish evidence about how well their tests operate with different kinds of people under a variety of circumstances.

An example of a published descriptive research study by Sears, Kennedy, and Kaye (1997) is titled "Myers-Briggs Personality Profiles of Prospective Educators." These researchers administered the Myers-Briggs personality test to 4,483 undergraduate university students who were considering majoring in education. Their major purpose was to provide descriptive information about prospective teachers based on the popular Myers-Briggs personality test. They also checked student records several years later to see which of the students graduated and what area of education they selected as their majors.

They found that the predominant personality profile of the prospective educators who later graduated with degrees in elementary education was SFJ (sensing, feeling, and judging). They describe SFJs as "warm, sociable, responsible, and caring about people" (p. 201). In contrast, the personality profile of the students who graduated with degrees in secondary education was NTJ (intuitive, thinking, and judging). They described NTJs as "oriented to the theoretical, disposed to investigate possibilities and relationships; and drawn to complexity, innovation, and change" (p. 201). Because of these personality traits, the researchers predicted that the secondary education majors would be more likely than the elementary majors to advance educational innovation and reform once they became teachers (p. 291). If the researchers tested this prediction in a future research study, they would have an example of predictive research, which we discuss next. Remember, the key to descriptive research is that the researchers collect data used for description.

Predictive Research

Predictive research
Research focused on predicting the future status of one or more dependent variables based on one or more independent variables

Predictive research is done so that we can predict the future status of one or more dependent (or criterion) variables based on one or more independent (or predictor) variables (Pedhazur, 1997). For example, college admissions officers may be interested in predicting student performance based on variables such as high school GPA, scores on admissions tests, gender, and type of school attended (e.g., public, private). Insurance companies are interested in predicting who will have auto accidents, who will get sick, who will be injured, and who will die of old age. (That's why auto insurance rates are higher for males and for adolescents.) Employers are interested in predicting who will be a happy and productive employee. An economist might want to predict the performance of the United States economy using "leading indicators." Educators are often interested in predicting who is at risk for problems like poor academic performance, drug use, dropping out of high school, and skipping class. The key point is that if a researcher suggests that he or she wants to see how well he or she can predict some outcome based on one or more independent or predictor variables, then the research study is labeled predictive research.

Dykeman, Daehlin, Doyle, and Flamer (1996) provide an example of predictive research published in a journal article titled "Psychological Predictors of School-Based Violence: Implications for School Counselors." The researchers wanted to find out whether three psychological constructs could be used to predict violence among students in grades five through ten. The first psychological predictor was a measure of impulsivity. The researchers' hypothesis was that the more impulsive children are, the more prone to violence they will be. The second predictor was a measure of empathy. The researchers believed that delinquents were less likely to have empathic skills, which would result in greater aggression. Their hypothesis was, therefore, that there would be a negative relationship between empathy and violence (i.e., the more empathy students have, the less prone they are to violence). The third psychological predictor variable was locus of control. People with an internal locus of control tend to view their own experiences as resulting from their own actions and decisions. People with an external locus of control tend to view their experiences as resulting from luck, chance, or destiny. The researchers hypothesized that people with internal locus of control would be less prone to violence than people who had more external locus of control. The researchers used a special case of the general linear model called multiple regression to determine how well the three variables predicted violence. It turned out that all three of the predictive hypotheses were supported. Impulsivity was the most important of the three predictor variables. The authors concluded that the aim of a violence prevention program might be "(a) to change group norms about violence, (b) to enhance family relationship characteristics, (c) to improve peer relationship skills, (d) to decrease substance abuse, (e) to lessen impulsivity, (f) to increase empathy, and (g) to engender internal locus of control" (p. 44). The last three points were directly based on the data from this research study.

Explanatory Research

Explanatory research Testing hypotheses and theories that explain how and why a phenomenon operates as it does

In **explanatory research,** researchers are interested in testing hypotheses and theories that explain how and why a phenomenon operates as it does (Pedhazur, 1997). The researcher's goal is to understand the phenomenon being studied. The researcher is also interested in establishing evidence for cause-and-effect relationships. Although experimental research is the strongest form of explanatory research for providing evidence of cause and effect, you have learned in this chapter that many important independent variables cannot be manipulated, which means that these variables must be investigated using nonexperimental explanatory research.

A good example of explanatory nonexperimental research is "A Prospective, Longitudinal Study of the Correlates and Consequences of Early Grade Retention," by Jimerson, Carlson, Rotert, Egeland, Sroufe (1997). It is important to understand the effects of early grade retention (not promoting a child). However, it would be unethical to manipulate this independent variable (i.e., you cannot randomly assign students to be either retained in their grade or promoted). Therefore, nonexperimental explanatory research must be used to study the effects of grade retention.

In the Jimerson et al. study, a retained group was identified from the participants in a larger, long-term study of at-risk children and their parents. A group of similar low-achieving promoted students (the nonretained group) was also identified from the project participants for a comparison group. The retained and nonretained groups were matched on academic ability and academic performance because the researchers wanted to compare retained students who are low achieving with promoted students who are low achieving in order to learn about the effects of retention/promotion. The researchers also used the control technique called statistical control (discussed earlier in this chapter) when making some of their comparisons to further equate the groups on additional variables. The practical question driving the research was whether a low achieving student should be retained or promoted.

Key results from the research study include the following. The retained students showed a short-term improvement in math achievement. However, that improvement disappeared once new material was taught. The retained and nonretained students did not differ on most measures of social and personal adjustment or on a measure of behavior problems. The one difference found was that the promoted students were more emotionally adjusted several years after being promoted. The researchers concluded that "Essentially, the retained and low-achieving promoted students did not differ . . . despite an extra year, and [they] continued to remain comparable years after the promotion or retention" (p. 18). In short, this research study confirmed the results of many additional studies suggesting that elementary grade retention produces few if any of its promised effects. In general, retention appears to be an ineffective strategy for improving the achievement levels or psychological adjustment of children or for reducing behavior problems.

Causal modeling A form of explanatory research in which the researcher hypothesizes a causal model and then empirically tests the model

Another form of explanatory research increasing in popularity is called causal modeling (Asher, 1983; Maruyama, 1998; Pedhazur, 1997; Schumacker & Lomax, 1996). Although many of the details of causal modeling are beyond the scope of this book, we cover some of the basic conceptual ideas here. **Causal modeling** is a procedure in which a researcher hypothesizes a causal model and then empirically tests the model to determine how well the model fits the data. The researcher develops or constructs the causal model based on past research findings and on theoretical considerations. Causal models depict the interrelationships among two or more variables and are used to explain how some theoretical process operates. Some synonyms for the term *causal model* are *path model, structural model,* and *theoretical model.* Many researchers use these terms interchangeably.

A hypothetical causal model with four variables is shown in Figure 10.4. The four variables in the causal model are parental involvement, student motivation, teaching quality (of the school teachers), and student achievement. You can understand this model by realizing that each of the arrows stands for a hypothesized causal relationship. The type of causal relationship between any two variables connected by an arrow is known as a **direct effect,** which is the effect of the variable at the origin of an arrow on the variable at the receiving end of the arrow. For example, look at Figure 10.4 and you will see that there is an arrow going from parental involvement to student motivation (parental involvement → student motivation). This means that parental involvement is hypothesized to have a direct effect on student motivation. It is important to realize that the assumption that parental involvement affects student motivation (rather than student motivation affecting parental involvement) is based on theory. In the absence of experimental research data, assumptions like this will always be tentative.

The numbers on the arrows are called **path coefficients,** and they provide quantitative information about the direct effects based on the data collected in a research study. If the coefficient is positive, then the relationship between the two variables is positive (i.e., as one variable increases the other variable increases). If the coefficient is negative, then the relationship is negative (i.e., as one variable increases, the second variable decreases). You can interpret the strength of the relationship by looking at the size of the coefficient, just as with correlation coefficients (i.e., coefficients that are close to +1.00 or –1.00 are very

Direct effect
The effect of the variable at the origin of an arrow on the variable at the receiving end of the arrow

Path coefficient
A quantitative index providing information about a direct effect

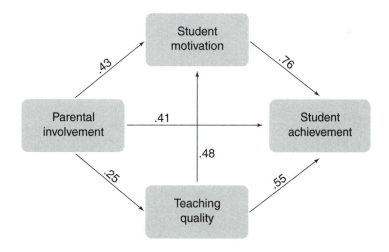

FIGURE 10.4 A causal model of student achievement.

strong, and coefficients that are near zero are very weak). Looking at Figure 10.4, you see the number .76 on the path from student motivation to student achievement. This suggests that there is a strong positive relationship between student motivation and student achievement.

Take a moment now to look at the other arrows in the causal model. Try to answer these questions. First, what two variables are hypothesized to have direct effects on student motivation? Second, what variable is hypothesized to have a direct effect on teaching quality? Third, what three variables are hypothesized in the model to have direct effects on student achievement? [The answers are (1) student motivation is shown to be influenced by parental involvement and teaching quality; (2) teaching quality is influenced by parental involvement; and (3) student achievement is influenced by parental involvement, teaching quality, and student motivation.]

In addition to showing hypothesized direct effects, causal models also show hypothesized indirect effects. An **indirect effect** occurs when one variable affects another variable indirectly; that is, an indirect effect occurs when a variable affects another variable by way of an **intervening variable.** We defined intervening variables (which are also called *mediator variables*) and indirect effects in Chapter 1. According to the causal path A → B → C, variable B is an intervening variable (it occurs in between A and C). Furthermore, variable A has an indirect effect on variable C by way of the intervening variable B. Whenever a variable falls in between two other variables in a causal chain, it is called an intervening variable.

Now that you know what an indirect effect is, see if you can find some indirect effects in the causal model shown in Figure 10.4. As you can see, teaching quality has an indirect effect on student achievement through student motivation. In this case, student motivation is the intervening variable. You can see that teaching quality also has a direct effect on student achievement because there is an arrow going from teaching quality to student achievement. In other words, a variable can have both a direct effect and an indirect effect. Also, parental involvement indirectly influences student achievement through teaching quality and through student motivation. There are quite a few relationships (indirect and direct) in even a relatively small causal model.

Figure 10.5 shows another example of a causal model, which was reported in the *Journal of Educational Psychology.* This model was developed and tested by Karabenick and Sharma (1994). It shows the effects of several variables on the likelihood of students asking questions during lectures. Look at the model and see if you think they have done a good job explaining what factors cause students to ask or not ask questions. The researchers collected data to test their model from 1,327 undergraduate college students. After collecting the data, they used a statistical program called LISREL to calculate the path coefficients (the numbers on the arrows).

The original theoretical model developed by the researchers looked like the model shown in Figure 10.5 except that it included an arrow from Perceived teacher support of questioning to Ask a question. Because this particular path turned out to be unimportant based on the data collected in the research study (it was not statistically significant), the researchers eliminated it from the final model shown in Figure 10.5. It is a common prac-

Indirect effect
An effect occurring through an intervening variable

Intervening variable
A variable occurring between two other variables in a causal chain

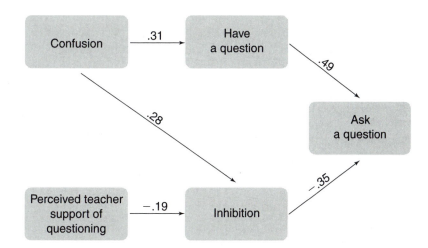

FIGURE 10.5   A causal model of question asking. (Adapted from Karabenick and Sharma, 1994, p. 98. Copyright © 1994 by the American Psychological Association. Adapted with permission.)

tice in the field of causal modeling to exclude arrows that turn out to be unimportant based on the data. This process of eliminating arrows is sometimes called *theory trimming*. The other arrows in the model in Figure 10.5 were correctly predicted by the researchers to be important.

You can determine the strength and direction of the direct effects by looking at the path coefficients on the arrows. For example, the path coefficient from inhibition to asking a question is –.35. This means that the effect of inhibition on asking a question (controlling for having a question) is small to moderate in size and the relationship operates in the negative direction. Recall from your study of correlation that a negative relationship exists when two variables move in opposite directions. In this case, the more inhibition students feel, the less likely they are to ask questions. Not surprisingly, the relationship between confusion and having a question (+.31) is moderately small in size, and the relationship is positive (i.e., the more confusion students have, the more likely they are to have questions). You can interpret the other path coefficients in the model in a similar way.

You can also find the indirect effects in Figure 10.5 by noting when variables affect other variables through intervening variables. For example, perceived teacher support of questioning does not affect students asking questions directly (i.e., there is no direct arrow). However, it does affect asking questions indirectly by way of the intervening variable called inhibition. Likewise, confusion indirectly affects asking questions through having a question and through inhibition. In other words, confusion has two indirect effects on asking questions. This is complex, but its complexity is also a strength because it more closely approximates how a small part of the real world actually operates. Also, researchers can communicate all of the relationships suggested by their theory in a picture.

We discussed causal modeling in this chapter because causal models are usually used in nonexperimental research, although they are occasionally tested in experimental research. Note also that although causal models are most frequently based on cross-sectional data (data collected at a single time), they are more and more frequently being based on longitudinal data (data collected at two or more time points). As a general rule, causal models based on experiments provide the most solid evidence for cause and effect; causal models based on longitudinal data are second best; and causal models based on cross-sectional data are the weakest. Even when based on cross-sectional data, however, causal models represent drastic improvements over the simple cases of causal-comparative and correlational research.

SUMMARY

The researcher does not manipulate independent variables in nonexperimental research. The researcher does study relationships among variables. If the researcher's questions concern independent variables that cannot be manipulated, nonexperimental research is the logical choice. A few independent variables that cannot be manipulated are gender, parenting style, grade retention, ethnicity, and intelligence. Researchers must be very careful when using the nonexperimental research method, however, if they wish to obtain evidence of cause-and-effect relationships. The three necessary conditions for concluding that the relationship between variable A and variable B is causal are (1) there must be a relationship between variable A and variable B, (2) variable A must occur before variable B, and (3) alternative explanations must be eliminated. Unfortunately, the third necessary condition is virtually always a problem in nonexperimental research. Researchers must attempt to control for any extraneous, or third, variables that may potentially explain the relationship between two variables when they want to obtain evidence that the relationship is causal. The three key techniques of control used in nonexperimental research are (1) matching, (2) restricting the study to a subpopulation, and (3) statistical control.

Nonexperimental research is sometimes classified based on the time dimension. If the data are collected at a single time point or data-collection period, it is a cross-sectional study. If the data are collected at multiple time points over time, it is a longitudinal study. If the data are collected backwards in time, it is a retrospective study. Nonexperimental research is also classified based on the researcher's primary research objective. The purpose of descriptive research is to provide an accurate description or picture of the status or characteristics of a situation or phenomenon. The purpose of predictive research is to predict the future status of one or more dependent or outcome variables based on one or more independent or predictor variables. The purpose of explanatory nonexperimental research is to test hypotheses and theories explaining how and why a phenomenon operates as it does. Causal modeling is a form of explanatory research in which the researcher develops a causal model and empirically tests the model to determine how well the model fits the data.

STUDY QUESTIONS

1. Why is experimental research much stronger than nonexperimental research when the researcher is interested in making cause-and-effect statements?
2. Why must a researcher sometimes conduct nonexperimental research rather than experimental research?
3. Why must researchers watch out for the post hoc fallacy?
4. Name a potential independent variable that cannot be manipulated.
5. Explain the problems with the simple cases of causal-comparative and correlational research. Why is a researcher *not* justified in making a cause-and-effect claim from these two cases?
6. Explain exactly how strong experimental research fulfills each of the three necessary conditions for cause and effect.
7. On which of the three necessary conditions for cause and effect is nonexperimental research especially weak? On which one of the three necessary conditions is nonexperimental research strong?
8. Explain why you cannot make a defensible causal claim based on an observed relationship between two variables (e.g., gender and achievement) in nonexperimental research.
9. What is the purpose of the techniques of control in nonexperimental research?
10. Which form of nonexperimental research tends to be the best for inferring cause and effect: cross-sectional research, trend studies, cohort studies, panel studies (i.e., prospective studies), or retrospective research studies? Why?
11. Explain the difference between a direct effect and an indirect effect.
12. List an advantage and a disadvantage of causal modeling.

EXERCISES

1. It is helpful to examine published examples of nonexperimental research so that you can see more concretely how to carry out nonexperimental research. As an exercise, read and write up a two-page review of *one* of the following nonexperimental research articles:

   Martinez-Pons, M. (1996). Test of a model of parental inducement of academic self-regulation. *Journal of Experimental Education, 64*(3), 213–227.
   Eckenrode, J., Laird, M., & Doris, J. (1993). School performance and disciplinary problems among abused and neglected children. *Developmental Psychology, 29*(1), 53–62.

   When you write up your article review, organize it into the following general sections:

1. Purpose	3. Results
2. Methods	4. Strengths and weaknesses of the research.

KEY TERMS

analysis of covariance (ANCOVA) (296)

causal modeling (304)

cohort (298)

cohort study (298)

cross-sectional research (297)

descriptive research (302)

differential attrition (299)

direct effect (305)

explanatory research (304)

general linear model (GLM) (295)

indirect effect (306)

intervening variable (306)

longitudinal research (297)

matching variable (293)

method of working multiple hypotheses (288)

nonexperimental research (282)

panel study (298)

partial correlation (295)

partially spurious (290)

path coefficient (305)

post hoc fallacy (283)

predictive research (303)

probabilistic cause (287)

prospective study (298)

retrospective questions (301)

retrospective research (301)

simple case of causal-comparative research (285)

simple case of correlational research (285)

simple cases (285)

special case of the general linear model (295)

spurious relationship (290)

statistically significant (285)

third-variable problem (288)

three necessary conditions (287)

trend study (298)

ENDNOTES

1. The only thing that changes is the type of statistical analysis used after the data are collected.
2. If the quantitative independent variable has more than ten levels, then we recommend that you collapse it into fewer categories for the purposes of matching.
3. Panel studies can also be used in experimental research. A panel study with manipulation is more powerful than a panel study without manipulation when you are interested in studying cause and effect.
4. There is a type of panel study, called the revolving panel design, in which new people are added to the panel (see Menard, 1991).
5. When you examine published research articles keep in mind that some research studies may have more than one objective.

CHAPTER 11

Qualitative Research

LEARNING OBJECTIVES

To be able to

- list the major characteristics of qualitative research.
- compare and contrast the four main approaches to qualitative research: phenomenology, ethnography, case study, and grounded theory.
- define and explain phenomenology.
- define and explain ethnography.
- define and explain case study research.
- define and explain grounded theory.

Qualitative research
Research relying primarily on the collection of qualitative data

In Chapter 1 we defined **qualitative research** as research relying primarily on the collection of qualitative data (nonnumerical data such as words and pictures). Qualitative researchers tend to rely on the inductive mode of the scientific method, and the major research objective of this type of research is exploration or discovery. This means that qualitative researchers generally study a phenomenon in an open-ended way, without prior expectations, and they develop hypotheses and theoretical explanations that are based on their interpretations of what they observe. Qualitative researchers prefer to study the world as it naturally occurs, without manipulating it (as in experimental research). While observing, qualitative researchers try not to draw attention to themselves. That is, they try to be unobtrusive so that they will have little influence on the naturally occurring behavior being studied. Qualitative researchers view human behavior as dynamic and changing, and they advocate studying phenomena in depth and over an extended period of time. The product of qualitative research is usually a narrative report with rich description (vivid and detailed writing) rather than a statistical report (a report with a lot of numbers and statistical test results).

In Figure 11.1 we have listed the six common steps in a qualitative research study. In a simple qualitative research study, the researcher may move directly through the steps, and the study will be completed. It is important that you understand, however, that the qualitative researcher does not always follow the six steps in a linear fashion (i.e., step 1, then step 2, then step 3, and so on). Typically, the qualitative researcher selects a topic and generates preliminary questions at the start of a research study. The questions can be changed or modified, however, during data collection and analysis if any of the questions are found to be naive or less important than other questions. This is one reason that qualitative research is often said to be an emergent or fluid type of research. During the conduct of a qualitative research study the researcher acts like a detective or novelist and goes wherever interesting and enlightening information may be.

Data collection and analysis (steps 3 and 4) in qualitative research have a longitudinal character because qualitative research often takes place over an extended period of time. The researcher purposely selects people to interview and/or observe at early points as well as at later points in a research study. Data collection and data analysis (steps 3 and 4 in Figure 11.1) are often done concurrently or in cycles in qualitative research (e.g., the researchers collect some data, analyze those data, collect more data, analyze those data, and so on). The researcher also attempts to validate the data and his or her interpretations throughout the research study (step 5). For example, the researcher should attempt to establish the kinds of qualitative research validity you learned about in Chapter 7 (descriptive

FIGURE 11.1 Common steps in a qualitative research study.

1. Select research topic and determine preliminary research questions or issues.
2. Select research participants and settings using purposive sampling techniques.
3. Collect the data (e.g., enter the field and observe and interview participants).
4. Analyze the data (e.g., determine themes and patterns occurring in the data).
5. Generate and validate conclusions.
6. Write the research report.

validity, interpretative validity, theoretical validity, internal validity, and external validity). At the end of the research study, the researcher finishes the research report (step 6).

For further extension of your knowledge about qualitative research, we include Patton's (1990) list of ten major characteristics of qualitative research in Table 11.1. Patton did a good job of succinctly summarizing what he saw as the ten key characteristics of qualitative research, and the list should be helpful as you learn about qualitative research. Although all qualitative research studies will not have all of the characteristics mentioned by us and by Patton, they are very typical of qualitative research.

TABLE 11.1   Ten Major Characteristics of Qualitative Research

1. Naturalistic inquiry	Studying real-world situations as they unfold naturally; nonmanipulative, unobtrusive, and noncontrolling; openness to whatever emerges—lack of predetermined constraints on outcomes.
2. Inductive analysis	Immersion in the details and specifics of the data to discover important categories, dimensions, and interrelationships; begin by exploring genuinely open questions rather than testing theoretically derived (deductive) hypotheses.
3. Holistic perspective	The *whole* phenomenon under study is understood as a complex system that is more than the sum of its parts; focus on complex interdependencies not meaningfully reduced to a few discrete variables and linear, cause-effect relationships.
4. Qualitative data	Detailed, thick description; inquiry in depth; direct quotations capturing people's personal perspectives and experiences.
5. Personal contact and insight	The researcher has direct contact with and gets close to the people, situation, and phenomenon under study; researcher's personal experiences and insights are an important part of the inquiry and critical to understanding the phenomenon.
6. Dynamic systems	Attention to process; assumes change is constant and ongoing whether the focus is on an individual or an entire culture.
7. Unique case orientation	Assumes each case is special and unique; the first level of inquiry is being true to, respecting, and capturing the details of the individual cases being studied; cross-case analysis follows from and depends on the quality of individual cases.
8. Context sensitivity	Places findings in a social, historical, and temporal context; dubious of the possibility or meaningfulness of generalizations across time and space.
9. Empathic neutrality	Complete objectivity is impossible; pure subjectivity undermines credibility; the researcher's passion is understanding the world in all its complexity—not proving something, not advocating, not advancing personal agendas, but understanding; the researcher includes personal experience and empathic insight as part of the relevant data, while taking a neutral nonjudgmental stance toward whatever content may emerge.
10. Design flexibility	Open to adapting inquiry as understanding deepens and/or situations change; avoids getting locked into rigid designs that eliminate responsiveness; pursues new paths of discovery as they emerge.

Adapted from M. Q. Patton, *Qualitative Evaluation and Research Methods,* 2nd ed., pp. 40–41, copyright © 1990 by Sage Publications, Inc. Reprinted by Permission of Sage Publications, Inc.

As you can see, qualitative research is not a linear and orderly form of research, but this does not mean that it is not useful when it is well done. Doing qualitative research well requires a lot of time and effort. If you have the time and perseverance, and if you are open to learning and adventure and you do not mind dealing with a lack of structure, then qualitative research may be for you. If you are wondering whether quantitative or qualitative research is the best, the answer is that they are both very important types of research in education, and you will be in excellent shape by understanding both of them!

The purpose of the remainder of this chapter is to introduce you to the different types of qualitative research. Although you already understand qualitative research as a general type of research, *qualitative research* is actually a very general term because there are many different types of qualitative research. We discuss what we believe to be the four most important types: phenomenology, ethnography, case study, and grounded theory. A list showing the major characteristics of these four approaches is given in Table 11.2. You may want

TABLE 11.2 Characteristics of Four Qualitative Research Approaches

Dimension	Qualitative Research Approach			
	Phenomenology	*Ethnography*	*Grounded Theory*	*Case Study*
Research purpose	To describe one or more individuals' experiences of a phenomenon (e.g., the experience of the death of a loved one).	To describe the cultural characteristics of a group of people and to describe cultural scenes.	To inductively generate a grounded theory describing and explaining a phenomenon.	To describe one or more cases in-depth and address the research questions and issues.
Disciplinary origin	Philosophy.	Anthropology.	Sociology.	Multidisciplinary roots, including business, law, social sciences, medicine, and education.
Primary data-collection method	In-depth interviews with up to 10 people.*	Participant observation over an extended period of time (e.g., one month to a year). Interviews with informants.	Interviews with 20 to 30 people.* Observations are also frequently used.	Multiple methods are used (e.g., interviews, observations, documents).
Data analysis approach	List significant statements, determine meaning of statements, and identify the essence of the phenomenon.	Holistic description and search for cultural themes in data.	Begin with open coding, then axial coding, and end with selective coding.	Holistic description and search for themes shedding light on the case. May also include cross-case analysis.
Narrative report focus	Rich description of the essential or invariant structures (i.e., the common characteristics, or essences) of the experience.	Rich description of context and cultural themes.	Description of topic and people being studied. End with a presentation of the grounded theory. May also list propositions.	Rich description of the context and operation of the case or cases. Discussion of themes, issues, and implications.

*The number of participants is based on Creswell (1998).

to preview the list now and then review it again after you finish reading this chapter. Each approach has a different history, and each is currently used in the field of education.

Because the four research approaches discussed in this chapter fall under the heading of qualitative research, the characteristics of qualitative research reviewed earlier will usually apply. This means that the approaches will have much in common. At the same time, each approach is different and distinct from the others in important ways (e.g., compare the four research purposes shown in Table 11.2). We describe the four major qualitative research approaches in detail now so that you can understand qualitative research articles and books based on these approaches and so that you can consider which approach you would choose to use if you ever wanted to conduct a qualitative research study on your own.

PHENOMENOLOGY

Phenomenology
The description of one or more individuals' consciousness and experience of a phenomenon

Life-world
An individual's inner world of immediate experience

Phenomenology refers to the description of one or more individuals' consciousness and experience of a phenomenon, such as the death of a loved one, viewing oneself as a teacher, the act of teaching, the experience of being a minority group member, or the experience of winning a soccer game. The purpose of phenomenological research is to obtain a view into your research participants' life-worlds and to understand their personal meanings (i.e., what something means to them) constructed from their "lived experiences." **Life-world** is the translation of the German term *Lebenswelt* used by the founder of phenomenology, philosopher Edmund Husserl (1859–1938), to refer to the individual's "world of immediate experience." It is the individual's inner world of consciousness and experience. You are in your life-world right now as you read this chapter and as you exist wherever you are. In other words, your life-world is in your mind. It is your combination of feelings, thoughts, and self-awareness at any moment in time. The purpose of phenomenology is to gain access to individuals' life-worlds and to describe their experiences of a phenomenon.

To experience phenomenology first hand, try describing your own personal experience of a phenomenon. To do this effectively, you must give it your full attention—the following poem by Moffitt[1] makes this point quite eloquently (cited in Moustakas, 1990):

> To look at any thing
> If you would know that thing,
> You must look at it long:
> To look at this green and say
> "I have seen spring in these
> Woods," will not do—you must
> Be the thing you see:
> You must be the dark snakes of
> Stems and ferny plumes of leaves,
> You must enter in
> To the small silences between
> The leaves,
> You must take your time
> And touch the very place
> They issue from.

When you want to experience something to its fullest, you must stop what you are doing, focus on what you are experiencing at that meaningful moment, and experience the thoughts, sensations, and feelings associated with that experience. To experience something in its purest form, phenomenologists point out that you need to **bracket,** or suspend, any preconceptions or learned feelings that you have about the phenomenon. This is because they want you to experience the phenomenon "as it is." When you bracket your preconceptions, you set aside your taken-for-granted orientation toward it and your experience of the phenomenon becomes part of your consciousness.

Bracket
To suspend your preconceptions or learned feelings about a phenomenon

Examples of Phenomenology

Here are brief descriptions of a few phenomenological research studies, any of which you can look up and read if you need to learn more about phenomenological research. Only one of these articles was based on a single individual's experiences (Green, 1995). First, Cross and Stewart (1995) studied what it is like being a gifted student in a rural high school in an article titled, "A Phenomenological Investigation of the Lebenswelt of Gifted Students in Rural High Schools." Cross and Stewart also compared rural students' experiences with the experiences of urban school students based on previous research. This is an exemplary phenomenological research article if you want to read one article. Green (1995) studied a teacher's meaning and experience of utilizing an experiential learning approach with her students in an article titled, "Experiential Learning and Teaching." Brown (1996) examined children's experiences of being in a mathematics classroom in an article titled, "The Phenomenology of the Mathematics Classroom." Finally, Muller (1994) studied the meaning and experience of empowering other people from the perspective of the person doing the empowering, in this case, six women who had been identified as leaders in the article titled, "Toward an Understanding of Empowerment: A Study of Six Women Leaders." Again, we remind you that one of the best ways to learn about qualitative research is to read qualitative research journal articles.

Types of Phenomenology

Phenomenology can be used to focus on the unique characteristics of an individual's experience of something. We all know that events, objects, and experiences can mean different things to different people. For example, different individuals may view a single event differently. The hiring of a new principal at a school may mean the school is moving in the right direction and offer solace to one teacher, while, to another teacher, the change may arouse anger and result in restlessness because of its uncertainty. In counseling, the phenomenological method is often used to understand each client's unique perspective of some life event or personal condition. The counselor assumes that each client's perspective is unique to that individual and attempts to empathetically understand that perspective. In education, a tenet of constructivist teaching is that teachers need to understand the unique perspective of each student in order to be in touch with the students and to better understand each individual student and his or her needs. Thus, there is a phenomenological component to this theory.

Phenomenological researchers do not, however, generally assume that individuals are completely unique. More technically speaking, phenomenological researchers do not

Essence
An invariant
structure of the
experience

just study the variant structures of an experience (the unique part of an individual's experience that varies from person to person). Phenomenologists generally assume that there is some commonality in human experience and they seek to understand this commonality. This commonality of experience is called an **essence,** or invariant structure, of the experience (a part of the experience that is common or consistent across the research participants). An essence is an essential characteristic of an experience. It is universal and is present in particular instances of a phenomenon (van Manen, 1990). Consider the experience of the death of a loved one. Certainly each of us reacts to and experiences this event somewhat differently (i.e., the idiosyncratic or variant structure). However, there are probably essences to this experience that are common to everyone (i.e., the common or invariant structures). For example, in the case of the death of a loved one, grief and sorrow would probably be elements of the common experience. You can search for the essential structures of a phenomenon by studying multiple examples of it and finding what experiences the different people have in common. An essence will often be more abstract than literal descriptions of the particular experiences (e.g., general sorrow is more abstract than being "sad that your Uncle Bob is no longer around" to provide love and friendship).

The search for the essences or invariant structures of a phenomenon is probably the defining characteristic of phenomenology as a research technique. An example of a rich description of the essences of the experience of guilt is given in Exhibit 11.1. Are your experiences of guilt similar to the ones described in the Exhibit? The description is from Yoder's (1990) doctoral dissertation.

Data Collection, Analysis, and Report Writing

In a typical phenomenological research study, the researcher collects data from several individuals and depicts their experience of something. The data are usually collected through in-depth interviews. Using the interview data, the researcher attempts to reduce the statements to the common core or essence of the experience as described by the research participants. In order for research participants to explore their experience they must be able to relive it in their minds, and they must be able to focus on the experience and nothing else. This is what you must get your research participants to do if you conduct a phenomenological research study.

One effective strategy for eliciting data from participants is to tell each participant to recall a specific experience he or she has had, to think about that specific experience carefully, and then to describe that experience to you. You might use the following general question to get participants talking about their experience: "Please carefully describe your experience with _____." You might also say: "When you think of your experience with _____ what comes into your mind?" You may find that you need to prompt the respondent during the interview for greater detail, and you should do so. Remember that your goal is to get your participants to think about their specific experience and to describe it in rich detail. Rather than having each research participant describe the meaning and structure of his or her experience to you in an in-person interview you can also have them write about their experience and then give you their written narrative. Both approaches work well.

During data analysis the researcher searches for significant statements. These are statements (a few words or phrase, a sentence, or a few sentences) that have particular

---

EXHIBIT 11.1   The Essence of Guilt

Feelings of guilt are signs of significant turbulence, flaring up within the person. They come like a storm with lightning and cold winds. "It felt like mists, cold wind, dark streets, uncomfortable things. Stormy clouds in the sky. Occasional flashes of lightning. Empty beaches on a cold day. A cold wind from the water."

Guilt feelings close in. They are an imprisonment in which there is no way out. "You feel closed in when you are really feeling guilty. You feel cramped, very claustrophobic, limited, constricted, walled in."

The feeling of guilt is sharp and jagged. It is "being on the hook," a "knife," a pain as sharp as a surgical incision. The feeling of guilt is fast. "I'm thinking of lightning because it is a jab."

Guilt feelings are "a heavy weight." They are experienced as a "crushing blow." The feeling of guilt pushes, removes, evokes withdrawal, a sinking enormously heavy feeling. It comes in waves. "This intense push that jolts me back." "I'm gonna sink down. It's like this weight is on me."

Feeling guilty is "being in a shell," an invisible agent in a "world of strangers." Guilt feelings send one adrift into space where time is unending and the link with others is severed and closed. There is no hope of repair, renewal, belonging, no chance of even recognizing a genuine self.

The experience of feeling guilty is the experience of being forcibly removed from the flow of everyday life, from the world of ordinary human sharing and warmth. When we feel guilty, we are cast into a painful, frozen, inner-focused world that takes over the self and creates a reality of its own. Guilt feelings sever our sense of connectedness with everyday things, with other people and with ourselves. In the experience of feeling guilty, time

stands still. All exits are closed. We are isolated and trapped within ourselves.

In guilt feelings, self-respect deteriorates, a sense of physical ugliness often awakens. Real emotions are hidden. Masked ways of being show themselves in pleasing others. In everyday and in ultimate moments, "The real me is not good enough. Not ever."

Time is experienced as slowed down and unchangeable. Clock time goes haywire. Everything churns and then freezes. Only the crystallized moment of guilt endures. The past is relived over and over again, an endless recycling, a movie that repeats itself without any genuine change or realization.

In guilt feelings, the relationship to the body is also affected. The body becomes distant, moves like a robot. It is in pain, anxious to move somehow, yet, at the same time, fearful that any action will reawaken the scenes of guilt.

In spite of the torturous feelings and helpless, endless, sense of guilt, there is still within the self, the possibility of recovering oneself and regaining the sense of harmonious flow with life. There is the potential to come to terms with the guilt, accept it, share it with another and, in this acceptance, find a way to peace. What is required is the courage to take the first step and risk scornful judgment and the pain of acknowledging one's limitations. There is no guarantee that if one freely and honestly expresses the guilt, and recognizes the vulnerability and limitedness of the self, that the guilty feelings will be excised permanently, but for some of my co-researchers this acceptance and sharing enabled them to reclaim themselves and reestablish inner tranquility.

Reprinted from Yoder, 1990.

---

relevance to the phenomenon being studied. For example, perhaps you asked a kindergarten student to describe what school is like and one of her statements was that "We are all like a family at my school." If this statement seemed to fit her other statements, then the statement is probably a significant statement. In general, to determine whether a statement is "significant" you should ask yourself, Does the statement seem to have meaning to the participant in describing his or her experience? Is the statement descriptive of the experience? Does the statement tap into the participant's experience? Many researchers like to record the significant statements verbatim (i.e., in the actual words of the participants). Some researchers also like to interpret and describe the meanings of the significant statements at this point by making a list of the *meanings*. For example, in the case of the kindergarten student's statement, you might conclude that the child sees school as like a family because there is a teacher (the head of the family) and other students (family members) at school, and the family does things together as a unit (play, eat, take naps). This is an interpretative process done by the researcher and should be verified by the participants (i.e., use the member checking technique discussed in the research validity chapter).

After constructing the lists of significant statements and meanings, the researcher searches for *themes* in the data. In other words, what kinds of things did the participants tend to mention as being important to them? The researcher may find that certain individuals or groups (e.g., males and females) tend to describe an experience somewhat differently. This information is useful in understanding individual and group differences. However, the phenomenological researcher is usually most interested in describing the fundamental structure of the experience (the essence) for the total group. It is here that the researcher describes the fundamental features of the experience that are experienced in common by virtually all the participants. Finally, researchers should use member checking as a validity check whenever possible in this process. This means that the researcher should have the original participants review the interpretations and descriptions of the experience, especially the statement of the fundamental structure of the experience.

In a research chapter titled, "The Essential Structure of a Caring Interaction: Doing Phenomenology," Riemen (1986) reported hospital patients' experiences of "caring" and "noncaring" nurses. We have included Rieman's description of the "essential structure" of her hospital patients' experiences of caring and noncaring nurses in Exhibits 11.2 and 11.3. Riemen also compared males' and females' significant statements and meanings. This is an excellent example of phenomenological research and a good model to follow.

The final report in a typical phenomenological study is a narrative that includes a description of the participants in the study and the methods used to obtain the information

---

EXHIBIT 11.2   Description of a Caring Nurse

In a caring interaction, the nurse's existential presence is perceived by the client as more than just a physical presence. There is the aspect of the nurse giving of oneself to the client. This giving of oneself may be in response to the client's request, but it is more often a voluntary effort and is unsolicited by the client. The nurse's willingness to give of oneself is primarily perceived by the client as an attitude and behavior of sitting down and really listening and responding to the unique concerns of the individual as a person of value. The relaxation, comfort, and security that the client experiences both physically and mentally are an immediate and direct result of the client's stated and unstated needs being heard and responded to by the nurse.

From Creswell (1998), p. 289.

EXHIBIT 11.3   Description of a Noncaring Nurse

The nurse's presence with the client is perceived by the client as a minimal presence of the nurse being physically present only. The nurse is viewed as being there only because it is a job and not to assist the client or answer his or her needs. Any response by the nurse is done with a minimal amount of energy expenditure and bound by the rules. The client perceives the nurse who does not respond to this request for assistance as being noncaring. Therefore, an interaction that never happened is labeled as a noncaring interaction. The nurse is too busy and hurried to spend time with the client and therefore does not sit down and really listen to the client's individual concerns. The client is further devalued as a unique person because he or she is scolded, treated as a child, or treated as a nonhuman being or an object. Because of the devaluing and lack of concern, the client's needs are not met and the client has negative feelings, that is, frustrated, scared, depressed, angry, afraid, and upset.

From Creswell (1998), p. 289.

---

from the participants (usually interviews), a rich description of the fundamental structure of the experience, and a discussion of the findings. The researcher may also describe any interesting individual or group differences. A well-written report will be highly descriptive of the participants' experience of the phenomenon, and it will elicit in the readers a feeling that they understand what it would be like to experience the phenomenon themselves. This kind of feeling is called a vicarious experience.

ETHNOGRAPHY

Ethnography
The discovery and comprehensive description of the culture of a group of people

Ethnography is an approach to qualitative research that originated in the discipline of anthropology around the turn of the twentieth century. Ethnography literally means "writing about people" (*ethnos* means people, race, or cultural group, and *graphia* means writing or representing) (LeCompte & Preissle, 1993). Because of the importance of the concept of culture to the discipline of anthropology, **ethnography** is traditionally or classically defined as the discovery and comprehensive description of the culture of a group of people. Educational ethnographers also focus on cultural description as done in classical ethnography. The main difference is that anthropologists usually describe small cultures across the world (especially in less developed nations), and educational ethnographers usually study the cultural characteristics of small groups of people or other cultural scenes as they relate to educational issues.

Before going further, we want to point out that the word *ethnography* is used in two discrete ways. Ethnography is used to refer to the type of qualitative research that focuses on cultural description. It is also used to refer to the report or written product of an ethnographic study, which is called "the ethnography." In other words, the word *ethnography* is used to refer to a specific qualitative research method and the product of that method. Because of the importance of the concept of culture in understanding ethnographic research, we now explain this important concept in more detail.

The Idea of Culture

Culture
A system of shared beliefs, values, practices, perspectives, folk knowledge, language, norms, rituals, and material objects and artifacts that members of a group use in understanding their world and in relating to others

Culture is a system of shared beliefs, values, practices, perspectives, folk knowledge, language, norms, rituals, and material objects and artifacts that members of a group use in understanding their world and in relating to others. So that you can better understand this definition, here are the definitions of several important words in it. **Shared beliefs** are the specific cultural conventions or statements that people who share a culture hold to be true or false. **Shared values** are the culturally defined standards about what is good or bad or desirable or undesirable. **Norms** are the written and unwritten rules that specify appropriate group behavior (e.g., "Raise your hand when you have a question" is a common norm in a classroom).

If you look at the definition of culture, you will notice it includes a nonmaterial component (the shared beliefs, values, norms, and so forth of the members of a group) and a material component (the material things produced by group members, such as buildings, books, classroom bulletin boards, and art). Ethnographers sometimes refer to these two components as *material culture* and *nonmaterial culture.* Although ethnographers do not usually specify whether they are referring to the material or nonmaterial component of culture, or both, the intention is usually clear from the context of the statement. When attempting to understand and explain human behavior, the nonmaterial component is usually the focus of attention.

Shared beliefs
The specific cultural conventions or statements that people who share a culture hold to be true or false

Individuals become members of a culture through the socialization process by which they learn and are trained about the features of the culture. During socialization they usually internalize the culture; that is, they take the values and beliefs to be their own. Over time, people identify so strongly with their culture that the ways of doing things in their own culture may seem natural to them and the ways of doing things in other cultures may seem strange. You may have heard the term *culture shock,* which refers to an experience people have when they observe different cultural practices. Cultures are maintained over time through socialization and through a social sanctioning process through which members of a culture stigmatize people who break group norms, and they praise and associate with the members who follow the appropriate cultural norms. In general, as people become members of any new group, they learn the culture of that group so that they can become fully functioning and accepted members of the group. The people who follow the norms of a group or society are often called normal and those who deviate from the cultural norms are called deviant.

Shared values
The culturally defined standards about what is good or bad or desirable or undesirable

Norms
The written and unwritten rules that specify appropriate group behavior

Although we often think of a culture as being associated with a very large group such as a society (e.g., the culture of the United States), the concept of culture can be used on a much smaller scale. In fact, culture can be viewed as varying on a continuum, with macro culture on one end and micro culture on the other end. At the macro level we might study the cultural characteristics (the shared values, beliefs, and norms) of United States citizens, Japanese adolescents, or the Ohio Amish. On a more micro level, we might study the cultural characteristics of a group of Sikh immigrants (first-generation Americans originally from a province in India) attending an American high school. Other micro-level groups we might study include the members of the Chicago Bears football team, the band members at a local high school, Spanish-speaking students at a local middle school, or the students in Mrs. Smith's first-grade classroom. Educational ethnographers are most likely to study cultures or the cultural characteristics of groups much smaller than an entire nation like the United States or Japan. That is, they usually (but not always) study relatively small or micro cultures.

In an educational ethnography conducted at a clearly micro level, a researcher might choose to study a classroom culture. For example, the researcher might want to study the culture of one elementary schoolteacher's home room students to find out how and why the teacher has been successful in helping these students learn to read. Ethnographic concepts (shared values, beliefs, group norms, etc.) and procedures (observations and interviews) will be very useful in understanding this classroom. You might ask questions such as, What norms do the students follow while they are in this classroom? What values do they adopt while they are in the classroom? How does the teacher interact with the students? How do the students interact with one another? Are all of the students usually doing the same thing or are there several clusters of interacting students at a time? What seems to motivate the students to work so hard? What classroom values have the students internalized? What teaching practices and strategies does the teacher use to teach? This list of questions is un-limited because an ethnography should be a relatively comprehensive description of the group's culture and the important cultural scenes.

Sometimes the term *subculture* is used to refer to a culture that is embedded within a larger culture. For example, a high school can be viewed as containing several subcultures (e.g., a teacher culture and various student group cultures). However, researchers usually continue to use the more general term *culture* even for these smaller groups (i.e., they say the school is composed of several cultures) rather than using the more specific term *subculture*. If you want to make the point that a group of people is composed of two or more smaller but distinct groups, then you may use the term *subculture*. Otherwise, using the more general term *culture* is fine. In general, humans are members of and are affected by multiple cultures or subcultures simultaneously. For example, the members of the school band at a suburban high school are probably affected by the overall United States culture, by the adolescent culture within the United States, by a suburban culture, by their own school culture, and by any cultural characteristics they share by virtue of their membership in the band.

Examples of Ethnographic Research

Now that you know what ethnography and culture are, we briefly describe several published research articles that use ethnographic techniques. As with all of the qualitative research approaches discussed in this chapter, the best way to learn more about them is to read some published articles or book-length examples. In "An Ethnographic Study of Norms of Inclusion and Cooperation in a Multiethnic Middle School," Deering (1996) studied the culture in a middle school that was known to be supportive of inclusion. Deering defined inclusion as "the degree to which all persons and their aspirations and interests are incorporated into a given social context" (p. 22). Deering studied the school over a two-year period by observing and talking to teachers, administrators, students, parents, and other community members. He described the school culture, the peer culture, and parent and community involvement. It was remarkable how well students from different groups got along at this particular school. Some reasons were the leadership provided by the principal, a norm of respect applied to everyone in the school, and an expectation of positive involvement by all groups in the school.

In "The Content of Conversations about the Body Parts and Behaviors of Animals During Elementary School Visits to a Zoo and the Implications for Teachers Organizing Field Trips," Tunnicliffe (1995) observed and listened to children while they were at a zoo. She provided a description of what the children said, she classified those statements by topic, and she provided some quotes from the children (e.g., "It's showing its teeth." "Miss Wicks, look! Their hands are like ours!" "There's a baby one."). This study took the reader into a small part of the children's culture and described it to the reader. It is an example of a cultural scene.

In "An Ethnographic Study of Cross-Cultural Communication with Puerto Rican–American Families in the Special Education System," Harry (1992) observed and interviewed parents from twelve Spanish-speaking Puerto Rican American families who had children in the special education system. She also interviewed several educators. She found that cultural differences seemed to lead to communication breakdowns between the educators and the Puerto Rican American parents. For example, the parents expected the educational professionals to treat them as friends (i.e., as *mi amiga* or "my friend") as in Puerto Rico, but they did not perceive this to be happening. They felt the American school system was impersonal, and they did not trust it. Much of the communication about their children and the Individual Education Plan (IEP) was written and this tended to further alienate the parents. Sometimes the parents didn't understand the language and jargon used by the educators (e.g., the term IEP was sometimes misunderstood). Feeling a lack of power, the parents often withdrew from the communication process and deferred to the professionals who, as a result, felt the parents were apathetic. In sum, the educators and the parents tended to come from different cultures and they often misunderstood one another.

Types of Ethnographic Research

Ethnology
The comparative study of cultural groups

There are two other types of ethnographic work that are closely related to classical ethnography. These are called ethnology and ethnohistory. An **ethnology** is the comparative study of cultural groups. It involves conducting or comparing a series of separate ethnographic studies of the same or different cultural groups to uncover general patterns and rules of social behavior. For example, ethnology might involve the comparison of family practices or educational practices in several different cultures. The ethnologist would look for similarities and differences among the groups. As an example, sociologists and anthropologists have found that all societies have some form of the family institution. However, the extended family pattern, in which parents, children, and other kin such as grandparents and aunts and uncles interact a great deal, is more common in traditional agrarian societies (e.g., El Salvador and Bangladesh) and the nuclear family pattern, in which one or two parents and their children interact the most, is more common in modern industrial societies (e.g., the United States and Sweden). Because there is greater interest in general patterns (what many people have in common) in ethnology than in particular patterns (the unique characteristics of each group), this form of research tends to have greater external validity than a single ethnography.

An example of an educational ethnology is LeCompte and Preissle's (1992) chapter titled, "Toward an Ethnology of Student Life in Schools and Classrooms: Synthesizing the Qualitative Research Tradition." LeCompte and Preissle have been conducting educational ethnographies for two decades, and in this ethnology they compare the findings from a large number of ethnographic studies over that time period. Their goal was to find some common themes across the educational ethnographies. We mention only three of their findings. First, they found that children's focus of attention changes over time (e.g., from kindergarten to high school). "Younger children conceptualize school experience as types of activity [e.g., work and play] and the structures that support them. Older students shift their attention from structures, tasks, and schedules to relationships with people" (p. 823). Not surprisingly, students' and teachers' perspectives about what is important tended to be different. Second, they also found that teacher expectations for different kinds of students tended to affect student behavior. Third, they found that "Students who are better integrated into their home culture achieve higher success in school, even if they are members of stigmatized minority groups" (p. 846).

Ethnohistory
The study of the cultural past of a group of people

The other form of ethnographic research is **ethnohistory,** which is the study of the cultural past of a group of people. An ethnohistory is often done during the early stages of an ethnography to uncover the group members' cultural roots and to study how the group has changed (or not changed) over time. This information provides the researcher with a deeper sense of the people being studied. The researcher relies on data such as official documents, oral histories, journals and newspapers, and information gathered from talking with the older people in the group to learn about how things used to be and how things are different now. The ethnohistory can be the end purpose of a research study, but it is usually part of a larger ethnographic study.

Data Collection, Analysis, and Report Writing

Ethnography relies on extended fieldwork. This means that the researcher spends a lengthy amount of time in the field with the people being studied. The researcher typically becomes a participant or nonparticipant observer. In fact, extended fieldwork and "participant observation" are the most distinguishing characteristics of a classical or ideal type ethnography. Spending six months to a year in the field is not at all uncommon. As you can see, this type of research can be quite demanding!

Data collection and data analysis in ethnography are said to be concurrent, or alternating. This means ethnographers typically collect some data and analyze those data, then return to the field to collect more data and analyze those data, and so on. This process cycles during most of the time spent in the field. The researcher needs to look at the data and analyze them while he or she is still fresh out of the field, and also in order to know where and what kinds of data need to be collected next.

Ethnography is an emergent, fluid, and responsive approach to qualitative research because the original research questions frequently change. For example, Holland and Eisenhart (1990) spent several years studying females attending college. They were originally interested in the influence of peer groups on females' role identities and how peer groups affected the women's choices of college majors. They realized over time that the women's peers knew very little about how or why they chose their college major. The researchers decided that the more important questions emerging from their study were how the women responded to their college culture, how they specifically responded to the patriarchal conditions that they faced, and what important subcultural differences existed among the women. Although an ethnographer may think he or she knows exactly what to study in the field, it is always possible that it becomes clear during extended fieldwork that the original research questions were naive, unimportant, or not researchable, or that other issues and questions were more important.

The researcher collects any kind of data during fieldwork that may help in understanding the group of people. Ethnographers talk to people, observe their behavior in their natural day-to-day environments, and examine documents kept by the group members. They also take extensive field notes of what they see on an ongoing basis and they write memos to themselves, recording their thoughts and interpretations about the developing ethnographic description. Video and audio recording devices are frequently helpful because of their accuracy and because the tapes can be reviewed at a later time.

Ethnocentrism
Judging people from a different culture according to the standards of your own culture

One of the cardinal rules in doing ethnographic research is not to be ethnocentric toward the people you are studying. **Ethnocentrism** means judging other people from a different culture or group according to the standards of your own culture or group. An example of ethnocentric behavior would be going to another country and being judgmental about what they eat (e.g., Why would anyone eat snails?!). When we are being ethnocentric we don't try to understand people who are different from us. Therefore, when doing ethnographic research you must take a nonjudgemental stance toward the people you are studying in order to gain useful information.

Emic perspective
The insider's perspective

Ethnographers also try to take on the emic and etic perspectives during data collection and analysis. The **emic perspective** is the insider's perspective. It includes the meanings and views of the people in the group being studied. Taking the emic perspective also means considering questions and issues for study that are important to insiders. The researcher documenting the emic perspective, must try to get inside of the heads of the group members. Therefore, this aspect of ethnography is very phenomenological in approach. In order to understand the emic perspective, it is helpful if you can learn the local language and forms of expression used by the people being studied. Special words or terms used by them are called **emic terms.** Some emic terms used by high school students in a middle-sized southern city to refer to the more academic-type students were *brains, advanced, intellectuals, nerds, geeks, dorks,* and *smarties* (Smith, 1997). A larger list of emic terms identified by Smith for various groups in high schools is shown in Table 11.3.

Emic terms
Special words or terms used by the people in a group

Etic perspective
An external, social scientific view of reality

Ethnographers use the term **etic perspective** to refer to an external, social scientific view of reality (Fetterman, 1998). This is the perspective of the objective researcher studying a group of people. The goal is to move beyond the perspectives of the people being studied and use social science concepts, terms (i.e., **etic terms**), and procedures to describe the people and explain their behavior. Researchers using the etic perspective also bring their research questions from the outside (e.g., issues are considered important based on a review of the research literature). They tend to take an instrumental view, wanting to study the participants in order to answer a specific question or to produce a specific product.

Etic terms
Outsider's words or special words that are used by social scientists

TABLE 11.3   Selected Emic Terms Used by High School Students.

Losers	Rebels	Skanks	Jocks	Prep	Holy Rollers
Retards	Rednecks	Bubbas	Mechanics	Vo Techs	Goody-Goodies
Hippies	Peacers	Gangsters	Druggies	Burnouts	Clowns
Grubbies	Loners	Roaches	Wannabes	Woodies	Azalea Trail Maids
Surfers	Whammers	Punks	Airheads	Rockers	Brains
Geeks	Dorks	Duds	Book worms	Grunge	Band

From Smith, Heather J. 1997. *The Role of Symbolism in the Structure, Maintenance, and Interaction of High School Social Groupings.* Masters Thesis. University of South Alabama Department of Sociology and Anthropology. Used by permission.

Going native
Identifying so completely with the group being studied that you can no longer remain objective

Effective ethnographers are able to utilize both perspectives. If a researcher only took the emic perspective, he or she would risk what is called **going native,** which means that the researcher identifies so completely with the group that he or she can no longer remain objective. When someone goes native, they have basically become an insider. They have overidentified with the group and they can only view things from the viewpoint of the insiders. On the other hand, if researchers only took the etic viewpoint, they would risk not understanding the people from the native perspective. They would also risk imposing their own predetermined beliefs and categories on their interpretations about the participants. We believe that effective researchers must walk the fine line between the emic and etic perspectives, and they must periodically delve into the world of each perspective in order to gather insights and produce a good ethnography.

Because of the reliance on observational and interview data, ethnographers should constantly triangulate their observations and data sources in order to corroborate their research findings. For example, if a participant or informant says some event took place, the ethnographer does not take that single participant's account at face value. Instead, the ethnographer searches for other participants who experienced (or observed or heard about) the same event and listens to their accounts and interpretations. In this way, evidence for research validity is improved. During the later months in the field, ethnographers frequently begin composing and writing their final report. This way the written description and interpretation can be shown to the participants for their review and validation. Recall that this process is called participant review or member checking.

When writing the final report, ethnographers contextualize their study. That is, they carefully examine the context in which the group is situated and they write this up in the report. For example, ethnographers describe the particulars of the physical and social settings, including the time, the place, and the situation in which a study was conducted. Contextualization helps make the ethnographer more aware of the relationship between the context and the observed behavior, and it helps readers of the research report to know where and to whom they can apply the research results.

When describing a group, ethnographers also try to be holistic. Holism was discussed briefly in Chapter 1 and also in Table 11.1 (characteristic 3). Although the concept of holism is summed up in the statement "the whole is greater than its parts," holistic description does not ignore the parts of the whole because an analysis of the parts is essential to understanding the whole. For example, a high school band is composed of individuals who come together as a unit and create a holistic product (music). In a typical ethnography holistic description involves examining the characteristics of the individuals in a group (e.g., what the individuals are like); it involves examining how the individuals in the group interact with one another (e.g., when they interact and what they do); and it involves examining how the individuals come together to form the group (e.g., what they have in common, what their group norms and rituals are, and what the group identity is). In short, when conducting a holistic description, you must study the parts of the whole in addition to describing the whole. The final ethnographic report typically includes rich and holistic description of the group. It also usually includes many verbatims (direct quotations from group members).

CASE STUDY RESEARCH

Merriam (1988) tells us that "case study research is nothing new" (p. xi), pointing out that the idea of studying cases has been around for a long time and across many different disciplines (e.g., medicine, law, business, the social sciences). During the late 1970s and the 1980s, however, authors such as Robert Stake (1978), Robert Yin (1981), and Sharan Merriam (1988) delineated case study research as a specific type of research. Although Stake and Merriam have a qualitative orientation to case study research and Yin has a more quantitative orientation, what these case study researchers have in common is that they choose to call their objects of study cases, and they organize their research efforts around the study of those cases (e.g., Merriam, 1988; Stake, 1995; Yin, 1998). Although case study research can clearly be quantitative or qualitative (or both), we take a more qualitative approach in this chapter. We define **case study research** simply as research that provides a detailed account and analysis of one or more cases.[2]

Case study research Research that provides a detailed account and analysis of one or more cases

Case A bounded system

What Is a Case?

A **case** is defined as a bounded system. In the words of one prominent case study researcher, Robert Stake (1997), "Lou Smith used a fancy name, 'bounded system,' to indicate that we are going to try to figure out what complex things go on within that system. The case study tells a story about a bounded system" (p. 406). Note that a "system" is a set of interrelated elements that form an organized whole. Using the system metaphor, cases are seen as holistic entities that have parts and that act or operate in their environments. "Bounded" is added to emphasize that you should identify the outline or boundaries of the system—you must determine what the case is and what it is not.

Typical cases are a child with a learning disability, a pupil with a special need, a language arts classroom, a charter school, and a national program (e.g., Head Start Program). Some case study researchers are very inclusive in what they call cases (e.g., Cresswell, 1998; Merriam, 1988; Yin, 1998). For them a case is not just an object or entity with a clear identity (e.g., a group, a person, a classroom, or an organization), but can also include an event (e.g., a campus protest), an activity (e.g., learning to play softball), or a process (e.g., becoming a professional teacher during one's first year of teaching). When you read case study articles, you should check early on to see what kind of case the authors are examining.

For example, Gallo and Horton (1994) conducted a case study of one high school in East Central Florida. Here the high school was the case. The research focused on the process and results of having access to the Internet at the high school. The authors concluded that Internet access could have many positive effects on teachers (e.g., incorporation of technology into the classroom, increased self-esteem, development of positive attitudes toward computers), especially if the teachers were given adequate training in how to use the Internet and how to incorporate it into their classrooms. Valentine and McIntosh (1990) examined the characteristics of an organization (the case) in which women held all the positions of power. They found that the organization took on a *gemeinschaft* (a local community) type of character rather than a *gesellschaft* (citylike, impersonal) character. Van Haneghan and Stofflett (1995) conducted case studies of four fifth-grade teachers (four cases). They determined how each teacher implemented an innovative videodisc curriculum focused on problem solving. These authors developed a heuristic model based on their observations that could be used to train teachers to implement the new curriculum into their classrooms.

Because case study researchers define a case as a bounded system it should not be surprising that they study how the system operates. As a result, they are interested in holistic description. Almost all systems are made up of components or parts, and it is important to understand how the parts operate in order to understand the system (i.e., the case). For example, a high school is made up of teachers, buildings, students, classrooms, and books (among many other things). You can also view an individual as being composed of many different components or parts (e.g., cognitive, emotional, physiological).

Case study researchers also view each case as having an internal and an external context. Take a school as an example. Internally, a researcher might examine the organizational climate at a school, the leadership style used by the principal, and the condition of the physical and instructional facilities. Externally, the school will be situated in a geographical area with specific social, economic, and demographic characteristics. If the school is a public school, it will be situated within a public school system with additional characteristics. The point is that case study researchers carefully examine the contexts of the case in order to better describe and explain the functioning of the case.

Types of Case Study Research Designs

Intrinsic case study Interest is in understanding a specific case

There are three different kinds of case studies according to Stake (1995): intrinsic case studies, instrumental case studies, and collective case studies. In an **intrinsic case study** the researcher's primary interest is in understanding a specific case. This design is the classic, single-case design. Here the researcher describes, in-depth, the particulars of the case in order to shed light on the case. For example, a researcher might want to understand a student who is having difficulty in class or a researcher might want to understand how the local PTA operates. The goal is to understand the case as a holistic entity as well as to understand its inner workings. A secondary goal is to understand a more general process based on an analysis of the single case.

The intrinsic case study is very popular in education. It is also popular with program evaluators whose goal is to describe a program and to evaluate how effectively the program is operating (e.g., an evaluator might evaluate a local drug education program for at-risk middle and high school students). Finally, the intrinsic case study is often used in exploratory research in which the researcher attempts to learn about a little-known phenomenon by studying a single case in depth. The advantage of the intrinsic case study is that researchers can put all their time and resources into the study of a single case and can, therefore, develop an in-depth understanding. A weakness is that generalizing from a single case can be very risky.

Instrumental case study
Interest is in understanding something more general than the particular case

In an **instrumental case study,** the researcher's primary interest is in understanding something other than the particular case. The case is seen as important only as a means to an end. In other words, the researcher studies the case to learn about something more general (e.g., teenage drug use in general rather than teenage drug use at a particular high school, or discipline in general rather than discipline in a particular teacher's classroom). The goal tends to be less particularistic and more universalistic. That is, researchers doing instrumental case studies are less interested in making conclusions that are specific to the case and its particular setting than they are in making conclusions that apply beyond a particular case.

In the instrumental case study design, the researcher is usually interested in how and why a phenomenon operates as it does. That is, the researcher chooses the case in order to develop and/or test a theory or to better understand some important issue. Explanation is a key goal. The specific case can be selected because it is extreme or unique in some way (and can be used to test theoretical predictions) or because it is typical (and can be used to understand the general case). The instrumental case study is popular with many academic researchers when they are interested in generalizing and extending the findings in research literatures on various topics.

Collective case study
Studying multiple cases in one research study

In the **collective case study,** the researcher believes that he or she can gain greater insight into a research topic by concurrently studying multiple cases in one overall research study. The collective case study is also called the multiple-case design (e.g., Yin, 1994). Several cases are usually studied in a collective case study. For example, two or three cases might be studied when a relatively in-depth analysis of each case is required and when resources are limited. When less depth is required and when greater resources are available, collective case studies of around ten cases are common. The cases in the collective case study are usually studied instrumentally rather than intrinsically. For example, a researcher might select several cases to study because he or she is interested in studying the effects of inclusion of children with mild mental retardation in general education classes. Rather than studying the outcomes in a single classroom, the researcher studies the impact in several different classrooms.

There are several advantages to studying more than one case. First, a comparative type of study can be conducted in which several cases are compared for similarities and differences. For example, a public school might be studied and compared with a private school. Second, one can more effectively test a theory by observing the results of multiple cases. Third, one is more likely to be able to generalize the results from multiple cases than from a single case. Yin (1994) points out that replication logic can be used when one has multiple cases. In experimental research we have more confidence in a finding when it has been replicated many times. Here is what Yin says about this idea and its relevance for case study research:

> Thus, if one has access only to three cases of a rare, clinical syndrome in psychology or medical science, the appropriate research design is one in which the same results are predicted for each of the three cases, thereby producing evidence that the three cases did indeed involve the same syndrome. If similar results are obtained from all three cases, replication is said to have taken place. (p. 45)

In Yin's example mentioned in this quote, the theory that predicted the same result for each case was supported. Therefore, compared to a single case study, the researcher would have greater confidence that a similar result would happen in a new case.

A disadvantage of studying multiple cases is that depth of analysis will usually have to be sacrificed because of the breadth of analysis obtained from studying more than one case. This is the classic "depth versus breadth tradeoff," and it is a common tradeoff in case study research. In other words, because of limited resources (e.g., money and time) available in most research studies, you will be forced to make a choice between "depth and detail" and "breadth and comparative information." It takes considerable time to study one case in depth, but you end up with a deep understanding of the case. On the other hand, if you are going to study multiple cases, you will have to reduce the amount of time spent on each case but you get important comparative information. As you can see, there are advantages and disadvantages to both sides of this tradeoff. You will ultimately have to make the final judgment about how to deal with this tradeoff if you conduct a research study.

Data Collection, Analysis, and Report Writing

Case study research methodologists (those researchers who write books about doing case study research) tend to be pragmatic and advocate the use of multiple methods and multiple data sources (i.e., methods and data triangulation). These methodologists recommend that you take an eclectic approach and rely on any data that will help you understand your case and answer your research questions. Any of the methods of data collection (observation, interviews, questionnaires, documents) discussed in Chapter 5 can be used. Qualitative versions of these methods (participant observation, in-depth interviews, open-ended questionnaires) do, however, tend to be the most popular in education.

The final report is usually written to present a rich (vivid and detailed) and holistic (i.e., describes the whole and its parts) description of the case and its context. An example of rich description is given in Exhibit 11.4. Research questions (or research "issues" according to Stake) and the relevant findings are presented. The findings should be related back to similar findings in the research literature when possible. When people or groups of people are studied, an attempt is usually made to reconstruct the participants' realities and portray the multiple viewpoints existing in the case (e.g., you might portray the different viewpoints of the teachers in a school). When a collective case study is conducted (i.e., studying multiple cases), the report may be organized case by case with a separate section integrating the findings from all of the cases.

EXHIBIT 11.4   An Example of Rich Description in a Case Study

---

That first morning, I reached Harper [School] a few minutes after 8 A.M., in time to see most of the students arriving. It was a nippy morning, the day following Martin Luther King's birthday. Many youngsters were bundled in Chicago Bulls gear. All were walking, almost all from the adjacent high-rise housing. Residents called it "The Place."

A middle-school youngster wearing a crossing-guard sash courteously escorted me to an unmarked door. Also unmarked—by graffiti or weather—was the white brick face of the building, lettered simply Frances Harper School. Just inside the door, Mr. Carter, the security captain, pointed the way to the office. A janitor and several kids took notice of my arrival.

The office clerk, with a large smile, introduced me to "the boss." Principal Lyda Hawkins's greeting also was warm. We moved into her room for a lengthy conversation—in spite of mounting traffic. First we commented on yesterday's Denver confrontation between King marchers and Klansmen. I said, "How could it be?" She said, "Some things don't change."

Lyda Hawkins had taught in this part of Chicago since the 1950s and had been principal of this school for over 16 years. She knew her neighbor-hood. We talked about change, about the Chicago school reform plan, about its orientation to governance more than to teaching and learning. "To many, it was license to get the principal," she said with feeling. She spoke of Local School Councils, noting that she had a good council. She spoke of unrealistic expectations of reform groups about readiness of parents to assume school governance responsibilities, the lack of experience before election, the insufficiency of orientation after. One of her council members had said, "How do you expect us to understand a $2 million budget? I can't manage $460 a month!"

Community involvement in Harper School was not high. Only a few parent volunteers worked with teachers. It was even difficult to get Local School Council members to come to council meetings. In the words of Mattie Mitchell, teacher and school community representative, "Who wants to make decisions? Who is ready to make decisions? Not many."

Reprinted from R. E. Stake, *The Art of Case Study Research,* pp. 138–139, copyright © 1995 by Sage Publications, Inc. Reprinted by Permission of Sage Publications, Inc.

GROUNDED THEORY

Barney Glaser and Anselm Strauss wrote a book in 1967 on what they called grounded theory. These two sociologists contended that theory should emerge, inductively, from empirical data. They said we need to "discover theory from data" (p. 1). Although this was not an entirely new idea in the field of research, Glaser and Strauss wanted to counter what they saw as a tendency in their field to focus on *theory confirmation* (testing hypotheses developed from previous theories) rather than on *theory generation* and construction (developing new theories grounded in new data). They felt that the discipline of sociology had stagnated because of a reliance on older theories. They also felt that current research was too quantitative and had become too far removed from the empirical reality that it sought to explain. They believed that many of the popular theories at that time were not grounded in real data but were, instead, based on the thinking of a few famous theorists. Since Glaser and Strauss's important book was published in 1967, grounded theory has become a popular approach to qualitative research in many different disciplines, including education, counseling, and nursing.

Grounded theory
A general
methodology
for developing
theory that is
grounded
in data
systematically
gathered and
analyzed

"**Grounded theory** is a *general methodology* for developing theory that is grounded in data systematically gathered and analyzed" (Strauss & Corbin, 1994, p. 273). The product of the grounded theory methodology is frequently called a grounded theory. Therefore, when you do grounded theory research, your goal is to construct a grounded theory. It is important to understand that *a grounded theory is not generated a priori* (i.e., based only on reasoning). Rather, a grounded theory is based on concepts that are generated directly from the data that are collected in one or more research studies. This is another way of saying that the theory is inductively derived. Figuratively speaking, you can think of inductive analysis as "getting into your data" (during data collection and analysis), "living there" or "hanging out there for a while," and developing an understanding of the phenomenon based on the data. For example, if someone outside of education wanted to learn about teaching, this person could go to a real classroom, observe a teacher for several weeks, and then draw some tentative, data-based conclusions about teaching. Induction is a bottom-up approach based on original data (i.e., you start with the data and then make your generalizations after looking at your data). Strauss and Corbin (1990) point out the inductive nature of grounded theory research when they say that "One does not begin with a theory, then prove it. Rather, one begins with an area of study and what is relevant to that area is allowed to emerge" (p. 23). During a particular grounded theory research study, some data are collected and analyzed and, as the theory is being developed, additional data are collected and analyzed to further clarify, develop, and validate the theory.

Characteristics of a Grounded Theory

Glaser and Strauss (1967) list four important characteristics of a grounded theory. They are fit, understanding, generality, and control. First, the theory must fit the data if it is to be useful. Glaser and Strauss make an important point when they say that a researcher "often develops a theory that embodies, without his realizing it, his own ideals and the values of his occupation and social class, as well as popular views and myths, along with his deliberate efforts at making logical deductions from some formal theory to which he became committed as a graduate student" (p. 238). The point is that theory must correspond closely to the real-world data, not to our personal wishes or biases. Second, the theory should be clearly stated and readily understandable to people working in the substantive area, even to nonresearch types. One reason for this is that practitioners may need to use the theory or employ someone else to use the theory one day. If the theory is not understandable to them, it may never be used. Glaser and Strauss point out that "Their understanding the theory tends to engender a readiness to use it, for it sharpens their sensitivity to the problems that they face and gives them an image of how they can potentially make matters better" (p. 240).

Third, the theory should have generality. This means that the scope of the theory and its conceptual level should not be so specific that the theory only applies to one small set of people or to only one specific situation. Such a theory would rarely be of use. Furthermore, it would be practically impossible to develop a new theory for every single person and situation. A strategy for avoiding such specificity is to conceptualize the concepts in the theory at a level abstract enough to move beyond the specifics in the original research study. The fourth characteristic of a good grounded theory as discussed by Glaser and Strauss is control. If someone uses the theory, he or she should have some control over the phenomenon that is explained by the theory. In their words, "The substantive theory must enable the person who uses it to have enough control in everyday situations to make its application worth trying" (p. 245). As a result, it is a good idea to identify controllable variables and build them into your grounded theory.

As you can see, meeting the criteria of fit, understanding, generality, and control is a lot to expect from a grounded theory, especially if the theory is developed from a single research study. That is why the development of a grounded theory is a neverending process. In a single research study the researcher should try to collect as extensive data as feasible. During the study the researcher will interact with the data and collect additional data when questions arise and need answering. A grounded theory should be further elaborated and modified in future research studies—the key strategy, again, is that the developing theory should be grounded in the data. Practitioners who attempt to use the theory should also be involved in making suggestions for theory modifications. As Glaser and Strauss say, "The person who applies the theory becomes, in effect, a generator of theory" (p. 242).

Example of a Grounded Theory

So that you will have a better idea about a real grounded theory research study, we will now describe a study conducted by Creswell and Brown (1992) titled, "How Chairpersons Enhance Faculty Research: A Grounded Theory Study." The article is easy to read, and it is a good example of a grounded theory based on a single research study.

Creswell and Brown studied how college and university department chairpersons interact with their faculty members. They conducted "semi-structured telephone interviews with thirty-three chairpersons" (p. 42). They found that the chairpersons actually performed many different roles. The roles identified were labeled "providing, enabling, advocating, acting as a mentor, encouraging, collaborating, and challenging." They also found that the chairpersons performed different roles at different times, depending on the level of the faculty member they were interacting with. The important levels identified in the study were beginning faculty (faculty who had been in the department from one to three years), pre-tenured faculty (faculty who had been in the department from three to five years), post-tenured faculty (faculty who had not yet been promoted to full professor), and senior faculty (faculty who were full professors). They found, for example, that beginning faculty needed extra time for writing and publishing, and the chairperson would provide additional resources and try to enable the faculty member by providing a favorable schedule and a reduction in committee work. If this strategy were successful, the outcome would be more publications by the faculty member, which would help improve the faculty member's chance of getting tenure. You can see Creswell and Brown's depiction of their grounded theory in Figure 11.2. As shown there, the type of faculty issue that a chairperson is concerned with depends on the career stage of the faculty member and other signs such as a lack of productivity. Given a faculty member who is at a specific stage and the presence of

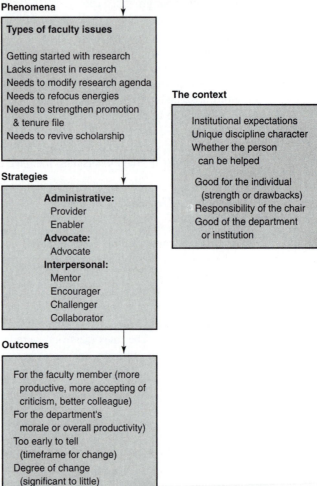

Causal conditions

Signs

Who identifies the problem
  (chair or faculty member)
Overt signs
  (e.g., lack of tenure,
  lack of productivity)
Problems in other areas
  than research

Stages of career

Beginning faculty member
  (1–3 years)
Pretenure faculty member
  (3–5 years)
Posttenure faculty member
  (before full professor)
Senior faculty member
  (full professor to retirement)

Phenomena

Types of faculty issues

Getting started with research
Lacks interest in research
Needs to modify research agenda
Needs to refocus energies
Needs to strengthen promotion
  & tenure file
Needs to revive scholarship

The context

Institutional expectations
Unique discipline character
Whether the person
  can be helped

Good for the individual
  (strength or drawbacks)
Responsibility of the chair
Good of the department
  or institution

Strategies

Administrative:
  Provider
  Enabler
Advocate:
  Advocate
Interpersonal:
  Mentor
  Encourager
  Challenger
  Collaborator

Outcomes

For the faculty member (more
  productive, more accepting of
  criticism, better colleague)
For the department's
  morale or overall productivity)
Too early to tell
  (timeframe for change)
Degree of change
  (significant to little)

FIGURE 11.2   Creswell and Brown's model for chairs' role in enhancing faculty research performance. (From: J. W. Creswell and M. L. Brown. "How Chairpersons Enhance Faculty Research: A Grounded Theory Study." *Reviews of Higher Education,* vol. 16(1), p. 57. © 1992. The Association for the Study of Higher Education. Reprinted by permission of the Johns Hopkins University Press.)

certain signs, the department chairperson performs certain roles (strategies) to help the faculty member develop. These actions result in specific outcomes (e.g., improved productivity, an improved attitude toward the department). Finally, the general process operates within a context, which can also affect how the chairperson works with the faculty member.

Data Collection, Analysis, and Report Writing

Data analysis in grounded theory starts at the moment of initial contact with the phenomenon being studied, and it continues throughout the development of a grounded theory. In other words, data collection and analysis in grounded theory are concurrent and continual activities. The most popular data-collection method in grounded theory is the open-ended interview, although other strategies, especially direct observations, are often used to collect original data. Technically, any data-collection method is allowed in developing a grounded theory. Remember that what is always required in a grounded theory research study is that the theory be grounded in the data.

Constant comparative method
Data analysis in grounded theory research

Data analysis in grounded theory is called the **constant comparative method,** and it involves the constant interplay between the researcher, the data, and the developing theory. Because of the active role of the researcher in this process, it is important that the researcher have **theoretical sensitivity,** a characteristic of the researcher that is present when the researcher is effective at thinking about what kinds of data need to be collected and what aspects of the already collected data are the most important for the grounded theory. It involves a mixture of analytic thinking ability, curiosity, and creativity. The theoretically sensitive researcher is able to continually ask questions of the data in order to develop a deeper and deeper understanding of the phenomenon. Over time the theoretically sensitive researcher will be able to develop a grounded theory that meets the criteria discussed earlier (i.e., fit, understanding, generality, and control). The more research experience you get, the more theoretically sensitive you will become. If you like to ask questions, then it is very possible that you have what it takes!

Theoretical sensitivity
When a researcher is effective at thinking about what kinds of data need to be collected and what aspects of already collected data are the most important for the grounded theory

The theoretically sensitive researcher attempts continually to learn by observing and listening to research participants and by examining and thinking about the data. As just mentioned, the researcher must constantly ask questions of the data in order to learn what the data are saying. During analysis, ideas and hypotheses are generated and then provisionally tested, either with additional data that have already been collected or by collecting more data. When a grounded theory study involves extended fieldwork (spending many months in the field), there will be plenty of time to collect additional data to fill in gaps in the developing grounded theory. There will also be time to verify and test propositions based on the theory. As you can see, extended fieldwork is a optimal situation because you can continue to collect important data. If all the data have to be collected in one short period of time, then the conditions for developing a convincing grounded theory are not nearly as favorable. Nonetheless, you still may be able to develop a tentative grounded theory that can be further developed in later research.

One of the most unique parts of the grounded theory research approach is its approach to data analysis. The three types or stages of data analysis are called open coding,

Open coding
The first stage in grounded theory data analysis

axial coding, and selective coding (Strauss & Corbin, 1990). **Open coding** is the first stage in grounded theory data analysis. It begins after some initial data have been collected, and it involves examining the data (usually reading transcripts line-by-line) and naming and categorizing discrete elements in the data. In other words, it involves labeling important words and phrases in the transcribed data. For example, let's say that you have collected interview data from twenty participants. You are reading an interview transcript and it says, "I believe that two important properties of a good teacher are caring about your students and motivating them to learn." From this phrase, you might generate the concepts teaching techniques, caring about students, and motivating students. Open coding means finding the concepts like this in your data. As you continue open coding you would continue to see whether teaching techniques are reflected again in future comments by the same person or by another person in another interview.

Axial coding
The second stage in grounded theory data analysis

Axial coding follows open coding. During **axial coding** the researcher develops the concepts into categories (i.e., slightly more abstract concepts) and organizes the categories. The researcher then looks to see what kinds of things were mentioned by the participants many times (i.e., what themes appeared across the interviews). The researcher also looks for possible relationships among the categories in the data. A goal is to show how the phenomenon operates (i.e., showing its process). The researcher also asks questions like, How is the phenomenon manifested? What are its key features? What conditions bring about the phenomenon? What strategies do participants use to deal with the phenomenon? What are the consequences of those strategies? Creswell and Brown addressed many of these questions in their grounded theory. For example, looking at Figure 11.2 you will see that the characteristics of the phenomenon are listed under the title "Phenomena." The conditions that bring about the phenomenon are listed under "Causal conditions." Strategies are listed under "Strategies." And the consequences of the strategies are listed under "Outcomes."

Selective coding
The final stage in grounded theory data analysis

Selective coding is the stage of data analysis in which the researcher puts the finishing touches on the grounded theory for the current research study. In particular, this is where the grounded theorist looks for the story line of the theory (i.e., the main idea) by reflecting on the data and the results that were produced during open coding and axial coding. The researcher will usually need to continue to analyze the data, but with more focus on the central idea of the developing theory. Ultimately, it is during selective coding that the researcher writes the story, explaining the grounded theory. It is here that the researcher fleshes out the details of the theory. Selective coding also involves rechecking the theory with the data to make sure that no mistakes were made. The researcher also goes to the published literature during selective coding for additional ideas to consider in developing the grounded theory and in understanding its broader significance. The grounded theorist has

Theoretical saturation
Occurs when no new information or concepts are emerging from the data and the grounded theory has been validated

finished analyzing the data when **theoretical saturation** occurs. This occurs when no new information or concepts are emerging from the data and when the grounded theory has been throughly validated with the collected data.

A grounded theory research report reflects the process of generating a grounded theory. The major research question or topic is discussed first. The participants selected for the study and why they were selected are also discussed early in the report. Then the methods of data collection are discussed. As you know, interviews and observations are the most popular data-collection methods. The results section is the most lengthy section in the report because a grounded theory is usually based on extensive information learned in a research study. Ultimately, the final grounded theory is discussed. Glaser and Strauss, the founders of grounded theory, usually wrote book-length expositions of their grounded theories. Today, grounded theories are commonly reported in journal articles. By way of summary, we have provided an example of a grounded theory in Exhibit 11.5.

EXHIBIT 11.5   A Grounded Theory of Instructional Leadership

Harchar and Hyle (1996) were interested in the process of instructional leadership by administrators in elementary schools. They studied known leaders (most were principals who were nominated because of their leadership abilities), and they determined what these leaders did when they were leading. Although there is much more to this journal article, we provide a quote in which they discuss their procedures first, and then we provide a quote in which they summarize their grounded theory.

> Grounded Theory served as both the theoretical structure and research design. Data collection, analysis and theory development followed Strauss and Corbin's Grounded Theory. Loosely-structured, open-ended interviews **served** as the primary data collection strategy. Following transcription, we subjected the data to three coding procedures: open, axial and selective. In open coding, the information was labeled, classified, named, and categories developed in terms of their properties and dimensions, simultaneously and, at times, randomly. Through axial coding, the researcher arranged the data in new ways through the exploration of elements of context, intervening conditions, action/interaction strategies and consequences to those strategies. Selective coding, the last analytic process, resulted in the development of a story line, the gist of the phenomenon under study. On the basis of these related concepts, a theory was developed which described elementary instructional leadership. (p. 16)

Here is Harchar and Hyle's final description of their grounded theory.

Through collaborative power, instructional leaders balance power inequities in the school and school community. . . . School environments are fraught with power inequities, both experiential and knowledge-based, ranging from educational and district/building experience to knowledge and preparation expertise. Within this environment, the elementary instructional leader works to develop a common vision across staff and throughout the community. Through visioning, each organizational and community supporter is empowered with direction and purpose. The principal recognizes and supports positive behaviors and confronts and defuses negative behaviors. Trust, respect and collegiality form the foundation of the school environment as all work for the development of a quality school where staff, students and community share and work toward common, dynamic goals. The importance of all organizational members is recognized and an even playing field developed from which all can and must contribute. Consistency, honesty, and visibility are key constants. The principal must demand that all teachers voice their opinions and ideas, thus fostering problem solving, constructive discourse and ownership in an equitable school environment. Even though all principals did not use the same strategies, there were general tactics used to balance power. The strategies are not linear; they occur both simultaneously and at varying times, building on each other. (pp. 26–27)

SUMMARY

We started by summarizing the major characteristics of qualitative research. Next we discussed the four most prominent approaches to qualitative research in education. These approaches are phenomenology, ethnography, case study, and grounded theory. Although each approach follows the qualitative research paradigm, the focus of each approach is different from the others. In a phenomenology, the researcher is interested in obtaining a vivid description of individuals' experiences of some phenomenon. In ethnography, the researcher is also interested in getting into the heads of the people being studied. However, ethnographers are specifically interested in studying cultural groups, and they focus on cultural description and on relating cultural characteristics to human behavior. Case study research is a very general and inclusive approach to qualitative research. What case study researchers have in common is that they choose to call their objects of study "cases," and they organize their research efforts around the study of those cases. The focus is usually on describing the characteristics of one or more cases, describing how the case or cases operate, and answering specific research questions about the case(s). In the grounded theory approach to qualitative research, researchers focus on generating a grounded theory to explain some phenomenon. Important characteristics of a grounded theory are fit, understanding, generality, and control.

STUDY QUESTIONS

1. What are the key characteristics of qualitative research?
2. Explain the role of induction in qualitative research.
3. Why is it said that qualitative research does *not* follow a series of steps in a linear fashion?
4. Why is qualitative research important for educational research?
5. What are the key characteristics of phenomenology?
6. How does the researcher analyze the data collected in a phenomenology?
7. What are the key characteristics of ethnography?
8. What is the difference between a macro and a micro culture?
9. How do people become members of cultures?
10. What is the difference between the emic and the etic perspective?
11. What are the key characteristics of case study research?
12. What is a case?
13. Define intrinsic case study, instrumental case study, and collective case study.
14. What are the key characteristics of grounded theory?
15. What are the four important characteristics of grounded theory according to Glaser and Strauss?
16. When does the researcher stop collecting data in grounded theory research?

EXERCISES

1. We have pointed out repeatedly that one of the best ways to learn about research is to read published research articles. Here are several good examples of qualitative research articles. Go to the library and look at each article. Then choose *one* article to review.

    Ethnography example (*Note:* this article is included in Appendix B in this book.)

    Deering, P. D. (1996). An ethnographic study of norms of inclusion and cooperation in a multiethnic middle school. *The Urban Review, 28*(1), 21–39.

    Case study example

    Abell, S. K., & Roth, M. (1994). Constructing science teaching in the elementary school: The socialization of a science enthusiast student teacher. *Journal of Research in Science Teaching, 31*(1), 77–90.

    Phenomenology example

    Cross, T. L., & Stewart, R. A. (1995). A phenomenological investigation of the *lebenswelt* of gifted students in rural high schools. *The Journal of Secondary Gifted Education, 6*(4), 273–280.

    Grounded theory example

    Neufeldt, S. A., Karno, M. P., & Nelson, M. L. (1996). A qualitative study of experts' conceptualization of supervisee reflectivity. *Journal of Counseling Psychology, 43*(1), 3–9.

2. This exercise will help you to "experience" phenomenology. Think about a time in your past when your were afraid. For example, you might have been afraid of the dark when you were a child. You might have been accosted by a stranger. You might have been in an accident. Try to remember how you felt and then write this down in rich detail. Compare your description with some others, and search for the essential characteristics of the phenomenon of being afraid.

KEY TERMS

axial coding (336)

bracket (316)

case (327)

case study research (327)

collective case study (329)

constant comparative
  method (335)

culture (321)

emic perspective (325)

emic terms (325)

essence (317)

ethnocentrism (325)

ethnography (320)

ethnohistory (324)

ethnology (323)

etic perspective (325)

etic terms (325)

going native (326)

grounded theory (332)

instrumental case study (329)

intrinsic case study (328)

life-world (315)

norms (321)

open coding (336)

phenomenology (315)

qualitative research (312)

selective coding (336)

shared beliefs (321)

shared values (321)

theoretical saturation (336)

theoretical sensitivity (335)

ENDNOTES

1. Reprinted by permission of John Moffitt Papers, Special Collections, University of Virginia Library.
2. Don't be surprised if you see journal articles in which the authors claim to be performing case study research as well as another research method. The term *case study* is not used consistently. For example, it is not uncommon for ethnographers to refer to their groups as "cases" (LeCompte & Preissle, 1993). Similarly, other qualitative researchers may call the individuals or groups in their study "cases."

CHAPTER 12

Historical Research

LEARNING OBJECTIVES

To be able to

- explain what is meant by historical research.
- explain the various reasons for conducting historical research.
- explain how historical research is conducted.
- differentiate between primary and secondary sources.
- explain the meaning of external and internal criticism and why they are important when conducting historical research.
- differentiate between positive and negative criticism.
- recognize and explain the methodological problems that must be avoided when synthesizing the data collected and preparing the narrative account of this data.

In reading the title of this chapter, you may wonder why a chapter on historical research is included in a textbook on educational research methods. Historical research obviously has to focus on events occurring in the past, and our primary concern is with improving the current and future educational process. Throughout this book we discuss research methods that enable us to answer research questions that focus on current educational issues. This would seem to further indicate that focusing on past events has little, if any, relevance to the solution of current educational problems. However, as we discuss later in this chapter, the past does have significance for present and future events, and historical research provides a means for capitalizing on the past. In this chapter we discuss the methodology of historical research, how it is useful to professional educators, and the relevance it has to current educational problems.

WHAT IS HISTORICAL RESEARCH?

Historical research
The process of systematically examining past events or combinations of events to arrive at an account of what happened in the past

Historical research is the process of systematically examining past events or combinations of events to arrive at an account of what has happened in the past (Berg, 1998). In constructing this account, it is important to realize that historical research involves much more than an accumulation of facts, dates, figures, or a description of past events, people, or developments. Historical research is interpretative. Its presentation is much more than the mere retelling of past facts. Instead it is a flowing, fluid, dynamic account of past events that attempts to recapture the complex nuances, individual personalities, and ideas that influenced the events being investigated (Berg, 1998). This does not mean that the historical researcher does not use incidents, facts, dates, and figures. Rather, the historical researcher uses this type of information but also attempts to reconstruct and present the facts and figures in a way that communicates an understanding of the events from the multiple points of view of those who participated in them. In presenting these multiple points of view, the historian's own interpretation is also very much a part of history. In fact, that is the very heart of historical interpretation. Historians openly acknowledge their own biases in a way few other scholars do. Whether the historian is liberal or conservative, black or white, male or female matters a great deal in the account of the historical event being investigated and the interpretation of the facts and incidents surrounding that event.

To illustrate this use of facts and data, look at Fultz's (1995) account of the African American schools in the south from 1890–1940.

> 93.4 percent of the 24,079 African American schools in fourteen southern states in 1925–26 were rural. Of the total, more than three-fourths (82.6 percent) were one-teacher (63.8 percent) or two-teacher (18.8 percent) facilities. Moreover, almost three-fourths (73.9 percent) of the African American teachers in these states taught in rural schools. (p. 402)

Now look at the way in which Fultz (1995) continued this discussion of African American schools by moving into the interpretative phase, which provides a dynamic and fluid account not only of the condition of the schools, but also of the effect that these conditions had on the delivery of instructional services.

> In addition, the literature is replete with references to the deplorable physical condition of many African American schools, a pervasive state of disrepair that potentially undermined the delivery of instructional services. Among the signs of neglect were rickety benches with and without backs, holes in the floor and the roof, inadequate heating, poor lighting, unpainted walls, dilapidated steps, unkempt surroundings, and a lack of desks and other educational supplies and materials. (p. 403)

This narrative account of events and accompanying interpretations presented as a story provides far more than just a retelling of the facts. It provides a rich account of the development of the historical events and gives the reader an idea of the circumstances that shaped the events of the past.

SIGNIFICANCE OF HISTORICAL RESEARCH

Why should we want to study the history of education? If you are a history buff, you realize that events that happened in the past are often very interesting. For example, it is very interesting to read an account detailing the educational system that existed in rural America in the 1800s and the difficulties that children and families of that time had to endure to receive even a minimal education. Berg (1998) has identified five reasons for conducting historical research:

1. To uncover the unknown
2. To answer questions
3. To identify the relationship that the past has to the present
4. To record and evaluate the accomplishments of individuals, agencies, or institutions
5. To aid in our understanding of the culture in which we live

Some of these reasons may seem very apparent and logical and others may not. For example, uncovering the unknown may seem somewhat strange because historical research focuses on past events and past events should already be known. For any of a variety of reasons, however, significant events often go unrecorded. For example, Fultz (1995) observed that the content of the journals devoted to information about African Americans in the early 1900s virtually ignored any discussion of black teachers and their social roles and community contributions. Without the systematic investigation and documentation of these events and roles, we would have little knowledge or appreciation of the contributions made by black teachers in the early part of the twentieth century.

Providing answers to questions is probably one of the most logical and apparent reasons for conducting historical research. As a teacher or student you may have wondered what it was like to go to school in the 1800s or just how severely teachers disciplined children in the early part of the twentieth century. These are obviously questions that require historical research. Many other questions could be asked about past educational practices, policies, or events.

Historical research is also conducted to identify the relationship that the past has to the present. It may seem strange that we should conduct historical research to find out something about the present. However, the past can give us a perspective for current decision making and help avoid the phenomenon of trying to reinvent the wheel. The past can also provide information as to what strategies have and have not worked. In other words, it allows us to discover those things that have been tried and found wanting and those things that have been inadequately tried and still might work. For example, a neighbor of one of the authors (Christensen) was a historian engaged in documenting the history of one of the banks in Houston, Texas. Christensen inquired about why the bank would want someone to record its history. The neighbor stated that prior historical analysis of various banks has indicated that bank officials tend to repeat mistakes and having a record of their history and the mistakes they had previously made should help them avoid such mistakes in the future. Kaestle (1997), in his discussion of the history of American education, pointed out school decentralization—making community boards responsible for making many of the decisions involved in the operation of regular elementary and secondary education rather than having these decisions made at a central education agency—was debated vigorously in the 1960s. Advocates of decentralization used information from the past to point out that centralization was used by the social elites in the early twentieth century to control urban education, protect the social structure, and impose certain values on the children of that time. Decentralization, it was argued, was an undemocratic means of social control. This is just one example of individuals using past experience as an argument for present policy on the assumption that the experience of the past would be repeated if similar policies were implemented again. Educational policy and planning may be able to profit by knowing what has and has not worked in the past. Frequently, past events can be used in the formulation of current policy and procedure by allowing individuals to capitalize on what has and has not been effective.

Historical research is frequently conducted to record the accomplishments of a noted individual or the history of an agency or institution. For example, an educational researcher might be interested in documenting development and growth of private, church-supported schools. Historically, Catholic churches have operated schools and provided education primarily for children of the Catholic faith. However, other denominations have increasingly moved into the educational field and participated in the education of the youth of America. Other educational researchers may be interested in recording the accomplishments of a noted individual in the field of education. Jonathan Messerli (1972), for example, profiled the life of Horace Mann, the individual who has been viewed as the founder of public education.

Historical research is also conducted to assist us in understanding the culture in which we live. Education has always been a part of our history. It is as much a part of our culture as anything we could possibly imagine. In discussing the history of American education, Kaestle (1997) points out that prior to the 1950s, individuals writing about the history of American education focused almost entirely on the public school system. However, the history of education is a broader phenomenon that must include the history of schooling, which includes agencies of instruction other than schools, such as the family, the workplace, and the churches (Kaestle, 1997). In the broadest definition of education, it includes every aspect of socialization, which means it is a cultural event.

HISTORICAL RESEARCH METHODOLOGY

How is historical research conducted? The uninformed individual seems to think that historical research is divided into two phases (Carr, 1963), collecting and reading material related to the topic of the research and writing the manuscript or book from the notes taken on the material that was collected. Carr (1963) points out that this is a very unrealistic picture of the methodology followed. For Carr (1963) the process is one of back-and-forth between reading and writing. After reading some of the primary sources, Carr begins writing, and not necessarily at the beginning. After writing a certain amount, he returns to reading about additional sources relating to his chosen topic. Carr finds that the writing helps direct the reading because the more he writes, the more he knows what he is looking for and what he needs to read.

This is an overview of just one person's approach, and Carr acknowledges that others probably use a somewhat different approach. Other individuals conduct an exhaustive search for historical information and read and digest this information prior to organizing and writing the historical account. Kaestle (1992, 1997) has even stated that there is no agreed on methodology for conducting historical research and historians are constantly looking to other disciplines for methods or theories. This does not mean that there is no consistency in the way in which historical research is conducted. Its general methodology has much in common with the other research methods we have discussed in this book. In general, historical research adheres to the following steps, although there is overlap and a movement back and forth between these steps.

1. Identification of the research topic and formulation of the research problem or question
2. Data collection or literature review
3. Evaluation of materials
4. Data synthesis
5. Report preparation or preparation of the narrative exposition

We discuss each of these steps in some detail.

IDENTIFICATION OF THE RESEARCH TOPIC AND FORMULATION OF THE RESEARCH PROBLEM OR QUESTION

As with any type of educational research, the first step is to identify a topic you wish to investigate and then formulate the research problem or question you wish to answer. The research topics chosen by investigators can be stimulated by any of a variety of sources. Current issues in education are frequently the stimulus for a research study. For example, during the decade of the 1990s there was a movement away from affirmative action policies in college admission. You may want to know what led to the affirmative action policy in the first place and why this policy, which was implemented for decades, is now being reversed.

A research topic could also result from an interest in the impact of a specific individual, institution, or social movement on educational policy and/or reform. For example, you may know of someone that has spent his or her professional life working for the improvement of the education of children from the ghetto. If this individual made significant strides in this direction in the face of continued adversity, a record of his or her accomplishments and the process of gaining these accomplishments may be of significance to the field of education and worthy of investigation.

You may also be interested in exploring the relationship among different events. For example, during the decade of the 1960s busing—moving children from one neighborhood school to another in an attempt to create a specific racial/ethnic mix of children in each public school—was initiated. There are a number of questions that could be asked about the effect of implementing this policy. What effect did busing have on the quality of education that the children received? Did busing have any effect on the decisions that many parents made regarding where their children were educated? Parents could, for example, go along with the busing decision or they could send their children to private school. Why is busing no longer being implemented?

You may even think that past events that have been presented by educational historians can be interpreted in a different and more appropriate way. Kaestle (1997), for example, has observed that during the past twenty-five to thirty years, the traditional methods and assumptions of American historians have increasingly come under attack. Until about 1950, the assumption of most American educational historians was that the history of education was almost exclusively related to the history of public school systems and that public universal schooling was a good thing. Since that time this view has increasingly come under attack as more recent American educational historians have focused on education being delivered by agencies (e.g., church, family) other than the public school. Additionally, some American educational historians have questioned the notion that public education was universally good.

Research topics leading to historical research can come from a variety of sources and can focus on many different topics and events. Table 12.1 lists examples of a number of research studies conducted by educational historians. As you can see, these topics cover many diverse areas in the field of education.

TABLE 12.1 Examples of Research Studies Conducted by Educational Historians

Cleverly, J. (1991). *The schooling of China: Tradition and modernity in Chinese education.* North Sydney, Australia: Allen and Unwin.

Fultz, M. (1995). African American teachers in the south, 1890–1940: Powerlessness and the ironies of expectations and protest. *History of Education Quarterly, 37,* 401–422.

Galenson, D. W. (1995). Determinants of the school attendance of boys in early Chicago. *History of Education Quarterly, 37,* 371–400.

Mitch, D. F. (1992). *The rise of popular literacy in Victorian England: The influence of private choice and public policy.* Philadelphia: University of Pennsylvania Press.

Osgood, R. L. (1997). Undermining the common school ideal: Intermediate schools and ungraded classes in Boston, 1838–1900. *History of Education Quarterly, 37,* 375–398.

Reuben, J. A. (1997). Beyond politics: Community civics and the redefinition of citizenship in the progressive era. *History of Education Quarterly, 37,* 399–420.

Rosner, L. (1991). *Medical education in the age of improvement: Edinburgh students and apprentices, 1760–1826.* Edinburgh: Edinburgh University Press.

Tomiak, J., ed. (1991). *Schooling, educational policy, and ethnic identity: Comparative studies on governments and non-dominant ethnic groups in Europe, 1850–1940,* vol. 1. New York: New York University Press.

DATA COLLECTION OR LITERATURE REVIEW

Once you have decided on a research topic, the next step is to identify the sources that will contain information about your research topic and then locate these sources. The identification, location, and collection of related information is the data collection or literature review stage of historical research. As such, it is similar to the literature review you would conduct for other types of educational research, because in qualitative and quantitative studies you conduct a literature review to locate studies that have been conducted in the past. These studies tell you what is known about your given research topic. In historical research, a similar process takes place. However, the sources containing the information you need are quite different from those of other types of educational research. In historical research, the information you seek may be contained in documents, records, photographs, relics, and interviews rather than in professional journals and books.

The documents or records of interest to the educational historian typically consist of written or printed materials such as diplomas, cartoons, diaries, memoirs, newspapers, yearbooks, memos, periodicals, reports, files, attendance records, census reports, budgets, maps, and tests. Actually, just about anything that is printed or written down and relating to the chosen research topic would represent a document or record that you would want to obtain and, perhaps, use in your final narrative account of your chosen topic.

Oral histories
Interviews with
a person who
has had direct
or indirect
experience with or
knowledge of the
chosen topic

Oral histories or oral records are another source of information the educational historian may want to use. **Oral histories** or records consist of interviews that the educational historian may conduct with a person who has had direct or indirect experience with or knowledge of the chosen topic. A psychological historian, Rand Evans, who was gathering information on E. B. Titchener, an individual influential in the development of the field of psychology, had gathered a wealth of information from available records and documents. However, he also wanted to talk to someone who knew Titchener personally. The only problem was finding this person. Based on the information Evans had collected, he knew where Titchener resided at the time of his death, so he placed an advertisement in that city's newspaper asking any relative of Titchener to contact him. After placing several of these advertisements and getting no response, Evans was discouraged and assumed that he was not going to make contact with a relative of Titchener. A friend of Evans encouraged him to try one more time, which he did. This time one of Titchener's relatives saw the advertisement and contacted Evans, much to his delight. Evans then proceeded to set up a time and place when he could interview this individual and obtain an oral record of information about Titchener. Oral records are not, however, limited to interviews with people. They may also consist of stories, tales, songs, or other forms of oral expression.

Relics can also be used as a source of information. A relic is any object whose physical or visual characteristics can provide information about the past. Relics, therefore, may be articles of clothing, buildings, books, architectural plans, desks, or any other object that may provide information about the past.

HOW TO LOCATE HISTORICAL INFORMATION

Libraries, particularly the larger university libraries such as the one that exists at the University of Texas, are good sources of information because they typically have collections of things such as rare books, letters, periodicals, personal papers, and old maps. Once in such a library, you can make use of reference books such as *Reference Sources in History: An Introductory Guide,* by Fritze, Coutts, and Vyhnanek (1990); *Guide to Historical Literature* by Norton (1995); and *Biographical Dictionary of American Educators* by Ohles to locate relevant information.

If you are not close to a large library, you may want to first identify a repository that may contain the information you desire. The National Historical Publications and Records Commission publishes the *Directory of Archives and Manuscript Repositories in the United States* (1988), which contains a list of repositories in the United States. Additionally, the *National Inventory of Documentary Sources in the United States* provides a list of federal documents and libraries.

One very good source of historical information is the National Archives, which contains records of the U.S. government. The National Archives is an extremely valuable resource containing documents, cartographic items, video and sound recordings, photographs, and reels of motion picture film all created by various govenmental agencies since the creation of our nation. These documents and other historical items exist in various record centers, presidential libraries, and regional archives.

In locating historical information about a given topic, you must remember that you are conducting an educational study. Therefore, you should also consider local courthouses and school board central offices as well as individual schools as possible information sources. Additionally, oral histories should not be forgotten, because they can provide information that frequently cannot be obtained in any other way (Yow, 1994). Oral histories can provide insight and an understanding of the cause or motive for an event that may not be accessible in any other form because the information was not recorded. However, there are limitations in the use of oral histories. Oral histories tend to focus on personal experiences, but these experiences take place in the larger context of a specific sociopolitical climate. It is important to consider the local, national, or international trends taking place at the time of the targeted event and consider the relationship between these events and the personal experiences reported by the individual or individuals providing the oral history.

Oral histories are naturally limited to individuals who are still alive, and these individuals tend to be older people. The oral history is, therefore, confined to the experiences, memory, and interpretations of a selected group of individuals who must rely upon their memory to relay past events. Recall of events changes with the passage of time and every individual selectively remembers past events. To overcome some of these biases, Yow (1994) recommends interviewing a range of individuals from the most confident and articulate to those with compromised verbal skills. In conducting this interview Yow (1994) recommends that you include questions such as the following:

- If you were writing this study, what would you include?
- Who would you recommend I interview?
- If you were writing this history, what would you consider important?
- Who was present at that event?
- Who was instrumental in making this happen?
- Who was affected by this?

Although these are obviously not all the questions you would want to ask, they do represent some of the ones that may be overlooked and can lead to focusing on important issues and interviewing other individuals who may provide important insights and information.

Primary versus Secondary Sources

Primary source
A source in which the creator was a direct witness or in some other way directly involved or related to the event

As you locate and acquire the documents, records, oral histories, or other sources needed to prepare your narrative of the topic or event you have selected to research, you need to classify these sources as primary or secondary. A **primary source** is a source in which the creator was a direct witness or in some other way directly involved or related to the event. Examples of primary sources are a diary, an original map, a song or ballad, a transcript of an oral interview conducted with a person who participated in an event, the minutes of a board meeting, court decisions and the arguments that accompany them, and a photograph

Secondary source
A source that was
created from
primary sources,
secondary
sources, or some
combination of
the two

of a World War II battle scene. A **secondary source** is a source that was created from primary sources, other secondary sources, or some combination of primary and secondary sources. A secondary source is, therefore, a source that is at least one step removed from direct contact, involvement, or relationship with the event being researched. The most useful and accurate secondary sources are probably those that have been created by scholarly historians using primary sources. Scholarly historians have written articles and books about all types of events ranging from battles and court decisions to accounts of ethical violations such as the Tuskegee experiments that we discussed in the chapter on ethics. Other secondary sources are history textbooks or encyclopedias. However, history textbooks and encyclopedias are secondary sources that are even more removed from the actual event being described and frequently viewed as the least useful source of information.

EVALUATION OF HISTORICAL SOURCES

An educational researcher engaged in a historical study must evaluate every source of information obtained for its authenticity and accuracy regardless of whether that source is a document, map, photograph, or oral history. Every piece of material has to be tested for its truthfulness because any source can be affected by factors such as prejudice, social or economic conditions, political climate, and religious background. These are the kinds of biases that color the interpretation of every historian. This means that a document may be slanted to reflect a particular bias of its author. An old photograph or document may appear to represent a given event when, in fact, it has been forged, deliberately altered, or even falsified. Even if a document has not been deliberately altered or falsified, it could be affected by the particular bias a person may have or the political or economic climate existing at the time. For example, an educational historian writing about an educational event during the Depression would probably have his or her view and interpretation of the event colored by the depressed economy of that time. Educational historians must therefore view every source with a critical eye, and every source must pass two kinds of evaluations before it is used to construct the narration of the event being researched. Every source must be evaluated in terms of external and internal criticism.

External Criticism

External criticism
The validity,
trustworthiness,
or authenticity
of the source

External criticism refers to the validity, trustworthiness, or authenticity of the source. In other words, was the document, diary, or memo really created by the author to whom it was attributed? Was the photograph or map really produced at the time specified and does it depict the events occurring at that time? In other words, the historian has to determine whether the document, record, or other source is what it claims to be or has been falsified in some way. Unfortunately, throughout history there have been notable examples of hoaxes. For example, in the early 1980s two men sold sixty volumes of what was supposed to be Adolf Hitler's diaries to the German magazine *Stern* for the tidy sum of $3 million dollars. Several years later the *Stern* discovered that the diaries were false and sued the sellers, resulting in their returning the money and being sent to prison (Hitler diaries, 1985). Obviously, if the *Stern* had been more diligent about checking the authenticity of the volumes they would never have purchased the forged diaries. Hoaxes such as this are quite rare and, as is evident from the case just mentioned, typically motivated by financial gain.

Sometimes the validity of documents or other sources can be easily established by handwriting; age of the paper on which the documents are written; signatures; and, particularly, if they have been filed, collected, and archived under the name of the author(s) (Christy, 1975). In other instances it is more difficult to validate a source because, for example, a document could be ghostwritten. Although you can never be completely certain about the validity of your sources, you can attempt to acquire information that will maximize the probability that the sources used are valid. For example, you can attempt to get answers to questions such as who wrote a particular document, when the document was written, and whether different versions of the document exist. At times it may be necessary to obtain the services of specialists such as handwriting experts or linguists knowledgeable of the dialects or writing style of a given period. You may even want to carbon date a particular source to ensure that it was produced during a given era. In most instances it is not necessary to go to such extremes because, as with other areas of research, authors attempt to be as accurate and valid as possible. In most instances the documents and other information sources used by the educational historian are authentic, which means that historians typically spend little time focusing on the phase of external criticism.

Internal Criticism

Internal criticism
The reliability or accuracy of the information contained in the sources collected

Positive criticism
Ensuring that the statements made or the meaning conveyed in the various sources is correct

Vagueness
Uncertainty in the meaning of words or phrases

After the educational historian has done everything possible to ensure that his or her documents and other sources are valid and authentic and, if secondary sources are used, that they are true to the original, the researcher is ready for the process of internal criticism. **Internal criticism** refers to the reliability or accuracy of the information contained in the sources collected. In making an assessment of reliability or accuracy, the educational historian must first engage in positive criticism (Christy, 1975). By **positive criticism** we mean that the educational historian must be sure that he or she understands the statements made or the meaning conveyed in the various sources. For example, Supreme Court decisions must frequently be converted into policy at the local level. This means that the agencies and people affected by a decision must interpret its text and meaning. The words, terms, and phrases of the decision must be interpreted properly for the decision to be carried out appropriately. This interpretation becomes even more difficult for the historian because words and colloquialisms may take on new meanings over time or be foreign to the investigator. Kaestle (1997) states that this is a problem of vagueness and presentism. **Vagueness** refers to uncertainty in the meaning of words or phrases. As an example of vagueness, Kaestle (1997) points out that it is commonplace in educational history to see the notion that industrialization caused educational reform. However, this statement has the potential of communicating different things to different people unless the terms *industrialization* and *educational reform* are defined. Additionally, it is difficult to assess and document the relationship between industrialization and educational reform without a strict definition of these terms.

Presentism
The assumption that the present-day connotations of terms also existed in the past

Presentism refers to the assumption that the present-day connotations of terms also existed in the past. It is not uncommon for the meaning of terms to change over time. There are examples of terms that have a specific present-day meaning or connotation that either did not exist in the past or was something totally different. For example, a person who was called "square" in the early 1900s was considered to be honest, upright, or trustworthy. The current connotation is that a "square" person is someone who is unsophisticated or has conservative tastes (Christy, 1975). Similarly, in the eighteenth century, a public educational institution was an institution where children learned collectively, and the educational endeavor was for the public good as opposed to selfish gain. The educational institutions of that time were financed by tuition and were considered and called "public" institutions. Present-day terminology would have labeled them "private" institutions (Kaestle, 1997) because they were financed by tuition rather than being state supported.

Negative criticism
Establishing the reliability or authenticity and accuracy of the content of the documents and other sources used by the researcher

Once the researcher has satisfied the criterion of positive criticism, he or she moves to the phase of negative criticism (Christy, 1975). **Negative criticism** refers to establishing the reliability or authenticity and accuracy of the content of the documents and other sources used by educational historians. The negative criticism phase is the more difficult because it requires the educational historian to make a judgment about the authenticity and accuracy of what is contained in the source. Although most authors attempt to be as accurate as possible in their production of documents, photographs, maps, or other sources of evidence, there are times when inaccurate statements are made. For example, in June 1974 (Holy Horatio, 1974) a brief article appeared in *Time* magazine revealing that the biography Herbert Mayes had written of Horatio Alger in the 1920s was filled with contradictions, absurd fabrications, and invented events and occurrences derived totally from his imagination. This biography had served as the standard reference work on Alger for more than forty years and was quoted by historians and scholars during this time. Fortunately, such inaccurate statements are rare because historians typically make every effort possible to avoid making inaccurate statements.

Firsthand accounts by witnesses to an event are frequently assumed to be the most reliable and accurate. However, eyewitness accounts can be biased and there is a tendency for memory to fade over time and the gaps in memory to be filled in with plausible details. To get an example of the differences that can exist in memory, all you have to do is ask two or more people to recall the details of some event such as an automobile accident or a school board meeting. This does not mean that there is any deliberate attempt to distort the event witnessed. Rather, each person has different motivations and attends to different components of an event.

Just think of a physician, a law enforcement officer, and an insurance agent witnessing a car accident and then making a report on it. The physician will probably focus on the severity of the injuries sustained by the passengers. The law enforcement officer will most likely focus on the speed the car was traveling, road conditions, and traffic conditions, and the insurance agent will probably focus on the amount of damage the automobile sustained. Each person will, because of his or her training, prejudices, or prior experience, focus on different aspects of the event, which will lead to very different reports. The educational historian attempts to take this background and prior experience that colors a report of an event into account when establishing the accuracy of the contents of a document.

If eyewitness accounts may represent a biased account, how does the educational historian establish the accuracy of his or her source material? Wineburg (1991), in his analysis of the way in which historians handle evidence, concluded that three heuristics—corroboration, sourcing, and contextualization—were used in evaluating documents. **Corroboration** refers to comparing documents to each other to determine whether they provide the same information or reach the same conclusions. For example, several of the documents used in Wineburg's (1991) study focused on the size of the colonial force that assembled on Lexington Green in Massachusetts. One document listed the size of the force at 300 to 400 men. This document was compared with other documents that provided indirect information about the size of the colonial force, but this information suggested that the size of the force was considerably smaller.

Sourcing, the second heuristic identified by Wineburg (1991), refers to information that identifies "the source or attribution of the document" (p. 79). In other words, sourcing refers to identifying the author, the date of creation of the document, and the place it was created. This information allows the historian to dismiss information created by a novelist or from a secondary source such as a textbook written long after the event occurred. Additionally, it allows the historian to identify the distance in time between the documentation of an event and its actual occurrence. For example, a historian may well consider an account of a battle recorded as the battle was being fought as more accurate than a participant's account several days after the battle was fought. Sourcing, therefore, provides information that is used in judging the trustworthiness and accuracy of the content of a document.

Contextualization, the third heuristic identified by Wineburg (1991), refers to the identification of when and where an event took place. The "when" component of this heuristic involves placing events in chronological order and requires historians to focus on the sequencing of events. The "where" component of this heuristic involves identifying where an event took place as well as identifying the conditions that existed at the time of occurrence, such as the weather, landscape, and geography of the surrounding area. The contextualization heuristic is very important because it not only identifies order of the events that took place, but it also assists in the interpretative phase of the narration of the event. For example, one of the historians in Wineburg's (1991) study used information about the time of occurrence of an event in one of the documents "to reconstruct the intelligence network of the Minutemen, making inferences about when the colonists must have learned that the British were setting out from Boston" (p. 82).

The three heuristics identified by Weinburg (1991) are important in the evaluation of historical documents. Although historians probably do make use of methods and procedures other than those identified by Weinburg, his study did identify three important characteristics of the historical method. In evaluating documents, historians compare information sources, give critical attention to the sources of their documents, and attend to the chronological and geographical context in which the event took place.

Corroboration
Comparing documents to each other to determine whether they provide the same information or reach the same conclusion

Sourcing
Information that identifies the source or attribution of the document

Contextualization
The identification of when and where an event took place

DATA SYNTHESIS AND
REPORT PREPARATION

Synthesis
The selection,
organization, and
analysis of the
materials
collected

The last task the educational historian must accomplish is synthesizing, or putting together the materials collected, and writing the narrative account of the topic or event selected. **Synthesis,** therefore, refers to the selection, organization, and analysis of the materials collected. The information that has passed the test of internal and external criticism is sorted and categorized into topical themes and central ideas or concepts. These themes and ideas are then pulled together so that there is a continuity between them. A chronological ordering of events is frequently helpful.

As the researcher is synthesizing the material collected, he or she will typically begin the narrative account of the topic or event selected. This will consist of a narration of the patterns, connections, and insights uncovered from the synthesis of the documents and other source materials collected. In synthesizing the material collected and preparing the narrative account, the educational researcher should always be aware of four methodological problems that must be avoided (Kaestle, 1997). The first problem is the confusion of correlation and causation. In statistics courses and methods courses such as this one, you will repeatedly hear the admonition to make sure that you do not try to infer causation from correlational evidence. Just because two phenomena occur together or that one proceeds another does not mean that one caused the other. For example, urban Irish families in America during the 1800s did not send their children to school as often as did parents of other ethnic groups (Kaestle, 1997). However, this does not mean that being Irish caused low school attendance. Obviously, many other factors, such as socioeconomic status, could have contributed to the low school attendance. Whenever we deal with correlational evidence we must avoid the temptation of inferring causation regardless of how tempting it may be or how logical it seems.

A second problem that must be attended to is the problem of defining and interpreting key words, terms, and phrases. As we discussed earlier in this chapter, this boils down to the dual issues of vagueness and presentism. Not only must terms be defined so as to avoid ambiguity, but close attention should be paid to the connotation of terms as they existed during the time in which the historical event took place.

A third problem identified by Kaestle (1997) is that educational historians should make sure that they differentiate between evidence indicating how people should behave and evidence indicating how they did in fact behave. For example, Kaestle (1997) points out that educators and physicians in the late 1830s in the northeastern part of the United States encouraged parents to keep children under five or six at home. These professionals believed that school attendance of children this age was unwise, dangerous to their health, and a nuisance to teachers. This evidence may lead one to infer that children began school at age five or six. However, such an inference would be incorrect, because census data and statistical school reports revealed that parents sent three and four-year-old children to school until local regulations enacted in the 1850s and 1860s forced them to keep these children at home. This example demonstrates that there was a lag between the opinion of the professionals and popular behavior, and educational historians must be alert to such differences.

The final problem that educational historians must avoid when constructing their narrative account is maintaining a distinction between intent and consequences. Historians, because they conduct their research after events have taken place, run the risk of assuming that the historical actors were aware of the full consequences of their ideas and actions. In other words, there is the risk of assuming that the consequences observed from some policy or activity were the consequences intended. For example, school busing for racial/ethnic balance, which was implemented in the 1960s, led to the growth of private schools in many parts of the United States. To assume that this consequence was one of the intents of busing would be totally inaccurate. This is the type of inappropriate connection that must be avoided by the educational historian.

Constructing the narrative account of a historical event is a difficult process requiring the synthesis of a wealth of information. In reading and synthesizing this information the educational historian must not only make judgments regarding the accuracy and authenticity of his or her information, but he or she must also avoid making certain assumptions such as those just discussed.

When writing the narrative account of a historical event, you should adhere to the style presented in *The Chicago Manual of Style* (1993). Most quantitative and qualitative research reports make use of the writing style presented in the *Publication Manual of the American Psychological Association* (1994), although some of these journals will accept research reports prepared according to either style. Historical studies, however, are usually prepared following *The Chicago Manual of Style*. One of the biggest differences between *The Chicago Manual of Style* and the style presented in the *Publication Manual of the American Psychological Association* is that *The Chicago Manual of Style* makes use of numbered footnotes or endnotes to document or expand on ideas presented in the text. The endnotes or footnotes identify the sources used in the study and provide information that supplements the material in the text. The *Publication Manual of the American Psychological Association* uses an author-date style to indicate sources used and minimizes the use of footnotes, as will become apparent in Chapter 16, which discusses this style in some detail.

SUMMARY

Historical research attempts to arrive at an account of what has happened in the past by systematically examining past events or combinations of events. This account represents a flowing, fluid, and dynamic account of facts, dates, people, and figures as well as an interpretation of them to capture the nuances, personalities, and ideas that influenced the events being investigated.

Historical research is conducted for multiple reasons. It is conducted to uncover the unknown; to answer questions; to identify the relationship that the past has to the present; to record and evaluate the accomplishments of individuals, agencies, or institutions; and to aid in our understanding of the culture in which we live. Conducting historical research involves a series of activities, including the identification of the research topic and formulating the research problem or research question, reviewing the available literature or collecting the information related to the research topic, evaluating the collected information, synthesizing the information, and preparing the narrative exposition.

Historical research topics can originate from any of a variety of sources, such as a current educational issue or the impact of an individual, institution, or social movement on the field of education. Research topics can also originate from an interest in investigating the relationship between several historical events or from a desire to look at a different way of interpreting a historical event. The point is that historical research topics can originate from many different sources.

Collecting information on a historical topic involves locating documents, records, and relics. This information can generally be found in university libraries or repositories such as the National Archives. Oral histories are also valuable sources of information about many historical topics. They can provide insight and an understanding of the cause or motive for an event that may not be available from other sources. Oral histories are, however, confined to the experiences, memory, and interpretations of the individuals who provide them and may be biased by the passage of time and the selective memory for events.

The information sources collected are classified as primary or secondary. Primary sources are those in which the creator was a direct witness, or in some other way directly involved in or related to the event. A secondary source is one that was created from primary sources. Primary sources are generally viewed as the more valuable sources of information.

Regardless of whether an information source is primary or secondary, it must be evaluated for its accuracy and authenticity. This means that each information source must pass the test of external criticism and internal criticism. External criticism refers to the validity, trustworthiness, or authenticity of the source. Internal criticism refers to the reliability or accuracy of the information contained in the material collected. In making this assessment of reliability and accuracy, the educational historian must engage in positive and negative criticism. Positive criticism means that the educational historian must be sure he or she understands the statements made and the meaning conveyed in the source material. Negative criticism refers to the accuracy or authenticity of the statements made, or the content of the source materials. In establishing the accuracy of his or her source material, historians use the three heuristics of corroboration, sourcing, and contextualization.

The final task of the educational historian is to synthesize the data collected and write the narrative account of the historical event or issue researched. In preparing this narrative account, the educational historian must avoid the methodological problems of confusing correlation and causation, misinterpreting key terms, words, and phrases, failing to differentiate between evidence indicating how people should behave and how they did behave, and failing to maintain a distinction between intent and consequences.

STUDY QUESTIONS

1. Define historical research.
2. Why would a person want to conduct historical research?
3. What are the two phases of historical research? Explain each one.

4. What is an oral history?
5. Where would you locate historical information?
6. What is the difference between a primary and a secondary source?
7. What is the difference between external and internal criticism?
8. What is meant by the terms *vagueness* and *presentism*?
9. What is negative criticism and how is it established?
10. What is positive criticism and how is it established?
11. What are the three heuristics used by historical researchers to establish the accuracy of their evidence? Explain each one.

EXERCISES

The following article is one that is representative of the type of research conducted by educational historians. Get this article from the library and read it to gain some idea of historical research conducted in the field of education.

Murphy, M. F. (1997). Unmaking and remaking the "One Best System." London, Ontario, 1852–1860. *History of Education Quarterly, 37,* 291–309.

After reading this article, answer the following questions.

1. What was the author's purpose in conducting this historical research?
2. How does the presentation of this historical research differ from the presentation of quantitative research?
3. Identify at least one primary and one secondary source used by the author.

KEY TERMS

contextualization (353)	negative criticism (352)	secondary source (350)
corroboration (353)	oral histories (348)	sourcing (353)
external criticism (350)	positive criticism (351)	synthesis (354)
historical research (342)	primary source (349)	vagueness (351)
internal criticism (351)	presentism (352)	

CHAPTER 13

Descriptive Statistics

LEARNING OBJECTIVES

To be able to

- explain the purpose of descriptive statistics.
- distinguish between inferential and descriptive statistics.
- explain the difference between a frequency distribution and a grouped frequency distribution.
- read and interpret bar graphs, line graphs, and scatterplots.
- calculate the mode, median, and mean.
- list the strengths and weaknesses of the mode, median, and mean.
- explain positive skew and negative skew.
- explain the impact of skewness on the measures of central tendency.
- describe and interpret the different measures of variability.
- calculate the range, variance, and standard deviation.
- explain percentile ranks and z-scores.
- explain how to construct and interpret a contingency table.
- explain the difference between simple and multiple regression.
- explain the difference between the Y-intercept and the regression coefficient.

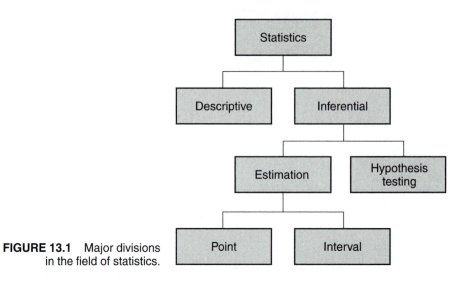

FIGURE 13.1   Major divisions in the field of statistics.

Descriptive statistics
Statistics that focus on describing, summarizing, or explaining data

Inferential statistics
Statistics that go beyond the immediate data and infer the characteristics of population based on samples

The field of statistics is a branch of mathematics that deals with the analysis of numerical data. It is generally divided into two broad categories called descriptive statistics and inferential statistics. In **descriptive statistics,** the goal is to describe, summarize, or make sense of a particular set of data. The goal of **inferential statistics** is to go beyond the immediate data and to infer the characteristics of populations based on samples. As you can see in Figure 13.1, inferential statistics may be subdivided into estimation and hypothesis testing, and estimation may be divided into point and interval estimation. In this chapter we focus on descriptive statistics, and in the next chapter we focus on inferential statistics. Our discussion requires very little mathematical background, so don't worry! We focus more on interpretation than on calculation. We do, however, show you how to perform a few basic calculations, so get your calculator handy.

DESCRIPTIVE STATISTICS

Data set
A set of data

Descriptive statistics starts with a set of data sometimes called a **data set**. The researcher attempts to convey the essential characteristics of the data by arranging the data into a more interpretable form (e.g., by forming frequency distributions and generating graphical displays) and by calculating numerical indexes such as averages, percentile ranks, and measures of spread. The researcher can summarize the variables in a data set one at a time. He or she can also examine how the variables are interrelated (e.g., by examining correlations). The key question in descriptive statistics is how we can communicate the essential characteristics of the data. An obvious way would be to supply a printout of the complete set of data. However, we can do much better than that!

We have included a data set (i.e., a set of data) in Table 13.1 that we will use in several of our examples in this chapter and the next. We refer to this data set as the "college

TABLE 13.1   Hypothetical Set of Data for Twenty-Five Recent College Graduates*

Person	Starting Salary	GPA	College Major	Gender	GRE Verbal
1	31,000	2.9	2	1	520
2	32,000	3.6	1	1	600
3	33,000	3.7	1	1	610
4	28,000	2.4	2	0	450
5	37,000	3.4	3	0	500
6	32,000	3.0	3	0	500
7	33,000	3.1	2	0	520
8	25,000	2.5	1	1	450
9	38,000	3.0	3	0	650
10	33,000	2.7	2	0	490
11	30,000	3.0	2	1	500
12	32,000	2.6	1	0	580
13	32,000	3.1	2	1	480
14	31,000	3.1	1	1	530
15	24,000	2.5	1	1	460
16	40,000	3.3	3	0	630
17	31,000	3.3	1	1	510
18	38,000	3.2	2	1	620
19	35,000	3.1	3	1	680
20	32,000	3.2	2	0	550
21	41,000	3.5	3	0	680
22	34,000	3.0	3	1	590
23	28,000	3.0	1	1	650
24	30,000	2.9	2	0	480
25	36,000	3.5	2	0	570

*Note: For the categorical variable college major, the value labels are 1 = education, 2 = arts and sciences, 3 = business. For the categorical variable gender, the value labels are 0 = male and 1 = female.

student data set." The hypothetical data are for twenty-five recent college graduates. Data values are provided for three quantitative variables—starting salary, grade point average, and GRE:Verbal scores—and for two categorical variables—college major and gender. Take a look at Table 13.1 now to see what a data set looks like. Notice that the data set is structured so that the cases (i.e., individuals) are represented in rows and the variables are represented in columns. This cases-by-variables arrangement is the standard way of organizing data after data collection has been completed.

FREQUENCY DISTRIBUTIONS

Frequency distribution
Arrangement in which the frequencies of each unique data value are shown

One of the most basic ways to describe the data values of a variable is to construct a frequency distribution. A **frequency distribution** is a systematic arrangement of data values in which the data are rank ordered and the frequencies of each unique data value are shown. Just follow these steps and you can construct a frequency distribution for the data values of any variable:

1. List each unique number in ascending order in column 1. If a particular number appears more than once, remember to list it only once. For example, even if the number 3 appears five times, list it only once. If a number does not appear in the data, you don't need to list it.
2. Count the number of times each number listed in column 1 occurs and place the results in column 2.
3. (Optional). Construct a third column by converting column 2 into percentages by dividing each number in column 2 by the total number of numbers.

The first column shows the unique data values, the second column shows the frequencies, and the third column shows the percentages.

Grouped frequency distribution
The data values are clustered or grouped into separate intervals and the frequencies of each interval are given

For example, look at Table 13.2. This frequency distribution is for the variable starting salary from the college student data set provided in Table 13.1. You can see in column 1 that the lowest starting income is $24,000 and the highest starting income is $41,000. The frequencies are shown in column 2. For example, the most frequently occurring starting income for our recent college graduates was $32,000. Percentages are shown in column 3. For example, 20 percent of the students started at $32,000 per year, and 4 percent started at $41,000 per year.

When a variable has a wide range of data values, interpretation may be facilitated by collapsing the values of the variable into intervals. The result is called a **grouped frequency distribution** because the data values are clustered, or grouped, into intervals. Re-

TABLE 13.2 Frequency Distribution of Starting Salary*

(1) Starting Salary (X)	(2) Frequency (f)	(3) Percentage (%)
24,000	1	4.0
25,000	1	4.0
28,000	2	8.0
30,000	2	8.0
31,000	3	12.0
32,000	5	20.0
33,000	3	12.0
34,000	1	4.0
35,000	1	4.0
36,000	1	4.0
37,000	1	4.0
38,000	2	8.0
40,000	1	4.0
41,000	1	4.0
	$n = 25$	100.0%

*Column 2 shows the frequency distribution. Column 3 shows the percentage distribution.

TABLE 13.3   Grouped Frequency Distribution of Starting Salary

Starting Salary (X)	Frequency (f)	Percentage (%)
20,000–24,999	1	4.0
25,000–29,999	3	12.0
30,000–34,999	14	56.0
35,000–39,000	5	20.0
40,000–44,999	2	8.0
	n = 25	100.0%

Mutually
exclusive
Property that
intervals do not
overlap

Exhaustive
Property that a set
of intervals covers
the complete
range of data
values

searchers typically construct around five to eight equal-size intervals. We constructed a grouped frequency distribution for starting income, which you can see in Table 13.3. Column 1 shows the intervals. As before, the frequencies are shown in column 2 and the percentages are shown in column 3. You can see that the most frequent interval is $30,000–$34,999. This interval includes fourteen of the data values, which make up 56 percent of all starting income data values.

When constructing a grouped frequency distribution, it is important that the intervals are **mutually exclusive.** This means that there should not be any overlap among the intervals. (The intervals $20,000–$25,000 and $25,000–$30,000 are not mutually exclusive because a person earning $25,000 can be placed into two intervals.) It is also important that the intervals are **exhaustive.** A set of intervals is exhaustive when it covers the complete range of data values. If all the data values fall into the set of intervals, the intervals are exhaustive.

GRAPHIC REPRESENTATIONS OF DATA

Graphs are pictorial representations of data in two-dimensional space. Many graphs display the data on two dimensions or *axes.* These two axes are the X- and Y-axes, where the X-axis (also called the abscissa) is the horizontal dimension and the Y-axis (also called the ordinate) is the vertical dimension. If you are graphing the data for a single variable, the values of this variable are represented on the X-axis and frequencies or percentages are represented on the Y-axis. If you are examining two variables, the values of the independent variable are put on the X-axis and the values of the dependent variable are put on the Y-axis. Graphs can also be constructed for more than two variables. What symbols are placed in a graph depends on the type of graph you want to construct.

Bar Graphs

Bar graph
A graph that uses
vertical bars to
represent the data

A **bar graph** is a graph that uses vertical bars to represent the data. You can see a bar graph of college major in Figure 13.2. The data are from Table 13.1, our college student data set. Notice that the X-axis represents the variable called college major and the Y-axis represents

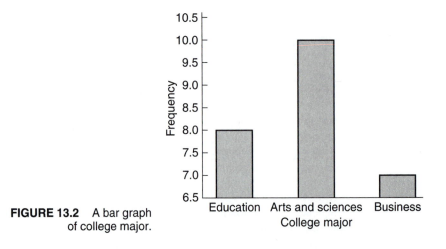

FIGURE 13.2   A bar graph
of college major.

frequency of occurrence. The bars provide graphical representations of the frequencies of the three different college majors. Arts and sciences was the most common major ($n = 10$), education the second most common ($n = 8$), and business the least common ($n = 7$).

Line Graphs

Line graph
A graph that relies on the drawing of one or more lines

One useful way to draw a graphical picture of the distribution of a variable is to construct a **line graph.** A line graph is a format for illustrating data that relies on the drawing of one or more lines. You can see a line graph of grade point average (from the college student data set) in Figure 13.3. GPA data values around 3.0 are near the center of the distribution and they occur the most frequently (i.e., low B grades occur the most frequently). You can also see that there are quite a few GPA data values that are higher and lower than 3.0. In other words, the GPA data values are somewhat spread out.

In the previous example, the line graph was given for a single variable, grade point average. It is important to understand that line graphs can also be used with more than one variable. For example, look back at Figure 8.15(b) (page 245), and you will see the type of line graph that is commonly constructed in factorial research designs. The dependent variable is placed on the vertical axis, one of the independent variables is placed on the horizontal axis, and the categories of a second independent variable are represented by separate lines.

Another common use of line graphs is to show trends over time. In this case, the variable you wish to observe changing over time is placed on the vertical axis and time is placed on the horizontal axis. The key point is that there is not just one type of line graph. Line graphing is a versatile tool that you may want to use in the future.

Scatterplot
A graph used to depict the relationship between two quantitative variables

Scatterplots

A **scatterplot,** or scatter graph, is a very useful way to visualize the relationship between two quantitative variables. The dependent variable is represented on the vertical axis, and

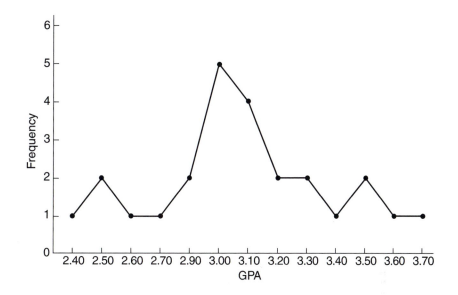

FIGURE 13.3   A line graph of grade point average.

the independent variable is represented on the horizontal axis. Dots are plotted within the graph to represent the cases (i.e., individuals).

A scatterplot of grade point average by starting salary is shown in Figure 13.4. These quantitative variables are from our college student data set. There are a total of twenty-five data points in the graph (i.e., one data point for each of the twenty-five individuals in the data set). If you examine the graph in Figure 13.4, you will clearly see that there is a positive relationship between GPA and starting salary. We calculated the correlation coefficient and found that it is equal to +0.628. This moderately strong, positive correlation coefficient confirms our observation that as GPA increases, starting salary also tends to increase. In short, there is a clear linear relationship between GPA and starting salary.

When you examine a scatterplot, it is helpful to consider the following questions:

- Does there appear to be a relationship between the two variables?
- Is it a linear relationship (a straight line) or a curvilinear relationship (a curved line)? (Linear relationships are much more common than curvilinear relationships.)
- If there is a linear relationship present, then is it a positive relationship or is it a negative relationship? The relationship is positive if the data points move in a southwest to northeast direction. The relationship is negative if the data points move in a northwest to southeast direction.
- If there is a relationship, then how strong does it appear to be? The more the data points look like a straight line, the stronger the relationship. The more they look like a circle or the more dispersed the data are, the weaker the relationship.

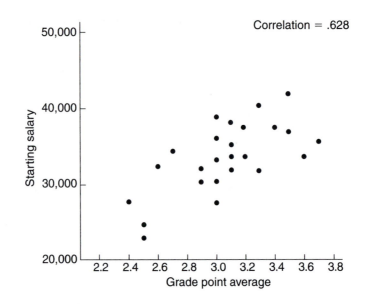

FIGURE 13.4   A scatterplot of starting salary by grade point average.

MEASURES OF CENTRAL TENDENCY

Measure of central tendency The single numerical value considered most typical of the values of a quantitative variable

A **measure of central tendency** is the single numerical value that is considered the most typical of the values of a quantitative variable. For example, if someone asked a teacher how well his or her students did on their last exam, a measure of central tendency would provide an indication of what score was typical. If someone wanted to know how much money people tend to earn annually in the United States, a measure of central tendency would again be called for. Finally, in an experiment a researcher may be interested in comparing the average performance (which is a measure of central tendency) of the experimental group with the average performance of the control group. Measures of central tendency are, perhaps, the most commonly used of all the descriptive statistics. We now discuss the three most commonly used measures of central tendency: the mode, the median, and the mean.

Mode

Mode The most frequently occurring number

The **mode** (Mo) is the most frequently occurring number. For example, if you had the numbers

1, 2, *3, 3,* 4

the mode is 3 because 3 occurs more often than any other number. The number 3 occurs twice, and the other numbers only occur once. Therefore, the number 3 is the most frequently occurring number. What if you had this set of numbers:

1, 1, 3, 3, 4

In this case you have two modes, 1 and 3. When you have two modes like this, you can use the term *bimodal* to describe the data. (If you have three or more modes, some researchers use the term *multimodal* as a descriptor.) If you had this set of numbers:

1, 3, 5, 8

you would conclude that you have multiple modes because all the numbers occur an equal number of times. For practice, what is the mode in this set of numbers:

1, 4, 6, 7, 7, 7, 9, 9, 11, 11, 30

The mode is 7 because 7 is the most frequently occurring number. For a more challenging exercise, find the mode of the variable called starting salary in our earlier data set. You will see that the mode is equal to $32,000.

Median

Median
The fiftieth
percentile

The **median** (Mdn), or fiftieth percentile, is the middle point in a set of numbers that has been arranged in order of magnitude (either ascending order or descending order). If you have an odd number of numbers, the median is defined as the middle number. Here is a simple example. If you had the numbers

2, 9, 1, 7, 10

you would first put them in ascending order of magnitude as follows:

1, 2, 7, 9, 10

Now you can easily see that the median is equal to 7 because 7 is the middle number. (If you "slice" the number 7 down the center, you have the middle point.)

If you have an even number of numbers, the median is defined as the average of the two innermost numbers. For example, if you had the numbers

3, 4, 1, 10

you would first put them in ascending order:

1, 3, 4, 10

Since there is no center number, you take the average of the two innermost numbers (i.e., take the average of the numbers 3 and 4). You can see that the median is 3.5 because that is the average of the two innermost numbers [i.e., $(3 + 4)/2 = 3.5$].

If you have many numbers, you can save some time by using a simple formula that tells you the **median location** (i.e., the numerical place to find the median in your set of ordered numbers). The formula is

Median location
The numerical place where you can find the median in a set of ordered numbers

$$\text{Median location} = \frac{n + 1}{2},$$

where
n is the number of numbers in your set of data.

We now apply this formula to the data from our earlier example: 1, 2, 7, 9, 10. There are five numbers in this set of numbers, right? Also, the numbers have been put into ascending order. Now, just insert the number 5 into the formula to find the median location:

$$\text{Median location} = \frac{5 + 1}{2} = \frac{6}{2} = 3$$

You now know the location of the median. The median is the third number in the set of five numbers (1, 2, 7, 9, 10). You can easily locate the third number. It is 7.

Now we apply the median location formula to our other set of numbers: 1, 3, 4, 10. Since we have four numbers this time, insert 4 into the formula:

$$\text{Median location} = \frac{4 + 1}{2} = \frac{5}{2} = 2.5$$

This value of 2.5 means that the median is halfway between the second and third numbers. You can see that the average of 3 (the second number) and 4 (the third number) is equal to 3.5. Therefore the median is 3.5.

Before moving on, check yourself to make sure that you can find the median in a set of numbers. Here an easy one: What is the median of 1 and 2? Right, it is 1.5. Now find the median for this set of numbers: 1, 5, 7, 8, 9. The median is 7, because 7 is the middle number. As a more challenging check on your understanding, find the median of starting salary in the college student data set, Table 13.1. The median is equal to $32,000. (Here is a helpful hint: The median location of the starting salary numbers, after they have been placed in order, is $(25+1)/2 = 13$. The location of the median is the thirteenth number.)

Mean

Mean
The arithmetic
average

The **mean** is the arithmetic average, or what most people call the average. You probably already know how to get the average. For example, find the average of these three numbers: 1, 2, and 3. The average is 2. That wasn't hard, was it! Here is what you did, according to the formula for the mean:

$$\text{Mean} = \frac{\sum X}{n}$$

This formula is not hard to use once you learn what the symbols stand for. The symbol X stands for the variable whose observed values are 1, 2, and 3 in our example. The symbol $\sum$ (the Greek letter sigma) means "sum what follows." Therefore, the numerator (the top part) in the formula says "sum the X values." The n in the formula stands for the number of numbers. You get the average by summing the observed values of your variable and dividing that sum by the number of numbers. If the numbers are 1, 2, and 3, you would use the formula as follows:

$$\text{Mean} = \frac{\sum X}{n} = \frac{1 + 2 + 3}{3} = \frac{6}{3} = 2$$

Now, don't say you can't do this because you already know how to get the average of these three numbers. You do need to carefully note the symbols used, however, since they are probably new to you. For practice, use the formula now and get the average of 2, 3, 6, 7, and 2. (The average is 4.) You could also calculate the mean of starting salary from the college student data set (Table 13.1). If you add up all the numbers and divide by the total number of numbers, you will find that the mean starting salary is equal to $32,640.

A Comparison of the Mean, Median, and Mode

In this section we are going to introduce the normal distribution and the concept called skewness. Afterward we show the impact that the shape of a distribution of scores has on the mean, median, and mode. We also provide some commentary on the properties of the mean, median, and mode. Let's start with the idea of the normal curve.

Normal
distribution
A unimodal,
symmetric,
bell-shaped
distribution that
is the theoretical
model of many
variables

The **normal distribution,** or normal curve, is a unimodal, symmetric, bell-shaped distribution that is the theoretical model used to describe many physical, psychological, and educational variables. You can see an example in Figure 13.5(b). The normal distribution is unimodal because it has only one mode. It is symmetrical because the two sides of the distribution are mirror images. It is said to be bell-shaped because it is shaped somewhat like a bell (i.e., the curve is highest at the center and tapers off as you move away from the center). The height of the curve shows the frequency or density of the data values. Now, remember this important characteristic of the normal distribution: the mean, the median, and the mode are the same number.

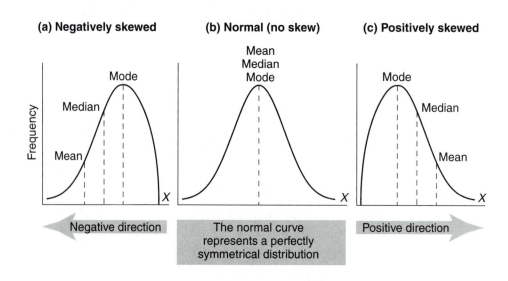

FIGURE 13.5 Examples of normal and skewed distributions.

Skewed
Not symmetrical

The other two distributions shown in Figure 13.5 are not normally distributed [see the distributions in (a) and (c)]. These two distributions are **skewed,** which means they are not symmetrical. A distribution is skewed when one tail is stretched out longer than the other tail, making the distribution asymmetrical. The numbers in the longer tail occur less frequently than the numbers in the "mound" of the distribution. If one tail appears to be stretched or pulled toward the left, the distribution is said to be skewed to the left, or **negatively skewed** (i.e., stretched in the negative direction where numbers are decreasing in numerical value). The scores on an easy test will tend to be negatively skewed. If a tail appears to be stretched or pulled toward the right, the distribution is said to be skewed to the right, or **positively skewed** (i.e., stretched in the positive direction where numbers are increasing in numerical value). The scores on a very difficult test will tend to be positively skewed.

Negatively skewed
Skewed to the left

Positively skewed
Skewed to the right

Something interesting happens when a distribution is skewed. In particular, the mean, the median, and the mode are different when a distribution is skewed. In the negatively skewed distribution shown in Figure 13.5, the numerical value of the mean is less than the median, and the numerical value of the median is less than the mode (i.e., mean < median < mode). In the positively skewed distribution shown in Figure 13.5, the numerical value of the mean is greater than the median, which is greater than the mode (i.e., mean > median > mode).

Why does the mean change more than the other measures of central tendency in the presence of a skewed distribution? The answer is because the mean takes into account the magnitude of all of the scores. In contrast, the median only takes into account the number of scores and the values of the middle scores.

Here is a demonstration. If you have these five numbers,

1, 2, 3, 4, 5

you can see that the median and the mean are both equal to 3. However, look at what happens if the last number is changed from 5 to 1,000. Here are the new numbers:

1, 2, 3, 4, 1,000

This time the mean is equal to 202 rather than 3. That is quite a dramatic change. The median, however, is unchanged. The median is still equal to 3. The point is that the mean uses the magnitude of all the scores and is affected by the scores in the tails of a distribution (i.e., by the large numbers and by the small numbers), whereas the median is affected only by the middlemost scores. This means that the mean is pulled more to the left in a negatively skewed distribution (the small values pull the mean down) and the mean is pulled more to the right in a positively skewed distribution (the large values pull the mean up). Because of this pattern, you should remember this general rule:

- If the mean is less than the median, the data are skewed to the left.
- If the mean is greater than the median, the data are skewed to the right.

This rule is helpful because it allows you to obtain a rough indication of skewness simply by comparing the mean and the median. If they are very different, the data are probably skewed.[1]

You may wonder which measure of central tendency is the best. As a general rule, the mean is the best measure because it is the most precise. The mean takes into account the magnitude of all scores. The median and the mode do not do this. The mean is also the most stable from sample to sample. As you know, the median takes into account only the number of scores and the values of the middle scores. The mode is usually the least desirable because it provides information only about what data value occurs the most often. Therefore you should only use the mode when you believe that it is important to express which single number or category occurs the most frequently. Otherwise, the mean or the median are usually the preferred measures of central tendency.

There is one situation in which the median is preferred over the mean. The median is usually preferred when your data are highly skewed. This is because the median is less affected by extreme scores. We use measures of central tendency when we want to describe what is typical for a set of numbers.

Here is an example in which the median would be preferred. Assume that the annual incomes for the ten families living in a small residential neighborhood are

$16,000
$18,000
$18,000
$18,000
$19,000
$19,000
$20,000
$21,000
$21,000
$500,000

Outlier
A number that is very atypical of the other numbers in a distribution

Nine of the families earn somewhere between $16,000 and $21,000. There is, however, an **outlier,** a number that is very atypical of the other numbers in a distribution. One family in the neighborhood earns $500,000. (Think of it like this: if Bill Gates lived in your neighborhood, his income would certainly be an outlier!) The median income in this example is $19,000, and the mean income is $67,000. Which of these two numbers do you believe best describes the "typical family income"? Many would argue that the median better represents these ten families. The median is much closer than is the mean to the actual incomes of 90 percent of the people in this example. Ninety percent of these families are basically under some financial constraints because of low income levels. The mean provides an overly optimistic assessment of the income levels by suggesting that the average or typical family income is $67,000. This is why researchers usually use the median rather than the mean when they are reporting annual income and, more importantly, why they often use the median when their data are highly skewed.

MEASURES OF VARIABILITY

Measure of variability
A numerical index that provides information about how spread out or how much variation is present

A **measure of variability** is a numerical index that provides information about how spread out or dispersed the data values are or how much variation is present. In other words, measures of variability tell you how similar or different people are with respect to a variable. For example, do the individuals in our earlier data set tend to have very similar or very different grade point averages? The variability in grade point average in our data set was visually shown by the line plot in Figure 13.3. Measures of variability provide a numerical indication of the amount of variability and therefore provide another type of information when you are describing a set of numbers.

If all the numbers were the same, there would be no variability at all. For example, if the set of numbers was

7, 7, 7, 7, 7, 7, 7, 7

you would conclude that there was no variability for the simple reason that there is no variation in the data: All the numbers are the same. On the other hand, the following set of numbers does have some variability present:

1, 3, 7, 10, 12, 15, 17, 20

Homogeneous
A set of numbers with little variability

Heterogeneous
A set of numbers with a great deal of variability

When there is very little variability in a set of numbers, we sometimes say the numbers are **homogeneous.** If, on the other hand, there is a great deal of variability, we describe the numbers as being **heterogeneous.** When a set of numbers is relatively homogeneous, you can place more trust in the measure of central tendency (mean, median, or mode) as being typical. Conversely, when a set of numbers is relatively heterogeneous, you should view the measure of central tendency as being less typical or representative of the data values.

Following are examples of relatively low variability and relatively high variability:

Data for group A: 53, 54, 55, 55, 56, 56, 57, 57, 58, 59
Data for group B: 4, 8, 23, 41, 57, 72, 78, 83, 94, 100

You can see that the numbers for group B are more spread out (and have higher variability) than the numbers for group A. You may be surprised to learn that the mean is actually the same in both of these sets of data! The mean is 56 for both. When the numbers are not very spread out, the mean is more representative of the set of numbers than when the numbers are quite spread out. Therefore, a measure of variability should usually accompany measures of central tendency. We now discuss the three most commonly used indexes of variability: the range, the variance, and the standard deviation.

Range

Range
The difference
between the
highest and lowest
numbers

The **range** is simply the difference between the highest and lowest numbers. In the following formula, the range is the highest (i.e., largest) number minus the lowest (i.e., smallest) number in a set of numbers:

$$Range = H - L$$

where

H is the highest number, and
L is the lowest number.

Find the range for the distributions for group A and group B shown in the previous section. The range in distribution A is 6 (i.e., $59 - 53 = 6$). The range in distribution B is 96 (i.e., $100 - 4 = 96$). The range seems to work in this case because we knew that distribution B had more variability than distribution A. Although the range is very easy to calculate, its use is limited. In fact, the range is not used very often by researchers. One problem with the range is that it takes into account only the two most extreme numbers. A related problem is that it is severely affected by the presence of a single extreme number. To see this problem, change the highest number from 59 to 101 in distribution A shown in the previous section. The range changes from 6 to 48; it became eight times larger based on changing a single number.

Variance and Standard Deviation

The two most popular measures of variability among researchers are the variance and standard deviation, because these measures are the most stable and are the foundations of more advanced statistical analysis. These measures are also based on all the data values of a variable and not just the highest and lowest numbers, as was the case with the range. They are essentially measures of the amount of dispersion or variation around the mean of a variable.

Variance
A measure of the average deviation from the mean in squared units

The **variance** is a measure of the average deviation from the mean in squared units. In order to turn the variance back into more appealing units, you just take the square root. When you take the square root of the variance, you obtain the standard deviation. You can view the **standard deviation** as an approximate indicator of how far the numbers tend to vary from the mean. The variance and standard deviation will be larger when the data are spread out (heterogeneous) and smaller when the data are not very spread out (homogeneous).

Standard deviation
The square root of the variance

We show you how to calculate the variance and standard deviation in Table 13.4. We also explain it to you in words here. To get the variance and standard deviation, follow these five steps:

1. Find the mean of a set of numbers. As illustrated in Table 13.4, add the numbers in column 1 and divide by the number of numbers. (Note that we use the symbol "X-bar" (i.e., $\bar{X}$) to stand for the mean.)
2. Subtract the mean from each number. As illustrated in Table 13.4, subtract the mean from each number in column 1 and place the result in column 2.
3. Square each of the numbers you obtained in the last step. As illustrated in Table 13.4, square each number in column 2 and place the result in column 3. (To

TABLE 13.4   Calculating the Variance and Standard Deviation

(1)* X	(2) $(X-\bar{X})$	(3) $(X-\bar{X})^2$
1	−2	4
2	−1	1
3	0	0
4	1	1
5	2	4
15	0	10
↑	↑	↑

Sums	$\sum X$	$\sum (X-\bar{X})$	$\sum (X-\bar{X})^2$

$$**(4)\ \text{Variance} = \frac{\sum (X-\bar{X})^2}{n} = \frac{10}{5} = \frac{2}{1} = 2$$

$$(5)\ \text{Standard deviation} = \sqrt{\text{variance}} = \sqrt{2} = 1.41$$

*The mean of column 1 = $\bar{X} = \dfrac{\sum X}{n} = \dfrac{15}{5} = \dfrac{3}{1} = 3$

**Note:* If the variance is used in inferential statistics (i.e., where the sample variance is used as the estimate of the population variance), then you need to use $n-1$ rather than n in the denominator for technical reasons. When you use $n-1$, the variance is referred to as the sample variance.

square a number, multiply the number by itself. For example, 2 squared is 2×2, which is equal to 4.)

4. Put the appropriate numbers into the variance formula. As illustrated in Table 13.4, insert the sum of the numbers in column 3 into the numerator (the top part) of the variance formula. The denominator (the bottom part) of the variance formula is the number of numbers in column 1. Now divide the numerator by the denominator and you have the *variance*.

5. You obtained the variance in the previous step. Now take the square root of the variance and you have the *standard deviation*. (To get the square root, type the number into your calculator and press the square root [$\sqrt{\ }$] key.)

Standard Deviation and the Normal Distribution

Now that you understand the idea of standard deviation, we can point out another important characteristic of the normal distribution that we did not mention earlier. The following will be true *if* the data follow a normal distribution:

- 68.26 percent of the cases fall within *one* standard deviation,
- 95 percent fall within 1.96 standard deviations,
- 95.44 percent fall within *two* standard deviations, and
- 99.77 percent fall within *three* standard deviations.

A good rule for approximating the area within one, two, and three standard deviations is what we call the "68, 95, 99.7 percent rule" (Figure 13.6). Don't forget, however, that you can only use this rule when you know that the data are normally distributed. The rule is a

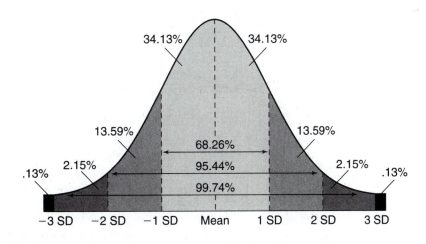

FIGURE 13.6   Areas under the normal curve. SD = standard deviation.

useful approximation, for example, when you are talking about things like height, weight, and IQ. You should be careful, however, when you have collected your own data, because a distribution usually does not become normally distributed (even if the underlying distribution is normal) until many, many cases have been collected. If you want to apply the 68, 95, 99.7 percent rule, check to see that the data are normally distributed. Do not automatically assume that the rule is applicable.

MEASURES OF RELATIVE STANDING

Measures of relative standing Provide information about where a score falls in relation to the other scores in the distribution of data

Percentile ranks Scores that divide a distribution into 100 equal parts

Standard scores Scores that have been converted from one scale to another to have a particular mean and standard deviation

Percentile rank The percentage of scores in a reference group that fall below a particular raw score

Reference group The norm group used to determine the percentile ranks

The raw scores of many research and assessment instruments are not inherently meaningful. How would you feel, for example, if someone told you your raw scholastic aptitude score was 134? Likewise, how would you compare your score to a score of 119? Without more information, you obviously would not know exactly how to interpret your raw score of 134. This is why standardized test makers rarely report raw scores. Instead, they report various **measures of relative standing,** which provide information about where a score falls in relation to the other scores in the distribution of data. We focus on two types of relative standing: **percentile ranks** (scores that divide a distribution into 100 equal parts) and **standard scores** (scores that have been converted from one scale to another so that they have a particular mean and standard deviation that are believed to be more interpretable). Our following discussion of standard scores focuses on z-scores, although two additional types of standard scores are shown in Figure 13.7. We have included IQ scores (which usually have a mean of 100 and a standard deviation of 15) and SAT scores (which have a mean of 500 and a standard deviation of 100) for your comparison.

Percentile Ranks

A **percentile rank** is interpreted as the percentage of scores in a reference group that fall below a particular raw score (Crocker and Algina, 1986; Cronbach, 1984; ETS, 1998). Percentile ranks help individuals interpret their test scores in comparison to others. The reference group is often referred to as the norm group or the standardization sample. A **reference group** is the group of people that is used to determine the percentile ranks. A reference group might be a national sample, a sample of a particular aged child, or composed of all of the students in a school district. As a general rule, percentile ranks should be used only when the reference group is quite large.

To interpret the meaning of a score using a percentile rank, let's say that you made a raw score of 680 on the Graduate Record Examination Verbal Test. This score of 680 corresponds to a percentile rank of 95, which means that 95 percent of the individuals in the norm group made scores less than your score. For another example, assume that a friend of yours got a raw score of 420. Since this score corresponds to a percentile rank of 32, only 32 percent of the individuals made a score lower than your friend. You can see the list of other GRE Verbal Test standard scores and the corresponding percentile ranks in Table 13.5. As a final example, how would you interpret a score of 580? As you can see in Table 13.5, this score corresponds to the percentile rank of 79.

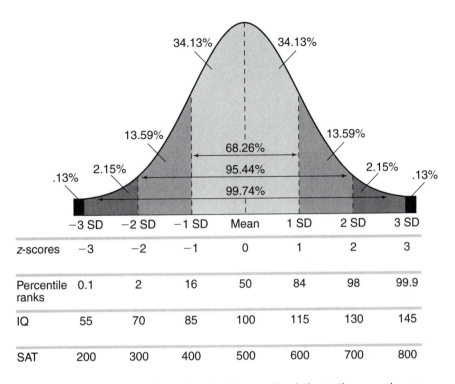

FIGURE 13.7   Percentile ranks and standard scores in relation to the normal curve.

z-Scores

z-score
A raw score
that has been
transformed into
standard deviation
units

A **z-score** is defined as a raw score that has been transformed into standard deviation units. This means that *a z-score tells you how many standard deviations a raw score is from the mean.* If a raw score is above the mean, the z-score will be positive; if a raw score is below the mean, the z-score will be negative; if a raw score is equal to the mean, the z-score will equal zero (because the mean of a set of z-scores will always be zero).

The z-score standardization transforms any set of raw scores into a new set of scores that has a mean of zero and a standard deviation of one. *The z-score transformation does not impact the overall shape of the data distribution.* If the data are normal (not skewed) before the z-score transformation, then they will still be normal after the z-score transformation, and if the data are skewed before the z-score transformation, then they will still be skewed after the z-score transformation. The new, transformed scores are called "z-scores."

For example, let's say that Jenny has a z-score of +2.00 on some standardized test (e.g., the GRE, the MAT, the SAT). This means that Jenny scored two standard deviations above the mean. Remember, z-scores tell you where a person's score stands in relation to the mean. Jenny obviously did better than the average person. Let's say that Jay has a z-score of –2.00; therefore, Jay scored two standard deviations below the mean. In other words, Jay did worse than average. John's z-score is zero; therefore, John's raw score is equal to the mean (i.e., the overall average). John was exactly average. Jean's z-score is

TABLE 13.5   GRE General Test Interpretive Data

	Percentile Ranks*		
Scaled Score	Verbal Ability	Quantitative Ability	Analytical Ability
800	99	99	99
780	99	95	97
760	99	92	95
740	99	88	93
720	98	84	90
700	96	80	87
680	95	77	83
660	93	73	78
640	90	68	73
620	87	64	67
600	84	59	62
580	79	54	56
560	75	50	50
540	69	45	45
520	64	40	39
500	58	35	34
480	52	31	29
460	45	26	25
440	39	22	21
420	32	18	18
400	26	15	14
380	20	12	11
360	15	9	9
340	10	6	7
320	7	4	5
300	5	3	3
280	3	2	2
260	2	1	1
240	1		
220			
200			
Mean	476	555	546
Standard deviation	115	139	130
Number of examinees	1,163,460	1,162,650	1,156,081

*Based on the performance of all examinees tested between October 1, 1993 and September 30, 1996. From *GRE 1997–98 Guide to the Use of Scores,* p. 12. Reprinted by permission of Educational Testing Service, the copyright owner. Permission to reprint GRE materials does not constitute review or endorsement by Educational Testing Service of this publication as a whole or of any other testing information it may contain.

+3.50. Jean's raw score falls 3½ deviations above the mean, which is far above the average and better than Jenny's score, which was two standard deviations above the mean.

If the underlying data are normally distributed, then z-scores communicate additional information. In Figure 13.7 we show the normal distribution along with percentile ranks and several standard scores (z-scores, IQ scores, and SAT scores). Because we are now assuming that the scores are normally distributed, we have additional information about Jenny's score of +2.00. Since a z-score of +2.00 has a percentile rank of 98 when the data are normally distributed, we know that Jenny's score is better than 98 percent of the people taking the standardized test. Jay's score has a percentile rank of 2, which means that he did better than only 2 percent of the people. John was right at the median (i.e., the fiftieth percentile). Jean did better than virtually everybody, including Jenny.

You can compute a z-score by taking the difference between a particular raw score and the overall mean and then dividing by the standard deviation. You would use this formula:

$$z\text{-score} = \frac{\text{raw score} - \text{mean}}{\text{standard deviation}} = \frac{X - \bar{X}}{SD}$$

In order to use this formula, you need the raw score that you wish to transform into a z-score, and you need to know the mean and standard deviation of all of the scores. Most IQ tests have a mean of 100 and a standard deviation of 15. Therefore, the z-score for Maria, who scored 115 on an IQ test, would be determined as follows:

$$z\text{-score} = \frac{115 - 100}{15} = \frac{15}{15} = 1$$

We put Maria's IQ of 115 into the formula, along with the IQ mean (100) and standard deviation (15). The resulting z-score is equal to one (+1.00), which means Maria's IQ is one standard deviation above the mean. That's all you do if you want to use the z-score formula!

An advantage of z-scores is that they can be used to compare raw scores between two different tests that have different means and standard deviations. To compare a person's scores on two different tests, you simply convert the two raw scores into z-scores and compare them. For example, assume that Maria got an SAT score of 700. Did Maria do better on the SAT or on the IQ test? You already know that Maria's IQ score results in a z-score of one. An SAT score of 700 results in a z-score of +2.00. (If you want to calculate the z-score for an SAT score of 700, put these values into the formula: raw score = 700, mean = 500, and standard deviation = 100. The result will be a z-score of +2.00). Obviously, a z-score of +2.00 is better than a z-score of +1.00, which means Maria did better on the SAT than she did on the IQ test.

EXAMINING RELATIONSHIPS
AMONG VARIABLES

Throughout this book we have been talking about relationships among variables. This is because researchers are seldom satisfied with describing the characteristics of single variables. Research becomes much more interesting when the relationships among variables are also described. We have already talked about comparing means (e.g., see discussion of analysis of variance in Chapter 8) and about interpreting correlation coefficients (e.g., see discussion of correlation coefficients in Chapter 1) in earlier chapters. There are two more topics, however, that you need to know about. These topics are contingency tables and regression.

Contingency Tables

Contingency table
A table displaying information in cells formed by the intersection of two or more categorical variables

A **contingency table** (also called a cross-tabulation) displays information in cells formed by the intersection of two or more categorical variables. In a two-dimensional contingency table, the rows represent the categories of one variable and the columns represent the categories of the other variable. Various kinds of information can be put into the cells of a contingency table (e.g., observed cell frequencies, row percentages, column percentages). You can see a contingency table with cell frequencies in Table 13.6(a). You can see a contingency table with column percentages in Table 13.6(b).

Look at the contingency table in Table 13.6(a). You can see that the row variable is political party identification and the column variable is gender. The numbers in the cells are the observed cell frequencies, which indicate the number of people in each cell. For exam-

TABLE 13.6 Party Identification by Gender Contingency Tables

(a) Contingency Table Showing Cell Frequencies (Hypothetical Data)

Political Party Identification	Gender		Total
	Males	*Females*	
Democrat	92	390	482
Republican	16	169	185
Total	108	559	667

(b) Contingency Table Showing Column Percentages (based on the data in Part (a)*

Political Party Identification	Gender	
	Males	*Females*
Democrat	85.2%	69.8%
Republican	14.8%	30.2%
Total Column %	100%	100%

*The column percentage 85.2 percent was obtained by dividing 92 by 108 (and multiplying by 100 to get a percentage); 14.8 percent was obtained by dividing 16 by 108; 69.8 percent was obtained by dividing 390 by 559; 30.2 percent was obtained by dividing 169 by 559. Note that both columns in part (b) sum to 100 percent. [If you want to obtain row percentages, just divide the number of cases in each cell in part (a) by the corresponding row total. Then each row will sum to 100%.]

ple, 92 people in the hypothetical set of data were Democrat and male and 390 were Democrat and female. A table with cell frequencies is a good starting point when constructing a contingency table, but you should not stop there because it is very difficult to detect a relationship between the variables when you examine only the cell frequencies.

Look at the contingency table in Table 13.6(b). This table was constructed in the following way. We made the independent or predictor variable the column variable; we made the dependent variable the row variable; and we obtained column percentages by calculating the percentages down the columns. This is an appropriate table construction because it will allow us to make our comparisons across the levels of the independent variable (gender). We explain exactly where the numbers came from in a footnote to the table. Whenever you obtain *column* percentages, each column will sum to 100 percent, just as the columns do in (b). After you construct your table this way, you should make your comparisons across the rows.

Now we are going to try to trick you! Based on the data you see in Table 13.6(a), who do you think is more likely to be a Democrat, a man or a woman? A few people will incorrectly assume that women are more likely than men to be Democrats because there are 390 females who are Democrats but there are only 92 males who are Democrats. (After all, 390 is bigger than 92, right?) Now we show you how to make the correct interpretation.

You can make the correct interpretation of our hypothetical data by looking at the table in Table 13.6(b). Remember to make your comparisons across the rows when you are reading the column percentages. You can now clearly see that 85.2 percent of the males are Democrats but only 69.8 percent of the females are Democrats. Therefore, *males are more likely than females to be Democrats*! Furthermore, 30.2 percent of the females are Republicans and only 14.8 percent of the males are Republicans. Therefore, *females are more likely than males to be Republicans.* Although both males and females are more likely to be Democrats than Republicans, there is also a clear relationship between gender and party identification (these two categorical variables are related). Males are more likely than females to be Democrats, and females are more likely than males to be Republicans. (Obviously these data are hypothetical.) When you hear percentage comparisons in the news, they are usually calculated this way. That is, you will often hear a report that one group is more likely than another group to have some characteristic. The group percentages are being compared.

Here is a simple rule for you to use whenever you want to see whether the variables in a contingency table are related:

- If the percentages are calculated down the columns, compare across the rows.
- If the percentages are calculated across the rows, compare down the columns.

This simple rule will help you to see, very quickly, whether there is a relationship between two variables in a contingency table. It is also easy to memorize.

You can extend the ideas presented here by adding more categorical variables to the mix. If you have three categorical variables, the basic strategy is to examine the original two-dimensional table separately for each level of the third categorical variable. If you want to see an example of this process or learn more about higher level contingency tables (i.e., tables based on three or more variables), we recommend reading Babbie (1998, pp. 378–383 and Chapter 16) and Frankfort-Nachmias and Nachmias (1992, pp. 403–412). Now we introduce a technique called regression analysis.

Regression Analysis

Regression analysis
A set of statistical procedures used to explain or predict the values of a dependent variable based on the values of one or more independent variables

Regression analysis is a set of statistical procedures used to explain or predict the values of a dependent variable based on the values of one or more independent variables. In regression analysis, there is always a single quantitative dependent variable. Although the independent variables can be either categorical or quantitative, we discuss only the case in which the independent variables are quantitative. The two main types of regression are called **simple regression,** where there is a single independent variable, and **multiple regression,** where there are two or more independent variables.

Simple regression
Regression based on one dependent variable and one independent variable

The basic idea of simple regression is that you obtain a **regression equation.** The regression equation defines the **regression line** that best fits a pattern of observations. The two important characteristics of any line (including a regression line) are the slope of the line and the Y-intercept of the line. The slope of a line basically tells you how steep the line is. The Y-intercept tells you where the line crosses the Y-axis. These are the two key components of the regression equation. Here is the simple regression equation formula:

$$\hat{Y} = a + bX$$

where

Multiple regression
Regression based on one dependent variable and two or more independent variables

$\hat{Y}$ (called y-hat) is the predicted value of the dependent variable,
a is the Y-intercept,
b is the regression coefficient or slope, and
X is the single independent variable.

Regression equation
The equation that defines the regression line

Researchers rarely calculate regression equations by hand. Most researchers use a computer program such as SPSS or SAS. All of this might seem complicated, but it will become clearer with an example. Let's use our college student data set (Table 13.1) to see whether we can predict starting salary using our knowledge of grade point average. If you look at Figure 13.8, you can see the regression line that resulted when we used the computer program SPSS to fit the regression line to the data. You can see from looking at the regression line that the relationship is positive (i.e., as grade point average increases, starting salary increases). You can also use the regression line to make approximate predictions.

Regression line
The line that best fits a pattern of observations

Here is what to do if you want to use the regression line to make an approximate prediction. You can visually examine the regression line to see what value of Y (the dependent variable) corresponds to a particular value of X (the independent variable). For example, first find the value 3.00 for grade point average on the horizontal axis. Then mark the point on the regression line that corresponds to this grade point average of 3.00. Third, determine what starting salary (i.e., what point on the vertical axis) corresponds to this point on the regression line. It looks like the predicted starting salary is about halfway between $30,000 and $35,000, so our guess is that the predicted starting salary is about $32,000.

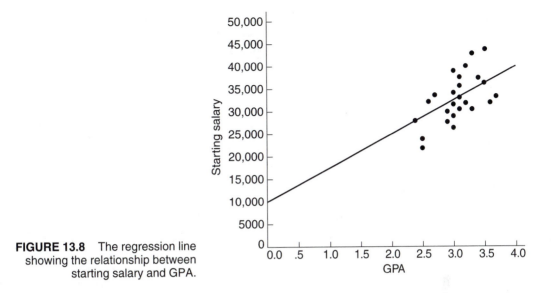

FIGURE 13.8 The regression line showing the relationship between starting salary and GPA.

Rather than making predictions by visually examining the regression line, we usually obtain the regression equation and insert values of X and obtain the predicted values of Y. We will show you how to insert values in a moment. Now look at the regression equation that was provided by the computer program:

$$\hat{Y} = 9{,}239.08 + 7{,}689.60(X)$$

Y-intercept
The point where the regression line crosses the Y-axis

The Y-intercept is equal to $9,239.08. The **Y-intercept** is defined as the point where the regression line crosses the Y-axis. In Figure 13.8 the X-axis is grade point average and the Y-axis is starting salary. The value of Y at the point where the regression line touches the Y-axis is $9,239.08. It is the value of the Y variable (the dependent variable) that would be predicted if the independent variable (X) were equal to zero.

Regression coefficient
The predicted change in Y given a one-unit change in X

The regression coefficient in the regression equation is equal to $7,689.60. The regression coefficient, or slope, tells you how steep the regression line is. The **regression coefficient** is more formally defined as the predicted change in Y given a one-unit change in X. A large regression coefficient implies a steep line, and if a line is very steep, Y will change quite a lot given a one-unit change in X. A small regression coefficient implies a line that is not very steep, and if a line is not very steep, Y will not change much given a one-unit change in X. In our example, the regression equation tells us that if someone's GPA increased by one full unit (it went from a C to a B or it went from a B to an A), then we would expect his or her starting salary to increase by $7,689.60. In sum, you can see in Figure 13.8 that the variables starting salary and grade point average are related, and the regression coefficient tells you how much, on average, starting salary increases given a one-unit increase in grade point average.

Now we will show you something you will probably find interesting—you can use a simple regression equation to make predictions. In our example, the dependent variable Y is starting salary. We can obtain a predicted value of starting salary by inserting a value for grade point average into the equation and solving. Let's find the predicted starting salary for someone who has a B grade point average (for someone whose grade point average is 3.00). First we write down the equation:

$$\hat{Y} = 9,239.08 + 7,689.60(X)$$

Now we insert the value for X (grade point average) and see what predicted value for Y we obtain:

$\hat{Y} = 9,239.08 + 7,689.60(3.00)$	We inserted the GPA value of 3.00.
$\hat{Y} = 9,239.08 + 23,068.80$	We multiplied $7,689.60 and 3.00.
$\hat{Y} = 32,307.88$	We added $9,239.08 and $23,068.80.

Our predicted value of starting salary is $32,307.88 when grade point average is a 3.00 (i.e., B). In short, based on our hypothetical college student data, we expect B students to have a starting salary of $32,307.88. We have now used our regression equation to make a prediction.

You should try to make a prediction now. Determine what starting salary you would predict college students with a grade point average of 3.8 to have based on our data. All you need to do is take the equation $\hat{Y} = 9,239.08 + 7,689.60(X)$ and insert the value of 3.8 where it says X. Then do the arithmetic and find the result. You will find that the predicted value is $38,459.56. You can insert other grade point averages into the equation to find other predicted starting salaries.

When you use a regression equation such as the one we just used from our college student data set, you need to remember that you should use it only for values of X that are in the range of the X values in your data set. In our case, we should *not* use our equation for grade point averages that are below a C or higher than an A because we do not have any data on these grade levels. All the students in our data set had grades in the C to A range. In fact, it is impossible for a student to get a grade higher than an A, so you would never insert a value greater than 4.00 into the equation. Researchers must be very careful when using a regression equation to make predictions.

Multiple regression is similar to simple regression except that there are two or more independent variables. The main difference is that the regression coefficients in multiple regression show the predicted change in Y given a one-unit change in the independent variable *while controlling for the other independent variable(s) in the equation.* The regression coefficients still show the relationship between an independent variable and the dependent variable. However, the multiple regression coefficients also take into account the fact that other independent variables are included in the regression equation. Multiple regression coefficients are similar to partial correlation coefficients, discussed in Chapter 11.

Let's use our college student data set one more time. We let starting salary be our dependent variable and we use two independent variables, grade point average and GRE

Verbal scores. Here is the multiple regression equation that was provided by our statistical program, SPSS:

$$\hat{Y} = 4{,}246.58 + 4{,}496.45(X_1) + 26.65(X_2)$$

where

X_1 is grade point average, and
X_2 is GRE Verbal.

According to this equation, starting salary increases by \$4,496.45 for a one-unit increase in grade point average, when you control for GRE Verbal performance. Also, starting salary increases by \$26.65 for a one-unit increase in GRE Verbal performance when you control for grade point average.

You can also use the multiple regression equation to find the predicted starting salary for a set of values for the two independent variables that you choose. Let's say you want to know the predicted starting salary when a student is a B student (i.e., the student's GPA is 3.00) and the student earned a 500 on the GRE Verbal test. All you have to do is insert 3.00 for GPA and 500 for GRE Verbal and then find the predicted value for Y, the predicted starting income:

$\hat{Y} = 4{,}246.58 + 4{,}496.45(3.00) + 26.65(500)$ We inserted the two values.

$\hat{Y} = 4{,}246.58 + 13{,}489.35 + 26.65(500)$ We multiplied 4,496.45 times 3.00.

$\hat{Y} = 4{,}246.58 + 13{,}489.35 + 13{,}325$ We multiplied 26.65 times 500.

$\hat{Y} = 31{,}060.93.$

If a recent college graduate has a grade point average of 3.00 and a GRE Verbal score of 500, we predict his or her starting salary will be \$31,060.93. You can put any other valid values into the regression equation and obtain the predicted starting salary. For example, you might want to know the predicted starting salary for someone with a GPA of 3.8 and a GRE Verbal of 700. All you need to do is insert these two values into the equation and get the predicted salary.

SUMMARY

The goal of descriptive statistics is to describe or summarize a set of data. Typically, variables are summarized one at a time. Some common ways to describe the values of a variable are to construct a frequency distribution or a grouped frequency distribution. Graphical representations, such as bar graphs and line graphs, are also useful in describing data. Scatterplots are useful when you want to examine the relationship between two quantitative variables. Measures of central tendency (mean, median, and mode) provide the numerical value considered most typical of the values of a quantitative variable. The mean takes into account the magnitude of the scores and is usually considered the best measure of central tendency. However, the median is sometimes the preferred measure of central tendency if the data are severely skewed (not symmetrical). Measures of variability tell you how spread out or dispersed the data values are. The most useful measures are the variance and the standard deviation. When data are normally distributed, you can apply the following approximate rule: 68 percent of the cases will fall within one standard deviation; 95 percent of the cases will fall within two standard deviations; and 99.7 percent of the cases will fall within three standard deviations. Measures of relative standing tell you where a score falls in relation to other scores. The most important measures of relative standing are percentile ranks and z-scores. Some important ways to examine and describe the relationships among variables are scatterplots, contingency tables, and regression analysis.

STUDY QUESTIONS

1. What is the difference between descriptive statistics and inferential statistics?
2. List the three steps in constructing a frequency distribution.
3. What types of graphical representations of data were discussed in the chapter?
4. Which graphical representation is used to examine the correlation between two quantitative variables?
5. What is a measure of central tendency, and what are the common measures of central tendency?
6. When is the median preferred over the mean?
7. If the mean is much greater than the median, then are the data skewed to the right or skewed to the left?
8. What is a measure of variability, and what are the common measures of variability?
9. How are the variance and standard deviation mathematically related?
10. If a set of data is normally distributed, then how many of the cases fall within one standard deviation? How many fall within two standard deviations? How many fall within three standard deviations?
11. What is a measure of relative standing, and what are the common measures of relative standing?
12. How do you calculate a z-score?
13. What are some of the different ways to examine the relationships among variables?
14. If you calculate percentages in a contingency table down, then should you make your comparisons down the columns or across the rows?
15. What is the difference between simple and multiple regression?
16. How is the regression coefficient interpreted in simple regression?
17. How is the regression coefficient interpreted in multiple regression?

EXERCISES

1. What are the mean, median, and mode of the following numbers: 1, 2, 2, 2, 3, 3, 3, 3, 4, 4, 4, 9, 1650? Are these data skewed to the left (negatively skewed) or skewed to the right (positively skewed)? Which measure of central tendency do you think best represents the central tendency of the data?

2. In Table 13.4 we calculated the standard deviation of the following set of numbers: 1, 2, 3, 4, 5. Now calculate the z-score for each of the five numbers. You will recall that we claimed that the mean is zero and the standard deviation is one for any complete set of z-scores. Is this true for your set of z-scores?

3. If someone tells you that his or her IQ is 145, then how rare is this event? (*Hint:* calculate the z-score and interpret it in relation to the normal curve.)

4. In the chapter we provided a simple regression equation showing the relationship between grade point average and starting salary. The regression equation is: $\hat{Y} = 9,239.08 + 7,689.60(X)$. What starting salary would you predict (using the regression equation) for someone who has a GPA of 4.00 (a student who has all A's)?

5. In Table 13.6(a) we showed a contingency table with cell frequencies. In part (b), we showed a contingency table that had been percentaged down the columns. There is a new set of cell frequencies in the table that follows.

Party Identification	Gender		
	Males	Females	Total
Democrat	390	920	1310
Republican	569	160	729
Total	959	1080	2039

Calculate percentages in this new table down the columns and interpret the results. Who are more likely to be Democrats according to your new contingency table, males or females? Who are more likely to be Republicans?

KEY TERMS

bar graph (363)

contingency table (380)

data set (360)

descriptive statistics (360)

exhaustive (363)

frequency distribution (361)

grouped frequency distribution (362)

heterogeneous (372)

homogeneous (372)

inferential statistics (360)

line graph (364)

mean (369)

measure of central tendency (366)

measure of variability (372)

measures of relative standing (376)

median (367)

median location (368)

mode (366)

multiple regression (382)

mutually exclusive (363)

negatively skewed (370)

normal distribution (369)

outlier (372)

percentile rank (376)

percentile ranks (376)

positively skewed (370)

range (373)

reference group (376)

regression analysis (382)

regression coefficient (383)

regression equation (382)

regression line (382)

scatterplot (364)

simple regression (382)

skewed (370)

standard deviation (374)

standard scores (376)

variance (374)

Y-intercept (383)

z-score (377)

ENDNOTES

1. Note that you cannot necessarily conclude that the data are normal when the mean and the median are the same.

CHAPTER 14

Inferential Statistics

LEARNING OBJECTIVES

To be able to

- define inferential statistics.
- explain the difference between a sample and a population.
- explain the difference between a statistic and a parameter.
- recognize the symbols used for the mean, variance, standard deviation, correlation coefficient, proportion, and regression coefficient.
- provide the definition of sampling distribution.
- compare and contrast point estimation and interval estimation.
- explain how confidence intervals work over repeated sampling.
- list and explain the steps in hypothesis testing.
- explain the difference between the null hypothesis and the alternative hypothesis.
- explain the difference between a nondirectional and a directional alternative hypothesis.
- explain the difference between a probability value and the significance level.
- draw the hypothesis testing decision matrix and explain the contents.

- state how to decrease the probability of Type I and Type II errors.
- explain the purpose of hypothesis testing.
- explain the basic logic of significance testing.
- explain the different significance tests discussed in the chapter.
- explain the difference between statistical and practical significance.

Inferential statistics
Use of the laws of probability to make inferences and draw statistical conclusions about populations based on sample data

In descriptive statistics, researchers attempt to describe the numerical characteristics of their data. In **inferential statistics** researchers attempt to go beyond their data. In particular, they use the laws of probability to make inferences and draw statistical conclusions about populations based on sample data. In the branch of inferential statistics known as estimation, researchers want to estimate the characteristics of populations based on their sample data. In order to make valid statistical estimations about populations, they use random samples (i.e., "probability" samples). In the branch of inferential statistics known as hypothesis testing, researchers test specific hypotheses about populations based on their sample data. You can see the major divisions of the field of statistics by reviewing Figure 13.1 (page 360).

Sample
A subset of cases that is drawn from the population

Let's start with four important points about inferential statistics. First, the distinction between samples and populations is essential. You will recall that a **sample** is a subset of cases drawn from a population, and a **population** is the complete set of cases. A population might be all first-grade students in the city of Ann Arbor, Michigan, and a sample might consist of 200 first-grade students selected from this population. The researcher should always define the population of interest.

Population
The complete set of cases

Second, a **statistic** (also called a sample statistic) is a numerical characteristic of a sample, and a **parameter** (also called a population parameter) is a numerical characteristic of a population. Some examples of numerical characteristics that interest researchers are means (averages), proportions (or percentages), variances, standard deviations, correlations, and regression coefficients. Here is the main idea: if a mean or a correlation (or any other numerical characteristic) is calculated from sample data, it is called a statistic; if it is based on all the cases in the entire population (such as in a census), it is called a parameter.

Statistic
A numerical characteristic of a sample

Parameter
A numerical characteristic of a population

Third, in inferential statistics we study samples when we are actually much more interested in populations. We don't study populations directly because it would be cost prohibitive and impossible to study everyone in a population for every single research study. Because we study samples rather than populations, our conclusions will sometimes be wrong. The solution provided by inferential statistics is that we can assign probabilities to our statements, and we can make conclusions that are very likely to be correct.

Fourth, random sampling is assumed in inferential statistics. You will recall from our earlier chapter on sampling that random sampling produces representative samples (i.e., samples that are similar to the populations from which they are selected). The assumption of random sampling is important in inferential statistics because it allows researchers to utilize the probability theory that underlies inferential statistics. Basically, statisticians have studied the behavior of sample statistics when these statistics are based on random samples.

Now you need to become familiar with some symbols that are used to represent several commonly used statistics and parameters. Researchers and statisticians use different symbols for *statistics* and *parameters* because they want to communicate whether their research is based on sample or population data. Statisticians usually use Greek letters to symbolize population parameters and Roman letters (i.e., English letters) to symbolize sample statistics. (This is probably why some students say, "Statistics is like Greek to me!") This convention goes quite far back in the history of statistics. Please take a moment now and examine the symbols shown in Table 14.1. In the next paragraph we are going to ask you a few questions about the symbols shown in Table 14.1.

Let's say that you have calculated the average reading performance of a sample of 100 fifth-grade students. What symbol would you use for this sample mean? The most commonly used symbol is $\bar{X}$ (it's called *X*-bar). Now assume that you have conducted a census of all fifth-grade students in the United States, and you have calculated the average reading performance of all these students. What symbol would you use? As you can see in Table 14.1, the correct symbol for the population mean is μ (mu). The average is calculated in exactly the same way for both a sample and a population. The only difference is the symbol that is used to stand for the mean.

Now assume that you also calculated the correlation between math performance and reading performance for the 100 students in your sample of fifth graders. What symbol would you use? The correct symbol for the sample correlation is r. If you conducted a census of all the fifth-grade students in the U.S. population and calculated the correlation between math performance and reading performance, what symbol would you use? The appropriate symbol is ρ (it's called rho). The important point is that when you calculate numerical indexes like means, percentages, and correlations, you should use the appropriate symbol, and the correct symbol depends on whether you are analyzing sample data or population data. Statistics and parameters are *usually* calculated in exactly the same way. For example, the mean is calculated the same way for sample and population data. The key exception to this rule is that researchers use $n-1$ rather than n in the denominator of the variance and standard deviation formulas when they are analyzing sample data. (You don't need to worry about the technical reason for this exception to the rule.[1])

TABLE 14.1 A List of Symbols Used for Statistics and Parameters*

Name	Sample Statistic	Population Parameter
Mean	$\bar{X}$	μ (mu)
Variance	SD^2	σ^2 (sigma squared)
Standard deviation	SD	σ (sigma)
Correlation	r	ρ (rho)
Proportion	p	π (pi)
Regression coefficient	b	β (beta)

Note: Statistics are usually symbolized with Roman letters and parameters with Greek letters.

SAMPLING DISTRIBUTIONS

Sampling distribution
The theoretical probability distribution of the values of a statistic that results when all possible random samples of a particular size are drawn from a population

The theoretical notion of sampling distributions is what allows researchers to make probability statements about population parameters based on sample statistics. The **sampling distribution** of a statistic is defined as the theoretical probability distribution of the values of a statistic that results when all possible random samples of a particular size are drawn from a population. More simply, a sampling distribution is the distribution of a sample statistic that comes from **repeated sampling** (i.e., drawing a sample, calculating the statistic, and putting the sample back into the population, drawing *another* sample, calculating the statistic, and putting the sample back into the population, drawing *another* sample, and so forth, until *all* possible unique samples have been selected). The sampling distribution is an important idea to know about because it explains how sample statistics operate over repeated sampling.

Repeated sampling
Drawing many or all possible samples from a population

The idea of a sampling distribution is a very general one because a sampling distribution can be constructed for any sample statistic. For example, a sampling distribution can be constructed for the mean (the sampling distribution of the mean), a percentage (the sampling distribution of the percentage or proportion), a correlation (the sampling distribution of the correlation coefficient), a variance (the sampling distribution of the variance), and even for the difference between two means. Can you guess what this last type of sampling distribution is called? (It's called the sampling distribution of the difference between two means.) You will be glad to know that you will never have to actually construct a sampling distribution! Mathematical statisticians have already constructed the sampling distributions for every common statistic that educational researchers currently use. You need to know only the definition of a sampling distribution given above and to understand the concept of sampling distributions.

It is important that you remember the following point: researchers do *not* actually construct sampling distributions when they conduct their research. A researcher typically selects only *one* sample, not all possible samples, from a population, and then he or she uses a computer program such as SPSS or SAS to analyze the data collected from the people in the sample. Remember that a sampling distribution is based on all possible samples, not the single sample that the researcher studies. The computer program does, however, use sampling distributions. In particular, the computer uses the idea of a sampling distribution to determine certain probabilities that we will discuss shortly. You should, therefore, think of a sampling distribution as a theoretical distribution because there is a sampling distribution underlying each inferential statistical procedure that a researcher uses.

Sampling error
The difference between a sample statistic and the corresponding population parameter

A sampling distribution demonstrates that *the value of any sample statistic* (such as a mean or a correlation coefficient) *varies from sample to sample.* Think of it like this: if you selected several random samples from a population and calculated the value of a statistic (such as a mean) for each of the samples, wouldn't you expect the sample values to be a little different from one another? You would *not* expect all of your sample values to be *exactly* the same number. This chance variation from sample to sample results in sampling error.

Sampling error is the difference between a sample statistic and the corresponding population parameter, and it is virtually always present in research because researchers rarely study everyone in a population. The presence of sampling error does not mean that random sampling doesn't work or that a researcher has made a mistake. It simply means that the values of statistics calculated from random samples will tend to vary because of chance fluctuations.

Standard error
The standard
deviation
of a sampling
distribution

Researchers sometimes need an indicator of the amount of sampling error (i.e., variation) present in a sampling distribution. That is, they need to know what is called the standard error of a sampling distribution. The **standard error** is nothing more than the standard deviation of a sampling distribution. Recall from Chapter 13 that the standard deviation tells you how much variation there is in a distribution of data. The variation of a sampling distribution can also be described by determining the standard deviation. However, statisticians like to call this special type of standard deviation (the standard deviation of a *sampling distribution*) the standard error. It tells you how much variation there is in the scores that make up a sampling distribution. Whenever you hear the word *standard error,* you should therefore think of the variation in a sampling distribution.

When there is a lot of sampling error in a sampling distribution, the standard error will be large, and when there is not much sampling error, the standard error will be small. For example, if a sampling distribution is based on large random samples (e.g., all possible samples of size 1500), the standard error will be smaller than if the sampling distribution is based on small random samples (e.g., all possible samples of size 20). That's because, on average, large samples provide values closer to the population parameter than small samples. In short, researchers prefer a small standard error, and a good way to get a small standard error is to select a large sample.

There is one more characteristic of sampling distributions to remember. If you construct a sampling distribution, you see that *the average of the values of the sample statistic is equal to the population parameter.* For example, if you took all possible samples from a population and calculated the correlation for each sample, the average of all those sample correlations would equal the correlation in the entire population. The reason is that a sample statistic value will sometimes overestimate the population value and it will sometimes underestimate the population value. Most importantly, a sample statistic will not be consistently too large or too small. The result is that the average of all the possible sample statistic values is equal to the population parameter.

Sampling Distribution of the Mean

Now let's make things a little more concrete by considering the sampling distribution of a particular statistic. Let's think about the sampling distribution of the mean. Let's say that you just drew a random sample of 100 people from the population of a city. *For the purpose of this example, we are telling you that the average income of the population is $50,000.* (In practice you would *not* know the population mean.) What value would you expect to obtain if you calculated the mean income of the 100 people in your randomly selected sample? You would expect the sample mean to be around $50,000 (since you happen to know that the population mean is $50,000). Let's say, however, that your sample mean turns out to be $45,600. Your mean is a little less than the population mean, and the amount of sampling error is $4,400 (i.e., $50,000 – $45,600 = $4,400). Your sample mean is not exactly the same as the population mean.

Now assume that you select *another* random sample of 100 people from the same city population. What value would you expect for the sample mean this time? Again, you would expect the sample mean to be about $50,000. This time, however, the sample mean is equal to $52,000. Now draw *another* random sample of 100 people. Let's say this sample mean is $49,800. Now, let's say, hypothetically speaking, that *you continued this process (of selecting a random sample of a specified size and calculating the sample mean on each sample) until all possible samples have been examined.* You would obviously have a lot of sample means resulting from your exercise in repeated sampling! The line graph constructed from all of these means would form a normal curve, and the overall average of this sampling distribution would be $50,000 (which is the same as the population parameter). The name of this theoretical distribution of sample means is the **sampling distribution of the mean.**

You can see a picture of our hypothetical sampling distribution of the mean in Figure 14.1. We assume that the standard error is $10,000. This means that the standard deviation of our hypothetical sampling distribution of the mean is $10,000. If you look at the line graph in Figure 14.1, you see that the sampling distribution of the mean is normally distributed. Because the distribution is normally distributed, we know that most of the randomly selected sample means will be close to the population mean, but a few of them will be farther away. Basically, random sampling works well most of the time, but not all of the time.

Sampling distribution of the mean
The theoretical probability distribution of the means of all possible random samples of a particular size drawn from a population

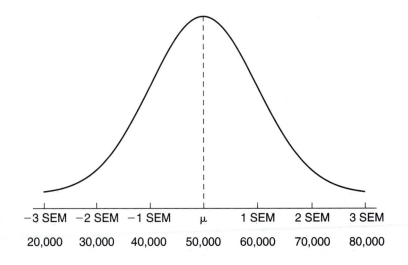

FIGURE 14.1   The sampling distribution of the mean. SEM stands for standard error of the mean. *Standard error* is the term used to refer to the standard deviation of a sampling distribution.

The mean of the sampling distribution of the mean is equal to the true population mean because random sampling is an unbiased sampling process (i.e., random sampling does not produce sample statistics that are systematically larger or smaller than the population parameter). If you take all possible random samples and calculate the mean of each sample, the means will fluctuate randomly around the population mean and they will form a normal distribution. Some of these means will fall above the population mean and some will fall below the population mean, but the average of all of these sample means will equal the true population mean. That's how random sampling operates. It is a chance process. You now have the important ideas of sampling distributions. Sampling distributions are important in estimation and hypothesis testing, the major divisions of inferential statistics.

ESTIMATION

People often make estimations. For example, if your best friend asks you what time you're coming to his house Sunday for a visit, you will provide an estimate. You might say to your friend, "I'll probably come over about two o'clock." In other words, your estimate is "two o'clock." Researchers use inferential statistics to make an estimation of a population parameter. The key question in the field of statistical estimation is

• Based on my random sample, what is my estimate of the population parameter?

There are two different kinds of estimation procedures in inferential statistics. If you use a single number (the value of your sample statistic) as your estimate (as your best guess) of the population parameter, then you are engaged in point estimation. If you use a range of numbers that you believe includes the population parameter, then you are engaged in interval estimation. As an analogy, let's say that you take your car in for a repair and the service manager gives you an estimate of how much the repair will cost. If the manager says the cost will probably be $300, then the manager has provided a point estimate (a single number). If the manager says the cost will probably be "somewhere between $250 and $350" then the manager has provided an interval estimate (a range of numbers that is likely to include the true cost). That's the basic idea. Now we will explain these two ideas a little further.

Point estimation
The use of the value of a sample statistic as the estimate of the value of a population parameter

Point estimate
The estimated value of a population parameter

Point Estimation

Point estimation is defined as the use of the value of a sample statistic as the estimate of the value of a population parameter. You might use the sample mean to estimate the population mean, or the sample percentage to estimate the population percentage, or the sample correlation to estimate the population correlation. The specific value of the statistic is called the **point estimate,** and it is the estimated value of the population parameter. The point estimate is your best guess about the likely value of the unknown population parameter.

Let's see whether you can now engage in point estimation. Let's say that the average income of the people in a random sample of 350 teachers from San Antonio, Texas, is $39,000. What is your point estimate of the population mean? You would estimate the value in the population of teachers in San Antonio to be $39,000 because that was the mean in your random sample. Now let's say that 59 percent of the 350 teachers in your sample say that they support bilingual education. What is the point estimate of the population percentage? You would estimate the percentage in the population of teachers in San Antonio to be 59 percent because that was the percentage in your random sample. In sum, your point estimates are $39,000 (for income) and 59 percent (for bilingual education).

Point estimation is used whenever a researcher uses the value of the sample statistic as his or her estimate of the population parameter. Because of the presence of sampling error, however, a point estimate will rarely be exactly the same value as the population parameter. Think of it like this. If the average income in a population is $35,000, would you expect your sample value to be exactly $35,000, or would you expect it to be some number near $35,000? You should expect that it would be a number near but not exactly equal to $35,000. An insight from our earlier study of sampling distributions is that *the value of a statistic varies from sample to sample.* That's why a point estimate is usually wrong. Because of the presence of sampling error, many researchers recommend the use of interval estimation.

Confidence interval
A range of numbers inferred from the sample that has a certain probability of including the population parameter

Interval Estimation

Confidence limits
The endpoints of a confidence interval

When researchers use interval estimation, they construct confidence intervals. A **confidence interval** is a range of numbers inferred from the sample that has a certain probability or chance of including the population parameter. The endpoints of a confidence interval are called **confidence limits,** where the smallest number is called the **lower limit** and the largest number is called the **upper limit.** In other words, rather than using a point estimate (which is a single number), the researcher uses a range of numbers, bounded by the lower and upper limits, as the interval estimate. This way, researchers can increase their chances of capturing the true population parameter.

Lower limit
The smallest number on a confidence interval

Upper limit
The largest number on a confidence interval

Researchers are able to state the probability (called the **level of confidence**) that a confidence interval to be constructed from a random sample will include the population parameter. We use the future tense because our confidence is actually in the long-term process of constructing confidence intervals. For example, 95 percent confidence intervals will capture the population parameter 95 percent of the time (the probability is 95 percent), and 99 percent confidence intervals will capture the population parameter 99 percent of the time (the probability is 99 percent). This idea is demonstrated in Figure 14.2.

Level of confidence
The probability that a confidence interval to be constructed from a random sample will include the population parameter

In the top part of Figure 14.2, you see a hypothetical sampling distribution of the mean. Recall from our earlier discussion that the sampling distribution of the mean is normally distributed and its mean is equal to the population mean. Also, a key idea of the sampling distribution of the mean is that the values of individual sample means vary from sample to sample because of sampling error. Now look at the twenty sample means (the dots) surrounded by their confidence intervals below the sampling distribution in Figure 14.2. These twenty means randomly jump around the population mean just as you would expect. Notice, however, that nineteen out of the twenty confidence intervals covered the population

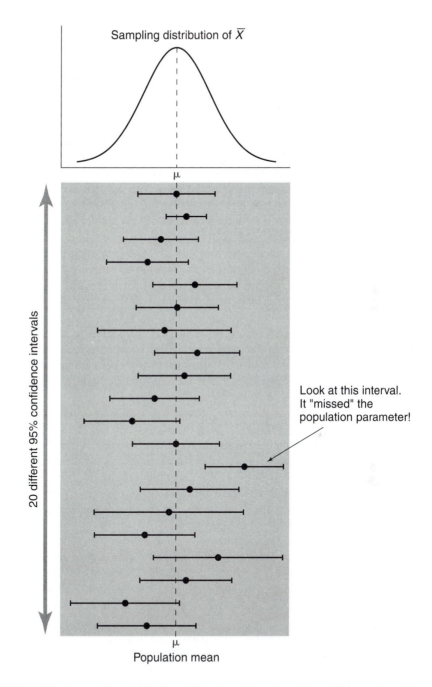

FIGURE 14.2   A sampling distribution of the mean (based on all possible samples of size 100) and an illustration of the 95 percent confidence intervals for twenty possible samples. The width of the intervals will be slightly different because they are estimated from different random samples. In the long run, 95 percent of confidence intervals will capture the population mean.

mean. Only one of the confidence intervals missed the true population mean. The process worked as we would expect for these twenty samples.

Most of the time confidence intervals will include the population parameter, but occasionally they will miss it. In Figure 14.2 the process worked nineteen times out of twenty. Since the intervals were 95 percent confidence intervals, that is exactly what we expected would happen. We expected to be right about 95 percent of the time, and we were (nineteen out of twenty is 95 percent). The bottom line is that if you construct 95 percent confidence intervals then you will capture the population parameter 95 percent of the time in the long run.

You are probably wondering why a researcher would use 95 percent confidence intervals rather than 99 percent confidence intervals. After all, the researcher will make a mistake 5 percent of the time with 95 percent confidence intervals but only 1 percent of the time with 99 percent confidence intervals. The reason is because 99 percent confidence intervals are wider than 95 percent confidence intervals, and wider intervals are less precise (e.g., the interval from 20 to 80 is wider and less precise than the interval from 45 to 55). That is the tradeoff. Fortunately, there is a way out of it. *An effective way to achieve both a higher level of confidence and obtain a more narrow (i.e., more precise) interval is to increase the sample size.* Bigger samples are, therefore, better than smaller samples. As a general rule, most researchers use 95 percent confidence intervals, and as a result they make a mistake about 5 percent of the time. Researchers also attempt to select sample sizes that produce intervals that are narrow (i.e., precise) enough for their needs.

Now we want to give you an intuitive explanation of how a confidence interval is constructed. Here is the general formula for a confidence interval:

Confidence interval = point estimate ± margin of error

Margin of error
One-half the
width of a
confidence
interval

where the symbol ± means plus or minus. As you can see, a confidence interval is a point estimate (a sample mean, a sample percentage, a sample correlation, and so forth) plus or minus the margin of error. The **margin of error** is simply one-half the width of the confidence interval. A confidence interval is constructed by taking a point estimate and surrounding it by the margin of error. For example, if you wanted a confidence interval for the mean, you could find the sample mean and surround it on each side by the margin of error. To find out how to calculate the margin of error, you will need to consult a statistics book (e.g., Moore & McCabe, 1993, p. 503). Fortunately, researchers rarely need to calculate their confidence intervals by hand because confidence intervals are easily obtained through the use of statistical computer programs such as SPSS and SAS.

Now we will show you an example of a confidence interval based on the college student data set that we introduced in Table 13.1. Using the statistical computer program called SPSS, we obtained the point estimate and the 95 percent confidence interval for starting salary. The average starting salary for the twenty-five recent college graduates in our data set was $32,800. Therefore, $32,800 is the point estimate. (If we had to pick *one* number as our estimate, $32,800 is the number we would pick.) We found that the margin of error for the 95 percent confidence interval was $1,722.70. Therefore, the 95 percent confidence interval is the range of values from $31,077.30 to $34,522.70. We conclude that we are 95 percent confident that the interval from \$31,077.30 to \$34,522.70 includes the population mean. Now you know how to interpret a confidence interval correctly!

HYPOTHESIS TESTING

In the last section we introduced you to estimation, where the goal was to use sample statistics to estimate population parameters. You learned that you can use a single number as the estimate (a point estimate) or you can construct a confidence interval around the point estimate, allowing you to estimate the parameter with a certain level of confidence. The key question in estimation is

- Based on my random sample, what is my (point or interval) estimate of the true population parameter?

Hypothesis testing
The branch of inferential statistics concerned with how well the sample data support a null hypothesis and when the null hypothesis can be rejected

In this section, we introduce **hypothesis testing,** the branch of inferential statistics concerned with how well the sample data support a particular hypothesis called the null hypothesis and when the null hypothesis can be rejected. Unlike estimation, in which the researcher usually has no clear hypothesis about the population parameter, in hypothesis testing the researcher constructs *a priori* null and alternative hypotheses and uses inferential statistics to help make a decision about these hypotheses (*a priori* hypotheses are hypotheses that are stated by the researcher before the data are collected). For now, just think of the null hypothesis as the hypothesis that states "there is no effect present," and the alternative hypothesis as the hypothesis that states "there is an effect present."

This is the key question that is answered in hypothesis testing:

- Is the value of my sample statistic unlikely enough (*assuming* that the null hypothesis is true) for me to reject the null hypothesis and tentatively accept the alternative hypothesis?

For example, a researcher might do an experiment to compare a new method of counseling (given to the experimental group) to no counseling at all (the control group). In this case, the null hypothesis says that there is no effect (i.e., the treatment group is *not* any better than the control group after the treatment) and the alternative hypothesis says that there is an effect (i.e, the treatment and control groups do differ after the treatment). If the two groups are very dissimilar after the treatment, the researcher may be able to reject the null hypothesis and accept the alternative hypothesis.[2] The goal of hypothesis testing is to help a researcher make a probabilistic decision about the truth of the null and alternative hypotheses. Ultimately, the researcher hopes the research data will allow him or her to reject the null hypothesis and support the alternative hypothesis.

In the next section we carefully explain the null hypothesis and the alternative hypothesis because these two hypotheses are the foundation of hypothesis testing. In Exhibit 14.1 we show you that hypothesis testing has some similarities to the courtroom. The material in Exhibit 14.1 provides a preview of the material that follows.

EXHIBIT 14.1   An Analogy from Jurisprudence

The U.S. criminal justice system operates on the *assumption* that the defendant is innocent until proven guilty beyond a reasonable doubt. In hypothesis testing, this assumption is called the null hypothesis. That is, researchers assume that the null hypothesis is true until the evidence suggests that it is not likely to be true. The researcher's null hypothesis might be that a technique of counseling does not work any better than no counseling. The researcher is like a prosecuting attorney, who brings someone to trial when he or she believes there is some evidence against the accused; the researcher brings a null hypothesis to "trial" when he or she believes there is some evidence against the null hypothesis (i.e., the researcher actually believes that the counseling technique does work better than no counseling). In the courtroom, the jury decides what constitutes rea-

sonable doubt, and it makes a decision about guilt or innocence. The researcher uses inferential statistics to determine the probability of the evidence under the *assumption* that the null hypothesis is true. If this probability is low, the researcher is able to reject the null hypothesis and accept the alternative hypothesis. If this probability is not low, the researcher is not able to reject the null hypothesis. No matter what decision is made, things are still not completely settled, because a mistake could have been made. In the courtroom, decisions of guilt or innocence are sometimes overturned or found to be incorrect. Similarly, in research, the decision to reject or not reject the null hypothesis is based on probability, so researchers sometimes make a mistake. However, inferential statistics gives researchers the probability of their making a mistake.

Null and Alternative Hypotheses

Null hypothesis
A statement about a population parameter

The starting point for hypothesis testing is to state the null and the alternative hypotheses. The **null hypothesis,** represented by the symbol H_0, is a statement about a population parameter and states that some condition concerning the population parameter is true. In most educational research studies, the null hypothesis (H_0) predicts no difference or no relationship in the population. It is the null hypothesis that is the hypothesis directly tested using probability theory. In particular, hypothesis testing operates under the *assumption* that the null hypothesis is true. Then, *if the results obtained from the research study are very different from that expected under the assumption that the null hypothesis is true, the researcher rejects the null hypothesis and then tentatively accepts the alternative hypothesis.* The null hypothesis is the focal point in hypothesis testing because it is the hypothesis that is directly tested.

Alternative hypothesis
Statement that the population parameter is some value other than the value stated by the null hypothesis

The **alternative hypothesis,** represented by the symbol H_1, states that the population parameter is some value other than the value stated by H_0. The alternative hypothesis typically asserts the opposite of the H_0 and usually represents a statement of a difference or a relationship that is consistent with what the researcher actually believes is true. The null and the alternative hypotheses are logically contradictory because the null and alternative cannot both be true at the same time. Remember that the alternative hypothesis is consistent with the researcher's research hypothesis, which means that the researcher is interested in supporting the alternative hypothesis, not the null hypothesis. You can see several examples of research questions, null hypotheses, and alternative hypotheses in Table 14.2. Later in this chapter, we will test several of these null hypotheses using our college student data set from Table 13.1.

Many students are curious why researchers use the term null hypothesis. It was developed by a famous statistician, Sir Ronald Fisher (1890–1962), who invented the procedure of hypothesis testing. The idea is to set up a hypothesis to be "knocked down" or rejected. Researchers do this because the convention is to assume no effect or no difference from the hypothesized null value until sufficient evidence to the contrary is provided. You can, therefore, view the null hypothesis as the no change or the no effect hypothesis. You can also view it as the status quo or the "nothing new" or the "business as usual" hypothesis. The key point is that the null hypothesis is what researchers *assume* until they can demonstrate otherwise.

Here is how Harnett (1982) explains the null hypothesis:

> The term "null hypothesis" developed from early work in the theory of hypothesis testing, in which this hypothesis corresponded to a theory about a population parameter that the researcher thought did *not* represent the true value of the parameter (hence the word "null," which means invalid, void, or amounting to nothing). The *alternative hypothesis* generally specified those values of the parameter that the researcher believed did hold true. (p. 346)

TABLE 14.2   Examples of Null and Alternative Hypotheses in Inferential Statistics

Research Question	Verbal Null (H_0) Hypothesis	Symbolic H_0 Hypothesis	Verbal Alternative (H_1) Hypothesis	Symbolic H_1 Hypothesis
Do teachers score higher on the GRE Verbal than the national average?	The teacher population GRE Verbal mean is equal to the national average of 476.	H_0: $\mu_{\text{GRE V}} = 476$	The teacher population GRE Verbal mean is different from the national average of 476.	H_1: $\mu_{\text{GRE V}} \neq 476$
Do males or females tend to score better on the GRE Verbal?	The male and female population means are not different.	H_0: $\mu_M = \mu_F$	The male and female population means are different.	H_1: $\mu_M \neq \mu_F$
Do education, arts and sciences, and business students have different starting incomes?	The education, arts and sciences, and business student populations have the same mean starting incomes.	H_0: $\mu_E = \mu_{A\&S} = \mu_B$	At least two of the three population means are different.	H_1: Not all equal
Is there a correlation between GPA (X), and starting salary (Y)?	The population correlation between GPA and starting salary is equal to zero.	H_0: $\rho_{XY} = 0$	The population correlation between GPA and starting salary is not equal to zero.	H_1: $\rho_{XY} \neq 0$
Is there a relationship between GRE Verbal (X_1), and starting salary (Y), controlling for GPA (X_2)?	The population regression coefficient is equal to zero.	H_0: $\beta_{YX_1 \cdot X_2} = 0$	The population regression coefficient is not equal to zero.	H_1: $\beta_{YX_1 \cdot X_2} \neq 0$

According to the logic of hypothesis testing, you should assume that an effect is *not* present until you have good evidence to conclude otherwise. The researcher states a null hypothesis, but ultimately hopes to be able to reject it. In other words, the null hypothesis is the hypothesis that the researcher hopes to be able to nullify by conducting the hypothesis test.

As an example, let's assume that we are interested in knowing which teaching method works best, the discussion teaching method or the lecture teaching method. Here are the null and alternative hypotheses:

Null hypothesis: $H_0: \mu_D = \mu_L$
Alternative hypothesis: $H_1: \mu_D \neq \mu_L$

where

μ_D is the symbol for the discussion group population mean, and
μ_L is the symbol for the lecture group population mean

This null hypothesis says that the average performance of students in discussion classes is equal to the average performance of students in lecture classes. This null hypothesis is called a point or exact hypothesis, because it contains an equals sign (=). As you can see, the alternative hypothesis states the opposite of the null hypothesis (i.e., that the discussion and lecture population means are *not* equal).

It is a good idea to remember the following three points about hypothesis testing. First, the alternative hypothesis can never include an equals sign (=). Second, the alternative hypothesis is based on one of these three signs: $\neq$ (not equal to), $<$ (less than), or $>$ (greater than). Third, the null hypothesis is based on one of these three signs: = (equal to), $\leq$ (less than or equal to), or $\geq$ (greater than or equal to). As you can see, the equality sign is always a part of the null hypothesis.

Directional Alternative Hypotheses

Nondirectional alternative hypothesis
An alternative hypothesis that includes the not equal to sign, $\neq$

Sometimes the researcher will state an alternative hypothesis in a directional form rather than in a nondirectional form. A **nondirectional alternative hypothesis** includes a not equal to sign ($\neq$). A **directional alternative hypothesis** contains either a greater than sign ($>$) or a less than sign ($<$).

For example, the researcher in our previous example could have stated this set of hypotheses:

Directional alternative hypothesis
An alternative hypothesis that contains either a greater than sign, $>$, or a less than sign, $<$

Null hypothesis: $H_0: \mu_D \leq \mu_L$
Alternative hypothesis: $H_1: \mu_D > \mu_L$

You can see that the alternative hypothesis states that the discussion group population mean is greater than the lecture group population mean. In other words, a directional alternative hypothesis was stated. The null hypothesis was also changed so that all possible outcomes were included in the two hypotheses. Note that the null hypothesis still has the equality in it (i.e., the sign $\leq$ means less than or *equal* to).

The researcher could have also stated this set of hypotheses:

Null hypothesis: $H_0: \mu_D \geq \mu_L$

Alternative hypothesis: $H_1: \mu_D < \mu_L$

Once again, a directional alternative hypothesis is given. This time, however, the alternative hypothesis states that the discussion group population mean is less than the lecture group population mean. In other words, it is hypothesized that students learning by lecture do better, on average, than students learning by discussion.

Although the use of directional alternative hypotheses may seem attractive, there is a major drawback. If a researcher uses a directional alternative hypothesis and a large difference in the *opposite* direction is found, the researcher must conclude that *no* relationship exists in the population. That is the rule of hypothesis testing. Therefore, when you read journal articles, the vast majority of the alternative hypotheses will be nondirectional. In fact, if a researcher has used a *directional* alternative hypothesis, he or she is obliged to tell you (Pillemer, 1991). If a researcher does not state the type of alternative hypothesis used, you can assume that it was a nondirectional alternative hypothesis.

Examining the Probability Value and Making a Decision

Now you are going to learn how the researcher makes the decision to reject or fail to reject the null hypothesis. As we told you earlier, it is the null hypothesis that is directly tested in the hypothesis testing procedure. When a researcher states a null hypothesis, the researcher is able to use the principles of inferential statistics to construct a probability model about what would happen *if the null hypothesis were true*.[3] This probability model is nothing but the sampling distribution that would result for the sample statistic (mean, percentage, correlation) over repeated sampling if the null hypothesis were true. In practice, the researcher uses a computer package, such as SPSS or SAS, that automatically selects the correct sampling distribution for the particular statistical test. For example, if you tested a null hypothesis about the mean, SPSS would use information about the sampling distribution of the mean for your statistical test. All you have to do is know what null hypothesis you want to test and then select the appropriate statistical test.

After the researcher states the null hypothesis, collects the research data, and selects a statistical test using SPSS, the computer program analyzes the research data and provides something called a probability value as part of the computer output. The **probability value** is the probability of the result of your research study or an even more extreme result *assuming that the null hypothesis is true. Obtaining the probability value is a key idea in hypothesis testing because the researcher uses this value to make a decision about the null hypothesis.* In particular, the researcher uses the probability value that is based on his or her research results to determine whether the observed value of the sample statistic (mean,

Probability value
The probability of the result of your research study, assuming that the null hypothesis is true

percentage, correlation, and so forth) is probable or improbable, *assuming that the null hypothesis is true.*

For example, suppose a researcher wants to determine who has the higher starting salary, recent male college graduates or recent female college graduates. Let's say that you construct these two statistical hypotheses for your research study:

Null hypothesis: H_0: $\mu_{\text{Males}} = \mu_{\text{Females}}$

Alternative hypothesis: H_1: $\mu_{\text{Males}} \neq \mu_{\text{Females}}$

As you can see, you want to test the null hypothesis that the average starting salaries for the males and females are the same in their respective populations. The alternative hypothesis says the average starting salaries are *not* the same. You have randomly selected samples of males and females and you have calculated the starting salaries for these individuals in your research study.

If the average starting salary was $43,000 for the males and $27,000 for the females in your research study, the probability value would be small because such a large difference would be unlikely if the null hypothesis were true. When the probability value is small, the researcher rejects the null hypothesis because the research results call into question the null hypothesis. When the researcher rejects the null hypothesis, the researcher decides to accept the alternative hypothesis. (We will explain in a moment when you should consider a probability value to be small.) If you did reject the null hypothesis and, therefore, tentatively accepted the alternative hypothesis, you would also make the claim that the finding is **statistically significant.** Researchers claim their finding is statistically significant when they do *not* believe their observed result was due to chance or sampling error.

On the other hand, if the average starting salary was $33,000 for the males in your study and $31,000 for the females in your study, the difference between $33,000 and $31,000 could simply be due to chance (i.e., sampling error). In this case, the probability value would be larger than in the previous example because this time the difference is not so unlikely under the assumption that the null hypothesis is true. If the probability value is large, the researcher will fail to reject the null hypothesis. The researcher will also make the claim that the research finding is not statistically significant (i.e., the observed difference between the two means may simply be a random or chance fluctuation).

We told you that you can use a computer program such as SPSS to find out how likely or unlikely your sample result is *assuming that the null hypothesis is true.* You make this determination using the probability value that you get from the computer printout. If the probability value is small, then your sample result is unlikely (assuming the null hypothesis is true). If the probability value is large, then your sample result is not unlikely (assuming the null hypothesis is true). You are probably wondering, "When do I consider a probability value to be small?" and "When do I consider a probability value to be large?" The answer is that most researchers consider a probability value that is less than or equal to .05 to be small and a probability value that is greater than .05 to be relatively large.

For example, assume that the probability value (based on your computer analysis of the research data) was .03 when the male and female incomes were very different ($43,000 versus $27,000). Since this probability value is less than .05, the researcher would reject the

Statistically significant Claim made when the evidence suggests an observed result was probably *not* due to chance

null hypothesis that the two population means are the same (H_0: $\mu_{\text{Males}} = \mu_{\text{Females}}$), and the researcher would accept the alternative hypothesis that the two population means are different (H_1: $\mu_{\text{Males}} \neq \mu_{\text{Females}}$). The researcher would also claim that the difference between the two sample means is statistically significant.

On the other hand, assume that the probability value (based on your computer analysis of the data) was .45 when the male and female incomes were similar ($33,000 versus $31,000). In this case, the probability value is greater than .05. Therefore, the researcher would *fail to reject the null hypothesis.* The researcher would also claim that the difference between the two sample means is not statistically significant. Note that the researcher cannot claim that the two population means are the same. The researcher can only claim that he or she has failed to reject the null hypothesis. Basically, whenever the researcher is unable to reject the null hypothesis, he or she is left in an ambiguous situation.

This number .05 that we just used is the significance level that we chose to help us decide when the probability value was small or large. In other words, a researcher selects a significance level to aid in making the decision about the size of the probability value obtained from the analysis of the research data. The **significance level** (also called the alpha level) is the cutoff that the researcher uses for deciding when to reject the null hypothesis: (1) when the probability value is less than or equal to the significance level, the researcher rejects the null hypothesis, and (2) when the probability value is greater than the significance level, the researcher fails to reject the null hypothesis. It is important to understand that a significance level does not always have to be .05. The researcher can select any significance level to use in a research study as long as he or she can justify why a particular significance level was used.

You may wonder why educational researchers *usually* select a significance level of .05 and why they believe that a probability value that is less than or equal to .05 is small enough to reject the null hypothesis and that a probability value greater than .05 is not small enough (is too large) to reject the null hypothesis. There are no ultimate answers to these questions. Basically, the significance level of .05 has become a widespread convention among researchers in education and every other social and behavioral science. In other words, it is the significance level that researchers have decided to adopt. Historically, Sir Ronald Fisher originally used the .05 significance level, and ever since then the .05 significance level has been popular with many researchers. Remember, however, that the .05 significance level is not used by all researchers; it is only the most commonly used significance level.

What exactly does a significance level of .05 mean? A significance level of .05 means that if the observed sample result occurs only 5 percent of the time or less (when the null hypothesis is true), *then the researcher will consider the observed sample result to be an unlikely event, and, therefore, the researcher will make the decision to reject the null hypothesis.* Remember this point: The significance level is the value that the researcher compares the probability value with.

Be careful not to get the probability value and the significance level mixed up! First, the researcher gets the probability value from the computer printout. The probability value is based on the statistical analysis of the research data. It tells the researcher how likely the observed value of the sample statistic is, under the *assumption* that the null hypothesis is true. Remember that the probability value is based on the empirical research data collected

Significance level
The cutoff the researcher uses to decide when to reject the null hypothesis

by the researcher and analyzed by the computer program. Second, the researcher selects a significance level that he or she wants to use in the research study. The significance level is a value (such as .05) that the researcher chooses to use in deciding when the probability value is small enough to call into question the null hypothesis.

When you engage in hypothesis testing, you follow these two rules:

- *Rule 1:* If the probability value (which is a number obtained from the computer print-out and is based on your research results) is *less than or equal to* the significance level (the researcher usually uses .05), then the researcher rejects the null hypothesis and tentatively accepts the alternative hypothesis. The researcher also concludes that the observed relationship is statistically significant (e.g., the observed difference between the groups is *not* due to chance fluctuations).
- *Rule 2:* If the probability value is *greater than* the significance level, then the researcher cannot reject the null hypothesis. The researcher can only claim to fail to reject the null hypothesis and conclude that the relationship is not statistically significant (e.g., any observed difference between the groups may be due to chance fluctuations).

If you memorize rule one and rule two, then the rest of the material in this chapter is going to be easier than you may expect! These two rules are stated more concisely in Table 14.3. At this point you should review the steps in hypothesis testing summarized in Table 14.3 so that you can remember the logic of hypothesis testing (also called the logic of significance testing).

Understanding Probability Value and Significance Level

The ideas of probability value and significance level are extremely important. A coin-tossing example may help you to gain a deeper understanding of the ideas of significance level and probability value.

Let's suppose that your research teacher decides to test the null hypothesis that a particular coin is fair. A fair coin has an equal chance of coming up heads or tails on a given toss. The coin looks like a normal coin, but you can see it only from a distance. Next, your research teacher tells you she is going to check to see whether the assumption that the coin is fair seems to be justified. The two hypotheses in this example are as follows:

Null hypothesis:	H_0: The coin is fair.
Alternative hypothesis:	H_1: The coin is biased.

Your teacher tells you she is going to flip the coin ten times and record the number of heads. Obviously if the coin is fair, you would expect to get about as many heads as tails over the ten flips of the coin. Your teacher flips the coin for the first time, looks at it, and says, "It was heads." She puts a check on the board to record the result. She flips the coin again, looks at it, and says, "It was heads." She puts another check on the board. Once

TABLE 14.3   Steps in Hypothesis Testing

1. State the null and alternative hypotheses.

2. Set the significance level before the research study.
(Most educational researchers use .05 as the significance level. Note that the significance level is also called the *alpha level* or, more simply, *alpha*)

3. Obtain the probability value using a computer program such as SPSS.

4. Compare the probability value to the significance level and make the statistical decision.

Step 4 includes two decision-making rules:

Rule 1:

If: Probability value ≤ significance level (i.e., probability value ≤ alpha)

Then: Reject the null hypothesis.

And: Conclude that the research finding is statistically significant.

In practice, this usually means:

If: Probability value ≤ .05

Then: Reject the null hypothesis.

And: Conclude that the finding is statistically significant.

Rule 2:

If: Probability value > significance level (i.e., probability value > alpha)

Then: Fail to reject the null hypothesis.

And: Conclude that the research finding is not statistically significant.

In practice this usually means:

If: Probability value > .05

Then: Fail to reject the null hypothesis.

And: Conclude that the research finding is not statistically significant.

5. Interpret the results. That is, make a substantive, real-world decision and determine practical significance.
This means that you must decide what the results of your research study mean. Statistics are only a tool for determining statistical significance. If you obtain statistical significance, you now interpret your results in terms of the variables used in your research study. For example, you might decide that females perform better, on average, than males on the GRE Verbal test, or that client-centered therapy works better than rational emotive therapy, or that phonics and whole language in combination work better than phonics only.
You must also determine the *practical significance* of your findings. A finding is practically significant when the difference between the means or the size of the relationship is big enough, in your opinion, to be of any practical use. For example, a correlation of .15 would probably not be practically significant, even if it was statistically significant. On the other hand, a correlation of .85 would probably be practically significant.

again, your teacher flips the coin, looks at it, and says, "It was heads." She puts yet another check on the board. Your teacher continues this coin-flipping exercise seven more times, and each time she tells you that the coin flip resulted in heads! Is this coin fair? The teacher flipped the coin ten times, and it came up heads every single time. That is ten heads in a row. Does this seem like a likely or an unlikely result?

Most students reject the null hypothesis that the coin in this exercise is fair, and they claim that the coin must be biased. Some students will start questioning the assumption that the coin is fair after only three or four heads have come up in a row. By the time heads has come up ten times in a row, virtually everyone rejects the null hypothesis that the coin is fair. Basically, each student has the concepts of significance level and probability in his or her head. The cutoff point (the point where the student decides the coin is not fair) is the student's significance level. The student's perception of how likely the particular observed result would be assuming the coin is fair is the probability value. Students compare this probability value to the significance level. When the probability value reaches the student's significance level (the point where the student decides that the fair-coin hypothesis appears to be too improbable to believe), the student rejects the null hypothesis. The student rejects the original assumption that the coin is fair.

In Table 14.4, you can see the actual probability values of getting heads under the assumption that the coin is fair. The probability of getting ten heads in a row is .00098. What this probability value means is that if the coin is fair, the rules of probability inform us that we will get ten heads in a row only about once every thousand times. That means getting ten heads in a row is quite unlikely. *Formal hypothesis testing works a lot like this coin-tossing example.* Researchers compare the actual probability value (which they get from the computer printout) to the significance level that they choose to use. As you know, researchers usually use a significance level of .05. In our coin-tossing example we would have rejected the null hypothesis (that the coin is fair) because the probability value (.00098) is clearly less than the significance level (.05). Remember that the *probability value* is the mathematical probability of an observed result, under the assumption that the null hypothesis is true. The *significance level* is the cutoff point that the researcher chooses to use when deciding how unlikely an event must be in order to reject the null hypothesis.

TABLE 14.4   Coin Toss Probabilities

Number of Tosses		Probability Value of Consecutive Heads
1	.50000	Probability of heads
2	.25000	Probability of two heads in a row
3	.12500	Probability of three heads in a row
4	.06250	Probability of four heads in a row
5	.03125	Probability of five heads in a row
6	.01563	Probability of six heads in a row
7	.00781	Probability of seven heads in a row
8	.00391	Probability of eight heads in a row
9	.00195	Probability of nine heads in a row
10	.00098	Probability of ten heads in a row

The Hypothesis Testing Decision Matrix

Because samples are studied in inferential statistics rather than complete populations, hypothesis testing is based on incomplete data. Because hypothesis testing is based on sample data, it relies on probability theory to inform the decision-making process. As a result, decision-making errors will inevitably be made some of the time. The four possible hypothesis testing outcomes are illustrated in Table 14.5.

Across the top of Table 14.5 are the two possible conditions that can exist in the population: the null hypothesis is true or the null hypothesis is false. Across the rows of the table are the two possible decisions that a researcher can make: a researcher can reject the null hypothesis or a researcher can fail to reject the null hypothesis. You will see in Table 14.5 that these two sets of conditions result in four possible outcomes. Two of the outcomes are good (they are correct decisions), and two of the outcomes are bad (they are incorrect decisions).

Can you locate the two correct decisions in Table 14.5? Type A correct decisions occur when the null hypothesis is true and you do not reject it (i.e., you fail to reject the null hypothesis). This is exactly what you hope to do when the null hypothesis is true. Type B correct decisions occur when the null hypothesis is false and you reject it. Again, this is exactly what you hope to do when the null hypothesis is false. If the null hypothesis is false, you always want to reject it. Researchers hope for a Type B correct decision because they hope to reject their null hypotheses and be able to claim that their research findings are statistically significant.

Now look at the two "errors" in Table 14.5. These errors are called Type I errors and Type II errors. A **Type I error** occurs when the researcher rejects a true null hypothesis. Remember: if the null hypothesis is true it should *not* be rejected. Type I errors are called false positives because the researcher has falsely concluded that there is a relationship in the population. The researcher has claimed statistical significance in error. Here is an analogy. In medicine, the null hypothesis is "the patient is not ill." Therefore, a false positive occurs

Type I error
Rejecting a true
null hypothesis

TABLE 14.5   The Four Possible Outcomes in Hypothesis Testing

		The True (but unknown) Status of the Null Hypothesis	
		The null hypothesis is true (It should not be rejected.)	The null hypothesis is false (It should be rejected.)
Your Decision*	Fail to reject the null hypothesis	Type A Correct decision!	**Type II Error** (false negative)
	Reject the null hypothesis	**Type I Error** (false positive)	Type B Correct decision!

*Remember if the null hypothesis is true, it should *not* be rejected, but if the null hypothesis is false, it *should* be rejected. The problem is that you will not know if the null hypothesis is true or false. You only have the probabilistic *evidence* obtained from your sample data.

when a medical test says you have a disease, but you really don't. As another analogy, in the criminal justice system, the defendant is presumed to be innocent until found guilty by a judge or jury. Hence, a Type I error occurs when an innocent person is found guilty.

Type II error
Failing to reject
a false null
hypothesis

A **Type II error** occurs when the researcher fails to reject a false null hypothesis. Remember: If the null hypothesis is false, it is supposed to be rejected. Type II errors are sometimes called false negatives because the researcher has falsely concluded that there is no relationship in the population. That is, the researcher has claimed it to be not statistically significant in error. In a medical analogy, a false negative occurs when a medical test says you do not have a disease, but you really do. In the courtroom, a Type II error occurs when a guilty person is found to be innocent.

Traditionally, researchers have been more concerned with avoiding Type I errors than Type II errors. In fact, the significance level that we have been discussing is defined as the probability of making a Type I error that the researcher is willing to tolerate. If a researcher uses .05 as the significance level, the researcher is saying that he or she is only willing to tolerate making a Type I error 5 percent of the time. In other words, the researcher is willing to tolerate making false positives (claiming there is an effect when there is none) only 5 percent of the time. This attitude suggests that researchers are conservative people when it comes to making claims from their research data. They are willing to *incorrectly* claim that they have an effect only 5 percent of the time.

Controlling the Risk of Errors

We pointed out in the previous section that the significance level used by a researcher is the probability of making a Type I error that a researcher is willing to accept. When a researcher uses the .05 significance level, for example, the researcher is willing to make Type I errors only 5 percent of the time. You may wonder, therefore, why researchers don't just use a smaller significance level. For example, why don't researchers just use a significance level equal to .01 rather than a significance level equal to .05? After all, if a researcher uses this smaller level, he or she will make fewer Type I errors.

The problem with using a smaller significance level is that Type I errors and Type II errors tend to be inversely related. In other words, when you try to *decrease* the likelihood of making a Type I error, you usually *increase* the likelihood of making a Type II error. For example, if you use a smaller significance level, say, .01 rather than .05, you will make it harder to reject the null hypothesis. This reduces the frequency of Type I errors. However, when you make it harder to reject the null hypothesis this way, you are also more prone to making Type II errors. That is, you are more likely to fail to reject the null hypothesis when you should have rejected it. That is the tradeoff. In short, when you try to make a false positive less likely, you tend to make a false negative more likely.

You will be glad to know that there is a way to reduce the likelihood of making *both* Type I and Type II errors! The solution is to include more participants in your research study. In other words, you need to *increase your sample size.* Larger samples provide a more sensitive or powerful test. If you increase the sample size, *both* Type I and Type II errors are less likely, and that is exactly what we all want! So remember, "the bigger the sample size, the better."[4] Larger sample sizes are better than smaller sample sizes because you will be less likely to make a Type I or a Type II error, and you are therefore more likely to draw the correct conclusion.

If you are able to use large sample sizes and you also happen to obtain statistical significance (you reject the null hypothesis), you must also make sure that your finding is **practically significant** (the difference between the means is large or the correlation is strong enough to be of practical importance). This is because *even small deviations from the null hypothesis are sometimes found to be statistically significant when large sample sizes are used.* For example, perhaps you compared two techniques for teaching spelling, and the two means in your study turned out to be 86 and 85 percent correct on the spelling test after the intervention. The difference between these two means is quite small and is probably not practically significant; however, this difference might end up being statistically significant if you have a very large number of people in each of the two treatment groups. Likewise, a small correlation might be statistically significant but not practically significant if you have a very large number of people in your research study. This does *not* mean that larger samples are bad. The bigger the sample size, the better the rule still applies. It simply means that you must always make sure that a finding is practically significant in addition to being statistically significant.

Practical significance A conclusion made when a relationship is strong enough to be of practical importance

A useful tool for helping you to determine when a finding is practically significant is to examine an effect-size indicator. An **effect-size indicator** is a statistical measure of the strength of a relationship. It tells you how big an effect is present. Some effect-size indicators are Cohen's standardized effect size, eta squared, omega squared, and the correlation coefficient squared. (If you want to learn more about effect-size indicators, you can refer to a statistics book such as Hays, 1994; Howell, 1997; or Huck and Cormier, 1996.) All you need to know now is that *effect-size indicators tell you how big or how strong an effect is.* You also need to understand that hypothesis testing is only a tool that the researcher uses to determine whether the null or the alternative hypothesis provides the best explanation of the data. Hypothesis testing does *not* tell you anything about the effect size or the practical importance of a research finding. Hypothesis testing only tells you whether a finding is statistically significant.

Effect-size indicator A measure of the strength of a relationship

HYPOTHESIS TESTING IN PRACTICE

When you read educational journal articles, you will quickly notice that researchers frequently test hypotheses and therefore report on the statistical significance of their findings. You will recall that when a null hypothesis is rejected, the finding is said to be statistically significant, and when a null hypothesis is not rejected, the finding is said to be not statistically significant. Researchers do this to add credibility to their conclusions. *Researchers do not want to interpret findings that are not statistically significant because these findings are probably nothing but a reflection of sampling error (i.e., chance fluctuations).* On the other hand, researchers do want to interpret research findings that are statistically significant. A commonly used synonym for the term *hypothesis testing* is the term **significance testing,** because when you engage in hypothesis testing you are also checking for statistical significance.

We now show some examples of several commonly used significance tests. Keep in mind that we use the .05 significance level for all of our statistical tests. For a more exhaustive introduction to significance testing, you will need to examine a statistics textbook (e.g., Glass and Hopkins, 1996; Hays, 1994; Howell, 1997; Huck and Cormier, 1996; Knoke and Bohrnstedt, 1994; Moore and McCabe, 1993).

Before we get started, you need to review the two hypothesis testing rules discussed earlier and shown in Table 14.3.

- *Rule 1.* If the probability value is less than or equal to the significance level, then reject the null hypothesis, tentatively accept the alternative hypothesis, and conclude that the finding is statistically significant.
- *Rule 2.* If the probability value is greater than your significance level, then you must fail to reject the null hypothesis and conclude that the finding is not statistically significant.

All you really have to do when conducting a significance test is set your significance level (most people use .05) and get the probability value. The significance level is selected by the researcher (we will use .05). The probability value is based on the computer analysis of the data from your research study, and the researcher gets the probability value from the computer printout. Finally, *you compare the probability value to the significance level and determine whether rule 1 or rule 2 applies.* In all of the following examples, we will simply follow these two rules.

We use the same college student data set that we used in Table 13.1. The data set includes the hypothetical data for twenty-five recent college graduates on several variables (starting salary, gender, GRE Verbal, GPA, and college major). Because we will use these data for inferential statistics in this chapter, we *assume* that the twenty-five individuals are a random sample from a larger population of recent college graduates. In practice, a sample of only twenty-five people would be quite small. However, our data set is for illustration only.

The t-*Test for Independent Samples*

One of the most common statistical significance tests is called the *t*-test for independent samples. The *t*-**test for independent samples** is used with a quantitative dependent variable and a dichotomous (i.e., composed of two levels or groups) independent variable. The purpose of this test is to see whether the difference between the means of two groups is statistically significant. The reason this test is called a *t*-test is that the sampling distribution used to determine the probability value is known as the *t*-distribution. The *t*-distributions (there is a separate *t*-distribution for each sample size) look quite a bit like the normal curve shown in the last chapter. The main difference is that, for relatively small sample sizes, the *t*-distribution is a little flatter and a little more spread out than the normal curve. The mean of the *t*-distribution is equal to zero. Just like the normal curve, the *t*-distribution is symmetrical, it is higher at the center, and it has a "right tail" and a "left tail" that represent extreme events.

The *t*-distribution is the sampling distribution under the *assumption* that the null hypothesis is true. Therefore, the researcher rejects the null hypothesis when the value of *t* is large (i.e., when it falls in one of the two tails of the *t*-distribution). Typically, *t* values that are greater than +2.00 (e.g., +2.15) or less than –2.00 (e.g., –2.15) are considered to be large *t* values. When we say large, we mean that the value is not near the center of the distribution; instead, the value is in a tail of the distribution. As an analogy, think about the normal curve. Values that are more than two standard deviations out from the center of the normal curve are considered to be extreme because less than 5 percent of the cases fall beyond these points. It is exactly the same way with the *t*-distribution. That is, when the *t* value of the sample result falls in one of the two tails of the *t*-distribution (i.e., in the left tail or in the right tail), it is considered to be an unlikely event (under the assumption that the null hypothesis is true). Therefore, the researcher rejects the null hypothesis and claims that the alternative hypothesis is the better explanation of the results.

We used the sample data in our college student data set (Table 13.1) to examine the following research question: Is the difference between the average starting salary for males and the average starting salary for females statistically significant? The dependent variable is starting salary and the independent variable is gender. The two statistical hypotheses are

Null hypothesis: $H_0: \mu_M = \mu_F$

Alternative hypothesis: $H_1: \mu_M \neq \mu_F$

As you can see, the null hypothesis states that the male and female population means are the same. The alternative hypothesis states that the male and female population means are different (i.e., they are not equal). Assuming that our male and female data were randomly selected, we can legitimately test the null hypothesis.

The average starting salary for the males in our data set was $34,500, and the average starting salary for the females in our data set was $31,230.80. Obviously these two sample means are different. Remember, however, that whenever sample data are used, sampling error will be present. This means that the observed difference in the sample means *could* be due to sampling error. The key question is whether the sample means are different enough for us to conclude that the difference is probably not due to sampling error, and that there is a real difference between male and female starting salaries in the population from which the data came.

Using SPSS (a very popular computer package used to analyze data), we conducted the *t*-test for independent samples on our student data. The *t* value was 2.09, and because this *t* value falls in the right tail of the *t*-distribution, it is an unlikely value. (If the *t* value had been –2.09, then it would have fallen in the left tail of the *t*-distribution, which would have also been an unlikely value.) Because the *t* value is relatively unlikely, assuming that the null hypothesis is true, the probability value was small. We got the probability value from the computer printout based on the analysis of our data. The probability value was equal to

.048. Because this probability value (.048) is less than the significance level (.05), we reject the null hypothesis and we accept the alternative hypothesis (using rule 1 from Table 14.3).

We conclude that the observed difference between the male and female means is statistically significant. We do not believe that the observed difference between our sample means was due to sampling error. Rather, we believe that there is a real difference between the starting salaries of males and females in the population. We look at the two means and because the male mean is higher than the female mean, we conclude that males have a higher starting salary, on average, than females.

One-Way Analysis of Variance

One-way analysis of variance
Statistical test used to compare two or more group means

One-way analysis of variance (one-way ANOVA) is used to compare two or more group means. It is appropriate whenever you have one quantitative dependent variable and one categorical independent variable. (Two-way analysis of variance is used when you have two categorical independent variables; three-way analysis of variance is used when you have three categorical independent variables; and so forth.) Analysis of variance techniques use what is called the F-distribution. This is the name of the sampling distribution that is used in analysis of variance techniques. Don't be surprised if you sometimes hear analysis of variance techniques referred to as F-tests. The F-distribution looks like the distribution shown in Figure 13.5, which was skewed to the right (i.e., the tail was pulled or stretched out to the right). You don't have to worry much about the F-distribution because the statistical computer programs take care of that for you.

Here is the research question that we were interested in for our example: Is there a statistically significant difference in the starting salaries of education majors, arts and sciences majors, and business majors? The dependent variable is starting salary, and the independent variable is college major.

The two statistical hypotheses are

| Null hypothesis: | H_0: $\mu_E = \mu_{A\&S} = \mu_B$ |
| Alternative hypothesis: | H_1: Not all equal |

The null hypothesis states that the education, the arts and sciences, and the business student populations all have the same mean starting income. The alternative hypothesis states that at least two of the population means are different from one another. The alternative hypothesis does not state which two of the population means are different from one another.

Once again we used SPSS to obtain our results. The F value was equal to 9.02, which is quite an extreme value. (When there is no relationship, the F value is theoretically equal to 1.0.) Our F value of 9.02 is quite a bit bigger than 1.0, which means our sample result falls in the right tail of the F-distribution. Therefore, the probability value was small (i.e., the sample result was unlikely *assuming* the null hypothesis is true). The probability value, which we got from the SPSS printout, was equal to .001. Since we are using a significance level of .05, we reject the null hypothesis and conclude that the relationship between college major and starting income is statistically significant. That's because our probability value (.001) was less than our significance level (.05) (from rule 1). We can conclude that at least two of the college major means are significantly different.

Post Hoc Tests in Analysis of Variance

One-way analysis of variance tells the researcher whether the relationship between the independent and dependent variables is statistically significant. In our example, college major and starting income were significantly related. We therefore concluded that at least two of the means were significantly different. If you want to know which means are significantly different, you have to use what is called a **post hoc test,** a follow-up test to analysis of variance that is used to determine which means are significantly different. If an independent variable has only two levels, you don't need a post hoc test. You just need to look to see which mean is bigger. *If an independent variable has three or more levels, you will need post hoc testing.*

Post hoc test
A followup test
to the analysis
of variance

There are many different post hoc tests available to a researcher. All of them provide appropriate probability values for a researcher to use in determining statistical significance. Some of the popular post hoc tests are the Newman-Keuls Test, the Tukey Test, the Scheffe Test, and the Bonferroni Test. We used the Bonferroni procedure to see which of the means in our previous example were significantly different.

Here are the mean incomes for our example:

- Average starting salary for education majors is $29,625.
- Average starting salary for arts and sciences majors is $32,600.
- Average starting salary for business majors is $36,714.

These are the sample means. The question is, Which of these means are significantly different from each other? We must check for statistical significance because the differences between our sample means *could be* due to chance (i.e., sampling error).

First, we checked to see whether the education and the arts and sciences means were significantly different. The Bonferroni-adjusted probability value (obtained from the SPSS printout) was .196. Our significance level is .05. As you can see, our probability value (.196) is greater than the significance level (.05). Therefore, we use rule 2. We fail to reject the null hypothesis (that the population means are the same), and we conclude that the difference between the two means is *not* statistically significant. We can't really say whether the education or the arts and sciences mean is larger in the population.

Second, we checked to see whether the education and the business majors' means were significantly different. The Bonferroni-adjusted probability value was .001. Our significance level is .05. You can see that our probability value (.001) is less than the significance level (.05). Therefore, we use rule 1. We reject the null hypothesis (that the population means are the same), and we conclude that the difference between the two means is statistically significant. We believe that business majors have a higher starting salary than education majors.

Third, we checked to see whether the arts and sciences and the business majors' means were significantly different. The Bonferroni-adjusted probability value was .051.

Our significance level is .05. Therefore, we use rule 2. We fail to reject the null hypothesis (that the population means are the same), and we conclude that the difference between the two means is *not* statistically significant. We can't really say whether the arts and sciences or the business major mean is larger in the population.[5]

The t-Test for Correlation Coefficients

t-test for correlation coefficients Statistical test used to determine whether a correlation coefficient is statistically significant

Correlation coefficients are usually used to show the relationship between a quantitative dependent variable and a quantitative independent variable. In inferential statistics, the researcher wants to know if an observed correlation coefficient is statistically significant. The *t*-test for correlation coefficients is the statistical test used to determine whether a correlation coefficient is statistically significant. We called this procedure a *t*-test for correlation coefficients because the sampling distribution used to test the null hypothesis (that the population correlation coefficient is zero) is the same *t*-distribution that we used earlier. The *t*-distribution is used for many different statistical tests.

Using our college student data set, we decided to answer this research question: Is there a statistically significant correlation between GPA (X) and starting salary (Y)? The statistical hypotheses are

Null hypothesis: H_0: $\rho_{XY} = 0$

Alternative hypothesis: H_1: $\rho_{XY} \neq 0$

The null hypothesis says there is no correlation between GPA and starting salary in the population from which the data were selected. The alternative hypothesis says there is a correlation in the population.

Our sample correlation between GPA and starting salary was +.63, which suggests that there is a moderately strong positive correlation between GPA and starting salary. However, we wanted to know whether this correlation was statistically significant. Our probability value (based on the analysis of our data and obtained from the SPSS printout) was equal to .001. Once again, we are using a significance level of .05. Because the probability value is less than the significance level, our correlation is statistically significant. We conclude that GPA and starting salary are correlated in the population.

The t-Test for Regression Coefficients

t-test for regression coefficients Statistical test used to determine whether a regression coefficient is statistically significant

We point out in Chapter 13 that simple regression is used to test the relationship between one quantitative dependent variable and one independent variable. We also point out that multiple regression is used to test the relationship between one quantitative dependent variable and two or more independent variables. The *t*-test for regression coefficients uses the *t*-distribution (sampling distribution) to test each regression coefficient for statistical significance.

Since we introduced you to simple and multiple regression in Chapter 13, we do not repeat that material here. Rather, we take the multiple regression equation discussed in

Chapter 13 and now test the two regression coefficients in that equation for statistical significance. Look at the equation from Chapter 13 once again:

$$\hat{Y} = 4{,}246.58 + 4{,}496.45(X_1) + 26.65(X_2)$$

where

$\hat{Y}$ is predicted starting salary,
X_1 is grade point average,
X_2 is GRE Verbal,
4,246.58 is the Y-intercept,
4,496.45 is the value of the regression coefficient for X_1. It shows the relationship between starting salary and GPA (controlling for GRE Verbal), and
26.65 is the value of the "regression coefficient" for X_2. It shows the relationship between starting salary and GRE Verbal (controlling for GPA).

The key point for you to understand is that researchers usually test their regression coefficients for statistical significance. A researcher will not trust a coefficient that is not statistically significant because the coefficient may simply be due to chance (sampling error). If a coefficient is statistically significant a researcher can conclude that there is a real relationship in the population from which the data came.

Our first research question relates to the first regression coefficient (4,496.45):

- *Research question 1.* Is there a statistically significant relationship between starting salary (Y) and GPA (X_1) [controlling for GRE Verbal (X_2)]?

The two statistical hypotheses for this first research question are

Null hypothesis: H_0: $\beta_{YX_1 \cdot X_2} = 0$
Alternative hypothesis: H_1: $\beta_{YX_1 \cdot X_2} \neq 0$

The null hypothesis says that the population regression coefficient is equal to zero (i.e., there is no relationship). The alternative hypothesis says that the population regression coefficient is not zero (i.e., there is a relationship).

Using SPSS, the t-test was computed and we obtained the probability value corresponding to the regression coefficient, showing the relationship between starting salary and GPA. The probability value was equal to .017. Because this probability value (.017) is less than our significance level (.05), we reject the null hypothesis and accept the alternative hypothesis. We conclude that the relationship between starting salary and GPA (controlling for GRE Verbal) is statistically significant.

This is the research question for the second regression coefficient (26.65):

- *Research question 2.* Is there a statistically significant relationship between starting salary (Y) and GRE Verbal (X_2) [controlling for GPA (X_1)]?

The two statistical hypotheses for research question two are

Null hypothesis: $H_0: \beta_{YX_2 \cdot X_1} = 0$

Alternative hypothesis: $H_1: \beta_{YX_2 \cdot X_1} \neq 0$

Using SPSS, the t-test was computed and we obtained the probability value corresponding to the regression coefficient showing the relationship between starting salary and GRE Verbal. The probability value was equal to .048. Because this probability value (.048) is less than our significance level (.05), we reject the null hypothesis and accept the alternative hypothesis. We conclude that the relationship between starting salary and GRE Verbal (controlling for GPA) is statistically significant.

The Chi-Square Test for Contingency Tables

Chi-square test for contingency tables
Statistical test used to determine whether a relationship observed in a contingency table is statistically significant

The **chi-square test for contingency tables** is used to determine whether a relationship observed in a contingency table is statistically significant. In Chapter 13, we taught you how to construct and interpret the numbers in contingency tables. We told you that contingency tables are used when both variables are categorical. The two categorical variables in our college student data set are gender and college major. Therefore, let's see whether these two variables are significantly related. We used the computer package called SPSS to produce the contingency table shown in Table 14.6. The row variable is college major and the column variable is gender. Within the body of the table are the counts (the number of people in each cell), the expected counts (the number of people that would be expected to be in each cell *if the variables were not related*), and the "percent of gender" (the column percentages).

How can you determine whether the variables in this contingency table are related? These are the rules from the last chapter:

- If the percentages are calculated down the columns, compare across the rows.
- If the percentages are calculated across the rows, compare down the columns.

You can see that we calculated the percentages down the columns in Table 14.6. Therefore you can determine whether college major and gender are related by reading across the rows. If you do this, you will see that the variables appear to be related. Looking at the first row, you can see that 53.8 percent of the females were education majors but only 8.3 percent of the males were education majors. Obviously females were more likely to be education majors. Can you determine who is more likely to be an arts and sciences major in Table 14.6? Males are more likely. In particular, fully 50 percent of the males were arts and sciences majors, but only 30.8 percent of the females were arts and sciences majors. Finally, because 41.7 percent of the males were business majors and only 15.4 percent of the females were business majors, it is clear that males were more likely than females to be business majors.

The inferential statistics question is, Is the observed relationship between college major and gender in the contingency table statistically significant? The null hypothesis

TABLE 14.6   Contingency Table of College Major by Gender

			Gender		Total
			Male	Female	
College Major	Education	Count	1	7	8
		Expected count	3.8	4.2	8.0
		% of gender	8.3%	53.8%	32.0%
	Arts and sciences	Count	6	4	10
		Expected count	4.8	5.2	10.0
		% of gender	50.0%	30.8%	40.0%
	Business	Count	5	2	7
		Expected count	3.4	3.6	7.0
		% of gender	41.7%	15.4%	28.0%
Total		Count	12	13	25
		Expected count	12.0	13.0	25.0
		% of gender	100.0%	100.0%	100.0%

says that college major and gender are *not* related in the population from which the data were selected. The alternative hypothesis says that college major and gender *are* related in the population. The sampling distribution used for contingency tables is called the chi-square distribution. The computed value of chi-square in our example is 6.16. The probability value is .046. Our probability value of .046 is less than our significance level of .05. Therefore, we reject the null hypothesis (there is no relationship) and accept the alternative hypothesis (there is a relationship). We conclude that there is a relationship between college major and gender, and that relationship is statistically significant. (We used rule 1.)

Other Significance Tests

Believe it or not, you have come a long way! There are many additional significance tests that we could discuss. In fact, we mentioned several other statistical analyses in earlier chapters. For example, we discussed two-way analysis of variance in Chapter 8, we discussed analysis of covariance in Chapter 7 and in Chapter 10, and we discussed partial correlation coefficients in Chapter 10. If you ever need to refresh yourself on any of these procedures, you can review that material. The key point is that the ideas that you have learned in this chapter apply to any significance test (including two-way ANOVA, AN-COVA, and partial correlation). In other words, you can determine whether the observed relationship is statistically significant.

Logic of significance testing
Understanding and following the steps shown in Table 14.3

Here is some good news. You now understand the fundamental **logic of significance testing.** You state the null and alternative hypotheses. Then you determine the probability value and compare it to the significance level. You decide whether the finding is statistically significant or not statistically significant using the two rules shown in Table 14.3. This fundamental logic will carry you quite a long way when you read journal articles or begin conducting your own research. If you run across a significance test not mentioned in this book, you can consult a textbook focused on statistics (e.g., Glass and Hopkins, 1996; Hays, 1994; Howell, 1997; Huck and Cormier, 1996; Knoke and Bohrnstedt 1994; Moore and McCabe, 1993). However, the idea of statistical significance will remain the same.

SUMMARY

The purpose of inferential statistics is to estimate the characteristics of populations and to test hypotheses about population parameters. Randomization (random sampling or random assignment) is required when using the probability theory underlying inferential statistics, which is based on the idea of sampling distributions. A sampling distribution is the theoretical probability distribution of the values of a statistic that results when all possible random samples of a particular size (e.g., all possible samples of size 100 or all possible samples of size 500) are drawn from a defined population. Sampling distributions make it clear that the value of a sample statistic varies from sample to sample. The sampling distribution constructed for the sample mean is called the sampling distribution of the mean. It shows the distribution of the sample mean when many samples are taken. Other sample statistics (e.g., proportions, correlation coefficients) also have their own sampling distributions.

There are two types of estimation. In point estimation, the researcher uses the value of a sample statistic as the estimate of the population parameter. In interval estimation, the researcher constructs a confidence interval (a band of numbers) that will include the population parameter a certain percentage of the time in the long run. For example, 95 percent confidence intervals will capture the population parameter 95 percent of the time.

Hypothesis testing is the branch of inferential statistics concerned with testing hypotheses about population parameters. Hypothesis testing follows a very specific logic, called the logic of significance testing. Basically, the researcher sets up a null hypothesis that he or she hopes to ultimately reject in order to accept the alternative hypothesis. It is the null hypothesis (not the alternative hypothesis) that is directly tested using probability theory. In order to engage in hypothesis testing, you must understand the difference between the probability value and the significance level. The *probability value* is the probability of the sample results under the assumption that the null hypothesis is true. The *significance level* is the cutoff point that the researcher believes represents an unlikely event. Using these ideas, the researcher follows these decision-making rules:

- *Rule 1.* If the probability value is less than or equal to the significance level, then reject the null hypothesis, tentatively accept the alternative hypothesis, and conclude that the finding is statistically significant.
- *Rule 2.* If the probability value is greater than the significance level, then you must fail to reject the null hypothesis and conclude that the finding is not statistically significant.

A statistically significant finding is a finding that the researcher does *not* believe is due to chance. A finding is statistically significant when the evidence supports the alternative hypothesis rather than the null hypothesis. The logic of significance testing will carry you a long way because the basic logic applies to all significance tests, and significance tests are frequently reported in published research.

STUDY QUESTIONS

1. What is the difference between a statistic and a parameter?
2. What is the symbol for the population mean?
3. What is the symbol for the population correlation coefficient?
4. What is the definition of a sampling distribution?
5. How does the idea of repeated sampling relate to the concept of a sampling distribution?
6. Which of the two types of estimation do you like the most, and why?
7. What is a null hypothesis?
8. Whom is the researcher similar to in hypothesis testing, the defense attorney or the prosecuting attorney? Why?
9. What is the difference between a probability value and the significance level?
10. Why do educational researchers usually use .05 as their significance level?
11. State the two decision-making rules of hypothesis testing.
12. Do the following statements sound like typical null or alternative hypotheses? (a) The coin is fair. (b) There is no difference between male and female incomes in the population. (c) There is no correlation in the population. (d) The patient is not sick (i.e., is well). (e) The defendant is innocent.
13. What is a Type I error? What is a Type II error? How can you minimize the risk of both types of errors?
14. If a finding is statistically significant, then why is it also important to consider practical significance?
15. How do you write the null and alternative hypotheses for each of the following? (a) The *t*-test for independent samples, (b) one-way analysis of variance, (c) the *t*-test for correlation coefficients.

EXERCISES

1. Many quantitative research articles in education do not provide the exact probability values. Rather, they include statements of probability values such as $p < .05, p < .01, p < .03, p < .001$, and so forth. Remember that the significance level used in most articles is .05. For each of the following possible probability values, indicate whether the result would be statistically significant or not statistically significant. Assume that the significance level is set at .05. (*Hint:* If a probability value is less than or equal to the significance level, the result is statistically significant. Otherwise, it is not statistically significant.) Place a check in the box to the left of each of your answers.

Probability Value	**Your Statistical Decision**	
$p > .05$	☐ Statistically significant	☐ Not statistically significant
$p < .05$	☐ Statistically significant	☐ Not statistically significant
$p < .03$	☐ Statistically significant	☐ Not statistically significant
$p < .01$	☐ Statistically significant	☐ Not statistically significant
$p < .001$	☐ Statistically significant	☐ Not statistically significant
$p < .0001$	☐ Statistically significant	☐ Not statistically significant

2. Let's now assume that the researcher is using a more conservative significance level. In particular, assume that the researcher is using the .01 significance level rather than the .05 significance level. For each of the following probability values, indicate whether the result would be statistically significant or not statistically significant.

Probability Value	**Your Statistical Decision**	
$p > .05$	☐ Statistically significant	☐ Not statistically significant
$p < .05$	☐ Statistically significant	☐ Not statistically significant
$p < .03$	☐ Statistically significant	☐ Not statistically significant
$p < .01$	☐ Statistically significant	☐ Not statistically significant
$p < .001$	☐ Statistically significant	☐ Not statistically significant
$p < .0001$	☐ Statistically significant	☐ Not statistically significant

3. Find a quantitative journal article (you can use the one in Appendix A if you want to) and note where the author(s) talk about statistical significance. (*Note:* Some researchers still say significant when they actually mean statistically significant.) Did the author(s) report probability values when they claimed that a finding was statistically significant? Were any of the findings in the research article you examined *not* statistically significant? Did the author(s) adequately address the issue of practical significance in addition to statistical significance?

KEY TERMS

alternative hypothesis (400)

chi-square test for contingency tables (418)

confidence interval (396)

confidence limits (396)

directional alternative hypothesis (402)

effect-size indicator (411)

hypothesis testing (399)

inferential statistics (390)

level of confidence (396)

logic of significance testing (420)

lower limit (396)

margin of error (398)

nondirectional alternative hypothesis (402)

null hypothesis (400)

one-way analysis of variance (414)

parameter (390)

point estimate (395)

point estimation (395)

population (390)

post hoc test (415)

practical significance (411)

probability value (403)

repeated sampling (392)

sample (390)

sampling distribution (392)

sampling distribution of the mean (394)

sampling error (392)

significance level (405)

significance testing (412)

standard error (393)

statistic (390)

statistically significant (404)

t-test for correlation coefficients (416)

t-test for independent samples (412)

t-test for regression coefficients (416)

Type I error (409)

Type II error (410)

upper limit (396)

ENDNOTES

1. In case you are curious, researchers use $n - 1$ because statisticians have shown that the use of n provides an underestimate of the population parameter.
2. Although we sometimes say that you "accept" the alternative hypothesis, remember that whenever you reject the null hypothesis, you can only tentatively accept the alternative hypothesis because you could have made a mistake.
3. Don't forget that the research participants must be randomly selected or randomly assigned whenever inferential statistics is used. That is, without randomization, the probability model will have no meaning.
4. At some point, a sample size becomes large enough. In other words, it would become wasteful to include more participants in the research study. You may want to review our discussion in Chapter 6 on how big a sample is big enough.
5. Some statisticians suggest *not* following the procedure we just explained (i.e., conducting an analysis of variance and following it up with post hoc tests). Instead, they suggest that researchers should conduct what are called *planned comparisons*. That is, they suggest that researchers plan, before they collect their data, the exact hypotheses that they want to test.

CHAPTER 15

Data Analysis in Qualitative Research

LEARNING OBJECTIVES

To be able to

- understand the terminology surrounding qualitative data analysis.
- describe the process of coding.
- list the different types of codes.
- know what it means to analyze data inductively.
- code some text data.
- know some of the common types of relationships found in qualitative data.
- describe the procedures used to analyze qualitative data.
- list the three most popular computer programs used to analyze qualitative data.
- know the advantages and disadvantages of using computer programs for qualitative data analysis.

Formal qualitative research has been conducted since the early twentieth century. Qualitative data analysis, however, is still a relatively new and rapidly developing branch of research methodology. Writing in 1984, two pioneers in qualitative data analysis, Matthew Miles and Michael Huberman, noted that "we have few agreed-on canons for qualitative data analysis" (p. 16). By 1994 they noted that "Today, we have come far from that state of affairs. . . . Still, much remains to be done." (Huberman & Miles, p. 428). Over recent years, many qualitative researchers have realized the need for more systematic data analysis procedures, and they have started to write more about how to conduct qualitative research data analysis (e.g., Bryman & Burgess, 1994; Dey, 1993; Huberman & Miles, 1994; LeCompte & Preissle, 1993; Lofland & Lofland, 1995; Miles & Huberman, 1994; Patton, 1990; Silverman, 1993; Strauss & Corbin, 1990). In this chapter we introduce you to the terminology surrounding qualitative data analysis, show you the basics of qualitative data analysis, and briefly discuss the use of computer software in the analysis of qualitative data.

INTERIM ANALYSIS

Interim analysis
The cyclical
process of
collecting and
analyzing data
during a single
research study

Data analysis begins early in a qualitative research study, and during a single research study qualitative researchers alternate between data collection (e.g., interviews, observations, focus groups, documents, physical artifacts, fieldnotes) and data analysis (creating meaning from raw data). This cyclical process of collecting data, analyzing the data, collecting additional data, analyzing those data, and so on throughout the research project is called **interim analysis** (Miles & Huberman, 1994).

Interim analysis is used in qualitative research because qualitative researchers usually collect data over an extended time period, and they need to continually learn more and more about what they are studying during this time frame. In other words, qualitative researchers use interim analysis to develop a successively deeper understanding of their research topic and to guide each round of data collection. This is a strength of qualitative research. By collecting data at more than one time, qualitative researchers are able to collect data that help refine their developing theories and test their inductively generated hypotheses (i.e., hypotheses developed from examining their data or developed when they are in the field). Qualitative researchers basically act like detectives when they carefully examine and ask questions of their data and then reenter the field to collect more data to help answer their questions.

MEMOING

Memoing
Recording
reflective notes
about what you
are learning from
the data

A helpful tool for recording ideas generated during data analysis is called **memoing** (writing memos). Memos are reflective notes that researchers write to themselves about what they are learning from their data. The content of memos can include notes about anything, including thoughts on emerging concepts, themes or patterns found in the data, the need for further data collection, a comparison that needs to be made in the data, and virtually anything else. Memos written early in a project tend to be more speculative, and memos written later in a project tend to be more focused and conclusive. Memoing is an important tool to use during a research project to record insights gained from reflecting on data. Because qualitative data analysis is an interpretative process, it is important that you keep track of your ideas. You should try to record your insights as they occur so that you do not have to rely on your memory later.

DATA ENTRY AND STORAGE

Transcription
Transforming
qualitative data
into typed text

In order to carefully analyze qualitative data, we (along with many other qualitative researcher methodologists) recommend that you transcribe your data. **Transcription** is the process of transforming qualitative research data, such as audio recordings of interviews or field notes written from observations, into typed text. The typed text is called a transcript. If the original data source is an audio recording, transcription involves sitting down, listening to the tape recording, and typing what was said into a word processing file. If the data are memos, open-ended questionnaires, or observational field notes, transcription involves typing the handwritten text into a word processing file. In short, transcription involves transferring data from a less usable to a more usable form. After you transcribe your data, you should put your original data somewhere for safekeeping.

Some qualitative researchers use one of the voice recognition computer programs available on the market, which can make transcribing relatively easy. These programs create transcriptions of data while you read the words and sentences into a microphone attached to your computer. Two popular programs are IBM's Simply Speaking and ViaVoice. These and similar programs do require fairly powerful computers with a lot of internal memory. However, if you plan on doing a lot of qualitative data analysis, you will want to be on the lookout for a program that fits your particular needs. The main advantage of voice recognition software is that it makes transcribing easier. For most people it is easier to talk into a microphone than it is to type. Time savings are not currently large compared with typing, but the efficiency of these programs will continue to improve over time.

CODING AND DEVELOPING CATEGORY SYSTEMS

Segmenting
Dividing data
into meaningful
analytical units

Segmenting involves dividing the data into meaningful analytical units. When you segment text data, you read the text line by line and continually ask yourself the following kinds of questions: Do I see a segment of text that has a specific meaning that might be important for my research study? Is this segment different in some way from the text coming before and after it? Where does this segment start and end? A meaningful unit (i.e., segment) of text can be a word, a single sentence, several sentences, or it might include a larger passage such as a paragraph or even a complete document. The segment of text must have meaning that the researcher thinks should be documented.

Coding
Marking segments of data with symbols, descriptive words, or category names

Coding is the process of marking segments of data (usually text data) with symbols, descriptive words, or category names. Here is how Miles and Huberman (1994, p. 56) explain it: "*Codes* are tags or labels for assigning units of meaning to the descriptive or inferential information compiled during a study. Codes usually are attached to 'chunks' of varying size—words, phrases, sentences, or whole paragraphs. . . . They can take the form of a straightforward category label or a more complex one." When a researcher finds a meaningful segment of text in a transcript, he or she assigns a code or category name to signify or identify that particular segment. As you can see, segmenting and coding go hand-in-hand because segmenting involves locating meaningful segments of data, and coding involves marking or labeling those segments with codes or categories.

An example of a coded interview transcript is shown in Table 15.1. The narrative in the transcript is from an interview with a college teacher (CT) by a researcher (R). If you look at Table 15.1, you can see that the researcher read the text line by line and placed descriptive words or phrases in the left-hand margin next to the segments of text. The researcher also placed brackets around the segments of data to make it clear where each segment started and ended. Some other ways to mark segments are to use line numbers or

TABLE 15.1   Example of Coded Text Data

	R: Well, let's start with the impact of early field experiences in the schools for undergraduate education majors. What kind of an impact do you see these experiences having on your students?
Book learning	**CT:** I think it gives them a needed view into the classroom in the real world. [It's one thing to read about teaching in books;] [it is another to actually go into a real classroom, with real students, and actually try to teach them something. Basically, I think that there
Experiential learning Classroom management Teaching strategies	is something to learning by experience.] [My students can try out the classroom management principles] and the [teaching strategies] I teach them about in my educational psychology course. My students can also learn that all elementary students are
Common student needs Individual student needs	not alike. [The kids have a set of common needs], but [they also have a set of needs unique to each individual in the classroom].
	R: Are there any other results from going into the classroom?
Career choice	**CT:** Yes. Most of my students have not been in a real classroom since they were in school themselves. Things have changed in the schools in many ways since then. [The vocational experience of going into the classroom has helped some of my students decide that teaching really was not for them.] I hate to lose potential
Timing of vocational learning	teachers, but [it is probably better that they decide now than wait until they have completed four years of education learning to be a teacher and then decide they don't want to be in a classroom.]

to underline the relevant text rather than using brackets as in Table 15.1. In this example, a college teacher was asked about the experiences her students had when they visited elementary school classrooms as a course requirement in an educational psychology course. The teacher believes the visitation experiences provide experiential learning and provide her students (potential future teachers) with information that helps them to make career choices.

Master list
A list of all the codes used in a research study

As new codes are developed during coding, they must be added to the master list of codes if they are not already on the list. A **master list** is simply a list of all the codes used in the research study. The master list should include each code followed by the full code name and a brief description or definition of the code. A well-structured master list will enable other researchers working on the project to readily use the list.

During coding, the codes on the master list should be reapplied to new segments of text each time an appropriate segment is encountered. For example, one category from the master for the data in Table 15.1 would be "career choice." Therefore, when the data analyst for this research study encountered another segment of data where the same or a different person being interviewed made a comment about career choice, the researcher would reapply the label "career choice." Every time a segment of text is about career choice, the researcher would use the code career choice to refer to that segment.

Here is an example of coding based on data from a consulting project done by one of this book's authors. The members of a public organization filled out an open-ended questionnaire in which one of the questions asked, What are some specific problems needing action in your organization? The participants' responses are shown in Table 15.2. Take a look at the responses for a moment and decide whether you notice any meaningful categories of information. Then, look at Table 15.3 and see how the data were coded. As you can see, the answers to the open-ended question are segmented into six categories in Table 15.3. The codes are shown in the left hand margin. The members of the organization listed a number of problems in their organization, and these problems fell into the categories of management issues, physical environment, personnel practices, employee development, intergroup and interpersonal relations, and work structure. These six categories were determined by examining the responses and sorting them into these inductive categories.

Intercoder reliability
Consistency among different coders

Intracoder reliability
Consistency within a single individual

If you think you or someone else may have coded the responses from the previous example differently, you are probably right. When you have high consistency among different coders about the appropriate codes, you have **intercoder reliability.** Intercoder reliability is a type of inter-rater reliability (discussed in Chapter 4; also see Miles & Huberman, 1994, p. 64). Intercoder reliability adds to the objectivity of the research, and it reduces errors due to inconsistencies among coders. Achieving high consistency requires training and a good deal of practice. **Intracoder reliability** is also important. That is, it is also important that each individual coder be consistent. To help you remember the difference between intercoder reliability and intracoder reliability, remember that the prefix inter- means "between" and the prefix intra- means "within." Therefore, intercoder reliability means reliability, or consistency, between or across coders, and intracoder reliability means reliability within a single coder. If the authors of qualitative research articles that you read address the issues of inter- and intracoder reliability, you should upgrade your evaluation of their research.

TABLE 15.2   Unordered List of Responses to the Open-Ended Question, What are some specific problems needing action in your organization?

Participant Responses

There is not enough space for everyone.
Our office furniture is dated and needs replacing.
We need a better cleaning service for the office.
We need more objective recruitment and hiring standards.
We need objective performance appraisal and reward systems.
We need consistent application of policy.
There are leadership problems.
Nonproductive staff members should not be retained.
Each department has stereotypes of the other departments.
Decisions are often based on inaccurate information.
We need more opportunities for advancement here.
Our product is not consistent because there are too many styles.
There is too much gossiping and criticizing.
Responsibility at various levels are unclear.
We need a suggestion box.
We need more computer terminals.
There is a lot of "us and them" sentiment here.
There is a lack of attention to individual needs.
There is favoritism and preferential treatment of staff.
More training is needed at all levels.
There needs to be better assessment of employee ability and performance so
     that promotions can be more objectively based.
Training is needed for new employees.
Many employees are carrying the weight of other untrained employees.
This office is "turf" oriented.
There is a pecking order at every level and within every level.
Communication needs improving.
Certain departments are put on a pedestal.
There are too many review levels for our product.
Too many signatures are required.
There is a lot of overlap and redundancy.
The components of our office work against one another rather than as a team.

If you want to code your own data and develop category names, you should start with words that describe the content of the segments of data. You will often want the category name to be more abstract than the literal text so that the same category name can be applied to other similar instances of the phenomenon that you encounter as you read more text. For example, in Table 15.3 the category name "physical environment" was used rather than "office furniture" so that other aspects of the physical environment, in addition to office furniture, could be included in the category. This ability comes with practice. You might not get the best category name on your first try. If you don't, all you have to do is generate a new category name and use the new category name on the transcripts. When you actually code some written text, you will find that this process of coding is easier than you might think.

TABLE 15.3   Categorization of Responses to the Open-Ended Question, What are some specific problems needing action in your organization?

Inductive Categories	*Participant Responses*
Management issues	There are leadership problems.
	We need a suggestion box.
	There is a lack of attention to individual needs.
	There is favoritism and preferential treatment of staff.
	Decisions are often based on inaccurate information.
	We need consistent application of policy.
Physical environment	We need a better cleaning service for the office.
	Our office furniture is dated and needs replacing.
	We need more computer terminals.
	There is not enough space for everyone.
Personnel practices	We need more objective recruitment and hiring standards.
	We need objective performance appraisal and reward systems.
	Nonproductive staff members should not be retained.
	There needs to be better assessment of employee ability and performance so that promotions can be more objectively based.
Employee development	More training is needed at all levels.
	Training is needed for new employees.
	Many employees are carrying the weight of other untrained employees.
	We need more opportunities for advancement here.
Intergroup and interpersonal relations	This office is "turf" oriented.
	There is a lot of "us and them" sentiment here.
	There is a pecking order at every level and within every level.
	Communication needs improving.
	There is too much gossiping and criticizing.
	Certain departments are put on a pedestal.
	Each department has stereotypes of the other departments.
Work structure	There are too many review levels for our product.
	Too many signatures are required.
	Responsibility at various levels are unclear
	The components of our office work against one another rather than as a team.
	There is a lot of overlap and redundancy.
	Our product is not consistent because there are too many styles.

Full descriptive words or phrases are not always used in coding. Some researchers prefer to use abbreviations of category names as their codes. Using abbreviations can save time as compared to writing out full category names every time a category appears in the data. Other researchers develop complex symbol systems for coding their data. When you code some data for yourself you must decide whether you want to use full words, phrases, abbreviations, or a complex symbolic coding system.

An example of data coded using a symbolic coding system is shown in Table 15.4. The transcript is an excerpt from an observational study done by educational ethnographer Margaret LeCompte, who was studying norms in the elementary school classroom. LeCompte placed the time in the left column every five minutes or when an activity changed. She placed teacher talk in quotes and placed student talk and information recorded by the researcher in parentheses. The type of activity is indicated in the left margin. The code R stands for teacher talk that establishes rules; the code T stands for teacher talk focused on organizing a time schedule for the students; and the code W stands for teacher talk that is focused on student tasks or student work. Although the codes used in the table are not very clear to the outside reader, they had very precise meaning to LeCompte. LeCompte inductively developed her coding system early in her research study and she used it in her later data analysis.

TABLE 15.4   Symbolic Coding System Used on Field Note Transcript

(Children are playing outside the classroom; a few are standing on the porch. The teacher arrives.)

8:55			"Come in, girls first." (There's some messing
8:57			around before they line up.) (They come in and
		T2A	move toward their seats.) (T2A) "Mrs. Smith is
	Getting		ready to start." (She's sitting on the desk in the
	settled	R1A	front of the room.) (R1A) "Mrs. Smith is
		R2B	waiting." (R2B) "I like the way Bernie is sitting
		R1A	down, and Atocha." (R1A) "Please, people, do
		R4B	not throw snowballs at one another." (R4B)
			"There isn't enough snow on the ground and you
			pick up rocks with it. If we have a lot of snow
			we'll have a snowball fight, but please don't
			throw the snow when there isn't much . . ."
		R4A	(R4A) "If you go along with me and don't throw
			now, as soon as there's good stuff we'll have a
		R4B	snowball fight." (R4B) "It isn't just that you hurt
			people, but you'll get in trouble too."
		T2A	(T2A) "All right, the girls will go to bake cookies
9:03		W1B	at recess." (W1B) "Boys, come back here if you
			aren't done; if you can't work alone you can go
	Getting	W2B	into Mrs. Dvorak's game room." (W2B) "I expect
	organized		if you come in here to work I expect you to
		R1A	work." (R1A) "I want everybody to bring a nickel
			by Monday." (Is it for the girl's surprise?) "No,
			it's for everybody."

Note: Teacher talk is recorded in quotations; pupil talk and locational description are enclosed in parentheses. From M. D. LeCompte, J. Preissle, and R. Tesch, *Ethnography and Qualitative Design in Educational Research,* p. 260, copyright © 1993 by Academic Press. Reprinted by permission of Academic Press and the authors.

Inductive and A Priori Codes

Inductive codes
Codes generated by a researcher by directly examining the data

Because of the inductive nature of most qualitative research, qualitative researchers typically generate their codes or category names directly from their data. When you develop codes this way, you are actually generating **inductive codes,** which are defined as codes that are generated by the researcher by directly examining the data during the coding process. Inductive codes can be based on emic terms (terms that are used by the participants themselves). For example, high school students might use the emic term "jocks" to refer to students who play sports. Inductive codes can also be based on social science terms that a researcher is familiar with. For example, a social science term for "jocks" might be "athletic role." Finally, inductive codes may be good, clear descriptive words that most people would agree characterize a segment of data (e.g., we might agree that the segment of data refers to athletes).

A priori codes
Codes developed before examining the current data

Sometimes researchers bring an already developed coding scheme to the research project. These codes are called **a priori codes** because they were developed before or at the very beginning of the current research study. A priori codes are used when a researcher is trying to replicate or extend a certain line of previous research. Researchers may also establish some a priori codes before data collection based on their relevance to the research questions. When researchers bring a priori codes to a research study, they come in with a start list of codes—an already developed master list that they can use for coding. During coding, however, the researcher should apply these codes only when they clearly fit segments of data. The codes should not be forced onto the data, and new codes should be generated when data segments are found that do not fit any of the codes on the list.

Co-Occurring and Facesheet Codes

Co-occurring codes
Codes that partially or completely overlap

In our discussion so far we have used just one descriptive category for any given segment of data. If you code transcripts, however, it is very possible that the codes will overlap. In other words, more than one topic or category may be applied to the same set of data. If the categories are intertwined, you simply allow the codes to naturally overlap, and the result is what is called co-occurring codes. **Co-occurring codes** are sets of codes (i.e., two or more codes) that partially or completely overlap. Co-occurring codes may merely show conceptual redundancy in coding (i.e., the two codes mean basically the same thing). More interestingly, co-occurring codes may suggest a relationship among categories within a set of text for a single individual (e.g., an interview transcript) or across multiple sets of text for different individuals (i.e., across several interview transcripts).

An example of co-occurring codes within an individual's transcript is shown in Table 15.5. If you look at the text in the table, you will see that "mood" is the category marking lines 8–13, "positive" is the category for lines 11–20, "like" is the category for lines 16–20, "don't like" is the category for lines 21–29, "miss" is the category for lines 30–40, and "they" is the category for lines 32–34. As you can see, some of these categories overlap. More specifically, lines 32 through 34 are coded with two co-occurring codes. The two codes "miss" and "they" co-occur for these three lines. Also, lines 16–20 are coded with the codes "like" and "positive." Therefore, these are also co-occurring codes. The key point to remember is that you can allow codes to overlap when coding data.

TABLE 15.5   Text with Overlapping Codes

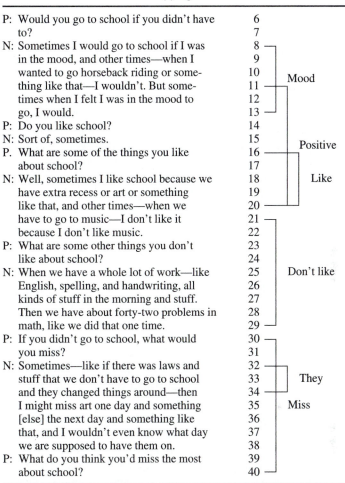

P: Would you go to school if you didn't have	6
to?	7
N: Sometimes I would go to school if I was	8
in the mood, and other times—when I	9
wanted to go horseback riding or some-	10
thing like that—I wouldn't. But some-	11
times when I felt I was in the mood to	12
go, I would.	13
P: Do you like school?	14
N: Sort of, sometimes.	15
P. What are some of the things you like	16
about school?	17
N: Well, sometimes I like school because we	18
have extra recess or art or something	19
like that, and other times—when we	20
have to go to music—I don't like it	21
because I don't like music.	22
P: What are some other things you don't	23
like about school?	24
N: When we have a whole lot of work—like	25
English, spelling, and handwriting, all	26
kinds of stuff in the morning and stuff.	27
Then we have about forty-two problems in	28
math, like we did that one time.	29
P: If you didn't go to school, what would	30
you miss?	31
N: Sometimes—like if there was laws and	32
stuff that we don't have to go to school	33
and they changed things around—then	34
I might miss art one day and something	35
[else] the next day and something like	36
that, and I wouldn't even know what day	37
we are supposed to have them on.	38
P: What do you think you'd miss the most	39
about school?	40

Codes in the right margin: Mood (lines 8–13), Positive (lines 16–20), Like (lines 16–20), Don't like (lines 21–29), They (lines 32–34), Miss (lines 30–40).

From M. D. LeCompte, J. Preissle, and R. Tesch, *Ethnography and Qualitative Design in Educational Research,* p. 294, copyright © 1993 by Academic Press. Reprinted by permission of Academic Press and the authors.

A researcher can also attach codes to an entire document, interview, or set of lines. For example, lines 6–40 in Table 15.5 (i.e., all the given lines) could have been given a code such as "school" because that was the topic of discussion in all of the lines. If you had several interview transcripts, you might decide to attach the code "female" or "male" to each transcript to signify the participant's gender. Codes that apply to a complete document or case (e.g., to an interview) are called **facesheet codes.** The origin of the term facesheet probably comes from researchers attaching a sheet of paper to each transcript with codes listed that apply to the whole transcript. Demographic variables are frequently used as

Facesheet codes
Codes that apply
to a complete
document or case

facesheet codes (e.g., gender, age, race, occupation, school). Researchers may later decide to sort their data files by facesheet codes to search for group differences (e.g., differences between older and younger teachers) or other relationships in the data.

ENUMERATION

Enumeration
The process of
quantifying data

We have talked about the importance of transcribing data, and we have shown you the basics of assigning codes to qualitative data. At this point, a data analyst may decide to determine how frequently words or coded categories appear in the data. This process of quantifying data is called **enumeration.** Weber (1990), for example, reports the word frequencies used in the 1980 Democratic and Republican platforms. The five most common words in the Democratic platform were *our* (430 occurrences), *must* (321), *Democratic* (226), *federal* (177), and *support* (144). The most common words in the Republican platform were *our* (347), *their* (161), *administration* (131), *government* (128), and *Republican* (126). Word or code frequencies can help researchers determine the importance of words and ideas. Listing frequencies can also help in identifying prominent themes in the data (e.g., What kinds of things did the participants say many times?).

When numbers are reported in qualitative research reports, you must always be sure to check the basis of the numbers being used or you may be misled. For example, in the Democratic and Republican platform example, the basis was all words in the document (e.g., 144 of the words in the Democratic platform were *support*). A number such as this simply points out the emphasis placed on a word by the writer of the document. If several interview transcripts are analyzed, the basis of a reported number might be the number of words mentioned by all of the participants. If a word had a high frequency in this case, you might be inclined to believe that most of the participants used the word frequently. However, a high frequency of a particular word could also mean that a single participant used the particular word many times. In other words, a word might have a large frequency simply because one or two research participants used the word many times, not because a large number of different participants used the word. So remember this warning: all numbers are not created equally. Enumeration can be helpful in qualitative data analysis, but always be careful to recognize the kinds of numbers that are being reported.

CREATING HIERARCHICAL CATEGORY SYSTEMS

Categories are the basic building blocks of qualitative data analysis because qualitative researchers make sense of their data by identifying and studying the categories that appear in their data. You can generally think of the set of categories for a collection of data as forming a classification system characterizing those data. Rather than having to think about each sentence or each word in the data, the researcher will, after coding the data, be able to focus on the themes and relationships suggested by the classification system. You learned earlier how to find categories in qualitative data, and you also learned that you may want to count these categories for suggestive themes.

Sometimes categories can be organized into different levels. That is, a set of subcategories may fall beneath a certain category, and that certain category may itself fall under an even higher level category. Think about the category called fruit. In this case some possible subcategories are oranges, grapefruit, kiwi, apples, and bananas. These are subcategories of fruit because they are "part of" or "types of" the higher level category called fruit. The category fruit may itself be a subcategory of yet a higher category called food group. Systems of categories like this are called hierarchies because they are layered or fall into different levels.

An example of a hierarchical classification system can be found in a research article by Frontman and Kunkel (1994). These researchers were interested in when and how counselors believed a session with a client was successful. They interviewed sixty-nine mental health workers from various mental health fields, including counseling psychology, clinical psychology, marriage and family therapy, social work, and school psychology. After an initial session with a client, the participants filled out an open-ended questionnaire asking them to describe what they felt was successful in the session. A team of researchers analyzed the transcripts and came up with a rather elaborate hierarchical classification system. Frontman and Kunkel report that they developed their hierarchy in a bottom-up fashion, which means that the lowest level categories are the closest to the actual data collected in the study. This bottom-up, or inductive, strategy is the most common approach used by qualitative researchers (Weitzman & Miles, 1995).

We have reproduced a small part of Frontman and Kunkel's classification system in Figure 15.1 to give you a feel for hierarchical coding. When looking at the figure, be sure to realize that many of the categories in Frontman and Kunkel's hierarchical system are left out; the downward arrows indicate where additional levels and categories were excluded. All forty-four categories in their full hierarchical classification system are given in the article.

You can see that the higher levels of the hierarchy shown in Figure 15.1 are more general than the lower levels. That is, a higher level category includes or subsumes the categories falling under it. The highest level of the hierarchy in Figure 15.1 includes the very general categories called positive awareness and collaboration. Frontman and Kunkel tell us that they decided near the conclusion of their research project that these two general categories subsumed the sets of categories falling below them. At the second highest level of the hierarchy in Figure 15.1, you can see that the researchers categorized counselors' construal of success into five categories. The five categories with brief explanations are as follows.

1. Client display of strengths ("The skills, actions, and characteristics expressed by the client that the counselor connotes as indication of success.")
2. Counselor self-evaluation of performance ("Counselor assesses success through evaluating the quality of his or her performance during the session.")
3. Adherence to desired interactional norms ("Success is determined by the presence of particular interactional patterns in the session.")
4. Establishment of rapport ("Success defined as indication that rapport between counselor and client is being established.")

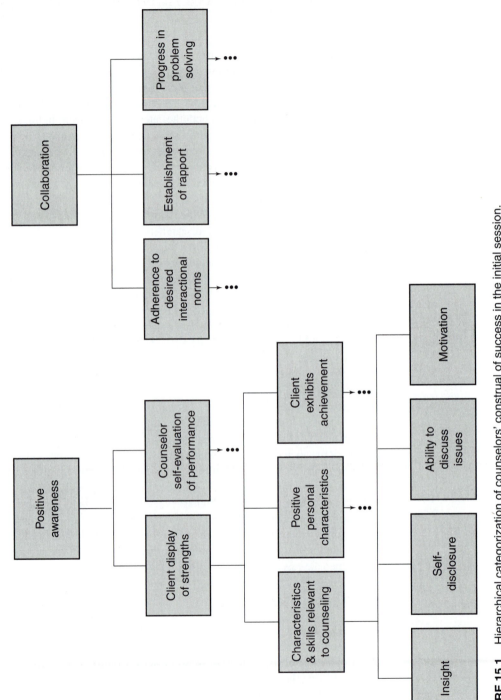

FIGURE 15.1 Hierarchical categorization of counselors' construal of success in the initial session.

5.   Progress in problem solving ("Success is attributed to client making progress toward establishing and implementing direct steps in solving a problem.") (Frontman & Kunkel, 1994, pp. 498–499).

The first two of the five categories we just listed are part of positive awareness, and the last three are part of collaboration. At the second lowest level of the hierarchy, we provide the categories falling under client display of strengths. At the lowest level of the hierarchy we show the categories falling under characteristics and skills relevant to counseling. As you can see, there are a total of four levels in the hierarchy shown in Figure 15.1. We find Frontman and Kunkel's hierarchy interesting because it provides a direct picture of the hierarchical structure of their data. Plus it is interesting to see what counselors believe makes therapy successful.

SHOWING RELATIONSHIPS AMONG CATEGORIES

In this section we show you some ways to explore relationships in qualitative research data. When qualitative researchers use the term *relationship,* they have a slightly different meaning than when quantitative researchers use the term. You learned in earlier chapters that quantitative researchers focus their efforts on examining the relationships among variables. Qualitative researchers, however, attach a much broader meaning to the term *relationship*. They use the term to refer to many different kinds of relations or connections between things, including but not limited to variables. This is not better or worse, it is just different.

A summary of several kinds of relationships identified by one well-known qualitative researcher named James Spradley (1979) is given in Table 15.6. Take a moment to examine the nine relationships because you might identify some of these relationships when you are reading transcripts or when you are examining categories generated from your data. Spradley's list is not exhaustive, but it is suggestive. You will undoubtedly find additional kinds of relationships if you analyze some transcribed data.

Suppose you were reading an interview transcript and you came across the following text: "When I just ignore Johnny's acting out, he becomes more aggressive toward the other

TABLE 15.6   Spradley's Universal Semantic Relationships

Title	*Form of Relationship*
1. Strict inclusion	X is a kind of Y
2. Spatial	X is a place in Y; X is a part of Y
3. Cause-effect	X is a result of Y; X is a cause of Y
4. Rationale	X is a reason for doing Y
5. Location for action	X is a place for doing Y
6. Function	X is used for Y
7. Means-end	X is a way to do Y
8. Sequence	X is a step (stage) in Y
9. Attribution	X is an attribute (characteristic) of Y

Adapted from J. P. Spradley, 1979, p. 111. Used by permission.

students in my classroom. But if I walk over and stand beside him, he will usually quiet down for a little while." This text suggests a possible causal process operating among several categories. (In Table 15.6, this is called a cause-effect relationship.) It is suggested, in particular, that ignoring Johnny's behavioral outbursts results in aggressive behavior, and proximity results in less aggressive behavior. Obviously, two sentences like this in a transcript do not provide solid evidence of a general cause-and-effect relationship; however, statements like this do have a causal form, and they may suggest that you do additional analysis and data collection to further explore the relationship.

Now recall the hierarchical categorization we showed you in Figure 15.1. If you look at the figure again you will see that one of the categories was "characteristics and skills relevant to counseling." That category has four characteristics falling under it. They are insight, self-disclosure, ability to discuss issues, and motivation. You can view these four subcategories as following Spradley's strict inclusion relationship because they are "kinds of" characteristics or skills. Strict inclusion is a very common form of relationship in qualitative data analysis.

Typology
A classification system that breaks something down into different types or kinds

Educational researchers often use the term *typology* to refer to categories that follow Spradley's strict inclusion form of relationship. A **typology** is a classification system that breaks something down into its different types or kinds. A typology is basically the same thing as a taxonomy. You may remember what a taxonomy is from your high school or college biology class. (Okay, I know it has been a long time!) In biology, the levels of the animal taxonomy are kingdom, phylum, class, order, family, genus, and species. (Here's a memory aid: **K**ings **P**lay **C**hess **O**n **F**iber **G**lass **S**tools.) Bailey (1994) points out that "the term *taxonomy* is more generally used in the biological sciences, while *typology* is used in the social sciences" (p. 6). Typologies are useful because they help make sense out of qualitative data.

Typologies can be simple or complex. You might, for example, be interested in the different types of cliques in schools, types of teaching strategies used by teachers, or types of student lifestyles. These would be fairly simple, one-dimensional typologies. At a more complex level, you could view the hierarchical classification in Figure 15.1 as one big typology, showing the types of counselors' construal of success. To construct a typology it is helpful to construct mutually exclusive and exhaustive categories. **Mutually exclusive categories** are categories that are clearly separate or distinct; they do not overlap. **Exhaustive categories** classify all the relevant cases in your data. Exhaustiveness of categories can be difficult in qualitative research because some cases simply don't fit into a typology. However, the more cases that fit into your typology, the better.

Mutually exclusive categories
A set of categories that are separate or distinct

Exhaustive categories
A set of categories that classify all of the relevant cases in the data

Another interesting typology was constructed by Patton (1990) when he was helping a group of high school teachers develop a student dropout prevention program. Patton observed and interviewed teachers, and here is what he found.

> The inductive analysis of the data suggested that teachers' behaviors toward dropouts could be conceptualized along a continuum according to the extent to which teachers were willing to take direct responsibility for doing something about the problem. This dimension varied from taking responsibility to shifting responsibility to others. The second dimension concerned the teachers' views about the effective intervention strategies. The inductive analysis revealed three perspectives

among the teachers. Some teachers believed that a rehabilitation effort was needed to help kids with their problems; some teachers preferred a maintenance or care-taking effort aimed at just keeping the school running, that is, maintaining the system; and still other teachers favored finding some way of punishing students for their unacceptable and inappropriate behaviors, no longer letting them get away with the infractions they had been committing in the past. (pp. 411–412)

You can see from this quote that Patton found two simple or one-dimensional typologies that were related to dropout prevention: (1) teachers' beliefs about how to deal with drop-outs, and (2) teachers' behaviors toward dropouts.

Patton then decided to cross these two simple typologies into a two dimensional matrix to relate the two dimensions. When he did this, he found a typology that made a lot of sense to the teachers in the research study. The typology included six types of teacher roles in dealing with the high school dropout problem. The roles are shown in the six cells of the matrix in Figure 15.2. The different types of teacher roles shown in the figure are counselor/

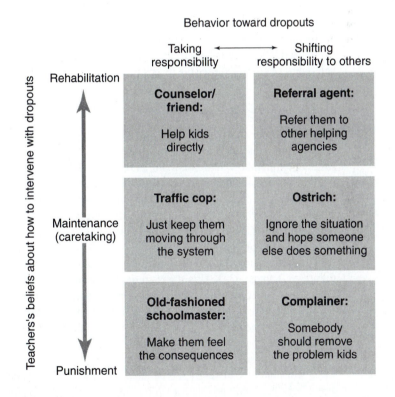

FIGURE 15.2 Patton's typology of teacher roles in dealing with high school dropouts. (Reprinted from M. Q. Patton, *Qualitative Evaluation and Research Methods,* p. 413, copyright © 1990 by Sage Publications, Inc. Reprinted by Permission of Sage Publications, Inc.)

friend, traffic cop, old-fashioned schoolmaster, referral agent, ostrich, and complainer. You may know some of these kinds of teachers at your own school. Remember: when analyzing qualitative data, you can sometimes find new and interesting information by cross-classifying two or more dimensions.

Now let's look at an example of Spradley's "sequence" type of relationship (Table 15.6). This example comes from an article titled, "A Framework for Describing Developmental Change among Older Adults," by Fisher (1993). Fisher pursued this research because he was interested in determining whether older adulthood could be categorized into a set of meaningful stages. He decided not to rely on the stages presented in popular developmental psychology books because many of these lists were dated. Also, some of these lists lumped all older people into a single developmental stage called old age. Fisher decided that he wanted to explore the concept of old age using qualitative research.

Fisher conducted in-depth interviews with seventy-four older adults whose ages ranged from sixty-one to ninety-four years old. Using in-depth, open-ended interviews, he asked his participants what kinds of experiences they had in their lives. An interesting theme in his research findings was a tendency by all of the older adults toward adaptation to their life circumstances, no matter what the circumstances were. Fisher also generated five core categories from his data that could be ordered by time. These categories resulted in the following sequence of old age: (1) continuity with middle age, (2) early transition, (3) revised lifestyle, (4) later transition, and (5) final period. You can see the defining characteristics of each of these five stages in Table 15.7.

Drawing Diagrams

Diagraming
Making a sketch, drawing, or outline to show how something works or to clarify the relationship between the parts of a whole

A useful tool for showing the relationships among categories is called **diagramming** (i.e., making diagrams). A diagram is "a plan, sketch, drawing, or outline designed to demonstrate or explain how something works or to clarify the relationship between the parts of a whole" (American Heritage Dictionary). Figures 15.1 and 15.2, which we discussed in the previous section, are examples of diagrams. Diagrams are very popular with visually oriented learners and can be used to effectively demonstrate relationships for the readers of reports. The use of diagrams can also be helpful during data analysis when you are trying to make sense out of your data.

An easily understood example of a diagram showing a complex process appears in Figure 11.2 (page 334). This diagram depicts a grounded theory about how departmental chairpersons at universities facilitate the growth and development of their faculty members. The diagram shows that the career stage of the faculty member determines the type of faculty issue chairpersons are concerned with, and the faculty issue determines the specific strategy a chairperson uses in working with a faculty member. The diagram also lists the outcomes resulting from applying the strategies.

Network diagram
A diagram showing the direct links between variables or events over time

A similar type of diagram is called a network diagram. A **network diagram** shows the direct links between variables or events over time (Miles & Huberman, 1994). An example of a network diagram is the path analysis diagram that appears in Figure 10.4 (page 305). The path analysis diagram was based on quantitative research. However, network diagrams can also be based on qualitative data. Qualitative researchers often use these diagrams to depict

TABLE 15.7   Categories Ordered by Time

Category I: Continuity with Middle Age

Characteristics: Retirement plans pursued
Middle-age lifestyle continued
Other activities substituted for work

Category II: Early Transition

Characteristics: Involuntary transitional events
Voluntary transitional events
End of continuity with middle age

Category III: Revised Lifestyle

Characteristics: Adaptation to changes of early transition
Stable lifestyle appropriate to older adulthood
Socialization realized through age-group affiliation

Category IV: Later Transition

Characteristics: Loss of health and mobility
Need for assistance and/or care
Loss of autonomy

Category V: Final Period

Characteristics: Adaptation to changes of later transition
Stable lifestyle appropriate to level of dependency
Sense of finitude, mortality

Adapted from Fisher, J. C. (1993). A framework for describing developmental change among older adults. *Adult Education Quarterly 43*(2), 81.

their thinking about potential causal relationships. We included an example of a part of a network diagram based on qualitative data in Figure 15.3. This diagram is based on a school innovation and improvement study by Miles and Huberman (1994). According to the diagram, low internal funds in school districts resulted in high environmental turbulence in those districts (e.g., a shortage of money resulted in uncertain operating conditions for principals). This resulted in low stability for the leaders of the various school improvement programs and in low stability for the program staff. As a result of this instability, job mobility was high.

To learn more about causal network diagrams, you should take a look at Miles and Huberman (1994). They provide an extensive discussion of the issues surrounding causal analysis in qualitative research, and they discuss how to develop causal networks based on a single case or on multiple cases. If you are interested in cause-and-effect relationships with qualitative data, you should also review Chapter 7 on research validity in this book, especially the section on validity in qualitative research. Miles and Huberman (1994) also discuss how to construct many different kinds of interesting matrices (i.e., classifications of two or more dimensions) to aid in the analysis and presentation of qualitative research data.

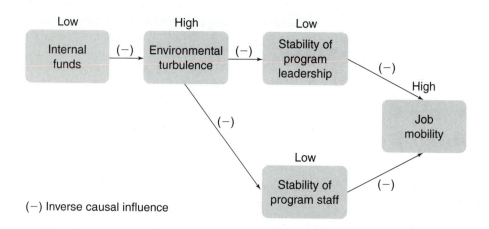

FIGURE 15.3   Network diagram for job mobility. (Reprinted from M. B. Miles and A. M. Huberman, *Qualitative Data Analysis: An Expanded Source Book,* p. 231, copyright © 1994 by Sage Publications, Inc. Reprinted by Permission of Sage Publications, Inc.)

COMPUTER PROGRAMS FOR QUALITATIVE DATA ANALYSIS

Qualitative researchers are just beginning to capitalize on the possibilities for computer use in the analysis of qualitative data. Although qualitative researchers have been using word processors for transcribing and editing their data for quite some time, it has been only during the last decade that a number of qualitative data analysis computer programs have readily become available. The developers of these programs examined the procedures that qualitative researchers follow when making sense of their data and then developed programs that help automate these procedures. Before we examine the potential of using qualitative data analysis programs, we will look at how qualitative researchers have traditionally made sense of their data without these programs.

Qualitative researchers traditionally use a filing system approach to data analysis. They begin their data analysis by transcribing their data and making copies of the various data documents. Then they hand code the data in the left margin of these copies. After this, researchers make copies of the coded data and cut the data into segments of text with the marked codes. Then a filing system is created and used, with one folder reserved for each code. The segments of text are placed into their appropriate folder. If a segment of text has more than one code then more than one copy of the segment is made, and a copy of the segment is placed in all the relevant folders. This way, all the folders contain all the appropriate data segments. At this point researchers can reread the segments of text in each folder, looking for themes occurring in the data.

More complex analyses require even more work when done by hand. For example, searching for two co-occurring codes typically requires making a folder with the two codes as its title, locating the two individual code folders, and then checking the text segments in those folders to see whether they include both codes in the left margin. If both codes are present, the segment of text is copied and placed into the new two-code folder. As you can see, complex data analysis by hand can be time consuming and quite difficult. Perhaps this is one reason why qualitative data analysis has not advanced as rapidly as has quantitative data analysis. Because of the increasing use of computer programs, however, we predict that the analysis of qualitative data will take a giant step forward during the next decade. One reason for our prediction is that procedures that are highly time consuming when done by hand are available with just a few keystrokes on the computer. So that you have a basic idea about the potential of computer data analysis, we list a few of the capabilities of qualitative data analysis computer programs.

Qualitative data analysis programs can be used to do virtually everything discussed in this chapter. They can, for example, be used to store and code your data. During coding, most programs allow complex hierarchical classification systems such as the one shown in Figure 15.1 to be developed. Most programs allow the use of many different kinds of codes, including co-occurring and facesheet codes. Enumeration is easily done with just a few clicks of the computer mouse. Many programs allow you to attach memos or annotations to the codes or data documents so you can record the important thoughts you have during analysis. Some programs will produce graphics that can be used in presenting the data. Finally, the heart and soul of most qualitative data analysis programs is their searching capabilities, the topic to which we now turn.

You can perform simple or complex searches using computer packages that use Boolean operators. **Boolean operators** are words used to create logical combinations based on basic laws of thought. We all use Boolean operators every day when we think and talk about things. Some common Boolean operators we all use are AND, OR, NOT, IF, THEN, and EXCEPT. Qualitative data analysis computer programs are written so that you can search your data or a set of codes using these and many other operators.

Boolean operators
Words used to create logical combinations

You might, for example, search the codes or text in a set of interview transcripts concerning teacher satisfaction using the following string of words: "male AND satisfied AND first grade." The Boolean operator AND is called the intersection operator because it finds all intersections of the words or codes. This search would locate all instances of male, first grade teachers, who were satisfied. Similarly, you could search for female teachers using this string of words: "female AND teacher." You can find disconfirming cases (instances that do not have any of the characteristics) by adding the word NOT to the search command (e.g., NOT teacher will find all nonteacher instances).

Another operator is the OR, or union, operator. This operator finds all instances that take on any one of the provided words or codes. For example, if you searched a document with the command "female OR first grade" you would come up with instances that are either "female" or "first grade" or both. Another kind of search command is called FOLLOWED-BY in one popular program. Using this you can find instances in which two codes occur in a specific order in the data (e.g., punishment FOLLOWED-BY quiet behavior). As you can see, you can do a lot of different kinds of searches using Boolean operators.

There are many qualitative data analysis computer programs currently available. The three most popular programs are NUD*IST (this stands for **N**onnumerical, **U**nstructured

Data **I**ndexing, **S**earching, and **T**heorizing, not what you were thinking about!), the Ethnograph, and ATLAS. There are many others. If you ever need to learn more about these or related programs, take a look at the book by Weitzman and Miles (1995), titled *Computer Programs for Qualitative Data Analysis.* Weitzman and Miles describe the features of many different programs, list the program costs, and include the addresses, phone numbers, and Internet addresses of the companies selling the programs. Most of the companies will also send you a demonstration copy or allow you to download one from their Internet site free of charge.[1] If you decide you are interested in a qualitative data analysis program, testing out a demonstration copy is an excellent way to find out which program best suits your particular needs. Most programs are available for the Mac or IBM-compatible computers.

We conclude by listing some of the advantages and disadvantages of using computer programs for the analysis of qualitative data. The advantages are that qualitative data analysis computer programs can help in storing and organizing data, they can be used for all of the analyses discussed in this chapter plus many more, they can reduce the time required to analyze data (e.g., an analysis procedure that takes a lot of time by hand may take virtually no time with a computer program), and they can make procedures available to you that are rarely done by hand because they are either too time consuming or too complex. Some disadvantages are that computer programs can take time to learn, they cost money and require computer availability, and they can become dated. The biggest disadvantage is startup time. Nonetheless, if you are planning on doing a lot of qualitative data analysis for an extended period of time, we recommend the use of computer programs.

SUMMARY

Qualitative data analysis typically involves the analysis of text from interview or field note transcripts. Some basic procedures in qualitative data analysis are transcribing data, reading and rereading transcripts (i.e., immersing yourself in your data to understand what is going on), segmenting and coding the data, counting words and coded categories (enumeration), searching for relationships and themes in the data, and generating diagrams to help in interpreting the data. The goal of data analysis is to be able to clearly summarize your data and generate inductive theories based on the data. Some questions you might ask of your data are: What themes occurred in your interviews or field notes? What topics were mentioned most often? What issues were most important to the people in your study? What are the cultural characteristics of the people in your research study? How do your participants view the topic of your research? What kinds of relationships (e.g., strict inclusion, cause-effect, function, sequence) are apparent in your data? How can the categories identified in the data be ordered into meaningful grounded theories? The questions you can ask are virtually unlimited and they will vary depending on your research problem, the type of qualitative research you are conducting (e.g., phenomenology, ethnography, case study, grounded theory, historical), and your own theoretical perspective based on your disciplinary training. Qualitative data analysis computer programs can aid in the analysis of qualitative data but they do take quite a bit of time to learn.

STUDY QUESTIONS

1. What is interim analysis?
2. What is memoing?
3. Why is it important to transcribe qualitative data when possible?
4. What is the difference between segmenting and coding?
5. What is the difference between inductive and a priori codes?
6. What is the difference between co-occurring and facesheet codes?
7. Explain the process of enumeration.
8. What is a hierarchical category system, and why can it be useful to construct hierarchical systems?
9. How do qualitative researchers show relationships among categories?
10. How are network diagrams used in qualitative research?
11. What are some of the capabilities of computer programs for data analysis?
12. What are two of the leading qualitative data analysis computer programs?

EXERCISES

1. Analyze the following data. The data are transcribed field notes from a classroom observation done in Mexico City by Robert Stake. As you code the data, be on the lookout for answers to the following questions: What topics appeared in the text? What was the context of the classroom like? What teaching style did the instructor use? Explain this teaching style. What were some of the norms of the classroom (e.g., arrival to class, speaking out in class)? What was the content of the lesson? What was the political persuasion of the students and/or teacher? What kinds of instructional materials were used in the classroom? After you finish coding the text, write a brief summary report on the observation, answering the questions just posed and adding any additional insights that emerge as you code the data.

    Class Notes, October 23[2]
    The temperature will climb into the 70's today, but now it is chilly in this white tile and terrazzo classroom. Eleven students (of 29 still on the roster) are here, each in a jacket or sweater. No doubt it was cooler still when they left home. The instructor, Senor Pretelin, reminds them of the topic, the Origins of Capitalism, and selects a question for which they have prepared

answers. An answer from the back row is ventured. Two more students arrive—it is ten past the hour—now four more.—Senor Pretelin undertakes a correction of the answer, but asks for still more of an answer. His style is casual. He draws long on a cigarette. His audience is alert.—Marx is a presence, spoken in name, and looming from the cover of the textbook. Two books only are in sight. Several students have photocopies of the chapter assigned.—The chalkboard remains filled with last class's logic symbols, now unnoticed. Some students read through their answers, most concentrate on what Pretelin says about answers that are offered.—The first answers had been volunteered by males, now one from a female. The instructor draws her out, more of her idea, then improves upon the explanation himself.

—The coolness of the space is warmed by the exchanges.—Outside a power mower sputters, struggling with a thickness of grass for which it probably was not designed.—It is 20 past the hour. Another student arrives. Most are around 20, all have black hair. These are incoming freshmen in the social studies and humanities program, enrolled in a sociology course on political doctrines. Still another arrives. She pushes the door closed, and jams it with a chair, to thwart the breeze from the squared-out plaza.—Senor Pretelin is expanding an answer at length. He then turns to another question, lights another cigarette while awaiting a volunteer—again he asks for improvement, gets a couple of tries; then answers the question to his satisfaction. Another question. He patiently awaits student initiative. The students appear to think or read to themselves what they had written earlier.

—The haze of Mexico City shrouds the city-center several miles to the southeast. Yesterday's downpour did not long cleanse the sky.—Quiet again while awaiting a volunteer. The first young woman offers her answer. She is the only female of the seven or so students who have ventured forth. Heads nod to her reference to the camposinos, and to Pretelin's amplification. There seems to be an empathy for these abstract, at least distant, camposinos. If capitalistic advocacy exists in this classroom it does not speak out. A half hour has passed. The recital continues. Only a few students are correcting their notes (or creating them belatedly), most try to read or listen. Minds are mobilized, not idling. Finally a small wedge of humor.

—The air may relax a bit.—Four observers are dispersed about the room, little noticed even as they write. The instructor maintains his task, not ever stopping to take roll. Pretelin is a slight man, perhaps 40. He wears a smart jacket, a dark shirt buttoned high, a gold neck-chain. His fingers are long and expressive.—For several minutes, the dragging of heavy objects outside the room interferes.—For a last time the students are sent to their answers, even asked to look further. Few have books. Then the students are invited to pose questions. The exchange becomes more good natured, but business-like still. The engagement goes on, minds "full on," provoked sociably, heads nodding agreement.—More immediate camposinos, now drawn 17 million strong to the streets below, make the noises of the city. A poster admonishes: "Admon. Vota. Platestda." Near the door the graffiti begins "La ignorancia mata. . . ." The hour draws to a close, a final cigarette, a summary, a warm smile.

KEY TERMS

a priori codes (432)

Boolean operators (443)

coding (427)

co-occurring codes (432)

diagramming (440)

enumeration (434)

exhaustive categories (438)

facesheet codes (433)

inductive codes (432)

intercoder reliability (428)

interim analysis (425)

intracoder reliability (428)

master list (428)

memoing (425)

mutually exclusive
   categories (438)

network diagram (440)

segmenting (426)

transcription (426)

typology (438)

ENDNOTES

1. The Internet address for the Ethnograph is *http://www.qualisresearch.com.* The address for QSR
   NUD*IST and ATLAS/ti is *http://www.scolari.com.*
2. Reprinted from Robert E. Stake, "Class Notes, October 23," *The Art of Case Study Research,*
   pp. 88-90, copyright © 1995 by Sage Publications, Inc. Reprinted by Permission of Sage Publications, Inc., and the author.

6
PART

WRITING THE RESEARCH REPORT

CHAPTER 16

Preparation of the Research Report

Throughout this book, we have been discussing the issues that must be considered while conducting both quantitative and qualitative research. If you follow the guidelines and suggestions we have presented, you should be able to conduct a good research study. However, researchers have a responsibility not only to conduct well-designed and well-executed research studies, but also to communicate the results of their study. You may have conducted a study that provides an answer to a very important research question, such as identifying the best way of teaching children with dyslexia to read, but its results are of no value unless they are made public and can be used by other educators. The primary mechanism for communicating the results of research studies is through professional journals. Table 16.1 lists some of the journals in which educational researchers publish.

After you have conducted a research study, you should consider preparing a research report and submitting it to a journal for publication. Prior to preparing the research report you should ask yourself whether the study is important enough to justify publication. Would others be interested in the results, and would it influence their work or have some educational impact? As a general rule you should never conduct a study you don't think is publishable. If the study is important and free from flaws that would preclude drawing unambiguous conclusions, you should proceed with the preparation of a research report.

The preparation of research reports differs somewhat depending on whether you conducted a quantitative or a qualitative research study. Remember that quantitative studies

TABLE 16.1 Journals Publishing the Results of Educational Research

American Educational Research Journal	Journal of Curriculum Studies
American Journal of Education	Journal of Education
Anthropology and Education Quarterly	Journal of Education for Students Placed at Risk
Applied Measurement in Education	
Art Education	Journal of Educational and Behavioral Statistics
Cambridge Journal of Education	
Child Development	Journal of Educational Research
Cognition and Instruction	Journal of Information Technology for Teacher Education
Creativity Research Journal	
Cross Cultural Psychology	Journal of In-service Education
Curriculum Studies	Journal of Literacy Research
Curriculum/Technology Quarterly	Journal of Negro Education
Early Childhood Education Journal	The Journal of Research in Science Teaching
Education and Urban Society	Journal of Vocational Education and Training
Education Action Research	
Educational Assessment	Kappa Delta Pi Record
Educational Evaluation and Policy Analysis	New Teacher Advocate
The Educational Forum	Oxford Studies in Comparative Education
Educational Policy	Phi Delta Kappan
Educational Psychologist	PROSPERO
Educational Psychology Review	Reading Research Quarterly
Educational Research and Evaluation	Research in Post-Compulsory Education
Educational Researcher	Research in the Teaching of English
Elementary School Journal	Review of Educational Research
FORUM: for promoting 3–19 comprehensive education	School Leadership and Management
	Teacher Development
Harvard Educational Review	Teacher Education Quarterly
International Studies in Sociology of Education	Teachers and Teaching: theory and practice
	Teachers College Record
Journal for Research in Mathematics Education	Teaching and Teacher Education
	Theory into Practice
Journal of Classroom Interaction	Urban Education
Journal of Curriculum and Supervision	The Urban Review

focus on hypothesis testing and are epitomized by experimental research studies focusing on objective observation under controlled conditions, with the data collected being reduced to numerical data. Qualitative studies are more often exploratory and bridge a variety of approaches or methods from ethnography to historical research. The qualitative data collected are frequently words, impressions, and discourse that are analyzed in terms of themes, hypotheses, or theories that often attempt to portray the fluid and dynamic aspect of behavior. Because of the different goals and approaches of quantitative and qualitative research, the approach to writing quantitative and qualitative research reports differs. We therefore focus first on quantitative research report writing and then on qualitative research report writing. However, prior to this discussion, we want to cover a number of general principles that must be adhered to when writing either type of research report.

GENERAL PRINCIPLES RELATED TO WRITING THE RESEARCH REPORT

Perhaps the overriding general principle that must be followed in writing the research report is that it must be prepared in a manner that clearly communicates to the reader. Good writing is a craft that requires thoughtful concern for the presentation and language used. Good writing is usually a developmental process acquired over time. Instruction in developing good writing is obviously not the purpose of this textbook or the course you are taking.

We discuss some of the general principles you should adhere to when preparing a research report, which are elaborated on in more detail in the APA publication manual (1994). If you have difficulty with writing, there are several books that can be very helpful. W. Strunk, Jr., and E. B. White's *The Elements of Style* is a classic and has the virtue of being short. Gage's *The Shape of Reason* and Rosnow and Rosnow's *Writing Papers in Psychology* are excellent and can be of assistance in writing clearly, as can the APA publication manual. Hult's book, *Researching and Writing in the Social Science,* and Becker's book, *Writing for Social Scientists,* are also excellent references.

Clear communication requires an orderly presentation of ideas. There must be a continuity of words, concepts, and thematic development from the beginning to the end of the report. This continuity can be achieved by the use of punctuation marks to show the relationship between ideas and by the use of transitional words, such as *then, next, therefore,* and *however.* Some transition words (for example, *while* and *since*) can create confusion and should be used cautiously. Because you are so familiar with the material you are reporting, objectivity is frequently lost and problems in clarity of communication are not immediately apparent. One good technique to use is to write the research report and then put it aside for several days before reading it again. A later reading of the report can uncover difficulties in clarity of communication.

Preparation of the research report requires a clarity of expression. This means that you should say only what needs to be said and avoid jargon, wordiness, and redundancy. For example, rather than using "at the present time," use "now." The phrase "absolutely essential" is redundant and can be reduced to "essential." These are only a few of the issues that need to be considered when preparing a clearly presented report. Other issues, such as the use of correct grammar, are presented in the APA publication manual.

Language

The language used to communicate the results of research should be free of demeaning attitudes and biased assumptions. There are three guidelines that should be followed to achieve this goal.

Specificity   When referring to a person or persons, you should choose accurate and clear words that are free from bias. When in doubt, err in the direction of being more rather than less specific. For example, if you are describing age groups, it is better to provide a specific age range (for example, *ages eight to twelve*) instead of a broad category such as *under twelve. People at risk* is also too broad. Instead, identify the risk and the people involved (e.g., children at risk for sexual abuse). Similarly, *gender* is preferred when referring to men and women as a social group rather than *sex,* as *sex* can be confused with sexual behavior.

Labels   Labels such as *sexually abused children* or *attention-deficit children* can, over time, acquire negative connotations and can offend the target group. Therefore, it is preferable to avoid labeling people when possible. An effective option is to place the subject first followed by a descriptive phrase (e.g., *children with a diagnosis of attention-deficit disorder*). Similarly, sensitivity should be given to any suggestion that one group is better than another or is the standard against which another is to be judged. For example, it would be inappropriate to contrast *abused children* with *normal children,* thus stigmatizing the abused children. A more appropriate contrast would be between *abused* and *nonabused* children.

Participation   You should write about the participants in your study in a way that acknowledges their participation. In the past, research reports have used the term *subjects.* This impersonal term should, and is, being replaced with more descriptive terms such as *research participants, children,* or *high school students,* as we have done in this book. You should also use the active voice when writing the research report (e.g., "the students completed"). In general, tell what the research participants did and do so in a way that acknowledges this participation.

These are the guidelines that need to be followed to avoid writing in a way that reflects demeaning attitudes and biased assumptions. Keeping these in mind, specific attention should be given to the following issues.

Gender   Participants should be described in such a way that avoids ambiguity in sex identity or sex role. This means that you should avoid using *he* to refer to both sexes or *man* or *mankind* to refer to people in general. The words *people, individuals,* or *persons* can be substituted without losing meaning or clarity of expression

Sexual Orientation   The sexual orientation of individuals should be used because there is no indication of sexual preference unless there is some deliberate indication of choice. This means that terms such as *homosexual* should be replaced with terms such as *gay men, lesbians,* and *bisexual women or men.* Terms such as *same gender, male-male, female-female,* and *male-female,* should be used to indicate specific instances of sexual behavior regardless of sexual orientation.

Racial and Ethnic Identity   Researchers should ask participants about their preferred designations because nouns referring to racial and ethnic groups change and can become dated and, sometimes, negative. When referring to a specific racial or ethnic group, remember to make sure that the first letter of the noun, such as Black, is capitalized.

Disabilities   When describing handicapped individuals, it is important to maintain their integrity as human beings. Language equating them with their condition, such as describing participants as *stroke victims* or *depressives,* should be avoided. Instead, describe a participant as *a person who has a stroke* instead of a *stroke victim.*

Age   The general rule to follow regarding age is to be specific in describing the age of participants and avoid open-ended definitions, such as *over 65.* People of high school age and younger can be referred to as *boys* and *girls.* Call people eighteen and older *men* and *women. Older person* is preferred to *elderly.*

Italics

As a general rule, use italics infrequently. Underline any words that are to appear in italics instead of using the italics function of your word processor.

Abbreviations

Use abbreviations sparingly. In general, abbreviate only when the abbreviations are conventional and likely to be familiar to the reader (such as IQ), or when it is necessary to abbreviate to save space and avoid cumbersome repetition. In all instances, the Latin abbreviations *cf.* (compare), *e.g.* (for example), *etc.* (and so forth), *i.e.* (that is), *viz.* (namely), and *vs.* (versus, against) are to be used only in parenthetical material. The exception to this rule is the Latin abbreviation *et al.,* which can be used in the text of the manuscript. The unit of time *second* is abbreviated *s* rather than *sec.* Periods are omitted with nonmetric measurements such as *ft* and *lb.* The only exception is inch, which is abbreviated *in.* with the period. Units of time such as *day, week, month,* and *year* are never abbreviated. There are many other abbreviations, identified in the APA publication manual, that can be used in a research report. Note that they should appear in Roman type in your report, not in italics or underlined.

Headings

The headings used in a manuscript serve to indicate the importance of each topic as well as the organization of the manuscript. There are five different levels of heading in a manuscript that have the following top-down progression: (level 1) centered main heading in uppercase letters, (level 2) centered main heading in upper- and lowercase letters, (level 3) centered main heading in underlined upper- and lowercase letters, (level 4) flush side heading in underlined upper- and lowercase letters, and (level 5) indented paragraph heading in underlined lowercase paragraph heading ending with a period. However, all headings are not used in every manuscript. If only one level of heading is needed in an article, use level 2. If two levels are needed, use level 2 and 4 as follows:

```
                        Method
```

```
Procedure
```

If three levels of heading are needed, use levels 2, 4, and 5 as follows:

Method

Procedure

    Instruments.

If four levels of headings are needed, use levels 2, 3, 4, and 5 as follows:

Experiment 1

Method

Procedure

    Instruments.

If five levels of headings are needed, use all of the headings in the order specified earlier.

Numbers

Use words to express numbers that begin a sentence as well as any number below ten. Use figures to express all other numbers. Exceptions to this rule are specified in the APA publication manual. When you express numbers, make sure that you use arabic and not roman numerals.

Physical Measurements

State all physical measurements in metric units. If a measurement is expressed in nonmetric units, put its metric equivalent in parentheses.

Presentation of Statistical Results

When presenting the results of statistical tests in the text, provide enough information to allow the reader to corroborate the results. Although sufficient information depends on the statistical test and analysis selected, in general it means including information about the magnitude or value of the test, the degrees of freedom, the probability level, and the direction of the effect. For example, t- and F-tests could be reported as follows:

$t(28) = 4.67, p < .05$

$F(3,32) = 8.79, p < .01$

When reporting a chi-square value, you should report the degrees of freedom and the sample size in parentheses as follows:

$\chi^2(3, N = 52) = 8.72, p < .05$

Common tests such as the *t-* and *F*-tests are not referenced, and the formulas are not included in the text. Referencing and formulas are included only when the statistical test is new, rare, or essential to the manuscript, as when the article concerns a given statistical test.

After the results of a statistical test are reported, descriptive statistical data, such as means and standard deviations, must be included to clarify the meaning of a significant effect and to indicate the direction of the effect.

Reference Citations in the Text

In the text of the research report, particularly in the introductory section, you must reference other works you have cited. The format is to use the author-date citation method, which involves inserting the author's surname and the publication date at the appropriate point, as follows:

```
Smith (1999) found that . . .
It has been demonstrated (Smith, 1999) . . .
```

With this information, the reader can turn to the reference list and locate complete information regarding the source. Multiple citations involving the same author are arranged in chronological order:

```
Smith (1987, 1993, 1998, 1999)
```

Multiple citations involving different authors are arranged alphabetically, as follows:

```
Several studies (Adams, 1997; Cox, 1994; Smith, 1998;
Thomas, 1999) have revealed that the developmental
changes . . .
```

If a citation includes more than two but fewer than six authors, all authors should be cited the first time the reference is used. Subsequent citations include only the name of the first author, followed by the abbreviation *et al.* and the year the article was published as follows:

```
Smith et al. (1998)
```

If six or more authors are associated with a citation, only the surname of the first author followed by *et al.* is used for all citations.

Reference List

All citations in the text of the research report must be accurately and completely cited in the reference list so that it is possible for readers to locate the works. This means that each entry should include the name of the author, year of publication, title, publishing data, and any other information necessary to identify the reference. All references are to appear in alphabetical order and typed double-spaced on a separate page with the word *References* centered at the top of the page in upper- and lowercase letters.

The general form of a reference is as follows for a periodical, book, and book chapter:

```
    Canned, I. B., & Had, U. B. (1999). Moderating
violence in a violent society. Journal of Violence and
Peace Making, 32, 231-243.
    Breeze, C. (1997). Why children kill. New York:
Academic Publishers.
    Good, I. M. (1998). Moral development in violent
children. In A. Writer & N. Author (Eds.), The anatomy
of violent children (pp. 134-187). Washington, DC:
Killer Books.
```

There are items that could be included in the reference list such as reports, brochures, and monographs. However, they are infrequently referenced and we do not present the style of documenting them. You should consult the APA publication manual for the specifics in presenting these items.

Typing

In typing the manuscript, double-space all material. There should be 1-inch margins at the top, bottom, right, and left of every page. Words should not be divided at the end of the page, and each page should contain no more than twenty-seven lines of text. Space once between the end of one sentence and the beginning of the next one.

WRITING QUANTITATIVE RESEARCH REPORTS USING THE APA STYLE

In order to facilitate clear communication, most journals specify that researchers follow a specific format or writing style when preparing their research reports. The style most journals of interest to educational researchers either recommend or specify that authors follow is the style specified in the *Publication Manual of the American Psychological Association* (American Psychological Association, 1994). We refer to this manual as the APA publication manual. It is the style we will discuss because it is so prevalent among the journals of interest to educational researchers.

There are seven major parts to the research report. These include the following:

1. Title page
2. Abstract

3. Introduction
4. Method
5. Results
6. Discussion
7. References

We discuss each of these parts in some detail, explaining the content of each and the material that should be included. We have also included a study (see Appendix A) titled, "Where Should 'You' Go in a Math Compare Problem?" conducted by Hsiao H. d'Ailly, Jacque Simpson, and G. E. MacKinnon of the University of Waterloo and published in the *Journal of Educational Psychology,* to illustrate each part of the research report.[1] We have selected this article because it is published by an educational researcher on an issue that should be of interest to educators, and it contains the major parts of a research report. As we discuss each part of the research report, you should read that section in the appended article to make the material we are presenting more meaningful. In doing so, realize that the preparation of the research report differs from the way it appears in the published form, as you will see in the following discussion.

Title Page

The title page contains a running head, title, author(s) name, and institutional affiliation of the author(s). The running head, which is an abbreviated title, is typed flush left at the top of the page in uppercase letters. It should be a maximum of 50 characters, counting letters, punctuation, and spaces between words. The title is centered on the page and typed in upper- and lowercase letters. It should summarize the main topic of the paper and concisely identify the variables or theoretical issues under investigation. The title should be 10 to 12 words in length and should inform the readers about the study. The names of authors who have made a substantial contribution to the study should appear immediately below the title typed in upper- and lowercase letters and centered on the page. The preferred form is to use the author's first name, middle initial, and last name with titles and degrees omitted. The institutional affiliation where the author(s) conducted the study is centered under the author(s) name(s).

The title page and each subsequent page of the paper also have a shortened title and page number appearing in the upper right-hand corner. The shortened title should consist of the first one to three words of the running head, which allow for identification of the page of the manuscript if the manuscript pages are separated during the review process. All pages should be numbered consecutively, beginning with the title page.

Abstract

The abstract is a comprehensive summary of the contents of the research report. It should not exceed 960 characters, which is about 120 words, and be typed on a separate page with the word *Abstract* centered at the top of the page in upper- and lowercase letters and no paragraph indentation. The abstract should be self-contained and include a brief statement of the problem, a description of the research participants, a summary of the method used, including a description of the instruments and the procedure used for data collection, the findings or results of the study, including statistical significance levels, and any conclusions and implications.

Introduction

The research report begins with the introduction, which is not labeled because of its position in the paper. The introduction presents the specific problem being investigated in the context of prior research and describes the research strategy. The introduction generally begins with a general introduction to the problem area and, perhaps, a statement of the point of the study. The introduction continues with a review of prior studies that have been conducted in the area and relating to the specific issue being investigated. This review is not exhaustive but cites only studies that are directly pertinent to place the current study in the context of prior work and to give an appropriate history and recognition of the work of others. An exhaustive review of the literature would be more appropriate for a thesis or dissertation.

After introducing the research problem and reviewing prior literature, you should tell what you did in the study you are reporting. This may take the form of stating the purpose of the study and any hypotheses that would give clarity to the paper. Overall, the introduction should specify the purpose of the study, show how it relates to prior work in the area, and identify hypotheses to be tested.

Method

The method section follows the introduction. It does not start on a separate page. The purpose of the method section is to tell the reader exactly how the study was conducted. It permits the reader to evaluate the appropriateness of the design of the study and be able to make an assessment of the reliability and validity of the results. If the method is presented well, another researcher can replicate the study. Actually, if another researcher can read the method section and replicate the study, you have adequately described it.

To facilitate communication of the method section, it is typically divided into subsections: participants, apparatus or materials, and procedure. Additional subsections may be included if the design of the experiment is complex to help communicate specific information. For example, a complex experiment may require a design subsection that explicitly describes the design of the study. Additional subsections should be used sparingly and only where needed to communicate essential information.

Participants   The participants subsection should identify the major demographic characteristics of the participants such as their age and gender as well as how they were selected. Any other pertinent information should also be included, such as how they were assigned to the experimental treatment conditions, the number of participants that were selected for the study but did not complete it (and why), and any inducements given to encourage participation.

Apparatus or Materials   This subsection tells the reader what apparatus or materials were used and why they were used. Sufficient detail should be included to enable the reader to obtain comparable materials or equipment. Commercially marketed equipment should be accompanied by the supplier's name and location as well as the model number of the equipment, or, in the case of a measuring instrument such as an achievement test, a reference that will enable the reader to obtain the same test. Custom-made equipment should be described and illustrated with a photograph.

Procedure   The procedure subsection tells the reader exactly how the study was executed, from the moment the participant and the researcher came into contact to the time the participant leaves the study. This subsection represents a step-by-step account of what the experimenter and participant did during the study, including any instructions, stimulus conditions presented to the participants and the responses they were to make, and any control techniques that were used, such as randomization or counterbalancing. In other words, in the procedure subsection, you are to tell exactly what both you and the participants did and how you did it.

Results

The results section follows the method section. It does *not* start on a separate page. The purpose of the results section is to summarize the data collected and their statistical treatment. In making this presentation, remember that any discussion of the results takes place in the discussion section. This section is limited to presenting the data and the analysis of the data. It should tell the reader how the data were analyzed and the results of this analysis. In presenting the results of statistical analysis, always state the alpha level used because the alpha level determines whether the results are statistically significant. This can be accomplished by stating the alpha level selected for all statistical tests conducted. For example, you could state that

```
The .05 alpha level was used for all statistical tests.
```

Then, when reporting the results of each statistical test, you could report the actual probability value of the computed statistic, which might be .006. If you do not make a general statement of the alpha level used for your statistical tests, you should specify this alpha level when reporting the results of each statistical test.

Results of any inferential tests (e.g., *t*-tests, *F*-tests, and chi-square) should be accompanied by the magnitude of the obtained value of the test, along with the accompanying degrees of freedom, probability level, and direction of the effect. There is also an increasing tendency and encouragement to report effect size whenever the results of a statistical test are reported because effect size provides an indication of the importance or magnitude of the effect. We strongly encourage you to make it a routine practice to report effect size.

In reporting and illustrating the direction of a significant effect (nonsignificant effects are not elaborated on for obvious reasons), you should decide on the medium that will most clearly and economically serve your purpose. Generally, tables illustrate main effects most efficiently and figures illustrate interactions most effectively. If you use a figure or table, make sure that you tell the reader, in the text of the report, what data it depicts. Then give a sufficient explanation of the presented data to make sure that the reader interprets them correctly. When means are reported always include an associated measure of variability, such as standard deviation or mean square error. In writing the results section you should not include individual data unless a single-participant study is conducted. Statistical formulas are not included unless the statistical test is new, unique, or in some other way not standard or commonly used.

Discussion

The discussion section has the purpose of interpreting and evaluating the results obtained, giving primary emphasis to the relationships between the results and the hypotheses of the study. Begin the discussion by stating whether the hypotheses of the study were or were not supported. Follow this statement with an interpretation of the results, telling the reader what you think they mean. In doing so, you should attempt to integrate your research findings with the results of prior research. Note that this is the only place in the research report where you are given any latitude for stating your own opinion, and even then you are limited to stating your interpretation of the results and what you think the major shortcomings of the study are. In general, the discussion should answer the following questions:

1. What does the study contribute?
2. How has it helped solve the study problem?
3. What conclusions and theoretical implications can be drawn from the study?

When discussing the shortcomings of the study you should mention only the flaws that may have had a significant influence on the results obtained. You should accept a negative finding as such rather than attempt to explain it as being due to some methodological flaw, unless, as may occur, there is a good reason why a flaw did cause the negative findings.

References

The reference section provides a list of all references cited in the text of the research report. In preparing the list of references, you should begin on a new page with the word *References* typed in the top center of the page. All entries are double-spaced although some theses and dissertations specify that the reference list be single-spaced. Indent the first line of each entry five to seven spaces.

Author Notes

Author identification notes appear with each printed article and are for the purpose of identifying the departmental affiliation of each author, acknowledging the basis of a study (such as a grant or a dissertation), acknowledging assistance of colleagues contribution to the conduct or preparation of the manuscript, and designating the address of the author to whom reprint requests are to be sent. These notes are typed on a separate page, with the words *Author Notes* at the top center of the page in upper- and lowercase letters. Each note should start with a paragraph indentation. The order is author names and departmental affiliations, then any special circumstances (e.g., study based on a dissertation) and acknowledgments, and finally the author's address for correspondence. These notes are not numbered or cited in the text and appear on the title page if the report is to be blind-reviewed (reviewed in the absence of any information that would identify the author).

Footnotes

Footnotes are numbered consecutively, with a superscript arabic numeral, in the order in which they appear in the text of the report. Most footnotes are content footnotes, containing material needed to supplement the information provided in the text. Such footnotes are typed on a separate page, with the word *Footnotes* centered in upper- and lowercase letters. The first line of each footnote is indented five spaces, and the superscript numeral of the footnote should appear in the space just preceding the beginning of the footnote. Footnotes are typed in the order in which they are mentioned in the text. Most research reports, such as the d'Ailley et al. (1997) article, do not contain footnotes.

Tables

Tables are expensive to publish and therefore should be reserved for use only when they can convey and summarize data more economically and clearly than can a lengthy discussion. Tables should be viewed as informative supplements to the text. Although each table should be intelligible by itself, it should also be an integral part of the text. As a supplement, only the table's highlights should be discussed. If you decide to use tables, number them with arabic numerals in the order in which they are mentioned in the text.

Each table should have a brief title that clearly explains the data it contains. This title and the word *Table* and its number are typed flush with the left margin and at the top of the table. Each column and row of data within the table should be given a label that identifies, as briefly as possible, the data contained in that row or column. Columns within the table should be at least three spaces apart. The APA publication manual should be consulted for a list of the various types of headings that can be used in tables. When placing data in the rows and columns, carry each data point out to the same number of decimal places, and place a dash to indicate an absence of data.

If you report the results of ANOVA statistics in a table, make sure that you include degrees of freedom and F-ratios for each source and mean square errors. Mean square errors are enclosed in parentheses and explained in a general note to the table. The APA publication manual should be consulted for the specifics of other tables such as regression tables and path and LISREL tables. These statistical analyses and accompanying tables require more advanced knowledge than exists among many students taking an introductory methods course and are not discussed here.

When writing the manuscript, you should refer to the table somewhere in the text. This reference should tell what data are presented in the table and briefly discuss the data. When referring to a table, identify it by name, as in "the data in Table 2." Do not use a reference such as "the above table" or "the table on page 12."

Figure Captions

Each figure has a caption that not only provides a brief description of the contents but also serves as a title. However, these captions are not placed on the figure but are typed on a separate page that precedes the figures with the words *Figure Captions* centered and typed in upper- and lowercase letters at the top of the page. Flush with the left margin of the page, each caption should begin with the word *Figure* and the number of the figure, both of which are underlined, followed by a period. The caption is typed on the remainder of the line. If more than one line is needed, each subsequent line also begins flush left.

Figures

Figures are very time consuming and expensive to produce and should be used only when they complement the text or eliminate a lengthy discussion of the data. Figures may consist of charts, graphs, photographs, drawings, or other similar means of representing data or pictorial concepts. Figures can be mechanically produced but most are computer generated. Computer-generated figures should be on high-quality paper and produced by software and hardware that produces smooth curves and crisp lines showing no jagged areas.

Once the figures have been prepared, number them consecutively with arabic numerals in the order in which they are used in the manuscript. On the back and also near the edge of the figure, write the number of the figure and a short title in pencil. Also write the word *top* on the back to designate the top of the figure.

WRITING QUALITATIVE RESEARCH REPORTS

We agree with Sharon Merriam (1998) that "There is no standard format for reporting qualitative research" (p. 227). Lofland (1974) stated two and a half decades ago that diversity in style was rampant in qualitative research. Diversity is still common today. For example, Richardson (1994) lists many nontraditional and creative styles that are sometimes used by qualitative researchers (e.g., such as incorporating stories, poems, essays, drawings, and photographs in qualitative reports). At the same time, we, and a growing number of scholars (e.g., Berg, 1998; Merriam, 1998) also believe that some structure to qualitative journal articles can be helpful because readers will know what information to expect and where that information will be located, and some structure can aid in the comparison of separate qualitative research reports. In short, when you write a qualitative research article you need to find a balance between the creative end of writing and the structured end of writing that works best for you and for the outlet in which you plan on disseminating your qualitative research (a journal, dissertation, thesis, evaluation report).

Unfortunately, the APA publication manual currently offers few specific guidelines for the structuring and writing of qualitative research articles. Additionally, the American Educational Research Association offers few if any guidelines for the construction of a qualitative research report. As a result, the best way to learn how to write the qualitative research report is to examine published examples and to use ideas learned there to aid you in writing your own article. If you want to examine some well-organized and well-written qualitative research reports, we recommend the following: phenomenology (Cross & Stewart, 1995; Riemen, 1986), ethnography (Deering, 1996; Wolcott, 1994), grounded theory (Cresswell & Brown, 1992; Frontman & Kunkel, 1994), case study (Alkin, 1979; Stake, 1995), and historical research (Fultz, 1995; Galenson, 1998).

We have included a qualitative research article in Appendix B for you to read (Deering, 1996). This article is an example of an ethnography, which is a commonly used approach to qualitative research in education. In this article, Paul Deering reports on his extensive study of the culture of a middle school that was successful in adopting inclusive norms and was characterized by positive intergroup relations. Deering was interested in documenting the characteristics of this successful school. This article is a shortened version of Deering's doctoral dissertation. Take a moment now to scan the article so you will have an overall view of what this qualitative research journal article looks like (e.g., take a look at the abstract and look at the headings that Deering used to organize the contents of the report).

Earlier in this chapter we discussed some general principles related to writing the research report. These principles apply to both quantitative research and to qualitative research. We would like to add to that discussion two points that are especially relevant in qualitative research. First, qualitative researchers tend to view the use of the "first person" (i.e., *I* rather than *the researcher*) and the active voice ("I interviewed the teachers" rather than "the teachers were interviewed by the researcher") very positively. They feel that this helps situate the qualitative researcher in his or her research and encourages qualitative researchers to take responsibility for their active role in their research. This makes sense because of the central role that the qualitative researcher must play in virtually every step during the conduct of a qualitative research study (e.g., the researcher is the "data collection instrument" because the researcher must make on-the-spot decisions about what is important and what should be noted and recorded, the researcher must manually code transcripts rather than using a statistical analysis program to provide an output of standard statistical results, the researcher must make interpretations throughout the research study, and so on).

Second, pseudonyms (i.e., fictitious names) are commonly used in qualitative research. Because of the small number of participants common to qualitative research and the in-depth information obtained about these individuals, qualitative researchers must be cautious to ensure that the identities of their research participants are adequately concealed. The guarantee of confidentiality may not be sufficient if the readers of a report are able to identify individuals based on descriptive information given about them in the report. For example, if you are conducting an ethnography of an elementary school, everyone in the school will know the principal, the librarian, and so forth. It may not be enough to use pseudonyms just for the individuals. You may also need to give a pseudonym to the school or city in the published version of the report. A last resort strategy is to withhold certain revealing information about an individual to make him or her less identifiable. In most cases, you will be able to obtain written permission from the participants in your study to use pseudonyms without any additional effort to conceal their identities. These ethical issues are especially critical in qualitative research.

Earlier in this chapter we discussed the seven major parts to the quantitative research report as recommended in the APA publication manual (the title page, abstract, introduction, method, results, discussion, and references). These seven sections can also be used quite effectively with qualitative research reports. Most of the earlier comments about these seven sections also apply to the qualitative research report. We do not repeat those ideas here; however, we highlight several important issues surrounding these seven sections in relation to writing a qualitative research report.

The title page is essentially the same for quantitative and qualitative research reports. You should always try to write a title that is clear and descriptive, regardless of the type of report. The abstract is also very similar for quantitative and qualitative research reports. When writing an abstract, your goal is always to succinctly describe the key focus of the article, its key methodological features, and the most important findings.

In the introduction, you should clearly explain the purpose of your research and then report any research literature that is relevant to your study. (Deering used the term *background* rather than *introduction*.) For example, if you are hoping to fit your study into a larger body of research, much of this material will be placed in the introduction. The qualitative research introduction section does, however, differ somewhat from the quantitative research introduction. For example, the qualitative report will usually not include any deductive hypotheses (tentative predictions about the relationships between variables based on prior literature and theory) because qualitative research is usually done more for exploratory than confirmatory reasons. Research questions and issues are often reported in the qualitative report introduction. However, they are usually stated in open-ended and general forms (e.g., the researcher hopes to: "discover," "explore a process," "explain or to understand," or "describe the experiences") rather than in the form of highly specific questions, which is more common in quantitative research (Cresswell, 1994, p. 71).

The methods section is sometimes incorporated into the introduction of the qualitative research report. However, it is becoming more common for qualitative research authors to include a separate section on methods. We believe that a separate methods section should be included in all qualitative journal articles. The author may wish to relegate the methods to an appendix in a more popularized version of a report, but even here it is essential that the researcher describes the methods used to carry out the research study. Otherwise, the reader is left hanging, without sufficient information to evaluate the quality of the research study.

The methods section needs to include information telling how the study was done, where it was done, with whom it was done, why the study was designed as it was, how the data were collected and analyzed, and, importantly, what procedures were carried out to ensure the validity of the arguments and conclusions. It is becoming common today for qualitative researchers to also include a section in the report in which they reflect on their personal biases and their disciplinary backgrounds and how this may affect the validity of their research. Researchers should also discuss what strategies they used to ensure qualitative research validity (e.g., see our discussion of triangulation, low-inference descriptors, extended fieldwork, and reflexivity in Chapter 7). When you read the methods section of a qualitative research report, a key question will be, Did the authors convince you that they conducted their study effectively and appropriately?

Perhaps the most important section in a qualitative research report is the results section (sometimes called the findings section in qualitative research reports). This is where the researcher provides the bulk of the evidence supporting his or her arguments. The overriding concern when writing a results section is to provide sufficient and convincing evidence. Assertions made by the researcher must be backed up with empirical data. You do not want the reader to go away saying, "I'm not sure that I agree with this writer's contentions." Qualitative researchers should try to minimize the situation where their readers must take their word for their arguments. We should all keep in mind the following point when working on our results sections: "It's about evidence." As Bogdan and Biklen (1998) point out: "The qualitative researcher, in effect, says to the reader, 'Here is what I found and here are the details to support that view' " (p. 195). If we follow this advice, we are likely to produce a results section that is convincing and defensible.

The qualitative researcher needs to find an appropriate balance between description and interpretation in order to write a convincing results section. On the one hand, you don't need to overkill with extensive descriptive detail and little interpretative commentary. For example, you don't want to provide pages and pages of interviews and fieldnotes with no interpretation. Keep in mind that such information may very well seem important to you because you are immersed in your research data; however, such detailed information is probably not important for your reader, and in journal articles, space is always limited. On the other hand, you do need to provide sufficient descriptive detail to support your conclusions and interpretative commentary. If you don't provide sufficient descriptive detail, the reader will be forced to rely too heavily on your word without supportive evidence, and if you don't provide enough interpretative commentary, your reader will end up lost in the details. Finding the best balance between description and interpretative commentary takes time and practice in writing qualitative research reports. It also depends on the audience and the outlet for your report. For example, space will be more plentiful in a book or a dissertation than in a journal. Also, the readers of journal articles are usually less willing to take your word for your interpretations than are readers of a best-selling nonfiction book version of your qualitative research.

One strategy for writing a results section is to provide quotes from your research participants and to include short sections from your field notes and your other data to get your reader close to your research participants and to the real-world situations described in your report. You should provide some rich and vivid description of the context, setting, participants, cultural scenes, and interactions among the participants. This way the reader can *vicariously* experience what it is like to be in the same situation as the research participants. The use of vignettes (e.g., detailed examples) and low-inference descriptors (e.g., quotes from the participants) are helpful for this purpose. Another way to present your data is to make interpretative statements and follow each statement with one or more illustrative examples. Intermixing your descriptive data with interpretative commentary throughout your results section helps your reader to follow your line of reasoning. Regardless of the specific format of your results section, remember that *you must always provide data (descriptions, quotes, data from multiple sources, and so forth) that back up your assertions.*

The results section of a qualitative report will usually include more subheadings than the results section of a quantitative report. The particular organization identified by the subheadings will vary depending on the type of qualitative research conducted and the results of the data analysis. For example, the qualitative research results may be organized around the research questions or research issues examined in the research, they may be organized around an a priori literature-based conceptual scheme applied to the research data, they may be organized around a typology that is developed during data analysis, they may be organized according to the key themes found in the data, or they may be organized around a conceptual scheme based on a grounded theory generated from the research data. Regardless of the exact format, remember that you must convince your reader of your arguments. That is the key for effective report writing.

In the discussion section (sometimes called the conclusion), the qualitative researcher may state the overall conclusions and offer additional interpretation of the findings. The researcher may also determine whether the results are consistent with other results published in the research literature. Even if the research is exploratory, it is important to fit your findings back into the relevant research literature in your discussion section. It is also helpful to provide suggestions for further research, because research is rarely done in a vacuum. Virtually all research can and should be related to the big picture of where we have been and where we are going in our efforts to increase research-based knowledge.

The references section is the same in a quantitative and qualitative report. If the APA referencing style is used, the references will follow the APA format described earlier in this chapter. Finally, the ancillary components discussed earlier (charts, tables, figures, and so forth) also have an important place in qualitative research reports. For example, a data chart or matrix is very helpful when it would take a great deal of narrative text to convey the same information. An excellent source for learning more about displaying qualitative research data is Miles and Huberman's (1994) book titled, *Qualitative Data Analysis: An Expanded Source Book.*

ENDNOTES

1. H. H. d'Ailly, J. Simpson, and G. E. MacKinnon, "Where Should 'You' Go in a Math Compare Problem?" *Journal of Education Psychology, 89,* 562–567. Copyright © 1997 by the American Psychological Association. Reprinted with permission.

APPENDIX A

Quantitative Research Article

Where Should "You" Go in a Math Compare Problem?

Where Should "You" Go in a Math Compare Problem?

Hsiao H. d'Ailly, Jacque Simpson, and G. E. MacKinnon
University of Waterloo

This study examined the cognitive effects of self-referencing in math word problems in 100 3rd, 4th, and 5th graders. Two types of compare problems were used: compare unknown (CU) and referent unknown (RU). The word *you* was placed in the problems either as the known or the unknown term. For the CU problems, self-referencing facilitated students' performance regardless of the position of the *you* term. When self-referencing was applied, students asked for fewer repeats and solved these CU problems faster and with greater accuracy. For the RU problems, however, students benefited from self-referencing only when the self term was placed as the compare (known) term. When the *you* term was placed as the referent term, the facilitative effect of self-referencing disappeared. The position of the *you* term in a RU problem apparently has an impact on the translation procedure required in solving the problem. Further research on the cognitive processing issues raised by these data is suggested and the educational implications of the findings are discussed.

Personalizing mathematics word problems, such as incorporating personal information (e.g., the child's favorite pet, movie, etc.), into the problem text can lead to improvements in performance (Wright & Wright, 1985). Students are more motivated and learn faster when personalized problems or examples are used in mathematics instruction (Anand & Ross, 1987). In previous studies, different questions incorporating personal information were generated for each student by means of computer technology. In the present study, we examined one personalization technique that can be readily generated and applied by classroom teachers. The technique is to insert a self-referencing term, the word *you,* in the problems.

Self is considered a rich schema where a lot of daily life experience, including informal math knowledge, is instantiated. Involving *self* in a problem may indeed help children to activate this knowledge and consequently help them to construct the problem representation. Moreover, d'Ailly, Murray, and Corkill (1995), demonstrated that self-referencing can also change the way information is processed. In their study, university students were tested on a linear ordering task (e.g., John is taller than Tom, Tom is taller than Paul, Paul is taller than you. Is John taller than you?). They found that it took students less time to answer questions containing a self-referencing term (e.g., the word *you*). In particular, an anchor shift effect was found such that students organized information differently according to the position of the *you* term in the problem text. Of interest in the present study was whether, and if so how, self-referencing may affect young children's cognitive processing in solving mathematics word problems.

Hsiao H. d'Ailly, Jacque Simpson, and G. E. MacKinnon, Department of Psychology, University of Waterloo, Waterloo, Ontario, Canada.

This study was supported in part by a postdoctoral fellowship award from the Social Science and Humanities Research Council of Canada and a grant from the University of Waterloo/Social Science and Humanities Council Grant Fund. A version of this article was presented at the 104th Annual Convention of the American Psychological Association, Toronto, Canada.

Correspondence concerning this paper should be addressed to Hsiao H. d'Ailly who is now at Renison College, University of Waterloo, Waterloo, Ontario, Canada N2L 3G4. Electronic mail may be sent via Internet to hdailly@renison.watstar.uwaterloo.ca

Two types of one-step mathematics word problems were used in this study: compare unknown (CU) problems (e.g., John has 5 marbles. Peter has 2 marbles more [less] than John. How many marbles does Peter have?) and referent unknown (RU) problems (e.g., John has 5 marbles. John has 2 marbles more [less] than Peter. How many marbles does Peter have?). These compare problems are generally more difficult for children to solve than other types of problems, such as combine and change problems (Briars & Larkin, 1984; Carpenter & Moser, 1982; Kintsch & Greeno, 1985; Riley, Greeno, & Heller, 1983). Of the two compare problems applied in this study, RU problems are more difficult than CU ones. Several explanations for this difference in difficulty have been offered by researchers (e.g., Lewis & Mayer, 1987; Riley & Greeno, 1988). As Lewis and Mayer pointed out, unlike the CU problems, the relational term in the second sentence (e.g., more than) in a RU problem is inconsistent with the necessary arithmetic operation (e.g., subtraction). Thus, when solving a RU problem, one needs to transform the statement by interchanging the subject and object of the sentence and reverse the relational term (e.g., John has 2 marbles more [less] than Peter → Peter has 2 marbles less [more] than John). This translation procedure appears to be difficult for young children and is error prone for adults. Stern (1993) reported that Grade 1 children had difficulty understanding that the quantitative difference between the same sets could be expressed in parallel ways with both the terms *more* and *fewer*. The lack of knowledge about the symmetry of language about quantitative comparison makes it difficult for young children to perform the translation procedure. Lewis and Mayer (1987) showed that college students are also more likely to make errors when the translation procedure is required in solving a problem.

In the present study, the cognitive effects of self-referencing were examined by measuring children's accuracy rates and reaction times as they solved CU and RU problems. The theory is that our short-term memory buffer (or working memory capacity) is lim-

ited. Therefore, problems that require heavy cognitive resources to process will be difficult to solve (Kintsch & Greeno, 1985). We hypothesized that self-referencing in word problems is an effective way to decrease the working memory load because it facilitates general encoding processes as well as the construction of a mental representation of the problem. Such facilitation should be reflected in higher accuracy rates and shorter reaction times for self-referenced problems.

The self-referencing word *you* was placed as either the unknown or the known term in this study. In addition, a control condition was included where no self-referencing term was used in the problems. On the basis of d'Ailly et al.'s (1995) study, we hypothesized that placing the self-referencing term at different positions in a problem will affect children's cognitive processing in solving the problem. For example, there might be a preferable mode of placing the self-referencing term in a problem that will facilitate the encoding process or the translation procedure better. Placing the self-referencing term as the known term or the unknown term in a problem may facilitate general encoding processes. Only RU problems require a translation procedure. Thus, if the position of the self-referencing term has an impact on the translation process, one would expect any effect of self-referencing to interact with problem type. Finally, the role of working memory and development level (grade) on children's performance were also examined.

METHOD

Participants

One hundred students in Grades 3, 4, and 5 from a local elementary school participated in this study. There were 16 girls and 16 boys in the Grade 3 sample, 21 girls and 13 boys in the Grade 4 sample, and 13 girls and 21 boys in the Grade 5 sample. Children's ages ranged from 7 years 11 months to 11 years 11 months. The mean age of Grade 3 children was 8 years 11 months, of Grade 4 children, 9 years 5 months, and of Grade 5 children, 10 years 0 months.

Materials and Apparatus

The working memory task was similar to those developed by Swanson (1992). Children were first presented orally with a string of numbers (e.g., 3, 5, 6) and then were asked to determine whether a given digit (e.g., 4) was one of the numbers in the string. After answering the question, children were then asked to recall the original number string. We started from 2 numbers in one string and increased the length of the string by one after every four sets of same-length strings. A ceiling rule was developed such that testing was discontinued when a child failed to recall two consecutive number strings correctly. The number of strings recalled correctly was taken as a measure of the child's working memory capacity. A computer program generated the random number strings used in the working memory task.

Two types of math problems (RU and CU) with three different self-referencing conditions (You-known, you-unknown, and control) were presented. Table 1 shows example problems for each condi-

tion. The numbers used in the problems ranged from 2 to 9 with a final answer not exceeding 10 for all problems.

A computer program was designed to generate the math problems. The program was designed in such a way that the order of presentation of problem types and self-referencing, as well as the names, numbers, and objects used within the problems were randomized. The computer program also incorporated a timing program designed by Graves and Bradley (1988), which provided millisecond timing. Reaction times were recorded by pressing a key on the computer to start timing and again pressing a key to stop the timing.

During the testing, the experimenter sat in front of the child with a Twinhead Slim Note 486 computer (Twinhead International Corp, Taiwan). The questions generated by the computer program were read by the experimenter, who kept the monitor away from the child to avoid distraction. Reaction times (accurate to milliseconds) were recorded by the experimenter, who pressed a key on the computer after reading the problem and again as soon as the child responded. Children's answers were then typed into the computer. Children were allowed to ask for a problem to be repeated. When a child requested for a repeat of the problem, the experimenter pressed a re-

TABLE 1 Example Questions Illustrating the Conditions of Self-Referencing and Problem Types

Self-Referencing	Problem Type	
	Compare Unknown	Referent Unknown
You-known	You have 3 balls. Bob has 2 more (less) balls than You. How many balls does Bob have?	You have 3 balls. You have 2 more (less) balls than Bob. How many balls does Bob have?
You-unknown	Bob has 3 balls. You have 2 more (less) balls than Bob. How many balls do You have?	Bob has 3 balls. Bob has 2 more (less) balls than You. How many balls do You have?
Control	Tom has 3 balls. Bob has 2 more (less) balls than Tom. How many balls does Bob have?	Tom has 3 balls. Tom has 2 more (less) balls than Bob. How many balls does Bob have?

peat key and the same question was presented on the screen again for the experimenter to read. The number of times a problem was read to the child was also recorded.

Procedure

All children were tested individually twice. In the first session they were given the working memory task first. The working memory task took approximately 5 min to complete; then the math problems were presented. In the second session, children were given math problems only. Both sessions took less than 30 min to complete.

All math problems were presented orally to the children. Each child received each problem with each condition twice in the first session and again twice in the second session. Therefore, four different questions in total were presented to the children for each of the experimental conditions.

RESULTS

Data Analyses

There were three major dependent measurements for the problem solving sessions: the number of repeats requested, accuracy, and reaction time. The total number of repeats and the accuracy rate for the four questions were calculated for each condition. In the analysis of reaction times, only those reaction times from accurate and nonrepeated problems were used. In addition, reaction times longer than 15,000 ms or less than 250 ms were excluded because of the extreme values. The reaction times from the four questions in each condition were averaged.

As to the independent variables, in addition to problem type, self-referencing, and grade, working memory was included as a factor in the analyses. The overall mean working memory score was 9.59 (SD = 1.81), with mean scores of 9.18 (SD = 2.82), 9.05

(SD = 2.57), and 10.53 (SD = 2.86) for Grade 3, 4 and 5 children, respectively. For Grade 3 and 4 students, children who had a working memory score of 10 or above were classified as high in working memory, those with working memory scores below 10 were classified as low in working memory. For Grade 5 students, the cutoff score for the high-working memory group was 11.

A 2 (problem type) × 3 (self-referencing) × 3 (grade) × 2 (working memory) ANOVA with self-referencing and problem type as within-variables and grade and working memory as between-variables was applied to analyze the number of repeats, accuracy rate, and reaction time data. All the significant effects reported below remain significant under a more conservative F test with adjustment on the degrees of freedom using Greenhouse-Geisser epsilon. For the sake of simplicity, the original degrees of freedom are reported. Following a significant interaction, a simultaneous test procedure using Dunn's procedure to control for Type I error (Kirk, 1982) was applied in simple main effect testings. For any significant self-referencing effects, Tukey's HSD test was applied to test the contrasts among the three self-referencing conditions.

Number of Problem Repeats Requested

During the testing sessions, students were allowed to ask for repeats if needed. In general, students with lower working-memory scores asked for repeats significantly more often (M = .55, SD = .47) than those with higher working-memory scores (M = .34, SD = .30), $F(1, 94)$ = 6.33, $p < .05$, MSE = .97. Students asked for significantly more repeats for RU problems (M = .53, SD = .52) than for CU problems (M = .38, SD = .37), F (1, 94) = 14.79, $p < .001$, MSE = .21. Self-referencing also had a significant main effect on students' request for repeats, $F(2, 188)$ = 18.87, $p <$ .001, MSE = .23. The mean number of repeats for the you-known, you-unknown, and control problems were .31 (SD = .40), .44 (SD = .42), and .61 (SD = .63), respectively.

A significant two-way interaction between problem type and self-referencing on the number of repeat requests is shown in Figure 1, $F(2, 188) = 4.69$, $p < .05$, $MSE = .02$. The self-referencing effect was significant for both CU, $F(2, 198) = 9.3$, and RU, $F(2, 188) = 13$ problems (critical $F = 4.5$), $MSE = 23$. For CU problems, the average number of repeats for you-known questions ($M = .30$, $SD = .44$) and you-unknown questions ($M = .29$, $SD = .39$) were both significantly lower than the control questions ($M = .56$, $SD = .62$); ψ (honestly significant difference [HSD] = .14, $MSE = .17$. The two self-referenced conditions did not differ significantly. On the other hand, for the RU problems, only the you-known questions ($M = .34$, $SD = .52$) had fewer number of repeats than the control questions ($M = .67$, $SD = .78$), ψ (HSD) = .16, $MSE = 24$. Students also asked for significantly more repeats on the you-unknown RU problems ($M = .58$, $SD = .64$) than on the you-known RU problems ($M = .34$, $SD = .52$). In short, compared with standard control problems, students asked for fewer repeats on all self-referenced questions with only one exception,

that is, when the *you* word was placed as the referent (unknown) term in a RU problem.

Accuracy Rate

In general, students' performance improved with grade level: Mean accuracy rates are .52 ($SD = .28$), .62 ($SD = .21$), and .67 ($SD = .21$) for Grade 3, 4, and 5 students, respectively; $F(2, 94) = 4.31$, $p < .05$, $MSE = .28$. Students with high working memory scores ($M = .69$, $SD = .21$) outperformed students with low working memory ($M = .53$, $SD = .24$); $F(1, 94) = 15.51$, $p < .001$, $MSE = .28$. RU problems ($M = .41$, $SD = .29$) were found to be more difficult than CU problems ($M = .75$, $SD = .2 1$); $F(1, 94) = 139.26$, $p < .001$, $MSE = .08$. There was also a significant main effect of self-referencing on performance, $F(2, 188) = 41.39$, $p < .001$, $MSE = .02$. The mean accuracy rates for the you-known, you-unknown, and control conditions were .67 ($SD = .26$), .60 ($SD = .26$), and .54 ($SD = .25$), respectively.

As shown in Figure 2, there was a significant interaction in accuracy, between working memory and grade, $F(2,94) = 4.16$, $p < .05$, $MSE = .28$. Only for Grade 3 students did working memory have a significant effect on performance, $F(1, 94) = 20.11$ (critical $F = 8.67$), $MSE = .28$.

There was also a significant interaction in accuracy between self-referencing and problem type, $F(2, 188) = 8.09$, $p < .001$, $MSE = .02$ (see Figure 3). Self-referencing had a significant effect on CU problems, $F(2, 188) = 14$, as well as on RU problems, $F(2, 188) = 38$, critical $F = 4.5$, $MSE = .02$. The pattern of this effect, however, was different for these two types of problems. For the CU problems, both you-known ($M = .78$, $SD = .26$) and you-unknown problems ($M = .78$, $SD = .27$) were solved better than the standard ones ($M = .69$, $SD = .29$), ψ (HSD) = .04, $MSE = .02$, and the two different self-referent conditions did not result in different performance. For the RU problems, however, only when the *you* term was placed as the known term ($M = .56$, $SD = .34$) did the performance improve over the control condition

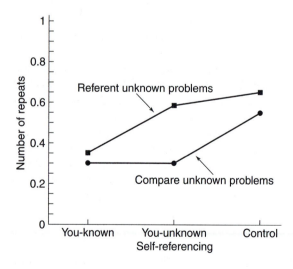

FIGURE 1   Mean number of problem repeats as a function of self-referencing and problem type.

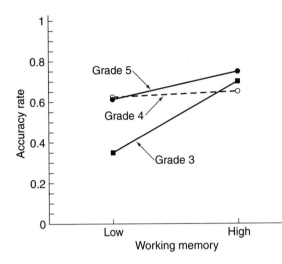

FIGURE 2 Mean accuracy rate as a function of working memory and grade.

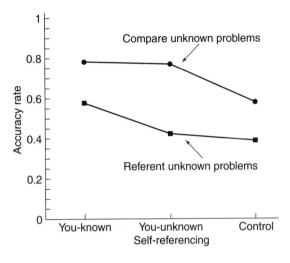

FIGURE 3 Mean accuracy rate as a function of self-referencing and problem type.

($M = .39$, $SD = .3$ 1), ψ (HSD) = .05, $MSE = .03$. Moreover, when the *you* term was placed as the unknown term, students' performance ($M = .43$, $SD = .31$) was significantly worse than when it was placed as the known term.

In short, the results observed in accuracy rates correspond to that of the number of repeats. Students generally could answer the self-referenced questions better except for one condition, that is when the *you* term was placed as the unknown term in a RU problem.

Reaction Time

A 2 (problem type) × 3 (self-referencing) × 3 (grade) × 2 (working memory) ANOVA was applied to analyze the reaction time data. There was a significant main effect of problem type, $F(1, 4\ 1) = 16.8$, $p < .001$, $MSE = 1764443.45$, and self-referencing, $F(2, 82) = 4.81$, $p < .05$, $MSE = 733218.82$. The interaction effect between self-referencing and problem type was also significant, $F(2, 82) = 5.03$, $p < .01$, $MSE = 747878.48$. As shown in Figure 4, in general, the re-

action times were longer for the RU problems ($M = 2442.89$, $SD = 1578.89$) than for the CU problems ($M = 1744.80$, $SD = 2442.89$). The effect of self-referencing appeared to differ for the two problem types. For CU problems, both of the two self-referenced conditions resulted in shorter reaction times than the control condition, with the mean reaction time for the self-known, self-unknown, and control conditions being 1651.76 ($SD = 1159.89$), 1536.29 ($SD = 1131.45$), and 2046.35 ($SD = 1437.52$) respectively; ψ (HSD) = 351.49, $MSE = 507868.11$. The you-known condition and the you-unknown condition did not differ significantly. On the other hand, for the RU problems, neither of the two self-referenced conditions resulted in a significant difference in children's reaction times from the control condition. When the *you* term was placed as the unknown term, however, it took children significantly longer ($M = 2722.69$, $SD = 1679.37$) to solve the problems than when the *you* term was placed as the known term ($M = 2075.05$, $SD = 1552.05$), ψ (HSD) = 486.57, $MSE = 973230.19$. These results also correspond to those obtained from the other two dependent

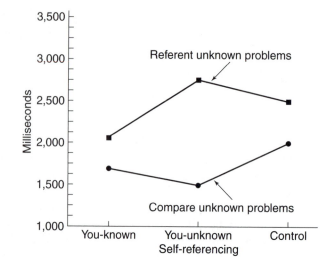

FIGURE 4 Mean reaction time as a function of self-referencing and problem type.

measures: That is, when the *you* term is placed in a RU problem, it is more difficult for the children to have it as the unknown term than as the known term.

DISCUSSION

As in previous studies (Briars & Larkin, 1984; Carpenter & Moser, 1982; Kintsch & Greeno, 1985; Riley et al., 1983) we found that RU problems are indeed more difficult for children to solve than the CU problems and that children's performance on these mathematics word problems improve as a function of grade level. In addition, for Grade 3 children working memory proved to be an important factor in solving the problems.

The major purpose of present study was to test whether and how self-referencing affects children's cognitive processing in solving simple mathematics word problems. The findings from analyses of number of requests for repeats, accuracy rate, and reaction times are clear and consistent. In general, self-referencing does have a significant facilitative effect on children's encoding processes in solving these prob-

lems. When a *you* word was involved in the problem, children asked for fewer repeats for the problems, and could solve the problems in a shorter amount of time and with a higher accuracy. For the CU problems, this facilitative effect of self-referencing was evident regardless of the positions of the "you" term in the problems. We consider these results a clear indication that self-referencing facilitates general encoding processes and decreases the load on working memory load during problem solving.

As described earlier, the major difference between solving RU and CU problems is that a translation procedure is required to solve RU problems (Lewis & Mayer, 1987). The significant interaction between problem type and self-referencing found in this study indicates that the position of self-referencing affected this translation procedure. Specifically, when the *you* term was placed as the unknown term (referent term), the facilitative effect of self-referencing disappeared.

These results provide support for the previous finding by d'Ailly et al. (1995). They found that self-referencing changes the way students process information and that participants appear to shift anchor point in a linear ordering task to wherever the *self* term is positioned. In the present study, during the translation procedure, one of the main tasks is to change the *referent* term into the *compare* term. We postulate that it may be that children tend to "anchor" or "fix" at the *self* term as suggested by d'Ailly et al.'s study (1995). This anchoring or fixing effect may have made it more difficult to perform the translation procedure, particularly when the *you* word is placed as the referent term in a RU problem. Further cognitive studies are needed to test this speculation.

Self-referencing clearly facilitates children's performance in solving math word problems. Moreover, translating "John has 3 dollars more than you" to "You have 3 dollars less than John" is more difficult than translating "You have 3 dollars more than John" to "John has 3 dollars less than you." These findings have implications in teaching. Teachers can use the intervention described in the present study easily by placing the *you* word in a problem in the classroom whenever it is appropriate. According to the results from the present study, in most cases students can solve self-referenced problems better in a shorter amount of time. Placing the *you* word in a problem also affects how students process the information. It appears that self-referencing may have differential effects on the translation procedure required in solving a RU problem. Students do not benefit from self-referencing when the *you* term is placed as the referent term. Thus, when placing the *you* term in a RU problem, it is preferable to place it as the known term in the problem.

REFERENCES

Anand, P. G., & Ross, S. (1987). Using computer-assisted instruction to personalize arithmetic materials for elementary school children. *Journal of Educational Psychology, 79,* 72–78.

Briars, D. J., & Larkin, J. S. (1984). An integrated model of skill in solving elementary word problems. *Cognition and Instruction, 1,* 245–296.

Carpenter, T. P., & Moser, J. M. (1982). The development of addition and subtraction problem-solving skills. In T. P. Carpenter, J. M. Moser, & T. Rombert (Eds.), *Addition and subtraction: A cognitive perspective* (pp. 9–24). Hillsdale, NJ: Erlbaum.

d'Ailly, H., Murray, H. G., & Corkill, A. (1995). The cognitive effects of self-referencing. *Journal of Contemporary Educational Psychology, 20,* 88–113.

Graves, R., & Bradley, R. (1988). More on millisecond timing and tachistoscope applications for IBM PC. *Behaviour Research Methods, Instruments, & Computers, 20,* 408–412.

Kintsch, W., & Greeno, J. G. (1985). Understanding and solving word arithmetic problems. *Psychological Review, 92,* 109–129.

Kirk, R. E. (1982). *Experimental design: Procedures for the behavioral sciences* (2nd ed.)., Monterey, CA: Wadsworth.

Lewis, A. B., & Mayer, R. E. (1987). Students' miscomprehension of relational statements in arithmetic word problems. *Journal of Educational Psychology, 79,* 363–371.

Riley, M. S., & Greeno, J. G. (1988). Developmental analysis of understanding language about quantities and of solving problems. *Cognition and Instruction, 5,* 49–101.

Riley, M. S., Greeno, J. G., & Heller, J. I. (1983). Development of children's problem-solving ability in arithmetic. In H. P. Ginsberg (Ed.), *The development of mathematical thinking* (pp. 153–196). New York: Academic Press.

Stern, E. (1993). What makes certain arithmetic word problems involving the comparison of sets so difficult for children? *Journal of Educational Psychology, 85,* 7–23.

Swanson, H. L. (1992). Generality and modifiability of working memory among skilled and less skilled readers. *Journal of Educational Psychology, 84,* 473–488.

Wright, J. P., & Wright, C. D. (1985). Personalized verbal problems: An application of the language experience approach. *Journal of Educational Research, 79,* 358–362.

Qualitative Research Article

An Ethnographic Study of Norms of Inclusion and Cooperation in a Multiethnic Middle School

An Ethnographic Study of Norms of Inclusion and Cooperation in a Multiethnic Middle School

Paul D. Deering
University of Hawaii, Manoa

This study used ethnographic methods to examine cultural norms regarding inclusion and cooperation at Banner Middle School, in a Western United States metropolitan area. Banner's students were predominantly working class Caucasians and Chicanos. Much middle-school and multicultural educational literature calls for inclusion of students of diverse abilities and race or ethnicity in school and classroom contexts, and for cooperative rather than competitive norms. There was generally powerful and consistent support at Banner for inclusive and cooperative norms at the sociocultural levels of the school as an institution, peer groups and parents. Two factors stand out in explaining the high degree of inclusion and cooperation: the strong, effective leadership provided by the principal, and the cultural congruity of these norms. This study supports the theoretical compatibility of middle school and multicultural educational philosophy.

BACKGROUND

The literatures on middle school education (e.g., Beane & Lipka, 1987; Johnston, 1992; Stevenson, 1992) and multicultural education (e.g., Banks, 1991; Cummins, 1986; Trueba, 1988) are highly congruent in their call for school cultures characterized by norms of inclusion and cooperation. "Middle school" is a general approach to educating early adolescents (10–14 year olds) that attempts to meet these students' distinct needs. Early adolescents undergo profound developmental changes in all realms—social, psychological, and physical—leaving them highly vulnerable to getting "lost in the system" at school. The daunting challenges of adolescence are compounded for minority and working-class students in American schools, as they often face heightened threats to their physical well-being in school and in the community and come to school with cultural capital that is often devalued in schools (Lewis, 1990; Scales, 1991; Trueba, 1988). Consequently, the middle-school ideal of a caring, inclusive, cooperative school culture is especially important in minority and low-income contexts. This ideal calls for a fundamentally different school culture from that of the traditional departmentalized, impersonal junior high school. As Oakes, Quartz, Gong, Guiton, and Lipton (1993) state:

> We argue that to achieve fundamental change [in early adolescent schooling] it will not be enough to reform existing technical practices; rather, norms of community and integration will need to replace many of the competitive, individualistic and bureaucratic norms embedded in current practice. (p. 460)

Inclusion, Cooperation, and School Culture

The concept of culture can help illuminate the ways in which middle schools construct inclusion and cooperation. As used in this article, the concept *culture* derives from a symbolic interactionist perspective,

Paul D. Deering is assistant professor, College of Education, University of Hawaii, Manoa. Address correspondence to Paul D. Deering, Ph.D., University of Hawaii, Manoa, College of Education, Department of Curriculum and Instruction, 1776 University Ave., Honolulu, HI 96822.

An earlier version of this paper was presented at the Annual Meeting of the American Education Research Association, Atlanta, 1992.

referring to the shared frame by which a people make meaning from their and others' perceptions, beliefs, and actions (Erickson, 1986; Geertz, 1973). Social interactions are the medium within which meaning—or culture—is constructed. When applied to a school, the concept of culture includes the obvious elements of schedules, curriculum, demographics, and policies, as well as the social interactions which are enacted within those structures. Thus school culture encompasses patterns of behavior and belief that give a school its feel and substance as "friendly," "elite," "competitive," "inclusive," and so on (e.g., Kapferer, 1981). Erickson (1982) notes that learning, or enculturation, occurs on an explicit level, observable to the eyes and ears, and also on an implicit level, perceptible only through an analysis of the underlying structure of what is observed. The values and norms of a school and its participants are subtly and pervasively manifest at the implicit level of social interaction, shaping the learning environment, and, ultimately, the learning of participants.

Inclusion and cooperation are important cultural norms for middle schools and multicultural educational contexts according to numerous theorists (Beane & Lipka, 1987; Clark & Clark, 1993; Carnegie Council on Adolescent Development [CCAD], 1989; Cummins, 1986; Little Soldier, 1989; Oakes et al., 1993; Johnston, 1992; Stevenson, 1992; Trueba, 1988). *Inclusion* can be conceived as a continuum which reflects the degree to which all persons and their aspirations and interests are incorporated into a given social context (Figure 1). A sports team with a no-cut policy is highly *inclusive,* while one with tryouts for a limited number of slots is *exclusive.* Mainstreaming of special program students (e.g., learning-disabled,

gifted and talented) into the regular instructional routine is an example of an inclusive school policy. Students' socializing readily with any and all peers is an example of an inclusive peer cultural norm.

Cooperation denotes the degree to which participants' likelihood of achieving their aspirations in a given situation are mutually reinforcing (see Figure 2; Johnson & Johnson, 1987; Slavin, 1983). A basketball team is *cooperative,* in that its players' chances of winning are positively correlated. However, the team is *competitive* toward its opponent, in that the two teams' chances of winning are negatively correlated and, in fact, mutually prohibitive. An example of a cooperative school practice would be having students work together in small groups on a project, as in cooperative learning (Johnson & Johnson, 1987; Slavin, 1983). Youngsters engaging in collaborative activities such as jumping rope or group dances would be examples of cooperative cultural peer norms. Students working alone toward fixed criteria of success, where there are no limitations on the number of rewards (such as high grades), would be an example of a school practice with an *independent* structure. Note that the continua of inclusion and cooperation may intersect at any two points (e.g., inclusive-cooperative, exclusive-competitive, individualistic-competitive). The one exception is that, by definition, any cooperative situation must involve at least some inclusion, since it is impossible to cooperate by oneself.

Middle Schools and Multicultural Education

Middle schools promote inclusion by frequently bringing together students of diverse abilities, inter-

Figure 1 Continuum of inclusion.

Figure 2 Continuum of cooperation.

ests, and backgrounds in instructional and social contexts. This pattern addresses early adolescents' need for interaction with a broad range of others as they attempt to expand on their social identities (Spear, 1992; Stevenson, 1992). Inclusive school grouping policies are also consistent with Allport's (1954) call for face-to-face interaction among students of different race and ethnicity as a precondition for enhanced intergroup relations. Another inclusive norm of middle schools is the promotion of close relationships between adults and students. This norm addresses early adolescents' need for varied adult role models and helps to provide the greater guidance, supervision, and nurturing that they need during these potentially chaotic years (Stevenson, 1992; Van Hoose & Strahan, 1991). Work by Dillon (1989) and Heath (1983), among others, has illustrated the power of close, positive teacher–student relationships in working-class and minority educational contexts. Inclusive curriculum is also a major emphasis within the middle-school movement, as theorists call for learning to focus on students' interests and concerns (e.g., Beane, 1990; Stevenson & Carr, 1994). Similarly, multicultural educational literature calls for schools to include students' cultural heritage in the curriculum (e.g., Cummins, 1986; Banks, 1991).

Middle-school theorists advocate cooperative school and classroom environments over competitive ones to allow students, with minimal pressure, to teach and learn from each other, and to explore their varied and changing interests (Alexander & George, 1981; Van Hoose & Strahan, 1991). By contrast, Wheelock (1986, 1992) has found that competitive, exclusive school policies such as tracking and suspension contribute to adolescent school dropout. Middle schools' advocacy of a cooperative school culture is quite compatible with a large body of multicultural educational literature which suggests that cooperation is a far more compatible norm than competition for African Americans (Fordham & Ogbu, 1986; Fordham, 1988), Hawaiians (Tharp & Gallimore, 1988), Latinos (Kagan, 1984; Ramirez & Castaneda, 1974; Trueba, 1988), Native Americans (Little Soldier, 1989; Philips, 1972), and females (Gilligan, 1982).

Both middle-school literature and multicultural educational literature also call for inclusion of and cooperation with parents (CCAD, 1989; Cummins, 1986; Kochan, 1992; Stevenson, 1992; Trueba, 1988). As Cummins (1986) states, "When educators involve minority parents as partners in their children's education, parents appear to develop a sense of efficacy that communicates itself to children, with positive academic consequences" (p. 26).

It cannot be assumed that attempts to build inclusive, cooperative middle school cultures will be met with enthusiasm or understanding by any of those involved: educators, students, parents, and the community. As Merten (1994) cautions in his recent ethnography of a middle-level school, "The community emphasis on individualism, competition, and achievement makes Fern Hills [School] part of mainstream America" (p. 31). Indeed, much of the mainstream American educational reform rhetoric focuses on making American students competitive with perceived foreign rivals (National Commission on Excellence in Education, 1983; United States Department of Education, 1991). In such a social and political climate, competitive, exclusive norms may well manifest themselves in middle schools. A school which appears to have explicitly caring, inclusive, cooperative rhetoric and policies could be fraught with undercurrents of indifference, hostility, and stratification at the implicit level of school culture. Such norms are highly likely to disadvantage minority and low-income students. Therefore, it is vital to examine norms of inclusion and cooperation in middle-school culture at both explicit and implicit levels (Erickson, 1982; Kapferer, 1981).

METHODS

This article is drawn from a larger dissertation study which focused on the instructional approach of cooperative learning (Johnson & Johnson, 1987; Slavin, 1983) as embedded in its social and cultural context. I used ethnographic methods (Goetz & LeCompte,

1984; Spindler, 1982) to develop a holistic picture of the sociocultural system within which cooperative learning and the middle-school culture were constructed. Participant and nonparticipant observation, ethnographic interviews, audio recording of verbal interactions, surveys of the physical environment, and document analysis were the primary data collection methods.

I selected Banner Middle School[1] from among three sites, as it appeared to offer the greatest number of examples of the criteria of interest: cooperative learning instruction and ethnic diversity. Banner was located in the town of Industry, on the edge of a large city in the western United States. Industry consisted of modest houses, apartments, and trailer courts interspersed with heavy industries, highways, and numerous bars and liquor stores. The population of 19,000 was primarily working-class, with nonskilled and semiskilled trades as the predominant occupations, and unemployment running considerably higher than in surrounding communities. Banner had approximately 700 students in sixth through eighth grades, with 60 percent qualifying for federal lunch support. The school population comprised 52 percent Caucasians, 42 percent Latinos (predominantly of Mexican ancestry), 3 percent African Americans, 2 percent Native Americans, and 1 percent Asian Americans.

I began data collection during Spring 1990 and ended in January 1992, with most of the fieldwork occurring during the 1990–1991 school year. I was in the field for a total of 77 days conducting observations in classrooms, throughout the school and its grounds, and in the community. I typically recorded written field notes during observations and then typed out and elaborated on them nightly. I made over 40 audio recordings of various events, including classroom lessons, interviews, meetings, and ceremonies. I conducted 30 formal, nonscheduled, standardized interviews with adults, and 28 with students (Goetz & LeCompte, 1984). All audio recordings were transcribed for analysis. I acquired

---

[1]All names of persons and local institutions are pseudonyms.

hundreds of documents, including school bulletins, memos, classroom handouts, textbook passages, tests, and quizzes, plus a large number of school and district records, curriculum guides, and policy statements. I took several rolls of still photos and drew maps of contexts in which I observed frequently. I continued to collect data until I found consistent repetition, indicating saturation (Erickson, 1986). All qualitative data were entered into HyperQual (Padilla, 1991), a Macintosh computer program which permits coding of data at an unlimited number of levels, thus facilitating gradual refinement of inductive and deductive categories of data.

My role in the field was designed to facilitate the greatest possible rapport with the various members of the cultural system. I chose a modification of Mandell's (1988) *least-adult* protocol for my role with students. I told them I was working on a college project to find out what it is like going to middle school. I interacted with them as a peer more than an adult authority figure by being on a first-name basis, eating lunch with them, and avoiding assuming authority over them. Students tested my nonauthority status with gradually escalating misbehavior in my presence, and by sharing the latest sexual and scatological humor with me. With educators, I fully disclosed my professional background. My middle-school teaching experience provided important credibility and access to them. I presented myself as a "graduate student" with parents to avoid any aura of authority.

Data analysis was guided by Erickson's (1982; Deering, 1992) multilevel theoretical framework for examining learning in its social context: (1) the general sociocultural system; (2) the immediate learning environment; and (3) individual functioning. Interactions among individuals occur in immediate learning environments, which, in this study, consisted of contexts such as classrooms, the school grounds, the cafeteria, meetings, dances, and so on. The general sociocultural system is the greater "surround" and, in this case, consisted of the community of Industry and Banner School as a whole. Individual functioning relates to individuals' development of identities in a social and cultural context (Eisenhart, 1990) and is only minimally touched on in this article. Erickson posits that norms and beliefs from the general sociocultural system manifest themselves at the implicit level in immediate learning environments, for example, through patterns of social interaction. Ogbu's (1988) work helps to illuminate a mechanism by which this can occur. He notes that historical oppression and cultural myths regarding success can shape the way students and their families interact with and in schools. He has found some African American youths and their families to hold myths of success that involve avenues other than, and in conflict with, schooling—hence they actively oppose school achievement.

Analysis in the project was both deductive and inductive. I employed deduction via the theoretical framework (Erickson, 1982) and the *a priori* concepts of cooperation and inclusion. I also used inductive processes in seeking emergent patterns and categories in the data (Goetz & LeCompte, 1984). I continuously developed tentative assertions about the nature and relationships of categories of data and subsequently sought refinement in them (Strauss & Corbin, 1990). One such refinement that emerged was conceiving of inclusion and cooperation as continua rather than static concepts. I first used the terms as broad coding categories, with the initial level of differentiation being whether the data related to people's actions or words, followed by coding by participant and framework level. The emergence of the continua helped to explain the data that were neither inclusive nor exclusive, nor cooperative nor competitive.

I actively sought disconfirming evidence and triangulation for my analytical assertions through varied data types (e.g., observations, documents, and interviews) and sources (e.g., students, parents, and educators; Goetz & LeCompte, 1984). I constructed numerous vignettes—low-inference, narrative representations of data during the course of the study (Erickson, 1986), portions of which are included below in the findings. I shared the vignettes and field notes with the participants in order to elicit feedback regarding accuracy and representativeness. I made

several formal presentations of findings to groups of educators and parents, and to the Industry Board of Education during the course of the study. These presentations provided participants with potentially useful insights, and provided me with important feedback on my work. On numerous occasions, input from participants prompted me to revise tentative assertions or to examine new data sources.

FINDINGS

The findings regarding inclusion and cooperation in Banner's school culture are presented in three sections: school culture, peer culture, and parent and community involvement and expectations. Most of the findings are derived from an analysis of the general sociocultural system of the study.

School Culture

Seventh graders pour out of wood shop and head for science class. Tina, a Chicana with the popular "high hair" look, and Ann, a Caucasian, walk together. They stop to check the Student of the Week display in the main hall. They can't believe that Rico won for the seventh grade. "He always goofs around in class!" exclaims Tina.

Lots of kids wave to Gloria, the secretary, as they pass by the office. She smiles and calls "Hi!" and "¡Hola!" to them by name. A couple eighth-grade girls stop to tell her about their continuation [graduation] dresses. Farther down the hall, the principal, Ms. Kramer, is talking to the now-famous Rico. She congratulates him on making it to school for three straight weeks and staying out of trouble. They make plans to go out for pizza with the sixth- and eighth-grade winners on Friday.

Tina and Ann turn down D Hall and pass Ms. Pacheco, the short, stout sixth-grade math teacher. She's in the center of the hall telling kids to stay out of their lockers. She occasionally grabs a boy or a girl and gives him or her a big, ridiculous hug or kiss. Roland Madison, an African American Crips-wannabe,[2] gets this treatment as he enters her room. He scowls sheepishly while trying to suppress a grin. A couple of boys hang around talking to Mr. McAndrews about the Outdoors Club, and about bringing in some of their pet snakes and turtles to science class. Just then, a loud, vicious dog bark explodes through the air. Several students jump in terror before they realize that it was only Mr. Brewer, one of the eighth-grade teachers goofing around. They laugh and begin throwing playful insults at him. (BMS, 9/15/90 and 1/16/91)

Such events were typical at Banner. Presiding over the sometimes-three-ring-circus was Ms. Kramer, in her third year as the principal. A Caucasian in her mid-40s, and a former bilingual education teacher and activist, she approached her job with vision, toughness, caring, and humor. Ms. Kramer was passionate about making Banner a school in which all students were included and cared for:

One thing is crucial and that's that teachers have to want to work with the kids at this level. . . . You have to have a lot of tolerance for the fact that the kids are going through lots of emotional turmoil, developmentally and physically and socially. Emotionally, they are in chaos, often, day by day. Minute by minute, they change. And so you have to really know about early adolescence and transescence, and to understand that and have the ability to work with it, and to tolerate it and not lose your temper, but to find strategies to help these kids to grow into young adulthood, to make some wise decisions. . . .

Middle school has to have . . . a lot of opportunity for self-expression. You know, they [students] will talk about what they are thinking, and what is upsetting to them, what is going on in their minds. . . . I think you really need a team of teachers that are real caring and concerned and work together well. Because everybody has to kind of be a big net around these kids. . . . And the kids need collectively to have everybody working and surrounding them together to help them make it through. . . . This policy has to be a real team effort. (BMS 7/26/90)

Ms. Kramer regularly included and collaborated with teachers and parents on important decisions. Among these were designing a curricular blueprint for the school, prioritizing budget items, scheduling, and implementing a schoolwide emphasis on writing. Ms. Kramer frequently presented issues and parameters and then delegated responsibility to groups of teachers and/or parents to generate solutions or plans. Banner staff meetings were typified by give and take and were sometimes quite contentious. Ms. Kramer described her approach to leadership as follows:

I try not to have real strict boundaries. It is a real dichotomy in a lot of ways, because my style is to involve people in decision making. I would really treat teachers as professionals always, unless they give me reason not to. That is just the way I operate. . . . I will always give them a chance to do it [make a decision] first, and work with them to try to resolve their issues, and to reach a decision. And if they can't, then they put the monkey in my lap, and I say, "OK, fine." . . . [Afterward], unless they can show me a reason why to change it, I usually don't. . . . On a couple of occasions I can think of, they convinced me that "OK, you are probably right; that is better for kids," so I back off on that. . . . That [what is best for kids] is like rule number one, or I always want it to be. I don't like teachers

---

[2]"Crips" are one of the local gangs. A "wannabe" is an official gang hopeful, much like an apprentice.

making decisions based on what's in their comfort zone, or what they are used to, or why they like to come to work every day. (BMS 7/26/90)

Discussion of policies that were "better for kids," occurred repeatedly at Banner, coming from faculty and administration, and appearing in school documents, meetings, and memos. Banner had a warm, family feel, much of which came from Ms. Kramer, and from Gloria and Paloma, the two Chicana secretaries. Each took an active role in nurturing and guiding students with hugs, advice, listening, and—for special accomplishments—a pizza. Banner's counseling staff and many of the teachers reached out to students in formal and informal ways with programs for at-risk students, a new peer-tutoring program, a wide array of discussion and support groups, clubs, and intramural and interscholastic sports programs. Many teachers and teams had their own student recognition programs as well. Further evidence of the caring culture at Banner could be found in the willingness of faculty to spend their own time and money to support student guidance, co- and extra-curricular activities, and classroom instruction. Ms. Klein, a language arts teacher, and Mr. Gallo, a math and social studies teacher, estimated that they each spent $1,500 to $3,000 of their own money annually on classroom supplies, curricular materials, and small rewards for their students.

Banner's school culture was also inclusive in more subtle ways. The composition of the faculty and their competencies illustrated a high degree of inclusiveness. Ms. Kramer and the secretaries, plus Mr. Ramos, the assistant principal, and eight teachers spoke Spanish with some degree of proficiency. This gave the school a degree of linguistic inclusiveness, as each of them could converse with Spanish-speaking students and family members. Another element of inclusiveness could be found in the numerous employees in nontraditional positions. For example, the school had nontraditional leadership in its female principal and its Latino assistant principal. There

were also female math teachers at every grade level, and both computer teachers were women. Material culture at Banner was also inclusive, as the great majority of commercial posters hanging around the school depicted multiracial groups. There was also an impressive display in the main hall for Black History Month.

One of the most striking examples of caring and inclusiveness at Banner occurred when a popular seventh-grader, María Suárez, was killed in an auto accident. Students were given freedom to roam the school grounds, to talk with others or to grieve alone. Banner and outside personnel talked with and listened informally to students all over the school grounds, including hallways, classrooms, and the bleachers. Boys, girls, Latinos, African Americans, and Caucasians walked arm in arm, crying, talking, and consoling each other throughout the day. Quite impressively, there were no incidents of students taking excessive advantage of their day's freedom.

There were some inconsistencies regarding inclusion and cooperation at Banner as well. Despite the substantial number of Spanish-speaking faculty and students, the Spanish language was rarely used outside the English-as-a-second language (ESL) classrooms—basically on an as-needed basis. This detracted from the school's ethnic and linguistic inclusiveness. Nevertheless, when I presented this finding to both the faculty and a parent organization, it was met with great concern. Plans were immediately discussed in both forums to make the Spanish language and Latino culture a much greater focus.

Another way in which Banner's inclusiveness was undermined was in the staffing of the seventh grade's two clusters (teams). Cluster A's completely minority teaching staff and 60 percent minority-student population contrasted markedly with Cluster B's all Caucasian teaching staff and 60 percent Caucasian student population. This created a "brown track" and a "white track," in the words of one teacher. A series of policies and decisions combined to create this imbalance. For one, the special-program students were concentrated by cluster to lessen the amount of running around by support personnel. All of the Latino ESL students were in Cluster A, while all other special-program students were in Cluster B. Both the compensatory special-education students,[3] and gifted-and-talented (GT) students were predominantly Caucasian, hence the great ethnic disparity between the clusters. The teachers were all aware of the ethnic skewing of students and teachers, and the Cluster A teachers in particular were quite upset about it. Ms. Kramer was aware of the ethnic imbalance of the seventh-grade staff but not of the GT program. She noted that she had mandated the program and staff assignments of the seventh-grade clusters after the teachers had remained in a prolonged deadlock over these issues. She said that, in retrospect, she was dissatisfied with the results and would seek a different approach for next year. She explained that one of the Cluster A minority teachers had been hired over the summer after the clusters had been formed, thus exacerbating the ethnic imbalance of the faculty. Ms. Kramer also said that she would initiate a reexamination of selection criteria for the GT program to determine why so few minority students were involved.

Banner's school culture, in addition to its elements of exclusion, contained limited elements of competition. The school and individual teachers held some formal and informal competitions, for example, the Student of the Week mentioned in the vignette. Several teachers used extra-credit points or "bonus bucks" (redeemable for small prizes) for students who behaved well or could answer a recitation question first. More talented and assertive students were disproportionately likely to win these rewards, though not extremely so. For the most part, however, rewards and recognition were quite evenly distributed at Banner. For example, the school and individual teachers made the recognition of student accomplishment a regular, and relatively noncompetitive, cultural feature. Approximately half of the students

received some kind of recognition at the quarterly awards ceremonies for academic, athletic, and service accomplishments. The distribution of awards was proportional by ethnicity but favored girls by about a 60:40 ratio. Caucasians and boys were disproportionately likely to receive failing grades for the first semester of the 1990–1991 school year. I pointed out this higher failure rate for Caucasians to Ms. Kramer and asked her if she had any theories to explain it. She speculated that it was due to more Caucasian students' coming from "dysfunctional families," while the Latino students were more likely to come from "traditional nuclear families" (BMS, 7/26/90). This assessment was later echoed by a central office administrator who described the local Caucasian population as being "stuck" in Industry, with no prospects of moving on, while the Latinos were upwardly mobile and headed for neighboring middle-class communities. In contrast to the low-key response to Caucasians' higher failure rate, Ms. Kramer requested in a memo after the third grading period of 1990–1991 that faculty examine the high rate of D and F grades given to African American students.

Peer Culture

Banner's peer culture was characterized by moderate competition and limited tendencies toward exclusion. Students regularly separated themselves into same-gender groups except when making a brief foray into the other sex's territory, usually for the purpose of flirting. Ethnicity was much more limited as a factor in peer-grouping tendencies. Students generally congregated in ethnically diverse groups, whether in the classroom or other school or nonschool contexts. Romantic couples were almost as likely to be mixed-ethnic as not. When I asked students what kinds of kids there were in the school, I got answers such as "cool, nerds, jocks, nice, mean," but almost never any reference to ethnic or racial groups, as illustrated in the following dialogue. Davey was a Caucasian boy prone to discipline problems; Nina was a Chicana who was well behaved and got good grades.

---

[3]Developmentally Disabled (DD); Emotionally and Behaviorally Disabled (EBD); English as a Second Language (ESL); Learning Disabled (LD); Multiple Handicapped (MH); Severe Learning Handicapped (SLH)

Author: What kinds of kids are there in this school?

Davey: Snooty—they think they're better than people. . . . Cool kids—they hang around with me. . . . We go get into trouble. Preps—people that dress up like they're rich. . . . Nerds—they walk around with their head down. They've got no friends except for nerds. (BMS, 2/21/91)

Author: What kind of kids are there in the this school?

Nina: GT kids. And there's mentally retarded. They're the slow learners. . . . There's smart kids, like with a B average and a little higher. . . . There's not-so-smart kids. They don't understand what's going on. . . . Nice kids are willing to help you when you need it. . . . There's snobs—they think they're number one. . . . Mean kids knock books outa your hands. (BMS, 3/5/91)

Despite the seeming ethnicity-blindness of Banner students, there was ethnic sorting, much of it quite subtle. Latina girls, especially the high-status ones, tended to stick together. The handful of African American students in the school were very likely to be with at least one other member of their race and gender subgroup at any given time, though they mixed quite readily with other students as well. Students in some of the special programs also tended to group together. The ESL students invariably congregated in a mixed-gender group talking in Spanish. Few non-ESL students interacted with them despite many students' being bilingual. Additionally, the DD, MH, and SLH students stuck together, eating in the cafeteria with the MH aides, and congregating together in other settings as well. The GT students gravitated to each other but were far from exclusive about this. The LD and EBD students mixed quite randomly with their peers.

Banner's peer culture had a highly competitive ritual which was enacted at school dances. Only the very best dancers ever danced, and when one of them did so, he or she was immediately challenged by a peer. The dancers would then try to outdo each other at intricate, MTV-style dances while a dense throng of onlookers crowded around. Jesse, a popular eighth-grade Chicana explained dance competitions as follows:

Jesse: Each one of them does their dance till one of them wins.

Author: How do you know who wins?

Jesse: You can tell! The crowd knows too! One of them just *wastes* the other one! Then the loser just quits. (BMS, 9/13/90)

The majority of the dance stars were Latinos or Latinas, with a couple of African Americans and Caucasians; about two thirds were boys. Interestingly, these students interacted quite readily with less socially prestigious students in classroom contexts (see Deering, 1992).

The most overt form of peer competition at Banner consisted of fighting, which was a fairly rare occurrence. Most fights revolved around romantic triangles and verbal putdowns, and at no point during field work was there any evidence of fighting related to race or ethnicity. Overt interracial or interethnic antagonism was conspicuously absent from the peer culture. I heard only one racial or ethnic joke, in contrast to large numbers of "dirty" jokes and blond jokes. The one time I heard a student use a racial or ethnic slur regarding peers was a Caucasian girl's reference to Mexican Americans as "beaners." A friend immediately scolded her, and she quickly repented.

Gangs were a frequent topic of students' conversations but showed limited overt activity—mostly the occasional wearing of gang colors by students. This behavior was always immediately confronted by the school staff. The great majority of opinions I heard from students were very negative toward gangs, as several described losing relatives or friends to gang violence. Mr. Ramos, who was chair of a gang task force, stated that there were only three or four actual gang members at the school, plus a number of wannabes. There were also several girls, mostly Latinas, who were members of the Pretty Girl

Posse, something like the Little Sisters of the Bloods. An interesting feature of gangs in Industry and the general metropolitan area was that they were "equal-opportunity gangs" in the words of the police chief, that is, racially and ethnically mixed.

Parent and Community Involvement and Expectations

Banner was highly inclusive in its relations with parents, families, and community members. Several parents said that this was a result of Ms. Kramer's arrival as principal, as the former administration had been quite hostile to parents. As noted, Banner parents were involved in a wide variety of school governance functions. In addition, parents, families, and community members participated in parent–teacher conferences, open house, service activities, school performances, athletic events, and awards ceremonies. The majority of these events attracted ethnically diverse but mostly female participants. A particularly noteworthy example of parent involvement was the Parent Involvement Team (PITs), a small, tight-knit, raucous group composed mostly of women. Ms. Kramer attended PITs meetings as a participant, adding ideas and swapping jokes with other members, but not leading nor dominating. The PITs had a substantial voice in strategic planning, such as in drawing up the school's curricular blueprint. One event which resulted from the PITs' involvement in school planning was the Ethnic Cookbook and Potluck project, which combined literacy activities and sharing of ethnic heritage. Another highly salient form of parent and family involvement was the year-end awards ceremonies. These were warm, festive potluck dinners attended by hundreds, ranging from grandparents to newborns. By contrast, open house and conferences attracted about one-fourth of the students' parents.

Banner parents were strongly supportive of cooperation and inclusion in interviews and conversations. When asked to choose between having their children learn to strive to be number one in school or to learn to get along with others, all but one parent chose getting along with others. Most noted that working with other kinds of children was good preparation for the world of work. The comments of a working class Caucasian couple exemplified this outlook:

> Stepfather: I think it would be group [that I prefer]. Learning how to relate, you could say, with other people, learning how to cooperate with other people.
> Mother: Because you are going to have to work with different people all your life.
> Stepfather: Because, like I keep telling him, "You're going to have to go through this all your life. . . . You're going to get up, you get a job, you're either going to have to work with this person or you're going to not work." *You* know. (BMS, 5/16/91)

The only parent among the 15 whom I interviewed at length who spoke against cooperation and inclusion was the mother of a Caucasian GT student. She felt that her son was being held back by being forced to work in the same classroom and in cooperative groups with less capable students.

DISCUSSION

Two factors stand out in explaining the generally high degrees of inclusion and cooperation at Banner Middle School: the strong leadership provided by Ms. Kramer and the cultural congruity of these norms.

Ms. Kramer contributed to the development and maintenance of a cooperative and inclusive school culture in two ways. First, she steadfastly advocated the implementation of cooperative and inclusive middle-level educational principles, such as widespread recognition of student success, equal opportunity, and providing caring and guidance for all. In addition, Ms. Kramer used a very inclusive and cooperative approach to leadership, thus providing a powerful model of these principles. Her inclusion of teachers and parents in meaningful decision making greatly enhanced the legitimacy of her advocacy for an inclusive, cooperative school. However, Ms. Kramer's participatory management approach was time-consuming. Ironically, one of her rare mandates created the racially skewed seventh-grade cluster distribution when she intervened in the teachers' deadlock on scheduling. Nevertheless, Ms. Kramer's willingness to hear feedback on the cluster and program distributions boded well for an eventual resolution of those problems.

The power afforded to parents through the PITs was also a highly inclusive and cooperative cultural norm. This contrasts sharply with Ogbu's (1987) findings of minority parents' being treated with hostility and contempt by school officials. Banner's openness toward parents was also largely attributable to Ms. Kramer, although she could not have created such a norm without the support of her staff. Another noteworthy element of parent and family inclusion was the great turnout at the school's nontraditional, family-oriented rituals. This suggests that they offered a more culturally congruent form of participation than the more traditional conferences and open house. Schools in other working-class contexts, and perhaps elsewhere, might emulate such family-style events.

The congruity between the explicit and implicit levels of Banner's school culture regarding inclusion and cooperation suggests that these were deeply held values. For example, at the explicit level, school documents and Ms. Kramer's pronouncements about inclusion, caring, and cooperation were consistent with the staff's myriad ways of reaching out to students. Cooperation and inclusion were congruent cultural norms for the students, and for the parents as well. The generally positive, noncompetitive, nonexclusive interethnic relations among students offer evidence of this congruency. So, too, did the parents' support of their children learning how to get along with others different from themselves. The linking of their support for these norms with their career aspira-

tions for their children suggests a sort of cooperative-inclusive folktale of success (Ogbu, 1988), in contrast to the traditional American myth of competitive, independent striving. This holds promising implications for middle-school and multicultural educators, as it suggests that working-class and minority parents may be particularly supportive of the cooperative, inclusive norms which are such an integral part of middle-school and multicultural educational philosophy (Cummins, 1986; Johnston, 1992; Van Hoose & Strahan, 1991).

The rather modest amount of competition promoted at Banner did not seem to undermine cooperative norms. Indeed, Banner was quite "warm and fuzzy" in comparison with the intensely competitive school cultures described in ethnographic studies by Goldman and McDermott (1987) of white, affluent "Allwin School," and by Merten (1994) of "Fern Hills Junior High." Banner's widely distributed awards and recognition promoted a sense that all could succeed. However, it appeared that Caucasians, African Americans, and boys were at a disadvantage, with their higher academic failure rates and the high proportion of Caucasians in compensatory special-education programs. The educators' apparently greater concern with the academic inequities experienced by minority students versus those experienced by Caucasians is a troubling phenomenon. It suggests that working-class Caucasian students are vulnerable to some of the same low expectations that have historically plagued minority students, for example, cultural deficit theories (Trueba, 1988), or at least, that their problems are not as likely to attract attention and concern. Educators in multicultural and/or low-income schools should be on the alert for such discrimination, as it would be terribly ironic to simply turn the racial tables in educational inequity.

The consistent tendency of Banner students to congregate with peers in the same special-education programs is testimony to the power of these ascribed identities. Similarly, the students' choice of same-gender groupings illustrates the social power of gender. Sorting by gender is a common developmental tendency of early adolescents (Stevenson, 1992) and probably not a cause for concern as manifested in this study. However, the students' exclusivity by special program stands as a challenge to the middle-school movement's advocacy of heterogeneous grouping and diverse social interaction (Beane & Lipka, 1987; Spear, 1992). Cooperative learning approaches have shown considerable promise in breaking down such barriers through prolonged, active, face-to-face interaction (Johnson & Johnson, 1987; Slavin, 1983). However, these approaches are no panacea for promoting positive intergroup relations, as other analyses from this project and work by others have demonstrated (Davis, 1984; Deering, 1992; Johnson, Johnson, Scott, and Ramolae, 1985; Gonzales, 1979; Slavin & Oickle, 1981; Webb, 1984, 1989; Weigel, Wiser, & Cook, 1975).

The generally strong, consistent support for norms of inclusion and cooperation at the explicit and implicit levels of school culture offer hope that middle schools can indeed be environments where *all* have a place. The principal's commitment to these norms, her collaborative leadership approach, and the congruity of inclusion and cooperation with peer culture and parents' expectations made them a very real part of the school's culture—at both explicit and implicit levels. This offers empirical evidence to support the theoretical compatibility of middle-school and multicultural educational philosophy. In addition, this study illustrates that examining multiple levels of social organization and culture can shed light on how the middle-school and multicultural educational ideals of inclusion and cooperation come to be constructed, the better to promote and nurture them.

Acknowledgments. I wish to thank the people of "Banner Middle School" and the community of "Industry" for welcoming me among them. I would also like to thank Margaret A. Eisenhart, Michael S. Meloth, Evelyn Jacob, and the University of Colorado School of Education's Anthropology Group for helping me to develop this line of research. The responsibility for all content lies solely with me.

REFERENCES

Alexander, William M., and George, Paul S. (1981). *The Exemplary Middle School.* New York: Holt, Rinehart & Winston.

Allport, Gordon W. (1954). *The Nature of Prejudice.* Cambridge, MA: Addison-Wesley.

Banks, James A. (1991). Multicultural education: For freedom's sake. *Educational Leadership* 49: 32–36.

Beane, James A. (1990). *A Middle School Curriculum: From Rhetoric to Reality.* Columbus, OH: National Middle School Association.

Beane, James A., and Lipka, Richard P. (1987). *When the Kids Come First: Enhancing Self Esteem.* Columbus, OH: National Middle School Association.

Carnegie Council on Adolescent Development. (1989). *Turning points: Preparing American Youth for the 21st Century.* New York: Author.

Clark, Sally N., and Clark, Donald C. (1993). Middle level school reform: The rhetoric and the reality. *Elementary School Journal* 93: 447–460.

Cummins, James (1986). Empowering minority students: A framework for intervention. *Harvard Educational Review* 56: 18–36.

Davis, B. R. (1984). *Evaluation of the Race/Human Relations Program: A Study of Cooperative Learning Strategies.* San Diego: San Diego City Schools, Division of Planning, Research and Evaluation. Washington, DC: Eric Document Reproduction Service, ED 256 862.

Deering, Paul D. (1992). *An ethnographic study of cooperative learning in a multiethnic working class middle school.* Unpublished doctoral dissertation, University of Colorado, Boulder.

Dillon, Deborah R. (1989). Showing them that I want them to learn and that I care about who they are: A microethnography of the social organization of a secondary low-track English-reading classroom. *American Educational Research Journal* 26: 227–259.

Eisenhart, Margaret A. (1990). Learning to romance: Cultural acquisition in college. *Anthropology and Education Quarterly* 21: 19–40.

Erickson, Frederick (1982). Taught cognitive learning in its immediate environments: A neglected topic in the anthropology of education. *Anthropology and Education Quarterly* 13: 149–180.

Erickson, Frederick (1986). Qualitative methods in research on teaching. In M. Wittrock (ed.), *Handbook of research on teaching,* 3rd ed., pp. 119–161. New York: Macmillan.

Fordham, Signithia (1988). *Peer-Proofing Academic Competition Among Black Adolescents: "Acting White" Black American Style.* Paper presented at the annual meeting of the American Anthropological Association, Phoenix, AZ.

Fordham, Signithia, and Ogbu, John U. (1986). Black students' school success: Coping with the "burden of 'acting White.' " *The Urban Review* 18: 176–206.

Geertz, Clifford (1973). *The Interpretation of Cultures.* New York: Basic Books.

Gilligan, Carol (1982). *In a Different Voice.* Cambridge: Harvard University Press.

Goetz, Judith P., and LeCompte, Margaret L. (1984). *Ethnography and Qualitative Design in Educational Research.* Orlando, FL: Academic Press.

Goldman, Shelley V., and McDermott, Ray (1987). The culture of competition in American schools. In George D. Spindler (ed.), *Education and Cultural Process: Anthropological Approaches,* 2nd ed., pp. 282–300. Prospect Hts., IL: Waveland Press.

Gonzales, A. (1979). *Classroom cooperation and ethnic balance.* Paper presented at the annual convention of the American Psychological Association, New York City.

Heath, Shirley B. (1983). *Ways with Words: Language, Life, and Work in Communities and Classrooms.* Cambridge: Cambridge University Press.

Johnson, David W., and Johnson, Roger T. (1987). *Learning Together and Alone: Cooperative,* *Competitive and Individualistic Learning,* 2nd ed. Englewood Cliffs, NJ: Prentice-Hall.

Johnson, Roger T., Johnson, David W., Scott, L. E., and Ramolae, B. A. (1985). Effects of single-sex and mixed-sex cooperative interaction on science achievement and attitudes and cross-handicap and cross-sex relationships. *Journal of Research in Science Teaching,* 22: 207–220.

Johnston, J. H. (1992). Climate and culture as mediators of school values and collaborative behavior. In Judith L. Irvin (ed.), *Transforming Middle Level Education: Perspectives and Possibilities,* pp. 77–92. Boston: Allyn & Bacon.

Kagan, Spencer (1984). Interpreting Chicano cooperativeness: Methodological and theoretical considerations. In J. L. Martinez and R. H. Mendoza (eds.), *Chicano Psychology,* 2nd ed. New York: Academic Press.

Kagan, Spencer (1986). Cooperative learning and sociocultural factors in learning. In Bilingual Education Office, California State Department of Education, *Beyond Language: Social and Cultural Factors in Schooling Language Minority Students,* pp. 231–298. Los Angeles: Author.

Kapferer, Judith L. (1981). Socialization and the symbolic order of the school. *Anthropology and Education Quarterly* 12: 259–274.

Kochan, Frances K. (1992). A new paradigm of schooling: Connecting school, home and community. In Judith L. Irvin (ed.), *Transforming Middle Level Education: Perspectives and Possibilities,* pp. 63–71. Boston: Allyn & Bacon.

Lewis, Anne C. (1990) *Making It in the Middle: The Why and How of Excellent Schools for Young Urban Adolescents.* New York: Edna McConnell Clark Foundation.

Little Soldier, L. (1989). Cooperative learning and the Native American student. *Phi Delta Kappan* 71: 161–163.

Mandell, Nancy (1988). The least-adult role in studying children. *Journal of Contemporary Ethnography* 16: 433–467.

Merten, Don E. (1993). The cultural context of aggression: The transition to junior high school. *Anthropology and Education Quarterly* 25: 29–43.

National Commission on Excellence in Education. (1983). *A Nation at Risk: The Imperative for Educational Reform: A Report to the Nation and the Secretary of Education, United States Department of Education.* Washington, DC: Author.

Oakes, Jeannie, Quartz, Karen H., Gong, Jennifer, Guiton, Gretchen, and Lipton, Martin (1993). Creating middle schools: Technical, normative, and political considerations. *Elementary School Journal* 93: 461–480.

Ogbu, John U. (1987). Variability in minority school performance: A problem in search of an explanation. *Anthropology and Education Quarterly* 18: 312–334.

Ogbu, John U. (1988). Class stratification, race stratification, and schooling. In Lois Weiss (ed.), *Class, Race and Gender in American Education,* pp. 163–182. Albany: State University of New York Press.

Padilla, Raymond V. (1991). *HyperQual Version 4.0.* Chandler, AZ: Author.

Philips, Susan U. (1972). Participant structures and communicative competence: Warm Springs children in community and classroom. In Courtney Cazden, Vera P. John, and Dell Hymes (eds.), *Functions of Language in the Classroom* pp. 370–394. New York: Teachers College Press.

Scales, Peter (1991). *A portrait of Young Adolescents in the 1990's.* Carrboro, NC: Center for Early Adolescence.

Slavin, Robert E. (1983). *Cooperative learning.* New York: Longman.

Slavin, Robert E., and Oickle, E. (1981). Effects of cooperative learning teams on student achievement and race relations: Treatment by race interactions. *Sociology of Education* 54: 174–180.

Spear, Robert C. (1992). Appropriate grouping practices for middle level students. In Judith L. Irvin (ed.), *Transforming Middle Level Education: Perspectives and Possibilities,* pp. 244–274. Boston: Allyn & Bacon.

Spindler, George D. (ed.). (1982). *Doing the Ethnography of Schooling: Educational Anthropology in Action.* New York: Holt, Rinehart & Winston.

Stevenson, Christopher (1992). *Teaching Ten to Fourteen Year Olds.* New York: Longman.

Stevenson, Christopher, and Carr, Judy F. (1993). *Integrated Studies in the Middle Grades.* New York: Teachers College Press.

Strauss, Anselm, and Corbin, Juliet (1990). *Basics of Qualitative Research: Grounded Theory Procedures and Techniques.* Newbury Park, CA: Sage.

Tharp, Roland G., and Gallimore, Ronald (1988). *Rousing Minds to Life: Teaching, Learning, and Schooling in Social Context.* Cambridge, MA: Cambridge University Press.

Trueba, Henry T. (1988). Culturally based explanations of minority students' academic achievement. *Anthropology and Education Quarterly* 19: 270–287.

U.S. Department of Education. (1991). *America 2000: An overview.* Washington, DC: Author.

Van Hoose, John, and Strahan, David (1991). *Young Adolescent Development and School Practices: Promoting Harmony.* Columbus, OH: National Middle School Association.

Webb, Noreen M. (1984). Sex differences in interaction and achievement in cooperative small groups. *Journal of Educational Psychology* 76: 33–44.

Webb, Noreen M. (1989). Peer interaction and learning in small groups. *International Journal of Educational Research* 13: 21–40.

Weigel, R. H., Wiser, P. L., and Cook, S. W. (1975). Impact of cooperative learning experiences on cross-ethnic relations and attitudes. *Journal of Social Issues* 31: 219–245.

Wheelock, Anne (1986). Dropping out: What the research says. *Equity and Choice* 3: 7–11.

Wheelock, Anne (1992). *Crossing the Tracks.* New York: New Press.

Correlations of Different Strengths and Directions

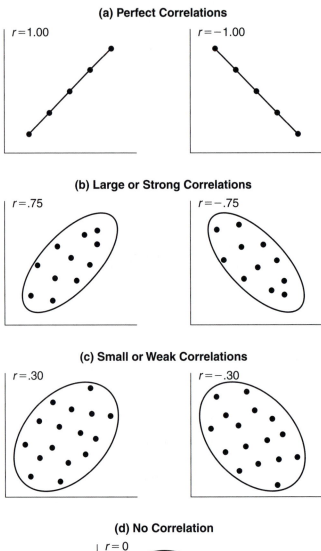

FIGURE 1 Correlations of different strengths and directions.

References

Adler, P. A., & Adler, P. (1991). *Blackboards and black-boards: College athletes and role engulfment.* New York: Columbia University Press.

Alkin, M. (1979). *Using evaluations: Does evaluation make a difference?* Beverly Hills, CA: Sage.

American Association for the Advancement of Science. (1990). *Science for all Americans: Project 2061.* New York: Oxford University Press.

American Educational Research Association (AERA). (1992). Ethical standards of the American Educational Research Association. *Educational Researcher, 21,* 23–26.

American Psychological Association (APA). (1994). *Publication manual of the American Psychological Association* (4th ed.). Washington, DC: Author.

Anderson, J. R. (1995). *Cognitive psychology and its implications.* New York: W. H. Freeman.

Angeles, P. A. (1992). *Philosophy.* New York: Harper-Collins.

Asher, H. B. (1983). *Causal modeling.* Beverly Hills, CA: Sage.

Babbie, E. R. (1990). *Survey research methods.* Belmont, CA: Wadsworth.

Babbie, E. (1998). *The practice of social research* (8th ed.). Belmont, CA: Wadsworth.

Baer, R. A., Tishelman, A. C., Degler, J. D., Osnes, P. G., & Stokes, T. F. (1992). Effects of self- vs. experimenter-selection of rewards on classroom behavior in young children. *Education and Treatment of Children, 15,* 1–14.

Bailey, K. D. (1994). *Typologies and taxonomies: An introduction to classification techniques.* Thousand Oaks, CA: Sage.

Baloche, L. (1994). Creativity and cooperation in the elementary music classroom. *The Journal of Creative Behavior, 28*(4), 255–265.

Bandalos, D. L., Yates, K., & Thorndike-Christ, T. (1995). Effects of math self-concept, perceived self-efficacy, and attributions for failure and success on test anxiety. *Journal of Educational Psychology, 87,* 611–623.

Barlow, D. H., & Hersen, M. (1992). *Single-case experimental designs. Strategies for studying behavior change* (Rev. 2nd ed.). Boston: Allyn & Bacon.

Baron, R. M., & Kenny, D. A. (1986). The moderator-mediator variable distinction in social psychological research: Conceptual, strategic, and statistical considerations. *Journal of Personality and Social Psychology, 51*(6), 1173–1182.

493

Bass, R. R. (1997). Development of a pseudo aggression device. *Journal of Fictitious and Nonexistent Devices, 99,* 1–2.

Baumrind, D. (1985). Research using intentional deception: Ethical issues revisited. *American Psychologist, 40,* 165–174.

Becker, H. S. (1986). *Writing for social scientists.* Chicago: University of Chicago Press.

Berg, B. L. (1998). *Qualitative research methods for the social sciences.* Boston: Allyn & Bacon.

Bijou, S. W., Peterson, R. F., Harris, F. R., Allen, K. E., & Johnston, M. S. (1969). Methodology for experimental studies of young children in natural settings. *Psychological Record, 19,* 177–210.

Blackburn, S. (1994). *The Oxford dictionary of philosophy.* Oxford: Oxford University Press.

Borden, M., Bruce, C., Mitchell, M. A., Carter, V., & Hall, R. V. (1970). Effects of teacher attention on attending behavior of two boys at adjacent desks. *Journal of Applied Behavior Analysis, 3,* 199–203.

Box, G. E. P., Hunter, W. G., & Hunter, J. S. (1978). *Statistics for experimenters.* New York: Wiley.

Box, G. E. P., & Jenkins, G. M. (1970). *Time-series analysis: Forecasting and control.* San Francisco: Holden-Day.

Bracht, G. H., & Glass, G. V. (1968). The external validity of experiments. *American Educational Research Journal, 5,* 437–474.

Brewer, J., & Hunter, A. (1989). *Multimethod research: A synthesis of styles.* Newbury Park, CA: Sage.

Breznitz, Z. (1997). Effects of accelerated reading rate on memory for text among dyslexic readers. *Journal of Educational Psychology, 89,* 289–297.

Bro, R. T., Shank, L. L., McLaughlin, T. F., & Williams, R. L. (1996). Effects of a breakfast program on on-task behaviors of vocational high school students. *The Journal of Educational Research, 90,* 112–115.

Brody, J. E. (1973, October 29). New heart study absolves coffee. *New York Times,* p. 6.

Brown, R., Pressley, M., Van Meter, P., & Schuder, T. (1996). A quasi-experimental validation of transactional strategies instruction with low-achieving second-grade readers. *Journal of Educational Psychology, 88,* 18–37.

Brown, T. (1996). The phenomenology of the mathematics classroom. *Educational Studies in Mathematics, 31,* 115–150.

Bryman, A., & Burgess, R. G. (1994). *Analyzing qualitative data.* (Edited). London: Routledge.

Butler, R., & Neuman, O. (1995). Effects of task and ego achievement goals on help-seeking behaviors. *Journal of Educational Psychology, 87,* 261–271.

Campbell, D. T. (1969). Reforms as experiments. *American Psychologist, 24,* 409–429.

Campbell, D. T. (1979). Degrees of freedom and the case study. In T. D. Cook & C. S. Reichardt (Eds.), *Qualitative and quantitative methods in evaluation research* (pp. 49–67). Beverly Hills, CA: Sage.

Campbell, D. T., & Boruch, R. F. (1975). Making the case for randomized assignments to treatments by considering the alternatives: Six ways in which quasi-experimental evaluations in compensatory education tend to underestimate effects. In C. A. Bennett & A. A. Lunsdaine (Eds.), *Evaluation and experiment: Some critical issues in assessing social programs.* New York: Academic Press.

Campbell, D. T., & Fiske, D. W. (1959). Convergent and discriminant validation by the multitrait-multimethod matrix. *Psychological Bulletin, 56,* 81–105.

Campbell, D. T., & Stanley, J. C. (1963) *Experimental and quasi-experimental designs for research.* Chicago: Rand McNally.

Carr, E. H. (1963). *What is history?* New York: Knopf.

Carr, M., & Jessup, D. L. (1997). Gender differences in first-grade mathematics strategy use: Social and metacognitive influences. *Journal of Educational Psychology, 89,* 318–328.

Chamberlin, T. (1965). The method of multiple working hypotheses. *Science, 147,* 754–759.

Chaplin, W. F., John, O. P., & Goldberg, L. R. (1988). Conceptions of state and traits: Dimensional attributes with ideals as prototypes. *Journal of Personality and Social Psychology, 54,* 541–557.

Christensen, L. (1991). Issues in the design of studies investigating the behavioral concomitants of foods. *Journal of Consulting and Clinical Psychology, 59,* 874–882.

Christensen, L. (1993). Effects of eating behavior on mood: A review of the literature. *International Journal of Eating Disorders, 14,* 173–183.

Christensen, L. (1997). *Experimental methodology.* Boston: Allyn & Bacon.

Christy, T. E. (1975). The methodology of historical research: A brief introduction. *Nursing Research, 24,* 189–192.

Cliff, N. (1984). An improved internal consistency reliability estimate. *Journal of Educational Statistics, 9,* 151–161.

Cochran, W. G. (1977). *Sampling techniques.* New York: Wiley.

Cohen, J. (1968). Multiple regression as a general data-analytic system. *Psychological Bulletin, 70,* 426–443.

Cohen, J., & Cohen, P. (1983). *Applied multiple regression/correlation analysis for the behavioral sciences.* Hillsdale, NJ: Lawrence Erlbaum.

Cohen, R. J., Swerdlik, M. E., & Phillips, S. M. (1996). *Psychological testing and assessment: An introduction to tests and measurements* (3rd ed.). Mountain View, CA: Mayfield.

Collingwood, R. G. (1940). *An essay on metaphysics.* Oxford: Clarendon.

Converse, J. M., & Presser, S. (1986). *Survey questions: Handcrafting the standardized questionnaire.* Newbury Park, CA: Sage.

Cook, T. D., & Campbell, D. T. (1979). *Quasi-experimentation. Design and analysis issues for field settings.* Chicago: Rand McNally.

Cook, T. D. & Shadish, W. R. (1994). Social experiments: Some developments over the past fifteen years. *Annual Review of Psychology, 45,* 545–580.

Cosbie, J. (1993). Interrupted time-series analysis with brief single-subject data. *Journal of Consulting and Clinical Psychology, 61,* 966–974.

Creswell, J. W. (1994). *Research design: Qualitative and quantitative approaches.* Thousand Oaks, CA: Sage.

Creswell, J. W. (1998). *Qualitative inquiry and research design: Choosing among five traditions.* Thousand Oaks, CA: Sage.

Creswell, J. W., & Brown, M. L. (1992). How chairpersons enhance faculty research: A grounded theory study. *The Review of Higher Education, 16*(1), 41–62.

Crocker, L., & Algina, J. (1986). *Introduction to classical and modern test theory.* Fort Worth: Holt, Rinehart, and Winston.

Cronbach, L. J. (1951). Coefficient alpha and the internal structure of tests. *Psychometrika, 16,* 297–334.

Cronbach, L. J. (1982). *Designing evaluations of educational and social programs.* San Francisco: Jossey-Bass.

Cronbach, L. J. (1984). *Essentials of psychological testing* (4th ed.). New York: Harper & Row.

Cronbach, L. J., & Furby, L. (1970). "How should we measure change"—or should we? *Psychological Bulletin, 74,* 68–80.

Cross, T. L., & Stewart, R. A. (1995). A phenomenological investigation of the Lebenswelt of gifted students in rural high schools. *The Journal of Secondary Gifted Education, 6*(4), 273–280.

Dane, F. C. (1990). *Research methods.* Pacific Grove, CA: Brooks/Cole.

Davis, J. A. (1985). *The logic of causal order.* Beverly Hills, CA: Sage.

Davis, J. A., & Smith, T. W. (1992). *The NORC General Social Survey: A user's guide.* Newbury Park, CA: Sage.

Denzin, N. K. (1989). *The research act: Theoretical introduction to sociological methods.* Englewood Cliffs, NJ: Prentice Hall.

Deering, P. D. (1996). An ethnographic study of norms of inclusion and cooperation in a multiethnic middle school. *The Urban Review, 28*(1), 21–39.

Dey, I. (1993). *Qualitative data analysis: A user-friendly guide for social scientists.* London: Routledge.

Deyhle, D. M. (1992, January). Constructing failure and maintaining cultural identity: Navajo and Ute school leavers. *Journal of American Indian Education,* 24–47.

Diener, E., & Crandall, R. (1978). *Ethics in social and behavioral research.* Chicago: The University of Chicago Press.

Drew, N. (1986). Exclusion and confirmation: A phenomenology of patients' experiences with caregivers. *IMAGE: Journal of Nursing Scholarship, 18,* 39–43.

Dworkin, A. G. (1987). *Burnout in the public schools: Structural causes and consequences for children.* Albany, NY: State University of New York Press.

Dykeman, C., Daehlin, W., Doyle, S., & Flamer, H. S. (1996). Psychological predictors of school-based violence: Implications for school counselors. *The School Counselor, 44,* 35–44.

Educational Testing Service. (1997). *GRE 1997–98 Guide to the Use of Scores.* Princeton, NJ: Author.

Farreil, E., Peguero, G., Lindsey, R., & White, R. (1988). Giving voice to high school students: Pressure and boredom, ya know what I'm sayin'? *American Education Research Journal, 25*(4), 489–502.

Festinger, I. (1957). *A theory of cognitive dissonance.* New York: Harper & Row.

Fetterman, D. M. (1998). Ethnography. In L. Bickman, & D. J. Rog (Eds.), *Handbook of Applied Social Research Methods.* Thousand Oaks, CA: Sage.

Finkel, S. E. (1995). *Causal analysis with panel data.* Thousand Oaks, CA: Sage.

Fisher, J. C. (1993). A framework for describing developmental change among older adults. *Adult Education Quarterly, 43*(2), 76–89.

Flannery, D. D. (1991). Adults' expectations of instructors: Criteria for hiring and evaluating instructors. *Continuing Higher Education Review, 55.*

Flynn, J. R. (1987). Massive IQ gains in 14 nations: What IQ tests really measure. *Psychological Bulletin, 101,* 171–191.

Forness, S. R., & Kavale, K. A. (1996). Treating social skill deficits in children with learning disabilities: A meta-analysis of the research. *Learning Disability Quarterly, 19,* 2–9.

Fraenkel, J. R., & Wallen, N. E. (1996). *How to design and evaluate research in education.* New York: McGraw-Hill.

Frankfort-Nachmias, C., & Nachmias, D. (1992). *Research methods in the social sciences* (4th ed.). New York: St Martin's Press.

Fritze, R. H., Coutts, B. E., & Vyhnanek, L. A. (1990). *Reference sources in history: An introductory guide.* Santa Barbara, CA: ABC-CLIO.

Frontman, K. C., & Kunkel, M. A. (1994). A grounded theory of counselors' construal of success in the initial session. *Journal of Counseling Psychology, 41*(4), 492–499.

Fuertes, J. N., Sedlacek, W. E., & Liu, W. M. (1994). Using the SAT and noncognitive variables to predict the grades and retention of Asian American university students. *Measurement and Evaluation in Counseling and Development, 27,* 74–84.

Fultz, M. (1995). African American teachers in the South, 1890–1940: Powerlessness and the ironies of expectation and protest. *History of Education Quarterly, 35,* 401–422.

Gage, J. T. (1991). *The shape of reason* (2nd ed.). New York: Macmillan.

Gail, M. H. (1996). Statistics in action. *Journal of the American Statistical Association, 91*(433), 1–13.

Galenson, D. W. (1998). Ethnic differences in neighborhood effects on the school attendance of boys in early Chicago. *History of Education Quarterly, 38,* 17–35.

Gallo, M. A., & Horton, P. B. (1994). Assessing the effect on high school teachers of direct and unrestricted access to the Internet: A case study of an East Central Florida high school. *ETR&D, 42*(4), 17–39.

Gay, L. R. (1996). *Educational research: Competencies for analysis and application.* Englewood Cliffs, NJ: Prentice-Hall.

Gentile, J. R., Voelkl, K. E., Mt. Pleasant, J., & Monaco, N. I. (1995). Recall after relearning by fast and slow learners. *The Journal of Experimental Education, 63*(3), 185–197.

Glaser, B. G. (1978). *Theoretical sensitivity.* Mill Valley, CA: Sociology Press.

Glaser, B. G., & Strauss, A. L. (1967). *The discovery of grounded theory: Strategies for qualitative research.* New York: Aldine De Gruyter.

Glass, G. (1976). Primary, secondary, and meta-analysis of research. *Educational Research, 5,* 3–8.

Glass, G. V. & Hopkins, K. D. (1984). *Statistical methods in education and psychology* (2nd ed.). Englewood Cliffs, NJ: Prentice-Hall.

Glass, G. V., & Hopkins, K. D. (1996). *Statistical methods in education and psychology.* Needham Heights, MA: Allyn & Bacon.

Glass, G. V., Willson, V. L., & Gottman, J. M. (1975). *Design and analysis of time series.* Boulder, CO: Laboratory of Educational Research Press.

Glenn, N. D. (1977). *Cohort analysis.* Beverly Hills, CA: Sage.

Goffman, E. (1959). *The presentation of self in everyday life.* Garden City, NY: Anchor Books.

Gold, R. (1958). Roles in sociological field observations. *Social Forces, 36,* 217–223.

Goldenberg, C. (1992). The limits of expectations: A case for case knowledge about teacher expectancy effects. *American Educational Research Journal, 29,* 517–544.

Green, A. J. (1995). Experiential learning and teaching: A critical evaluation of an enquiry which used phenomenological method. *Nurse Education Today, 15,* 420–426.

Grisso, T., Baldwin, E., Blanck, P. D., Rotheram-Borus, M. J., Schooler, N. R., & Thompson, T. (1991). Standards in research: APA's mechanism for monitoring challenges. *American Psychologist, 46,* 758–766.

Guba, E. G., & Lincoln, Y. S. (1981). *Effective evaluation.* San Francisco: Jossey-Bass.

Guba, E. G., & Lincoln, Y. S. (1989). *Fourth Generation Evaluation.* Newbury Park, CA: Sage.

Guilford, J. P. (1936). *Psychometric methods.* New York: McGraw-Hill.

Guilford, J. P. (1959). *Personality.* New York: McGraw-Hill.

Gunter, P. L., Shores, R. E., Jack, S. L., Denny, R. K., & DePaepe, P. A. (1994). A case study of the effects of altering instructional interactions on the disruptive behavior of a child identified with severe behavior disorders. *Education and Treatment of Children, 17,* 435–444.

Hall, C. S., & Lindzey, G. (1970). *Theories of Personality.* New York: Wiley.

Hall, R. V., & Fox, R. W. (1977). Changing-criterion designs: An alternative applied behavior analysis procedure. In C. C. Etzel, G. M. LeBlanc, & D. M. Baer (Eds.), *New developments in behavioral research: Theory, method, and application* (in honor of Sidney W. Bijou). Hillsdale, NJ: Lawrence Erlbaum.

Harchar, R. L., & Hyle, A. E. (1996). Collaborative power: A grounded theory of administrative instructional leadership in the elementary school. *Journal of Educational Administration, 34*(3), 15–29.

Harnett, D. L. (1982). *Statistical methods* (3rd ed.). Reading, MA: Addison Wesley.

Harry, B. (1992). An ethnographic study of cross-cultural communication with Puerto Rican-American families in the special education system. *American Educational Research Journal, 29*(3), 471–494.

Hays, W. L. (1994). *Statistics.* New York: Holt, Rinehart, and Winston.

Henry, G. T. (1990). *Practical sampling.* Newbury Park, CA: Sage.

Hersen, M., & Barlow, D. H. (1976). *Single case experimental designs: Strategies for studying behavioral change.* New York: Pergamon.

Hersen, M., & Bellack, A. S. (1988). *Dictionary of behavioral assessment techniques.* New York: Pergamon.

Hilgartner, S. (1990). Research fraud, misconduct, and the IRB. *IRB: A Review of Human Subjects Research, 12,* 1–4.

Hitler diaries trial stirs judge to disbelief and ire. (1985, January 6). *New York Times,* p. A14.

Holden, C. (1987). NIMH finds a case of "serious misconduct." *Science, 235,* 1566–1567.

Holland, D. C., & Eisenhart, M. A. (1990). *Educated in romance: Women, achievement, and college culture.* Chicago: University of Chicago Press.

Holy Horatio. (1974, June 10). *Time, 103,* 18.

Howe, K. R. & Dougherty, K. C. (1993). Ethics, institutional review boards, and the changing face of educational research. *Educational Researcher, 22,* 16–21.

Howell, D. C. (1997). *Statistical methods for psychology.* Belmont, CA: Duxbury Press.

Huber, G. P., & Van de Van, A. H. (1995). *Longitudinal field research methods: Studying processes of organizational change.* Thousand Oaks, CA: Sage.

Huberman, A. M., & Miles, M. B. (1994). Data management and analysis methods. In *Handbook of Qualitative Research,* N. K. Denzin & Y. S. Lincoln (Eds.). Newbury Park, CA: Sage.

Huck, S. W., & Cormier, W. H. (1996). *Reading statistics and research.* New York: HarperCollins.

Hult, C. A. (1996). *Researching and writing in the social sciences.* Boston: Allyn & Bacon.

Humphreys, P. (1989). *The chances of explanation: Causal explanation in the social, medical, and physical sciences.* Princeton, NJ: Princeton University Press.

Hyde, J. S., Fennema, E., & Lamon, S. J. (1990). Gender differences in mathematics performance: A meta-analysis. *Psychological Bulletin, 107*(2), 139–155.

Imich, A. J. (1994). Exclusions from school: Current trends and issues. *Educational Researcher, 36,* 3–11.

Isaac, S., & Michael, W. B. (1995). *Handbook in research and evaluation: For education and the behavioral sciences.* San Diego, CA: Educational and Industrial Testing Services.

Jaeger, R. M. (1984). *Sampling in education and the social sciences.* New York: Longman.

Jenkins, J. J., Russell, W. A., & Suci, G. J. (1958). An atlas of semantic profiles for 360 words. *American Journal of Psychology, 71,* 688–699.

Jimerson, S., Carlson, E., Rotert, M., Egeland, B., & Sroufe, L. A. (1997). A prospective, longitudinal study of the correlates and consequences of early grade retention. *Journal of School Psychology, 35*(1), 3–25.

Johnson, R. B. (1994). Qualitative research in education. *SRATE Journal, 4*(1), 3–7.

Johnson, R. B. (1995). Estimating an evaluation utilization model using conjoint measurement and analysis. *Evaluation Review, 19*(3), 313–338.

Johnson, R. B. (1997). Examining the validity structure of qualitative research. *Education, 118*(2), 282–292.

Jones, J. H. (1981). *Bad blood: The Tuskegee syphilis experiment.* New York: Free Press.

Jones, P. M. (1997, January 8). Results mixed in cities where mayors took over schools. *Mobile Press Register,* p. 1D (Newhouse News Service).

Judd, C. M., Smith, E. R., & Kidder, L. H. (1991). *Research methods in social relations.* Fort Worth, TX: Harcourt Brace Jovanovich.

Kalton, G. (1983). *Introduction to survey sampling.* Newbury Park, CA: Sage.

Karabenick, S. A., & Sharma, R. (1994). Perceived teacher support of student questioning in the college classroom: Its relation to student characteristics and role in the classroom questioning process. *Journal of Educational Psychology, 86*(1), 90–103.

Kazdin, A. E. (1973). The role of instructions and reinforcement in behavior changes in token reinforcement programs. *Journal of Educational Psychology, 64,* 63–71.

Kazdin, A. E. (1978). Methodological and interpretive problems of single-case experimental designs. *Journal of Consulting and Clinical Psychology, 46,* 629–642.

Keastle, C. F. (1992). Standards of evidence in historical research. *History of Education Quarterly, 32,* 361–366.

Keastle, C. F. (1997). Recent methodological developments in the history of American education. In R. M. Jaeger (Ed.), *Complementary methods for research in education* (pp. 119–132). Washington, DC: American Educational Research Association.

Keith, T. Z., & Reynolds, C. R. (1990). Measurement and design issues in child assessment research. In C. R. Reynolds & R. W. Kamphaus (Eds.), *Handbook of psychological and educational assessment of children: Intelligence & achievement* (pp. 29–61). New York: Guilford Press.

Kendall, M. G., and Smith, B. (1954). *Tables of random sampling numbers, tracts for computers No. 27.* Cambridge: Cambridge University Press.

Kerlinger, F. N. (1986). *Foundations of behavioral research.* Fort Worth, TX: Harcourt Brace Jovanovich.

Keyser, D. J. & Sweetland, R. C. (1984–1994). *Test Critiques* (Vols. I–X). Austin: Pro-Ed.

Kiecolt, K. J., & Nathan, L. E. (1985). *Secondary analysis of survey data.* Newbury Park, CA: Sage.

Kish, L. (1965). *Survey sampling.* New York: Wiley.

Knapp, T. R. (1978). Canonical correlation analysis: A general parametric significance testing system. *Psychological Bulletin, 85,* 410–416.

Knight, J. A. (1984). Exploring the compromise of ethical principles in science. *Perspectives in Biology and Medicine, 27,* 432–441.

Knoke, D., & Bohrnstedt, G. W. (1994). *Statistics for social data analysis.* Itasca, IL: F. E. Peacock.

Kuder, G. F., & Richardson, M. W. (1937). The theory of the estimation of reliability. *Psychometrika, 2,* 151–160.

Kusche, C. A., & Greenberg, M. T. (1983). Evaluative understanding and role taking ability: A comparison of deaf and hearing children. *Child Development, 54,* 141–147.

Lance, G. D. (1996). Computer access in higher education: A national survey of service providers for students with disabilities. *Journal of College Student Development, 37*(3), 279–288.

LaPiere, R. T. (1934). Attitudes vs. Actions. *Social Forces, 13,* 230–237.

Lasee, M. J., & Smith, D. K. (1991). *Relationships between the K-ABC and the Early Screening Profiles.* Paper presented at the Annual Meeting of the National Association of School Psychologists, Dallas, TX.

LeCompte, M. D., & Preissle, J. (1992). Toward an ethnology of student life in schools and classrooms: Synthesizing the qualitative research tradition. In M. D. LeCompte, W. L. Millroy, & J. Preissle (Eds.), *The handbook of qualitative research in education* (pp. 815–859). San Diego, CA: Academic Press.

LeCompte, M. D., & Preissle, J. (1993). *Ethnography and qualitative design in educational research.* San Diego, CA: Academic.

Leikin, S. (1993). Minors' assent, consent, or dissent to medical research. *IRB: A review of human subjects research, 15,* 1–7.

Leland, J. & Joseph, N. (1997, January 13). Hooked on ebonics. *Newsweek,* pp. 78–79.

Lewin, K. (1946). Action research and minority problems. *Journal of Social Issues, 2,* 34–46.

Likert, R. (1932). A technique for the measurement of attitudes. *Archives of Psychology, 140,* 5–53.

Lincoln, Y. S., & Guba, E. G. (1985). *Naturalistic inquiry.* Newbury Park, CA: Sage.

Linder, D. E., Cooper, J., & Jones, E. E. (1967). Decision freedom as a determinant of the role of incentive magnitude in attitude change. *Journal of Personality and Social Psychology, 6,* 245–254.

Lofland, J., & Lofland, L. H. (1995). *Analyzing social settings: A guide to qualitative observation and analysis.* Belmont, CA: Wadsworth.

Manthei, R. and Gilmore, A. (1996). Teacher stress in intermediate schools. *Educational Research, 38,* 3–18.

Martinez-Pons, M. (1996). Test of a model of parental inducement of academic self-regulation. *Journal of Experimental Education, 64*(3), 213–227.

Maruyama, G. M. (1998). *Basics of structural equation modeling.* Thousand Oaks, CA: Sage.

Maxwell, J. A. (1992). Understanding and validity in qualitative research. *Harvard Educational Review, 62*(3), 279–299.

Maxwell, J. A. (1996). *Qualitative research design.* Newbury Park, CA: Sage.

Mayer, G. R., Mitchell, L. K., Clementi, T., Clement-Robertson, E., & Myatt, R. (1993). A dropout prevention program for at-risk high school students: Emphasizing consulting to promote positive classroom climates. *Education and Treatment of Children, 16,* 135–146.

McAlpine, L., Eriks-Brophy, A., & Crago, M. (1996). Teaching beliefs in Mohawk classrooms: Issues of language and culture. *Anthropology and Education Quarterly, 27*(3), 390–413.

McCullough, J. P., Cornell, J. E., McDaniel, M. H., & Mueller, R. K. (1974). Utilization of the simultaneous treatment design to improve student behavior in a first-grade classroom. *Journal of Consulting and Clinical Psychology, 42,* 288–292.

McGuigan, F. J. (1963). The experimenter: A neglected stimulus object. *Psychological Bulletin, 60,* 421–428.

McKelvie, S. (1978). Graphic rating scales: How many categories? *British Journal of Psychology, 69,* 185–202.

Menard, S. (1991). *Longitudinal research.* Newbury Park, CA: Sage.

Menninger, K. A. (1953). *The human mind* (3rd ed.). New York: Knopf.

Merriam, S. B. (1988). Case study research in education: A qualitative approach. San Francisco: Jossey-Bass.

Merton, R. K. (1948). The self-fulfilling prophecy. *Antioch Review, 8,* 193–210.

Merton, R. K., Fiske, M., & Kendall, P. L. (1956). *The focused interview.* New York: Free Press.

Merton, R. K., & Kendall, P. L. (1946). The focused interview. *American Journal of Sociology, 51,* 541–557.

Messerli, J. (1972). *Horace Mann.* New York: Knopf.

Messick, S. (1989). Validity. In R. L. Linn (Ed.), *Educational measurement* (3rd ed., pp. 13–103). New York: Macmillan.

Messick, S. (1995). Validity of psychological assessment: Validation of inferences from persons' responses and performances as scientific inquiry into score meaning. *American Psychologist, 50,* 741–749.

Miles, M. B., & Huberman, A. M. (1994). *Qualitative data analysis: An expanded source book.* Thousand Oaks, CA: Sage.

Miller, D. C. (1991). *Handbook of research design and social measurement.* Newbury Park, CA: Sage.

Moore, D. S. (1993). *Telecourse study guide for against all odds: Inside statistics and introduction to the practice of statistics.* New York: W. H. Freeman.

Moore, D. S., & McCabe, G. P. (1993). *Introduction to the practice of statistics.* New York: W. H. Freeman.

Morgan, D. L., & Krueger, R. A. (1998). *The focus group kit.* Newbury Park, CA: Sage.

Moustakas, C. (1994). *Phenomenological research methods.* Thousand Oaks, CA: Sage.

Muller, L. E. (1994). Toward an understanding of empowerment: A study of six women leaders. *Journal of Humanistic Education and Development, 33,* 75–82.

Murphy, L. L., Conoley, J. C., & Impara, J. C. (1994). *Tests in print IV.* Lincoln: University of Nebraska Press.

Neisser, U. (1979). The concept of intelligence. *Intelligence, 3,* 217–227.

Neufeldt, S. A., Karno, M. P., & Nelson, M. L. (1996). A qualitative study of experts' conceptualization of supervisee reflectivity. *Journal of Counseling Psychology, 43*(1), 3–9.

Norton, M. B. (1995). *Guide to historical literature* (3rd ed.). New York: Oxford University Press.

Nunally, J. (1978). *Psychometric theory.* New York: McGraw-Hill.

Ohles, J. F. (Ed.). (1978). *Biographical dictionary of American educators.* Westport, CT: Greenwood.

Okey, T. N., & Cusick, P. A. (1995). Dropping out: Another side of the story. *Educational Administration Quarterly, 31*(2), 244–267.

OPRR Reports. (1991). *Code of federal regulations 45* (Part 46, p. 5). Washington, DC: U.S. Government Printing Office.

Osgood, C. E., Suci, G. J., & Tannenbaum, P. H. (1957). *The measurement of meaning.* Urbana: University of Illinois Press.

Pasternak, D. & Cary, P. (1995, September 18). Tales from the crypt: Medical horror stories from a trove of secret cold-war documents (radiation experiments on U.S. citizens). *U.S. News & World Report, 119,* 70.

Patton, M. Q. (1987). *How to use qualitative methods in evaluation.* Newbury Park, CA: Sage.

Patton, M. Q. (1990). *Qualitative evaluation and research methods.* Newbury Park, CA: Sage.

Pedhazur, E. J. (1997). *Multiple regression in behavioral research: Explanation and prediction.* Fort Worth, TX: Harcourt Brace.

Pedhazur, E. J., & Schmelkin, L. P. (1991). *Measurement, design, and analysis: An integrated approach.* Hillsdale, NJ: Lawrence Erlbaum.

Pence, G. E. (1980). Children's dissent to research—a minor matter? *IRB: A Review of Human Subjects Research, 2,* 1–4.

Phi Delta Kappa. (1996, September). The 28th annual Phi Delta Kappa/Gallup poll. *Phi Delta Kappan.*

Phillips, S. R. (1994). Asking the sensitive question: The ethics of survey research and teen sex *IRB: A Review of Human Subjects Research, 16,* 1–6.

Popper, K. R. (1974). Replies to my critics. In P. A. Schilpp (Ed.), *The Philosophy of Karl Popper* (pp. 963–1197). La Salle, IL: Open Court.

Popper, K. R. (1985). Falsificationism versus conventionalism. In D. Miller (Ed.), *Popper Selections.* Princeton, NJ: Princeton Press. (Originally published in 1938)

Rech, J. F. (1996, winter). Gender differences in mathematics achievement and other variables among university students. *Journal of Research and Development in Education, 29*(2), 73–76.

Resnick, J. H., & Schwartz, T. (1973). Ethical standards as an independent variable in psychological research. *American Psychologist, 28,* 134–139.

Richardson, M. W., & Kuder, G. F. (1939). The calculation of test reliability based upon the method of rational equivalence. *Journal of Educational Psychology, 30,* 681–687.

Rieman, D. J. (1986). The essential structure of a caring interaction: Doing phenomenology. In P. M. Munhall & C. J. Oiler (Eds.), *Nursing research: A qualitative perspective* (pp. 85–105). Norwalk, CT: Appleton-Century-Crofts.

Roberson, M. T., & Sundstrom, E. (1990). Questionnaire design, return rates, and response favorableness in an employee attitude questionnaire. *Journal of Applied Psychology, 75,* 354–357.

Robinson, J. P., Shaver, P. R., & Wrightsman, L. S. (1991). *Measures of personality and social psychological attitudes.* New York: Academic.

Rogosa, D. (1988). Myths about longitudinal research. In K. W. Schaie, R. T. Campbell, W. Meridith, & S. C. Rawlings (Eds.), *Methodological issues in aging research* (pp. 171–210). New York: Springer.

Rosenberg, M. (1968). *The logic of survey analysis* (with forward by Paul F. Lazarsfeld). New York: Basic Books.

Rosenthal, R. (1991). Teacher expectancy effects: A brief update 25 years after the Pygmalion experiment. *Journal of Research in Education, 1,* 3–12.

Rosenthal, R., & Jacobson, L. (1968). *Pygmalion in the classroom.* New York: Holt, Rinehart & Winston.

Rosnow, R. L., & Rosnow, M. (1992). *Writing papers in psychology* (2nd ed.). New York: Wiley.

Russell, William (personal communication).

Salmon, M. H. (1984). *Logic and critical thinking.* San Diego, CA: Harcourt Brace Jovanovich.

Scheaffer, R. L., Mendenhall, W., & Ott, R. L. (1996). *Elementary survey sampling* (5th ed.). Belmont, CA: Duxbury Press.

Schafer, M. & Smith, P. K. (1996). Teachers' perceptions of play fighting and real fighting in primary school. *Educational Research, 38,* 173–180.

Schlenker, B. R., & Forsyth, D. R. (1977). On the ethics of psychological research. *Journal of Experimental Social Psychology, 13,* 369–396.

Schouten, P. G. W., & Kirkpatrick, L. A. (1993). Questions and concerns about the Miller Assessment for Preschoolers. *The Occupational Therapy Journal of Research, 13,* 7–28.

Schumacker, R. E., & Lomax, R. G. (1996). *A beginner's guide to structural equation modeling.* Mahwah, NJ: Lawrence Erlbaum.

Schuman, H., & Presser, S. (1981). *Questions and answers in attitude surveys: Experiments on question form, wording, and content.* New York: Academic.

Schwandt, T. A. (1997). *Qualitative inquiry: A dictionary of terms.* Thousand Oaks, CA: Sage.

Scriven, M. (1967). The methodology of evaluation. In R. E. Stake (Ed.), *Curriculum evaluation.* Chicago: Rand McNally.

Sears, S. J., Kennedy, J. J., & Kaye, G. L. (1997). Myers-Briggs Personality Profiles of prospective educators. *The Journal of Education Research, 90*(4), 195–202.

Shaffir, W. B., & Stebbins, R. A. (Ed.). (1991). *Experiencing fieldwork: An inside view of qualitative research.* Newbury Park, CA: Sage.

Sidman, M. (1960). *Tactics of scientific research.* New York: Basic Books.

Silverman, D. (1993). *Interpreting qualitative data: Methods for analyzing talk, text and interaction.* London: Sage.

Smith, H. J. (1997). *The role of symbolism in the structure, maintenance, and interactions of high school groupings.* (Masters thesis.) Mobile, Alabama: University of South Alabama.

Smith, J. K. (1984). The problem of criteria for judging interpretive inquiry. *Educational Evaluation and Policy Analysis, 6,* 379–391.

Smith, L. M. (1978). An evolving logic of participant observation, educational ethnography, and other case studies. In L. Shuman (Ed.), *Review of research in education* (Vol. 6, pp. 316–377). Itasca, IL: Peacock.

Snowling, M. J., Goulandris, N., & Defty, N. (1996). A longitudinal study of reading development in dyslexic children. *Journal of Educational Psychology, 88,* 653–669.

Society for Research in Child Development. (1993). *Ethical standards for research with children.* Directory of Members.

Solso, R. L., & Johnson, H. H. (1994). *Experimental psychology: A case approach.* New York: HarperCollins.

Spradley, J. P. (1997). *The ethnographic interview.* Fort Worth, TX: Holt, Rinehart and Winston.

Stake, R. E. (1978). The case study method in social inquiry. *Educational Researcher, 7*(2), 5–9.

Stake, R. E. (1995). *The art of case study research.* Thousand Oaks, CA: Sage.

Stake, R. E. (1997). Case study methods in educational research. In R. M. Jaeger (Ed.), *Complementary Methods for Research in Education* (2nd ed.). Washington, DC: American Educational Research Association.

Starch, D., & Elliot, E. C. (1912). Reliability of grading of high school work in English. *School Review, 20,* 442–457.

Sternberg, R. J., Conway, B. E., Ketron, J. L., & Bernstein, M. (1981). People's conception of intelligence. *Journal of Personality and Social Psychology, 41,* 37–55.

Stewart, D. W., & Shamdasani, P. N. (1998). Focus group research. In L. Bickman & D. J. Rog (Eds.), *Handbook of Applied Social Research Methods.* Thousand Oaks, CA: Sage.

Stolzenberg, R. M., & Land, K. C. (1983). Causal modeling and survey research. In P. H. Rossi, J. D. Wright, & A. B. Anderson (Eds.), *Handbook of survey research.* Orlando, FL: Academic.

Strauss, A. (1995). Notes on the nature and development of general theories. *Qualitative Inquiry, 1*(1), 7–18.

Strauss, A., & Corbin, J. (1990). *Basics of qualitative research: Grounded theory procedures and techniques.* Newbury Park, CA: Sage.

Strauss, A., & Corbin, J. (1994). Grounded theory methodology: An overview. In N. K. Denzin & Y. S. Lincoln (Eds.), *Handbook of qualitative research.* Thousand Oaks, CA: Sage.

Stringer, E. T. (1996). *Action research.* Newbury Park: Sage.

Strunk, W., Jr., & White, E. B. (1979). *The elements of style* (3rd ed.). New York: Macmillan.

Sudman, S. (1976). *Applied sampling.* New York: Academic.

Suen, H. K., & Ary, D. (1989). *Analyzing quantitative behavioral observation data.* Hillsdale, NJ: Lawrence Erlbaum.

Tabachnick, B. G., & Fidell, L. S. (1996). *Using multivariate statistics.* New York: HarperCollins.

Tallerico, M. (1993). *Gender and politics at work: Why women exit the superintendency.* Fairfax, VA: National Policy Board for Educational Administration.

Taylor, S. J., & Bogdan, R. (1984). *Introduction to qualitative research methods.* New York: Wiley.

Thompson, B. (1998 April 15). *Five methodology errors in educational research: The pantheon of statistical significance and other faux pas.* Invited address presented at the annual meeting of the American Educational Research Association, San Diego.

Thorkildsen, T. A., Nolen, S. B., & Fournier, J. (1994). What is fair? Children's critiques of practices that influence motivation. *Journal of Educational Psychology, 86,* 475–486.

Tryfos, P. (1996). *Sampling methods for applied research: Text and cases.* New York: Wiley.

Tryon, W. W. (1982). A simplified time-series analysis for evaluating treatment interventions. *Journal of Applied Behavior Analysis, 15,* 423–429.

Tunnicliffe, S. D. (1995). The content of conversations about the body parts and behaviors of animals during elementary school visits to a zoo and the implications for teachers organizing field trips. *Journal of Elementary Science Education, 7*(1), 29–46.

Turner, L. A., Johnson, R. B., & Pickering, S. (1996). Effect of ego and task instructions on cognitive performance. *Psychological Reports, 78,* 1051–1058.

University of Chicago Press. (1993). *The Chicago Manual of Style* (14th ed.). Chicago: Author.

University of Michigan, Survey Research Center. (1976). *Interviewer's manual* (Rev. ed.). Ann Arbor, MI: Institute for Social Research.

Valentine, P., & McIntosh, G. (1990). Food for thought: Realities of a women-dominated organization. *The Alberta Journal of Educational Research, 36*(4), 353–369.

Van Haneghan, J. P., & Stofflett, R. T. (1995). Implementing problem solving technology into classrooms: Four case studies of teachers. *Journal of Technology and Teacher Education, 3*(1), 57–80.

Van Manen, M. (1990). *Researching lived experience: Human science for an action sensitive pedagogy.* London, Ontario: State University of New York Press.

Wade, E. A., & Blier, M. J. (1974). Learning and retention of verbal lists: Serial anticipation and serial discrimination. *Journal of Experimental Psychology, 103,* 732–739.

Walster, E. (1964). The temporal sequence of post-decision processes. In L. Festinger (Ed.), *Conflict, decision, and dissonance.* Stanford, CA: Stanford University Press.

Wang, J., & Staver, J. R. (1997). An empirical study of gender differences in Chinese students' science achievement. *The Journal of Educational Research, 90,* 252–255.

Webb, E. J., Campbell, D. T., Schwartz, R. D., Sechrest, L., & Grove, J. B. (1981). *Nonreactive measures in the social sciences* (2nd ed.). Boston: Houghton Mifflin.

Weber, M. (1968). *Economy and society.* New York: Bedminster.

Weber, R. P. (1990). *Basic content analysis.* (2nd ed.). Newbury Park, CA: Sage.

Wechsler, D. (1989). *Wechsler preschool and primary scale of intelligence—revised.* San Antonio, TX: Psychological Corporation.

Weick, K. E. (1968). Systematic observational methods. In Lindzey, G., & Aronson, E. (Eds.), *The handbook of social psychology* (Vol. 2). Reading, MA: Addison Wesley.

Weiner, B. (Ed.). (1974). *Achievement motivation and attribution theory.* Morristown, NJ: General Learning Press.

Weis, L., & Fine, M. (1996). Narrating the 1980s and 1990s: Voices of poor and working-class white and African American men. *Anthropology and Education Quarterly, 27*(4), 493–516.

Weitzman, E. A., & Miles, M. B. (1995). *Computer programs for qualitative data analysis.* Thousand Oaks, CA: Sage.

Wilson, S. L., Thompson, J. A., & Wylie, G. (1982). Automated psychological testing for the severely physically handicapped. *International Journal of Man-Machine Studies, 17,* 291–296.

Wilson, V. L. (1981). Time and the external validity of experiments. *Evaluation and Program Planning, 4,* 229–238.

Wineburg, S. S. (1991). Historical problem solving: A study of the cognitive processes used in the evaluation of documentary and pictorial evidence. *Journal of Educational Psychology, 33,* 73–87.

Wolcott, H. F. (1994). The elementary school principal: Notes from a field study. In H. F. Wolcott, *Transforming qualitative data: Description, analysis, and interpretation* (pp. 115–148). Thousand Oaks, CA: Sage.

Woolf, P. K. (1988). Deception in science. In American Association for the Advancement of Science and American Bar Association Conference of Lawyers and Scientists, *Project of Scientific Fraud and Misconduct: Report on Workshop Number One.* Washington, DC: AAAS.

Worthen, B. R., Sanders, J. R., & Fitzpatrick, J. L. (1997). *Program evaluation.* New York: Longman.

Wurtman, R. J., & Wurtman, J. J. (1989, January). Carbohydrates and depression. *Scientific American,* 68–75.

Wynder, E. L., & Graham, E. A. (1950). Tobacco smoking as a possible etiologic factor in bronchogenic carcinoma. *Journal of the American Medical Association, 143,* 329–336.

Yin, R. K. (1981). The case study as a serious research strategy. *Knowledge: Creation, Diffusion, Utilization, 3,* 84–100.

Yin, R. K. (1994). *Case study research: Design and methods.* Thousand Oaks, CA: Sage.

Yin, R. K. (1998). The abridged version of case study research: Design and method. In L. Bickman & D. J. Rog (Eds.), *Handbook of applied social research methods* (pp. 229–259). Thousand Oaks, CA: Sage.

Yoder, P. (1990). Guilt, the feeling and the force: A phenomenological study of the experience of feeling guilty. (Doctoral dissertation, The Union Institute). *Dissertation Abstracts International, 50,* 5341B.

Young, C. H., Savola, K. L., & Phelps, E. (1991). *Inventory of longitudinal studies in the social sciences.* Newbury Park, CA: Sage.

Yow, V. (1994). *Recording oral history: A practical guide for social scientists.* Thousand Oaks, CA: Sage.

Zimney, G. H. (1961). *Method in experimental psychology.* New York: Ronald Press.

Index